SAVING AMERICA'S CITIES

SAVING AMERICA'S CITIES

Ed Logue and the Struggle to Renew
Urban America in the Suburban Age

LIZABETH COHEN

FARRAR, STRAUS AND GIROUX | NEW YORK

Farrar, Straus and Giroux
120 Broadway, New York 10271

Library of Congress Cataloging-in-Publication Data
Names: Cohen, Lizabeth, author.
Title: Saving America's cities : Ed Logue and the struggle to renew urban America
    in the suburban age / Lizabeth Cohen.
Description: First edition. | New York : Farrar, Straus and Giroux, [2019] | Includes
    bibliographical references and index.
Identifiers: LCCN 2019014944 | ISBN 9780374254087 (hardcover)
Subjects: LCSH: Logue, Edward J. | Urban renewal—Connecticut—New Haven. |
    Urban renewal—Massachusetts—Boston. | Urban renewal—New York
    (State)—New York.
Classification: LCC HT175.C58 2019 | DDC 307.3/41609746/8—dc23
LC record available at https://lccn.loc.gov/2019014944

Designed by Richard Oriolo

Our books may be purchased in bulk for promotional, educational, or business
use. Please contact your local bookseller or the Macmillan Corporate and
Premium Sales Department at 1-800-221-7945, extension 5442, or by e-mail at
MacmillanSpecialMarkets@macmillan.com.

www.fsgbooks.com
www.twitter.com/fsgbooks • www.facebook.com/fsgbooks

10   9   8   7   6   5   4   3   2   1

For Herrick

And those who continue to struggle to make cities a home for all

CONTENTS

SAVING AMERICA'S CITIES

Introduction: Cities in Crisis

n fall 1975, Edward J. Logue, a titan in the redevelopment of America's ailing cities for a quarter century after World War II, found himself subjected to intense interrogation. The previous winter he had been forced to resign as president of the New York State Urban Development Corporation (UDC), the powerful state agency that he and the former liberal Republican governor Nelson Rockefeller had created in 1968 to tackle the daunting problems of economic decline and inadequate and unaffordable housing encountered by New York State's cities. Now Logue was the star witness in the extraordinary public hearings that the state's newly elected Democratic governor, Hugh Carey, had convened to investigate malfeasance at the UDC. On the stand, Logue was confronted with tough questions about the financial practices, internal operations, and re-form agenda of this organization that had revolutionized urban renewal in New York State, inspired similar initiatives elsewhere in the nation, and proved the pinnacle of the veteran redeveloper Logue's already extensive career. After he led groundbreaking urban renewal efforts in the deterio-rating cities of New Haven, Connecticut, in the 1950s, and Boston, Mas-sachusetts, in the 1960s, Logue was hailed as the savior of New York State's troubled cities—until the UDC's sudden downfall.

In his defense, Logue stressed the UDC's undeniable accomplishments. Faced with an acute housing crisis and New York voters' repeated rejection of referenda to remedy it, the UDC had innovated a new public-private fund-ing approach. In place of old-style urban renewal, which depended on federal funds in ever shorter supply with the rising costs of the Vietnam War, Logue and Rockefeller had developed a new paradigm for urban revitaliza-tion. They had combined over a billion dollars' worth of bond sales to private investors, state appropriations, and still-available, if dwindling, federal dollars to build over 33,000 units of housing, mostly for moderate- and low-income New Yorkers, through 117 residential projects in 50 different com-munities. The UDC had also developed 69 commercial, industrial, and civic sites and established 3 substantial New Towns, a postwar planning con-cept that combined residences, workplaces, and cultural institutions within relatively autonomous communities. And it had generated tens of thousands of construction jobs while ensuring many more by promoting the state's in-dustrial development.[1] Seeking to avoid pitfalls in previous urban renewal efforts, the UDC had emphasized building on undeveloped land so as not to dislocate current residents and had used its unique authority as a state-level renewal agency to enlist entire metropolitan areas in housing low-income city dwellers.

Despite the UDC's successes, Logue was vulnerable. Nine months earlier the UDC had run out of money and defaulted on $104.5 million in matur-ing short-term notes and $30 million in bank loans. With Nelson Rockefel-ler now serving as President Gerald Ford's vice president, there was no one in Albany to come to the rescue.[2] This calamity created a crisis in New York

State that reverberated throughout the nation, shocking admirers that "the most powerful and best staffed housing delivery system ever assembled," according to a nationally prominent planner, had actually failed. As one journalist wrote, its default was "a shot heard round both the financial world and the political world of dozens of states that had patterned their own agencies after the pioneering example set in New York."[3]

The commission appointed to investigate the UDC deliberated for a year. Logue's personal culpability as its kingpin remained a primary focus. In the end, he was exonerated of any wrongdoing, although the UDC was faulted for lax financial oversight. But it soon became clear that the real subject of this inquiry was much bigger than Logue, and even the UDC. Rather, it was about how best to respond to a deepening crisis in American industrial cities that had been struggling economically since the Great Depression, if not before. After decades of dependence on the federal government's tool kit and bank account, first made available under the Housing Act of 1949, Washington's helping hand was now being withdrawn, most dramatically in 1973 when President Richard Nixon proclaimed a moratorium on all federal spending on housing.

Logue and Rockefeller's alternative model for funding urban renewal had endured many tests already. Tensions had grown over striking the right balance between government support and private investment; the respective authority of the mighty, state-authorized UDC, bondholders, and local communities; and how success should be measured. These conflicts were fully on display at the hearings. Logue's adversaries charged the UDC not only with fiscal irresponsibility and mismanagement but also with refusing to meet the requirements of the private-sector bankers and bondholders, who were increasingly picking up the tab for public needs. They likewise lambasted the UDC for its "big daddy government" intrusion into the property rights of individuals and the political autonomy of localities, particularly suburban ones.[4] Logue, in turn, angrily lashed out at the bankers who bought and sold UDC bonds for prioritizing their private profit and undermining the UDC's social mission.[5] As Logue confronted his accusers, he felt he was fighting to defend his personal reputation, the UDC's record, and, most basically, what he, as a die-hard New Deal liberal, viewed as government's fundamental responsibility to address society's ills. That bondholders and sellers were now providing capital, he argued, should make little difference.

In the end, these hearings exposed a deep divide between opposing conceptions of the respective roles of the public and private sectors in shaping the future of American cities. They marked the end of an era of confidence in the problem-solving capacity of government, particularly at the national level, and the dawn of a new era of more privatized solutions. Logue would continue to believe until the end of his life that "the basic responsibility for subsidizing housing for the low and lower income families is federal. It is everywhere in the developed world. Used to be with us."[6] But Logue would soon learn that the shift to solving urban problems through private-market strategies would only grow after the UDC's demise. And his dream of finding metropolitan solutions to urban inequities would stay stillborn.

A CAREER OF RENEWING CITIES

Ed Logue's lifetime of work provides an ideal lens through which to view postwar urban history, because from the early 1950s until his death, in 2000, his career tracked remarkably well with important shifts in approaches to revitalizing American cities. If Logue's name is relatively unknown today, he was all over the mainstream press in his own day, dubbed "the Master Rebuilder" by *The Washington Post* in 1967, "our top city saver" by *Look* magazine in 1969, and "Mr. Urban Renewal" by *The New York Times* in 1970. *Newsweek* in 1972, with tongue in cheek, anointed him "one of the most impressive movers and shakers of subsidized construction since the time of King Tut."[7] Logue got his start in the field at the age of thirty-three, when New Haven's just-elected reform Democratic mayor, Richard Lee, appointed him to lead the city's major new urban renewal effort. Like many other midsize, old industrial cities, New Haven had been declining since the 1920s, a situation only worsened by the Great Depression. Although war production had given its increasingly obsolete nineteenth-century-era industries a temporary boost, when World War II ended, the postwar future looked bleak. Moreover, increasing numbers of middle-class residents were moving into new suburban communities mushrooming outside New Haven's borders, with businesses and retail stores following suit. Downtown New Haven, once a regional hub, was becoming noticeably passé, threatening the city's stature—and its coffers, already diminished by having so many Yale University and county buildings off the tax rolls.

To complicate things further, while cities like New Haven were losing middle-class, tax-paying residents to booming suburban areas of the metropolis, they were attracting new poorer populations in their place, many of them African Americans from the South seeking opportunity in the industrial North. Sadly, these hopeful migrants were arriving just as the good industrial jobs were leaving town, some for suburban locations out of their reach, others to the American South and West (and eventually offshore to the still-cheaper developing world).

As urban leaders like Logue and Lee watched New Haven lose out in the decentralizing postwar metropolitan landscape, they undertook what they felt was a fight for their city's survival. Skillfully grabbing hold of the recently extended lifeline of new tools and dollars provided by the federal Housing Acts of 1949 and 1954—intended to encourage urban investment as a counterweight to the national government's generous incentives for suburban development—they managed to attract more redevelopment funds per capita to New Haven than any other American city received. Their goal was to make New Haven a national laboratory for physical urban renewal and for many of the social programs that would later undergird President Lyndon Baines Johnson's Great Society. Indeed, their work made New Haven exactly that: a laboratory exposing both the strengths *and* the limitations of this first phase of federal urban renewal.

After seven years in New Haven, a now nationally known Logue moved on to the larger New England city of Boston, lured there by another recently elected mayor to work his magic with federal stardust on this nearly bankrupt, fast-declining city. As the head of the newly strengthened Boston Redevelopment Authority (BRA), Logue implemented an ambitious plan for downtown and neighborhood renewal that sought to avoid many of the mistakes made in New Haven as well as in Boston's first disastrous foray into urban renewal under the previous mayor—the destruction of the immigrant West End. After seven years at the helm of the BRA, Logue received credit for orchestrating the city's turnaround into what was acclaimed as the "New Boston." Here he learned to preserve more of the historic fabric of this centuries-old city and eventually, after several bruising failures, to negotiate somewhat better with neighborhood groups. He remained in this job until summer 1967, when he resigned to run an unsuccessful campaign for mayor.

Soon thereafter, Governor Nelson Rockefeller recruited Logue to head his new pioneering statewide urban renewal agency, the New York State Urban Development Corporation, which Logue did with great drive and ambition—and, some would argue, hubris—until his very public downfall in 1975. Here, among other goals, he pursued the economically and socially mixed communities he had long sought and put his faith in the potential of good architecture to improve urban life, engaging leading architects to design innovative and livable subsidized housing all over New York State. The high point of his career in power and influence, the UDC era ended in a spectacular agency collapse and Logue's humiliating, forced resignation.

Logue's last major job, from 1978 to 1985, brought him to the destitute South Bronx in a more modest position as the president of the nonprofit South Bronx Development Organization, loosely affiliated with New York City's municipal government. The shrunken scale of Logue's South Bronx stage not only resulted from his personal fate in the aftermath of the UDC debacle but also reflected the dwindling role of government—particularly at the federal level—in urban development. In the South Bronx, Logue was forced to operate within a new urban policy regime, allying closely with small-scale community development corporations (CDCs) and squeezing what he could out of the private sector and an emerging new partner on the redevelopment scene, nonprofit organizations like the Local Initiatives Support Corporation (LISC), which liaised between private contributors and city builders on the ground. The private-market funding model would bring with it a host of new challenges, including abandoning the cutting-edge modernist housing made possible with public funding in favor of single-family, suburban-style homes preferred by lower-middle-class buyers and private-sector mortgage lenders. Nonetheless, these modestly priced, subsidized houses for purchase and their locally committed owners would prove themselves crucial anchors for the revitalization of the South Bronx.

URBAN RENEWAL IN HISTORY

The decline in government's role in subsidizing low-income housing, and solving urban problems more generally, has been accompanied by a prevailing historical treatment of urban renewal as an abject failure. Over the last half century, skeptics on the Right and the Left have advanced this critique. Conservatives have insisted that market-based solutions can be made to work, and they warn of the danger of replaying what they consider disastrous federal overreach from the 1930s through the 1960s. This position has been actively nurtured for decades by right-wing think tanks like the Manhattan Institute.[8]

Progressive critics have contributed to this dominant historical narrative as well. Although they may call in the abstract for more government investment at the federal, state, and municipal levels—acknowledging that private interests cannot sufficiently fund public goods—many share the Right's doubts about public housing and federal urban renewal. For these critics on the Left, public housing conjures up images of blocks of alienating high-rise towers. Less often do they blame years of poor maintenance for deteriorating conditions, admit the contradiction in building tall and profitably for luxury living, and acknowledge the true loss of community that public housing tenants often feel when their homes are deemed social failures and demolished. Given this broad lack of sympathy with public housing, abandoned units are rarely replaced; the country has lost a quarter million of them since the mid-1990s alone.[9] Similarly, liberals often share conservatives' dismissal of federal urban renewal as a scandalous chapter in American urban policy, misguided in concept and practice and displaying little evolution or improvement over time. Instead, they favor small-scale, neighborhood-based approaches like nonprofit CDCs over the more visible hand of government, feared as overly ambitious in scope and insensitive to community will. Although understandable, this reticence often comes at the cost of ignoring the need for citywide, to say nothing of metropolitan-wide, planning and of forgoing a larger share of the public purse.

Condemnation of urban renewal as practiced for a quarter century after 1950 stems in no small part, I would argue, from the unquestioning acceptance of a distorted, oversimplified depiction of it as a decades-long, undifferentiated, and unmitigated disaster. This book aims to present an alternative, more nuanced history of postwar American city building that does not dismiss the federal role in renewing cities and subsidizing housing as pure folly. It claims instead that there is a usable past of successful government involvement in urban redevelopment from which we can benefit today as we grapple with the current challenges of persistent economic and racial inequality, unaffordable housing, and crumbling infrastructure. This book will contend that policies and practices of urban renewal evolved and improved over time. Although many serious mistakes were made, important lessons were also learned. And as a result of ever-shifting approaches to urban renewal, many cities were brought back to economic, cultural, and commercial vitality, with increasing amounts of community participation in the process. Urban renewal as experienced in 1972 was far different from that in 1952. The small glimpse given into Logue's UDC reveals just how experimental these urban renewal strategies often were.

Although this book calls for a fresh reexamination of postwar urban renewal, I will in no way claim that it was always admirable in motive and effective in practice. Residents often were excessively and insensitively displaced from their homes. Flawed conceptions of the ideal city were all too common, such as when residences, work sites, and commerce were rigidly separated; when superblocks made downtown streets pedestrian-unfriendly; or when highways slashed through still viable neighborhoods. Seeking community involvement in planning was sometimes a pretense. Racial inequity proved stubbornly tenacious, even though—perhaps surprisingly—some urban renewers like Logue were deeply committed to the nation's racial progress and at times had backing from black leaders and organizations eager for resources and infuriated with the discriminatory status quo. Urban renewal at some moments encouraged what critics cynically labeled "Negro removal" and in other moments improved lives. The UDC, for example, insisted on substantial black participation in its projects, as workers and as residents, an admirable move that surely contributed to its growing unpopularity and ultimate defeat in New York State.[10]

Nor would I hold up Logue as any kind of hero. Even his admirers considered him a complicated character who could inspire with his utopian idealism of promoting the public good and could antagonize with his demanding, overly self-assured personal style. That tension was captured in a 1971 journalist's description of Logue as "a husky, energetic man of fifty who has achieved almost mythological status in the annals of urban renewal, as hero and ogre, by tearing down and rebuilding large sectors of New Haven and Boston."[11] Moreover, as much as Logue espoused a progressive view on race, he found it easier to work with an older generation of integrationist black leaders than their more demanding successors. And although he increasingly hired women onto his staff, his liberal social agenda did not prioritize their advancement.

At times Logue was a figure of Greek tragedy, whose good intentions were undermined by his own fatal flaws. One blind spot in particular he shared with other urban liberals of his era. Eager to achieve greater social and economic opportunity in American democratic society, he became deeply invested in an expert-driven activist government. So convinced was he of the righteousness of his goals and his own ability to deliver them, however, that he sometimes paid mere lip service to community input, sanctioning a less-than-democratic process that marginalized and alienated the very people whose lives he had set out to improve.[12] Indeed, Logue struggled with what it meant to live up to his signature slogan of "planning with people" throughout his career. In New Haven and into the Boston years, he embraced what I call pluralist democracy, content to give voice mostly to representatives of established community interests. Later in Boston, and much more so in the South Bronx, he would learn the limits of that approach and come to accept the importance of embracing a more grassroots participatory democracy. One could even argue that it was in Logue's bootstrapped South Bronx project, devoid of much government support and by necessity allied closely with neighborhood-based CDCs, where he came closest to actually planning with people.

A MULTIDIMENSIONAL STORY

I was drawn to a biographical approach to urban history, after many years of writing the social and political history of large groups of ordinary Americans, for the opportunity to investigate the experience of a person in a position of power during the postwar era. My career probing what has been called "history from the bottom up" left me eager to examine "history from the top down," but to bring to it social history's attentiveness to class, gender, race and ethnicity, profession, and other forms of identity that shaped how influential protagonists thought and acted. That Ed Logue was city-bred as a lower-middle-class Catholic in Philadelphia; that as a scholarship student he attended elite Yale College and Law School, where he became a progressive labor organizer, a civil rights activist, and an opponent of what would become known as McCarthyism; that he served as a bombardier in World War II with a bird's-eye view of European cities; that he brought an assertive, sometimes overly dismissive, hyper-male style to his redevelopment work—all these matter greatly in this story. Moreover, because Logue played a formative role in creating a new kind of postwar professional—the urban-redevelopment expert—who carried an expanding body of skills and knowledge from city to city, his personal experience illuminates a wider world. As Logue joked at a reunion celebrating his first mayoral boss, Richard Lee of New Haven, "Look at all of us. We have rebuilt half the East Coast."[13]

Too often the era of urban renewal is depicted as an abstract contest between unstoppable urban-growth machines and the defenseless communities that became their victims.[14] Following the career of someone like Logue allows us to grapple with the agency, motives, and constraints on all sides and, most importantly, to understand when and how conflicts or negotiations took place. The actions and attitudes of urban specialists on the one hand, and residents—mobilized and not—on the other, cannot easily be separated; they constantly interacted and shaped each other.

Although this book tells primarily an American postwar story, it will make many connections to the international context. The ambition to undertake the urban renewal of U.S. cities coincided with the rebuilding of many cities worldwide after the ravages of the Great Depression and the devastations of World War II. A young Logue found inspiring models in both the social housing experiments of European reformers dating back to the 1920s and the modernization schemes and community development programs he observed in the emerging new nation of India in the early 1950s, where he worked in the American embassy before he returned to New Haven. A more mature Logue became captivated by postwar European New Towns and imported the concept to New York State in the 1970s. Although every country put its own stamp on how it implemented innovations in architecture and planning, it is striking how widely ideas circulated among practitioners increasingly operating in globalizing professions.

The lack of subtlety that I have lamented in current historical understanding of postwar American urbanism stems partly from its frequent framing as a monumental battle between the clashing visions of the villainous Robert Moses and the saintly Jane Jacobs. Moses is frequently depicted as epitomizing government arrogance and the prioritizing of planners' projects over people. And Jacobs, in turn, is hailed for slamming planners' intrusions as disrupting the natural evolution of the street and neighborhood. This dichotomy is too simplistic and makes these two twentieth-century giants of urbanism into symbols of rigid orthodoxies. In truth, they were both more complex figures. Moses did not only bulldoze neighborhoods and build insensitively; he constructed crucially needed urban infrastructure.[15] In her influential 1961 critique of big planning, *The Death and Life of Great American Cities*, Jacobs taught the world important lessons in valuing the spontaneous life of the street, in allowing city neighborhoods to develop organically, and in viewing planners—with their top-down expertise—skeptically. But her sweeping repudiation of the planning profession and government intervention left few tools in place for delivering more equitable housing for those requiring it or for constructing badly needed public works.[16] No surprise that conservatives, particularly libertarians, have embraced Jacobs alongside her more left-leaning admirers, finding her criticism of urban renewal consistent with their own defense of individual property rights and discomfort with the "federal bulldozer" and other government actions deemed excessive. In fact, the conservative ideologue William F. Buckley, Jr., included Jacobs in his anthology *American Conservative Thought in the Twentieth Century*, while the libertarian magazine *Reason*, devoted to "free minds and free markets," named Jacobs one of its "thirty-five heroes of freedom."[17]

Logue knew Moses slightly. Both Yale men and avid football fans, they met up regularly in the parking lots of the Yale Bowl or Princeton's Palmer Stadium. While admiring some of Moses's accomplishments—parks and parkways, not public housing—Logue sought repeatedly to differentiate himself as less imperious and more committed to social change. As a close colleague at the UDC put it, Logue "was Robert Moses and the anti–Robert Moses all at once. He would think as large as Moses and had no less ability to implement . . . But unlike Moses, he was as committed to social transformation as he was to physical building."[18] Moses in turn was suspicious enough of Logue that when he heard reports that Mayor John V. Lindsay was trying to recruit him to New York City "as a super duper planner," Moses wrote to a Boston acquaintance—perhaps in jealousy, his own power already much diminished—to express his doubts and inquire how Logue was faring there. His correspondent gave him no satisfaction when he replied, "I think that Ed Logue has done a splendid job in Boston."[19] Comparisons between Logue and Moses continued long after their deaths. In 2008, the esteemed architecture critic Ada Louise Huxtable expressed her frustration with the slow rebuilding of the World Trade Center in a *Wall Street Journal* column, "New York's 9/11 Site Needed Not a Moses but a Logue."[20]

Logue dueled spiritedly and sometimes meanly with Jacobs. He rejected her stance, which he characterized sarcastically as "no more federal renewal aids; let the cities fend for themselves," an "approach [that] has won her many new friends, particularly among comfortable suburbanites" who liked being "told that neither their tax dollars nor their own time need be spent on the cities they leave behind them at the close of each work day." Nor, he pointed out, was her much-flaunted residence amid the Old World charms of New York's West Village a privilege easily shared by slum dwellers.[21] She returned the favor, once saying, "I thought he was a very destructive man . . . He thought that all should be wiped out and built new. Boy, in my books, he went down as a maniac." When her interviewer suggested a comparison between Logue and Adolph Hitler, however, she issued a caveat: "So we were lucky."[22]

A more subtle history of postwar urbanism must move beyond this stark and in many ways distorting dichotomy. Though Logue was quick to condemn what he considered excesses in both Moses and Jacobs, he learned from both of them. John Zuccotti, an admirer of both Logue and Jacobs and an important player in New York City's housing and planning circles before becoming a successful developer, recognized the need for more balance. "It's very hard to do what she [Jacobs] wants to do without some kind of government involvement. Excuse me, [but] if it wasn't for the government, the private developers would have annihilated every old building in the City of New York . . . [But] I don't blame them . . . That's what it's all about, right? Making money."[23] The urban renewal of American cities in the era of mass suburbanization deserves to be painted more in shades of gray than in black and white.

THE SIGNIFICANCE OF URBAN RENEWAL'S HISTORY

The relevance of this story of Ed Logue and the struggle over postwar urban renewal was constantly brought home to me as I worked on this book. I came to the project on the heels of the Hurricane Katrina catastrophe in New Orleans during August 2005, and I researched and wrote as Katrina raised complex and important questions about how a city rebuilds after such extreme devastation. As I watched events unfold in New Orleans, the debates that animated Logue's story—who's in charge, who should have a say, who benefits, and who pays the bill—took on real-life resonance before my eyes. Similarly, the Great Recession of a few years later, with its massive wave of foreclosures and talk of shrinking cities, gave me another ringside seat from which to watch urban decline and strategies of revival. As my writing of this book neared its end, the urban housing crisis of our own time became more pressing. And the United States elected a real estate developer for its forty-fifth president, with yet unknown long-term consequences for urban policy.

This history of making and keeping American cities viable remains relevant in the twenty-first century because many cities are still challenged by formidable problems. Today, urban America contends with a sharp contradiction. The good news is that after years of disinvestment and disinterest from middle-class metropolitan residents who preferred to head back to the suburbs at the end of every workday—the reality that Ed Logue battled—urban living appeals again. Whether young professionals employed at startups and tech firms increasingly locating downtown or formerly suburban empty nesters returning to the city, these new urbanites are willing to pay more and live smaller to be in the city, so long as it is the prospering kind that has successfully transitioned from a declining industrial to a flourishing postindustrial economy. New York, Boston, San Francisco, Atlanta, Chicago, Los Angeles, and their peers are considered attractive; Detroit, Baltimore, Milwaukee, Newark, and Memphis much less so.

But now for the bad news. Low-income residents have few prospects in economically declining cities, but their options are also worsening in more dynamic urban areas. Despite the fact that their labor often keeps these cities running, lower-income people find it increasingly difficult to survive as better-off residents are drawn there. They find a shrinking supply of available housing because of the transformation of existing rental units into condos, the gentrification of formerly working-class and immigrant neighborhoods, and community resistance to building new affordable residential projects. Meanwhile, working people's wages have stagnated as their rents continue to climb. The result is a severe national crisis. Increasing numbers of Americans are "rent-burdened." Traditionally that meant paying more than 30 percent of income on housing. In the 1960s, a bit more than one-fifth of renters bore that burden. By 2016, almost one-half did. In an expensive city like Los Angeles, nearly a third of renters paid more than 50 percent of their income for shelter.

Nationwide, evictions are epidemic. And on any given night, more than half a million men, women, and children are homeless. Waiting lists for subsidized apartments and housing vouchers intended to help low-income Americans "move to opportunity" grow ever longer, so long that some cities have even stopped taking new names. Despite a sharp rise in the number of very-low-income households qualifying for rental subsidies, the amount of assistance available has barely grown, reducing the beneficiaries among the eligible from 29 percent in 1987 to 25 percent in 2015.[24] The high levels of economic inequality that have exploded in the nation are even more extreme within its cities as market forces—little buffered in our neoliberal, anti-government age—reward the privileged and punish the rest. And inequality exists between cities as well. Wealthier cities command more resources than poorer ones to tackle their problems. But even thriving cities find it difficult to sustain efficient transportation, high-performing public services, and sound infrastructure, given the years of neglect and lack of government support. Internationally, the result of this American underinvestment is glaringly obvious simply by comparing mass transit systems in New York or Boston—among the most prosperous American cities—to Stockholm, Paris, or Shanghai, all places where a commitment to strong state subvention persists.

It is my hope that taking a deep dive into the long career of city redeveloper Edward J. Logue and the shifting regimes of urban policy within which he maneuvered will deepen our understanding of what it takes to make American cities dynamic and equitable. And it might just expand the repertoire of possibilities we can imagine for our own time, as we, too, continue to struggle to save America's cities for all their residents and to fulfill the still-elusive aspiration of the 1949 Housing Act to provide "a decent home and a suitable living environment for every American family."[25]

PART I

New Haven in the 1950s:
Creating a Laboratory for
Urban Renewal

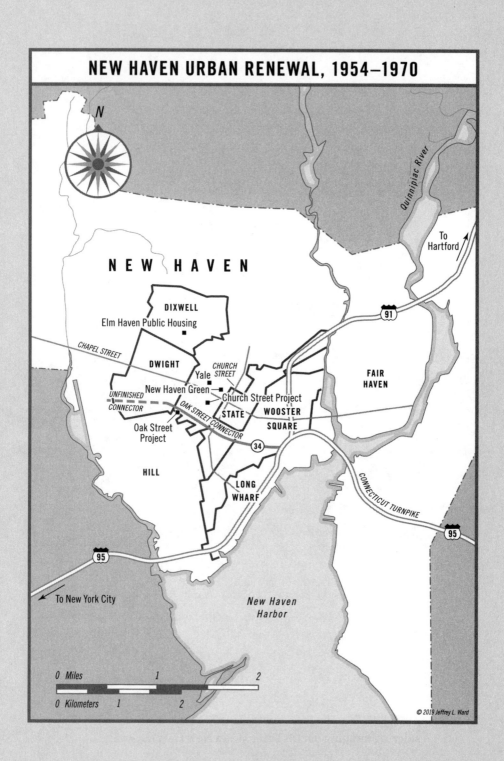

NEW HAVEN URBAN RENEWAL, 1954–1970

N

NEW HAVEN

Quinnipiac River

To Hartford

91

DIXWELL

Elm Haven Public Housing

CHAPEL STREET

DWIGHT

CHURCH STREET

Yale

New Haven Green

Church Street Project

UNFINISHED CONNECTOR

OAK STREET CONNECTOR

STATE

WOOSTER SQUARE

Oak Street Project

FAIR HAVEN

34

HILL

LONG WHARF

CONNECTICUT TURNPIKE

95

95

To New York City

New Haven Harbor

0 Miles   1   2

0 Kilometers   1   2

© 2019 Jeffrey L. Ward

1. The Making of an Urban Renewer

n September 1953, thirty-two-year-old Ed Logue returned to New Haven, Connecticut, with his wife, Margaret, to await the birth of their first child after six years away. They were resettling into a city that had launched Logue into adulthood. Here he had widened his horizons as a scholarship student at Yale College, had worked his first full-time job as a labor organizer, and had trained for a profession at Yale Law School. Here, too, he had met and married Margaret, the daughter of an influential couple in New Haven academic circles, the much-admired dean of Yale College William Clyde DeVane and his wife, Mabel Phillips DeVane. Casting about for his next career move after working in India for eighteen months as Ambassador Chester Bowles's special assistant, Logue was considering hanging out his shingle as a New Haven lawyer.

But then opportunity intervened. Logue had arrived just in time to help with the mayoral campaign of the Democratic reform candidate Richard Lee, who was mounting his third attempt to be elected mayor of New Haven. The determined, thirty-seven-year-old hometown boy, "Dick" Lee, currently the director of the Yale News Bureau, built his run around an ambitious promise to "renew" what was undeniably a deteriorating New Haven. Factories were closing, downtown retail was stagnating, and middle-class residents were decamping for the city's flourishing suburbs. These departures, furthermore, were fueling growing discontent among those remaining behind, who resented how the city's property tax rates kept climbing simply to sustain existing services. Logue, identifying himself as a "longtime admirer of Dick Lee," became a key player in Independents for Lee, an effort to position Lee as an alternative to business as usual as practiced by New Haven's Democratic Party machine. The third time was the charm, and Lee claimed victory on the night of November 3, 1953, with 52.3 percent of the vote.[1]

Within weeks of his election, Lee invited Logue to be his executive secretary, an ostensibly part-time post that Lee created to tap the unique combination of smarts, energy, and vision that he saw in Logue. Logue accepted, but it quickly became apparent that the job was much bigger, more like an unofficial deputy mayor. They lost little time collaborating on an ambitious plan to remake New Haven as "a slumless city—the first in the nation," as they liked to say.[2] In February 1955, Lee officially appointed Logue as the development administrator of the New Haven Redevelopment Agency. Logue's brilliance at garnering newly available federal urban renewal funds, combined with Lee's intimate knowledge of New Haven, made them an irrepressible and nationally admired team who could boast that they were attracting more federal dollars per capita to New Haven than any other American city was getting. The masterful politician and his bureaucratically savvy partner together piloted schemes in New Haven that other cities would watch and copy.

Medium-size New Haven, a struggling old industrial city in an increasingly suburban postindustrial age, became the model city of urban renewal, a laboratory for salvaging urban America. The problems that Dick Lee and

Ed Logue were addressing were faced by many American cities that had flourished with the rise of America's industrial might in the nineteenth century. Now, in the second half of the twentieth, these cities were atrophying as their manufacturing bases disappeared. Strategies to renew American cities would evolve continually for at least two more decades, in response to new ideas, mistakes made and learned from, the ebb and flow of funding, and political pressures exerted from many quarters, most notably policy makers in Washington and critics at the grass roots. The successes and failures of Dick Lee and Ed Logue's efforts in New Haven reveal how the urban renewal project fared in its first phase during the 1950s.

ED LOGUE, LIBERAL NEW DEALER

The charges brought against urban renewal by the mid-1960s as pro-business, undemocratic, and racially biased would have been anathema to the Ed Logue who joined forces with Dick Lee. He was by personal history and self-perception quite the opposite: a political progressive on many fronts who viewed urban renewal as the next worthy liberal cause demanding immediate government action.

Logue was born and raised in Philadelphia in a devoutly Irish Catholic and staunchly Democratic home, which he would recall later as being "without any racial prejudice."[3] Until his father died in 1934 when Ed was thirteen and his four siblings—John, Gordon, Frank, and Ellen—were eleven, ten, nine, and seven, respectively, the family lived comfortably in a rowhouse on Mount Vernon Street just north of Center City, Philadelphia. Ed's father earned a decent salary as a city tax assessor, good enough to send five children to the private Notre Dame Academy in Rittenhouse Square and to nearby Cape May for the summer. Logue's happiest early memories were linked to the excitement of downtown Philadelphia: "From childhood, I was always interested in cities."[4] He particularly prized the "walking trips" he made with his father around town.[5] He also enjoyed hearing his aunt, a Catholic nun named Sister Maria Kostka, discuss with his father an ambitious architectural design for Chestnut Hill College, a Catholic women's college she founded in 1924 and ran for her order, the Sisters of Saint Joseph.[6] But then Ed's father suddenly died during a routine hernia operation, leaving the family precariously dependent on a meager monthly insurance check of $134.84 and the charity of an uncle who bought them a semidetached house in the outlying Overbrook neighborhood. Renting out the third floor barely helped make ends meet.[7]

Yale College, where Logue matriculated in September 1938 as a bursary or scholarship student after rejecting the free ride at Catholic University arranged by his aunt the nun, shaped many aspects of Logue's adult life. Logue was a political science major who studied with Harvey Claflin Mansfield, Albert Galloway Keller, and the labor economist E. Wight Bakke, author of a remarkable eight-year study of unemployed workers and their families in Depression-era New Haven, published in 1940, that made a deep impression on Logue.

Yale influenced young Logue outside the classroom as well. The Yale College that Ed Logue entered in fall 1938 newly aspired to having a more diverse undergraduate community of academic as well as athletic and societal leaders, having lagged behind Columbia, Harvard, and the University of Chicago in this regard. Carrying the name of a traditional Yale family had been the best ticket to Yale admissions, so much so that the application requested a mother's maiden name to catch candidates with maternal rather than paternal connections.

As a striving, not-well-off, Irish Catholic graduate of a public high school in Philadelphia, Logue encountered a Yale that was beginning to break down social boundaries among its students but was still a bastion of elite Protestant prep schoolers. Only 213 students out of his freshman class of 855—about a quarter—had graduated from public high schools. Almost a third of the total matriculants were "Yale sons." At Yale, Catholic students historically had experienced less prejudice than Jewish students had. Interestingly, however, because Catholics were less oriented toward higher education in the first half of the century and Catholic colleges eagerly recruited those who were, the Catholic presence on campus lagged behind the proportion of Catholics in the general population. In contrast, Yale's

Jewish students far exceeded their numbers nationally. Moreover, many of the Jews and Catholics who attended Yale gained entrance because they grew up in New Haven and qualified for the scholarships Yale reserved for local boys to improve town-gown relations.

Yale's first residential colleges had opened in 1933, only five years before Logue arrived, thanks to a $16 million gift from the alumnus Edward Harkness aimed at improving the undergraduate residential experience. By 1940, Logue's junior year, the popular colleges had succeeded in decreasing the proportion of undergraduates living off campus to 13 percent from 38 percent in 1920, and the fraternities and exclusive senior societies that had fragmented the student body were declining in influence as well. But although the new colleges aimed to bring together students of different backgrounds, exclusionary policies still guided roommate matching. Rooming committees were told never to mix Jews and Catholics with Protestants, prep school with public school students, or the well-off with scholarship recipients. Not surprisingly, then, Logue's Yale friends were overwhelmingly Catholic and Jewish. Brother Frank Logue (Class of '48) well understood the Yale that he and his brothers entered: "A great WASPy university admitted those four sons of a widowed Irish kindergarten teacher" is the way he later put it, wryly noting that most of their Berkeley College roommates were Jews, a sign of how fully Yale segregated its students.[8]

Attending Yale at this moment in time made Ed Logue, his brothers, and his friends grateful for the liberalization of the university that was enabling their attendance but resentful of the still-powerful vestiges of privilege. Logue's good college and law school friend John Arcudi, an Italian Catholic whose parents owned a small grocery in nearby Westport, explained how, as a bursary student, he felt apart from what he called the "white shoe boys" from prep school. "We . . . the people who had been the waiters in Commons . . . were a separate part of the Yale society." The lower social status of students like Arcudi and Logue played out politically as well. Both recounted their alienation from a student body that in the presidential election of 1940 overwhelmingly supported the Republican candidate Wendell Willkie against their hero, the Democratic incumbent Franklin Delano

Roosevelt. They responded by inviting the Republican New York City mayor Fiorello La Guardia, an enthusiastic FDR supporter, to a rally to reassure New Haven's many Italians that the president bore no prejudice, despite his criticism of Mussolini. When Roosevelt won the election, Logue and a Jewish friend on scholarship, Allen "Bud" Scher, "celebrated quietly" and walked across a Yale campus that "was like a graveyard. There was no celebration for FDR by the Yalies," according to Scher, who derisively called them "the bloods."[9]

Watching so many of his peers shun Roosevelt made Logue only more combative. He joined the Labor Party in the Yale Political Union debating society (a more left alternative to the Liberal and Conservative Parties and the nexus for pro-union students) and devoted himself to supporting New Haven's working class, whether by leafleting at the nearby Winchester Repeating Arms Company plant or rallying behind Yale's own dining hall workers—many of whom he knew well from working in Freshman Commons—when they went on strike in 1941.[10]

A decade later, in 1951, when Logue needed security clearance to work in the American embassy in New Delhi, the FBI talked to a supervisor in the Yale dining services who remembered him as "not dependable" and "'sneaky' in all of his actions, including always eating the leftovers from the plates in the dining room." The FBI agent investigating continued, "She stated that he was in her opinion the poorest worker that was ever employed in the Yale Dining Room. She further advised that applicant was constantly spreading 'malicious rumors' about the management of Yale University, stating that 'they were dictators, slave drivers, and oppressing the employees of Yale.'" It was not clear how much of her condemnation was due to Logue's pro-labor politics, his incompetence as a worker, or his hearty appetite—most likely, a combination of all three. In any event, Logue was eventually fired for "inadequate effort."[11]

Logue didn't just connect to Yale's workers on campus. His social position and political sympathies made him more at home in their urban world outside the campus gates than most other Yale students were. When as a senior he showed a date around New Haven and "she was totally uninterested," he took that as grounds enough to end the relationship.[12]

Logue's bond with Yale's low-level employees, so appalling to his dining-services supervisor from freshman year, only grew over his college career and drew him into helping with a full-scale union-organizing drive mounted during his senior year, 1941–42. The 1930s and early 1940s were a dynamic period for labor in New Haven, as elsewhere in the United States. Garment workers, clock workers, metalworkers, and other local laborers succeeded in organizing unions for the first time. Even the drivers for the Chieppo Bus Company, hired by the university to drive students to the Yale Bowl and other sports fields, struck for union recognition. With so much local activity, Yale's janitors, maids, maintenance, and power and boiler room workers joined in, motivated by serious complaints of their own: miserably low wages, long hours (often seven days a week), and poor working conditions—no overtime, sick leave, holiday pay, job protection, or vacations other than a three-month summer layoff. With the arrival of a Congress of Industrial Organizations (CIO) organizer, long-simmering discontent boiled over and led to the chartering of a CIO local in May 1941, followed by an overwhelming electoral victory for the union in October. When negotiations with the university broke down the next month, four hundred workers went on strike—the first in Yale's history. Finally, in February 1942, came a favorable contract between Yale University and Local 142 of the United Construction Workers, affiliated with the United Mine Workers–CIO. Logue threw himself into this yearlong roller-coaster ride of a unionization struggle, which he later recalled as "a time with a lot of idealism, a lot of 'we're going to do what we can to make the world better.'" He was rewarded upon graduation with a full-time job as general organizer for the local.[13]

As an activist on the New Haven labor scene, Logue had a clear political position: pro-labor and anti-communist. Although he wasn't religious himself, Logue's Catholic upbringing propelled his anti-communism, just as it helped inspire his commitment to social justice.[14] But mostly, he was a New Dealer to the core, convinced that the best way to improve ordinary people's lives was to empower the federal government to be a force for good.[15] In New Haven, that approach meant much more than organizing workers. As Logue would have been aware, the New Haven Central Labor Council had advocated for the City-Wide Conference for Slum Clearance and Better

Housing in 1937. After publicizing the poor conditions in which many New Haveners lived, the city's labor leaders helped secure funding for Elm Haven Housing, New Haven's first federally funded low-rise public housing project. Two more much-needed public housing projects would soon follow. The New Haven labor movement taught the budding-activist Logue that enlightened government could play a key role in delivering decent, affordable homes, along with good jobs, to its citizens.[16]

Knowing it was only a matter of time until he was drafted into World War II, Logue decided in November 1942 to enlist in the navy, hoping to become a combat flyer. To his surprise and dismay, he was turned down. Throughout his life he remained convinced that his labor activism had made him unacceptable to the navy. He even wrote to President Roosevelt in outrage: "The Navy seems to have a policy on organizers. Keep 'em out." (The FBI found no evidence for Logue's suspicion in its security investigation of him in 1952. Nor did I in my Freedom of Information Act inquiry of 2009. But the recruitment officer at the Philadelphia Naval Aviation Selection Board, who recorded "lack of interest in Naval Aviation" as the official grounds for rejection, might privately have deemed Logue too politically unreliable.)[17] Logue then enlisted in the U.S. Army Air Forces, hoping to qualify as a pilot, and received orders to report for flight training in early 1943. His farewell message to Local 142's membership conveyed how much he connected the union struggle at Yale with the democracy he would soon be defending abroad. "Unions are the greatest single force today in preserving and strengthening our democracy on the home front. Do your part in our fight for democracy by being an active, loyal union member and by practicing that tolerance of your fellow man regardless of race, creed or color which is the core of democracy and the American labor movement."[18]

Before too long, Logue washed out of pilot training (not uncommon in this highly selective military division) and had to content himself with being a bombardier. He served in the Fifteenth Air Force in Italy from 1944 to 1945, flying seventeen missions, winning his share of medals and stars, and mustering out as a second lieutenant in summer 1945. On the ground, he was impressed with Florence, Siena, and Rome, but Logue most often mentioned how all that time in the "great glass bubble" gave him a valuable bird's-eye view of European cities, teaching him to "read" the physical layout to "get a feeling for how a city is put together." It was "the best possible city planning training I [could have] had."[19]

Although Logue was not likely aware of it, the famed French modernist architect Le Corbusier (the professional name of Charles-Édouard Jeanneret-Gris), whose dramatic schemes to remake cities would powerfully influence postwar urban renewers like Logue, also credited aerial views with inspiring him: "When one has taken a long flight over the city like a bird gliding, ideas attack you . . . everything became clear to me . . . I expressed the ideas of modern planning." Le Corbusier's signature linear radiant city, with its rational division of urban functions, towering skyscrapers, and lyrical flow of highways, apparently came to him while studying the problems of nineteenth-century cities from airplanes during the 1930s and 1940s. Likewise, Le Corbusier's own bold interventions on the landscape were easily discernible from the air.[20] This aerial perspective encouraged Logue, Le Corbusier, and other modernists, including the New Haven planner Maurice E. H. Rotival, to reimagine the city as made up of distinct, legible parts—residential neighborhoods, downtown cores, industrial and market districts, and connective roadways—that could be grasped from above and modernized in discrete sections as needed. Peering down on Europe, Logue learned "how a city's functions separated themselves and how they worked together."[21] From these heights, a city was like a complex machine whose interconnected parts required frequent recalibration for the full urban mechanism to work properly.

Once the European war ended and Logue returned to the United States, he took up his life again in New Haven, using the GI Bill to matriculate at Yale Law School. He also went back to working part-time as an organizer for Local 142, which continued to unionize Yale workers, concentrating now on the university's dining halls, library, and hospital.[22] At Yale Law, Logue was drawn to an iconoclastic group of law professors known as legal realists. They condemned the Harvard-based, case-method style of legal education, with its orderly rules to explain judicial decisions. Instead, they

argued that legal judgments were more idiosyncratic, more politically motivated, and more shaped by pressures from the larger society. Logue
particularly admired a member of this group, Fred Rodell, whom he had
met through the union struggle on campus before the war. Rodell became
a mentor, father figure, and close friend.[23]

Rodell was an irreverent political progressive, affectionately known as
"Fred the Red," who had scorned the mainstream legal academic culture
when at the age of twenty-nine he wrote an article published in the *Virginia
Law Review* titled "Goodbye to Law Reviews," denouncing the whole law review system as flawed and hypocritical. Three years later, in 1939, Rodell published a tract titled *Woe unto You, Lawyers*, which took aim at the law
profession itself as no more than hired guns of the privileged, wielding legal
jargon as ammunition. For decades Rodell annoyed the Yale University
Corporation and administration by being a persistent gadfly, most infu-
riatingly when he canceled his classes during the Local 142 strike of November 1941.[24]

With the encouragement of Rodell and other leftists on the law school
faculty, Logue and his friends worked energetically to challenge the university not only on its labor practices, but also for its racial and religious
discrimination—through quotas in admissions and prejudices in faculty
hiring—and for its weak defense of academic freedom in the increasingly
anti-communist atmosphere of the 1940s. As its president Charles Seymour
famously said, "There will be no witch-hunts at Yale because there will be no
witches. We do not intend to hire Communists." Logue may have personally
disliked communism, but he adamantly rejected red-baiting of any kind.[25]

On and off campus during these immediate postwar years, Logue developed a political identity as a pro-labor liberal and a committed racial
integrationist. He founded a Yale chapter of the national American Veterans Committee (AVC), a progressive movement of veterans committed to
challenging the conservative American Legion and Veterans of Foreign
Wars. When the AVC went through a bruising battle between its liberal and
communist wings, Logue characteristically chose the anti-communist
side.[26] But opting for the more moderate path in the AVC did not stop Logue

from bravely championing the cause of racial integration, raising havoc at the slightest hint of discrimination or injustice. In fact, Logue's very first publication, in 1946, was a book review of Robert C. Weaver's *Negro Labor* in the left-wing magazine *The Progressive*, in which Logue called for government pressure to deliver "social justice" to African American workers, "*now*, not *soon*." That same year he shot off an angry letter of complaint to the editor of the left-leaning Catholic *Commonweal* magazine, protesting that the article "Veterans on Campus" did not adequately treat the special problems of black veterans.[27]

In Logue's academic program at Yale Law School, which was condensed into two years to advance returning vets more quickly, he focused on labor and legislative law but also gained exposure to urban policy from two teachers, Myres McDougal and Maurice Rotival. McDougal taught a required first-year course on real property, which he introduced by saying, "If you are interested in deed transfers, if you are interested in mortgages, that's not my course. You will learn that stuff in the first or second year at work out of law school. My interest is to convey how the law can achieve appropriate public policies in the utilization of real property."[28] McDougal, who also teamed up with the political scientist Harold Lasswell to train Yale Law School students to advocate for more democratic social policies, would himself become the first chair of the New Haven Redevelopment Authority when it was established in 1950 to enable the city to compete for funding newly available under the Federal Housing Act of 1949.[29] From Rotival, a charismatic and prominent modernist planner who was on the faculty at the Yale School of Art and Architecture and had developed a renewal plan for New Haven in the early 1940s, Logue learned the latest thinking about urban redevelopment.

By the time Ed Logue left New Haven in late fall 1947, he had developed a political disposition best described as being a rebel in the belly of the establishment beast. At this stage, and arguably for the rest of his life, Logue thrived as an insider comfortable in the bastions of power who then fought hard to improve what he judged were damaging deficiencies. His combative stance did not always sit well with others. An unidentified Yale

University official with whom Logue interacted over labor issues—possibly R. Carter Nyman, appointed as Yale's first personnel director for service and clerical staff in 1939—admitted when interviewed by the FBI in 1951 that he had no grounds to doubt Logue's loyalty to the United States but, back in 1941–42, he had been incensed that as a scholarship student Logue "was doing everything in his power to upset the administration of the school that was giving him the opportunity for an education." When budget cuts had required the laying off of maids at Yale, Logue apparently thought, to this individual's outrage, that "they should be continued on the pay roll because he, LOGUE, felt it was the University's moral obligation to look after them."[30]

Logue brought this reformist zeal to his personal life as well. He met his future wife, Margaret DeVane, daughter of the powerful Dean DeVane, soon after he returned to New Haven for law school. She was only a sophomore at Smith College at the time, though emotionally mature for her age and as politically liberal and idealistic as her future husband. They would marry in June 1947, when she still had a year of college to go, which did not please her parents. They were no happier when their future son-in-law called a strike of workers at Grace–New Haven Hospital (later renamed Yale–New Haven Hospital) in April 1947, while his future mother-in-law lay on an operating table inside undergoing a minor procedure.[31] Marriage to Margaret, the dean's daughter, may have ensconced Logue deeper in the Yale establishment, but it did little to suppress his appetite for rebellion. A favorite family story captured the armed truce on matters political between Ed Logue and Dean DeVane. One day when Logue was making calls to schedule a union meeting from the DeVanes' living room, the dean walked in and said, "You know, Ed, I like you and I can respect what you're doing, but please don't do it from my telephone."[32]

Logue would practice "tough love" throughout his life, holding the people and institutions he most valued to what he considered to be higher standards. This commitment to productive engagement, however contentious, made him increasingly impatient with the cynical aloofness often displayed by his mentor Fred Rodell and other political skeptics given more to critique than to action. Appropriately, one of Logue's favorite sayings was

"Keep the left hand high," referring to the boxer's training to be ever vigilant in fending off counterpunches. His longtime colleague Allan Talbot explained what Logue meant: "public service as a form of combat" was to be welcomed, not avoided.[33]

After graduating Yale Law in October 1947, Ed Logue pursued his ambition to practice labor law by moving back to his hometown of Philadelphia to apprentice with a well-respected practitioner, Morris H. Goldstein, who represented the International Union of Marine and Shipbuilding Workers of America–CIO and other CIO and AFL union locals in Philadelphia.[34] It would turn out that returning to Philadelphia offered Logue much more than training in labor law. Most importantly, it helped direct his attention to city building as a cornerstone of progressive politics.

Logue had already visited and drawn inspiration from the influential "Better Philadelphia Exhibition," which in 1947 the planners Edmund Bacon and Robert Mitchell and the architects Oskar Stonorov and Louis Kahn had installed downtown in the top two floors of Gimbels department store to engage the public in imagining what Philadelphia might look like by its three hundredth anniversary in 1982—"if you support city planning."[35] Logue had been one of almost four hundred thousand people to attend this exhibition, which aimed to be both educational and entertaining. Here he observed the "shadow of blight" spreading ominously over the heart of Philadelphia as a pendulum swung back and forth. He watched sections of Center City flip over on a huge thirty-by-fourteen-foot scale model, synchronized with a narration, to show proposed improvements by 1982. He walked around a life-size reconstruction of what the exhibition's creators considered a "dingy and overcrowded" block in South Philadelphia badly in need of rehabilitation. Here, at the top of the Gimbels flagship store, Logue and many others were introduced—through novel, World's Fair–type exhibits—to fundamental concepts that would underlie urban renewal for decades to come.[36] "It was magic," Logue still mused nostalgically five decades later.[37]

The political connections that Logue already had in Philadelphia made it easy for him to find organizations and individuals who shared his view of urban redevelopment as a promising new frontier for liberal experimentation. In no time, he was attending meetings of the Philadelphia Housing Association, the Citizens' Council on City Planning (CCCP), the Philadelphia branch of the Americans for Democratic Action (ADA), and the progressive wing of the Democratic Party. Here he served as a Democratic committeeman for his district and as a dedicated campaign worker in the exciting 1949 "revolution" in Philadelphia politics when the Democratic reformers Joseph Clark and Richardson Dilworth successfully wrestled the city out of the almost century-long stranglehold of the GOP machine.[38] In the late 1940s, Logue's Philadelphia became his schoolroom for early instruction in both physical and political renewal. And he was not alone in this regard. Many individuals were involved in both struggles, including Molly Yard, who was a leader of the Clark-Dilworth team, a board member of ADA, and the executive secretary of the CCCP. (She would cap her long career in progressive politics with the presidency of the National Organization for Women in 1987.) Housing low-income Philadelphians and redeveloping "blighted" neighborhoods stood high on the reformist Democratic Party agenda.

As Logue's fascination with urban policy grew, so, too, did his impatience with the daily tedium of practicing law. As he wrote to Fred Rodell in July 1948, "The law is a whore's trade. I don't want a nice law practice for anything but the income, and I'm a son of a bitch if I'll throw away ten or twenty years of my life building up an income." Looking back a quarter century later, he also recalled becoming frustrated with the limited reach of a union attorney: "I discovered that being a labor lawyer was serving the interests of people who are in the labor unions and labor movement, but you weren't going to run it . . . I knew . . . that that was not for me."[39]

Casting about for alternatives, he came up with two job offers in politics. One was working for the recently elected U.S. senator Hubert H. Humphrey, who had made himself a liberal hero by proposing an enlightened civil rights plank for the 1948 Democratic Party platform. His passionate plea that "the time has arrived in America for the Democratic Party to get out of the shadow of states' rights and to walk forthrightly into the bright sunshine of human rights" precipitated the walkout of infuriated Southern Dixiecrats from the Democratic Convention in Philadelphia, which Logue had attended as a local Democratic committeeman. The other offer came from the new Democratic governor of Connecticut, Chester Bowles, an advertising tycoon who had brilliantly masterminded a national system of price controls during World War II for the Roosevelt administration.[40] In accepting the Bowles offer, Logue, for the first but not the last time, chose a local or state position over a federal one, because he felt he could make a greater impact more quickly at this level.

Logue became Bowles's labor secretary, part of a liberal administration that swept into office determined to create a "Little New Deal" to reform Connecticut state government after a long Republican reign. Here Logue first tested the waters of government service as a more rewarding way to improve the world than practicing law—and he liked it. He became involved in many of Governor Bowles's socially progressive initiatives in civil rights and social welfare, including coping with an acute postwar housing shortage, which further awakened Logue to the looming urban crisis: "His housing program . . . was the most farsighted and the most effective in any state at that time," Logue later recalled.[41]

Partners in a whirlwind pace of work in Hartford, Ed Logue and Chester Bowles forged a warm friendship that would last for four decades, with Bowles serving as another father figure whose political commitment, social compassion, and moral integrity won Logue's admiration.[42] The voters of Connecticut proved less smitten with Bowles and his liberal agenda, however, and they booted out the governor and his idealistic young crew after a two-year term. Soon thereafter, President Harry S. Truman appointed the defeated Bowles as ambassador to India and Nepal, the third American to serve since India had declared its independence from the British Empire in 1947. Bowles invited Logue to come along as his special assistant, and by January 1952, Ed and Margaret Logue were on their way to New Delhi for about eighteen months, until the newly elected Republican president, Dwight D. Eisenhower, sent both Bowles and Logue packing in spring 1953.[43]

India beckoned as a great adventure to thirty-year-old Ed and twenty-five-year-old Margaret, the only damper being questions raised by the State

Department under its Loyalty and Security Program that red-flagged Ed and his brother John's political activities. Ed was singled out for his labor organizing; for signing petitions sponsored by suspected communist-front organizations, such as one protesting the threatened deportation of the radical longshoreman Harry Bridges; and for other political actions that the State Department deemed suspicious. Logue responded at length to the chair of the State Department's Loyalty Board, infuriated to be charged with harboring communist sympathies. He defended himself not by citing his history of anti-communism but rather by taking the more principled position of claiming that all his actions were legal and proper exercises of his constitutional rights. He reserved his greatest anger for the "improper and offensive" attention to his brother John, a lifelong adherent of the idealistic, anti-fascist, antiwar World Federalist Movement, founded in 1947 to promote more effective world governance than the fledgling United Nations appeared to promise: "It seems to me that my brother should have a right to know that sort of malicious gossip not only exists but has been dignified with such notice as this by his government."

Years later, Margaret would shudder at memories of the incident. "Ed was terribly upset by it. Our first taste of McCarthyism."[44] Logue would reflect at greater length on the damage wrought by McCarthyism as he journeyed back to the United States in summer 1953. He blamed President Truman and his secretary of state Dean Acheson's loyalty program, "which includes every last janitor and was never able to focus on the problem—nor to separate treason, subversion and actual disloyalty from either fuzzy thinking or radical thinking, the first of which cannot be helped and the second of which is in my opinion, so long as it is not unreasonable, subversive or disloyal, a useful thing to have in government, on the campus and elsewhere."[45]

RURAL INDIA NURTURES AN URBANIST

Many aspects of Logue's experience in India profoundly affected him. He and Bowles became only more committed to improving civil rights in the United States when faced with mounting Indian criticism of American racial discrimination, particularly from the influential Communist Party of India. "The number one question at any press conference or forum was, 'What about America's treatment of the Negro?'" bemoaned Ambassador Bowles.[46] In early 1953, Logue composed and began circulating widely a proposal he called "Is One Hundred Years Long Enough?" in which he idealistically called for a vigorous national commitment over the next ten years, in anticipation of the centennial of the Emancipation Proclamation, to acknowledging that "the Negro problem in America today is not a Negro problem. It is a white problem." He urged "mak[ing] democracy meaningful for thirteen million Americans who are not yet full partners in our society, . . . an opportunity to show our friends abroad, particularly the darker-skinned peoples in Asia and Africa, that American democracy is genuine and not the hollow mockery it sometimes seems when the color line is drawn." Logue tried—unsuccessfully—to interest liberal organizations such as the Ford Foundation and the United Auto Workers in sponsoring a national, community-based campaign aimed at white Americans, "to examine ourselves to see the way to progress and to move toward it."[47]

Most important for Logue's later career in city building were his observations of the community development work that the U.S. government and the Ford Foundation were supporting across India. Focused on modernizing rural villages, assumed to be the bedrock of traditional Indian society, the State Department's Point Four Program promoted a holistic approach to improving a village's built environment, social welfare, and technical knowledge. Named for the fourth point in President Truman's inaugural address of 1949, the program was born out of the fires of the Cold War to, in Truman's words, "make the benefits of our scientific advances and industrial progress available for the improvement and growth of underdeveloped areas," so that the "free peoples of the world, through their own efforts" would be able to "lighten their burdens."[48] New physical infrastructure such as wells, roads, schools, clinics, and community centers were to accompany reforms in land ownership and tenancy, public health, and education in everything from literacy to improved farming methods. Thirty-five thousand "village workers" trained by the Ford Foundation provided expertise on the ground. The goal was a more modern, self-sufficient, and, not least, democratic India—an India that could be counted on as a solid anti-communist American ally in Asia.[49]

Soon after Bowles and Logue arrived in New Delhi, they became intrigued with a demonstration project already under way at Etawah, in the nearby state of Uttar Pradesh. Originally conceived by the American architect and planner Albert Mayer in 1948 at the encouragement of Prime Minister Jawaharlal Nehru, this model site, covering ninety-seven villages, combined an anti-colonial Gandhian commitment to village survival with the extension service techniques (improved seeds, tools, fertilizer, livestock, irrigation) of the U.S. Department of Agriculture. In just three years, food production had increased by 50 percent and the project's reach had extended to over three hundred villages. A more urban pilot project—the Indian government's new cities of Faridabad and Nilokheri, intended for refugees of the partition of British India into the separate nations of Islamic Pakistan and Hindu India—likewise practiced an integrated approach, combining construction of new infrastructure with improved economic and social programs. Every family received a house with running water, factory jobs, and access to a modern hospital and schools.[50]

Bowles immediately went to work encouraging Prime Minister Nehru's government and his own to partner in a much more ambitious, national-level undertaking. On the anniversary of Mohandas K. Gandhi's birthday, October 2, 1952, Nehru proclaimed the launch of a nationwide program of community development with fifty-five projects, covering sixteen thousand villages and more than eleven million people. Although Nehru famously adhered to a policy of nonalignment in the raging Cold War, he framed this approach to eradicating village poverty through individual and community self-help as the next step in India's democratic revolution. Nehru's linkage of development and democracy pleased the Americans, who were themselves operating with assumptions rooted in the modernization theory popular at the time that economic progress would yield political democratization. Nehru's American partner hoped that the result of its investment in community development would be not only more plentiful harvests and higher living standards but also an India that would serve as a bulwark of the "free

Asia" it sought against the threat of communism. Looming over the American agenda was the recent "loss of China" to the communists, who had built their political base among the suffering peasants of China's villages.[51]

While analysts now may debate the virtues and effectiveness of the massive American-supported efforts in rural development, there is little doubt that Bowles, Logue, and their colleagues felt that they were successfully applying modern Western science and democratic values to previously "backward" and exploitative rural conditions. But they also recognized the need to proceed cautiously. Bowles took special care to argue—particularly within his own State Department—that community development must be viewed as an Indian program that relied on a "grassroots, village-by-village attack upon poverty, *directed by and participated in by the Indian people themselves*." It could not be a top-down, colonial-style American imposition, despite the reliance on expert advisers. As he warned his Republican successor as ambassador, George Allen, "Any effort by the Administration or Congress to tie political strings to Indian Aid or to force us to go out to 'claim credit' which really belongs to the Indians, will be disastrous." Bowles was right to worry. For many reasons—including the Indian government's reticence to enforce true land reform and wrest control from the landholding rural elites, and Point Four's failure to adequately engage ordinary Indians in decision-making—community development was never as popular among villagers as Bowles had hoped.[52]

This Indian experience would stay with Logue for many years. By 1955, when he was working in New Haven, Point Four would provide a model for the kind of integrated physical and social reconstruction he was promoting at home. "As you may have heard, I am busy in a New England version of community development," he wrote to Douglas Ensminger, the Ford Foundation's representative in New Delhi. The following year, he tried to recruit Ensminger to speak to a seminar on urban renewal that he was co-teaching at Yale, convinced of the relevance of the community development experience in India. And in 1957, Logue was still claiming that his Indian community development work remained "very pertinent to the work I am now doing," including its pitfalls. When he sought to give Bowles a balanced view of New Haven's progress in urban renewal, he honestly admitted, without detailed elaboration, "New Haven has a good program. If our present plans mature by the end of the year, we will be one of the half dozen best in the country. However, you remember Nilokheri and Faridabad and Etawah. Their problems reappear here in other forms. We certainly have not found the panacea."[53]

The community development work in India that so inspired Logue was the brainchild of a very distinctive—and politically progressive—group of social scientists and agricultural experts, which helped convince Logue of the worthiness of the undertaking. They had been agrarian Social Democrats within the New Deal's Department of Agriculture, supported by its reformist secretary Henry Wallace and clustered in its Bureau of Agricultural Economics, Farm Security Administration, and land-grant college training programs. There they promoted all kinds of innovative projects to help family farmers—and even in some cases sharecroppers and farm workers—cope with the Great Depression and the growing threat from corporate agriculture. During World War II and its immediate aftermath, they found their cooperative county planning committees, state agricultural extension services, and other grassroots participatory schemes—what they called a "cultural approach to extension" for valorizing farmers' long-standing customs and traditions—suddenly under attack in an increasingly anti-communist Congress. Despite the fact that most of them, like Logue and Bowles, condemned communism, they were pushed out of government service as too radical. The growth of international rural development work in the late 1940s and 1950s in what was then called "the third world"—sponsored by Point Four, the Ford and Rockefeller Foundations, and the United Nations Food and Agriculture Organization—provided these agricultural reformers with an opportunity to practice their integrated program of agricultural modernization and agrarian democratization overseas.[54]

Among this group, Logue particularly admired Wolf Ladejinsky, a Russian Jew who had immigrated to the United States, studied at Columbia, worked in the Department of Agriculture in Washington, and after World War II became a skilled strategist for pushing reluctant Asian governments to widen land ownership as the best defense against communism. The Logues met Ladejinsky when he came to India to advise on land reform, and they then visited him in Japan for three weeks as the last stop on their return trek through India, Ceylon (now Sri Lanka), Singapore, and Hong Kong. As the architect of sweeping land redistribution under the American Occupation, Ladejinsky surely conveyed to the Logues how the reconstruction of Japan was successfully integrating a reeducation in democracy with the physical rebuilding of a nation devastated in war. At the end of the trip Logue enthused in a letter to Ford's Ensminger back in New Delhi: "This country could be the proving ground for democracy in all of Asia."[55]

Later, in 1954 and again in 1956, Logue rallied to Ladejinsky's defense when he was red-baited. First, Ladejinsky was forced to leave Japan when the Republican secretary of agriculture deemed his Russian origins a security risk. Then, two years later, when he was working on land reform in South Vietnam, the State Department dismissed him for a technical conflict of interest, as he had bought stock in a Taiwanese company that had a contract with the U.S. government. Logue was convinced that Ladejinsky was being politically targeted and was outraged. As he wrote to another associate from his India days, "Wolf is the leading democratic expert in the world on land reform. There is a certain irony in the fact that his resignation was forced because he was the only American publicly known to have invested a private dollar in private enterprise in Chiang Kai-Shek's Formosa." Logue tried to get the Ford Foundation to hire Ladejinsky, but it wouldn't touch him. Nor would other American organizations fearful of a communist taint. From 1956 to 1961 Ladejinsky worked directly for the South Vietnamese government, until the Ford Foundation and later the World Bank finally took him on as a consultant.[56] Historians have recognized that New Deal agricultural reformers carried many of their domestically tested ideas abroad to the developing world as the United States expanded its sphere of influence during the Cold War. But they have barely begun to track individuals like Ed Logue—or his American embassy colleague Bernard Loshbough, who helped direct development programs in India and then returned to the

United States to work in housing and redevelopment in Washington, D.C., and Pittsburgh. They brought many of those ideas back home again and applied them to America's urban problems in the 1950s and 1960s. "It is ironic—perhaps shocking," Loshbough mused in 1962, "that an urbanite like myself had to travel 10,000 miles to India to learn that a homegrown product like agricultural extension can likely be adapted for effective use in urban centers." Loshbough would launch a highly regarded, Ford-funded "urban extension" program in Pittsburgh that mimicked its model in India, deploying "urban agents" to organize "self-help renewal" projects in four neighborhoods.[57] The roots of Logue's lifelong concern with improving America's urban environment likewise grew deep in the soil of rural India, where, in the early 1950s, a complex alliance of different sorts of modernizing progressives—nonaligned Indian leaders, reformist agricultural experts, and a New Deal–inspired American embassy staff serving under a committed liberal ambassador—all embraced village renewal as the key to India's success with democracy.

Logue brought the excitement of helping to build a new India to his work in New Haven. When the opportunity arose to join Lee in creating a model of urban renewal for the nation, he felt that he was undertaking his own version of Etawah, Faridabad, and Nilokheri. His urban upbringing in Philadelphia, his years as a rebel at Yale, his commitment to labor organizing, his aerial perspective as a bombardier, his civil rights activism, his legal training, his government service, and, most recently, his nurturing of a more modern and democratic India—each of these experiences shaped the Ed Logue who in January 1954 threw himself into the challenge of addressing the urban crisis in America through remaking his adopted hometown of New Haven.[58] In the years ahead, Logue and his partner Mayor Dick Lee devoted themselves to what became an enormously ambitious, expensive—and ultimately controversial—undertaking. Redeveloping New Haven would be one of the most important testing grounds for federal urban policy in the 1950s and 1960s, and it would catapult Lee and his first lieutenant Logue into national prominence.

MULTIPLE CRISES IN NEW HAVEN

The city that Ed and Margaret Logue returned to from New Delhi was actually made up of at least four distinct New Havens—and none were faring well. First, there was Yankee New Haven, centered on the city's impressive Green, dating back to the Puritan colony's seventeenth-century settlement and originally containing its marketplace, burying ground, and meetinghouse. Later, it provided an anchor for Yale College's development directly to the west after its founding in 1701. By the Federal Period of the late eighteenth and early nineteenth centuries, the Green had become one of the finest public squares in the country, graced with three venerable Protestant churches built between 1812 and 1815 and lined with majestic elm trees that gave New Haven the moniker of "Elm City." But by the time of Lee's ascension to the mayoralty in 1954, the neighboring, private Yale University was dwarfing the public Green in size and national prestige, the picturesque site where town and gown converged barely masking the growing tension between them.[59] There were numerous fault lines, but the widest was the financial burden the city bore from having so much of nonprofit Yale's property off the municipal tax rolls. As the university's ambitions grew after World War II, so, too, had its real estate holdings. Every new building constructed on a previously occupied site increased the tax load on nonexempt taxpayers. This problem had already become obvious to Logue as a law student years earlier. In 1946, he wrote to his future wife, Margaret, "While it is true that Yale does wonders for New Haven, it still uses up a lot of tax-free land. Aside from the med school, Yale seems to have had a pretty casual attitude toward the government and the welfare of New Haven."[60]

At the Green's southern border sat a busy downtown commercial district, choked with local as well as long-distance traffic in the days before the Connecticut Turnpike (I-95) bypassed the city in 1958. The intersection of Chapel and Church Streets was its heart: there stood two major department stores, Malley's and Shartenberg's. For years, New Haveners met up "at the clock at Malley's." A third department store, Gamble-Desmond, had closed in September 1953, right before Lee's election as mayor, a disturbing sign of the city's growing commercial troubles. Surrounding these department stores, which had anchored downtown since the nineteenth century, were a dozen blocks of theaters, offices, and storefronts in conditions ranging from modestly modernized to comfortably dowdy to downright dilapidated. They housed pharmacies, luncheonettes, barbershops, and haberdasheries; jewelry, camera, and novelty stores; bowling alleys and billiard halls; and smoke, hat, and dress shops. Inexpensive office space—a worrisome amount of it empty—was for rent upstairs. Almost all these downtown businesses were locally owned, many by ethnic New Haveners, particularly Jews, for whom opening a store offered a promising route to upward mobility. For decades, downtown New Haven had served as the commercial center not just of the city but also for the surrounding Southern Connecticut region. More and more, however, brand-new suburban shopping centers were encroaching on New Haven's retail dominance, with their easier car access and acres of free parking.

New Haven as a political and administrative headquarters dominated a third side of the Green. Here were impressive structures—a Victorian Gothic city hall, a colonnaded neoclassical post office, and courthouses, law offices, and banks associated with the city's status as the seat of New Haven County. Not far away, in the city's better-off neighborhoods, bankers and lawyers from prestigious local firms, many of them Yale Law graduates, occupied stately homes and supported exclusive social institutions such as the Graduate Club and the New Haven Lawn Club. Gradually, though, counties were declining in importance in Connecticut—their governments would be officially abolished in 1960. And the city's elite were increasingly becoming New Haveners by day and residents of leafy, prosperous suburban communities like Woodbridge, Orange, Madison, North Haven, Branford, Guilford, and Hamden by night, thereby shifting their identities and allegiances from city to suburb.

By the mid-1950s, New Haven's fourth dimension of factory districts and working-class communities was showing the greatest fragility of all. New Haven had thrived as a manufacturing center for many kinds of goods in the nineteenth century—carriages, hardware, clocks, rubber boots, garments, and munitions. Since 1870, the Winchester Repeating Arms Company, maker of military and sporting weaponry, had been the city's largest employer, operating a mammoth plant not far from Yale's gates. But now its declining payroll was causing alarm. Although 21,000 had worked there during World War I and 13,700 during World War II, by the 1950s the plant employed just 5,000.[61]

For over a century, immigrants had poured into New Haven to take up plentiful jobs in factories and with the city's important railroad and telephone networks. First came the Irish and Germans, followed by the Italians and Jews from Russia and Eastern Europe. They crowded initially into immigrant districts like the Oak Street tenement neighborhood bordering downtown, and then, once established, moved on to stable working-class communities such as Wooster Square, Dixwell, and Fair Haven, settling on streets lined with modest but respectable brick rowhouses and clapboarded three-deckers. By 1953, African Americans from the South made up the latest stream of migrants looking for high-wage manufacturing jobs. Unfortunately, they were arriving just as the city's industries drastically retrenched. The consolidation of corporations nationally made New Haven's factories less valued outposts of major firms, their dated physical plants too hemmed in to allow expansion, and cheaper nonunion labor more easily found elsewhere. Moreover, as flexible trucking transport replaced domestic rail and water shipping, New Haven's superb access to both mattered less. With more and more New Haveners struggling to make a living, housing and neighborhoods deteriorated, as landlords were less willing to invest in their properties. These and other changes over the course of the twentieth century destabilized industrial New Haven and increased the number of city residents—old and new—searching for good jobs and decent homes.

ELECTING DICK LEE AS MAYOR

Dick Lee's victory in 1953 over the Italian Republican mayor William Celentano, after two failed challenges in 1949 and 1951, validated his decision to make the city's creeping decline his poster cause. In the previous two elections, Lee had charged Celentano, a successful funeral home operator, with the usual failure to deliver quality services. Both candidates had worried about the city's deterioration, but their proposed remedies had skirted the larger structural problems with quick fixes—more parking here, a traffic light there, better street paving everywhere. The Yale Law School professor Eugene Rostow, who recruited Logue to help with Independents for Lee in 1953, said that despite Lee's Yale connections, "very few of us at the university took any interest in Dick's first two attempts to become mayor . . . They were really ordinary affairs with Dick hitting conventional themes of efficiency and honesty."[62] What made 1953 so different was that after his second defeat in 1951, Lee said, "I began to tie in all these ideas we'd been practicing in city planning for years in terms of the human benefits that a program like this could reap for a city . . . And I began to realize that while we had lots of people interested in doing something for the city they were all working at cross purposes. There was no unity of approach."[63]

The excitement generated by Lee's third campaign was palpable, even among the usually blasé and locally disinterested Yale community, who were more invested in electing the nationally prominent fellow "egghead" Adlai Stevenson as president than a provincial politician named Dick Lee as mayor. "When he campaigned to rebuild the city in 1953, he struck a responsive chord," Rostow continued. "He was attacking fundamental ills of our time, the moral, economic, and social injustice of the slum . . . I believe the reason he finally won in 1953 is that he abandoned the stock clichés of electioneering and allowed his morality to come through. Voters sense this in a candidate. From 1953 . . . the people have understood that Dick means it when he says that slums are evil and the city must be rebuilt. They sense his commitment."[64] Ed Logue was only one of many idealistic liberals who signed up to work for Lee.

Logue and his ilk had good reason to believe that Lee might be just the one to pull off an audacious plan to revitalize the city. Lee was born in New Haven to a working-class English and Irish family (though he played up the Irish side for its greater political rewards), attended local public schools, and soon after graduating high school in 1934 found jobs locally, first as a reporter for the *New Haven Journal-Courier*, then as a staff member of the Chamber of Commerce, and, beginning in 1944, as the head of Yale's news bureau. Each job embedded lower-class Lee in another bastion of elite power in the city—the Republican newspapers of the locally powerful Jackson family, the organized business community, and Yale University. By 1953, Lee had already served for fourteen years as a New Haven alderman representing the Irish Democratic Seventeenth Ward, where he had grown up. With a foot in both town and gown and with a new, potentially more civic-minded Yale president, A. Whitney Griswold, at the university's helm, Lee seemed well positioned to overcome the difficult relations of the past and lead a collaborative effort to turn around New Haven.

Conservatively dressed in tweeds, button-down collars, and bow ties from Fenn-Feinstein and J. Press—New Haven men's clothiers selling a new-fangled Ivy look—townie Lee appeared as Ivy as the bluest of Yalies as he ran from wake to bar mitzvah to League of Women Voters tea, solidifying his ties with the city's many communities.[65] Explained one of his aides,

> When he is with the Irish, his ethnic background comes out and he looks like he grew up in Dublin. When he is at the university, he is a wise old man. Over at the Chamber he is a shrewd capitalist. With the unions he is a cigar-chomping tough guy. He's not just "acting" either. He really knows how to talk the language of each of those groups.[66]

Lee's aide might have added that in the 1953 election, Lee even gained the trust of the local chapter of the NAACP, to which he promised more blacks on the police force and an end to police brutality.[67] Logue, too, noted how broadly Lee could communicate: "Dick was a marvel . . . There wasn't anything or anyone in that town he didn't know or couldn't get a read on in five minutes—a good natural politician."[68] It was Lee's commitment to bringing multiple New Haven voices to the table, in fact, that would later propel him to work closely with Logue to design an innovative structure of community consultation for urban renewal, the Citizens Action Commission (CAC).

Lee was the first of three elected officials to partner with Logue in his career of rebuilding cities, providing the political cover that made Logue's work possible. Mayor John Collins of Boston and Governor Nelson Rockefeller of New York would follow. All shared Logue's conviction that rebuilding a city physically was a necessary part of revitalizing its economy and offering greater opportunity to its residents. The partnership that Lee and Logue forged in New Haven thus became the template for the kind of collaboration that Logue would repeatedly seek in his career: a committed elected official to run political interference while he, the administrative expert supported by a nationally recruited professional staff, determined what to do and how to pay for it.

GETTING TO WORK

Within weeks of Lee's inauguration in January 1954, the mayor and Logue began scheming how to structure their redevelopment agenda to take the greatest possible advantage of new federal programs aimed at revitalizing cities. They were also determined that the mayor's office would fully control the effort—and not leave it to the appointed Redevelopment Agency Board, with its ties to party regulars, or the city's current staff, whom they considered ineffective.[69]

Logue and Lee's ability to use federal funding for New Haven's urban renewal was made possible by the Housing Acts of 1937, 1949, and 1954 and the Federal-Aid Highway Act of 1956. The programs those acts created—put most simply as public housing in 1937, urban redevelopment in 1949, urban renewal in 1954, and massive interstate-highway construction in 1956, for the first time prioritizing urban rather than rural roads—made federal dollars available to cities to address the deteriorated housing, economic disinvestment, and suburban competition that cities like New Haven faced all over the country.[70] Historians have emphasized how federal actions like the Homeowners Loan Corporation of the New Deal era, designed to help people hold on to their homes during the Depression, and the GI Bill of Rights of 1944, which created many new homeowners after World War II, encouraged the exodus of people and capital from cities to suburbs. Both made mortgage money available only in areas deemed sound investments for banks, essentially redlining urban areas considered poor risks because their populations were too immigrant, black, or poor. The Highway Act, with its forty-one-thousand-mile network, similarly channeled the white middle class into suburbia.

Often missing in this telling, however, is the extent to which the U.S. government, pressured by city leaders, also supported urban revitalization, albeit in careful consultation with powerful real estate interests. In "writing down"—in other words, subsidizing—the costs of demolishing or rehabilitating areas deemed "blighted" (assumed to be unredeemable), they hoped to attract a reluctant private sector to invest in city rebuilding. Money was also made available to address the serious shortage of decent housing resulting from the cumulative deprivations wrought by years of depression and war.

It came naturally to Logue and Lee, as committed New Deal Democrats, to turn to the federal government to foot the bill for much of New Haven's redevelopment. They saw urban decline as no different from many other social problems—such as unemployment, labor strife, or security in old age—that the federal government had proved itself capable of tackling. Sure, the private sector would ultimately have to step up and invest in projects for the long-term health of a city. But public authorities should be firmly in control. As Logue said often, "[You] can't trust the private sector to protect the public interest."[71] Logue despaired of the self-interest he saw rampant around him in New Haven. "One of the freedoms Americans seem to value most is the freedom to use or abuse their privately owned property as they see fit, . . . regardless of its impact on . . . neighbors, or the whole neighborhood, or indeed the whole city." The result: "The public interest is a lonely, unattended, silent spinster."[72]

The approach that the New Haven leaders crafted put Logue's redevelopment operation squarely in charge of making renewal plans and applying for government assistance, which was doled out with a required one-third local match to two-thirds federal funds. Logue and his team's genius became minimizing the city's outright cash contribution to the required local one-third by counting already funded capital expenditures for schools, roads, and parking garages.[73] During Lee's years in office, New Haven would attract more than $130 million in federal aid (more than $1 billion in today's dollars), which in 1965 put it sixth among the twelve cities receiving the largest federal renewal grants, the smallest city by far on that list. New Haven easily ranked first among the twelve for grant money per capita: $745.38 for each of its 152,000 people—almost three times what the next highest, Newark, received. While John Lindsay's New York City was enjoying the moniker "Fun City" in the 1960s, its smaller, northern neighbor would become known in some circles as "Fund City."[74]

Logue and Lee's early enthusiasm for federally funded urban renewal gave them an advantage over many other cities. By the mid-1950s, when they got started, Congress had authorized $500 million but only $74 million had as yet been claimed. Meanwhile, New Haven's leaders were already geared up, according to Allan Talbot, who worked in New Haven's redevelopment operation. "They would unroll their maps, gesture magnificently, argue persuasively, and feign a professional assurance that created the impression they were direct descendants of Baron Von Haussmann," the master builder of Paris in the 1860s.[75]

THE IMPORTANCE OF A TOTAL PLAN

Lee and Logue were able to move so quickly because they had no problem meeting the federal government's requirement that a general redevelopment plan be made and approved before funds would be authorized. New Haven's leaders themselves favored having what they called a "total plan." Lee had campaigned on the idea. Logue elaborated the concept in an article he wrote for *The New York Times Magazine* titled "Urban Ruin—or Urban Renewal?" Here he rejected the old-style "master plan" that, he argued, was nothing more than a theoretical exercise by planners who "dream[ed] what the good city ought to be . . . and never seemed to have a section on how they were to be carried out."[76] Logue scolded, "Too many theoretical planners preferred the applause of elegant critics to the earthier appreciation of politicians who had to try to carry out the plans and get re-elected, too." New Haven had already endured that fate. In 1910 the New Haven Civic Improvement Association had hired the nationally prominent landscape architect Frederick Law Olmsted, Jr., and the architect Cass Gilbert to prepare an elaborate plan for the future of the city. It sat ignored for forty years. By contrast, the new approach advocated by Lee and Logue required pragmatic and comprehensive planning that "focuses on the city as a whole and treats all urban problems as interrelated."[77] The resulting "total plan" would ensure a rational coherence unachievable through the all-too-common small, scattered projects initiated by individuals, private enterprise, real estate developers, and government.

Lee and Logue felt that while all cities would benefit from more ambitious planning, New Haven especially needed it, given its double jeopardy of a steep economic decline and a long history of political paralysis that stymied effective action. From the start, Lee was constrained by a difficult political structure: a weak mayor facing reelection every two years; an unwieldy board of thirty-three elected aldermen, one of the largest of such boards in the country; and a "hodgepodge of boards and commissions which made efficiency impossible," as *The Saturday Evening Post* put it in 1949.[78] Twice over his sixteen years as mayor, Lee mounted a campaign to revise the city's charter, and twice he failed. Frustration with New Haven politics more than anything else propelled him to set up Logue in early 1955 as an independent, powerful development administrator reporting directly to the mayor and insulated from New Haven's calcified politics as usual by the enormous amount of federal money underwriting urban renewal.

Lee's move now gave Logue official oversight of all departments concerned with physical development, which long had operated independently or antagonistically toward one another. These included the New Haven Redevelopment Agency, the City Plan Department, the Housing Authority, the Building Inspector, Traffic and Parking, and relevant aspects of the Health Department.[79] Under Logue, the now supreme New Haven Redevelopment Agency became so powerful that locals jokingly referred to it, in this height of the Cold War, as the "Kremlin," with Logue as "czar." Frank O'Brion, the banker who chaired the New Haven Redevelopment

Authority, endorsed the importance of having someone like Logue at the helm: "We learned—and all cities doing this will learn—that it is essential to have a co-ordinator with power to get things done."[80]

The plan for physically redeveloping New Haven that Lee and Logue embraced had originally been commissioned from Logue's former professor at Yale, the planner Maurice Rotival, in 1941. A version had been distributed publicly in 1944 as a thirty-four-page pamphlet titled *Tomorrow Is Here* (cleverly referencing Le Corbusier's 1929 classic, *The City of Tomorrow and Its Planning*) and then had been updated by Rotival several times, most recently in 1953. Rotival's plan called for reversing the city's declining fortunes by substantially remaking its physical face. Such a call for dramatic action fit well with the times. After all, a herculean full-blown American effort had recently won World War II for the United States' floundering allies, and now, after the war, the nation was helping reconstruct severely damaged European cities. Logue made the analogy explicit when he urged that "the Marshall Plan has much to teach us about how to approach slums and blight."[81]

Logue's admiration for Rotival as his Yale Law School teacher contributed to his enthusiasm for utilizing *Tomorrow Is Here* as the basis for the city's required general plan. Back then, Margaret Logue had even tagged along to watch Rotival's fabled performances. "He would say, 'You've got this going up the coast, and then you've this going up the river valley, and they all converge here, and'—drawing with different colored markers—'see what could be done if you could do this?'"[82] The Logues often brought home the large paper sketches that Rotival dashed off in his lectures to adorn their student-apartment walls. Lee and Logue had dismissed other planners as useless theoreticians, but they trusted Rotival, who, Logue explained, "was unusual, . . . a planner who had seen his plans happen."[83]

AUTOMOBILITY FOR ECONOMIC SURVIVAL

Rotival's vision for a new New Haven that inspired Lee and Logue was heavily influenced by the sensibilities of Le Corbusier, with whom he had collaborated in the 1930s in Algeria. The French-born planner and engineer

Rotival went on to work extensively in the developing world, including in such cities as Baghdad and Caracas, giving him a shared experience with Logue.[84] A basic principle that Rotival drew from this background, and which he applied to New Haven, was that the modern city must be oriented around the car. Accordingly, Rotival's plan for New Haven tied the city's future to updating its historic role as a distribution center: whereas once ships and rails had dispersed New Haven's industrial products, now highways must serve as the lifeblood of the city's future development as a trade and service center for the entire southern New England region. "Fresh, healthy arteries," Rotival told *Architectural Forum* in 1958, "encourage all kinds of tissue to grow around them," conveying optimism about the future with the same bodily metaphors that at the time commonly portrayed slums as "diseased" and cities as "dying."[85]

From his first 1941 plan, Rotival had proposed positioning New Haven at the crossroads of highways, many of which became realities: a shoreline interstate that would eventually be I-95; the Connector (Route 34) that would transport people from there to a reinvigorated downtown and link the harbor to the Green; a north-south roadway (Route 91) that would tie New Haven to points northward; and a "circumferential route" to move traffic efficiently around the city, which would inspire much discussion but never be built. When the dramatic swirls of blue ink on his plans became new highways, Rotival promised, office buildings and retail stores would follow as the engine rooms for the city's new postindustrial economy. And classic Corbusian "towers in the park" would replace blighted neighborhoods, housing residents in more modern and sanitary homes surrounded by green space.[86]

New Haven's urban renewers unambivalently embraced Rotival's recommendation to improve road access. In a 1959 article published in *Traffic Quarterly* Logue asked, "Is it possible for a city, any city, to make its peace with the automobile and to provide an environment where car and man can get along together?" He answered by arguing that highways were the only way to protect cities from being destroyed or abandoned by the large quantity of cars flooding the nation. Highway planning had been in the works in Connecticut since the 1930s, and after the interruption of depression and war, massive construction—like it or not—was remaking the landscape. By 1950, this tiny state had more roads per square mile than any other.[87] The hugely expensive Federal-Aid Highway Act of 1956 only further fed the state's appetite for roads, providing as it did federal subsidies covering 90 percent of construction costs. Lee, Logue, and Rotival concurred that New Haven's future health would depend on shrewdly locating the city in Connecticut's emerging highway grid. Staff worked hard negotiating with state road planners in Hartford to place I-95, Route 91, and the Connector in locations that they felt would best serve the city.

The urban renewers also pinned their hopes on improving car mobility within New Haven. They had inherited a city laid out in the eighteenth and early nineteenth centuries with narrow streets for horses and carriages, later adapted to electric streetcars. New Haven had only recently given up its trolleys, the last city in Connecticut to do so.[88] When automobiles had arrived on the scene in the first decades of the twentieth century, congestion mounted. Motivated by Rotival's plan, Lee and Logue called for wider, straighter, faster-moving main streets; abundant—preferably off-street—parking; and secondary streets dead-ended to discourage drivers from threading their way through residential neighborhoods. Jane Jacobs, critic though she was of urban renewal, praised New Haven's traffic commissioner William McGrath in her *Death and Life of Great American Cities* in 1961 as "brilliant" for schemes that she felt would ultimately favor more efficient bus and truck service over automobiles.[89] Lee and Logue had no doubts that New Haven would have to be more motor-friendly to survive. Lee promised his constituents, "We are taking the town out of the eighteenth century and projecting it into the twenty-first."[90]

Adjusting New Haven to the automobile shaped new residential projects as well, in hopes that mimicking aspects of car-oriented suburbia would increase their appeal. New luxury apartment towers in the Oak Street area close to downtown were publicized as "town living in the modern manner," which meant plenty of parking on the landscaped grounds.[91] John Johansen designed the Florence Virtue Homes in the African American neighborhood of Dixwell as a modernist, concrete-block, garden apartment–type complex with buildings occupying only 16 percent of its landscaped site.

Front and back yards for each townhouse, curvy roads, and off-street parking contributed to a suburban feel.[92] The adjacent Dixwell Plaza extended
the anti-urban, village-like concept with a new K–4 school topped by a bell
tower, a church, a library, and a community center. A shopping arcade that
resembled a suburban-strip shopping center with parking was intended to
serve as the new commercial heart of the Dixwell neighborhood.

Improving automobile access to downtown New Haven became the
linchpin of the strategy. Although retaining and recruiting manufacturers
who offered good jobs to New Haven's large working class were top priorities for the urban renewers, they recognized that they must simultaneously
nurture a postindustrial economy. Businesses specializing in communications, television, hospitals, and medical research, they hoped, would eventually put down roots alongside the Connector, with its easy access to
downtown, Yale, and the world outside via I-95. For now, their best hope lay
with capitalizing on the city's traditional importance as a market town for
the region and reinvigorating its retail appeal. If mass consumption was
driving prosperity in postwar America, then it should work in New Haven
as well.[93]

Before the 1940s, New Haven had faced little commercial competition
from the surrounding area. In fact, since the early twentieth century,
Malley's department store had promoted itself as "the Metropolitan Store of
Connecticut." A manager of a large downtown clothing store, J. Johnson &
Sons, remembered back to the 1920s, when "New Haven was the leading
city in the state for shopping" and "we used to wait for the buses to bring
people in from [the] towns."[94] But times were changing: Gamble-Desmond
department store shut its doors in 1953, Sears Roebuck left its cramped
downtown New Haven home for a spacious new branch store in suburban
Hamden in 1956, Stanley Dry Goods Co. and Shartenberg's department
store closed in 1962, and shopping centers popped up one after another in
suburbs surrounding the city. Downtown's share of all retail sales in the
New Haven metropolitan area plunged from 88 percent in 1948 to only
48 percent by 1963. In the first year after the twenty-nine-store Hamden
Plaza Shopping Center opened in 1955, it did $33 million in sales, most of it

diverted from New Haven stores. By 1960, a new ninety-store complex, the Connecticut Post Shopping Center, opened in Milford a few miles southwest of New Haven, convenient to both the new Connecticut Turnpike and the Merritt Parkway. A smaller development would soon follow to the east. And Hamden Plaza to the north was doubling in size.[95] The City of New Haven was fast losing shoppers to fierce competition from its own suburbs.

But what really set off alarm bells was learning from a Louis Harris survey that Logue secretly commissioned in 1956 that not only were a growing number of suburbanites shunning downtown New Haven, but also city residents were increasingly patronizing the new suburban shopping centers. Forty percent of the respondents said they visited the central business district (CBD) less often than they used to, while only 12 percent claimed to go more frequently. Fifty-six percent testified to doing more shopping in nearby Hamden. They cited congested streets, inadequate parking, and old-fashioned stores as their reasons for heading out of town—not downtown—to shop.[96] A decline in downtown customers meant both lower profits for retailers and fewer tax dollars for the city, whether from falling downtown property values or, even worse, empty stores. By the mid-1950s, 17 percent of the floor space in the area that would become the Church Street Project, a modern retail center, was already vacant. Although the CBD made up less than 1 percent of the city's total land area, it contributed a quarter of all tax revenues. Continued retail deterioration, on top of the steady departure of manufacturing, would prove devastating to the city's coffers.[97]

Faced with this impending disaster, Lee and Logue hatched plans to demolish the three square blocks at the heart of downtown New Haven and replace them with the Church Street Project, consisting of new Malley's and Macy's department stores, the Chapel Square Mall with smaller specialty shops, and a huge attached parking garage. In many ways, it was an effort to beat the suburbs at their own game, to build a bigger, better "regional shopping center in the heart of the city," as Logue's office put it. The Redevelopment Agency carefully studied suburban shopping centers for models, going so far as taking staff on a field trip to Shoppers World in Framingham, Massachusetts. The goal was to introduce features into the

Church Street Project, such as interior walkways between the parking garage and stores, that made shopping in the city as comfortable—and safe—as shopping in the suburbs, particularly for women. One promotional brochure claimed that the shopper would be "protected from the elements wherever she may walk within the New Haven Center." Multiple images of a blond, middle-class consumer with shopping bag and purse in hand were superimposed on a baseball diamond–shape map of the New Haven metropolitan area, with all roads heading toward home plate.[98]

Prospective retail tenants confirmed that access to parking and the Connector mattered significantly in their decisions. Malley's, in fact, chose to move from its historic home facing the Green to a new location closer to the Connector and the new massive Temple Street Parking Garage. Macy's made it clear that it would use New Haven as a foothold for its planned expansion into the New England market only if its store enjoyed proximity to highways and parking. Soon after the garage was completed in 1963, Macy's officials congratulated Mayor Lee and acknowledged "the chief reason we are coming to New Haven is to tie into that structure." They also lauded the "spur connect[ing] the Connecticut Turnpike to the downtown section of New Haven" and "the ramps which lead directly to Macy's parking facilities." Jack I. Straus, chair of Macy's board, could not have been blunter: Macy's will go "where there is good ingress and egress to a city, plus inexpensive parking provided by municipally operated setups . . . We at Macy's will not build any store without this assurance."[99] Pressure was on closer to home as well. In a survey Lee commissioned of New Haven's voters before the November 1959 election, parking downtown emerged as their greatest concern.[100]

The importance that New Haven's postwar planners gave to the automobile was hardly surprising. Since the 1920s, depictions of what the city of the future would look like—in architectural circles as well as popular magazines and movies—centered on the wonders of the car. Le Corbusier famously imagined future urbanity as nodes on superhighways; drivers would speed from one "auto-port" of high-rise office towers or residential skyscrapers to another.[101] In the late 1930s, another prominent European modernist, Sigfried Giedion, argued that highways were "the new form of the city," requiring that "the actual structure of the city . . . be changed" to better suit the automobile. When, in the late 1950s—just as Lee and Logue were reinventing New Haven—the modernist architects Lucio Costa and Oscar Niemeyer had the opportunity to construct a new futurist city from scratch for Brazil's new capital of Brasilia, they designed it around two "radial arteries" to facilitate traffic flow that were lined with separate super-block sectors designated for civic life, commerce, and residences.[102] Even the utopian urbanism of homegrown American modernist Frank Lloyd Wright, Broadacre City, revolved around the automobile.[103]

Ordinary Americans encountered the same message that the future belonged to the car everywhere, but particularly at the enormously influential world's fairs mounted frequently during the interwar period in Chicago, San Diego, Dallas, and New York. These fairs introduced visitors to all forms of modernism—in architecture, industry, and domestic life—but the automobile took pride of place. Exhibitions, many sponsored by auto manufacturers eager to sell cars and, even more importantly, to sell Americans on the nation's need to invest heavily in massive highway construction, hammered home that the automobile was the key to social and economic progress. At the New York World's Fair of 1939–40, with its theme of "Building the World of Tomorrow," the biggest hit was the General Motors "Highways and Horizons" pavilion, featuring a sixteen-minute "Futurama" conveyor-belt ride. Twenty-eight thousand visitors a day peered down from moving armchairs onto a thirty-six-thousand-square-foot miniaturized model of the United States as imagined in 1960. In this America of tomorrow, multilane "Magic Motorways" traversed the landscape, safely accommodating automobile speeds up to a hundred miles an hour as they shot across elevated overpasses and wide-span suspension bridges, through rugged mountain passes, and around dramatic cloverleafs. Just to make sure they got the point, visitors received buttons reading "I Have Seen the Future" upon disembarking.[104] Given the persistent linkage of the car with progress, it was no wonder that a promotional brochure for Malley's new downtown New Haven store celebrated its proximity to the futuristic Connector with "We're a real Turnpike head-turner!"[105]

SEPARATING FUNCTIONS

Rotival's proposal for the physical renewal of New Haven introduced Lee and Logue to several other modernist planning principles, beyond the importance of accommodating the automobile. Among the most fundamental was the concept of separation of functions. As Rotival put it in *Tomorrow Is Here*, "Each section of the city would be defined so that housing will not interfere with industry, nor industry with the market, nor transportation with parks and playgrounds. Yet all are tied together so that each section operates efficiently."[106] Here was the city made up of parts of a well-calibrated machine that Logue had appreciated from his aerial perspective as a bombardier during World War II. With this ideal of separated functions in mind, the renewers targeted areas of mixed use—where residential, commercial, and light industrial overlapped—for renewal activity. In the immigrant gateway of Oak Street, the largely Italian Wooster Square, and the predominantly African American Dixwell, garment sweatshops or machine shops were often cheek by jowl with grocery stores or rows of tenement flats.

In these neighborhoods, Lee and Logue determined to separate uses, convinced that their proximity contributed to disorderly, run-down residential areas and overlooking how that mix might have kept them affordable. A disastrous fire in a Wooster Square garment factory in 1957, which killed fifteen people, helped the renewers make their case for the necessity of separating functions. When the developer of University Towers, the first high-rise apartment building slated for the Oak Street redevelopment area, tried to convince Lee and Logue to permit a supermarket and restaurant on-site, going so far as forwarding a newspaper article praising a Parisian-style eatery in a similar project in New York, Logue shot back, "Dear Pete, We love Paris, but we are not interested in a banquet facility for the University Towers area." They feared that any deviation from the purely residential character of this project could undermine the challenging task of selling apartments to middle-class New Haven residents already tempted by comfortable suburban living.[107]

The same commitment to dividing functions guided the relocation of the proposed north-south Route 91 so that it divided Wooster Square into a more purely residential quarter and an industrial district, which then was expanded to include a new 350-acre area named Long Wharf, built on reclaimed land along the harbor.[108] Long Wharf housed a new wholesale food distribution center, a modern reinvention of the outdoor street market that planners relocated from downtown. In the old market, just minutes from the stately Green, vendors had hawked fruits and vegetables from the open backs of trucks; butchers had weighed squawking poultry on open-air scales; and cars, trucks, handcarts, and shoppers all had competed for space on refuse-filled streets.[109] To those like Rotival, Lee, and Logue, who dreamed of a gleaming downtown New Haven, this market was an unfortunate vestige of a bygone era—inefficient, unsanitary, inaccessible to transportation, and an impediment to the retail and office development they considered more appropriate for an up-to-date CBD. Refrigerated units, well-ordered wholesalers' stalls, and ample parking away from downtown in Long Wharf seemed much more appealing.

Logue hoped that by consolidating industry and wholesale commerce at Long Wharf—convenient to I-95 and rail and water transport—the city's new industrial center would serve as a beacon attracting further investment and jobs. As a former labor man, Logue knew how dependent the city and its workers still were on industry. He watched with alarm how the proportion of New Haveners employed in manufacturing jobs was plummeting: 50 percent in 1950 and 31 percent in 1960; by 1971, it would be only 25 percent. If cities were to remain "the best sites for industry," Logue wrote in *The New York Times*, then their traditional attractions of "skilled workers" and "variety of suppliers and networks of communications and transportation" would not suffice. Cities must also encourage the replacement of "factory buildings which are obsolescent, or worse" with new-style, horizontally sprawling plants in proper industrial corridors, and not simply allow them to flee to the open stretches of suburbia. So it was considered a great victory when the Armstrong Rubber Company, Gant Shirtmakers, and C. W. Blakeslee, a long-time local manufacturer of pre-stressed concrete, all opened substantial new factories in the city's new Long Wharf industrial area.[110]

BUILDING MODERN

Although remaking the city to welcome cars and separate functions followed the rule book of modernist planning precepts, the third major goal of Lee and Logue's physical renewal of New Haven came more from their own inclinations than from Rotival's instruction. They decided that constructing architecturally modern buildings would send just the right message that New Haven was reinventing itself. Vincent Scully, a Yale architectural historian who was a native New Havener and later an apostle of postmodernism and a harsh critic of the city's urban renewal, recalled how around 1950 even he embraced modernism. "We wanted Modern Architecture. What did we mean by that? On the whole we meant that we wanted forms nobody had ever seen before . . . Somehow we wanted to wipe the present clean of the past, to sweep it pure of contaminating objects. Everything had to begin anew and be closed anew. We would brook no compromise."[111]

Modernism of the 1950s era fulfilled this ambition well, as one of its central tenets was that new standards of design were universally appropriate and superior to indigenous and historical styles. With their "curtain walls" of glass, shunning of ornament and other inessentials for a more austere "functionalism," and innovative use of steel, reinforced concrete, and other alternatives to the traditional building materials of wood, brick, and stone, modern structures worldwide would have more in common with one another than with their own particular local and national architectural traditions.[112] Scully connected New Haven's renewal to this larger modernist design project when he recalled, cynically in retrospect, that after Rotival returned to Yale from Caracas around 1950, he regularly encountered him at the college where they both were fellows: "He would often reappear in the common room after a long absence, rotund, genial, and well turned out, with the Legion of Honor in his buttonhole. I would normally say something like 'Ah, Maurice, where have you been?' and he would reply 'I have been planning—[pause]—Madagascar.' It was all very impressive and utterly destructive of places, and it achieved its full scope in the Redevelopment of New Haven."[113]

Making decisions about New Haven's architecture might well have reminded Logue of debates that had raged in India. Architects, employing an almost utopian, physical determinism, felt they could modernize the developing world through imposing "advanced" aesthetic concepts that would erase a more "primitive" or colonial past. So, for example, Le Corbusier's design for the new Punjabi capital of Chandigarh in India rejected Albert Mayer's original plan, which valorized indigenous materials and styles. Backed by the modernizer Nehru, who sought a city that expressed the nation's faith in the future, Le Corbusier insisted on "brut concrete" rather than local brick and stone and set out to expunge all references to Indian tradition, which Mayer had promoted as a way of being modern "without robbing the Indians of what is distinctly theirs."[114] Likewise, modern building in New Haven, the urban renewers thought, could help New Haven transcend its architectural—and thereby other sorts of—provincialism, so evident in the dreary, old-fashioned Victorian buildings and shabby storefronts downtown. Cutting-edge modern architecture would signal New Haven's embrace of the future as well as differentiate cosmopolitan New Haven from both middle-brow suburban Connecticut, overrun with ersatz colonial-style home building, and its rusting urban neighbor of Bridgeport.[115]

Lee and Logue also hoped that showcasing the work of prominent architects would lend prestige to New Haven's rebirth, particularly when combined with what was happening on Yale's campus, where President Griswold commissioned no fewer than twenty-six new buildings between 1951 and 1963.[116] As *Time* magazine noted, "In the past few years more advanced architecture has risen on Yale's 150 acres in New Haven, Conn., than in all of Manhattan." Rejecting traditional collegiate Gothic, *Time* continued, Griswold "turned to a number of the most lustrous and far-out contemporary master builders" who "adhered to no single style, only to the modern mood."[117] In particular, Griswold used modern architecture to mark Yale's newfound commitment to the future-oriented sciences, long an underfunded and underappreciated stepchild at a university with historic strength in the humanities.[118] Scully concurred that Griswold became "one of the greatest of architectural patrons" because "he built out of his own integral and long-standing passion to be modern."[119] Town and gown working together, the renewers thought, might put New Haven on the world's architectural map.

Lee and Logue came to their posts in 1954 already primed for modernist design because it fit well with their progressive cultural and political identities in the late 1940s and early 1950s. Ed and Margaret Logue had been attracted to modern styles when they fantasized in spring 1948 about furnishing their first apartment once Margaret graduated from Smith and joined Ed in Philadelphia. Margaret wrote to him excitedly about a feature she had read in *Life* magazine about homes by a modernist architect—"I want an Alden Dow house"—and a couple of weeks later, enthused, "I'm dying to be spending all our money getting some good furniture I can call ours. I want to go to the Museum of Modern Art before I get anything, 'cause I might get some good ideas there." A few days later she wrote that she was eager to "look into the all-modern furniture store." Margaret's keenness for modern design was interspersed in her letters with political commentary condemning racial segregation and endorsing liberal candidates in Smith's mock Democratic Party convention, indicating that all were a part of a consistent worldview. A year later, as Margaret contemplated their next move to Hartford, she wrote, "I'd love a Lustron home," referring to the innovative, prefabricated, porcelain-enameled steel houses developed to meet the housing crisis after World War II.[120]

Soon after the Logues returned to New Haven in 1953, they decided to build a new house in the modern style. They hired Chester Bowles's son Ches, who had recently graduated from the Yale School of Architecture, to design it. "We live in the only modern house in our part of town," Logue proudly reported to his Yale class secretary. A local paper described it as a "red-beamed, glass-walled house of somewhat Japanese design," and in fact many of its features were inspired by a Japanese home designed by the modernist architect Junzo Yoshimura that was exhibited at the Museum of Modern Art in 1953.[121] This was the first of three modern houses Ches Bowles would design for the Logues, the latter two built on Martha's Vineyard.

Lee brought a similar passion for modern design with him to the mayor's job. While working at Yale in the late 1940s, he did a part-time public relations stint for the Connecticut branch of the American Institute of Architects (AIA).[122] One of Lee's first symbolic acts upon becoming mayor was to redecorate his office in the modern style. He later urged the New Haven fire chief to put Danish modern furniture in purple and orange and bare concrete walls into his office in the new central fire station. The fire chief resisted, with, "Damn it, Mayor, the men will think I'm a fairy."[123]

Logue and Lee used modern design to make a cultural statement about themselves, and also about the city they were deeply engaged in revitalizing. Lee often bragged about the "panorama of greatest architects" who were remaking New Haven: "As we began to replace and rebuild after we had the blitz of demolition, I felt we were going to . . . rebuild our city once. We should build it [in] as beautiful a fashion as we could. And the answer to that was that we should get the best architects."[124] And indeed the New Haven lineup became a who's who of modernist designers, among them Edward Larrabee Barnes, Marcel Breuer, Gordon Bunshaft, John M. Johansen, Philip Johnson, Louis Kahn, Kevin Roche, Paul Rudolph, Eero Saarinen, Chloethiel Woodard Smith, and Mies van der Rohe.[125]

Despite their proclivity toward modernism, it took time for Lee and Logue to figure out how to incorporate good modern design into their urban renewal plans. Much of that learning happened on the job, often through disappointment. Their colleague Allan Talbot recalled how unhappy Lee and Logue were with the first buildings to go up alongside the Connector, particularly the prosaic, squat, ten-story, five-hundred-thousand-square-foot Southern New England Telephone Company headquarters. "During the construction phase, the project was a source of pride to the administration, but when the buildings were finished, their drab design and the generally sterile appearance of the new Oak Street [convinced] Lee and his staff . . . that more attention would have to be paid to design."[126] It was particularly humiliating to have the editor of *Architectural Forum* describe the telephone company building as "that great green hulk of a building which looks like it was designed by the janitor."[127] Lee also confided to close associates that the first two apartment towers on Oak Street were "the most God awful-looking things I ever laid eyes on."[128]

For his part, Logue was having deep reservations about the design of the Chapel Square Mall by summer 1958. He wrote to the developer Roger Stevens rather grandiosely that "the final reputation of the Stevens project as well as its commercial success will depend a good deal on the architectural quality of the finished product. The project will have a much greater impact on New Haven than even Rockefeller Center has on New York." When by mid-September he saw little improvement and had received a rebuke from the project's architects "that my staff was not competent to review and criticize their work," Logue insisted on hiring a design consultant for the city "who would assist with our review and who would be a man of such outstanding reputation that the question of our competence [to critique design work] could not be raised again."

After considering a wide range of prominent architects, including Norman Fletcher, Carl Koch, Eero Saarinen, Hugh Stubbins, Harry Weese, and Minoru Yamasaki, Logue settled on Paul Rudolph, whom he described as "young (39) and of a very flexible and practical temperament." This new chair of the Department of Architecture at Yale, Logue asserted, was not only "the best man in New Haven, but the best man in the United States."[129] It did not hurt that hiring Yale's Rudolph helped address—on paper if not in spirit, given Rudolph's national reputation—Lee's constant refrain, reinforced by pressure from Democratic Party regulars, to hire local (what he called "insiders") while still offering Logue the expertise of a prominent "outsider." Before Rudolph was chosen, Lee had instructed Logue: "I want you to employ a local architect as an associate on those Temple Street garages. I will not have it any other way . . . We are going to hire outside architectural firms—and I do approve this approach—to do the important architectural work on our projects, but we must have local firms."[130]

As design consultant to the Church Street Project, Rudolph made extensive plans and elevations, some of which influenced the final design.[131] The greatest prize he walked away with, however, was the commission to design the two-block-long, 1,300-car Temple Street Parking Garage, which has probably become his best-known urban renewal project. Margaret Logue recalled how excited Ed was about the distinctive—to his eye, almost sensual—

modernism of the garage. "He loved the line created and was excited by the beauty used in such a utilitarian way. That sort of structure was very unusual then."[132] *Architectural Forum* gave Rudolph's garage the imprimatur that Logue had hoped for when it devoted a six-page spread to its opening and proclaimed it "an enormous, unabashed piece of sculpture."[133] Similarly, *Vogue*'s feature on the garage and its architect—illustrated with a bird's-eye view of Rudolph standing confidently at military ease alongside a sports car on the garage's top deck—recognized the architectural sophistication the redevelopers sought.[134] Logue's experience in New Haven, working with Rudolph in particular, would encourage him to institutionalize professional design review by prominent architects thereafter in Boston and New York. Almost twenty years later, in 1972, Logue admitted, "I cringe every time I see it [the telephone company building]. But the memory of it has led me, over the years since its completion, to be appropriately demanding of good design when it hurts. That is the real test. Everybody . . . is for good design—until it hurts. It counts only when you insist on it all the way."[135]

Logue would develop strong relationships with many architects over his years in city building, some of whom—like Rudolph and Johansen from his New Haven days—he would employ repeatedly. But Ed Logue retained for life a special feeling for his first design partner, Paul Rudolph. Margaret Logue attributed their connection to "the chance occurrence of the two living in the same university community and sharing a focus on urban problems early in their careers and early in the recognition of urban decay."[136] Both Logue's and Rudolph's personal papers contained clippings about the other, suggesting that they kept track of their respective careers. At their last known public meeting, a conference at the New School in New York City titled "Rethinking Designs of the 60s," Logue acknowledged Rudolph with warm affection. "I had a long interest in design, but when I realized how ignorant I was, I called a friend, head of the Yale Architecture School, one Paul Rudolph. He is responsible for a lot of the sins I've committed I guess ever since."[137]

One of Rudolph's most important lessons for Logue was that modern structures should be of sufficient quality, scale, and grandeur to be considered monumental. Logue felt that Rudolph's garage qualified: "My friends like to rib me from time to time over my 'architectural monument' . . . dominating the Church Street project."[138] Rudolph himself considered his Temple Street Parking Garage a worthy civic gateway to a city being recalibrated to suit the automobile, a transformation he approved of.[139] The urban renewers also strove to give the full downtown an élan of monumentality. "The centers of our great cities are too often uninteresting," Logue lamented. "They lack the magic appeal of the western European cities. A city . . . must have a focus; it must have something that lifts the spirit."[140] Superblocks provided one common tool urban renewers used to achieve modernist monumentality. In merging small pieces of real estate into larger parcels conducive to big projects, planners encouraged long and broad avenues and large, open plazas for public space. Although critics would ultimately—and often rightfully—condemn superblocks for decreasing density and creating vacant and alienating urban space, in the 1950s they appealed to many planners as a way to break out of what they considered the confining grid of the nineteenth-century city and introduce more light, air, and grand scale into modern urbanity.[141]

Logue's dispute with the developer Roger Stevens over the Chapel Square Mall design partly revolved around Logue's desire to place monumental public space, not simply profitable commerce, at the heart of the rebuilt downtown. He wanted a setback at the corner of Church and Chapel and a pedestrian promenade with fountains, whereas Stevens resisted reducing rentable space, arguing that he needed every inch to make a profit on the city's high, at almost nineteen dollars per square foot, land cost. Ultimately, they compromised, and the city considered open spaces as non-income-producing public use, relieving Stevens of taxes and maintenance for them.[142] Creating impressive civic space would remain a top priority for Logue, evident a few years later when he put Government Center at the core of his downtown Boston renewal.

Modernist design also offered Logue a way of achieving the integration of new infrastructure and social improvement that had impressed him in the community development work he'd observed in India. This ambition can best be seen in the assault that Lee and Logue made on New Haven's poor-quality schools. Whenever Lee and Logue strategized about how best to thwart the suburban threat to New Haven, they fixed on the importance of improving the city's schools, which long had been underfunded, over-crowded, and physically deteriorated. Only two schools had been built in New Haven between 1920 and 1950, and many of the others bore the tell-tale signs of neglect.

A mounting exodus from the city's public schools had resulted. In 1959, one child out of five in New Haven attended private school—the wealthy in nonsectarian independent schools, the less-well-off in Catholic parochial schools. By 1964, one in four students was opting out.[143] Meanwhile, New Haven's suburbs were spending extravagantly on their schools, particularly for new construction, at a rate even faster than their enrollments were grow-ing. In a period when Branford's pupil population increased by 57 percent, its education expenditures went up by 291 percent; Milford's student enroll-ment soared by 115 percent, and its school budget by 440 percent.[144] Logue and Lee responded by launching a New Schools for New Haven initiative, which managed to construct twelve new schools, including two high schools, a replacement of about a third of the city's thirty-seven schools.[145] Logue's clever use of federal urban renewal funds made this massive overhaul pos-sible, as capital expenditures for school construction were counted as a non-cash credit toward fulfilling the required local contribution.

Most telling, however, was how the renewers used the opportunity to build new schools to innovate socially. For example, the Conté School in Wooster Square and the Hélène Grant School in Dixwell were experimen-tal "community schools" intended to serve neighborhood residents as well as schoolchildren during the long day and evening hours they stayed open. Both were designed by well-known architects—Conté by Gordon Bunshaft of Skidmore, Owings & Merrill; and Grant by John Johansen. The Conté School, which Logue considered "as fine as anything in the suburbs will offer," housed programs designed to benefit the entire Italian working-class community. In addition to the school, it included a senior citizens' center with card rooms and bocce courts, a branch library, social service offices, community meeting rooms, a swimming pool, and an auditorium. The K–4 Grant School in Johansen's Florence Virtue project received acclaim for its state-of-the-art design, with clusters of classrooms surrounding internal courts and a gardenlike central courtyard providing light to much of the school's interior. But the Grant School also had a social mandate to become a racially integrated school in a city that had few of them, an opening wedge into creating the racially mixed neighborhoods that Lee and Logue desired. An article in *Architectural Forum* in 1966, a year after the school opened, reported that the school "is as advanced in program as in design . . . The entire school has an atmosphere of experimentation." City officials considered the true test of its success that the white families moving into the neighboring Florence Virtue houses, who as a minority of residents had previously "talked about sending their children to private schools," were "now all enrolled at Grant for next fall."[146] In the years ahead, Logue would carry this awareness of the potential of school building for architectural and social innovation with him to Boston and then on to New York.

MODEL CITY ON DISPLAY

As early as 1958, thirty-four official delegations from cities all over the United States had trooped through New Haven to learn from its efforts in urban renewal. By 1966 that stream had become a "constant flow of engineers, planners, city officials, citizens and sociologists" from home and abroad who visited New Haven—more than any other city—"to see what can be accomplished when a full-scale attack on blight and poverty is undertaken," according to the newly created U.S. Department of Housing and Urban Development (HUD).[147] That same year, WNBC-TV broadcast a documentary titled *Connecticut Illustrated: A City Reborn*, celebrating "the spirit of New Haven," whose commitment to solving difficult urban problems has transformed it over the last ten years from one "choked with slums into a model *modern* city."[148]

Luminaries likewise gave their blessings. "New Haven is the greatest success story in the history of the world," proclaimed the U.S. secretary of labor Willard Wirtz rather hyperbolically. "I think New Haven is coming closest to our dream of a slumless city," echoed Robert C. Weaver, who was the first secretary of HUD—and the first African American presidential cabinet member in the United States.[149] Popular national magazines like *Time*, *Harper's*, *Life*, *Look*, and *The Saturday Evening Post* carried major features about how New Haven was miraculously reinventing itself—and these were only a small portion of the estimated 242 magazine articles and 8 books documenting the city's urban renewal by the late 1960s.[150] Awards mounted and praise reverberated everywhere, as the small, troubled city of New Haven, Connecticut, was touted as a significant site for innovation. Lee and Logue were particularly proud that when New Haven's example was acclaimed far beyond its borders, their achievements were understood to be much greater than the physical urban renewal visible to the eye.

2. Urban Renewal as a Liberal Project

R emaking New Haven with bricks and mortar, ambitious though it was, played only a part in Lee and Logue's approach to renewing their city. Three other commitments featured prominently. One they called "human renewal" for how it sought to attack the social problems of struggling New Haven residents caught in the city's economic decline. The second revolved around defining an appropriate relationship between government officials and the public to engage citizens democratically in urban renewal. And the third was their establishment of a new kind of urban administrator to oversee the renewal process, armed with professional expertise that would also affect how planners, architects, and developers participated in redevelopment. All three innovations expanded into the postwar-era commitments made during the New Deal and World War II to create a liberal welfare state suitable to the American context. As New Haven's leaders experimented with these new strategies for remaking New Haven socially and politically, as they had done with physical renewal, they promoted their city as "a national showcase" to which people "make pilgrimages . . . to see how it's done," according to *The New York Times*.[1]

HUMAN RENEWAL

Not long into his redevelopment work in New Haven, Logue became frustrated that New Haven's existing social agencies were not meeting the needs of the "multi-problem families," often minorities, that the Redevelopment Agency was encountering on a daily basis. So he invited an old acquaintance, Paul Ylvisaker of the Ford Foundation, to visit New Haven. Logue, who was home ill that day, said, "We sat outside at my house. I teased him about the fact that the Ford Foundation didn't know there were any blacks in America. He was somewhat startled and said that was absolutely not true. And I said, 'Well, you haven't got a single grant that has anything to do with black people in this report,'" referring to Ford's latest annual report.

Ylvisaker purportedly committed himself at that moment to what became the Gray Areas Program, ultimately established in New Haven and five other places.[2] This funding led to the creation in New Haven of a new social agency named Community Progress Inc., known locally as CPI, whose founding document, "Opening Opportunities," made the case for the necessity of interweaving social programs with infrastructural improvement, what Logue had observed with community development in India and had strived to achieve through school building in New Haven: "More and more the central cities of the metropolitan complexes are becoming places where much of the deprivation of our society is concentrated." It continued, "As New Haven has met the need for physical improvements in a manner as yet unequalled elsewhere, so also the city intends to tackle the social problems in a comprehensive manner."[3] Later, when some critics accused CPI of paternalism and ineffectiveness, in an effort to rid New Haven of poor people,

CPI's creators argued that, to the contrary, its very establishment testified to their commitment to improve poor New Haveners' lives, not remove them from the city.

Logue's version of the origins of CPI and Ford's Gray Areas Program more broadly may have exaggerated his own and New Haven's importance. In fact, Ylvisaker, a smart, charismatic, morally driven reformer, had been struggling for several years to figure out a way for Ford to intervene in the unfolding racial dimensions of the urban crisis despite the foundation board's reticence to address race outright. Most likely, Logue's clearly articulated desire for more comprehensive, better integrated social intervention into the lives of poor, often black, urban residents offered Ylvisaker a welcome opportunity.

New Haven's CPI would eventually spend $22 million, $5 million of it from Ford, most of the rest from the federal government, a collaboration that pleased Ford as evidence that the foundation's investment in "demonstration" was attracting additional support. At its peak, CPI would employ about three hundred workers. Experimenting with job training and placement, prekindergarten education, legal assistance, community schools and health centers, tutoring, adult literacy, juvenile delinquency prevention, and other programs, CPI was widely recognized as the incubator for many of the community action programs—such as the Job Corps, Head Start, and Neighborhood Legal Services—that would become signatures of President Lyndon Baines Johnson's (LBJ) national War on Poverty by the mid-1960s.

From its inception in 1962 until 1966, CPI was headed by Mitchell "Mike" Sviridoff, a pal of Logue's going back to his union-organizing days at Yale.[4] Born in the same working-class neighborhood of New Haven as Dick Lee, Sviridoff, like Lee, could not afford college upon graduating high school and so headed into the labor force, where he became a sheet metal worker on the assembly line of United Aircraft in Stratford, Connecticut. In no time, his reputation for being shrewd, pragmatic, and fair propelled him to head the United Auto Workers local. Within a few years he was president of the union statewide, and by age twenty-seven, president of the Connecticut Congress of Industrial Organizations, which in 1957 became a consolidated

AFL-CIO. Logue met Sviridoff when organizing workers at Yale, continued to collaborate with him while labor secretary to Governor Bowles, worked on voter registration for him in fall 1951 as he awaited his security clearance for India, and remained his friend and colleague throughout their prominent careers in urban affairs—Logue on the physical planning side, Sviridoff on the human services side. When New Haven first received Ford money to launch CPI, Sviridoff was off working for the Alliance for Progress, the U.S. State Department's new development program for Latin America. Convinced of Sviridoff's talent and deep social commitment, Logue proposed him for the CPI executive directorship.[5] Soon Sviridoff, like Logue and Rotival, was bringing experience in a third-world aid job to bear on solving the urban crisis in the first world.

Lee and Logue took great pride in the way CPI made New Haven's total planning even more comprehensive. When Lee appointed Sviridoff to New Haven's Board of Education, of which he soon became president, CPI became tied all the tighter to the mayor's overall reform efforts, making use of the city's community schools as outposts for delivering coordinated social services at the neighborhood level. Moreover, the renewers felt comfortable with CPI's approach of developing programs that helped clients overcome their personal problems—whether unemployment, illiteracy, or legal jeopardy. It fit well with their liberal ideology of maximizing individual opportunity, rather than transforming larger societal or economic structures. When Logue headed to Boston in 1961, he secured a promise from Ylvisaker to name Boston as another of the six sites to receive Ford's Gray Areas Program funding. Action for Boston Community Development (ABCD) was born as a close cousin to CPI, as Logue again aspired to weave physical and social renewal together.

PLURALIST DEMOCRATS

One of the greatest challenges New Haven urban renewers faced was finding a democratic way of implementing urban renewal that incorporated citizen input—valued by them as well as required by the federal government—without compromising the knowledge and authority of public officials. In New Haven, Logue would begin seeking what he considered an ideal balance, and it would remain a preoccupation throughout his career. Tellingly, by his next stop in Boston, he would arrive flaunting his signature slogan "planning with people."

Logue felt confident that he had long demonstrated a deep commitment to advancing democracy, in the United States and the world. It was omnipresent in his language and his goals, whether he was unionizing low-level Yale workers, fighting in World War II as a bombardier, organizing veterans for greater rights and benefits, working as a labor lawyer and Connecticut's labor secretary, helping a new Indian nation develop, promoting racial progress, or—now—redeveloping a city in crisis. All these efforts, he thought, fulfilled the political ideology that he had expressed to the State Department's Loyalty Board when he sought its approval to serve in India. Here Logue wrote that "every nation should have as its primary aim the development of conditions of life which will make it possible for every person living in that nation to achieve the maximum human dignity and individual fulfillment." He then described what he felt was the best route to achieving a democratic America: "I believe in a society which is pluralistic, . . . in which there are many centers of power."[6]

What Logue intimated here, and elaborated on during his years in New Haven, was a view of the world as divided between public and private interests, where the achievement of a more democratic and egalitarian American society lay in strengthening the public sector to mediate between diverse but often conflicting private interests. He felt that a redevelopment official like himself—independent, impartial, and public-spirited—had the responsibility to protect the public interest from entrenched politicians motivated by favoritism or private-sector actors pursuing their own self-interest.[7] Logue's like-minded successor as development administrator of New Haven, L. Thomas Appleby, and New Haven alderman William Lee Miller coauthored a piece in *The New York Times Magazine* in which they explained the danger of officials *not* actively protecting the public good from what today we would call narrow NIMBYism ("not in my backyard"): "What happens when a neighborhood says it wants no Negroes, no low income public housing, no site for a public high school? Sometimes that's exactly 'what the people in the area themselves want,' but it is . . . hard to work with on a community-wide basis."[8]

During the 1950s, as money was flowing abundantly from Washington to New Haven for federal urban renewal, the Yale political science professor Robert Dahl and his students decided to turn their city into a laboratory for confronting a key question facing Cold War America: How well was democracy functioning in the United States as it met challenges from communism and socialism? The result was Dahl's *Who Governs? Democracy and Power in an American City*, published in 1961, based on extensive interviews and other field study from 1957 to 1959. Two related works by Dahl's graduate students, who helped him with the research, appeared subsequently: Nelson Polsby's *Community Power and Political Theory* (1963) and Raymond Wolfinger's *The Politics of Progress* (1974).[9] Dahl and his students were engaged in a research project to test ideas about political elitism formulated by the Italian political theorists Gaetano Mosca and Vilfredo Pareto as well as the claims of the American sociologists C. Wright Mills and Floyd Hunter. Mills and Hunter had published books a few years earlier provocatively arguing that a small, cohesive, interlocking group of social, economic, and political elites had come to dominate American society and to exercise disproportionate and self-interested influence in decision-making.[10] They concluded that American democracy was not alive and well.

Dahl decided that the best way to investigate the validity of these arguments about the health of American democracy was to move beyond theory and observe practices on the ground—to track how decisions were made and who made them—in a high-stakes arena such as urban renewal, which was transforming his home base of New Haven at the time. He concluded that although clearly some people had more influence than others, the lack of a single homogeneous ruling elite undermined the claims of Mills and Hunter (and later G. William Domhoff, who would revive Hunter's analysis through his own investigation of New Haven in *Who Really Rules? New Haven and Community Power Reexamined*).[11] The dispersal of power through what Dahl labeled "pluralist democracy," which he insisted could be observed empirically, ensured that no small political or economic faction was all-powerful. *Who Governs?* would win the American Political Science Association's prestigious Woodrow Wilson Prize for the field's best book in 1962 and remains a classic. When Dahl died at the age of ninety-eight in February 2014, his *New York Times* obituary still described him as "his profession's most distinguished student of democratic government."[12]

Dahl and his students requested and received thorough cooperation from Mayor Lee and the redevelopment administrator Logue. Not only did they interview both Lee and Logue extensively, but Wolfinger also spent a year in city hall as a participant observer. From July 1957 through January 1958, he worked for Logue's agency. In February 1958, he moved next door to the mayor's office and spent the next five months watching Lee do his job. Throughout this period Wolfinger wrote detailed memos to Dahl, minutely dissecting how decisions were made, who influenced them, and how power was exercised in New Haven. Meanwhile, Dahl and Polsby were busy interviewing everyone involved in the city's activities, with particular attention to members of the Citizens Action Commission (CAC), the body the renewers created to engage a wide, bipartisan cross section of New Haven's citizens in their ambitious redevelopment plans. This advisory commission was, in Wolfinger's words, "designed to sell redevelopment to those groups that remained fairly aloof from redevelopment—professional men, middle-class do-gooders, liberals, and most important, big business— and to use their membership to lend an aura of prestige, nonpartisanship, and business community support to redevelopment."[13]

Dahl's pluralist analysis of urban renewal identified a complex collaboration between private and public interests. Private interests, he argued, were represented by the almost six hundred people involved in the CAC, including a high-powered executive committee and subsidiary action committees organized around problem areas: industrial and harbor development; the central business district; housing and slum clearance; health, welfare, recreation, and human relations; education; and the metropolitan New Haven region. Among these hundreds of participants were leading bankers

and businessmen, but also representatives of labor unions, civic associations, ethnic and racial organizations, and charities. The public interest, in
contrast, was embodied in the elected mayor and his administrators under
Logue, who managed the process from plan to implementation in what Dahl
labeled an "executive-centered order."

As Dahl and his students explained the process, the CAC and its committees heard about the redevelopment plans as they progressed, but rarely
if ever initiated, opposed, or altered proposals brought before them by Lee
and Logue. They were too divided and uninformed for that. But they were
plenty capable of expressing "vigorous opposition [that] might easily have
blocked a proposal." CAC members thus "represented and reflected the main
sources of articulate opinion in the political spectrum of New Haven," exposing the mayor and his redevelopment team to public attitudes. As a result, "members of the administration shaped their proposals according to
what they expected would receive the full support of the CAC and therefore
of the political spectrum."[14] A "litmus test," was how Logue's deputy H. Ralph
Taylor described it to Dahl. Max Livingston, a well-respected member of the
CAC who represented New Haven's Jewish community, explained how he
thought the process worked: ideas that "originate with the professionals"
need to be "sold" to the CAC, and then the CAC "takes a very vital role in
organizing the opinion of the community . . . so they have the political backing that they need in order to become reality." Livingston gave an example
of how he helped save a recreation budget for Dixwell from aldermanic
cutting by "contacting every organization and every person we could think
of . . . who would get up on their feet" and defend the program.[15]

To Dahl's mind, this complex process proved that there was no power
elite pulling the strings of New Haven's government. Rather, Lee and Logue's
need to anticipate the diverse concerns of organized community interests
represented on the CAC created a feedback loop that put a pluralist form of
democracy in place as the city remade itself with federal assistance. The
CAC's *Third Annual Report* in 1957 described itself accordingly as a "grassroots organization" that included "a cross-section of community life with
all its rich and varied character . . . These representative men and women

are the democratic foundation on which the success of urban renewal in New Haven depends."[16] As a member of the CAC executive committee told Dahl, they aimed to embrace "every darn organization in the city, PTA, church, labor, whatever and build on that organizational structure which is the life blood of your community."[17] Time and again, the political scientists found the urban renewers consciously acting within a framework of representational democracy. Wolfinger, for example, quoted a "major city official" defending even backroom negotiations as democratic if a wide range of voices were at the table: "People say in a democracy that you should not be secretive in any of your public acts, but, you know, . . . you have to realize that if you talk about wholesale relocation and demolition, then the people . . . would be filled with fear and frustrations . . . So, all in all, . . . while we explore very carefully all the implications of every project, we have to be careful not to have any public discussion until we are absolutely satisfied that we are right."[18]

In addition to the CAC, Logue often pointed to other democratic vehicles that provided crucial feedback from the community to the Lee administration. He cited proudly the appointed neighborhood renewal committees that vetted plans and the frequent public hearings, required by federal law, where opponents could raise objections. In addition, he claimed, the mayoral election every two years served as a kind of referendum on urban renewal, where the strength of Lee's mandate usually fluctuated with the ups and downs of the program.[19] As Logue told Dahl and Polsby in 1957, "As far as I'm concerned, you don't make such a joke of the democratic process—debate and discuss and everything else and nothing gets accomplished . . . Two years is a hell of a short time and if people don't like it, they can throw us out."[20]

To gauge public opinion even more frequently, Logue and Lee commissioned Harris polls about every six months, with particular attention to urban renewal. They were pleased with a 1957 Harris survey that showed 71 percent of the sample approving of the Oak Street project and only 6 percent disapproving, and they expressed concern over a 1959 survey that showed Jewish support for Lee slipping slightly over the dislocation of downtown merchants—many of whom were Jews—despite the group's generally strong support for redevelopment.[21] Logue's Redevelopment Agency also opened a temporary "Progress Pavilion" at the intersection of Church and Chapel Streets with scale models, wall panels, and a comment book that Lee famously scrutinized in search of public feedback.[22] Whenever critics charged New Haven's urban renewal with being undemocratic, its leaders argued that they had plenty of evidence to the contrary. The CAC gave input regularly; rarely was much opposition expressed at public meetings; Lee continued to get reelected, often in landslides; and urban renewal polled well.[23]

THE LEE-LOGUE TEAM

If the CAC and other mechanisms provided a way for private interests to influence New Haven's urban renewal, then Lee and Logue meant for Logue's powerful, well-endowed New Haven Redevelopment Agency—staffed by well-trained, impartial experts—to embody the public interest. And the responsibility to protect that general good began at the top, with the city's leaders. The development administrator Logue and the mayor shared a common vision for what a rebuilt New Haven should look like and the self-confidence that they could make it happen, frequently contrasting themselves favorably to their predecessors, the redevelopment director Sam Spielvogel and Mayor William Celentano. Their conviction that they were on the right track was reinforced when someone of the stature of Hubert H. Humphrey—ex-mayor of Minneapolis, senator, and later vice president from 1965 to 1969—confided, "Dick, you son of a gun, what we really ought to do is let the other mayors spend a day with you and your staff. Then they'd understand what we mean by creative federalism."[24]

Despite their shared ambition for New Haven, Lee and Logue played very different roles in its renewal. Lee was the "outside guy," responsible for cultivating support on the streets of New Haven, in the Connecticut legislature, and in multiple arenas nationally. Amid his constant campaigning for mayor, he also flirted with seeking higher office, in particular a Senate seat that many thought was his for the asking. Labeled "the hottest piece of political real estate in Connecticut" by *The Hartford Courant*, Lee nonetheless decided that he couldn't abandon New Haven's renewal. Others speculated that he feared leaving the safe harbors of New Haven, where he had no worries about his lack of a college degree or being considered provincial.[25] But even as he stuck close to home, Lee modeled himself after the era's prototype of the young, liberal, charismatic, Irish Catholic politician: the senator and then, in 1961, president John Fitzgerald Kennedy (JFK), with whom he had a political friendship. Lee felt that he was making New Haven the testing ground for Kennedy's national urban agenda.[26]

Ever the public relations man, Lee promoted New Haven's renewal brazenly, labeling everything he did—as minor as installing a traffic light—as "another step in our city-wide renewal program." Probably his most notorious sales job for urban renewal was widely disseminating photographs that documented the rooting out of some ten thousand rats he claimed had infested the Oak Street tenements. For a number of years Lee had his own local television show, where he discussed redevelopment plans, and he penned a regular Sunday column in the *Bridgeport Herald*. Lee testified in support of urban renewal before countless congressional committees, lobbied hard for changes in federal regulations to benefit cities, and turned his presidency of the U.S. Conference of Mayors into a bully pulpit for the cause.[27] When President Johnson signed an act establishing the new cabinet-level agency of Housing and Urban Development, he respectfully sent Lee one of the pens he had used, with the note, "You deserve a lion's share of the credit for efforts leading to the new department which will advance the progress of our cities."[28]

Logue, as New Haven's development administrator, was the "inside guy" whose job it was to make sure that their grand plans got formulated, funded, and implemented. With Lee providing political protection, Logue prided himself on being an innovative, tough-minded, effective administrator who ran an exemplary Redevelopment Agency. This included working his staff hard. Sixty- to seventy-hour weeks, with frequent evenings and weekends spent at the office, were de rigueur, leaving Margaret and other wives to

complain at times about being redevelopment widows.[29] Many staff responded well to Logue's high expectations, throwing themselves into the
work and learning how to handle his intense, demanding style. Harold
"Hal" Grabino recalled his own quick learning curve. Soon after he started
working as general counsel at the Redevelopment Agency, he was assigned
to complete a form for the Feds outlining all the Connecticut statutes relevant to urban renewal. "I did a lousy job," he said. When he handed it to
Logue, Grabino recalled, "He lace[d] into me, like Logue always did . . . and
he was right. So I took it back, and I redid it. And from that day on, I resolved
that that is never going to happen again."[30] For young professionals like
Grabino, Ed Logue became a mentor and a model of a self-assured, rigorous,
and principled public servant who knew how to get results.

Some subordinates, however, chafed at Logue's demanding management style. Soon after Allan Talbot arrived to work in the New Haven Redevelopment Agency, one of his first assignments was to prepare the annual
report for the agency. "He looked at my script and kind of threw it away, and
said some expletive, that this was totally inadequate, and [when] I began to
question what was inadequate about it, he took the chair from behind his
desk and threw it across the room," Talbot said. "So the techniques were one
of . . . intimidation . . . [to accomplish] what he wanted."[31] In time, Talbot came
to admire Logue, but for some others, the dressing-downs still remained
open wounds years later.

Logue worked best with thick-skinned employees who not only could
tolerate a demanding boss but also were willing and able to challenge him.
The Ed Logue who had styled himself a rebel in the belly of the establishment beast during Yale days responded well to other rebels in his midst, as
long as they were smart, savvy, and hardworking. After Grabino's humiliating lesson in the need for higher standards, he recognized, "If you were
sure of yourself, and you held your ground, and you screamed back at him
and didn't let him get away with it, you became friends. And that's the way
it worked with Ed."[32] In fact, later, when Logue was building a new staff in
Boston, he became frustrated with how deferential people seemed. He
claimed to sorely miss his New Haven underling Tom Appleby's "Goddam-

mit, Logue, you're wrong! Fucking wrong, WRONG, WRONG!"[33] Logue's dep-
uty in New Haven, Ralph Taylor, said that Logue went so far as to tell him,
"You son-of-a-bitch, if you lose the courage to tell me I'm wrong and I'm crazy,
I'll fire you."[34]

Allan Talbot captured well the Jekyll-and-Hyde aspect of Ed Logue in
his appreciative account of the Lee administration, written after working
there for five years: "[Logue was] a man who over the years has been vari-
ously described as 'a brilliant programmer,' 'the toughest man in the world,'
'a perfectly charming man,' 'an egotistical S.O.B.,' [and] 'one of the best
friends I ever had." Talbot concluded, "Logue's drive has been his most sa-
lient characteristic in public service. It has given him the image of a tough,
able, and often abrasive man of action."[35] Years later, Grabino still cherished
Talbot's imaginary myth about Logue: "Every summer, Logue goes up to the
Vineyard, takes a shovel out of the house, and digs in the sand. And he pulls
up something called self-doubt. And he looks at it for a few minutes, and he
puts it back, and that's the end of it for a year. And that's Logue. No self-doubt
whatsoever."[36]

Over time, Lee and Logue developed a productive partnership as the
politician and the redevelopment expert, where the mayor depended on
Logue's administrative talents to sustain his high national profile. In the late
1950s, when the Eisenhower White House threatened drastic cuts in urban
renewal appropriations, Logue organized a delegation of mayors to meet
with the president; Lee served as the spokesman and funds were restored.
When Lee became chair of the Urban Renewal Committee of the American
Municipal Association (now the National League of Cities), Logue became
its secretary and expertly steered the committee. And in 1959–60, at the platform committee chair Chester Bowles's bidding, Logue did much of the work
on his and Lee's jointly drafted urban platform for the 1960 Democratic
Convention—"the first," he boasted, "that any party ever had"—and organized a high-profile conference in Pittsburgh to showcase JFK's urban
agenda.[37]

Although Logue and Lee respected each other's distinctive contributions and recognized that together they made a winning combination, they

nonetheless could clash—at times harshly. Most of Lee and Logue's spats were petty, quickly forgotten disturbances in their otherwise effective—often affectionate—teamwork. Occasionally, these disputes flared into larger confrontations. The major ones were usually rooted in their very different ways of operating. Logue, the brash, goal-oriented Yale lawyer, sometimes struck Lee as insufficiently concerned with process and the effect he was having on others, particularly people with votes, money, or influence. Lee was not alone in this view. Even Logue's good friend Sviridoff, in a confidential interview with Yale's Dahl, conveyed his own fear that should Lee run for the Senate, "This program is likely to fall flat on its face . . . Logue is a brilliant guy, in his field . . . but Logue primarily is a doer. And he has no feel for just getting along with people."[38] Deputy Taylor likewise noted the risks in his boss's confrontational style. "I think he is doing it quite deliberately and I'm also not sure he needs to . . . This is my major criticism of Ed . . . I think he gets as far being tough as you possibly can get. Where he really overdoes it is with the outside public." As a result, Taylor saw no obvious successor to Lee, should he seek higher office.[39]

But Lee deserved blame as well, in particular for sometimes banishing Logue to the back office without adequate authority and recognition. As Logue explained the occasional tension, "I was ready to be a behind-the-scenes fella. But there's a difference between being a subordinate and a slave. Once Dick cut the ground under me in public . . . When he did that, I just got up and quit."[40] On another occasion, Logue made a public statement, informed by a secret Louis Harris survey of shoppers, that downtown New Haven was dying and required drastic life support, including a new department store. Although there was nothing surprising about that observation, Logue's statement infuriated executives at Malley's, who had no interest in attracting a competitor. Lee unleashed his wrath on Logue.[41] A misstep like that only reinforced Lee's conviction that he couldn't trust Logue's political judgment. "If given a free rein, in a week he would be run out of town," Lee confided to Dahl's graduate student researcher Wolfinger.[42] Lee's mistrust of Logue's instincts fed his considerable, and by many accounts, annoying, micromanaging tendencies. In one instance, Lee insisted on spreading around

the lucrative title-search business arising out of the property transfers frequent in urban renewal. When Logue resisted the mayor's dictate, Lee
responded tartly, "For God's sake, . . . start to be a little political in your
thinking!" Logue stood his ground, however, insisting, "Too much of you and
too much of me has gone into this program, and too much more hard work
lies ahead for both you or me[,] for either of us, or our wives, to be content
with anything less than the best people or the best method."[43]

THE NEW ADMINISTRATIVE EXPERT

Lee may have had periodic frustrations with his partner Logue, but he knew
that New Haven's—and his own—success in urban renewal rested on Logue's
assuming a new kind of administrative responsibility called for in the post–
New Deal environment of expanding federal power. Success as this kind of
expert depended not on mastery of a narrowly defined body of technical information, as had often been the case earlier in the twentieth century during the Progressive Era. Instead, it required broad skills to negotiate for the
resources available to cities from Washington and to oversee a wide range
of initiatives on the ground. That expansive portfolio included urban planning, real estate, design, construction, management, legal matters, public
relations, community organizing, and lobbying. A lawyer like Logue, who
emerged from legal training at Yale schooled in public interest law (long before the term became popular in the 1970s) with a focus on labor and legislation, was particularly well suited to engage with the growing government
bureaucracy of postwar America. Moreover, Logue had gained valuable
administrative experience working with Chester Bowles in Hartford and
New Delhi.[44]

Ambassador Bowles, in writing his final evaluation of Logue before
he departed India in March 1953, gave him the highest rating possible
and predicted future success, praising him for just this kind of broad mastery: "By academic training and job experience, as well as by temperament
and inclination, Mr. Logue is what is known as a 'generalist' rather than a
'specialist' . . . He is able to get into any new problem without specialized

knowledge and sort out the difficulties and recommend solutions."[45] Three years later, after Logue was ensconced in his new role as development administrator in New Haven, he explained his new position to the Ford Foundation's Doug Ensminger back in New Delhi—no stranger himself to the important role that experts were playing in Indian development: "Urban redevelopment and renewal in itself is a rapidly expanding career. Some of the leading people in it come from a public housing background and some from an administrative or planning background. In the course of time a new kind of 'area generalist' skill will be built up around this program." He added, "My own work, which is coordinating that program with all the related activities, is an even newer field, and I think the most challenging of all."[46]

Other observers at the time shared Bowles and Logue's recognition that a new kind of "generalist" expert was needed to manage the growing investment the federal government was making in many realms of American society, the nation's cities included. Although enthusiasm about statist solutions to economic and social problems ebbed and flowed with the party in power— with some retrenching, for example, when the Republican Dwight D. Eisenhower took the reins from the Democrat Harry S. Truman—the trend was still upward, as Eisenhower expanded government authority more than popular stereotypes often have it.[47] A New Deal agency like the Tennessee Valley Authority, created in 1933 to deliver hydroelectric power to the rural, multistate Tennessee River region, and the postwar Atomic Energy Commission, established in 1947 to manage atomic energy for military and civilian uses, required broadly trained managerial experts to oversee these pioneering activities of the federal government. That David Lilienthal, trained as a lawyer, headed both these innovative agencies testified to the increasing priority put on administrative skill rather than narrowly defined technical knowledge.[48]

Beyond the New Deal, World War II was pivotal in promoting more rational state planning and the greater administrative expertise needed to implement it. When Hubert Humphrey laid out a liberal social agenda for the United States in his 1964 book, *War on Poverty*, he urged a transfer of "our genius for planning and management," which had successfully met wartime "attacks from both sides of the globe," to "fight[ing] the war on poverty."[49] Logue shared Humphrey's conviction. As early as 1948, in a speech to the American Veterans Committee, he said, "To some people, planning is a bogey; but all veterans are familiar with it; it operates on all levels, sometimes it is good and sometimes bad, but all of us would agree it is necessary."[50]

Even as it became clear that a new kind of expert was emerging to oversee urban redevelopment, there was no common label for this budding role. *Time* magazine dubbed the new field of redevelopment "urbanology," which the journalist Fred Powledge defined as dominated by "educated, articulate men, who had training or experience, or both, in . . . disciplines bordering on the behavioral sciences, along with an appreciation for and understanding of practical politics, [and] were able to accumulate and use power in rebuilding cities."[51]

Dahl's graduate student Wolfinger invented the term "cosmopolitan professionals" to describe the same group of urban administrators, stressing how a national mandate and professional standards protected them from local, sometimes provincial, and often resistant municipal authorities. Working "in policy areas where federal grants provide a substantial part of the budget and where skill and national connections are the most important factors in obtaining such aid," these professionals enjoyed a remarkable degree of professional and political independence, Wolfinger argued. "Because these officials are oriented toward goals, norms, and publics beyond their city of current employment, . . . they can bring to bear resources of power somewhat independent of the contending local interests that often stymie progress." Wolfinger optimistically predicted that the public, particularly the needy poor, would benefit from the emergence of this new, independent urban policy elite. "These officials have a vested interest in maximizing the programs for which they are responsible," he hypothesized. "The likelihood is that such expansion will be in the direction of more services for the poor, improvement of the social and physical environment, and attempts to impose a greater degree of rationality and coordination on market processes."[52] Mike Sviridoff claimed that he was looking for just such staff members, whom he labeled "urban generalists," when he hired for New Haven's CPI. "There was no one professional road leading to this new program," he explained.[53]

Logue was excited that in assembling his redevelopment staff in New Haven, he was helping to define a new profession. Without it, "slum-fighting," he suggested, would be like "leaving firefighting in Times Square to a company of volunteer firemen."[54] But even if this new administrative role required general rather than narrow technical expertise, its authority must still be based in science. The Rotival plan had set out three stages of block development, three categories of roadways, and recommendations presented with color-coded and graphically patterned prescriptive maps. New Haven's officials created additional measures of their own, such as categorizing all existing structures in New Haven as "Standard" or "Substandard" and identifying all "Families to be displaced by proposed improvements" as "Multi-member," "Single-member," or "Roomers." The Redevelopment Agency also developed twelve criteria through which to concretize the amorphous category of blight, including population change and density, intermixture of land uses, room overcrowding, age of housing, dwelling-unit conditions, average monthly rent, welfare cases, and juvenile and tax delinquency. The presence of more than six characteristics, they calculated, indicated blight.[55] Beyond providing intellectual ballast to their expertise, these quantifiable measurements had the benefit of helping Lee and Logue render potentially controversial determinations of blight—and any actions taken to remedy them—as based on indisputable facts.

Logue's first rule in assembling his team of experts was to recruit nationally, not draw from the ranks of locals burdened with loyalties more personal than professional. One of New Haven's top Democratic Party bosses in fact never forgave Logue for spurning his candidates. "Logue would infuriate us," he recalled bitterly. "I'd send a guy over to Redevelopment for a job . . . The least I expected was that Logue would talk to him. Instead, the guy would come back to me complaining, 'What the hell is this city coming to? That damned Logue just about threw me out of his office.'"[56] Once qualified staff were recruited, Logue determined to keep them outside of civil service, which further aggravated local politicians. He wanted the freedom to set salaries competitive nationally, not locally, and to hire and fire at will. By origin, civil service had aimed at insulating public employees from the old patronage politics of party machines. But in most American cities by the post–World War II era, the job security offered through civil service employment had become integral to the reward structure of entrenched local politicians.[57]

By separating urban renewal staffing from the city's business as usual, Logue was able to bring top talent into city employment. Many of his hires would continue working at this jurisdictional level, even as they jumped from one professional opportunity to another over their careers. None of Logue's cosmopolitan and well-educated lieutenants arrived intending to spend his life in New Haven, and none in the end did.[58] But in the Eisenhower era, when national politics seemed stodgy and uninspiring, ambitious young liberals like Logue and his staff felt that city-level government, under the guidance of a reform mayor like Lee and backed by federal bucks, held the most promise for progressive innovation.[59] That urban renewal attracted this kind of professional redevelopment staff came in for attack by the politically conservative magazine *Human Events* in its special issue "The Case Against Urban Renewal." The Republican challenger to Dick Lee in the 1961 mayoral election was approvingly quoted as saying, "A cult of planners and redevelopers has sprung up; they move from city to city, from one fat public job to another."[60]

In recruiting nationally, Logue favored individuals broadly educated in public policy or law who took political science, economics, and philosophy seriously.[61] Grabino recalled, "Logue liked lawyers. He liked the way they operated . . . Ed always thought that properly educated and trained lawyers were good people to move programs."[62] One account of Logue's staff meetings captured what Grabino meant, with Logue described as a "brilliant synthesizer" who took stock of all the myriad issues in his agency's complex projects and combined them seamlessly into a "brief" that he would dictate, leaving spaces for others to fill in details.[63]

It is worth noting that despite Jane Jacobs's skepticism about top-down planning in her *Death and Life of Great American Cities*, she shared Logue's embrace of an administrative structure for cities in which expert staff members had broad, general knowledge rather than narrowly defined and isolated responsibilities in what she called bureaucratic "labyrinths." She even singled out New Haven as a knowable "little city" where "agency heads and their staff . . . can be experts . . . in their own responsibilities, and . . . on the subject of New Haven itself." Having observed the operation in New Haven as she researched her book, Jacobs appreciated its staff's avoidance of the "fractionated empires" that she complained dominated many larger cities.[64]

Logue's second rule favored hiring individuals with a track record in the redevelopment field: "I wanted people who either had good experience on their own or had worked in organizations that were accomplishing something."[65] In the early years when urban renewal was a new frontier, people with experience drafting and implementing key national housing acts were particularly valuable to have on staff. They knew all the fine print in these complex laws as well as how best to negotiate with the Urban Renewal Administration bureaucracy. Speaking on the television news show *Meet the Press* in 1966, Lee attributed New Haven's success to just this advantage: "I have an outstanding staff . . . We study the programs as they evolve in Washington. We help develop this, support the legislation, and in some cases write the legislation, and then when the money is passed out we are there with a bushel basket."[66] New Haven's success at negotiating for Paul Rudolph's garage and Yale's payment for the site of two former high schools to count as noncash local contributions, thereby increasing the total federal allocation, resulted directly from the skillful maneuvering of Washington veterans in the New Haven Redevelopment Agency.[67]

Logue's first major hire once he became the head honcho was for an executive director of the Redevelopment Agency, essentially his deputy. Ralph Taylor had trained at the Littauer School of Public Administration at Harvard, become a Massachusetts state housing administrator and an expert on the Housing Act of 1949, and then directed the redevelopment program in Somerville, Massachusetts, overseeing one of the first urban redevelopment projects in the nation.[68] Dahl noted that Taylor "was considered a professional by his peers throughout the country, . . . including those in the federal agencies." With that experience, Taylor "knew how to cut through the interminable delays . . . and he exploited statutes and rules to gain concessions for New Haven."[69]

Another key appointment was Tom Appleby, also an experienced redevelopment professional. He had earned a master's in public administration from the University of Minnesota, had previously worked in Washington, D.C., and at the local level in Norfolk, Virginia, and had a prominent administrative pedigree and contacts as the son of Paul Appleby, whom Logue had met in India when, as the dean of Syracuse University's Maxwell School of Citizenship and Public Affairs (the nation's first school of public administration, established in 1927), Appleby consulted on improving Indian administrative structures. Grabino likewise arrived that first year, having been drawn to New Haven, like Logue was, by Yale Law School. Grabino excelled as a law student and after a few years, bored in private practice, leapt at the opportunity to join the new adventure of urban renewal, to which he had first been introduced in law school by Myres McDougal and Maurice Rotival, much as Logue had.[70]

Requesting salary raises for Taylor, Appleby, and Grabino, Logue told Lee, "I consider them a team, and as such the finest in the country, . . . without which New Haven would not have the renewal reputation it now enjoys."[71] For Logue, high-performing experts deserved recognition in salary, a "price tag" that would register in a national professional market. The same day he wrote to Lee requesting raises for these staff, he was forthright in making a request for himself: "You know better than anyone else whether I have performed above and beyond the call of duty or not in the last two years since my last raise, and in particular in the last year. You also know how completely anonymous it has all been. If you stay [not run for the Senate], I want the recognition as well as the income that a salary of $15,000 provides. If you go, I want to go out not just with a lot of personal satisfaction in what has been accomplished and deep regret that the job will be left undone, but with a $15,000 price tag." Mindful that Lee's own salary was $15,000, Logue astutely proposed a raise for the mayor to $17,500 or $20,000.[72]

Logue expected his team of experts to participate in the emerging national community of urban renewers in other ways than the scale of their salaries: to network with peers in other cities, to attend professional meetings, and in time to move on to become part of the diaspora of New Haven veterans who for years populated the American urban renewal field. Later, he was proud that his staff "had gone on to bigger and better things."[73] Taylor was typical. He was first interviewed for the New Haven job at a national meeting, he introduced Logue and Lee to other specialists working in Washington and elsewhere, and although he left New Haven after four years to work for a private developer active in urban redevelopment, he soon returned to public service to head LBJ's Model Cities Program, doling out federal money to former colleagues working in cities around the nation. Tom Appleby had a similar story. He took over Taylor's position upon the latter's departure from New Haven and then moved on to head the District of Columbia Redevelopment Land Agency, where he hired a number of veterans of New Haven as staff and consultants, Logue among the latter.

A CPI publication articulated well the renewers' aspiration not simply to *be* expert but also to *propagate* experts: "The large number who have moved on to much higher-paying positions in the Northeast and elsewhere in the nation" made New Haven "one of the nation's most important training grounds for leaders in antipoverty and urban-improvement programs."[74] For decades Logue kept in close contact with former colleagues, often hiring them back as consultants and staffers when he moved into a new position. Few people ever disappeared from Logue's Rolodex. Most made repeated entrances and exits throughout his half-century-long career in urban redevelopment, members of a professional club with life membership.

Nationally networked urban renewers also took their expertise abroad, often back to the developing world, where many had gained crucial experience early in their careers. In a fascinating lap to the international circulation of planning ideas, in 1957 Ford's Ensminger wrote from New Delhi requesting material on New Haven's urban renewal and informed Logue, "We are as you might guess wanting to experiment . . . by transferring the community development experience to the Urban Community." Ensminger announced that, partly inspired by American-style urban renewal, a team had begun to create a long-range plan for the redevelopment of the Delhi area. Seven months later, he reported, "We are making good progress on the Delhi Plan. It is hard, slow work. I'm more and more attracted to the importance of giving increasing attention to India's worsening urban slums."[75] In February 1958, Ensminger sent Logue an overview of the master plan for New Delhi, to be carried out in collaboration with the local planning body responsible for the Delhi metropolitan area. And who should emerge as the "overall consultant on the project" but Albert Mayer, creator of the Etawah village demonstration project ten years earlier and currently engaged in urban renewal work in the United States.

Two years later, Logue received an update on the Delhi project, "Report of a Pilot Project in Urban Community Development," which he circulated to his own staff in New Haven.[76] Soon after that, in 1961–62, Logue was invited by Ensminger to join the Ford Foundation Advisory Committee on Community Development for Calcutta, working with the Calcutta Metropolitan Planning Organization. His colleagues in this undertaking included none other than Bernard Loshbough, his associate from the Delhi embassy who was now doing urban renewal in Pittsburgh, and Paul Ylvisaker, Logue's Gray Areas partner. Ylvisaker later remarked on the usefulness of this Indian experience, as Calcutta was undergoing "simply an exaggerated version of the same thing our cities were going through."[77] Here, American practitioners like Logue and Ylvisaker were assuming the universality of their expertise in solving urban problems, one more piece of the modernization process that they also felt gave common shape to economic development, political democratization, and contemporary architecture worldwide.

THE MASCULINITY OF EXPERTISE

The network of urban redevelopment experts that Logue took such pride in nurturing was reinforced by a powerful culture of masculinity. Of course, men dominated most white-collar work in the 1950s and 1960s and gave it a male character, even when a few women were thrown into the mix, as was always the case in Logue's urban renewal agencies in New Haven, Boston, and New York. Mary Hommann, one of the few women working in the New Haven Redevelopment Agency, acknowledged the male dominance of the operation: "I will be forever grateful for his courage in taking a chance on me," she wrote to Margaret after Ed's death, "even though I was a woman, which in the days before the woman's movement could be a decided hand-icap."[78] The great excitement and high stakes of this new venture only in-tensified powerful male bonds. Laboring long hours together in the trenches of urban renewal, Logue and his staff developed a workplace esprit de corps organized around being men with a common purpose—and sometimes common enemies. "We were like the Marines getting to Iwo Jima," recalled Grabino. "We were fighting the battle. We were all committed."[79]

Other forms of male camaraderie imbued Redevelopment Agency cul-ture. The bottle of whiskey that came out of Logue's bottom desk drawer at the end of the day lubricated relationships among those who were invited to linger.[80] Lunch meetings, often spiced with martinis, took place at all-male clubs like Mory's and the Graduate Club in New Haven (and later at the Tavern Club in Boston and the Century Association in New York City). Not only did these sociable lunches deepen relationships among colleagues; they also helped the urban renewers rub shoulders as peers with other powerful men—the lawyers, journalists, businessmen, and government officials who likewise lunched at these clubs, strengthening ties with other members of the city's male elite.

When Logue negotiated the terms of his position in Boston in 1960–61, in fact, he made membership in the prestigious Tavern Club part of the pack-age. Rooming at the club before his family relocated, he very quickly met up with a circle of well-connected young men who grew to admire him. Her-bert Gleason, a lawyer active in civic affairs, remembered, "I was captivated by him. He was stylish, he was fun. If you could get him to come to your house for a party or a dinner, that was a coup." Martin Nolan, a reporter with *The Boston Globe*, recalled that Logue "was such a dashing figure. He had dark Irish good looks and people thought he was very . . . impressive."[81] Years later, in the 1980s, Richard Kahan, an influential player in New York City's public life, was shocked to find Ed Logue, whom he had long admired as a social progressive and considered his "affirmative action hero" for leadership in hiring minority contractors, outspokenly opposed to admitting women into New York's Century Association—until he realized how important male collegiality had proved throughout Logue's career.[82]

What weekend leisure existed in the pressure cooker of New Haven redevelopment also reinforced male bonds. The young couples whose husbands worked for Logue partied together frequently. In typical fifties fashion, the men and women tended to congregate separately, even though Margaret Logue was hardly the stereotypical housewife of the era. Despite giving birth to a second child in 1957, she continued to teach part-time and would go on to have a serious career in education, with the full support of her husband. The agency staff also played regular Saturday touch football games against the prominent New Haven law firm employed as outside counsel, which Logue was said to take "deadly seriously," rarely missing a game.[83]

Logue's competitiveness on the football field, as on tennis and squash courts, ruled the office as well, where he was convinced that a male-style combative culture improved the quality of performance. Talbot was not alone in recalling how Logue made work into a contest. He routinely gave the identical assignment to several staff at the same time. "The man coming up with the best answer got the prize of following through under the direct supervision of the boss."[84] Logue's own competitive nature was rarely out of view. He loved boasting of the city's redevelopment successes—saying that "New Haven received twice as much urban renewal funding per capita than any other American city" and that Church Street "is one of the boldest projects in the United States."[85] Harold "Harry" Wexler, an observant young staff member of the Redevelopment Agency in those years, noted that Ed and Mike Sviridoff were close, but at times rivals for Dick Lee's affection and attention.[86] *Life*, in a special issue on the American city in December 1965, appropriately titled its profile of Logue "Bold Boston Gladiator." *Newsweek* that same year described Logue as a "vigorous, forceful man who glories in political brawls and has a temper as quick as his smile." Logue's defense: "I express positions rather strongly when people who have said they're going to perform fail miserably . . . It's my job to be impatient."[87]

The template for many of Logue's interactions at work was relations between men in families—as brothers, fathers, and sons. As the oldest of four boys in his own fatherless family, Ed was used to the easy mix of companionship, competition, and loyalty among brothers—as well as being the one who ruled the roost of a gaggle of guys. When Logue and Lee were asked about what Lee called their "awful, just plain ferocious fights," where "I'd fire him once a week, sometimes twice," they both independently asserted, "We fought like brothers." They also schemed like brothers, observed by others as having "the air of two brothers talking of family affairs, even of family pranks, with Lee usually taking the position of the older boy who would be held responsible for whatever trouble they might get into."[88] They sulked like brothers, too. When Logue wanted the title of development administrator, considering it commensurate with his responsibilities, and Lee initially hesitated, Ed gave Dick the silent treatment until he relented.[89] And they teased each other like brothers. Wolfinger reported to Dahl that Lee "calls Ed Logue 'Fatty' whenever Ed comes in. I don't know if this is a friendly nickname or if it's some kind of compensation for feelings of Ed's intellectual superiority."[90] Margaret pointed out one more way that they behaved like brothers: "They'd defend each other against anybody."[91] Other relationships were similarly charged with expectations of fraternal loyalty. When Taylor announced that he was resigning to work for a private-sector housing developer, Logue was so hurt that he called Ralph a "traitor to the program" and barely talked to him before he departed.[92]

Logue aspired to be a paternal as well as fraternal presence. He called the young, idealistic men his agency attracted "my boys."[93] In his thirties during the New Haven years, he tended to hire males in their twenties, recently graduated from college, public policy, or law school and eager to save the endangered American city. The national prominence of New Haven's program ensured that there was no shortage of applicants. Talbot observed that the "screening process was long and personal, much more like being looked over for a fraternity than being interviewed for a job."[94] Robert Hazen was widely recognized as Logue's favorite "fair-haired boy," whom he took under his wing and treated like a son. After working for two summers for the New Haven Redevelopment Agency while a student at nearby Wesleyan University and again while getting his master's in public administration at the University of Michigan, Hazen was hired in an entry-level position. This assistant job seemed to bring with it the license to hang out a great deal at the Logues' house—"like a son or a younger brother," Margaret recalled.[95] Following a stint in the army, Hazen would follow Logue to Boston, because, "for Christ's sake," Logue told an annoyed Lee, "he grew up with me."[96] Hazen would work alongside Logue again in New York. In Boston, Logue would hire a young architect right out of Harvard named Theodore Liebman, whom he would eventually make chief architect in New York. Liebman admired Logue as a mentor—"I did not want to disappoint him. And I thought we were doing god's work"—but more than that, he came to love him as "a surrogate father."[97]

The list could go on of impressionable young men attracted to the oftentimes gruff and demanding, but also inspiring and caring, Ed Logue. Taylor remembered with a chuckle how Ed's boys "all modeled themselves after Logue." He was particularly amused at Grabino, "this bright young guy," who became a miniature Ed "without the maturity of judgment. Grabino is truculent for the sake of being truculent. Ed is truculent when he wants to achieve an objective."[98] Howard Moskof (Yale Law '59) admitted his own susceptibility. He "caught the disease" of urban renewal after a lunch with Grabino and Logue—"two arrogant sons-of-bitches"—and before very long had joined the team, becoming "just like them—everyone became clones of Logue."[99]

New Haven urban renewal was not exceptional in its masculine culture. Urban renewal in many cities was associated with a strong male figure, whether Pittsburgh's David Lawrence, Newark's Louis Danzig, San Francisco's Justin Herman, Philadelphia's Edmund Bacon, or, the most overbearing of them all, New York's Robert Moses. This male culture of urban renewal contrasted sharply with Progressivism, which took on a strong female character through the imprint of social reformers and so-called urban housekeepers such as Jane Addams, Florence Kelley, and Lillian Wald, to name only the most prominent.[100] Whereas the female Progressives lobbied for new protective legislation for workers, particularly women and children, and organized female consumers to boycott goods produced under exploitative conditions, the male urban renewers controlled large amounts of money and used it to rebuild cities on a massive scale. Some architectural critics have taken the analysis even further and argued that the aesthetics of urban renewal carried the stamp of this male-dominated culture, with urban renewers like Lee and Logue attracted to a hard-edged, high-rise, brutalist modernist architecture that celebrated Cold War virility.[101] Even without taking that leap, it is possible to say that urban renewal was nourished in a male culture of expertise and sociability that encouraged big men to build big structures with big ambitions. This was not a world that welcomed women.

Mayor Lee appreciatively described his Citizens Action Commission, with its several hundred community members, in similar manly terms:

> We've got the biggest muscles, the biggest set of muscles in New Haven on the top C.A.C. . . . They're muscular because they control wealth, they're muscular because they control industries, represent banks. They're muscular because they head up labor. They're muscular because they represent the intellectual portions of the community. They're muscular because they're articulate, because they're respectable, because of their financial power, and because of the accumulation of prestige which they have built up over the years as individuals in all kinds of causes, whether United Fund, Red Cross, or whatever.[102]

As for Logue's team of urban experts back at the office, the fraternal intensity of the workplace, when combined with their nationally oriented professional identity, served to set them apart from other New Haven municipal employees as well as from the ordinary citizens in the neighborhoods they set out to improve—a divide that would ultimately jeopardize their cause.

THE CHANGING ROLE OF SPECIALIZED EXPERTS

With Logue and his staff considering themselves generalist experts, more specialized tasks in urban renewal were left to technical experts with mastery of specific forms of knowledge, such as planners, architects, and real estate developers. Much the way community development administrators like Doug Ensminger and Bernard Loshbough had recruited skilled technicians to work at the village level in India, broadly trained urban renewal professionals looked to those with more focused expertise and experience for help. The rise of powerful development administrators in this new era of federal urban renewal would change the nature of these other professions, as well as how they related to one another, constructing a new hierarchy of practitioners.

The power struggle between Logue as redevelopment administrator and the planners, architects, and developers he depended on shaped the reconstruction of downtown New Haven. In 1957, Taylor explained bluntly to Dahl that in the planning of the all-important Church Street Project, "the power on this whole thing is Ed."[103] Logue's assertion of authority over the centerpiece of New Haven's urban renewal effort marginalized city planners most of all, including Rotival. Employed on contract, Rotival griped about being brought in "piece-meal, on 'whistle-stop' commitments, mostly as an 'atelier' working from day-to-day," not doing the "general planning for which our firm is best known, and in which we have made the greatest contribution . . . both in the United States and abroad."[104] Logue had a ready answer. He sent Rotival a memorandum with the subject line "Your time and how you spend it?" which said bluntly, "It seems to me that your talents are not best employed in attending meetings and in concerning yourself with various administrative matters. We regard you as one of the greatest planners in all the world and one of the most experienced. That is why we are proud to have you working on this project. However, you are not an administrator skilled in the ins and outs of American bureaucracy at the local, state, and national levels and we did not retain you for this purpose." With a final slash of his sword, Logue closed, "If you stick to your job of planning and designing and leave the red tape to the rest of us, we will all get farther faster."[105] Lee concurred. He told *Architectural Forum* that "too many communities have assumed that renewal is a job for planners alone." Lee continued that the program is so "unbelievably complicated" that it calls for the most skilled administrators."[106]

The planning profession had emerged in the early decades of the twentieth century when urban residents and their local governments wanted more control over how their mushrooming cities were developing. Planners' role was strengthened when the crucial tool of zoning was upheld in 1926 by the United States Supreme Court in *Village of Euclid* v. *Ambler Realty*, which confirmed localities' constitutional authority to regulate private property in the broad public interest. The New Deal accelerated planning activity, but it was really the needs of World War II and the postwar boom that transformed a half-hearted, often Chamber of Commerce–dominated operation in most cities and towns into the responsibility of full-time professionals, employed in municipal government and armed with new zoning ordinances.[107] In keeping with these trends, New Haven had established its City Plan Commission early, in 1913, but the body had neither funds nor a professional staff until 1941. Soon thereafter, at Alderman Lee's encouragement, Rotival was hired to develop the city's first comprehensive plan. By the time Lee and Logue took over in 1954, the city's planning department had become a legitimate part of New Haven's municipal government.[108] But although its size grew under Lee's administration, "it had a curiously subordinate place," Wolfinger observed, as the new "cosmopolitan professionals" were "much more self-consciously pragmatic and accustomed to negotiation rather than subordination in their dealings with politicians and businessmen."[109]

In the 1960s, some planners—unhappy with how their profession had become subservient to redevelopment—responded by reinventing themselves as advocates for ordinary residents in the urban renewal process, positioning themselves to explicitly challenge their cities' redevelopment programs. "Advocacy planners," they called themselves, adopting the language of Paul Davidoff, a professor of planning at the University of

Pennsylvania and then Hunter College, who published a call to arms in the field's major journal in 1965: "Advocacy and Pluralism in Planning."[110] Although advocacy planners sought to salvage their profession from what they considered the taint of autocratic redevelopment, they in their own way, and quite intentionally, contributed to the decline in the planning profession's authority as experts, as they aspired to become "value-driven" rather than "value-neutral" public advocates. Planners came out of the urban renewal era with more work than ever but with an altered professional standing—weaker politically in elite urban policy circles and with a radical wing that explicitly challenged practitioners' claim to expertise.[111] Logue summed it up with his characteristic bluntness: "Planners are losing ground. Responsibility for the replanning of cities is moving into the hands of administrators." And he added, wishfully perhaps, "Surprisingly, the planners do not seem to mind."[112]

Architects fared somewhat better in urban renewal's new pecking order of professions. Rudolph's Temple Street Parking Garage became one of Logue and Lee's prime showplaces, and they put great effort into attracting other prominent architects to redesign downtown. These designers benefited from the new government patronage made possible with urban renewal, even as their work was constrained by strict federal regulations and cost limitations. Architects were partners in urban renewal, designing civic buildings and defining the aesthetics of this ambitious national program. The architect Ieoh Ming "I. M." Pei, who worked as a staff architect on urban renewal projects for the developer William "Big Bill" Zeckendorf in the 1950s (and did the plan for Boston's Government Center for Logue soon after forming his own firm in the early 1960s), explained that "after the war, there was a very difficult time. What little building other than that [urban renewal] was probably all captured by S.O.M. [Skidmore, Owings & Merrill, a major American architecture firm] . . . Those of us who were outside had to pick up just these little things, you know, like urban redevelopment, low-cost housing."[113]

The architect John Johansen, whose Florence Virtue Homes and neighboring school and church in the Dixwell section of New Haven were among his first civic commissions, poignantly recounted how getting the New Haven job changed his career. "Until I was forty years old [1956], only commissions for houses came my way. I may say for the solace of the young struggling architects of any generation that this was a long wait. I was filled with impatience and envy of established architects . . . I was bitter and in despair observing the inequities of my profession." Johansen also recalled how competing for urban renewal work made him by necessity more innovative with materials: "In the desperate effort to gain commissions for public buildings, the young architect promises and somehow produces designs for buildings at dangerously low budgets. One inexpensive material with some substance is concrete block. In three early commissions in New Haven, Connecticut, . . . a community development was realized in concrete block."[114] Pei, too, claimed that he learned a lot from the ten years he spent doing urban renewal projects, particularly "how to work within the constraints of a budget and a lot of other design demands that were very concrete and specific."[115]

Urban renewal work in New Haven changed the career trajectory of Paul Rudolph as well, giving him just the patronage he sought to design monumental civic buildings. An analysis of his oeuvre demonstrates that his publicly funded commissions clustered between 1956 and 1975, almost the exact bookends of government investment in urban renewal. Of Rudolph's forty publicly funded commissions over this period, twelve occurred under the direct oversight of Logue and another five originated from officials with close ties to Logue, such as Dick Lee, Tom Appleby, and Ed Logue's brother Frank, who became mayor of New Haven in the 1970s, together totaling 43 percent of Rudolph's lifelong public work.[116]

But as much as architects may have benefited, they still found themselves subject to redevelopment administrators' tight control. When Logue got wind that the developers of the University Towers project on the fringe of downtown had dropped the prominent modernist architect Hugh Stubbins of Cambridge and were substituting the New York firm of Kelly & Grutzen, he was furious and, in the words of eyewitness Wolfinger, "in violent, abusive and obscene language" he told them that K&G would never participate in any redevelopment program in New Haven. They finally compromised on another New York firm, Kahn & Jacobs.[117] Not far from downtown, the architects of the Conté School in Wooster Square also had to contend with Logue's strong views. Natalie de Blois, who as a young architect at Skidmore, Owings & Merrill worked with Gordon Bunshaft on the school, recalled a dispute with Logue over the siting of the building. Bunshaft's original scheme, which set it back from the street, met with Logue's "No way are we going to have a plaza in front of that building." She went on, "So Gordon had to listen to him . . . Logue said there had to be a building right on the building line. It was very important. I certainly thought it was a valid criticism."[118]

Although some architects would complain he was intrusive, working with architects remained one of Logue's favorite activities throughout his long career in urban redevelopment. As Ted Liebman, a staff architect for Logue in Boston and New York, put it, "He loved them [the architects]. He loved the architectural meetings . . . The picture of him that I thought was the best [has him] looking at that model, [thinking] this is something that's going to be a new idea. And you see the twinkle in his eye."[119] Logue would in fact work with many of the major architects and firms on the East Coast, most of them well-established second-generation modernists. And he would return repeatedly to proven architectural veterans of urban renewal, who accepted his authority as development administrator. He even prided himself on contributing to architects' maturation. "There are many good architects who have talent, who have not had the opportunity to show it prominently enough. And there are other architects who haven't been stretched enough, and we help to provide a little of that stretching."[120]

Logue was not alone in arguing that architecture and urban renewal mutually benefited each other. Charles Abrams, chair of the City Planning Division at Columbia University and at times a critic of urban renewal, applauded "its serious effort . . . to make design a major factor," citing in particular the "plazas and pedestrian malls, underground parking, and a better relationship between buildings." He even singled out New Haven for incorporating "schools as part of the project" and successfully convincing factory owners "to employ architects" rather than depend "on stock plans pulled out of a file by an industrial engineer." Delighted that prominent architects were working in urban renewal all over the country, Abrams concluded that redevelopment was teaching cities and developers "to add design to profit criteria."[121]

Not everyone, however, praised the architectural legacy of urban renewal. Robert A. M. Stern, already embarked on his own path toward postmodernism, accused urban renewal's architects of promoting "heroic" designs rigidly loyal to orthodox modernist principles rather than more flexibly responding to how people actually used a particular urban site. He singled out "piazza compulsion," obsession with towers, and technologically innovative "mega-structures" as common mistakes.[122] Even the Temple Street Parking Garage, designed by Stern's Yale professor Paul Rudolph, came in for criticism, with its "arbitrary" and "unbending geometry of stacks of identically sized structural elements"—the aqueduct-inspired arches much beloved by Logue and Lee—and for an accommodation to the automobile that was "perhaps too expensive and too prominent."[123] Logue, Abrams, and many other patrons of the era's urban architecture would not have agreed with Stern's critique. But both champion Abrams and critic Stern recognized that architects played a major role in shaping the aesthetic vision behind the urban renewal program.

Downtown New Haven's renewal also sheds light on how a third group—real estate developers—was affected by the federal government's effort to incentivize them to invest time and treasure in American cities. Once an urban renewal agency had planned, cleared (using its powers of eminent domain if necessary), and prepared the site, it hired a developer to purchase the land at the much-reduced price made possible by government subsidies. From there the developer's job involved arranging financing, overseeing design and construction, getting extensive approvals, and marketing the project. Many of the problems that Logue and Lee encountered with the Church Street Project—beyond the gross mismatch between their grand ambition and the declining appeal of downtown New Haven—could be traced to the inexperience of the developer Roger Stevens, with whom they began meeting in 1955 and employed in 1957. Stevens was a real estate investor who had bought the Empire State Building and "flipped" it for a hefty profit. He had also produced Broadway shows, was a bigwig in the national Democratic Party, and had close connections with Yale. From 1953 to 1955, Stevens had tried—and eventually failed—to develop a proposal for the Prudential site in Boston that shared with the Church Street Project the ambition to combine the shopping ease of the suburban mall with the appeal of the big city. That this New York sophisticate was interested in redeveloping downtown New Haven thrilled Lee and Logue—until they discovered, too late, that there was an enormous difference between being a successful real estate entrepreneur and having the kind of know-how required of a real estate developer working within the complex environment of urban renewal.

Logue acknowledged to Eugene Rostow, dean of Yale Law School, what a big mistake he had made with Stevens. "At every turn we have either had to club him or solve his problems for him."[124] Later, he reflected, "We overestimated his ability as a developer. Roger was a strong real estate man, and there were few who could match his ability to buy existing buildings, rearranging the financing, and turning a profit. But developing raw land . . ." Yale would temporarily bail Stevens out with a $4.5 million loan to the Church Street Project, but by early 1964, having concluded that he "just got tired of throwing money away," Stevens recruited two construction companies to take over and bowed out.[125] Two years later, in the pages of *Fortune* magazine, Logue and Stevens were still duking it out. Stevens complained of the excessive government bureaucracy. "All along the line you had to have five commissioners approving everything . . . I wouldn't go into another urban-development deal for anything." Logue retorted acidly, "That's a very wise decision."[126]

Other developers working in downtown New Haven proved more successful at figuring out how to make urban renewal work for them. The developers of the University Towers apartments—a partnership of Jerome Lyle Rappaport and Theodore Shoolman of Boston and Seon Pierre Bonan of Connecticut and New York—succeeded because they understood subtleties in the rules of federal urban renewal. (That sophistication would also help them in Boston, where they developed the controversial Charles River Park luxury apartment complex on the site of the city's leveled West

End neighborhood.) In New Haven, Rappaport, Shoolman, and Bonan made use of an esoteric provision allowing developers to lease with an option to buy rather than purchase the land outright. This stipulation limited the Rappaport group's financial exposure and allowed it to outbid Yale for the University Towers site, upsetting Logue and Lee's expectation that Yale and the developer Stevens would win the auction required by the federal government.[127] On the morning of May 8, 1957, in the aldermanic chambers of New Haven's city hall, the bidding mounted to $1.15 million— far above the $700,000 minimum bid set and squeaking past Yale's authorized limit of $1.14 million. Logue described the startling turn of events as "an auction that would probably chill your soul." It certainly chilled the friendship between Dick Lee and the Yale president Whitney Griswold for a long while.[128]

Excluding developers from early planning gave enormous power to redevelopment agencies, but it also increased the risks of embarking on unfeasible projects and not attracting capable developers down the line. As late as 1971, a third of the projects begun nationally between 1950 and 1959 had property still lying empty; more than half of those started between 1960 and 1964 contained unsold land.[129] (These vacant plots, often left overgrown and strewn with junk, did little for urban renewal's reputation.) Like architects, those developers who did take on projects needed great skill and long patience to work with government agencies—and within government regulations and restricted budgets.

Ralph Taylor's decision to leave his job as executive director of redevelopment in New Haven to become CEO for the developer James H. Scheuer testified to the burgeoning opportunities urban renewal brought to those Taylor described as this "new breed of businessmen . . . concentrating on the redevelopment of areas cleared by the redevelopment process." Scheuer's impressive track record of promoting racial integration in housing attracted Taylor, and Taylor's considerable experience as a redevelopment official appealed to Scheuer. During the next seven years Scheuer and Taylor sponsored over $100 million worth (almost $835 million today) of housing in redevelopment areas, including a huge 1,739-unit project in Southwest Washington called Capital Park.

In 1964, Scheuer was elected to his first of thirteen terms as a liberal congressman from the Bronx, thereby moving from being a developer astute about federal legislation to a federal legislator. A couple of years later, Taylor followed Scheuer into government, becoming assistant secretary for model cities and governmental relations.[130] Scheuer's and Taylor's easy shuttling between the private and public sectors indicates how well integrated the realms of government and development became under federal urban renewal. Another developer, Pei's boss Zeckendorf, embraced redevelopment work once he figured out in 1952 "the kind of financing you can get—city and state participation and the [federal underwriting] of real estate," Pei recalled. "He told me that for the first time I don't need bankers! Uncle Sam's going to bank."[131]

In the reshuffling of professional standing that resulted from urban renewal, planners, architects, and developers all continued to play crucial roles, and many benefited greatly from lucrative opportunities. If scoring, one might say that architects and developers were winners as direct recipients of government largesse, planners much less so. "In the days of urban renewal," Pei confirmed, "the developer, the architect, and the city and state [were] really working together. I'm not saying all equal, but they are all important."[132] But there was no question that all three specialized experts became dependent on the favor of urban renewal administrators like Logue, who were empowered through federal funding, insulated from local politics as usual, and connected to peers nationally by strong professional ties.

Through the programs it initiated and the money it spent, federal urban renewal in cities like New Haven extended the liberal state-building of the Great Depression and World War II into the postwar era. In fact, one might say that, beginning as it did in the 1950s, urban renewal bridged the two great mid-twentieth-century reform movements of Franklin Roosevelt's New Deal and Lyndon Johnson's Great Society. A former New Haven alderman explained the work of the optimistic, "young, ambitious men" who undertook to renew New Haven in just this way. "They'd New-Dealed themselves to peace and prosperity, and they thought, 'Now we'll New-Deal ourselves to urban renewal.'"[133]

In time, the consequences—both positive and negative—of Logue and

Lee's approach to physical planning, social services, citizen engagement, and administrative strategy would become evident. Despite acknowledging some rough patches—such as a long-stalled Church Street Project—the renewers felt optimistic. Macy's finally signed on and the gaping big hole in downtown would soon open as the Chapel Square Mall. Neighborhood renewal was progressing in the Oak Street, Wooster Square, and Dixwell areas, and being planned elsewhere. Changes in the Housing Act of 1954 had enabled the renewal of Wooster Square to favor greater rehabilitation, not just demolition—proof, according to Logue, "that we could rebuild a neighborhood with a scalpel not a bulldozer."[134] As early as 1957, Logue wrote to Bowles, "Dick and I now believe that if the projected New Haven plan is carried through to completion, our position in 1976 will be stronger in every way than that of the suburbs around us."[135]

Nonetheless, there were frustrations. Limitations in the federal programs that enabled their work were one kind. The seemingly unstoppable flow of people and resources to the suburbs was another. But probably the most serious challenge of all came from within the New Haven community and grew out of a paradox at the heart of the renewers' own liberal agenda. Despite their conviction that what Dahl labeled pluralist democracy was a democratic mode of citizen engagement, their simultaneous championing of a new kind of urban professional to represent the public interest promoted a top-down structure that kept decision-making in the hands of experts. Although these experts may not have been the sort of dominating political elites whose existence Dahl set out to deny, they were elites of another sort. When Logue and his star staff, oriented toward the national stage, went to work, they inevitably measured their program's success by how it fared in grant competitions in Washington and in the eyes of their professional peers. How ordinary New Haveners felt inevitably mattered less. While residents grumbled some discontent throughout the 1950s, it would take until the 1960s—after Logue had left for Boston—for them to register the full extent of their complaints. By May 1967, when LBJ's National Commission on Urban Problems held hearings in New Haven, there was no mistaking the protests of at least some New Haveners.

Mayor Lee welcomed the commission hearings as a public relations opportunity for the city (and himself), a chance to show off spunky New Haven to a national audience. Logue would do the same in Boston when the commission visited there the next day. The commission members had put New Haven and Boston on their itinerary to pay homage to Lee and Logue's reputation over a dozen years for innovation in urban renewal and anti-poverty programs. But despite New Haven's finely tuned PR machinery, the commission hearings in New Haven developed in a way that the renewers hadn't planned on, making it clear that all was not quite so well. In fact, there was "trouble right here in Model City," to paraphrase the hit song "Ya Got Trouble," from a popular musical of the era, *The Music Man*. Invited speakers and commission members alike may have expected to watch a well-rehearsed performance of "New Haven, the Incubator of Urban Innovation," but they were in for a surprise. Uninvited speakers would demand the floor at those hearings to give voice to a very different perspective on New Haven's great experiment. Race, which had always been an issue in New Haven, now took center stage.

3. Trouble Right Here in Model City

On a Thursday morning, May 25, 1967, the well-known liberal Democrat and three-term Illinois senator Paul H. Douglas led his distinguished National Commission on Urban Problems to New Haven to hear testimony about how millions of federal dollars expended over more than a decade had underwritten a multifaceted attack on slums and poverty in this "model city." Chairman Douglas, a passionate advocate for urban America, and the commission's other members had been appointed by President Lyndon Baines Johnson the previous January. Their assignment: to investigate a myriad of technical problems faced by cities related to zoning and land use, building codes, taxation structures, and the like—pesky bugs in what Johnson believed was a challenging but improving urban picture, thanks to his ambitious Great Society programs. After undertaking inspections and hearings in twenty-two cities all over the United States, listening to testimony from hundreds of experts and ordinary citizens alike, the commission published its findings in December 1968 as *Building the American City*, accompanied by five volumes of hearing transcripts and numerous research reports. President Johnson was not pleased with the commission's conclusions. Months of bearing witness to the disturbing realities of urban life had led the commission to claim, "We found problems much worse, more widespread, and more explosive than any of us had thought." Its members decided that they "could not lose sight of the relationship between these technical matters and social problems. We agreed . . . not to duck the tough issues of poverty and race."

What Douglas's commission found was that despite Johnson's programs, American cities were in full-blown crisis, suffering most profoundly from an inadequate supply of decent, affordable housing, particularly the public housing that numerous housing acts had promised. Of the eight hundred thousand units authorized to be built in the six years after 1949, it had taken nearly two decades for only two-thirds to go up, more than half of them small apartments for the elderly. And the commission despaired of finding remedies, given the foot-dragging and timidity of the federal bureaucracy and Congress; antiquated fiscal structures overly dependent on the property tax; misconceived zoning and building codes; the ineffective and fragmented state of metropolitan government, ill-equipped to cope with the disturbing reality of "a white suburban noose" surrounding troubled, more racially diverse inner cities; stubborn, pernicious patterns of segregation within cities; and much more. Twenty-four months of immersion in the problems of urban America, punctuated by two rounds of urban riots—in the summer of 1967 and following Martin Luther King's assassination on April 4, 1968— had led the commission to see this urban crisis "as a test of our most fundamental beliefs," whether the nation had "faith in freedom, in equality, in justice, enough to make sacrifices in their cause." Exceeding President Johnson's charge, the commission called for even greater federal action, including the construction of more than two million housing units annually with half a million reserved for low- and moderate-income families. Johnson, incensed at what he perceived as an indictment of his substantial urban accomplishments, tried to suppress the report. Only Douglas's press savviness ensured its release in full.[1]

Many of these worrisome findings echoed what New Haven's officials had themselves experienced firsthand. In testifying to the commission, they certainly boasted of their achievements, but they also made no secret of the difficulties they had faced working within the limitations of federal urban renewal. In fact, they were likely among the commission's most outspoken tutors in what was going wrong, not just going right, in the nation's attack on its urban problems.[2]

New Haven was the second stop after Baltimore on the commission's ambitious fact-finding tour of American cities. Mayor Dick Lee, honored and excited to display the work that he and Ed Logue had masterminded in New Haven, decided to hold the hearing at one of the jewels of their urban renewal program, the modernist Conté Community School in the recently rehabilitated Wooster Square area. A lineup of practitioners and social scientists was carefully assembled to give expert testimony to the commission as it sought to learn from New Haven, because, as its chair explained, "This city illustrates as much, if not more, than any other city in the country, what an urban renewal program can do," and its mayor "has had more experience on the subject than almost any other man in the country." In traveling to New Haven, the commission's members flattered Mayor Lee that they were "bring[ing] the mountain to Mohammed."[3] The next day the commission would head north to Boston to hear from Logue about his work both there and earlier in New Haven, a city with which he was still very strongly identified. Acknowledging Logue's talents, Chairman Douglas complimented him as "one of the stars in the urban firmament, probably one of the most creative and original thinkers and also a man of action."[4]

The meeting began according to plan. Mayor Lee spoke first, submitting a written statement and then elaborating orally. He took pride in community schools like Conté, Community Progress Inc.'s pioneering Operation Head Start, the relocation of industry to Long Wharf, and the ongoing renewal of neighborhoods and downtown. But he also seized the opportunity to complain about imperfections in the federal laws and regulations that stymied his team. Three obstacles particularly frustrated them and, in turn, preoccupied the commission during this hearing: the inadequacy of federal funding available for renewal on the scale of New Haven's when there were so few local alternatives, the lack of sufficient provision for replacement housing for residents who were dislocated from redeveloped areas, and the difficulty of addressing the city's problems without having jurisdiction over the full metropolitan area.

Lee lost little time proclaiming, "We do not have . . . the kind of financial resources which we feel are necessary really to meet the programs on a broad enough basis." The lack of money for low-income housing and human resource programs was particularly galling when the need was so great and subsidies for agriculture and space exploration seemed to flow so generously.[5]

Lee and his colleagues depended so much on the Feds because they had few alternative sources of funding closer to home. Whereas the private sector had famously claimed to have orchestrated Pittsburgh's Renaissance through the corporate-dominated Allegheny Conference on Community Development, with minimal public expenditure, New Haven was smaller and enjoyed much less support from local business and industry. Lee and Logue had organized a field trip of two planeloads of New Haven's leaders to Pittsburgh in 1957 to show them how it had been done there, but New Haven (like most other American cities) could hardly rival Pittsburgh's extraordinary status as headquarters for Mellon Bank, U.S. Steel, Alcoa, Jones and Laughlin Steel, Pittsburgh Plate Glass, Westinghouse, and other major companies.[6]

In New Haven, as in many cities without deep-pocketed corporations or at least ones willing to empty them locally, the reality was quite different— and quite the opposite from what urban renewal's critics on the Left often charged: that the program was promoted by a "pro-growth coalition" uniting civic and corporate leaders in pursuit of their common interests in the urban economy, often at the expense of ordinary citizens.[7] That might have worked in wealthier places, but in New Haven and other struggling cities of the 1950s and 1960s, the challenge was simply to get businesses to care enough about revitalizing the city and not run for the exit.

Lee had learned this lesson early. When he campaigned for mayor in 1953, he promised to establish a Citizens Action Commission within sixty days of taking office. It took him nearly a year, because he had so much trouble finding someone willing to become chair. Typical, he said, was "one of the biggest men in the city" who had refused him so as not "to get tagged with a project that was so ethereal as to be doomed before it got off the ground."[8] The urban theorist Neil Brenner has argued persuasively, in fact, that the pro-growth coalition operated most importantly not on the municipal level, but rather on the national stage in promoting federal redevelopment legislation—what he calls the "national institutional envelope"—that protected large-scale corporate capital and put local political actors into "an iron cage of sorts" as they competed with other cities for private-sector investment.[9] Years later, Logue would reflect on the struggle to identify partners in the local business community: "Dick and I could never find standup businessmen in New Haven . . . They just weren't there."[10] When Jeanne Lowe published a comprehensive study of urban renewal in several cities, she particularly lamented the lack of initiative shown by New Haven's business community: "Almost everything of consequence that has taken place in New Haven in the past dozen years has been stimulated, put together and forwarded from City Hall, either directly or indirectly."[11] Aware of the private sector's reluctance, the Lee and Logue team tried knocking on the doors of nonprofit foundations. That led to important seed money from the Ford Foundation and small grants from the New Haven Foundation, but nothing on the scale of what they needed.

Local revenues were no more promising. The only major sources of income the city had were already fragile: property taxes and the sale of municipal bonds for capital improvements.[12] As New Haven's property values and population declined, sustaining property tax revenue became difficult. It didn't help that a third of all property in the city was tax-exempt, given Yale's extensive real estate holdings.[13] Lee hated to raise the tax rate to make up for the shortfall; that only encouraged more residents and businesses to flee—and cost him votes. Although he finally felt obligated to raise taxes in 1960 and 1962, he quickly reduced them in 1963. Lee preferred to raise tax assessments strategically on certain properties.[14]

The structure of taxation in Connecticut further constrained the city's revenue options. Although Governor Chester Bowles had courageously, to Logue's mind, tried in the late 1940s to repeal the sales tax and enact an income tax to increase state revenues and introduce more progressivity into how services were funded, it would take many more years, until 1991, for Connecticut to adopt an income tax.[15] At the time of the commission hearing in 1967, 75 percent of New Haven's revenue still came from the property tax.[16] With few alternatives, city officials promoted urban renewal as a way of increasing property tax revenue, even as they regretted their dependence on this tax.[17]

New Haven's reliance on federal funding required it to mold its programs to the laws' strict specifications, about which Lee also complained. When Lee and Logue came into office, the Federal Housing Act of 1949 was about to be amended as the Housing Act of 1954. Although the 1949 Act had promised to "remedy the serious housing shortage," the fine print about how that could be accomplished discouraged the public housing provided for in the 1937 Housing Act, written as it was with the blessing of a real estate industry wanting few public alternatives to the private market.[18] Lee and Logue were far from fans of public housing. Referring to Elm Haven Extension, a huge, high-rise public housing complex in Dixwell under way before he became mayor, Lee lamented that "public housing like that isolates people. You're a *project* family. Low-income public housing almost caused more problems than it solved. We are out of the business of that kind of concentration."[19] Logue would retain a similar dislike of public housing throughout his career, much preferring subsidized mixed-income projects.[20] But the two also recognized that in many cases—such as for African Americans and large families discriminated against in the private real estate market—public housing was the only option.

The 1954 Housing Act seemed to offer greater flexibility. Whereas its predecessor aimed redevelopment solely at "blighted" residential areas, stressed total clearance, and did not allow for the rehabilitation of existing buildings, this revised act made what was now labeled "urban renewal" more ambitious and varied. Lee and Logue took full advantage of the permission now to fund the redevelopment of "predominantly residential" areas, not just "solely residential" ones, such as New Haven's Church Street. They also embraced provisions permitting spot clearance for scattered site housing and, notably in Wooster Square, rehabilitation and stronger code-enforcement in older structures rather than requiring their replacement by new construction. In his testimony to the commission in Boston, Logue openly regretted the mistakes made during those early days of "bulldozer urban renewal that removed one population and replaced it with another." He assured the commission, "Let me just say we will never do that again," and promised that the sole high-rise housing being built in Boston was on the waterfront, where "the only creatures that are being displaced are fish."[21]

But even as the 1954 act broadened the scope of urban renewal to include downtowns like New Haven's, it also drew attention and resources away from the original, and still critical, goal of creating more affordable housing for low-income residents. Logue's difficulties providing decent relocation housing for those dislocated worsened as the building of low-income housing became a lower priority in federal urban renewal and harder to fund. Logue felt frustrated that the existing residential subsidies were so limited, primarily providing for elderly housing and moderate-income nonprofit co-ops.

Lee's second major complaint to the commission concerned this huge unmet need for replacement housing. He told them, "Relocation is our principal problem, not only residential or family relocation but also business relocation."[22] What Lee considered Logue's expert relocation operation too often met impossible obstacles.[23] Mike Sviridoff's wife, Doris, who served as deputy director of housing relocation, complained of difficulties like "having to deal with the same family now for the third time, because they'd be moved from Oak Street to the Hill, and from the Hill to some other declining neighborhood, and to not very good housing. But then the renewal program would enter that neighborhood."[24] Some of the problems came from

New Haven's redevelopers prioritizing other kinds of building projects, such as the luxury towers on Oak Street, that were never intended to rehouse low-income residents. They aimed instead to keep middle-class families in the city, thereby fulfilling the criticism frequently made of Title I of the Federal Housing Act that it took land from the poor, often minority, and gave it to middle- and upper-income residents, usually white.

But city officials also tried to tap federal programs to provide improved housing for those who were desperate for it. They made extensive use of the 221(d)(3) provision of the Federal Housing Act subsidizing cooperatives sponsored by nonprofit organizations such as churches, community groups, and labor unions. Sponsors received 100 percent Federal Housing Administration (FHA) loans with forty-year terms and below-market interest rates, which they used to build housing for moderate-income people who put $325 down, paid a below-market monthly fee, and ended up owning a home. If the units were rented instead, then tenants paid about 20 percent less than market price. In either case, tenants paid no more than 25 percent of income, with the difference subsidized by federal funds. The city also arranged with a local foundation to provide interest-free loans to help with the $325 down payment.

The Redevelopment Agency experimented with other approaches as well. It secured substantial funding to build housing for low-income senior citizens, who made up a significant portion of the poor but were often considered less threatening by white neighbors than minority families, particularly ones with teenagers. Where possible, the renewers constructed small clusters of affordable apartments scattered within middle-class neighborhoods. It experimented with supplementing rents of low-income tenants by paying the landlord the difference between what prospective occupants could afford and the market rent. And it developed what was called a "rent certificate" or "leased housing" program, in which the Housing Authority rented flats directly from private landlords and then subleased them to low-income families at the same cost as public housing. The "turnkey" housing program went even further. Here the city purchased low-income housing constructed by private developers and "turned the key over" for rental at subsidized rates.[25] With all these efforts to provide affordable housing, New Haven's urban renewers identified with the "housers" of the 1930s and 1940s, such as Catherine Bauer Wurster, whom they greatly admired for lobbying for European-style social housing in the United States and with whom they shared frustrations over a limited success.[26]

By the time the commission arrived in New Haven in 1967, it was quite clear that creating subsidized, racially integrated housing was nearly impossible at a scale even approaching the amount needed, particularly if high-rise public housing was shunned. By then, rehabilitation and new construction had swept across 30 percent of the city's land area. About 9,000 old dwelling units had been rehabbed and some 2,600 new publicly assisted units built.[27] Figuring out how well that met the need is difficult, but the analyst Douglas Rae estimates that during Lee's sixteen years in office, somewhere between 22,000 and 30,000 individuals, or about 10,000 households—approximately a fifth of the city's population—were forced to move. In 1969, close to the end of Lee's reign, the Redevelopment Agency would put the number of relocated households somewhat lower, at 6,970. The numbers were huge either way.[28]

Lee's final major complaint to the commission focused on an issue that he realized was not solely the responsibility of the federal government; states and localities had a role to play as well. As Lee put it bluntly to the commission, "The cities are not able to project their thinking beyond the borders of their own cities."[29] Witness after witness echoed the mayor's concern, lamenting the lack of any metropolitan governance to help cities share their problems with the wealthier suburban communities that increasingly surrounded them. By one alarming calculation, the population of the New Haven suburban ring increased by 51 percent between 1950 and 1960, while the city's population fell by 7.5 percent. Already by 1950, New Haven's population had slipped to 62 percent of its standard metropolitan statistical area (SMSA), down from 81 percent in 1920, and the downward trend was just gaining steam. By 1960 it was only 50 percent, and by 1970 it would reach as low as 39 percent. And to make matters worse, the wealthier were leading the exodus out of town. Whereas in 1950 New Haven's median income was

86 percent of its SMSA, by 1960 it was 80 percent and by 1970 would fall to 67 percent. At the low end of the income spectrum, 17 percent of the city's residents in 1960 had incomes of less than $3,000 a year, while only 7 percent in the SMSA did.[30]

Without metropolitan-scale resources, cities like New Haven were left holding a half-empty bag. Relocating tenants, for example, suffered for lack of access to the full metropolitan area. Racial integration of housing and schools was similarly constrained. Despite Lee's passionate hopes for a solution, however, he admitted to the commission, "I do not believe it is possible under the very strong traditions which New England has in maintaining the separate jurisdictions which these towns and cities have." Voluntary cooperation, maybe. By law, he concluded, "it is not only unlikely but impossible."[31] This absence of metropolitan-level problem solving would anger Logue throughout his career in urban renewal, including the very next day, when he told the commission in Boston: "The local suburban governments in America, in every metropolitan area I know, positively discourage low-income families of different races from coming out and sharing in the amenities of suburban life."[32] In the early 1970s, when working in New York State, Logue would finally find a way to take on the metropolitan issue—with dramatic results.

PROTEST FROM THE FLOOR

After the mayor finished speaking at the hearing, the commission prepared to move on to hear testimony from two prominent urban experts: Jack Meltzer, director of the Center for Urban Studies at the University of Chicago, and Mike Sviridoff, founding director of CPI from 1962 to 1966 and now vice president of national affairs at the Ford Foundation, replacing Paul Ylvisaker. Suddenly, an uninvited speaker, a local man named Fred Harris, burst out:

> You people have listened to the Mayor. How about listening to us?
> If this is supposed to be a public hearing, you should allow the

public that are involved in all this redevelopment area to speak their opinion . . . How are you people helping us when you listen to people like that, that decide what happens to our lives, and we are never given a chance to speak up and say what we think should help our neighborhoods? . . . You have got the man presenting a big whitewash up here.[33]

Harris was no stranger to New Haven's urban renewers, even if he was unknown to the commission members. The twenty-nine-year-old New Haven native was the leader of the Hill Parents Association (HPA), an organization he and his wife, Rose, had founded in 1965 to protest what they considered a racist curriculum and appalling physical conditions at their children's school in the Hill, one of the poorest neighborhoods in New Haven. After securing toilet paper for the students' restrooms, new paint and books, and a black principal at the school, the group had moved on to community issues: better police treatment; improved housing, particularly for the many newcomers to the neighborhood who had been displaced by urban renewal projects elsewhere; more parks and playgrounds; and a greater voice in New Haven's redevelopment and famed anti-poverty program, CPI. The HPA became the major opponent of the Redevelopment Agency's initiatives, its leaders speaking out boldly at public hearings and lobbying city agencies on behalf of the Hill neighborhood. Although Harris had not been asked to testify at the National Commission hearing—the urban renewers preferring to explain their program's deficiencies themselves—a friend in city hall apparently tipped him off and he and eleven other HPA members showed up at the Conté School, demanding to be heard. "We knew . . . that Mayor Lee was going to be speaking for the people of New Haven," Harris later recounted. "Now ain't that a bitch? He lives in good housing and sure as hell didn't get us good housing, so how was he going to speak about housing for us?" Harris and his colleagues had filed into the Conté School auditorium and, finding no open seats, sat down on the floor in front of the stage, from where he now rose to speak.[34]

Despite Harris's interruption, the commission stuck to its schedule.

Sviridoff submitted a written statement that praised "the vision and imagination of Mayor Richard Lee that shaped a new kind of urban renewal program in America" and recalled how "Ed Logue and I worked hand in hand under Dick Lee's direction in an attempt to tackle the total problem," as attentive to human renewal as physical renewal. With an irony Sviridoff did not seem to notice, given how his status as an expert had protected his spot in the speaker lineup while Harris was silenced, he went on to quote admiringly from Chairman Douglas's own call in 1933 for organizing the weak to give them what "the world respects, namely power," without which the "permanent benefits of Rooseveltian liberalism [will] be as illusory as were those of the Wilsonian era." Sviridoff then urged opening the New Deal door even wider in their own time: "Only the active and fullest possible participation of the neighborhood people in such a program [of renewal] can yield lasting and meaningful results." Soon Sviridoff, fulfilling his role as Ford Foundation urbanist, was supplying the kind of ammunition that would arm the commission in attacking Johnson's urban policies as too limited. He reminded the panel that the highly touted poverty program received only one-fifth of 1 percent of the gross national product, when in 1938 Roosevelt spent fifteen times that on public works alone—"and that was not enough." As national leaders called for domestic cuts to support the Vietnam War, Sviridoff feared "a mockery of our lofty goals." He concluded, "If our cities decay beyond repair, and if poverty undermines the very fabric of the country, what kind of society do we have left to defend?"[35]

Finally, the commission gave Fred Harris his turn. With his words, he transformed the focus of the meeting from the goals and challenges facing urban renewers to the impact their work was having on New Haven's poorest residents, the citizens they claimed to want to help. Unsurprisingly, Harris deplored how redevelopment had saddled New Haven's low-income residents with many years of evictions and exorbitant rents. But he directed his harshest criticism at the way urban renewal decisions were made, drawing a parallel with how the city and the commission had failed to invite "the people that are involved in the neighborhood . . . to speak for themselves" at this hearing. "The people don't have no voice here," he argued, referring to both exclusions. Echoing Sviridoff's call for neighborhood involvement but challenging the sincerity of his commitment, he urged, "If you involve the people in the neighborhoods, they feel as though they have a part. They feel as though they are helping to decide what is going to happen to their community." Harris made it clear that New Haven's poorest residents wanted what urban renewal promised: better housing, good schools, effective job training, and other kinds of government assistance. But they also wanted the opportunity to define those programs for themselves.

PARTICIPATORY DEMOCRACY

In making his case for the lack of community say in New Haven's urban renewal, Harris was expressing an alternative vision of how democracy should work to the pluralist democratic ideology and practice of the urban renewers. The political scientist Dahl had delineated their pluralist consultative process, with its roots in the New Deal era of the 1930s and 1940s and confidence that *public* officials—armed with administrative expertise, political muscle, and federal dollars—were best situated to represent the *public interest*, mediating between conflicting and often self-serving *private* interests. For Harris and community activists like him all over the country by the mid-1960s, however, democratic governance required much fuller participation by people at the grassroots—an ideal that I will label "participatory democracy." This more open, deliberative process, they contended, would give greater voice to those most affected by important decisions, who brought firsthand experience more useful than the knowledge of so-called experts or the establishment leaders they preferred to consult.

Harris had good reason to doubt that pluralist democracy was working well for his community. Vehicles of consultation that Logue and Lee claimed supported a democratic process of decision-making often discriminated against those with less access and power, more often than not lower class and minority. Many fell outside the organized interest groups represented on the CAC, which then removed their perspectives from Dahl's feedback loop. The voting and opinion polling that the renewers hailed as referenda on urban renewal discriminated against the displaced without stable addresses. The views of those caught in the crosshairs of redevelopment were rarely solicited more informally. In the forty-nine lengthy interviews that Dahl carried out in 1957–58 to test his pluralism theory, he never talked to any residents of the Oak Street neighborhood that was bulldozed for the Connector and luxury apartment towers.

These poorer citizens found it no easier to give testimony at the public meetings Logue championed. Wolfinger reported to Dahl how "the city customarily prepares very elaborate public hearings . . . in order to make a powerful case for the project."[36] The journalist Jeanne Lowe's largely sympathetic national investigation of urban renewal nonetheless described one such biased hearing on demolishing the Oak Street neighborhood in 1955. She observed the "six-foot Chief of Police in his dress uniform" testifying to more than six arrests in this area a day, the fire chief reporting that calls were "600 percent higher than the rest of the city," the city court judge claiming that prostitution was greater here than in any other neighborhood, and so on. After the redevelopment staff presented its case, "anyone opposed to redeveloping Oak Street would have been championing crime, disease, juvenile delinquency and higher taxes. Not a voice was raised in protest."[37] A critical perspective like this one, from a displaced black resident, had few public outlets: "Man, there used to be people—thousands of real, *live*, people living on Oak Street. It wasn't the classiest place in town, but it was home. Today you can't see a poor face on Oak Street, or a black face either."[38]

The HPA had singled out CPI for condemnation long before Harris arrived uninvited at the National Commission hearings. The growing tension was well captured in a participant-observer study by Russell D. Murphy, a Yale Ph.D. student who went on to teach at Wesleyan and publish *Political Entrepreneurs and Urban Poverty: The Strategies of Policy Innovation in New Haven's Model Anti-Poverty Project*. Murphy embedded himself in CPI from 1962 to 1966, years of both the agency's prominence under Sviridoff's pluralist democratic rule and its increasing vulnerability to attack by activists lobbying to give program participants greater authority. Ultimately, the HPA would file a formal complaint to the federal Office of Economic Opportunity, demanding that "at a minimum a majority of the Board of Directors of CPI . . . [must] be elected by the residents of the neighborhoods that CPI serves." Murphy showed how, in carrying out human renewal, Sviridoff and his staff mirrored the pluralist democratic approach that the city's physical renewal had undertaken. They established themselves as nationally acclaimed experts on urban poverty—creative and capable innovators of social renewal programs. They institutionalized community support not from consulting citizens directly, but by hiring hundreds of employees from the target neighborhoods to engage with clients. The CPI's nine-member board, moreover, was a mini-version of the elite CAC. It included "some of New Haven's most outstanding citizens," such as the minister of the Dixwell Avenue Congregational Church, the world's oldest African American United Church of Christ congregation, and other representatives of established community organizations like the Board of Education and the United Fund, along with Yale and local business leaders.

By the mid-1960s, however, this highly centralized, top-down CPI, run by what its deputy director would term a "democratic elite . . . taking a harmony of interest approach," found itself more and more under attack by those he described as promoting a "populist . . . conflict approach." To satisfy the Office of Economic Opportunity, CPI leaders reluctantly agreed to expand the board to sixteen to allow for the election of one additional member from each of the seven neighborhoods then being served, relieved to have warded off the more extreme demand of giving neighborhood representatives a board majority.[39]

Several other speakers during the contentious National Commission hearing confirmed Harris's message. Professor Herbert Kaufman, chair of the Yale Political Science Department, praised the renewers' success in "build[ing] what amounts to a new bureaucracy" with "new teams" of talented, professional experts in charge of both the redevelopment and human progress sides. But he warned that the political landscape of the nation was changing, with "a new form of fragmentation developing at the local level, represented by the claims of groups that hitherto have been unorganized."[40] Robert Cook, an assistant professor of sociology at Yale who headed a mostly white radical organization supportive of the Hill parents, the American Independent Movement (AIM), was more polemical, accusing Lee's urban renewal regime of taking a "totalitarian approach . . . antithetical to the American democratic tradition . . . We suggest dispersing the power, allowing the talents and abilities of the bulk of people in the city and country to be mobilized in a new way." Cook concluded on a note that echoed Harris's: "If you start to decentralize . . . you get more participation, more interest, and a growth of people's abilities to participate in a plan and work for themselves."[41]

What Kaufman and Cook did not need to say aloud because it was so well understood was that the increasingly militant social movements of the 1960s, particularly Black Power and the New Left, were now mounting a substantial challenge to the prevailing liberal pluralist democratic order. Yet despite their intense conflict, both sides articulated a commitment to democracy. Renewers and critics alike lived in a Cold War world where democracy was deeply valued, even if it took on variable meanings. Lee closed his statement to the commission with an exhortation to the entire nation to do more "to make our cities showplaces of democracy."[42] Harris, for his part, declared, "As long as we have officials sitting back drawing up plans for our neighborhoods," they are not "involving the people like it's supposed to be in a so-called democratic society."[43] President Johnson's Community Action Program, the centerpiece of his War on Poverty, had raised democratic expectations even higher for Harris and his peers by requiring "maximum feasible participation" of citizens in formulating social programs.

It is worth noting that another uninvited speaker at the hearings, a conservative New Haven resident named Stephen J. Papa, also called for more listening "to the people who know the needs of the people in New Haven" to stem the tide of the middle-class exodus to the suburbs. Papa and his fellow Republicans shared the Left's criticism of the Lee-Logue regime as undemocratic in violating majority rule, such as when its appointed Board of Education promoted school desegregation and its Redevelopment Agency built scattered-site affordable housing in neighborhoods hostile to it. They in fact anticipated how calls for a more grassroots democratic mobilization against mainstream liberalism would in time travel from the political Left to the political Right.[44]

RACE IN THE NEIGHBORHOODS

Harris's unexpected intervention at the National Commission hearing also changed the conversation about race. Sviridoff in his testimony boasted that the city "has succeeded in achieving a higher level of racial integration in housing than any other city in the State of Connecticut, and that probably means any city in the Nation." Sviridoff's assumption, shared with Lee, Logue, and the rest of their team, was that disturbing patterns of racial segregation were woven into the deteriorating neighborhoods of New Haven. If they managed to create a "slumless New Haven," then they could make it a more racially integrated one.[45] The urban renewers knew they could not leave this problem to New Haven residents to solve voluntarily. Fearful white residents had consistently resisted efforts to build subsidized housing in their neighborhoods, as they had protested busing for integration. The private real estate market left to its own devices would only perpetuate segregation by giving slumlords and mortgage lenders free rein to discriminate against blacks.

Heated charges in New Haven and elsewhere by the 1960s, however, argued that quite the opposite was happening: urban renewal was fueling "Negro removal." Since even the urban renewers didn't deny that some residential and highway projects dislocated those living in their paths, often racial minorities, it is imperative to understand how the likes of Lee and Logue reconciled their ostensible commitment to racial integration with the destruction of the neighborhoods where the city's most vulnerable populations lived.

When they launched New Haven's urban renewal in the mid-1950s, Lee and Logue found themselves charged with a city whose overall population was declining, while its nonwhite population (which at this time overwhelmingly meant African American) was simultaneously increasing.

The combination led to big jumps in the proportion of black residents—6 percent in 1950, 15 percent in 1960, 26 percent by 1970.[46] This expanding black population—poorer and less securely employed than the city's white population—was increasingly concentrated in slum neighborhoods. For example, when the Oak Street area was razed for the Connector in the late 1950s, this onetime port-of-entry for immigrants was now 50 percent black, whereas the city was barely 15 percent so. Part of the reason for this clustering was simply the uptick in numbers, but it also appeared that in contrast to the previous waves of immigrants who had moved into—and then out of—the Oak Street neighborhood as they made their way in New Haven, blacks got stuck there, without the options to move on that immigrants had enjoyed. Logue blamed "the unwillingness of most white Americans to share their neighborhoods with non-whites," so that "prejudice . . . piles the non-whites on top of one another into substandard housing wrung slowly and expensively from retreating whites. All too soon the overcrowding turns the neighborhood into a slum."[47] The renewers were not surprised when an investigation by the New Haven Human Rights Committee in 1964 revealed that nonwhites were almost twice as likely to live in substandard rental units as whites were—29 percent versus 15 percent—and on average they paid more for them, particularly the substandard ones.[48] Slum clearance seemed to hold the promise of eliminating these inequities along with the physical structures that sheltered them.

The problem became, however, that racially integrated neighborhoods did not result from urban renewal as much as the renewers hoped. The Yale political scientist Douglas Rae, who carefully analyzed population shifts in twentieth-century New Haven, concluded that the big demographic story in New Haven's urban renewal was less "Negro removal" than "white removal." Whites had been gradually leaving the city since the 1920s and the pace quickened between 1950 and 1970, not caused—but likely accentuated—by urban renewal. He identified three significant differences between the relocation fates of white and nonwhite families displaced by urban renewal projects. Nonwhites ended up in public housing more than three times as frequently as whites, often as their best option. Whites moved to purchased homes elsewhere in New Haven more than three times as frequently as nonwhites, because more whites had previously been homeowners and thus received financial compensation when their residences were condemned. And whites (mostly middle-class ones) were leaving the city at almost five times the rate of nonwhites, who could not afford—and were not welcome in—white suburbs. What was emerging by the late 1960s, according to Rae, was "the near-total Africanization of public housing, and . . . racial tipping in neighborhood after neighborhood."[49] The result was a New Haven that was becoming more and more racially segregated—not integrated.

During the 1950s, when Logue was most active in New Haven's redevelopment, African American community leaders had welcomed the urban renewers' integrationist efforts in housing and schooling.[50] In a world where inequities between blacks and whites were stark, racial integration seemed like a desirable, even radical, remedy. After all, Metropolitan Life's huge middle-income Stuyvesant Town opened in Manhattan in the late 1940s as whites-only and stubbornly resisted integration efforts through the 1950s. Given the overwhelming evidence that white New Haveners could not be enticed into black-dominated schools and neighborhoods, African Americans understandably sought access to white privileged spaces. As the local integrationist-oriented NAACP bluntly argued, "Urban renewal programs often present minority families with a long-awaited opportunity to move out of racial and economic ghettos into better neighborhoods with better housing."[51] After the Dixwell renewal plan was enthusiastically endorsed at a public hearing well attended by black community leaders and citizens in 1960, Logue elatedly called the assembly "far and away the best substantive solid support we have ever had."[52]

Indeed, New Haven's black population supported urban renewal enthusiastically. A 1957 Harris Poll documented that "Lee is widely praised in the Negro community for always having been a friend of the Negro people" and "for having sponsored and carried out integrated housing without incident."[53] Still by 1965, 83 percent of blacks polled—more than any other ethnic group—favored urban renewal.[54] Nor were whites blind to redevelopment's integrationist agenda. In a 1966 survey of public opinion on urban problems conducted in four Connecticut cities, white New Haveners frequently criticized urban renewal as a pro-black program that was leading to housing integration. The pollsters concluded, "Some say redevelopment has caused problems, but others are more frank and state that it favors Negroes and is threatening their property values."[55] New Haven's black leaders, working through established organizations and institutions, fit comfortably within the renewers' pluralist democratic political model. Through having a voice on the CAC and enjoying other forms of public visibility, they felt they were influencing redevelopment planning and pushing the city toward greater racial progress.

Convinced of the rightness of their cause, Lee and Logue and many established black leaders downplayed what was lost when neighborhoods were destroyed and intimate social bonds were broken—among neighbors and classmates, and between houses of worship and their congregations and tradesmen and their customers. They focused instead on the expected gains in housing quality and neighborhood racial integration.[56] With that mindset, the Redevelopment Agency early on made no secret of the numbers displaced from urban renewal projects. Calculations of displaced residents in fact provided a way of measuring success in moving slum dwellers out of substandard housing and, they hoped, into redeveloped, integrated neighborhoods.

But as time passed, and the renewers were faced with the enormous demand for housing and so many impediments in delivering it, the ideal of integration faded. Just finding adequate homes for displaced minorities proved challenging enough. As early as 1956, the first director of New Haven's Family Relocation Office resigned, despairing that "this job is impossible. There is more prejudice up North than there is in the South—only here it is often more subtle. When you answer an ad in the newspaper, all you hear is 'no children, no pets, and whites only'—so how is it possible to find a place for Negro families too large for public housing and unwanted by private landlords?"[57] More often than not, the relocation office resorted to moving minority tenants to another deteriorating but affordable black neighborhood or into public housing.

By the 1967 hearing, Harris's position on race signaled a significant shift from the stance taken by the black community's civil rights leaders during the previous decade. Harris was less concerned with integration and more interested in giving residents influence within the communities in which they lived: "We don't want to be going into white neighborhoods where we are not wanted. Let us stay in the slums, but fix it up so it will be decent, so we can live there. Sure, we should be integrated, but why force ourselves on people if it is going to create problems?"

Wooster Square, the redeveloped neighborhood where Logue felt that he "really learned to do the urban renewal business right" with more rehab than demolition and a high level of citizen engagement, proved Harris's point.[58] Although the Redevelopment Agency hoped to integrate this insular Italian community and took pride in putting up the Columbus Mall, a 221(d)(3) rental project where 24 percent of the residents were nonwhite and 33 percent of the families had been relocated from redevelopment elsewhere, Logue knew—and regretted—that there was a disturbing racial history to the neighborhood's urban renewal. He had been visited by a delegation of parishioners, led by their parish priest, to discuss how urban renewal might proceed in the Wooster Square community. The plan they advocated, for all its pioneering attractions like extensive residential rehab, the Conté Community School, and a new fire headquarters, came with the price of satisfying the neighborhood's desire to limit the growing number of African American residents. Highway 91 became a way to cut off the area where most blacks lived and develop it as the Long Wharf industrial district. Moreover, rehabilitation turned out to benefit homeowners, usually white, much more than racially diverse renters, who were often forced to move during renovation or could no longer afford the higher rents afterward.[59] No surprise that Harris found little to like in integrating a neighborhood such as Wooster Square.

The predominantly black Dixwell offered urban renewers and their allies within the black establishment a better shot at creating a racially integrated neighborhood. The plan called for substantial Wooster Square–type rehabilitation, for which loans arranged by the Redevelopment Agency would be crucial, given the paucity of residents' savings and rampant discrimination by private lenders. Complementing that rehab would be selective clearance and new construction of projects like Dixwell Plaza and the Florence Virtue Homes, a 221(d)(3) cooperative sponsored by the Dixwell Avenue Congregational Church, a community institution with deep roots and a serious commitment to the project. The church, too, got a new home on the Dixwell Plaza, next to the Grant School.[60]

Critics charged that strategies for selling the Florence Virtue co-ops—such as renaming them "University Park–Dixwell"—were blatant efforts to whiten a neighborhood close to Yale's campus and replace black tenants with white ones. But that accusation misses the more complex goal shared by white city officials and civil rights leaders alike to attract white families into a more integrated community—which then might be better positioned to demand higher-quality schools, stores, and other amenities for everyone. In fact, the architect John Johansen's prospectus for the 129-unit Florence Virtue Homes proudly hailed the project as "the first privately sponsored, FHA insured, cooperative development in the country providing integrated housing . . . a daring experiment in reverse integration."[61] When the homes opened with 55 percent black and 45 percent white residents, it was considered a victory, to be followed, it was hoped, by integration of the nearby park, community center, church, shopping center, and Grant School, where, to the Redevelopment Agency's relief, white children quickly enrolled.[62] Other co-ops, sponsored by the New Haven Human Relations Council and a neighborhood Catholic church, an elderly housing project, and a market-rate apartment building aimed at introducing class as well as racial diversity into Dixwell, were also constructed.

But Harris and his HPA would have recognized with some frustration that the racial and political realities of New Haven allowed Italian community leaders to use the resources of urban renewal to keep Wooster Square substantially segregated. In contrast, black leaders in Dixwell considered their best option to be inviting whites to integrate their community—which inevitably meant displacing less economically advantaged black residents. Many of those would find their way to Harris's Hill neighborhood.

Within the fragile racial environment of New Haven, the aspiration for racial integration that black leaders shared with the renewers often came at a greater cost to black than white residents.

Lee and Logue demonstrated their racial liberalism in other ways that aligned them more with the integrationists than with critics like Harris. Although some of their actions might be considered tokenism, they viewed them as symbolic racial politics much needed in their segregated city. Lee lived in Newhallville, a black neighborhood, until 1964. Soon after taking office, he appointed George Crawford (the namesake for the architect Paul Rudolph's Crawford Manor elderly housing) as the first black corporation counsel to the City of New Haven, and he desegregated New Haven's fire department as well as its housing projects, the latter at the encouragement of the civil rights organization Congress of Racial Equality (CORE).[63] The mayor also launched a front-page fight in 1963 by announcing publicly that the segregationist governor George Wallace of Alabama would be "officially unwelcome" in New Haven, despite his invitation from the Yale Political Union, Logue's old debating society.[64] That same year Lee forced notoriously racist building trade locals in New Haven to accept black members if they wanted any more city construction contracts.[65] And in what became a very controversial move, Lee, fed up with suburban blindness to the city's problems, encouraged black residents of New Haven to block late-afternoon rush-hour traffic with a "sit out" in the middle of one of the city's main arteries to convince homeward-bound suburban commuters "to walk through the slums and see the conditions which prevail."[66] What proved even more contentious was Lee's appointment of a human rights committee in June 1963 that, after a year of intense politics and public hearings, recommended passage of a nondiscrimination Equal Opportunities Ordinance, which the New Haven Board of Aldermen in turn approved.[67] The law provided the pressure needed to expand the controversial scattered-site housing effort that so outraged white middle-class homeowners.[68]

Intense as these conflicts proved, they paled when compared with the prolonged struggle to desegregate New Haven's schools. In 1958, when two new high schools opened, Lee quietly set the boundary between the two districts so as to equalize the black student population attending each.[69] But the next stage of school integration was harder to do sub rosa. In 1964, the school board announced, under pressure from the national NAACP, a plan to desegregate New Haven's neighborhood schools with extensive busing. In a district where 38 percent of the students were nonwhite, ten of the thirty-one elementary schools had nonwhite enrollments over 50 percent, as did two of the four junior-high schools. Six of those twelve schools were at least 79 percent nonwhite, four of them exceeding 90 percent. What followed was a vicious battle fought in racially charged public assemblies as well as emotional living room meetings. As one alderman from an embattled white ward described it, "The busing battle had a startling effect upon the social atmosphere, filling it with electricity and bringing out the worst in everybody . . . In private, no holds were barred, and even in the big public meetings the normal restraints of politeness dropped away. Pointed *ad hominem* attacks were standard procedure."[70]

The election of November 1965 became a referendum on school integration, with heated aldermanic contests and a fierce challenge to Lee by the Republican busing opponent Joseph Einhorn. Even *The New York Times* stepped into the fray, endorsing Lee and arguing that his defeat "would not only block progress for New Haven but would dishearten people working for reform and innovation in many other American cities." Prominent liberals made pilgrimages to New Haven to proclaim their support. The famed singer and racial activist Marian Anderson came to dedicate the Crawford Manor elderly housing, Vice President Hubert Humphrey lent his considerable credibility on civil rights to Lee's campaign, and Senator Robert Kennedy showed up "to help Mayor Lee" because if President Kennedy "were alive today, he would be here. What my brother hoped to do with the New Frontier, Dick Lee is doing in New Haven."[71] Lee ultimately won by his largest majority in seven successful campaigns—67 percent of the vote with a full sweep of the aldermanic races. Some of that enthusiasm for Lee surely came from a reawakened confidence in the urban renewal program after long delays. But the two initiatives could not be separated: reelecting Dick Lee the urban renewer and Dick Lee the racial integrationist came as one package, Einhorn having condemned them both with one stroke.

The aspiration for a more racially integrated city has often been over-looked in analyses of urban renewal. "Negro removal" is assumed to have been the goal of slum clearance and highway construction projects, confus-ing all-too-frequent outcomes with intentions and missing how at least some urban renewers committed themselves to creating a more racially integrated American society. Logue couldn't have made his own ambition clearer. In a letter to Chester Bowles in 1957, he reaffirmed what they had both learned in India about how social change and infrastructural improvement were en-tangled: "In the North, race relations and slums and blight are interwoven in such a way as to convince me that the only real hope of a solid, sustained improvement in race relations lies in an imaginative and vigorous urban renewal program." He went on to complain that labor unions could do so much more to advance both goals—and improve their image—by investing pension funds in building decent, integrated, moderate-cost housing, an idea he had floated to Walter Reuther of the United Auto Workers several years earlier.[72] Logue seemed not to recognize, however, that the effective-ness of his racial agenda was seriously compromised by the infrastructural choices the renewers had made to replace slums with less densely popu-lated, modernist alternatives like the Florence Virtue Homes in Dixwell. Such new buildings could never accommodate the scale and economic diversity of those demolished. Even if this modernist utopian ideal was achievable, a new New Haven could not be built with anything like the speed in which urban renewal was destroying the old one.

When Harris addressed the National Commission hearing in 1967, he was challenging the authority of the urban renewers, Mayor Lee, *and* the black establishment. Harris contended that Mayor Lee was a dictator who used CPI not to improve people's lives but to consolidate his power, includ-ing buying off "the black leadership"—older, more affluent, and more inte-grationist.[73] When Sviridoff protested that democracy was indeed at work—after all, Lee got reelected every two years, and with a strong black vote—Harris retorted that it was "because the people who have to eat work for him. That's why he wins."[74]

It turned out that Harris had a sensitive finger on the pulse of black

New Haven. His verbal disrupting of the National Commission hearings was one thing. A much greater racial challenge to Lee's urban renewal regime would follow three months later, in August 1967. The nonfatal shooting of a young Puerto Rican man by the white proprietor of Tony's Snack Bar in the Hill area, in what he claimed was self-defense against a knife attack, set off four nights of rioting in the city's low-income, predominantly black neighborhoods. Although observers differed in how tightly they tied the riot to the city's experience with urban renewal or linked it to the chain of urban uprisings across the country, it was hard not to hear echoes of the discussion at the Conté School the previous May. The turmoil of urban renewal and the failure to substantially improve conditions for many poor and minority residents had led to great frustration and anger, particularly among young men.

New Haven's civil disorders were not as violent as many that coursed through the nation's cities that summer. The rioters mostly were black teenagers who threw rocks at windows and passing cars, set fires, and looted neighborhood stores. No one was killed, and only three were seriously injured. But more than four hundred people were arrested (the number was disputed), and damage totaled $1.1 million. New Haven's worst day rated a B4 on the Kerner Commission's scale of riot intensity, which ranged from a high of A1 to a low of E1, putting it at a middling level. Yet this score was still devastating in a city that, as *Time* magazine put it, "has pioneered nearly every program in the Great Society's lexicon. Months and years before the Federal Government showed any interest in the cities, it had its own poverty and manpower-training projects, a rent-supplement demonstration, and a promising Head Start program. Washington had rewarded the city's imaginative urban-renewal administration with a greatly disproportionate share of federal renewal money."[75]

The close student of New Haven Douglas Rae has concluded that "the fundamental issue behind the city's incapacity to 'deliver' was the drying up of plant-gate opportunity for people without advanced education." But as neither city leaders nor struggling black residents of New Haven could control the labor market, they blamed one another. Harris and other activists felt betrayed by the mayor when the police chief—tied more closely to the traditional party machine than Lee's administration—ignored Lee's promises to reduce police provocations and lift curfews.[76] For his part, the mayor would remain disheartened by the riots and the city's generally more polarized political atmosphere. In 1969, he would decide not to seek a ninth term, even though polls indicated that his popularity remained high, particularly among the city's African American voters, where his approval hovered in the 80 to 90 percent range.[77] Lee's retreat paved the way for the return to power of the Democratic town committee chair Arthur T. Barbieri, marginalized for the better part of sixteen years as Lee built autonomous power bases with his federally funded urban renewal operation, CPI, and the CAC. Barbieri put his own man, veteran alderman Bartholomew Guida, in the mayor's office, officially bringing to a close Lee's urban renewal chapter.[78]

PROBLEMS OF THEIR OWN MAKING

Many of the difficulties that Lee and Logue encountered in successfully renewing New Haven could be attributed to factors outside their control: the unstoppable momentum of suburbanization and deindustrialization, limitations in what could be done under the housing acts, pernicious racism, a punishing tax structure, and political fragmentation in the metropolitan area. But they also made miscalculations that undermined their success in the long run. One of the most damaging was the way they went about redeveloping downtown New Haven. The renewers' image of what a modern downtown New Haven should look like required attracting major retailers that promised to offer the city economic stability, workers plentiful jobs, and consumers the latest merchandise. Old downtown New Haven's standard fare of dated stores, modest personal services, and cheap luncheonettes—many employing few staff beyond the owner's family— seemed a remnant of the provincial past, not a path to a modern future.

To be fair, the major chain and department stores that New Haven hoped to attract sent an unequivocal message rejecting having small local retailers

as neighbors. According to an official of Sears Roebuck, these merchants—
who rarely appealed to high-spending customers and often opposed changes
downtown—discouraged the big stores from expanding downtown just as
much as the better-known impediments of highway access, parking, and
project delays.[79] It also didn't help that the private-sector financiers, particularly insurance companies, whose investment was making the Church
Street Project possible, required that 65 to 70 percent of tenants have credit
ratings equivalent to AAA, meaning a million dollars in net assets, which
disqualified most Church Street merchants. Only the most financially secure could make the move to the Chapel Square Mall.[80]

Motivated by their ideal of a modern downtown and faced with these
external pressures, the urban renewers decided to marginalize small downtown retailers. Not surprisingly, Dahl identified them as the major opponents
to downtown urban renewal. In fact, a jeweler, Robert R. Savitt, unhappy
with the compensation the city offered for taking his store by eminent
domain—located as it was smack in the middle of the area being leveled for
the mall—embroiled the city in a suit that delayed the entire project for a
couple of years.[81] Savitt was not alone in fighting back. One hundred and
twenty small downtown merchants, fearing for their livelihoods, banded together in 1958 as the Central Civic Association (CCA), mockingly perhaps
inverting letters of the CAC.

Their president, Leo S. Gilden, also the president of "Gilden's, Inc., Jew-
elers for Four Generations," then sent a letter to Mayor Lee, bitterly outlining the group's grievances: They had not been informed of the Church Street
Project or consulted before the public announcement; they were not invited
to the Lawn Club celebratory luncheon disclosing the plans to the public but
instead "first learned of all this via radio and newspaper"; and they—as taxpayers and servants of the New Haven public for many years—took great offense at the mayor's recent statement "that you realize that perhaps some
of the smaller businessmen could not survive this change but that in the long
run the city would benefit from it." Reminding Mayor Lee in the common
parlance of the era "that this is a democracy that we live in," Gilden insisted
that "certainly the livlihoods [sic] and welfare of the thousands of people

involved in this must be considered before the interests of outside capital," referring to the project's New York developer Roger Stevens and the major New York department store that Logue and Lee hoped to attract.[82] The CCA then brought suit against the city. After a year, they got temporary quarters in prefabricated metal structures, with adjacent parking, and the promise of a 10 percent rental discount if and when they reopened in the Chapel Square Mall. But many dislocated businesses never made it to temporary headquarters, unable to foot the moving bill nor survive the long wait. And even some of the relocated fell by the wayside by the time the Chapel Square Mall finally opened in 1967, with its very high rents, almost a decade after the project's announcement.

Betting on big retail over small local merchants turned out to have been a questionable decision. Malley's closed in 1983, Macy's in 1993, and the Chapel Square Mall took a fatal dive not long thereafter. Department stores and national chains expected a certain margin of profit. When sales declined, they went under or abandoned downtown locations for more profitable suburban malls. In contrast, small-scale independent merchants might have survived better, with their lower expectations for profit, stronger ties to the city, and greater flexibility to diversify their merchandise to suit the local market.[83] The renewers' decision to redevelop Church and Chapel Streets to mimic the architecture of a suburban mall—with its solid-wall exteriors, interior-facing courts, and attached parking—also limited whatever spill-over effects might have benefited downtown more broadly, as customers arriving by car were contained inside the shopping center complex and not encouraged to venture beyond it. But Lee and Logue did not anticipate these obstacles to downtown's long-term success when they enthusiastically set out to rival neighboring suburban shopping centers and to satisfy the big retail fish they hoped to hook. When running for office in 1963, Lee reassured voters that a "very real, live, vital, dynamic, and prosperous central city" was just around the corner. After "a long haul," city residents could now look forward to much "better than what we had—a lot more than what my opponents wanted me to settle for, a hot dog stand and a Dairy Queen at Church and Chapel."[84]

ADAPTING TO A PARADIGM SHIFT

The same year that Logue's success in New Haven was rewarded with a job offer from Boston and Dahl clinched his reputation as a democratic theorist with the publication of *Who Governs?*, another influential treatise hit the bookstores, this one promoting a very different conception from Dahl's about how democracy should work in cities. In time it gave ballast to participatory democratic critics of urban renewal in New Haven and elsewhere. It was Jane Jacobs's *The Death and Life of Great American Cities*, not a book of academic scholarship but nonetheless a learned one that would help transform expectations about what the "public" side of the equation should consist of (government officials were not sufficient) and what it meant to have citizen involvement in planning (more than organized interests must participate).[85] The success of *Death and Life* would challenge urban renewers like Logue in new ways. By the end of the 1960s, any claims to a democratic city-building process would require tapping the local knowledge of neighborhood residents and giving them an explicit public role. Even in New Haven, citizen participation would gradually become more accepted and even expected, just when the funding faucets from Washington, it should be noted, were being shut off.

In 1968, with surprising candor, Mayor Lee acknowledged how dramatically the ground had shifted away from established and expert pluralist democrats and toward more community control by participatory democrats. He told an interviewer, "The important thing *now* is neighborhood and community participation. People become involved in planning their own destiny and working out their own problems, neighborhood by neighborhood, and this can be the most exciting and perhaps the most rewarding of all." Accordingly, CPI was decentralized into eight neighborhood corporations, and the CAC was quietly disbanded in 1969. Lee even admitted the CAC's limitations:

> We were *selecting* people who were members of the Establishment,
> I suppose in one sense to provide the leadership on the grounds

that we had no other leadership to turn to. And the people in the individual neighborhoods, to a certain extent, were accepting this passively . . . There were many participants in the neighborhood improvement programs, but there wasn't any *real sense* of involvement. Everything in a sense came from City Hall. The thrust today, which is just getting under way, is from the neighborhood to City Hall.

When pressed about whether this enormous change threatened him politically, Lee responded, "I'm more thoughtful than people appreciate, and I recognize the need for adaptation to different approaches."[86] Lee was surely also pushed to greater adaptability by a Ford Foundation report on CPI, carried out in June 1967 between the National Commission hearings and the riot but not made public until March 1968. While acknowledging CPI's achievements, it was highly critical. The Ford evaluators insisted on the inadequacy of what "Professor Dahl" had described as Lee's "executive-centered coalition" at "a time when urban people are demanding more of a voice in the decisions that control their lives." The Ford Foundation, founding parent of CPI almost a decade earlier, had also changed with the times and now called for "a more contemporary and aggressive strategy . . . in order to broaden resident participation in the decision-making of the organization." Speaking the language of participatory democracy, surely acquired through anxiously watching the upheavals in urban America during the 1960s, Ford concluded that "within a developing national climate of open urban democracy, no city can successfully keep to a control strategy in social development programming . . . No amount of technical expertise and public relations can make the control approach work."[87]

Much earlier, Ford had encountered similar pressures for greater popular participation in the community development work it funded in India. A Ford Foundation program letter from March 1960, titled "Grassroots Democracy Comes to Rajasthan," detailed how this Indian state had implemented "democratic decentralization" of community development, "a step recommended urgently by all students of community development programs in order to transfer initiative and power out of the hands of the bureaucracy into the hands of the people." Logue kept a copy of the Ford letter, written by a former colleague in Delhi, in his New Haven files, at the time surely unaware of how challenges in the development world would once again anticipate dynamics in his own.[88]

Although from here on, ordinary American citizens like the Hill parents would demand a decision-making role in matters of urban redevelopment, as in many other areas of social policy, they still expected the hand-up from the federal government that had empowered pluralist democrats in the past. As a New Haven black activist argued in 1968 when the HPA tried to convert black tenants of public housing into "equity-holding owners rather than powerless renters," they "should be assisted in this by the federal government which abetted whites in establishing lilywhite suburbia."[89]

But implementing a more decentralized participatory democracy in a city like New Haven raised challenges of its own. While it held out the promise of a more humane and equitable urban redevelopment, it did not offer easy answers to big structural problems, such as how the city might hold on to crucial property-tax payers and reinvigorate its economy to create more jobs when the winds of change were blowing them away. Or how it should judge whether those speaking the loudest in a community in fact represented the majority's will and not the self-interest of a vocal minority. Or what might be best for the city as a whole and not just the residents of one neighborhood like Wooster Square, where activist members of the community wanted to keep out African Americans. Or how to make sure that bold new architecture enlivened the city when many residents preferred the familiar styles of the past. Much that had seemed clearer and simpler in the era of top-down pluralist democracy would now become messier and more difficult as it became harder to differentiate between public and private interests, to define a singular "common good," and to assign distinctive roles to the expert and the citizen.

The New Haven that Dick Lee left behind when he stepped down as mayor in 1970 was a very different city from the one he and Ed Logue had eagerly and rather naively begun to renew sixteen years earlier. Physically, downtown had been modernized—or as some critics would complain, suburbanized—and it was attracting more retail business than it had in previous decades, though that success would not last too many more years. Neighborhoods had been rebuilt, some, like Oak Street, through drastic demolition; others, like Wooster Square, through more sensitive rehabilitation. The city was attracting new commerce and industry to its Long Wharf district, but not enough to stem the tide of departing manufacturers and their good working-class employment. About twelve thousand factory jobs disappeared between 1954 and 1967, about 43 percent of the almost twenty-eight thousand that had existed right after World War II. By 1997, only 10 percent of that total would remain. "The problem . . . was," Logue came to recognize, "we started to renew an old city without a secure economic base . . . We tried to solve it, but you don't solve it."[90] Yale complicated matters; it was as much a curse as a blessing to the city. Years later, when even Lee and Logue admitted to the failures of the city's urban renewal, they put much of that blame on Yale's lack of investment in improving the city.[91]

It should be evident that urban renewal was no one thing from 1954 to 1970. Rather, it was constantly evolving, due to changing ideas, successes and failures on the ground, the shifting power of allies and enemies, and new government legislation that repeatedly changed the rules of the game. One longtime New Haven resident noted that they used the tools available to them at the time. "If we had the Tax Credit Act of 1978 in 1958 [to encourage historic preservation] . . . Parisians would come here to look at all that stuff! But we didn't."[92] Logue and Lee made mistakes, but sometimes they learned from them. An ideal of rehabilitation replaced demolition, disappointing new architecture inspired higher design standards, and some top-down social programs devolved to more neighborhood control.

Probably the most important evolution over the decade and a half between when Dahl first asked, "Who governed?" and when Lee stepped down as mayor occurred in the locus of political authority. Experts—so central to the liberal pluralist democratic order—found themselves on the defensive as participatory democrats gained ground. Analysts like Ellen Herman and Fred Turner have argued for other professional realms—psychology and the media, respectively—that after the traumas of World War II and in the midst of the Cold War of the 1940s and 1950s, rule by experts was considered the best way to preserve democracy from the threat of authoritarianism, whether fascist mobs or communist dictators. Only the profound disillusionment that came with the Vietnam War, the prolonged struggle for civil rights, and the battles over other social causes unraveled that linkage between expertise and democracy.[93] Urban renewal likewise contributed to citizens' growing recognition that the most crucial kind of social knowledge required for democratic change resided with ordinary people, not just independent experts. Many participatory democrats actually recognized that some expertise was still needed to achieve their goals; as one Hill resident succinctly put it, "We do need 'experts,' but we must have experts who will plan what we want instead of what the people downtown want."[94] All these tough questions were raised in the years that Logue spent in New Haven, and in many ways the rest of his career in urban redevelopment would revolve around responding to their challenges.

But this reckoning all lay in the future. When Logue left for Boston in 1961, he thought New Haven's future looked bright. He had faith that a more economically viable and inclusive city was on the horizon and that it was time to put the skills he had developed over the past seven years to work in a bigger city with a higher profile on the regional and national stages. "I had done about as much as I could do in New Haven except stay the course and see it through. After a while there's not much challenge in that," he remembered later.[95] Confident of his own abilities and the great importance of this work, Ed Logue felt that his New Haven experience had made him all the wiser about what to do—and what not to—in the good fight to save America's cities. But he would soon discover that he still had a lot more to learn, as urban renewal in Boston thrust him into many of the same battles that would grip New Haven.

PART II

Boston in the 1960s:
Rebuilding the City on the Hill

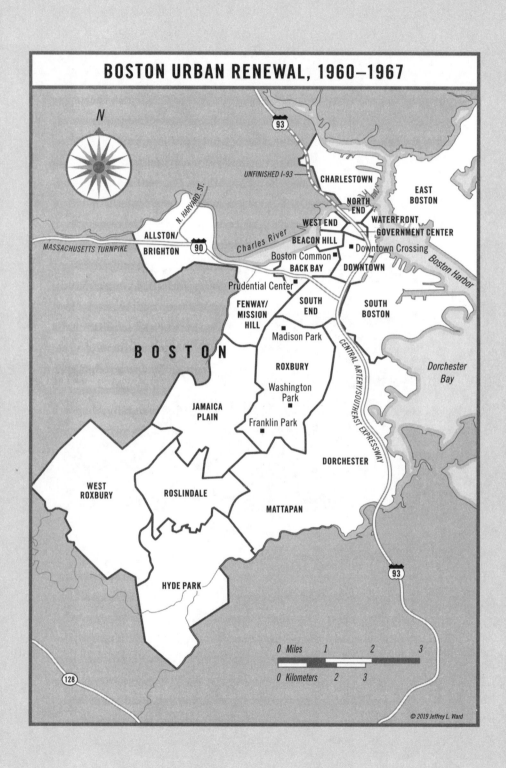

BOSTON URBAN RENEWAL, 1960–1967

N

UNFINISHED I-93

CHARLESTOWN

EAST BOSTON

NORTH END

WEST END

WATERFRONT

GOVERNMENT CENTER

BEACON HILL

Downtown Crossing

Boston Common

BACK BAY

DOWNTOWN

ALLSTON/ BRIGHTON

N. HARVARD ST.

Charles River

Boston Harbor

MASSACHUSETTS TURNPIKE

90

Prudential Center

FENWAY/ MISSION HILL

SOUTH END

SOUTH BOSTON

BOSTON

Madison Park

ROXBURY

Dorchester Bay

Washington Park

JAMAICA PLAIN

Franklin Park

DORCHESTER

CENTRAL ARTERY/SOUTHEAST EXPRESSWAY

WEST ROXBURY

ROSLINDALE

MATTAPAN

93

HYDE PARK

128

| 0 Miles | 1 | 2 | 3 |

| 0 Kilometers | 2 | 3 |

4. Sizing Up the Old Boston

The summons to come meet Boston's newly elected mayor, John Collins, arrived in December 1959. Ed Logue knew from his well-tuned professional network that Collins's people had been inquiring about him as a possible leader of Boston's revitalization. He might also have known they were investigating other candidates, including his former deputy Ralph Taylor, familiar to Bostonians from his work in neighboring Somerville before he decamped for New Haven. Logue accepted the invitation to visit. He met with the mayor-elect Collins, he looked around a city he barely knew outside of Harvard-Yale games, and he posed two key questions: Where's the comprehensive plan, and can an outsider do this job in a city notorious for its vicious political infighting?[1]

The answer to the first question was that there was no overall plan—only an inadequate and dated *General Plan for Boston* conceived back in 1950. Collins's predecessor as mayor, John Hynes, had launched Boston's urban renewal with two controversial and still-incomplete projects: redeveloping the West End and the New York Streets section of the South End. Hynes's next two ambitious moves—to persuade the Prudential Insurance Company to build a New England headquarters in the Back Bay and to construct the Government Center in downtown Boston—had stalled.

Collins's second answer was more encouraging: "Ed, *only* an outsider *can* do anything in this town. Around here they keep score on you from the time you're in short pants."[2] Anyone local, Collins believed, would inevitably be identified with one side or the other in the decades-long political feuds that divided the city. After meeting Logue and consulting with his advisers, Collins decided that in fact Logue *alone*—with his established track record in New Haven and Midas touch for attracting federal dollars, and without any compromising local affiliations—could head the much-invigorated Boston Redevelopment Authority (BRA). And he would be worth his shockingly high price tag of $30,000 a year, which was $10,000 more than the mayor himself, or indeed the Massachusetts governor, was earning.

Logue, who was intrigued by the Boston opportunity, had taken a risk and said that no lesser salary would motivate him to give up his satisfying work and comfortable life in New Haven, even if his pay there was only $13,500.[3] No one, including Logue, was exactly sure why he put such a high price on his own head, but the speculation of family members and colleagues ranged from a lifetime of insecurity about money traceable back to his fatherless youth to his high opinion of his own abilities to an ideological conviction that public service should not require financial sacrifice. Logue also knew from experience that federal urban renewal grants would cover most, if not all, of his salary. When he was asked by an intermediary for Collins, "What makes you think you're worth that?" Logue shot back, "When I was in the Fifteenth Air Force in Italy during the War, I got combat pay, and when I served in New Delhi in the Foreign Service, I got hardship pay . . . From what I hear about your town, it qualifies on both counts."[4] John Collins and

Ed Logue agreed that Logue would start as a per diem consultant that spring, learning about the city and developing a plan. They would see where it led.[5]

Where it would lead was to a seven-year run as the powerful development administrator of what became Boston's more than $200 million federally funded urban renewal. In no time, Boston would move from seventeenth to fourth in per capita dollars received from Washington, making Boston by far the largest investment the Feds made in a city of its size. Those funds would underwrite multiple projects under way simultaneously in the city's downtown and residential neighborhoods. This was an achievement greatly lauded by some and detested by others. Few kept their opinions to themselves. What became known as the "New Boston" provided almost daily front- and editorial-page copy for Boston's newspapers and juicy material for in-depth features in the national press. Major newspapers like *The New York Times* and *The Washington Post*; the newsweeklies *Life, Look, Time, Newsweek, National Review*, and *U.S. News and World Report*; business publications like *Fortune, The Economist*, and *Business Week*; and professional publications like *Architectural Forum*—all were fascinated by the question *Newsweek* aptly phrased as "What's happening to proper Old Boston?"

Logue himself attracted an outsize amount of attention. *Life*'s profile, "Bold Boston Gladiator—Ed Logue: Planner Stirs Up a Ruckus and Battles Opposition to Build the Place of His Dreams," proclaimed him "the most successful redevelopment boss in the country—and . . . the most controversial." *The Christian Science Monitor* introduced readers to "Boston's Mr. Urban Renewal, one of the top men in the renewal field." *The Washington Post* tagged him "the master rebuilder" in 1967.[6] Comparisons were frequently made with Christopher Wren's remaking of London in the seventeenth century, Charles Bulfinch's reenvisioning of Boston in the late eighteenth and early nineteenth centuries, and Baron Georges-Eugène Haussmann's reconstruction of Paris later in the nineteenth century.[7]

It was thus no mystery why the *Boston Herald* described Logue in 1965 as "more controversial, more discussed, more fervently admired and feverishly hated than any personality since James Michael Curley," referring to the Democratic Party machine boss who had dominated twentieth-century Boston politics.[8] If small-scale New Haven was a controlled laboratory experiment in urban renewal, then bigger Boston became the national testing ground for how to turn around a major American city—the tenth largest in the nation in 1950 at its population peak. In that effort, Logue would make allies and enemies as he grappled with the major dilemma that still confronts urban planners and public officials today: how to balance improving a city's economic profile as measured in the health of its tax base, its attractiveness to investors, and its success in providing jobs and services, against ensuring a decent—and equitable to the extent possible—quality of life for all its residents. In other words, how should a city's viability be assessed? From the very start in the contentious cauldron that was Boston, Logue faced choices and criticisms that propelled him to confront this question in ways that he had not needed to in New Haven, where citizens did not raise substantial challenges to Logue and Lee's agenda until the mid-1960s, several years after Logue had departed.

BECOMING THE BOSTON OF 1960

During that first spring and summer of 1960, Logue spent four days a week in Boston and weekends doing his New Haven work. He would walk from one end of this new city to another, scouting the territory around every Massachusetts Bay Transportation Authority, or "T," stop and talking to anyone who was willing. Finally, after three months of observations and three days of intense work holed up in his basement study in New Haven, doing "the most effective writing I have ever done," Logue was ready by June to present Mayor Collins with the first draft of an extensive plan. He did so at an intimate meeting in Collins's Jamaica Plain home, with only Collins and a few of his closest advisers in attendance. Logue took it as a high compliment to his sleuthing that Collins's first reaction was "Hell, I could have done that!"

By late September, his "$90 Million Development Program for Boston," encompassing downtown and ten neighborhoods—and potentially affecting a quarter of the city's acreage and half of its population over a ten-year period—was ready for public viewing. It was presented with great flourish at an evening meeting in the historic Old South Meeting House, "filled to the rafters," Logue recalled, with seven hundred invited neighborhood representatives and business, civic, and professional leaders.[9] Logue had taken the federal requirement of a "workable plan" to a whole new level of comprehensiveness, never doubting that his short, intense immersion in Boston and previous expertise in redevelopment were a sufficient-enough basis on which to recommend a massive reconfiguration of the city. He knew that public hearings and city and federal approvals would need to follow, but still, he (and Collins) considered it his job to launch the process with an ambitious vision for a New Boston.

That Boston was a city in crisis was obvious to everyone, even if they disagreed vehemently over what to do about it. The city was bleeding people and resources. Curley's conflicts with the national Democratic Party had deprived the city of its fair share of New Deal handouts, and its already declining manufacturing base got very little lift out of World War II.[10] Since 1950, Boston had lost 13 percent of its population, thinning out many of the city's neighborhoods. Good jobs were disappearing as well, with the loss of forty-eight thousand in manufacturing and fourteen thousand downtown, contributing to an 8 percent drop in city employment. Meanwhile, suburban jobs increased by 22 percent. This job loss gave Boston the lowest median family income of the nation's seven largest metropolitan areas. With slightly less than 10 percent of the city's population being African American in 1960—smaller than in many other major American cities—whites made up most of the city's poor.

Boston was also on the verge of bankruptcy. Its tax rate of $101 per $1,000 of assessed valuation, twice the rate in Chicago and New York and higher than in any other large American city, discouraged investors, who feared endlessly rising real estate taxes. As a result, only two new downtown office buildings had been constructed since 1930. The most dependable employer in town was city hall, bloating Boston's civil service payrolls by 50 percent higher than what was average for the nation's largest cities while draining Boston's coffers. It was no wonder that in 1959 Moody's had downgraded the city's bond rating from A to Baa, near junk level, making it the only city with a population over half a million to carry that stigma and borrowing burden.[11] WGBH, the local educational television station, regularly broadcast alarming programs like *City in Crisis*, a twenty-part series. While Logue was preparing to go public with his plan for a New Boston in August 1960, the Boston-based, politically progressive *Christian Science Monitor* wondered aloud, "Is Boston worth saving? The streets are choked with traffic, vast jungles of blighted housing, faded business districts . . . Is it all worth the effort to change this?"[12]

If anything became crystal clear to Logue from his initial, intense immersion in Boston, it was how the long arm of history had shaped the troubled city he now saw before him. Much of the current paralysis could be traced to the bitter, decades-long struggle between the Yankee Protestant (often referred to as "Brahmin") elite and the immigrant workers and their descendants—many of them Catholics and Jews—who labored in the city's once-flourishing ports, markets, shipyards, and manufacturing plants. It was "a confrontation," Logue was convinced, "of a deep nature" that did great "harm . . . to the city."[13] The Yankees had dominated the city economically and politically from its earliest days as a center of local fishing and global trade. They continued overseeing its transformation in the nineteenth century into a regional marketplace and the commercial heart of a thriving textile empire that stretched into the river-rich hinterlands of New England, including such mill towns as Lowell and Lawrence, Massachusetts, and Manchester, New Hampshire.

As the size of Boston's immigrant working class swelled—at first predominantly with the Irish but during the first decades of the twentieth century broadened to include substantial numbers of Italians and Eastern Europeans—the Yankees found their Republican hegemony threatened. By 1905, savvy Democratic politicians like John F. Kennedy's maternal grandfather John Francis "Honey Fitz" Fitzgerald, hailing from the city's then Irish and later Italian enclave of the North End, managed to turn the exploding numbers of ethnic voters into an engine powering a potent Democratic Party machine. From 1913 to 1949, the machine's undisputed leader, James

Michael Curley, dominated Boston politics, serving multiple terms as mayor, governor, and congressman—as well as two terms in federal prison. Curley's strategy was simple: milk downtown to feed the ethnic, working-class neighborhoods. With as much as 80 percent of the city's revenue coming from real estate taxes, he kept tax assessments low in the neighborhoods and sky-high and unpredictable—and, it was rumored, in pencil—downtown, to maximize the possibility of making tax abatement deals with business, one of his many party- and self-aggrandizing corruption schemes. A commanding orator, Curley took great delight in lampooning the Yankees as the "codfish aristocracy," who were "descended from rum runners and slave traders." He boasted that "it took the Irish to make Massachusetts a fit place to live."[14]

Not surprisingly with so fragile an economic base, citywide infrastructure and services—from sewers and streets to schools—deteriorated badly under Curley, while the Yankee elite retaliated with a roving eye. Some remained in the premier neighborhoods of Beacon Hill and the Back Bay, but many others left town. As Harvey Cox wrote in *The Secular City* in 1965, "The frontal collision between Yankees and Irish drove many people with money and civic interests to the suburbs. As Mr. Justice Brandeis reported, at the turn of the century the wealthy citizens of Boston told their sons: 'Boston holds nothing for you except heavy taxes and political misrule. When you marry, pick out a suburb to build your house in, join the Country Club, and make your life center about your club, your home, and your children.'" Cox proceeded to note that by midcentury, "the advice was taken not just by the sons of the wealthy, but by everyone with enough savings to flee to Newton or Belmont" or, "the most ludicrous anomaly of all," the town of Brookline, which, although "almost completely surrounded by the City of Boston, . . . nonetheless clings to its independent status, pretending to spurn all involvement with the corruption of The Hub."[15]

Businessmen similarly invested their substantial financial capital elsewhere—whether in Boston's suburbs, out west and down south, or halfway around the globe—leaving the city's factories, company headquarters, department stores, banks, and law firms languishing more and more with every passing decade. Boston took shabby-genteel to new heights. In a public speech as early as April 1960, when Logue was still a consultant, he openly criticized this disinvestment in the city: "Boston capital is at work all over the world. We need to create effective ways of putting it to work at home, on a business, not a charity, basis."[16]

The Yankee elite perhaps registered its greatest opposition by shifting its political ambitions from the city to the state, controlling the corruption at the Boston City Hall as much as possible from the Massachusetts State House only blocks away, in alliance with the state's western and suburban legislators. State aid to Boston was kept at a minimum and essentially the state deprived the city of home rule. It granted it no authority over revenue, other than collecting property taxes, and empowered the governor-appointed Finance Commission to monitor all city finances.[17] The controlling hand of the state even extended as far as the governor appointing the Boston police commissioner and overseeing his budget, a response spurred by the strike of the city's Irish Catholic–dominated police force in 1919.[18] Curley and his ilk might rule the Boston roost, but the Yankees were going to make damn sure they had few tools with which to do it.[19]

Whatever postwar prosperity Greater Boston enjoyed during the 1940s and 1950s took place outside the city's limits, particularly along the newly opened Route 128, the first high-speed circumferential highway built around an American city. Here an entrepreneurial electronics boom took off, spawned by experiments at MIT and other university labs—so much so that the roadway was nicknamed "America's Technology Highway" and then the "Space Highway," as transistor and semiconductor development gave way to aerospace (and eventually to computers). It was there, in fact, in 1951 that Boston's old-time Yankee real estate firm Cabot, Cabot & Forbes pioneered the industrial-park concept that guided its own local investing and created a national model. A few years later, the company vice president Robert H. Ryan likened Boston to "an apple with a shiny skin, rotten at the core."[20] Into the next decade, the local developer William Poorvu made sure to focus his own real estate investing on Harvard Square and Route 128, "markets [that] were outside the urban center."[21]

Route 128 and the Massachusetts Turnpike that followed it also opened up vast new suburban tracts for residential development, luring away the younger, more upwardly mobile of the city's population. Many were ex-GIs well supplied with VA mortgage loans usable only in white, middle-class suburbs, not in the inner-city neighborhoods of their parents and grandparents, which were redlined by banks.[22] They were also driven out by the city's poor services and deteriorating, outdated housing. Collins's deputy mayor, Henry Scagnoli, was not unusual for his generation in growing up during the 1920s and 1930s in a Jamaica Plain house without heat or hot water and with a toilet only in the cellar. A major goal when he returned from the war was to own a better house than his parents did.[23] Soon, department stores and other businesses followed the money out of town. Downtown lost an estimated $500 million in retail trade during the 1950s alone; by 1964, city retail sales would amount to less than half of the metropolitan area's total.[24]

The first break in the city's paralyzing stalemate came with the election in 1949 of John Hynes, an Irish Catholic Democrat like Curley but of a very different breed. Rather than grease the wheels of Curley's machine, Hynes challenged it—and won. Hynes had been Boston's city clerk when, in 1947, he suddenly found himself named acting mayor as Curley headed off to federal prison in Danbury, Connecticut, on a mail fraud conviction. A modest, mild-mannered, hardworking man, Hynes was furious when, on his return, Curley pronounced, "I have accomplished more in one day than has been done in the five months of my absence."[25] At that moment, Hynes decided to challenge Curley in the 1949 election, taking him on with the slogan "Restore Boston's Good Name" and the promise of honest government. He won by fifteen thousand votes in the highest election turnout ever. Hynes would get reelected handily in 1951 (required by a charter change) and again in 1955.

Hynes was supported by others who shared his deep concern about the city's future. Some critics of the status quo joined an organization called the New Boston Committee, founded in 1950 by an ambitious young reformer named Jerome Lyle Rappaport, who had come from New York to attend Harvard College and Harvard Law School and decided to stay and clean up his adopted city. He had founded the group Youth for Hynes in the 1949 election and became the mayor's chief assistant afterward. Others among the discontented responded to a bold move by Boston College to break the political and cultural deadlock by sponsoring the Boston College Citizen Seminars, aimed at bringing together Yankee businessmen, Irish politicians, and civic leaders of all stripes—"the people who owned Boston and those who ran it," as *U.S. News and World Report* so bluntly put it.[26] After a lively presentation and discussion on an urban problem, the assembled socialized. Logue was convinced that "a wide open bar" followed by dinner was "the key to the whole thing," given that "the Yankees and the Irish did not speak to and did not even know each other on a personal basis."[27]

Hynes's victory in 1949 was accompanied by a structural change in Boston's city government that would have a major impact on the urban renewal efforts of Collins and Logue a decade later. In an attempt to break the Curley machine's iron grip on the city, the New Boston Committee and other reformers proposed changing the city's charter to take authority away from the mayor and the city council and institute a professional city manager. The Curley machine responded with an alternate referendum, which passed, to strengthen the mayor's power but shrink the city council from twenty-two district representatives to nine elected at large, ostensibly to encourage more of a citywide consciousness among city councillors. But what the machine imagined would safeguard the autonomy of its mayor in the end strengthened the hand of victorious opponents, Mayors Hynes and Collins. With so much authority given to the mayor, the city council had little independent power to push back against executive ambitions. The council's input into the budget, for example, consisted only of the ability to delete items, not to add them, which kept the council from initiating programs.[28] The city council's influence on policy would mostly come through its efforts to shape public opinion, which invited obstreperous behavior aimed at attracting media attention. As it turned out, the new at-large city council may have been smaller, but its ethnic complexion and loyalties barely changed. It remained the mouthpiece of the neighborhoods, dominated by the Irish from South Boston and Charlestown and the Italians from the North End and East Boston.

Hynes recognized when he beat Curley that he had won a rather empty prize unless he solved the city's fiscal crisis. He cautiously reached out to the estranged business community and began strategizing how he might tap the new pots of federal funding becoming available through urban renewal. These funds promised to inject capital investment into his struggling city and to generate higher tax valuations on repurposed land, while also improving Boston's deteriorating physical face. Hynes took the initial step of creating a modest BRA operation, first as a division of the Boston Housing Authority (BHA) and then in 1957 as an independent agency. He named as its head Kane Simonian, a reliable supporter and a typical Boston civil servant from West Roxbury, who had worked up the ladder from a low-level post in the BHA to executive director of the BRA. Simonian was unusual only for being a Harvard graduate and Armenian rather than Irish. He was still heading the BRA when the newly elected Collins undertook his national search for a new chief.[29]

Hynes tried hard to make a success of urban renewal, but a combination of the city's limited resources; the top-down, clearance-oriented federal approach to urban renewal prevailing during the 1950s; and the long legacy of neighborhood suspicion of downtown conspired to make his record a mixed one that would haunt renewal initiatives far into the future. Hynes's efforts focused on both downtown and the neighborhoods. Downtown redevelopment moved two transportation projects forward. The first was the construction of what proved to be the disastrous John F. Fitzgerald Expressway, known as the "Central Artery," which sliced through downtown to whisk suburbanites in and out of the city. The other was a massive garage under the Boston Common where commuters could park upon arrival.[30]

Beyond that, Hynes's downtown strategy revolved around two projects that never came to fruition during his mayoralty: convincing the Prudential Insurance Company to build its New England regional headquarters on the site of the abandoned Boston & Maine railroad yards in the Back Bay and corralling the city, state, and federal governments to join forces to build Government Center on the location of Scollay Square, Boston's honky-tonk red-light district. When Hynes left office in 1960, having declined to run for another term, the Prudential Center was already designed—albeit in a corporate architectural style that was sized too large for its site and that garnered little praise—but the project was at an impasse because the city could not give Prudential sufficient assurances about its future tax liability.[31] And despite Hynes's shuttling between his own city hall, the Massachusetts State House, and the nation's capital, Government Center remained more of a hope than a reality, with the federal government preferring a less risky Back Bay site near Copley Square.[32]

Most problematic, however, was how these two simmering projects fell two miles apart, thereby diluting any effort to revitalize Boston's downtown economy with new offices, retail, and, in the case of Prudential, residences. The *Washington Post* architecture critic Wolf Von Eckardt, who dismissed "the Pru" as "so big and so bad," despaired at the "sad mistake of the Prudential [Center] and the Government Center going up at the same time and sort of tugging the city back and forth," both vying to be central. Von Eckardt's prediction would prove disturbingly true. Over time many fashionable stores would come to prefer the upscale Back Bay shopping area in and around Prudential to downtown locations, thereby contributing to the latter's decline.[33]

Whereas Hynes's legacy in downtown renewal held some promise on his departure from office, his neighborhood initiatives in the New York Streets area of the South End and in the West End were horrendous examples of 1950s-era demolition-style urban renewal. The New York Streets project bulldozed thirteen acres of run-down but still viable residences in the South End, home to a mixed ethnic and racial community of 850 families. They were replaced with light industry, such as a new headquarters and printing plant for the *Boston Herald Traveler* newspaper, intended to yield higher land values and tax revenues along with jobs. Melvin King, who would go on to become an important South End organizer and citywide activist, grew up happily as an African American in this diverse neighborhood and recalled his shock at hearing, while he was away at college, that the home territory he cherished was now branded a "skid row" and destined for replacement.[34]

A larger project to raze and rebuild the predominantly Italian and Jewish forty-eight-acre West End would reverberate locally and nationally as a symbol of urban renewal's destructive and hubristic approach in the fifties.[35] Hynes and Simonian's scheme involved condemning what they labeled a blighted slum, close enough to downtown to attract more lucrative uses, and replacing it with luxury apartment buildings designed to entice middle-class residents back to the city. It may have been ruthless but, unfortunately, it was not so out of sync with what other cities were doing at the time, including New Haven. But three factors distinguished Hynes's efforts. First, with a suspicious lack of transparency, the mayor gave the project to his former assistant Jerome Lyle Rappaport, who had spearheaded the New Boston Committee and was now a partner in a real estate development firm that also won the auction to develop the University Towers in New Haven.

Second, the atmosphere of distrust that had long divided neighborhoods and downtown in Boston was reinforced by the BRA's lack of responsiveness to residents' initial inquiries and growing protests. The project eventually became a cause célèbre for dislocating several thousand residents and dozens of small businesses. The BRA's anemic relocation operation, partly due to the minimal federal funding available for it, and the Rappaport group's reneging on its promise to include some low- and middle-income housing for former neighborhood residents in the new project, only made matters worse.[36]

Third, the West End became a textbook case, quite literally, of the toll urban renewal took on city residents, as social scientists such as the sociologist Herbert Gans, the psychologist Marc Fried, and the planner Chester Hartman launched important studies of the impact of West End redevelopment. They argued that where outsiders saw aging, substandard tenements on blighted blocks, those who called the West End home, even if poor, considered it a familiar and affordable neighborhood, interlaced with extensive familial, ethnic, and religious bonds whose destruction left them bereft. Gans's *The Urban Villagers: Group and Class in the Life of Italian-Americans* of 1962 would remain a touchstone for urban renewal opponents long thereafter, so much so that throughout his life, Logue went out of his way to deny involvement in the BRA's West End urban renewal.[37] The fact that the clearance was done by the time he arrived in Boston in 1960, however, did not spare Logue from the taint of this misconceived project. Its long shadow would color everything he tried to do in Boston's neighborhoods. And Rappaport, who had already frustrated Logue in New Haven by cleverly beating out Yale, would continue to exasperate him over the many years it took to complete the Charles River Park project.[38]

For all the hope that Hynes's election in 1949 had signaled for turning around Boston, he stepped down a decade later with only limited achievements, leaving it to his successor to run the next lap in revitalizing the city. The selection of Hynes's replacement would prove a surprising chapter in the annals of Boston elections, as John Francis Collins won a legendary upset against the powerful, well-connected Massachusetts state senate president John Powers of South Boston. Powers had lost against Hynes in 1955, but he seemed such a sure bet in 1959 that everyone, including the Kennedys and the cardinal, lined up behind him.

The forty-year-old Collins was an even more independent candidate than Hynes had been in 1949. A blue-collar kid who had grown up in Irish Catholic Roxbury, he had odd-jobbed his way through the working man's Suffolk Law School without pausing for a college degree he couldn't afford, fought in the wartime army, and served in both houses of the state legislature and the Boston City Council. Now he was occupying the sinecure of register of probate for Suffolk County, a well-paying position that he could have relaxed in for the rest of his career.[39] But that was not Collins's idea of a life worth living, particularly since surviving a devastating, near-death case of polio in 1955 while nursing his infected children back to health. They recovered fully. Collins spent the rest of his life in a wheelchair or occasionally using crutches or a cane.

The determination it took Collins to resume a public career—he ran for city council from his hospital bed—gave him political grit.[40] By making creative use of television—including plotting how best to present his disability—and by condemning Powers as a corrupt Curley rerun with the campaign slogan "Stop Power Politics," underdog Collins shocked the Boston bookies by winning nearly 56 percent of the vote. All but four of the city's twenty-two wards became his. Having made it to city hall with only the voters' mandate, Collins was a dark horse who owed no one for the ride—which gave him a rare independence as mayor to do things such as recruit an outsider like Ed Logue and give him enormous power.[41]

Urban renewal had not been a major issue in the campaign. After the West End debacle, no one in his right mind would want to raise it publicly. But candidates Powers and Collins were both being tutored on urban renewal, and in fact, they had the same teacher in Joseph Slavet, executive secretary of the clean-government, business-leaning Boston Municipal Research Bureau (MRB). Slavet was officially supporting Powers along with the rest of the establishment, but at the behest of his mentor, the MRB board chair Henry Lee Shattuck—a rare Brahmin lawyer who backed Collins— he started meeting with Collins to explain how other cities were coping with crises similar to Boston's.[42] By the time Collins took office in early January 1960, he had decided to make urban renewal the major priority of his administration. He began by extending a hand to the Yankee business and professional elite, who remained angry that tax assessments were unfair and the city was sinking deeper into deficit and decrepitude. Collins recognized that despite some early success, "Hynes spent the last few years of his term on a very defensive basis with the business community . . . They felt much more comfortable with Hynes than with Curley, but it was not a partnership by any means."[43]

The city's leaders had recently, in fact, formed the sixteen-member Coordinating Committee with representatives from the major business and civic organizations—soon to be popularly known as the "Vault" for their regular meetings in a conference room adjacent to the basement vault of the Brahmin banker Ralph Lowell's Boston Safe Deposit and Trust Company.[44] Soon after he was elected, Collins went to meet them, confident that they had no claims on him, and when they offered one—to pick up the tab on his $62,000 campaign debt—he unhesitatingly declined: "That's my debt; I'll take care of it."[45] But he also knew that he couldn't turn the city around without their assistance. Holding the line on property taxes and cutting municipal expenses and the public payroll would help, but it wouldn't be enough. Lobbying at the state house for other revenue-producing powers beyond the property tax, such as a long-sought sales tax, and other ways of loosening the noose that the state had tightened around Curley's Boston would require bigger guns than Collins carried on his own.[46]

The situation Collins faced was dire. As a case in point, the State of Massachusetts covered only 8 percent of city school costs, when the national average was 40 percent, making Massachusetts forty-sixth in state contributions to education.[47] It remained to be seen how generous Boston's Yankees would be with their influence and their wallets, but the idea of recruiting a pro like Logue with urban renewal expertise and experience attracting federal dollars appealed to them. Collins's inaugural address announcing Operation Revival to "restore, rebuild, and redevelop" generated much enthusiasm in downtown boardrooms, captured in a banner headline in *The Boston Globe* as "Business Leaders Hail Collins' Program for Hub."[48]

Such was the stage Logue entered when he began his work in Boston in March 1960, only a couple of months after Collins had gone public with Operation Revival. As Logue delved deeper that spring into Boston, he became more and more excited about the city's potential, particularly what he would dramatically call the "walk to the sea" from the Charles River through the Common to Boston Harbor. But he also became less and less sanguine about how to make it happen: "I scoured just about every inch of the city—and came to love it. But it was also easy to see that the problems were tremendous." Most disturbing, he felt, Boston was "a city without confidence in itself," despite its potential to seed a new economy built around technology and ideas. Logue decided that he could do the job only under the right conditions: "If this was going to be my show, it had to be pretty much my way."[49] But as he wrote to a professional colleague, housing reformer Catherine Bauer Wurster, in mid-June, "At this point I am not the slightest bit optimistic that the right set of conditions can be created."[50] His most important demand was to replicate the authority over planning *and* redevelopment that Mayor Dick Lee had given to him in New Haven. Integration, he was convinced, kept planning practical and redevelopment robust.

Given the short leash on which the state held the city, such a fundamental change in BRA structure required an amendment to Chapter 121A, the legislation by which the state had designated the BRA as the city's administrator of federal urban renewal funds. Logue made the passage of this amendment a nonnegotiable condition of accepting Collins's offer, and while he waited for the slow wheels of the state legislature to turn, he worked from October to December 1960 under a ninety-day contract. "I made it clear to the mayor and everyone else that I would not renew that arrangement. Either I got to run the show or not. No more extensions."[51]

GETTING APPROVED

When the amendment finally passed, Logue had orchestrated what *Architectural Forum* described as "the most massively centralized planning and renewal powers that any large city has ever voted to one man (other than New York's Robert Moses)." Or as *Fortune* magazine more succinctly phrased it, Logue "cooks and serves."[52] As part of this same amendment that empowered him, Logue wanted a legislative change that would allow the abandoned railroad yards to be ruled blighted and thereby eligible for special tax treatment, moving the Prudential project forward.[53] Logue also insisted on sufficient independence from the appointed BRA board, such as allowing them only up-or-down votes on projects, not the right to tinker with the details, "putting them in a straitjacket," as he described it. He likewise sought a free hand to recruit nationally and hire outside of civil service.[54] Logue wanted no part of what he jokingly called the "Irish social security system" for himself either. So he requested that the city pay $5,000 of his salary, instead of charging it all to federal urban renewal grants, to ensure that the mayor could fire him at will.[55] Ever since civil service workers in Connecticut had obstructed Governor Chester Bowles's reforms back in the late 1940s, Logue had taken a principled stand against tenure for high-level employees. He also hoped that a less protected status would "take care of any concern about a 'czar,'" so "completely different was it from the arrangements Bob Moses had made for himself in New York."[56] With all his demands now met, Logue's candidacy as development administrator was finally ready for approval by the BRA board, made up of five individuals charged with overseeing the city's redevelopment activities and affiliated with different powerful local interests—the Catholic Church, the local press, real estate, and labor.

Like everything in Boston, Logue's approval by this BRA board would surely be politically charged, no slam dunk. Rather, Logue predicted, "A Boston political battle royal loomed."[57] Collins had inherited the board from Hynes, who by law had appointed four members, with the governor naming the fifth. Collins's contribution—and it was a constructive one—was to move BRA member Monsignor Francis "Frank" Lally, the liberal editor of the Catholic Church's *Pilot* newspaper and a close confidant of Cardinal Richard Cushing's, into the chairmanship. Lally would prove a loyal supporter and helpful partner to Logue throughout his Boston career.[58] But there was only one other assured vote for Logue beyond Lally's—the real estate executive's—until some members of the Vault got wind of the board's resistance. Worried about a loss of momentum for change and the new Kennedy administration scooping up Logue, they pressured the editor of the *Record American* newspaper to force his photo editor, who was a BRA board member, to vote for Logue.[59]

In contrast to the board, a wide cross-section of Bostonians expressed enthusiasm for Logue. The Cambridge architect Carl Koch conveyed a common sentiment when he sent Logue a telegram the day before the vote: "For Boston's sake you must win."[60] The same day, Melnea Cass, the president of the NAACP's Boston Branch, mailed a letter to each member of the BRA board endorsing Logue's appointment "because of our basic interest in the improvement of our city, and because of the large number of Negroes living in deprived areas due to the discriminatory factors that tend to keep them there." As it had in New Haven, the local NAACP was hopeful that urban renewal would bring Boston's blacks long-awaited attention and was confident of Logue's "ability to implement this program in the best interest of Boston and all the people therein."[61] In expressing the NAACP's position so forthrightly and linking the fate of the black community to the larger city, Cass was claiming the NAACP's rightful place in Boston's pluralist democratic coalition, which Robert Dahl was describing for New Haven in his *Who Governs?* the very same year. On the morning of the vote, January 25, 1961, hundreds of people rallied outside the BRA offices to promote Logue's candidacy as the rescuer of "our distressed and sick city," as one advocate bluntly put it.[62] *The Christian Science Monitor*, which watched the showdown closely, concluded that "the real persuader, the real push, came with the outpouring of demands—in letters and phone calls—from virtually every section of the city . . . The extraordinary community support became articulate almost overnight."[63]

After meeting for nearly five hours, the BRA board begrudgingly voted 3 to 2 for Logue. It was hardly a mandate, but it was good enough for Logue, who by personality was more energized than undermined by a fight. One battle that would rage on was the Kane Simonian problem. With the encouragement of the BRA board member James Colbert, an influential newsman, the civil servant Simonian refused to accept Logue's hiring. In fact, as soon as Logue's appointment became official, Simonian brought suit, charging that he had been illegally demoted even though he retained the title of executive director. Although the case would be thrown out by the state's highest court in May, a compromise was reached whereby Simonian remained secretary of the BRA board and was responsible for the BRA's operations division—overseeing appraisals, land acquisition, site preparation, property maintenance, and the like. Simonian would also complete the already launched New York Streets and West End projects, from which Logue was more than happy to keep his distance.[64]

So began an unusual governance arrangement, where Simonian's division and Logue's much larger organization operated out of different offices a block apart and every BRA board meeting had two agendas, with the secretary and the development administrator taking turns presenting their business. John Ryan, a real estate man who joined the BRA board in 1961, recalled with amusement that Logue's shrewd strategy for coping with his less-than-supportive board members was "to deluge everyone with paperwork," giving them both everything and nothing.[65] There was never any doubt, however, who was really in charge. When queried about why he hadn't contented himself with the status of coordinator of redevelopment programs,

Logue retorted, "That's what you do when you don't have authority. I don't go into a job without power. Can you imagine [Secretary of Defense Robert] McNamara as coordinator of defense?"[66] After the vote on January 25, Logue headed back to his office, but, he said, "I stopped briefly, I confess, at the traffic island at Scollay Square," a spot that would soon become the centerpiece of the new Government Center. "I said to myself, 'The program, the money, the power, it is all there. And thanks to the mayor, I have it all.'" Later he reflected, with his characteristic confidence, "I don't remember any basic doubts on my part. I had been blessed with the opportunity to remake a rundown, somewhat dispirited city [and] had been given the resources to do the job."[67]

Logue made one more request in his negotiations with the Collins administration that, although relatively minor, provides some insight into his mind-set as he settled into Boston. He asked that it arrange for his admission to the Tavern Club, a fairly prestigious, invitation-only men's club that attracted the literary, artistic, and intellectual set among the city's elite but was not the ultra-exclusive Brahmin Somerset or Algonquin Clubs.[68] Here Logue got to know prominent local figures like the historian and Boston Athenaeum director Walter Muir Whitehill, a relationship that would prove useful to his work. When Collins heard this last demand of Logue's, he reputedly told him, "Are you crazy? I've lived here all my life and I've never even been *invited* to those places."[69]

Logue had been staying at the Tavern Club while doing his consulting work and wanted to join. As in New Haven, he valued male sociability. Undoubtedly, he thought membership would help him integrate into insular and standoffish Boston, giving him a place in the inner circles to which he'd had easy access in New Haven, having lived there most of his adult life since arriving as a Yale freshman and having benefited from connections through his wife's well-established family. An astute Logue had surely figured out that Boston was a clubby town. According to Cleveland Amory, a son of privileged Boston and the author of the satirical *The Proper Bostonians* in 1947, "The core of the Bostonian social system is clubdom; and here the status quo remains awe-inspiring."[70] Logue went on to join other clubs in Boston—the

Thursday Evening Club, the Examiner Club, the Saturday Club, and the Union Boat Club. All expanded his networks. "That's where he met the power players," explained Robert Campbell, *The Boston Globe*'s architecture critic (and a fellow Tavern Club member).

It is possible, too, that these clubs helped Logue navigate the tricky terrain of being an Irishman in the upper echelons of Boston society. Wife Margaret recalled his discomfort early on in Boston when "Ed encountered slurs from Yankees who didn't identify the name as Irish. He would let one remark go by but thereafter declare himself as Irish." She joked at the time that Logue should write a book called "Passing in Boston." Herbert Gleason, a mover and shaker in the city who befriended Logue early on, agreed that his Irishness mattered. "Tavern Club was status. Big status. I think he had . . . some Irish underdog element in his personality."[71] Perhaps, too, these clubs offered Logue new opportunities to perpetuate his old pattern of being a rebel in the belly of the establishment beast. It didn't escape him that the 1962 edition of the *Directory of Directors in the City of Boston and Vicinity*—of banks, insurance companies, law firms, and the like—documented "the monolithic Yankee character of the Boston business establishment." Not only were there no Irish, but "they didn't know anything about women. Italians didn't exist."[72] It had been a bruising battle to get named development administrator of the Boston Redevelopment Authority, and Logue was determined to make a success of it—without compromising who he was and what he set out to do.

SETTING UP SHOP IN BOSTON

When Logue's appointment finally became official in January 1961, he had seven years under his belt doing a similar job in New Haven. He was not quite forty years old, a young man to have just been given so much power. And it thrilled him to have this opportunity to move the practice of urban renewal to the next stage. Everyone in the business understood that cities like Boston were in desperate shape—and that the demolition-style urban renewal of the 1950s was not the answer. "The Cinderella dream of cities—to turn the old and shabby into the new and beautiful with the magic wand of Federal funds to live happily, urbanistically speaking, ever after," lamented the *New York Times* architecture critic Ada Louise Huxtable, had proved instead "a discouraging record of cross-country failures." What could be more exciting, Logue thought, than figuring out how to do the job right in the backyard of one of the worst abuses of urban renewal, the infamous West End project, described by Huxtable as "a definitive demonstration of how to destroy a community with a bulldozer."[73]

Logue's allies in Washington—including Robert Weaver, incoming administrator of the Housing and Home Finance Agency, and William Slayton, commissioner of the Urban Renewal Administration—were keeping a close eye on Logue's progress and stood ready to grant his requests for funds and special privileges, such as permitting early land acquisitions and relocations before the full approval processes were complete. (It didn't hurt that native son John F. Kennedy became president at the same time and that Boston's John McCormack was the number-two Democrat in the House.)[74] Long before Logue's plan was publicly announced in late September 1960 and his position made official the following January, a personal visit by Logue and Collins to the regional Housing and Home Finance Agency office in New York City had clinched an advance of $28 million on the first federal grant of $60 million, pending the plan's approval by local authorities.

Getting the required approval from the Boston City Council was not without its challenges. Weak in formal power, its members seized every opportunity to assert themselves, and they were no friend of urban renewal. City Councillors William F. "Bill" Foley, Jr., from South Boston, and Katherine "Kitty" Craven, from Hyde Park and a native of Charlestown, most visibly built their reputations during the 1960s around publicly drubbing Logue and Collins (who had given their man John Powers a thrashing in the 1959 mayoral race), but plenty of others joined in.[75] Logue bore the abuse stoically, buoyed by the support he received from professional colleagues, his large staff, and even ordinary citizens who wrote to him frequently to apologize for "the insults you are forced to take in the line of duty," as one city resident put it.[76] Given this treatment, Logue and the mayor delighted in having this early money securely in hand in time for the city council's hearing on the $90 Million Development Program. When Councilman Foley proclaimed dismissively, "John, the Feds will never approve it," Collins took pleasure in retorting, "Bill, they already have."[77] That sealed the deal, as the city council was in no position to give back federal dollars.

Logue brought experience building a redevelopment agency from New Haven to Boston—recruiting professional talent nationally, developing an organizational structure, and creating a dynamic esprit de corps, even as some staff protested, as they had in New Haven, that he could at times be too arbitrary and hard-driving as a boss. The BRA staffer John Stainton recalled that "he had a lot of charm" but he could "also be very abrasive and aggressive. 'Cruel' is a little strong, maybe, but he could really put people down." Logue was not oblivious to the charge. He claimed to have learned a lesson when his assistant, Janet Bowler, reported that Peter Riemer, whom he considered a "genius" as the Government Center project director, complained, "You know, I don't mind if he chews me out but he shouldn't chew me out in front of other people"—a reaction not unlike what Logue had expressed years earlier to Dick Lee.[78]

In time, Logue's redevelopment agency became much larger than New Haven's. When Logue arrived in 1960, Kane Simonian's office had sixteen staff members. By the time Logue stepped down in 1967, his BRA employed somewhere between five hundred and six hundred. (Totals varied, probably given the different ways of counting part-timers and Simonian's separate operations division. In any case, the payroll was huge, "probably the largest planning-renewal team in the nation," according to *Architectural Forum*.)[79] Many were young, idealistic, and well-educated at the nation's best planning, architecture, and law schools. Students at Harvard's Graduate School of Design (GSD) and MIT's School of Architecture and Planning eagerly pursued the BRA's plum jobs upon graduation.

In 1967, the average staff age was a young thirty-seven. The BRA was also known by African American professionals as a welcoming place to work. Black employment grew from 2 percent in 1961 to 13 percent by 1967 as a result of Logue's explicit commitment to recruiting minority staff, which took substantial effort given the small number of nonwhite professionals living in Boston in the 1960s. "He looked very hard to find black people with credentials who could run programs," recalled the BRA project director Robert Litke.[80] Few women served in the higher ranks of the BRA, however, with most female staff working as assistants and secretaries, typical of offices in the era. Esther Maletz, the only woman at a high managerial level—first as a lawyer experienced in housing and urban development and then as Government Center project director—felt that she "was not treated differently in any meaningful way [from] my male colleagues" while working closely with Logue for five years.[81] But Maletz's having few female peers suggests not only the paucity of candidates but also the fact that Logue's progressive hiring agenda during the 1960s put more emphasis on breaking down barriers of race than of gender. This was particularly striking because Logue's wife, Margaret, held jobs outside the home throughout their marriage, albeit in the female-dominated field of education. Upon moving to Boston with young children—eight-year-old Kathy and four-year-old Billy—Margaret secured employment, first as acting director of the Beacon Hill Nursery School and then as a teacher at the Winsor School, an independent school for girls.[82]

Logue sought ways to distinguish the BRA from the sluggish business as usual practiced in most Boston city departments. To bring good modern design to the office, Logue got help from the firm of the dean of Harvard's GSD, Josep Lluís Sert. When the elevator opened on the tenth and eleventh floors of City Hall Annex, observed a *Fortune* magazine writer, "suddenly the wall colors change" from the institutional green paint and bare bulbs below "to such vivid tones as mustard. Office doors are painted in bright primaries; lowered ceilings accommodate new lighting fixtures and acoustical surfaces," though he failed to mention that Logue playfully flaunted Corbusier's primary-colors palette with his Yale-blue door.

This journalist also admired the "zealous young multitude" that "walk[ed] swiftly in the halls." An MIT graduate student who was a participant-observer at the BRA for five months confirmed that in contrast to the first nine floors "staffed by elderly paper shufflers, . . . the immediate impression one gets of the BRA staff is of youth and vitality."[83] They may not have had the job security of Boston civil servants, but they were paid much better.[84] Not only were salaries higher, thanks to Uncle Sam picking up 90 percent of the payroll, but Christmas brought annual bonuses, creating, according to *Fortune*, "an envious shudder . . . through the other nine floors of City Hall Annex," as regular city employees asked, "Was Santa trapped on the top floors?" Arthur Reilly, who landed a job at the BRA through his family's political connections to Hynes and Collins, feared the consequences. Not only were other city employees resentful—"they've been working for the city for thirty years and were making $6,000 a year, and here's . . . some kid from New York, who's in upstairs, and he's making $16,000"—but also, as he predicted (rightly), the affront would come back to haunt the BRA's urban renewal efforts in a neighborhood like Charlestown, where many city workers lived.[85]

Organizationally, Logue developed an approach he liked to describe as "centralize in order to decentralize."[86] Much of the power was concentrated in the central BRA office and, in reality, in the charismatic if domineering Logue himself. By all reports, he was very hands-on and kept himself at the center of things, the sun around which all planets—divisions, departments, project teams—revolved. Even young staff members who did not know him well basked in the glow of his power. Years later, Reginald Griffith, an architect who had joined the BRA upon graduating from MIT, vividly recollected every major encounter with Logue. Boston native Frank Del Vecchio, hired right out of Harvard Law School, gloried in zipping Logue around town "at breakneck, white-knuckle speed" in his tiny Triumph TR4 sports car. Ted Liebman, a newly minted Harvard GSD grad, couldn't believe his luck when Logue personally asked him to make large, complicated drawings with overlays to present the Government Center plan to the city council. Rather than resent the onerous assignment, Liebman felt privileged to be among those getting direct requests from the big boss: "Ed Logue had brought together a bright group of people that were working their behinds off and we thought that we were the best in the world."[87] An organizational specialist might have faulted Logue for running such a flat organization with a large number of people reporting directly to him and no fixed hierarchy. Recalled Stainton, "He didn't . . . delegate specifically to different people. He sort of threw it out there . . . it ended up [that] everybody worked for Ed Logue."[88]

Decentralization, on the other hand, was meant to take place by locating teams in site offices within the various renewal areas, each headed by a project manager who had considerable discretion but also reported directly to Logue. Team members—consisting of planners, architects, relocation experts, social workers, rehabilitation advisers, and so forth—were responsible to managers on-site as well as to supervisors in the relevant department within the central BRA, such as design, planning, legal, transportation, rehabilitation, and relocation.[89] Logue hoped that embedding project teams in neighborhoods undergoing renewal would strengthen ties to residents, helping to carry out his trademark "planning with people." He liked to say, "It's a hell of a lot more fun to plan a neighborhood with the people who live in it than to plan for them as if you knew best."[90] But by many accounts, project managers often presented themselves as "mini Logues," replicating a phenomenon that had emerged in New Haven where impressionable and ambitious young men so strongly identified with their boss and his mission that they styled themselves after him.[91] Mini Logues adopted their boss's contradictions along with his more clear-cut strengths, including letting Logue's faith in professional expertise undermine his stated other goal of making the BRA collaborative with neighborhood residents.

MOVING BEYOND NEW HAVEN

As Logue threw himself into renewing Boston, he sought to replicate what had worked well in New Haven. Given that one of his top objectives was to expand on his success in Wooster Square promoting rehabilitation over demolition, the Logues' choice of Boston residence was symbolic. Whereas in New Haven they had built a new, modern house, in Boston they bought a renovated early nineteenth-century rowhouse on West Cedar Street in Beacon Hill, a historic urban neighborhood that Logue fell in love with. "I think it took him back," Margaret mused, to the golden part of his childhood when, before his father died, the family lived in an attached brick townhouse in central Philadelphia.[92] The Logues' most personal of decisions signaled greater flexibility in defining what it meant for a city to be modern.

More substantively, Logue knew he would need in Boston the same two foundations of his New Haven work: a committed mayor and federal funding. Logue frequently spoke admiringly of John Collins. He appreciated his intelligence ("one of the smartest guys I have ever known") as well as his political astuteness, his self-confidence, his managerial competence, and his fighter's commitment to turning around Boston.[93] They had a good working rapport where Logue met with the mayor often to brief him on progress and problems, a necessity given the political combustibility of urban renewal. But theirs was neither the father-son relationship Logue had cherished with Chester Bowles nor the sibling-like partnership he had experienced with Dick Lee. These men also shared Logue's political and cultural orientation as deeply committed Social Democrats and racial progressives. Collins was a reformer of a different stripe. He was culturally and morally conservative and a devout Catholic. After Collins stepped down as mayor, hot-button issues like abortion and Vietnam would push him further to the right and lead him to serve on the organizing committee of Texas governor John Connelly's Democrats for Nixon effort against George McGovern in 1972 and to chair its Massachusetts chapter. But as collaborators from 1960 to 1967, Logue and Collins respected each other and got along well. Collins wasn't threatened by Logue grabbing the headlines, and in fact he preferred to have Logue take the political heat as the public face of urban renewal at vicious city council hearings and contentious community meetings while he himself played "statesman-reformer," as one observer put it.[94]

Despite Collins's claims that he had brought Logue to Boston "for the purpose of doing the best possible professional job" and vowed "not [to] interfere in any political way whatsoever with the way he managed the department," the mayor nonetheless instructed his team to keep a close watch on Logue. He went so far as to install a well-seasoned political minder in BRA headquarters—John P. McMorrow, a former state representative, two-time member of the school committee, and competitor in the 1959 mayoral race—to approve all hiring and cast an attentive eye from his office across the hall from Logue's. Frank Del Vecchio, the recent Harvard Law School grad who had grown up in the West End, recalled McMorrow's blunt words during his "clearance interview" before any Logue offer could be made official: "Frank, I checked you out—Boston Latin, English High, Tufts. My job is to protect the mayor . . . There are grumblings in city hall that we are bringing in too many outsiders. You will help—you're a Bostonian and you have credentials."[95]

Federal dollars provided the other essential support that Logue needed in Boston, just as it had in New Haven. By the end, Logue's $90 million plan had grown to over $200 million—over $2 billion counting private investment. Once again, Logue proved a wizard in minimizing outright costs to the city— to do renewal "wholesale," as he liked to say. He also moved fast, knocking on Washington's door at a relentless pace. Logue believed that only high-speed momentum and a large-enough scale could pull Boston back from the physical and social brink, according to Langley Carleton Keyes, Jr., then a doctoral candidate in city and regional planning at MIT who wrote his Ph.D. dissertation on Boston's urban renewal, published in 1969 as *The Rehabilitation Planning Game: A Study in the Diversity of Neighborhood.*[96]

Logue saw an opportunity in Boston, however, to leverage the federal government's outlay to encourage greater private-sector investment. With potentially deeper corporate pockets here than in New Haven, Logue aimed not simply to attract real estate developers to a particular project by enticing them with the federal write-down of the land cost, as the housing acts intended. Even more ambitiously, he hoped to use publicly funded urban renewal to jump-start private-sector commitments in and around urban renewal areas. Logue's ambition for Government Center, for example, went far beyond attracting the city, state, and federal governments to build new headquarters. He intended to use that government expenditure to pressure businesses—long unwilling to spend money in Boston—to step up in a wholly new way.

Beyond mayoral support and federal funding, Logue imported two other dimensions of his New Haven work to Boston. First, before he left New

Haven, Logue secured Paul Ylvisaker's commitment to make Boston one of the six sites of the Ford Foundation's Gray Areas pilot program so that here, as in New Haven, human renewal could accompany physical renewal. With the help of a $1.9 million Ford grant, enriched by additional federal and local funding, Logue established Action for Boston Community Development (ABCD) along the same lines as New Haven's Community Progress Inc. (CPI). He personally sat on its board and recruited Joe Slavet—who had tutored Collins on urban renewal, had helped recruit Logue to Boston, and was ready for a new job after fourteen years at the Municipal Research Bureau—to be its executive director, eagerly anticipating having another Mike Sviridoff at his side.[97]

ABCD would run into many of the same kinds of challenges that CPI eventually encountered in New Haven—but even earlier. Logue envisioned ABCD as the BRA's social outreach into urban renewal areas, strengthening the agency's ties to citizens by aiding displaced residents, combating juvenile delinquency and unemployment, providing legal and educational assistance, and coordinating existing Boston agencies to deliver social services more effectively. As *Architectural Forum* explained it, ABCD "initially was to run interference for Logue's renewal program . . . Logue's feeling was that if ABCD first tackled some of each community's major social ills, physical renewal might be easier."[98] Logue hoped that ABCD could provide a viable pathway to engaging a neighborhood in planning and identifying local leadership for the BRA's program.

Slavet soon figured out, however, that allying his anti-poverty agency too closely with the BRA could prove damaging to its success. As he recounted later, "I said to him, 'There are things happening not only here but all over the country. There are trains leaving the station in connection with the anti-poverty program, you know, that I just can't stick in the areas that you have designated as urban renewal areas. There's a lot of pressure, particularly from the black community outside of urban renewal areas to get aboard.'"[99]

Logue and Slavet in time came to blows over the BRA-ABCD connection. When, for example, Logue urged Slavet to move ABCD's headquarters into the new Center Plaza office building across from City Hall Plaza, as the

BRA was desperate to prove Government Center's success and no paying tenants had yet surfaced, Slavet responded, "For Christ's sake, I'm running an anti-poverty program. For me to move into the most expensive place in Boston, they're going to kill me. What is the matter with you?"[100] Slavet's frustration was understood by Clifford Campbell, hired by Ford to review ABCD in February 1963. He told Ylvisaker, "Ed is of the view that for the most part ABCD should accommodate itself to, and maybe become the tool of urban renewal, whereas Joe sees, and rightly so, the larger objectives set for ABCD."[101] A year later, Campbell returned to Boston for a second round of reviewing and got another earful from Logue: "We were totally unprepared for his double-barreled onslaught on ABCD . . . He holds tenaciously to the point of view that ABCD is his instrument, created solely for the purpose of serving the ends of BRA." Campbell speculated that Logue's growing adamance was related to "his recognition of the role on the Boston scene that ABDC will play, if and when the Economic Opportunity Act of 1964 becomes a reality. You see, for the first time . . . the War on Poverty will provide a budget and program whose scope and depth will far exceed any program envisioned or executed under Urban Renewal. He is not about to give this up without a struggle." He concluded, "This is a struggle for power between two men."[102]

The same year, two other observers allied with Ford observed the same rift. Peter Marris and Martin Rein wrote that Logue believed so deeply that urban renewal was "an essential instrument of social justice" that he "felt increasingly betrayed. Gazing from the picture window of his office on the rising frame of Boston's new government centre [sic], he brooded on the bad faith of those to whom he had once shown the way."[103] As Community Action Program funds became available upon the passage of the Economic Opportunity Act, with its mandate of "maximum feasible participation," ABCD would indeed benefit—and become more independent of the BRA, as Logue had feared.[104]

Even as Slavet managed to guard ABCD's autonomy from the BRA for the sake of community credibility, he became personally embroiled in intense internal conflicts within the agency, not unlike Sviridoff's experience in New Haven. Slavet faced charges of too few black staff and board members, too little community control, and too much research-oriented piloting rather than broader impact programs. Slavet finally resigned in 1966. These tensions between ABDC and the BRA, and within ABCD as the pressures for more participatory democracy increased, strained the relationship between Slavet and Logue. But, notably, Campbell's candid reports to Ford did not undermine Paul Ylvisaker's admiration for Logue. When in 1973 Ylvisaker, then dean of Harvard's Graduate School of Education, was asked to supply a list of "the most creative and extraordinary people you have personally known," he provided twenty-nine names from his expansive career, of which "Ed Logue" was one.[105]

It didn't take long for Logue to identify a second dilemma that Boston shared with New Haven: the city faced problems metropolitan in scope with only the resources of one municipality to address them. Although Logue had been frustrated with New Haven's financial and political isolation from its flourishing suburban hinterlands, in Boston he became even more outspoken. He repeatedly proposed that the New Boston become the core of a metropolitan economy built around technological, scientific, and other knowledge-based innovation. This notion of the "City of Ideas," which was fully articulated in the BRA's *1965/1975 General Plan for the City of Boston and the Regional Core*, sought to turn the burden of having 42 percent of the city's land and buildings tax exempt as universities, hospitals, churches, and other public uses (the largest proportion of any major American city) into an economic advantage. Likewise, instead of viewing the research boom around Route 128 as a drain on the city, Logue argued that it should instead be welcomed—and cultivated—as nourishment for the growth of downtown lawyers, bankers, accountants, public relations firms, and the like.[106]

Logue's hope for a metropolitan-oriented New Boston did not stop there. He also forthrightly called for metropolitan-level solutions to two of the city's biggest social problems: the low-income housing crisis and the gross inequalities suffered by black children in Boston's notoriously segregated schools. Specifically, he advocated a "fair share" housing program whereby Boston suburbs would each construct a small number of subsidized units, a program he called "scatteration" in contrast to the current "concentration" of nonwhites in segregated, resource-starved communities. He also proposed building "New Towns," "planned for the whole income range spectrum and not for those who already have comfortable incomes."[107]

To remedy appalling educational inequities, Logue went very public in 1965 with a controversial proposal for a government program to bus four thousand fifth- through eighth-graders from underfunded black schools in Boston to twenty-one suburban districts.[108] As Logue testified before the U.S. Commission on Civil Rights when it held a hearing in Boston in October 1966, "The federal government, which bears such a very heavy responsibility for seeing that the suburbs were all white in the first place [has] some responsibility to redress the balance." Communities outside Boston have "some of the finest school systems in America and with insignificant numbers of nonwhite children [and] are not required to help." To attempt to solve the problem only within the city's limits was "unimaginative and cowardly."[109] Although Logue's advocacy of large-scale compulsory busing went nowhere, he was credited by many with spurring the creation of the Metropolitan Council for Educational Opportunity (METCO), a much smaller-scale voluntary busing program begun in 1966 that continues today to transport minority students from Boston to affluent suburban schools, making it the longest continually running voluntary busing program for school desegregation in the country. But it is worth noting that Logue's liberal fix-it instinct to address what he considered an outrage with a top-down, mandatory remedy was not only resisted by white suburbanites; it was also resented by some black parents who felt it rendered them and their children passive victims in need of saving.[110]

Not until Logue's next job as president of the New York State Urban Development Corporation, where he had the authority to operate on a statewide rather than mere city level, would he legally be in a position to implement metropolitan-level strategies intended to integrate communities and schools by race and class. Until then, the reality of urban responsibility and suburban retreat continued to frustrate Logue.[111] It played no small part in fact in his deepening feud with Jane Jacobs. Logue published an appreciative but critical review of Jacobs's *The Death and Life of Great American Cities* in *Architectural Forum* in March 1962, predictably taking umbrage at a text that began, "This book is an attack on current city planning and rebuilding."

Around the same time, Logue and Jacobs met up at a debate organized by the Museum of Modern Art in New York City, where he made many of the same points as in the review. While Logue claimed to share Jacobs's faith in community participation and housing rehabilitation and her frustration with some architects and planners, "who care more about what their colleagues think of their plans than the public," he rejected her primary message, which he phrased as "no more federal renewal aids; let the cities fend for themselves." That directive he considered the indulgence of someone living in the safe, well-off neighborhood of the West Village, an option not available to slum dwellers. He also expressed some skepticism about her ideal of urbanity, having paid a clandestine visit to her block one evening around 8:00 p.m. and noticed very few "eyes on the street" and other qualities she celebrated. And then, going for the jugular, he continued sarcastically, "Not surprisingly, this approach has won her many new friends, particularly among comfortable suburbanites. They like to be told that neither their tax dollars nor their own time need be spent on the cities they leave behind them at the close of each work day."[112] Although Logue concluded his review with "We need Jane Jacobs . . . to keep on giving us the needle," there was little doubt that in Logue's mind, Jacobs had let suburban residents of the metropolis off the hook.

Apart from his frustrations making human renewal and metropolitan governance work as he hoped, the move to Boston offered Logue exhilarating opportunities to innovate beyond what he and Mayor Lee had been able to do in New Haven. He now had the chance to pioneer a new model for the nation of how to revitalize a major city. In Boston, Ed Logue was determined to show Jane Jacobs that urban renewal could be done right.

5. Battling for a New Boston

One of Logue's greatest challenges when he arrived in Boston was figuring out new strategies for building strong citywide support for urban renewal. The West End's demolition had created a searing memory among Bostonians, and his own recent battle to get approved as development administrator of the Boston Redevelopment Authority only confirmed the importance of cultivating a diverse spectrum of allies. With memories still fresh of New Haven's reluctant corporate leaders and of suits brought by both jeweler Robert Savitt and the Central Civic Association's small retailers downtown, Logue was determined to avoid the delays that had slowed New Haven's urban renewal. This was time he felt he did not have in Boston.

Logue had seen enough of Boston to know that a pluralist democratic structure like New Haven's Citizens Action Commission—uniting a wide range of New Haven's constituencies in a singular, official mouthpiece of community support for urban renewal—would be impossible. Boston was too polarized and fragmented from years of bruising ethnic, racial, class, neighborhood, and political battles to speak in one voice. So Logue tried a different approach to building broad backing for the BRA that would engage representatives of key constituencies in the city—and in turn, he hoped, win their support. He would reach out to these parties separately to become his partners, appealing to how urban renewal might serve their particular interests. Aware that the redevelopers "were not going to accomplish anything" without far-reaching local backing, Logue admitted to seeking "a partner everywhere we went."[1] That was also the best insurance that the BRA would not be accused of favoring any one interest group. So it was that Logue's major allies in building the New Boston became the business leaders, the Catholic Church, the media—in particular *The Boston Globe*—and the architectural community. If flanked by leaders of these influential groups, bringing along their own rank and filers, Logue felt, then the BRA would be in a strong position to succeed with its two-prong attack to revive downtown economically and rejuvenate Boston's neighborhoods, there updating deteriorating infrastructure and improving residences that the U.S. Census of Housing in 1960 had found seriously wanting. One in four dwellings was judged substandard, more than in most large American cities.[2]

ALLIES IN BUSINESS

When Mayor John Collins first called on the Vault following his election, he simply opened a dialogue. Now the bigger challenge was to enlist the Yankee business elite's substantive support for urban renewal. Collins and Logue continued to meet with the Vault every two weeks, and in between, Logue spent time courting key business leaders, hoping to hook them.[3] At first, Logue recalled, "They were skeptical. They didn't think anything was going to happen. Why should they? Government Center had stalled for ten years.

[So] I gave them a present . . . I told them that I wouldn't do anything down-town without a business partner."[4] He also calculated that if local leaders became committed to the plan, then they—and not the BRA—would have to cope with more reticent peers fearing eminent domain takings and pressure for significant financial investment. Reserving the linchpin of downtown renewal—the Government Center project—for the BRA, Logue officially turned over two adjacent projects to business leaders for detailed planning: the waterfront and the retail core of the central business district (CBD). A key player in both endeavors was Charles Coolidge—Boston Brahmin, senior partner in the prestigious law firm Ropes & Gray, member of the Harvard Corporation, and president of the Greater Boston Chamber of Commerce—who agreed to lend his substantial credibility to promoting both initiatives.

Boston's waterfront, once a bustling center of fishing and shipping, had become virtually abandoned by the early 1960s, filled with rotting wharves and low-life dives made even more derelict by the unfortunate fate of being cut off from the rest of the city by the six-lane, elevated Central Artery, which opened in 1959—an inheritance from Mayor John Hynes that Collins called "that miserable expressway."[5] Given the waterfront's proximity to downtown and the absence of any controversial residential relocation problems, Logue gave the project, labeled the "Downtown Waterfront–Faneuil Hall Urban Renewal Plan," to the Chamber of Commerce to shepherd: "We'll set up a joint plan, it's your responsibility to make the plan, but you have to make it with me and together we'll carry it out."[6]

The Chamber created a Waterfront Redevelopment Division and raised $150,000 to fund two full-time professional staff members, assisted by part-time and student workers and many consultants, including two well-known planners: Kevin Lynch of MIT and Charles Abrams, then of City College of New York, soon to move to Columbia. State and federal agencies were also enlisted to study relocating the food markets and designating the Faneuil Hall area a historic district. Ideas for revitalization included relocating Atlantic Avenue to create more usable space alongside the harbor, constructing new recreational facilities on the waterfront, rehabilitating abandoned wharves as apartments for a diversity of income levels, renovating Faneuil Hall and adjacent Quincy Market for new uses, and attracting tourists to a world-class aquarium, hotel, and restaurants. Once the plan was approved by the BRA and the city council, it would become part of the BRA's overall program and subject to public hearings.[7]

The waterfront project would take many years to complete, and not all the grand schemes of broad access to housing and recreation would come to fruition. The Central Artery would remain a hated obstacle for many decades, until the roadway was finally moved underground with the Big Dig, completed in 2007. But the planners from the BRA and the Chamber nonetheless proposed imaginative reuses of the waterfront's once-impressive granite wharves and historic Faneuil Hall and Quincy Market to create "a range of residential and recreational opportunities for persons of all income levels" and to maximize "visual access" ("Boston's window to the sea") and "public access . . . to much of the water's edge."[8] Although the next mayor, Kevin White, would receive the credit for the adaptive reuse of Faneuil Hall and Quincy Market as the festival marketplace that opened under his watch, the origins of the project date back to the Collins and Logue era.[9]

Turning away from the water and toward the city's "very rundown shopping district," Logue sought another partner in the newly constituted Committee for the Central Business District (CCBD). The CCBD tackled rethinking the city's retail core with an executive board headed by Coolidge that included the heads of Boston's three major department stores: Jordan Marsh, Filene's, and Gilchrist's. Logue told them, "It will not work if you will not do it with us." *Fortune* noted the rarity of this collaboration between Jordan Marsh and Filene's: "These mighty two merchants put their renowned rivalry aside temporarily and together made the rounds of the stores, the banks, the newspapers, and other businesses in the area 'hat in hand' . . . and came back with a good hatful of funds—$250,000—for replanning the whole district."[10] *Fortune* may not have realized how alarming downtown retailers had found the closing in 1961 of four large stores doing $50 million annually, which motivated them to dig uncharacteristically deep into their pockets.[11]

Having learned a lesson from the resistance of many local New Haven merchants to redevelopment, Logue let Boston's retailers recommend to the BRA the extent of change in the retail district, the most desirable mix of large and small stores, and solutions to the always-sticky problem of temporary relocations. The CCBD used its quarter million dollars to hire a commercial architect and urban planner, Victor Gruen, and a Washington economist, Robert Gladstone, whom it charged with analyzing potential growth in the downtown Boston market.[12] Gruen was surprised at what he called the "pattern of cooperation" between the CCBD and the BRA. No stranger to the kind of conflicts that had wracked New Haven and his own Fort Worth, Texas, where he had struggled—unsuccessfully—to implement a futuristic downtown plan, Gruen appreciated the Boston agreement "that whatever is planned must be acceptable to both parties."[13] The *Boston Herald* likewise remarked on Logue's unusual restraint in approaching the planning of the retail core, with "a caution untypical of his usual drive to get things done, now if not sooner, as if there was a 'proceed cautiously' sign on the central business district so as to disrupt operations as little as possible."[14] Logue acknowledged to Monsignor Lally shortly before the public unveiling of the CCBD's proposal in May 1967 that while planning for the CBD had taken longer than he would have liked, he thought that "the result has been to get support and depth from the retailers."

Boston's business class clearly enjoyed more visibility in planning Boston's downtown urban renewal than New Haven's ever had, lending credence to the Left critics' claim that private capital used the New Boston to pursue its own interests.[15] Collins was in fact so sensitive to this charge that he went out of his way to insist that he alone set the agenda for his meetings with the Vault, not the other way around. And on Logue's instructions, BRA staffers kept a close eye on renewal projects delegated to business. Bob Hazen, Logue's assistant who had moved from New Haven to Boston with him, recalled how, as BRA liaison to the CCBD, he would sit in the offices of Jordan's Edward Mitton and Filene's Harold Hodgkinson at the end of many days and chat with them about how the planning effort was coming along. "The intent was to get an aggressive, comprehensive plan that you could execute, and Ed [Logue] guided that . . . As the planning staff, we worked very closely with it." According to a knowledgeable observer, BRA staff members had to "exercise the utmost tact in attempting to curb the enthusiasm of the CCBD for the most grandiose schemes."

The BRA's Robert Litke likewise oversaw the waterfront project from an office in Quincy Market. He orchestrated moving the produce market to Chelsea and the meat wholesalers to South Boston. When "Ed was not happy with the progress" being made by the chamber's operation—"it was taking forever, they were planning the hell out of it"—Litke said, "He sent me over there to make things happen. So I made things happen." Logue's staff consequently became deeply involved in planning the new waterfront.[16]

Despite the BRA's collaboration with the Vault, the Chamber of Commerce, and the CCBD, any assumptions about corporate capital's calculus must take into consideration how cautious, even unwilling, many local business leaders remained to invest in the New Boston. This proved true even after Collins delivered on his promise of decreases—albeit small ones—in real estate taxes. In a candid speech to his colleagues at the National League of Cities in August 1967, on the eve of stepping down as mayor and still smarting from the summer's racial tensions, Collins bitterly slammed "elements of our society that are not doing enough . . . to help cities and respond to mounting civic unrest," including "the private sector [that] has, by and large, stood by, . . . taking remarkably little initiative other than token [minority] hiring."[17] It was in fact a foreign firm, British Investors Ltd., that broke the investment boycott of downtown Boston and put up the first office skyscraper, the thirty-story State Street Bank Building, in 1966. This outsider appreciated more than locals that "Boston has some of the best bargains in real estate of any city in the U.S."[18] Casting forward to 1974, no local bank still would provide the financing to the Rouse Company to renovate historic Faneuil Hall and Quincy Market as a pioneering festival marketplace. Only enormous pressure from Mayor White's administration led a risk-averse consortium of ten Boston banks to agree to collectively match the New York–based Chase Manhattan Bank's $3.75 million investment. They were shocked when the project proved an enormous success almost immediately upon its opening during Boston's bicentennial in 1976.[19]

CRUSADING WITH THE CHURCH

If Boston's business community was an obvious, if reluctant, partner for Logue's urban renewal efforts, then a more surprising but enormously influential one was Boston's powerful Catholic Church. Boston was the most Catholic of major American cities—80 percent of the population throughout most of the twentieth century—and Boston's church was a very Irish one, with strong ties to James Michael Curley's neighborhood base. It had even managed to keep Italian Catholics marginalized. Cardinal Richard Cushing had made his support for Collins's opponent John Powers quite evident in the 1959 mayoral race. But for many reasons, the Church became one of Logue and Collins's staunchest allies in building the New Boston. To begin with, the archdiocese had a huge financial investment in Boston, with its many parish churches, parochial schools, hospitals, colleges, social service agencies, seminaries, and convents. So a decline in the city's population and attractiveness, particularly among the more affluent, suburban-bound middle class, translated quickly into empty pews, vacant school desks, and meager takes in Sunday collection baskets. In that way, the archdiocese, already coping with debt, differed little from any other Boston business, whether bank, manufacturer, or department store. Moreover, because church parishes were defined geographically, they were tied more tightly to their original locations than businesses or other religious institutions like Jewish synagogues, whose congregations could easily transplant when they moved to new neighborhoods or suburbs. For Catholic churches, survival meant making the most of where you were rooted.[20]

But beyond these considerations, the Boston Catholic Archdiocese—and in time the full American and indeed global Roman Catholic Church as well—was undergoing significant changes in its relationship to broader civil society that played to Logue's advantage. Cardinal Cushing had taken over at the death of his predecessor, Cardinal William O'Connell, in 1944.[21] Whereas Cardinal O'Connell had subscribed to the sectarian impulses of Curley and his Democratic machine, Cushing sympathized with the greater open-mindedness of the Irish Catholic reform mayor John Hynes and, once elected, John Collins as well. It was under Cushing that the Boston-born Jesuit priest W. Seavey Joyce, upon his assumption of the deanship of the Boston College School of Business Administration, created the Boston College Citizen Seminars, which opened a dialogue between the Yankee business elite and broader political, religious, and civic leaders.

The Church's fingerprints were all over Boston's urban renewal, back to the early Prudential project.[22] Cushing assigned his trusted adviser Monsignor Lally to serve as one of the original BRA board members in 1957 and then, in 1960, encouraged him to accept becoming chair. Lally was Cushing's right-hand man in matters of civil rights and interfaith relations, so it had been a progressive act to name him editor of the archdiocesan weekly newspaper, *The Pilot*, in 1952, and then to the BRA post. Throughout Logue's tenure in Boston, Lally's support, and through him the cardinal's— communicated through leadership on the BRA board, *Pilot* editorials, archdiocesan instructions to parish priests, and many other means—remained crucial. At every ribbon cutting or ground breaking, Lally was a dependable presence, donning a hard hat and wielding scissors or shovel, often joined by Cardinal Cushing himself.[23] Lally testified to the depth of the Cardinal's commitment. "He wanted everyone to stay in the city," he told an interviewer. "He made his investment in [Boston], saving parishes, supporting schools . . . If he could keep not just the Irish but the Catholic ethnic in the city, he would keep a coherence, a community."[24]

A characteristic statement of support for urban renewal from Cardinal Cushing came at the dedication of a new residence for retired priests in the West End in 1964, where he promised that this was but one of many contributions that the church would make to the New Boston, including building a new chapel in Government Center to be named for the city's namesake, Saint Botolph. "This is a time of change, and we cannot afford to be opposed against [sic] progress. We must move along with it," he asserted. He also made sure to remind his audience of the BRA's return favor to remove the hated Washington Street Elevated structure that overshadowed Boston's Mother Church, the Cathedral of the Holy Cross in the South End. The Yankee bosses of the Boston Elevated Railway (the "El") had callously put it there at the turn of the century—"a kind of finger to the Catholics," as the Boston transportation planner Frederick Salvucci described it—and it had long remained hated as "a symbol of oppression."[25]

From 1962 to 1965, the Roman Catholic Church thoroughly reinvented itself through the deliberations and decrees of the Second Vatican Council. Launched by Pope John XXIII and continued after his death by Pope Paul VI, the Ecumenical Council called for "updating" in multiple dimensions: in the nature of church liturgy, ritual, education, and relations within the hierarchy and between the clergy and laity; in attitudes and policies toward pluralism and religious freedom; in interactions between Catholics and other Christians and Jews; and in the realm most relevant to Logue's urban renewal project, the church's involvement in the world, including the complex social problems confronting the urban communities in which most dioceses were located. Boston's Cardinal Cushing had anticipated many of these changes. In fact, when *Time* magazine devoted an August 1964 issue to Catholicism, it singled out Cushing more than any other American bishop for epitomizing "the surge of church renewal."[26]

Already committed to many of its goals, Cushing and his Boston church used Vatican II to legitimate their partnering with other influential forces, such as the BRA, the Yankee Protestant business elite, and interfaith and interracial organizations. Without Rome's blessing, the Boston Archdiocese might have found it harder to defy internal and external pressures to define church business narrowly. Vatican II helped Cushing's archdiocese resist the call from parishioners who lived in some of the targeted neighborhoods to challenge urban renewal. Charlestown was a prime example. As the battle lines were drawn there from 1961 to 1965 and the Catholic Church took the BRA's side, Lally moved into the rectory of Saint Catherine's and parish priests at the other two Charlestown churches were instructed to sermonize about the benefits of urban renewal and how it would save their dwindling flocks. Logue also brought in as the BRA's Charlestown point person a Lithuanian Catholic from Chicago, Joe Vilimas, who had learned from the prominent community organizer Saul Alinsky how to tap into progressive elements in the Catholic Church. When, after two years of acrimony, the BRA triumphed at a raucous public hearing in March 1965, it was because a lo-cal priest brought hours of furious debate to an abrupt halt by suddenly calling for a vote, leading to a very close count. The Catholic Church would pay for advocating for urban renewal over the opposition of many parish-ioners, however, when a decade later these same communities became the heart of the opposition to mandatory busing for school integration. As the Church again took a more progressive stance than many of its congregants and endorsed the busing order of 1974, civil war broke out across the arch-diocese, fueling a resistance that built on habits of protest born in the fight against urban renewal.[27]

GETTING URBAN RENEWAL INTO PRINT

Another crucial ally with a mass constituency was the media, which in this era mainly meant daily newspapers, the most important being *The Boston Globe*. Logue recounted, "[Editor] Tom [Winship] and the *Globe* became our strongest supporters and that became more and more important, as the *Globe* itself did under Tom's leadership."[28] To the likely surprise of twenty-first-century Bostonians who know only two major city papers—*The Boston Globe* and *Boston Herald*—Boston in the 1960s had five newspapers, of which the *Globe*, today's premier city paper, was not the largest in circulation. Because newspapers depended on a thriving city economy for revenue—retail ad-vertising and classified ads providing their major source of income—it fol-lowed that they were invested in efforts to revitalize Boston. Some papers that depended on readers in Curley's Democratic, ethnic, working-class neighborhoods, such as Hearst's *Record American*, in fact struggled to ba-lance supporting reforms that might make Boston more economically viable and alienating their readers.[29]

The *Globe* had been an independent paper, family-owned by several gen-erations of Taylors and edited even more unusually by two generations of father-son Winships. Long a liberal voice in the city, it was now in the 1960s successfully reinventing itself as a metropolitan paper, with a substantial and like-minded readership residing in prospering middle-class suburbs.

These customers provided the *Globe* with a base for what were considered progressive causes, including improving the condition of downtown Boston, where many suburban readers worked.[30] By chance, Logue had met Tom Winship casually in Washington, D.C., almost a decade earlier, when he was visiting Yale classmates and Winship was a *Globe* correspondent in the capital. By the time Logue arrived in Boston, the younger Winship had returned to the city, first as metropolitan editor and then as managing editor. In 1965 he succeeded his father as editor in chief.

Logue encountered Winship again soon after he began consulting in Boston: "I walked into the *Globe* city room and Winship greeted me warmly, as if I were a long lost friend, which, in fact, was the way it worked out. Tom wanted action. I seemed to promise that."[31] The Logues and the Winships became close socially, sharing a liberal perspective on a constellation of issues—renewing the city, but also civil rights and in time opposition to the Vietnam War.[32] The *Globe* so obviously promoted Logue and Collins's urban renewal agenda, starting with endorsing Logue's appointment in January 1961 and continuing with huge, positive coverage of the BRA's activities, that critics cynically referred to it as the "Boston Logue."[33] Logue freely admitted that "Winship was the next person after the mayor to know of our plans," as they met frequently at their offices and homes.[34] On at least one occasion, Logue's nemesis on the city council, Bill Foley, angrily told him off with "You're gone! You're dead! You're beyond the reach of your newspaper friends to help you."[35]

Part of the reason the *Globe* could showcase Logue's New Boston so prominently was that at this time it had a structure rare among newspapers, where Winship oversaw both the news and the editorial pages of the paper.[36] Christopher Lydon, then a *Globe* reporter, remembers alerting Winship in 1966 to a critical report by Michael Appleby about Logue's Boston activities, commissioned by Jane Jacobs, Herbert Gans, and other determined opponents of the effort by the newly elected mayor, John Lindsay, to recruit Logue to New York City. To Lydon's dismay, Winship buried the tip, and no mention of the report ever made it into the *Globe*.[37]

Needless to say, the support of a newspaper as prominent and ambitious as *The Boston Globe* was a huge asset to Logue personally and to the larger BRA agenda. The *Boston Herald Traveler* and *The Christian Science Monitor* also enthusiastically promoted the city's urban renewal—and benefited directly from it, the *Herald Traveler* with a new plant in the South End's New York Streets renewal district, *The Christian Science Monitor* when a huge new Christian Science World Headquarters, designed by I. M. Pei's firm, rose in a cleared area of the South End.

REVIEW BY DESIGNERS

Logue actively cultivated a fourth ally for his renewal plans, Boston area architects, less for strategic political reasons and more to help him achieve the high-quality, forward-looking modernist design he eagerly sought. Logue's commitment to good architecture went back to his days in New Haven, where modern buildings served as a crucial marker of progressive change in that antiquated city. But the earliest structures had proved disappointing. Logue was determined to do better in Boston.[38] He developed a powerhouse design and planning department within the BRA under the direction of David A. Crane, a former professor of architecture and city planning at the University of Pennsylvania. Crane was headed for a position in Chicago in 1961 with a team of mostly recent Penn graduates to "enlarge upon Daniel H. Burnham's grand design" and get some "real world" experience when Mayor Richard Daley withdrew the offer to such a large group. As they were casting about for another option, a Penn colleague thought of an idea: "Ed Logue is the only urban development executive in this country with the scope of operation and personal moxy to feel secure hiring this much talent," is how Crane remembered it. Logue was also conveniently building a staff. Logue was called, Crane flew to Boston, and within a week Crane was appointed director of comprehensive planning and design and the whole team had BRA offers—to the consternation of some Boston locals who decried the invasion of "foreigners and academics." Crane thoroughly enjoyed informing City Councilman Foley that the "Chinaman" he was railing against was Tunney Lee, who, though trained as an architect at the University of Michigan, had grown up in Boston's Chinatown–South Cove neighborhood and had graduated from Boston Latin High School.

Crane and his colleagues brought high professional standards to the BRA's design work, introducing innovative—if not always practical—concepts like the "capital web," where government-sponsored public investments would create a spine from which residential growth and private development could branch, and "broken seams," empty areas between established settlements ripe for new initiatives. Crane's contribution found full expression in the BRA's *1965/1975 General Plan for the City of Boston and the Regional Core*.[39] When Jonathan Barnett went to work for the New York City Planning Department and was asked to set up an urban design capability within the staff, he looked to Boston as a rare model.[40]

This internal BRA design operation was complemented by an external design-review process that Logue enthusiastically implemented, with BRA board approval, for all major projects. Soon after he arrived, Logue institutionalized a volunteer Design Advisory Committee led by Hugh Stubbins, chair of Harvard's Architecture Department, and composed of the deans of Harvard and MIT—Josep Lluís Sert and Pietro Belluschi—and other well-respected local architects, including over time Nelson Aldrich, Henry Shepley, and Lawrence B. Anderson.[41] Additional architects with national reputations were paid to review specific projects, such as Vincent Kling and Harry Weese on a large commercial office building, Oskar Stonorov and Chloethiel Woodard Smith on moderate-income relocation housing, and Morris Ketchum and Dan Kiley on a neighborhood shopping center.[42] Although implementing the design review process was not always easy, Tunney Lee was convinced that "it raised the level of taste." It may not have worked in every case, "but just having it meant that developers would hire better architects to avoid having problems."[43] Serving as an architectural adviser to the BRA could also pay off, as Logue continued in the years ahead to hire architects he knew and respected.

Logue sought other ways of engaging with the Boston design community. He and his staff participated actively in major area architectural events such as the Harvard GSD's annual Urban Design Conference, most notably in May 1964 when the theme was "The Role of Government in the Form and Animation of the Urban Core."[44] And Logue supported experimentation with new technologies like prefabricated housing, which MIT's Carl Koch brought—not totally successfully—to Academy Homes in Roxbury. The design review panel for this project commended the BRA for "its initiative in sponsoring this research," as "precast concrete techniques are a promising direction for new low cost housing," but "industry is reluctant to experiment."[45] Figuring out how prefab housing might potentially solve the nation's affordable housing crisis remained a career-long pursuit for Logue.

With these allies and his initial $90 Million Development Program of 1960 in hand, Logue launched his two-prong renewal plan for Boston. He would soon learn, however, that having friends in high and low places and a comprehensive blueprint on paper was not sufficient to achieve his ambitions. Although Logue frequently spouted a commitment to "planning with people," the kind of cooperative process that he imagined rarely occurred. Instead, the result was more often a combative negotiation between renewer and renewed. Rarely was any side fully satisfied, but the new urban environment created in Boston long bore the visual imprint of intense contestation followed by compromise.

PUBLIC BUILDING TO SPUR PRIVATE SPENDING

Talk of creating Government Center had been in the air for decades, and early conceptual plans had even been drawn up under Mayor Hynes. But when Logue began investigating Boston as a consultant in March 1960, commitments were not yet firm and the city's preferred site of Scollay Square was still functioning as a dense, scruffy red-light district that spread over sixty prime downtown acres. Its small-scale eighteenth- and nineteenth-century buildings housed bars and nightclubs, burlesque theaters and striptease joints, pawnshops and tattoo parlors, flophouses and amusement arcades. A bustling destination for sailors reveling on shore leave during the war, it was by 1960 barely making it with out-of-town tourists, partying Harvard students, and local teenagers like Frank Del Vecchio, who snuck into the Old

Howard to gawk at a classic striptease act.[46] But Scollay Square's location seemed too promising to ignore, lying as it did between the retail CBD and the financial district, easy walking distance from both the Common and the waterfront, and in proximity to three subway lines and the Central Artery. Logue hoped that, if revitalized, the site could provide a missing focal point badly needed in downtown Boston.[47]

Even if Boston's substantial residential suburbanization could not be reversed, a thriving downtown that drew workers and shoppers would keep the city commercially viable. Logue laid out the strategy to Senator Abraham Ribicoff's subcommittee hearings in December 1966: "After thirty years [of] our suburban oriented national housing policy . . . weaken[ing] cities," leaving them "starving for revenue," and "with the much talked about federal cupboard fast emptying, . . . we are at work downtown trying to restore our economic and employment base and encourage private enterprise to participate in the renewal of the city downtown." He saw no choice. "We must create the jobs downtown. We must expand the tax base downtown, not to mention keeping it from eroding."[48]

When Logue stepped down as the BRA's development administrator eight months after testifying, the centerpiece of his strategy was almost complete. Scollay Square's maze of twenty-two narrow, crooked streets had been transformed into six superblocks on which the massive Government Center was rising, laid out by I. M. Pei and Associates and consisting of large-scale modernist buildings by major architectural firms, among them the John F. Kennedy Federal Building by Walter Gropius's the Architects Collaborative (1961–66); a new Boston City Hall by Kallmann, McKinnell, and Knowles (1962–68); Massachusetts's State Service Center by Paul Rudolph (1962–71); the Government Center Parking Garage, also by Kallmann, McKinnell, and Knowles (1962–71); and an expansive plaza binding these buildings together to ensure that Boston's new civic center became more than the sum of its parts.

Traditionally, public administrative buildings like these were constructed in brick and stone and decorated with classical motifs—columns, carvings, and other ornamentation—meant to invoke the grandeur and long legacy of republican government.[49] In contrast, in more prosperous American cities than Boston in the 1950s and 1960s, a Miesian-inspired International Style of steel and glass made corporate office towers modern symbols of power. Unlike the classical and the curtain wall, Boston's new Government Center was constructed mostly in concrete in a monumental modernist style, labeled by some as "brutalist" and—more recently—by others as "heroic," that aimed to convey through architecture the ambition, authority, and impact of the public sector.[50] A *Boston Globe* review of the city hall design in 1962 described it as "nothing but a whole-hearted affirmation of a new time, new social needs and the new technology and new aesthetics to declare faith in the civic instrument of government."[51]

From the start, the way that Logue and Collins planned and implemented Government Center signaled a new way of doing business in Boston. Once the federal government's commitment to build was finally locked in during November 1960, making the project feasible, Mayor Collins himself suggested to Logue hiring I. M. Pei's New York firm to rework the locally produced Adams, Howard & Greeley plan of 1950 to ensure that Government Center embodied the latest in urban design and avoided any taint of provinciality.[52] That the project was overseen by a transplanted Boston native, the Pei partner Henry N. "Harry" Cobb, was an added bonus.

Collins also urged holding an architectural competition for the centerpiece of the project, a new Boston City Hall, which would be the first one held for a major U.S. public building in more than fifty years. Initially, Logue resisted the suggestion as unnecessary, time-consuming, and possibly counterproductive to getting the best design.[53] But Collins persisted. Not only did he want city hall to be, as the BRA director of design Charles Hilgenhurst, put it, "the jewel of the Government Center" and an object of national attention, but also he was determined to remove the selection of architect from the culture of cronyism that he felt prevailed too often in Boston. Collins's commitment to selection by an impartial architectural jury held even when it was tested in front of an excited audience of four hundred assembled at the Museum of Fine Arts Boston at 4:00 p.m. on May 3, 1962. At that moment Collins lifted the sheet covering the model of the winning city hall design by Gerhard Kallmann, N. Michael McKinnell, and Edward Knowles, three young unknown architects from New York who had never built a major building before. What he saw shocked this man of conventional tastes.[54] Harold Hodgkinson, the head of Filene's department store and a member of the jury, later recalled "the surprise . . . evident in every line of his face, then amazement, and then executive composure" and finally the appropriate statement: "It is exciting and monumental. I believe in this century it is a really historic event, a design that will live for many years." Logue, as usual, cut right to the chase: "I could almost hear him thinking to himself, 'My God, what's that?' But he didn't blink, because he believed in the process."[55]

As *The Boston Globe*'s reviewer of the city hall design had understood, Logue and Collins wanted to use their Government Center project to send a message about the importance and integrity of government. McKinnell, one of the architects of city hall, remembered many years later that he and his partners too had a "tremendous feeling . . . that government was not just a benevolent institution, but was the institution for . . . social change," and they embedded that ideal in their design: "It should be the people's palace, and it should engage the people. It should be an open building, the symbol of open government." One way the architects conveyed this democratic vision was by placing the city council chamber in an open, easily accessible space where the public could come and go at will, not shutting it behind heavy closed doors. The amphitheater design of the chamber, with the councillors seated in the pit and the public assembled above them, sent a clear message, put succinctly by Deputy Mayor Henry Scagnoli as "you're working for me."[56]

The choice of brut concrete also embodied the architects' democratic ideals. "Brut concrete was an article of faith for us," McKinnell explained, as "Le Corbusier was our god" (and indeed his Sainte Marie de la Tourette Dominican monastery in France of a few years earlier clearly inspired them). But beyond that, he said, "We were absolutely opposed to the developer glass box" of New York's Park Avenue. We wanted to declare a resistance to that." In contrast, concrete seemed authentic and honest: "One material could do so much . . . It could be the structure. It could be the cladding. It could be the floors, it could be the walls. There's a kind of all-through-ness about it."[57] At Collins's insistence, Boston City Hall was built as designed—not always the case with competitions—to avoid any tampering with the jury's decision. Although opinion was divided, the avant-garde city hall was received with more enthusiastic praise than criticism, in contrast to Gropius's John F. Kennedy Federal Building, which was almost universally declared a disappointment.

Faith in the power of government was also captured architecturally in another Government Center building, the Massachusetts State Service Center.[58] Only in 1953 had the federal government's disparate but expanding activities in the realm of social provision been reorganized into the Department of Health, Education, and Welfare (HEW), the first cabinet department to be added since the Department of Labor was created in 1913. By the early 1960s, Kennedy and then Johnson's ambitious social agenda had fostered growing welfare activity at the state and national levels. The State Service Center complex began as three separate state buildings—for employment and social security; outpatient mental health services; and health, education, and welfare—each assigned to a different architectural firm. To Logue's frustration, the project "was poking along with a collection of architects who were sort of sniffing around at each other," making little progress on a plan "which looked like an Italian town, full of small buildings," in one critic's words.

The architect Paul Rudolph, brought in by one firm as a consultant, came to the rescue. He soon determined that the scheme was "too small for the site," the "manipulation of scale [being] the most important tool in the hands of the architect."[59] Logue had come to respect Rudolph greatly from their work together in New Haven, where Rudolph advised him on downtown renewal and designed one of the first buildings to go up, the huge Temple Street Parking Garage. So Logue seized Rudolph's entry into the project and named him coordinating architect for the whole State Service Center. Rudolph brilliantly figured out a way of integrating three fragmented, uninspiring designs into one cohesive, triangular, and sculptural complex enclosing a bowl-like central courtyard intended as a counterpoint to the convex dome on the Massachusetts State House several blocks away.[60] He gave the mega-structure the massiveness he felt its social importance required, prescribed ambitious design standards for all three units, planned a grand serpentine stairway entrance, and faced the entire surface with his distinctive corru-gated concrete, originally developed for the Yale Art and Architecture Build-ing. Much as social services were united in one all-encompassing HEW in Washington, D.C., so the Massachusetts State Service Center unified them in one monumental-scale building in Boston.

Logue and Collins aimed from the start to use Boston's Government Center to leverage private economic activity. They instructed Pei's firm to mark adjacent parcels for private development on all sides of Government Center. The final plan provided sites for four—later increased to five—major public buildings and at least ten private or other commercial structures, making it clear that the business of government was intended to stimulate the business of the private sector.[61] That was easier said than done, however, in tightfisted Boston. The first private project to go up—the Center Plaza office building across from City Hall Plaza—attracted only one bidder, the Leventhal brothers' Beacon Construction Company (later Beacon Compa-nies), which was brand new to the Boston development game. With little capital to play with and facing weak demand for new downtown office space, the firm could afford to construct the long, low, crescent-shaped building only in stages, famously mounting "To Be Continued" signs at the comple-tion of the first two out of three parts.[62]

The effort to have Government Center jump-start private development also led to a serious crisis: disputes and then legal suits over the BRA's tak-ing by eminent domain of two buildings occupying Parcel 8 at the corner of State and New Congress Streets. Logue, following Pei's plan, wanted to cre-ate a gateway from the business district to Government Center, more breath-ing space around Charles Bulfinch's landmark Old State House, and a larger lot on which to place a thirty- to forty-story office tower to rehouse the New England Merchants National Bank headquarters, which would bring in twice the tax dollars that the current building did. Logue's city council enemies made the suit into a cause célèbre, charging him with striking a "sweetheart deal" with the local real estate firm Cabot, Cabot & Forbes, whose newfound interest in building downtown rather than in the Route 128 corridor Logue hoped to encourage. Although the battle over Parcel 8 substantially delayed city council approval of Government Center until May 1965, ultimately the BRA prevailed in the state's highest court and a blue-ribbon panel appointed by the mayor to run a competition for the site ended up giving the project to Cabot, Cabot & Forbes anyway.[63] Not surprisingly, when the BRA laid out its major objectives in the *1965/1975 General Plan for the City of Boston and the Regional Core*, a top one was "Public Action for Private Change," meaning using government spending to "prime the pump."[64]

A very direct way of priming the pump involved instructing all designers of Government Center to push staff and the general public as much as possible out into the larger city to spend money as consumers. City hall, for example, was not to have a major cafeteria so that workers would patronize luncheonettes in the neighborhood; the subsidized dining rooms of Baltimore's Charles Center were known to have depressed pedestrian traffic nearby.[65] The city hall architects' original hope of animating the building and its plaza with a rathskeller restaurant, common in city hall basements in Kallmann's native Germany, thus came to naught. They were repeatedly told to exclude any commercial activity. McKinnell's understanding was that "a deal was struck with the local businessmen that . . . there would be no competition with the immediate area."[66]

The Government Center strategy worked. Despite all the nontaxable public buildings that went up in Government Center, the assessed valuation of taxed properties in the area jumped from about $17.5 million to $28 million upon completion. A district that had once employed six thousand soon had twenty-five thousand workers, who supported local businesses as consumers as well.[67] And as hoped, when Government Center became more of a concrete reality, the private investors who had once been so difficult to attract to downtown Boston started stepping up. First was the State Street Bank Building in 1966; then, after the release of the CCBD's plan to improve downtown retail in 1967, a spate of other buildings followed: the New England Merchants National Bank Building, the Boston Company Building, the First

National Bank Tower, the National Shawmut Bank, and adaptive use of Faneuil Hall and Quincy Market.[68] Symbolically, the former, ornate French Second Empire City Hall was repurposed as a French restaurant.[69] Logue thus fulfilled his prediction to the Boston City Council's Urban Renewal Committee in June 1962 that "private construction will follow rather than lead public building in the renewal of Scollay Square." Ironically, however, the crucial role that public investment had played in turning around Boston's flagging downtown economy in the 1960s has often been forgotten amid assumptions that credit for the city's dynamic twenty-first-century economy belongs to the risk-taking private entrepreneurs of more recent decades.

Although Logue and Collins encountered little organized opposition to Government Center other than the Parcel 8 kerfuffle—nostalgia for Scollay Square's honky-tonk charms arriving later—the major challenge to their plans came from defenders of the historic city who fought removal of old buildings they felt bore the imprint of the city's important past.[70] Logue was not insensitive to Boston's historical legacy. He chose to live in a nineteenth-century rowhouse on well-preserved Beacon Hill. He savored the old-world character of the North End. He worked hard to save the granite wharves, as well as Faneuil Hall and Quincy Market. And he loved much about the way Boston's history was woven into the contemporary city.[71] But when it came to turning around the deteriorating downtown with Government Center, Logue focused laser-like on constructing the new and the modern, going back on his promise to rehab, not demolish, by arguing that clearance in this case was unavoidable and would surely not happen at this scale again.

It didn't take long, however, before Logue was confronted by preservationists like the eminent Boston historian and fellow Tavern Club member Walter Muir Whitehill. He was horrified that Pei and Cobb's plan for Government Center called for removing the Sears Crescent, a curved, six-story, red-brick building constructed by Yankee merchant David Sears on Cornhill Street in 1816, and the Sears Block, its four-story granite neighbor dating from 1848. Cornhill had an important abolitionist history as the location of William Lloyd Garrison's *The Liberator* newspaper and had remained the heart of antiquarian bookselling in Boston. When Whitehill learned the fate planned for the "Cornhill Curve," he burst into Kane Simonian's office, demanding, "How dare you tear down the Sears Crescent!" When Simonian explained—gleefully, one can only imagine—that a decision like that rested solely with Ed Logue, Whitehill replaced his hat, stormed out, and headed for Logue's office. After letter-writing campaigns flooded city hall and delegations descended upon the mayor and the BRA, the decision was finally made—though not without a fight—to revise the original plan and incorporate the Sears Crescent and Block into Government Center.[72] Henry Scagnoli, Collins's deputy mayor, who sat on the Government Center commission officially responsible for the project, later recalled, "We wanted that thing down. We thought it was junk." But "Logue fought for it . . . And thank the Lord he didn't tear it down."[73] In 1964, Logue would get a personal thanks from George J. Gloss, owner of the Brattle Book Shop on Cornhill, for being "a certain man of integrity" who helped the shop "rise like a phoenix from the ashes."[74]

Over time, other historic buildings on the fringes of Government Center would also become part of the BRA's planning: the Old State House, Dock Square, the Blackstone Block, the Custom House and Tower, Quincy Market, and Faneuil Hall, which, as the site of Boston's first town meeting, was symbolically framed in a huge window in the new mayor's office.[75] Logue even agreed, under pressure, to save the Old Howard Theater in Scollay Square, which "had been closed for many years but had a sentimental hold on an older generation of Bostonians," and to explore turning it into a performing arts center—until a fire destroyed it. Logue pled innocent to preservationists' charges of arson.[76]

Logue summed up the status of historic preservation at an American Society of Planning Officials meeting in Boston in 1964. After "a wrestling match" over "what buildings we were going to save, . . . wherever possible we decided to try to keep them and work our new plans around them." And now, he pronounced proudly, the BRA has a "Historic Preservation Committee which examines every project area before the project plan is finished and makes recommendations to us about what kinds of buildings should be saved—where and how."[77] Not coincidentally, this was just the moment when the historic preservation movement was taking off nationally, with many advocates having been mobilized by the shocking destruction of New York's iconic Penn Station in 1964 as well as other losses resulting from overly aggressive urban renewal. The National Historic Preservation Act would follow in 1966, providing a way of inventorying significant historic buildings, protecting them from harm by federally funded projects, and making loans, grants, and tax incentives available to preserve worthy structures.[78]

Angry resistance to a thoroughly modern downtown city core had succeeded in forcing Logue and his BRA to begin negotiating with preservationists over acceptable compromises in their original downtown plans. It should be said that not everyone approved of this concession to history. Some, like Scagnoli, felt it would detract from Government Center's message that Boston was finally up-to-date. Others, like Logue's archenemy City Councillor Bill Foley, regretted the tax income that would be lost with less lucrative development.[79] But what resulted from this negotiation was a distinctive downtown cityscape—a vibrant collage of old and new buildings—that distinguished Boston from many other renewing cities and from cities defined by stringent architectural uniformity. In 1964, the *New York Times* architecture critic Ada Louise Huxtable expressed optimism that Boston, having "the only major urban renewal agency with an official architectural historian on its staff," was embracing "preservation and rehabilitation" with "specific plans and policy rather than pious announcements," "well aware of the sensitive problems of combining the old city with essential new construction."[80]

A dozen years later, soon after the restored Quincy Market reopened in August 1976, Huxtable would pronounce the experiment a success. "Twenty years is a short time to see a dream of a renewed city realized," she wrote, recalling how she "fell in love with Quincy Market" some two decades earlier, despite its "obvious state of terminal decline." Now, "exactly 150 years to the day after it originally opened, it reopened triumphantly. The restoration is one of the stellar features of Boston's exemplary downtown renewal, a remarkably sensitive synthesis of new and old, from Faneuil Hall to City Hall." With this proof that "there is no impossible dream," she credited Logue, assisted by Whitehill and other local historians, with determining "that the market complex was not expendable—one of his many bold, risky stands that paid off in Boston's brilliant downtown renewal."[81]

Although Logue at first only begrudgingly accommodated challenges from determined champions of the Old Boston, he eventually came to appreciate their perspective and even to advocate negotiating a cityscape that blended the historic and the modern. In a volume paying tribute to the first hundred years of the Boston Society of Architects, Logue wrote in 1967 of the necessity of "preserving our rich heritage" while also "bring[ing] Boston up to date," of having "a sensitivity to the relationship between the new and the old . . . that is all-important in maintaining the fabric of the city." He concluded, "While we must acknowledge history, we must avoid becoming enslaved by it."[82] By 1972 he went even further. At a symposium at New York's Museum of Modern Art, he reflected in a speech, "The Education of an Urban Administrator," on how he had learned to value the scale and intimacy of historic urban spaces and buildings, his own thinking evolving along with the broader society's greater embrace of historic preservation.[83]

Eventually, Logue would become so invested in the mix of modern and historic that distinguished downtown Boston's revitalization that in the 1980s he expressed concern about the impact of the decade-long economic boom that was decreasing the BRA's authority and increasing the influence of the private sector. Logue feared that too many massive "glass boxes" were undermining the visually exciting, delicate balance the city had previously struck between old and new.[84] He lamented how poorly the John Hancock Tower interfaced on the ground with "Henry Richardson's magnificently monumental Trinity Church" on nearby Copley Square. Logue even regretted that in the 1960s he had not used more red brick or stipulated more use of red "to echo and strengthen the original patina of the city."[85]

Boston's Government Center was far from perfect. Even the passage of time failed to blend this enormous development fully into the surrounding city, rendering the historic buildings saved on its periphery as quaint relics—too few, too small, and too precious. Crescent-shaped Cornhill was one thing as a two-sided street, quite another "with its nose exposed to this huge space . . . So we saved the building but we didn't save the experience," Cobb lamented.[86] Warnings about the danger of decontextualizing the Sears buildings had come early, in fact, through a notable exchange between Logue and his Design Advisory Committee. It recommended saving the Ames Building (1892), diagonally across from the Old State House, and the Sears Block, urging that if the latter could be "put in decent shape" and you do "not make it too unattractively clean but keep much of its dinginess as one of the historical second-hand bookshops of the City, we believe much interest would be added to the New City Hall setting." Logue agreed with their conclusions, but added, "If I may say so, I am somewhat dismayed at the way in which you choose to express your interest in the Sears Block. I doubt it will be helpful in achieving the objective."[87] Logue himself later recognized another limitation to Government Center, noting that it would have benefited from more mixed use—particularly the inclusion of housing to animate downtown during more hours of the day and days of the week than the offices did. But implementing that insight would have required abandoning faith in the modernist orthodoxy of separating functions, which the Logue of the 1960s was not yet ready to do.

Although the American Institute of Architects would name Boston City Hall the sixth greatest American building at the nation's bicentennial in 1976, many ordinary Bostonians and city workers came to hate it, culminating in a failed proposal from the former mayor Thomas M. Menino in 2006 to sell or tear it down and build a new city hall on his own redevelopment frontier of the South Boston Seaport.[88] Other criticisms mounted. The nine-acre brick-paved plaza proved windswept and inhospitable to the vibrant public life that its architects and planners had imagined. They had in mind St. Mark's Square in Venice, Piazza del Campo in Siena, and St. Peter's Square in Rome. Although Huxtable pronounced in 1972 that, thanks to the plaza, Boston's Government Center "can take its place among the world's great city spaces," her enthusiasm was not widely shared. Even the city hall architect McKinnell recognized the plaza's flaws, identifying it as a space that was too big, too uncontained at the edges, and too hard-surfaced, growing out of a "misplaced idealism that . . . there must be this civic place, this is where the crowds will meet. This is where the revolution will begin."[89] I. M. Pei shared McKinnell's regret that his and Cobb's original plan had specified too large a plaza, though they did call for grass rather than paving.[90] Over the years, endless schemes have been proposed to make City Hall Plaza less sterile.[91] In terms of the building itself, concrete turned out to be a material that in Boston's harsh climate required more maintenance than an increasingly cash-strapped city and state were willing or able to fund. Adding to the bill were cavernous interior spaces, designed in the energy-guzzling 1960s without attention to efficiency and cost.[92]

Despite these flaws, Government Center still stands as testament to a certain moment in time when Boston's urban renewers had faith that big government and the structures that housed it held the answer to the city's economic woes. It also reflects their growing awareness of the aesthetic and political need to carefully weave the rising monuments of the New Boston into one of the oldest cities in North America. Critics of urban renewal often fail to recognize that, at least in Boston, urban renewers did not remain at odds with historic preservation, but learned on the job to integrate it into their planning tool kit, albeit sometimes turning an authentic structure like the Sears Crescent into a static museum piece. When the Government Center Urban Renewal Plan, as revised May 29, 1963, was submitted, it acknowledged this complex negotiation between present and past in calling for the "creation of a symbol of democratic government and its related institutions in the physical context of the surrounding historical districts, thereby continuing and improving the important role this area has played in the political, social and cultural history of Boston and America."[93]

Once Government Center was substantially completed in 1968, it would help foster greater prosperity for downtown Boston in the decades ahead. Logue did not pretend the achievement had been easy. He made no secret of the challenging negotiations he had faced in pulling off Government Center—whether between the BRA and the multiple-level government agencies involved, with key local players including testy city councillors, with private-sector interests requiring badgering to invest downtown, or between proponents of a new modern Boston and those who feared losing too much of the old. As Logue explained at one meeting in 1962, "The Government Center is difficult to execute, because the problem of negotiation was not anticipated . . . I spent the last God damn nine months to get the Pei plan to work. The problem is negotiation. Complicated negotiations."[94]

But Logue had seen nothing yet. When he turned to renewing Boston's neighborhoods, heated negotiation would take place not only around competing visions of what revitalized neighborhoods should look like but also over questions of who should decide and through what processes. Logue had cavalierly promoted a philosophy of "planning with people" from his earliest days in Boston, but just how that collaboration should take place would become fraught with conflict, both between the BRA and the neighborhoods it targeted for renewal and within these communities themselves. Bostonians would teach the development administrator a thing or two about what it meant to plan with people. As one of his senior staff members bluntly put it, "When Ed turned to planning in some of the residential neighborhoods . . . war broke out. Ed was furious that his plan, which he fervently believed in, was being opposed by the very people he was trying to help. Ed knew how to swear and there was lots of swearing going on."[95] Logue may have left New Haven in time to escape the headwinds of participatory democracy there, but they would hit him with full force in Boston.

6. Negotiating Neighborhoods

Logue brought his own ideal of what a healthy residential community should look like to his urban renewal of Boston's neighborhoods. He described it to the U.S. Commission on Civil Rights on October 4, 1966, as "viable, stable neighborhood[s] in which people of all races and all creeds and varying levels of economic position can remain."[1] A city with a population decline as steep as Boston's, Logue reasoned, desperately needed to create appealing neighborhoods with housing stock and facilities of sufficient quality to attract the social mix that would prevent any district from being written off as a slum or dismissed as too marginal. Socially fragmented Boston faced a choice, Logue posited, between a "path of economic and racial integration" or "we can keep going as we are going," headed down "that path lead[ing] to segregation and second-rate status."[2]

Logue's neighborhood urban renewal of the 1960s was not the brash and brutal "Negro and poor removal" that frequently prevailed in the 1950s, most starkly in Boston's West End, and that many critics have assumed continued to underlie all urban renewal. It was more socially utopian than that. Outcomes, though, did not always match renewers' intentions. And what Logue considered a desirable aspiration was, understandably, often not shared by those facing the BRA's social reengineering on the ground. Logue's blueprint for a good neighborhood as socially integrated space—rather than the Boston he condemned of isolated ethnic, racial, and low-income islands floating in a sea of discrimination, disinvestment, and dilapidation—held little appeal for those residents who had loyal, deep roots in neighborhood enclaves that had long defined themselves through ethnic and class exclusivity. Moreover, many feared that the BRA's ideal of social integration would lead to their own dislocation.

What emerged from these tensions was an interaction between the BRA and Boston's neighborhoods that led to another form of "negotiated cityscape." Downtown renewal had been shaped by compromises between the modern and the historic and the public sector and the private. Neighborhood renewal not only took its own distinctive form but also varied from one neighborhood to another in ways that challenge the assumption that one urban renewal formula fit all communities. Rather, the outcome in each neighborhood resulted directly from how the renewers and the renewed interacted with each other, making the process much more of a negotiation than Logue originally intended and many skeptical Bostonians ever expected.

When Logue started investigating Boston's neighborhoods in 1960, he said to the head of the still-separate Planning Department, "Let's see what you've got." He was presented with a master plan from 1950, what Logue described as "a foolish plan done in the Corbusier mood which was all the rage then, all about 'towers in the park,' a sick formula for rebuilding cities which has had a baneful influence all over the world." Looking more closely at the South End and Charlestown district plans, he saw that they both called for total clearance, in the South End saving only the Roman Catholic Cathedral of the Holy Cross, the Cathedral public housing project, and Union Park; and in Charlestown, preserving Bunker Hill Monument (site of the historic Battle of Bunker Hill in 1775), Monument Square, the Bunker Hill public housing project, and a church or two. These plans, in the same vein as what had guided Hynes and Simonian's demolition of the West End, would have required the relocation of thirty thousand residents from the South End and fifteen thousand from Charlestown.[3] Logue knew this proposal was untenable and welcomed the opportunity to implement his newly awakened philosophy from New Haven's Wooster Square of "rehab don't demolish."

COMMON RENEWAL PATTERNS

The BRA's most substantial neighborhood renewal projects during the 1960s—in Roxbury, Charlestown, and the South End—shared many similarities. In developing neighborhood renewal plans to tackle the city's extensive deteriorated housing, the BRA gave all targeted communities three options to consider in determining how much existing housing should be cleared for new construction—a low (15 percent), a medium (20 percent), and a high amount (30 percent)—aiming on average for about 20 to 25 percent demolition. As Logue testified to President Johnson's National Commission on Urban Problems in May 1967, "As a rule of thumb we believe that 75 percent of the existing occupied structures must be kept and rehabilitated if you are going to do this on a large scale."[4] Where substandard buildings were kept, the BRA encouraged rehabilitation, to be achieved by offering advice, giving small loans, running a summer "work camp" for high school and college students to assist residents, and opening "pilot houses" to demonstrate affordable and acceptable methods of renovation.[5] New community amenities—YMCAs, schools, police and fire stations, shopping centers, and the like—were on the drawing board for cleared land.

Though Logue and the BRA were sincere in wanting to construct replacement housing for displaced tenants, they had limited tools at their disposal. A Ph.D. candidate at MIT who undertook research for her dissertation by working at the BRA for five months was convinced of "Logue's strong desire to assist in changing the prevailing public image of redevelopment by erecting low income housing," calling for as much of it "as possible, erected rapidly."[6] But providing sufficient relocation housing and making it available quickly became the BRA's Achilles' heel in Boston's neighborhoods, much as it had been for renewers in New Haven. Years later, Logue admitted that the BRA "couldn't keep pace with relocation."[7] Few if any federal funds existed beyond the 221(d)(3) program, which Logue had also made good use of in New Haven, where nonprofit organizations like churches and labor unions could secure low-cost, 100 percent financing as sponsors of small-scale housing complexes.

Logue bragged that Boston had the largest Section 221(d)(3) relocation housing program in the country. In Roxbury, for example, Academy Homes I and II (named for its site on the former campus of Notre Dame Academy, a Catholic girls' boarding school) were sponsored by the Building Services Employees Union Local 254. Marksdale Gardens I, II, and III were supported by Saint Mark Congregational Church. The largest project, Warren Gardens, was carried out by the Charlesbank Foundation. Charles Street AME Church created Charlame Park Homes I and II. Saint Joseph's Co-op was developed by the Roxbury Catholic church of the same name.

Though impressive, these efforts through the 221(d)(3) program proved inadequate to meet the great need for replacement housing, given limits in federal funding; the low density of the garden-type apartments that were preferred; and the challenge of attracting nonprofit sponsors or limited-dividend commercial developers as partners, who saw little promise of profit. (The average net profit on low- and moderate-income 221(d)(3) housing was in the 6 to 7 percent range, when the return on upper-income housing was at least twice that.) With all these obstacles, the "contagion effect" in new housing construction that the BRA hoped for never materialized in Boston, according to a close observer.[8]

Moreover, rents in the replacement units proved more expensive than in tenants' dilapidated former buildings. One calculation estimated that two-thirds of the 1,700 families being relocated in Roxbury's Washington Park as of 1964 could not afford the new 221(d)(3) rents.[9] Mayor Collins himself expressed frustration that a family with children might be paying $50 a month in a substandard apartment; "maybe it can afford to pay $75 a month—but not $95."[10] Inserting public housing into neighborhoods undergoing renewal was no solution either; Logue and the BRA were ideologically opposed to expanding this stigmatized housing type that would undermine, not advance, their vision of socially mixed communities.[11] Instead the BRA worked to secure funding for a pilot rent-supplement program—extended in some 221(d)(3) projects to 10 to 16 percent of the tenants, whose identities were kept confidential—but its reach was limited.[12] At every opportunity, whether testifying to a congressional committee or being interviewed by a reporter, Logue harangued about the inadequacy of government funding to create sufficient affordable housing.[13]

Criticism of the BRA's failure to provide a sufficient amount of replacement housing, which was forcing too many residents to leave neighborhoods where they had established roots, plagued Logue at every turn. He locked horns, for example, with the planner Chester Hartman, who excoriated the BRA's relocation record in a major planning journal, prompting a defensive response by Logue in a later issue.[14] Dislocation statistics are notoriously unreliable, but even the BRA's own accounting in 1967 conveys the extent of the upheaval. Of the 2,380 traceable families forced to move during Washington Park's renewal, 1,221 relocated within Roxbury, with only 581 remaining within the Washington Park area. One hundred and three Washington Park families headed for the suburbs, 35 families moved elsewhere in the state, and 36 moved out of state.[15] Very likely most of the families who left Washington Park were low income.

Realistically, the BRA's best relocation strategy took advantage of the city's severe population decline—of 172,000 between 1955 and 1965—to move dislocated families into available housing elsewhere in the city. This approach, of course, ignored the ties people felt to particular neighborhoods and contributed to their general sense of vulnerability.[16] According to one community activist, "There was an element of fear. People didn't know they could hold out for relocation to the place of their choice. They were told, 'Take it or leave it,' and they didn't know they could leave it."[17] With his eyes pinned on the prize of revitalizing neighborhoods, Logue chose not to dwell on those traumatized in the process.

The rehabilitation strategy came with its own limitations, even though it could make use of two additional federal programs—the Section 312 and Section 115 loans and grants.[18] As Logue had discovered in New Haven's Wooster Square, rehab inevitably favored homeowners over tenants, who often found themselves facing eviction during renovation and higher rents upon completion. And progress was slow. It was often hard to motivate private property owners to undertake rehabilitation. In Charlestown, a BRA project director recounted that many residents were too suspicious to take advantage of the 3 percent loans offered: "New heat, electricity. You'd be surprised how many people I couldn't convince to take it . . . They said we don't trust you."[19] Owners also felt little peer pressure from neighbors when much of the renovation went on inside.[20] The BRA's encouragement, advice, and small grants could help only so much. By May 1967 Logue had become so frustrated with the difficulty of getting landlords to rehab their buildings that he floated the idea of calling a one-day meeting of real estate professionals, tax lawyers and accountants, and Harvard Law and Business School professors to explore the possibility of imposing "tax penalties for failure to keep up rental properties."[21]

But even when property owners wanted to rehabilitate their property, they faced a huge problem: all these struggling neighborhoods were redlined by fire insurance companies and mortgage lenders, including the Federal Housing Administration, which provided crucial backing to banks extending loans. And owners needed to borrow, as the small-grant programs of the BRA were rarely sufficient for the major renovations required of seriously run-down properties. One of Logue's proudest achievements became taking on the FHA to reverse its discriminatory practices and become more lenient in its lending practices. He then pressured the Boston bankers who claimed to support the city's urban renewal to join forces in a consortium where each of twenty-one banks and thrift institutions would take a turn offering government-insured loans.[22] But still, it was not always easy for borrowers to get financing, and older residents were often reluctant to risk increasing their monthly carrying costs, even when the BRA insisted that, with FHA financing, many people's monthly expenses would decrease.[23]

Sadly, starting around 1968, after Logue had left Boston, this progress would backfire, as the Boston Banks Urban Renewal Group (known as B-BURG) shifted its willingness to lend in previously redlined neighborhoods to a rigid restriction *limiting* its lending to minority applicants in these areas *only*. The effect was to confine minority populations to certain Boston neighborhoods like Roxbury, parts of Dorchester, and Mattapan, predominantly Jewish neighborhoods now unprofitable to banks because so many mortgages were paid off. The B-BURG policy also encouraged blockbusting—scaring homeowners into selling cheaply out of fear that prices would plummet further when a minority racial group entered—and the resulting white flight. Unintentionally, Logue's aspiration to get mortgage money into the hands of marginalized homeowners to improve housing quality in socioeconomically diverse neighborhoods ended up contributing to the hardening of racial, ethnic, and economic lines within and between neighborhoods.[24]

The fate of the B-BURG program suggests the difficulties Logue faced in achieving his goal of greater class and racial mixing in Boston's neighborhoods undergoing renewal. Even beyond all the structural obstacles, Boston residents tended to reject the BRA's efforts to introduce diversity, whether they were middle-class black homeowners in Roxbury's Washington Park who resisted low-income housing as a threat to property values; or the working-class Irish in Charlestown who feared that urban renewal would open the floodgates to blacks; or low-income South Enders who equated a socioeconomic mix with the arrival of middle-class gentrifiers. Moreover, Logue's initiatives to place low- and moderate-income housing in stable neighborhoods not targeted for urban renewal failed as badly in Boston as they had in New Haven.

Publicly, Logue painted a rosy picture of neighborhood renewal as enjoying "a broad base of citizen support" and "the warm endorsement of most of the community's leaders, except for a few people in the local community who believe they can get some mileage by opposition."[25] The reality, however, proved much more complicated. Fortuitously, a participant-observer account provides an in-depth look at Boston's neighborhood urban renewal much the way Robert Dahl's *Who Governs?* did for New Haven. Langley Keyes, a Ph.D. candidate in planning at MIT, attended hundreds of community meetings and undertook dozens of interviews between 1962 and 1965 to understand what actually happened in Roxbury, Charlestown, and the South End. He published his findings four years later as *The Rehabilitation Planning Game: A Study in the Diversity of Neighborhood.*[26] Keyes concluded that each neighborhood engaged in negotiations within its own community and then with the BRA in a "game" where the victor was the group that mobilized sufficient support to position itself as chief negotiator with the BRA. The BRA, in turn, he argued, recognized that its best prospects for success depended on cooperating with the winning neighborhood team. As *The Washington Post*'s Nicholas von Hoffman explained: "[Logue] had to find a widely based group in every community that he could enfranchise as that community's bargaining agent with the Authority and which he could count on to support the project when it came time to shoot the rapids of City Council hostility."[27]

The winners of each neighborhood's rehabilitation planning game were often surprising and not nearly as predictable as the simple class analyses offered by many observers of urban renewal at the time. One school argued that urban renewal agencies consistently partnered with middle-class residents, wherever possible white, and excluded the lower-class and minority residents.[28] Others dismissed urban renewal's opponents in neighborhoods as "working-class authoritarians," tradition-bound and xenophobic. One particularly descriptive journalist portrayed them as "unsuccessful ethnic recidivists," a "calcified white proletariat," and "tribalists" who are "injured and aggrieved."[29] In truth, the victorious players varied from match to match, though, Keyes insisted, "in every case, the local [winning] team is composed of the neighborhood powerful—those local people who are able to negotiate for the future of their neighborhood."[30] Keyes's account provides insight into who won, how much, and why in each of Boston's major communities facing urban renewal.

ED LOGUE WITH SIBLINGS AT YALE, 1956. The five Logue children (left to right: Ed '42, Ellen, John '46, Frank '48, Gordon '47) grew up in Philadelphia with their widowed mother, having lost their father when Ed was twelve. With Ed leading the way, all four boys attended Yale College on scholarship. Ed, Frank, and Gordon also went to Yale Law School on the GI Bill. (COURTESY OF FAMILY OF EDWARD J. LOGUE)

A UNION ACTIVIST ON CAMPUS, 1942. Logue (with union button) expressed his liberal Democratic politics at conservative Yale by supporting unionization of the university's hourly workers during his senior year and becoming a full-time union organizer upon graduation. Agitating against the Yale administration launched a pattern in Logue's life of enjoying being a rebel in the belly of the establishment beast. (COURTESY OF FAMILY OF EDWARD J. LOGUE)

STUDYING EUROPEAN CITIES FROM THE AIR IN WORLD WAR II. Logue entered military service in early 1943 hoping to be a pilot but ended up a bombardier instead. He credited those cockpit hours with educating him in urban planning. (COURTESY OF FAMILY OF EDWARD J. LOGUE)

OBSERVING NEW TOWNS IN THE NEW NATION OF INDIA. India introduced Logue to an American government- and Ford Foundation–supported program of community development, in which infrastructural improvements and New Towns aimed to provide social benefits. He later applied these strategies to his urban renewal work in the United States. (COURTESY OF FAMILY OF EDWARD J. LOGUE)

ASSISTING AMBASSADOR CHESTER BOWLES IN INDIA, 1952–53. Logue served as special assistant to Bowles (shown here with Indian Prime Minister Jawaharlal Nehru). Logue considered Bowles a mentor, one of several father-like figures he looked up to as a young man. (MURALI / PIX INC. / THE LIFE IMAGES COLLECTION / GETTY IMAGES)

THE NEW HAVEN URBAN RENEWAL TEAM, 1954–61. Upon his return from India, Logue joined the reform Democratic administration of the new mayor Richard C. Lee (left) to help revitalize the city. Lee and Logue forged a dynamic partnership that attracted more federal dollars per capita to the "model city" of New Haven than to anywhere else in the nation. (COURTESY OF FAMILY OF EDWARD J. LOGUE)

SELLING URBAN RENEWAL TO THE NEW HAVEN COMMUNITY. This exhibition, *Time for Action*, was part of the campaign to promote urban renewal among the city's residents. (Logue is in the light jacket, with the planner Maurice Rotival to his left.) Mostly, however, New Haven's redevelopers reached out to leaders of established organizations, in an approach that the Yale political scientist Robert Dahl labeled "pluralist democracy." (COURTESY OF FAMILY OF EDWARD J. LOGUE)

DOWNTOWN APARTMENTS FOR THE MIDDLE CLASS. Lee here is proudly showing off a model of the new New Haven that he and Logue aspired to create. Closest to him are the luxury University Towers apartments, designed to keep middle-class residents from moving to the suburbs. In time, tearing down working-class neighborhoods for higher-income residences faced criticism everywhere. (ROBERT W. KELLEY / THE LIFE PICTURE COLLECTION / GETTY IMAGES)

CONNECTING DOWNTOWN NEW HAVEN TO THE INTERSTATE. Fearing that the new highway would sideline the city economically, the urban renewers built the Oak Street Connector from I-95 to downtown. The working-class Oak Street neighborhood, at the time considered a slum, was demolished to create this new gateway to New Haven, which included Malley's and Macy's department stores, attached to Paul Rudolph's parking garage, in the foreground. (NEW HAVEN MUSEUM)

URBAN RENEWAL BY DEMOLITION.
Desperate to improve the draw of
downtown as suburban residential
living and shopping increasingly
threatened New Haven's viability, the
urban developers leveled blocks of the
city's center to fill downtown with new
modern buildings, intended to signal
that New Haven was headed for a
successful future. (NEW HAVEN MUSEUM)

LOGUE WITH THE REDEVELOPMENT DEPUTY RALPH TAYLOR. Logue became a leader in creating a new national profession of urban redeveloper, an expert with general administrative know-how who then calls on others with more specialized, technical mastery. Visible out the office window is the intersection of Church and Chapel Streets before urban renewal demolition began. (COURTESY OF H. RALPH TAYLOR)

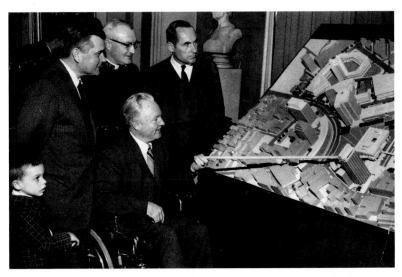

GOVERNMENT CENTER, CORNERSTONE OF BOSTON'S URBAN RENEWAL, 1963. This project sought to use the financial power and physical presence of government at every level to goad the reluctant Yankee-dominated private sector into financially investing in Boston. Here Logue (far left with his son Billy) is flanked by the Boston Redevelopment Authority (BRA) board chairman Monsignor Francis Lally, Mayor John Collins in the wheelchair, and Gerald Blakeley, president of the real estate firm Cabot, Cabot & Forbes. City, church, and private developers all shared a common interest in renewing Boston. (KARIN KEYSER FOR CALVIN CAMPBELL, PHOTOGRAPHER)

BOSTON'S CATHOLIC CHURCH, ALLY IN URBAN RENEWAL. From the earliest days, Cardinal Richard Cushing (left) and his archdiocese became the city's collaborators in redevelopment. The church was motivated by its substantial real estate holdings, a vested interest in keeping residents rooted in its geographically bounded parishes, and the injunction by the Second Vatican Council to participate more fully in civic life. (COURTESY OF BOSTON CITY ARCHIVES)

FROM RUN-DOWN ENTERTAINMENT DISTRICT TO SEAT OF GOVERNMENT. Despite promising not to repeat the demolition-style urban renewal that had leveled the immigrant West End, Logue's BRA constructed Government Center on the site of Scollay Square, Boston's red-light district. It faced minimal opposition, given that this downtown area was in decline and was more popular with tourists and students than residents. (PHOTO © IVAN MASSAR)

GOVERNMENT CENTER UNDER CONSTRUCTION, 1965. Logue and Mayor Collins are in front of the huge pit that will become the new city hall and plaza. A *Newsweek* article in April 1965 entitled "What's Happening to Proper Old Boston?" described the project as "the most ambitious civic rejuvenation program in the nation." Historic Faneuil Hall and Sears Crescent, bordering the site, survived but were soon dwarfed. (PHOTO © IVAN MASSAR)

GOVERNMENT CENTER SOON AFTER COMPLETION, 1971. The new brutalist-style city hall was surrounded by county, state, and federal buildings. As the renewers had hoped, this huge public expenditure jumpstarted more private investment—starting with the curved Center Plaza office building and the New England Merchants National Bank tower to the left of city hall. (AERIAL PHOTOS OF NEW ENGLAND, COURTESY OF PEI COBB FREED & PARTNERS)

NEGOTIATING BETWEEN OLD AND NEW. Logue came to recognize the importance of preserving some of Boston's historic buildings, such as the nineteenth-century Sears Block and Sears Crescent pictured here. A distinctive "negotiated cityscape" resulted, though critics still complained that too much of the historic city was lost to urban renewal. (COURTESY OF BOSTON CITY ARCHIVES)

MAKING THE CASE FOR URBAN RENEWAL TO CITY COUNCIL. This was one of the many hearings in which the BRA presented its redevelopment plans, making extensive use of models and graphics. (TED POLUMBAUM / NEWSEUM COLLECTION)

ENEMIES ON CITY COUNCIL. With little power to challenge the mayor, some city council members—rooted in the ethnic neighborhoods once tied to James Michael Curley's Democratic machine—contested the BRA's plans in raucous meetings and hearings. When *Life* magazine ran a feature in December 1965 entitled "Bold Boston Gladiator—Ed Logue," it included this photograph of "Mrs. Katherine Craven [who] once said 'the resemblances between Logue and Hitler are striking.'" (TED POLUMBAUM / NEWSEUM COLLECTION)

THE BRA WELCOMED IN ROXBURY'S WASHINGTON PARK NEIGHBORHOOD. Urban renewal was most enthusiastically welcomed by the home-owning black residents of Washington Park, who feared the deterioration of their middle-class neighborhood as whites moved out and poorer blacks moved in. Muriel Snowden (left) and her husband, Otto, were founders of the Freedom House Community Center, the local operating base for the BRA. Between Snowden, Collins, and Logue is Rev. Samuel Laviscount of Saint Mark Congregational Church, which partnered with the BRA to build subsidized housing. (COURTESY OF BOSTON CITY ARCHIVES)

GROUND BREAKING FOR THE FIRST NEW HOUSING IN WASHINGTON PARK, 1963. Surrounding Logue (second row, second from the right) are many local clergy, members of the sponsoring Saint Mark Congregational Church and its nonprofit development corporation, and other community activists in Roxbury. Notable is Paul Parks (back row, left), then a leader of the Boston chapter of the NAACP and later the Massachusetts Secretary of Education in the midst of the Boston busing crisis. (NORTHEASTERN UNIVERSITY LIBRARIES, ARCHIVES AND SPECIAL COLLECTIONS DEPARTMENT)

RESIDENTS OF ROXBURY'S MADISON PARK SUCCESSFULLY DEMAND HOUSING. Low-income residents of the Madison Park neighborhood of Roxbury organized in May 1966, as the Lower Roxbury Community Corporation, to pressure the BRA to incorporate critically needed housing into planning for a new high school. Much more combative than the middle-class Washington Park residents, they had recently forced the city to stop illegal dumping of everything from trash to cars in Madison Park. (COURTESY OF BOSTON CITY ARCHIVES)

REV. WALTER C. DAVIS DEDICATING CHARLAME PARK HOMES II IN ROXBURY, 1966. This moderate-income subsidized housing was sponsored by the Charles Street AME Church of which Rev. Davis, speaking here, was the pastor. The garden apartment–style design appealed to prospective tenants, but inadequate funding kept the rents out of reach for many families who had been dislocated by redevelopment, to Logue and Collins's great frustration. (NORTHEASTERN UNIVERSITY LIBRARIES, ARCHIVES AND SPECIAL COLLECTIONS DEPARTMENT)

WHOSE CHARLESTOWN? The isolated white working-class community of Charlestown proved the most challenging for the BRA to win over. Here, as elsewhere, Logue's BRA learned to play what one observer called the "rehabilitation planning game": negotiating with neighborhoods to give them more of what they want in return for their support. The tougher the neighborhood opposition, the greater its gains. Middle-class owners of historic homes surrounding Charlestown's Bunker Hill Monument were the

most enthusiastic. Here Mr. and Mrs. William F. Hennessy receive a citation for participating "in the forward march to progress now being made throughout the New Boston." (COURTESY OF BOSTON CITY ARCHIVES)

MILITANT SOUTH END ACTIVISTS CHALLENGE THE BRA. The South End neighborhood had been home to a skid row, lodging houses, and many poor Bostonians. But with an impressive supply of historic rowhouses surviving and the new Prudential Center opening nearby in 1964, it began to feel the pressure of gentrification. South End community activists, such as Mel King and his Community Assembly for a United South End, pushed the BRA for a more representative elected South End Urban Renewal Committee and substantially more subsidized housing. (COURTESY OF BOSTON CITY ARCHIVES)

A FAILURE TO NEGOTIATE IN NORTH HARVARD, 1965. The one place where Logue and Collins failed to negotiate at all was the North Harvard neighborhood of Allston. Their determination to condemn existing houses for an apartment tower infuriated the community, eventually forcing the BRA to back down. Logue later said this intransigence was the worst mistake of his career. (PHOTO BY BILL BRETT / *THE BOSTON GLOBE* VIA GETTY IMAGES)

CAMPAIGNING FOR BOSTON MAYOR, 1967. Only once in Logue's career did he venture out of the offices of a redevelopment agency—when he ran for mayor of Boston. Logue failed to win one of the two spots in the run-off election. (COURTESY OF JOHN STAINTON AND MICHAEL GRUENBAUM)

Monsignor Francis J. Lally congratulates Ed Logue

As with most of us, Ed Logue's personal life revolves around his family. Above left, Ed and Kathy. Above left center, Ed Logue, a decorated combat veteran of World War II. Above center right: Ed Logue talking with neighborhood residents. Bottom center: Ed, Billy, wife Margaret, Kathy. Right, Dad and son Billy take a walk.

BIOGRAPHY:

- Graduate of Yale College and Yale Law School.
- Combat Veteran, World War II.
- Married to the former Margaret DeVane, father of two children, Kathy, 13, and Billy, 9.
- Executive Director of the John F. Kennedy Conference on Urban Renewal. Nationally acclaimed authority on city affairs.

Ed Logue is not a Politician.
A hard-hitting go-getter who gets things *done*, Ed Logue became America's foremost Development Administrator, sought after by cities across the nation.

The building of the New Boston under Ed Logue's leadership has meant thousands of new jobs for the people of Boston.

Administrator, executive, family man, he has obtained more than $200 million from the federal government to improve our city of Boston.

Keep Boston moving ahead with the man who *knows* best how to solve Boston's problems... **ELECT Ed LOGUE MAYOR!**

ELECTORAL VICTORY IN ROXBURY, 1967.
The only election ward that Logue won outright was in the heart of Roxbury, where Washington Park residents repaid his commitment to their neighborhood's urban renewal. Here he is greeting Roxbury supporters (from left to right: Logue, Muriel Snowden, Kenneth Latimer). (NORTHEASTERN UNIVERSITY LIBRARIES, ARCHIVES AND SPECIAL COLLECTIONS DEPARTMENT)

KEEP THE BOSTON BULLDOZER OUT OF NEW YORK CITY !

The Citizens Housing and Planning Council is honoring two men who have helped destroy communities and provided middle-income and luxury housing at the expense of the poor: Robert F. Wagner and Edward J. Logue. Mayor Lindsay is considering Logue for the "Housing Czar" of New York. Logue's record indicates he would take over where Robert Moses left off. (Former Slum Clearance Administrator Moses is the man responsible for destroying many N.Y.C. communities by demolishing homes of the poor and building housing far too expensive for the people he evicted. Great numbers of those evicted and forced into ghettos were Negro and Puerto Rican.

Mayor Lindsay's task force, headed by Prof. Charles Abrams, stressed that the GREATEST NEED IN HOUSING WAS FOR THE LOW INCOME AND MINORITY GROUPS ... not the destruction of communities in a time of housing shortage.

New York needs genuine citizen participation in renewal areas, on behalf of the people involved— NOT FAKE COMMITTEES set up by city agencies to rubber stamp the city's real estate-oriented plans.

New York needs Vest-Pocket Housing on vacant land throughout the city – AT LOW RENTS!

NEW YORK NEEDS SOMEONE DEDICATED TO THESE PRINCIPLES!

ED LOGUE GO HOME !

Metropolitan Council on Housing - 219 Seventh Avenue - New York City 10011 - WA 4-9858

OPPOSING LOGUE'S HIRING IN NEW YORK CITY, 1966. When the newly elected mayor John V. Lindsay tried to hire Logue, local housing activists feared another destructive Robert Moses and campaigned actively against him. Lindsay extended the offer anyway, but Logue turned him down when the mayor would not grant him powers that were extensive enough. (COURTESY OF THE TAMIMENT LIBRARY, NEW YORK UNIVERSITY)

PLANNING WITH WHICH PEOPLE IN WASHINGTON PARK?

Roxbury's Washington Park was the first neighborhood renewal project to get off the ground and the one in which Logue took the greatest pride. Given his long-standing concern with improving American race relations, he was pleased to be partnering with leaders in Boston's African American community and, most importantly, to know that they were enthusiastic supporters of his neighborhood revitalization program. In fact, Muriel and Otto Snowden, the founding directors of the Freedom House Community Center, had reached out to Logue soon after he arrived, hoping to make their area a top priority in the BRA's new neighborhood urban renewal program— and to establish their Freedom House as a key player.[31] The day after Collins and Logue went public with the $90 Million Development Program in September 1960, the Snowdens—nervous that years of working to attract the city's attention to their neighborhood would now be neglected in grand plans for the New Boston—sent the mayor a telegram "urging that full consideration be given to our community in light of [your] recent announcement of broad scale neighborhood improvement."[32]

The Washington Park Urban Renewal Project turned out to be the BRA's largest single redevelopment initiative, encompassing 502 acres straddling Middle and Upper Roxbury. A hilly community of single-, two-, and three-family wooden houses centered on Washington Park, it had begun life as an upper-class Yankee area in the 1830s, become increasingly Irish in the 1870s and 1880s, and then for many decades served as the heart of Jewish Boston, home to many important Jewish institutions. (Irish Roxbury lingered, as John Collins grew up here in the 1920s and 1930s.) After World War II, Washington Park entered a new phase. Between 1950 and 1960, as Boston's black population grew larger with an influx of migrants from the rural South (though at 10 percent still small compared with that of other northern cities), Washington Park's population flipped dramatically from 70 percent white to 70 percent black. As Jews increasingly left for Boston neighborhoods farther south and western suburbs like Brookline and Newton, the Washington Park area remained one of the few parts of Boston where middle-class African Americans could buy homes. It became the mainstay of the Boston black elite.[33]

The Snowdens were prominent leaders of that community. Muriel Sutherland grew up as the daughter of a black dentist in the upper-middle-class, all-white suburb of Glen Ridge, New Jersey (where their home was purchased through a white "straw man"), and came to Boston to attend Radcliffe College, graduating in 1938. Otto, raised in Boston after his career army officer father retired, attended Howard University, where he graduated in 1937. Both Snowdens went into social work, married in 1944, and in 1949 founded Freedom House, soon to be located on the site of Hebrew Teachers College, to be a force for good and stability in Washington Park. That meant neighborhood improvement, social services, education, and keeping the neighborhood racially integrated.[34]

By the time Logue arrived in 1960, the dream of a mixed-race Washington Park was appearing increasingly doubtful, but the Snowdens and their neighbors looked to federal urban renewal to help them preserve as much integration as possible and to sustain a viable black middle-class community.[35] Eradicating "blight"—the goal of urban renewal agencies like the BRA—became their obsession as well, as did seizing other opportunities made possible by urban renewal, such as good BRA and ABCD jobs for blacks both downtown and on-site in Roxbury, where more than eighty were employed.[36] With their enthusiasm for urban renewal and a vision of an integrated Washington Park well aligned with Logue's, the Snowdens and Freedom House became the BRA's local clearinghouse for urban renewal from 1961 to 1968 and the pillar of the twenty-five member Washington Park Steering Committee that the Snowdens assembled. As Otto Snowden told *The Boston Globe* in 1962, "[The residents'] feeling has been that if the plans do not go through there will be no Roxbury. Many of them see this renewal program as the last chance to save the area."[37] When the architecture critic Wolf Von Eckardt visited the neighborhood a year later while writing a six-part series on urban renewal for *The New Republic*, he met hopeful homeowners who told him, "We are going to have a beautiful new neighborhood" when the charming old houses are renovated, the more hopeless ones replaced, streets and parks spruced up, and new schools and community facilities built.[38]

With little opposition expressed to the Washington Park urban renewal plan in the early to mid-1960s, the BRA felt confident that the Snowdens and their followers, working through a block-based organization called Washington Park Citizens Urban Renewal Action Committee (CURAC), were accepted as a legitimate voice of the community and a worthy BRA negotiating partner. One of Logue's favorite stories to tell was what happened when the Washington Park plan was presented at a big public meeting on January 14, 1963. Over twelve hundred Roxbury residents crowded into the auditorium at Boston Technical High School. One speaker after another praised the plan until finally the weary moderator, asked, "Look, isn't there anybody in this room opposed to this project?" Six people stood up.[39] In his remarks that evening, Logue praised in rather grandiose terms the momentous collaboration between "the people who live in the area and the BRA staff." Referencing two years of work and "countless meetings throughout the neighborhood," he said that "on December 18 the final plan was presented to his Honor the Mayor by more than forty citizens of Roxbury who, as individuals and through their organizations, had helped put the plan together. This has never happened before in the United States."[40] Beyond CURAC, a major help in rallying supporters was the Roxbury Clergy Committee on Renewal, though religious leaders kept a concerned eye on dislocations and were likely spurred to sponsor 221(d)(3) projects out of worry about retaining residents near their churches.[41]

Despite what seemed like overwhelming support for urban renewal, there were opponents to the plan for Washington Park, and their numbers grew over time. Generally these critics resented the ambition of urban renewal's neighborhood proponents to protect the middle-class character of Washington Park from poorer blacks spilling south into the neighborhood from Lower Roxbury and the South End. In the words of one letter to the editor in *The Boston Globe*, the urban renewers were failing "to meet their responsibilities to the city's low-income families . . . Those whose needs are the greatest, the community's low-income deprived segment, were never part of the planning process, only its victims."[42] Others cynically stated that the BRA planned with the "tea-drinking Negroes" in a Freedom House they caricatured as "Uncle Tom's Cabin." The community organizer Chuck Turner went further and charged that the Snowdens "ran cover for the BRA."[43]

But Washington Park's urban renewal leaders were pursuing their own agenda as much as the BRA's. Alarmed at the swift pace at which run-down houses were being carved into small apartments to house poor black newcomers to the neighborhood, they looked to the BRA's program for protection. Specifically, they tried to expand the urban renewal area to Franklin Park, more than doubling its size. They sought as much clearance of dilapidated buildings as they could get, not trusting owners of badly neglected structures to rehabilitate them. And they hoped that poor displaced residents would settle as far away from Washington Park as possible. To discourage them from sticking close, they fought construction of low-income housing. Instead, they hoped to attract whites to integrate new 221(d)(3) projects.

According to Keyes, when Logue presented the neighborhood steering committee with the usual three relocation options, "much to Logue's dismay the Committee was favorably impressed by the option that showed 60 percent relocation of residents. When the BRA at the next meeting . . . produced a plan that included all the same community facilities but only 40 percent relocation of residents [later reduced further to 35 percent, still higher than the BRA preferred], . . . the committee felt this plan represented a 'glorified ghetto.'"[44] Logue recounted another meeting where he tried to persuade the Urban Renewal Committee to put thirty-four units of public housing for large families on a site where churches were originally slated to go but none had stepped up. "We had a strenuous community debate . . . I was an ardent advocate for it and I lost. The Freedom House people, who had been accused in today's bitter parlance of being 'Uncle Toms' wound up against it. The NAACP was split."[45]

But from Muriel Snowden's point of view, more low-income and public housing "would lock the Negro community into Washington Park for the next forty years" and put "all responsibility for the serious social problems of the poor Negro" on this neighborhood alone rather than sharing it across the city. Moreover, the middle-class black property owners, the source of the community's stability, "had the most to lose," particularly since they had many fewer avenues of escape than the Irish and Jews who had been able to move on to other neighborhoods as their fortunes improved.[46] Even Fred Salvucci, at the time a BRA transportation planner who was becoming increasingly disenchanted with how Boston's urban renewal was unfolding, acknowledged the Washington Park situation as a tough call: "I mean those were the only home-owning blacks in the region. Shouldn't you support them . . . trying to make some stability?"[47]

The Snowdens remained the mediator between the BRA and the Washington Park neighborhood through Logue's era, albeit feeling increasingly challenged by more diverse voices in their community. Muriel Snowden had optimistically told a Boston College Citizen Seminar in 1963 that "the formula for the successful planning with people in Washington Park . . . is the personal commitment of the Mayor, the determination and dedication of the BRA, the Development Administrator and his staff, and the experience . . . which gives us, the citizens of the area, the sense that we are truly partners and not *pawns* in urban renewal."[48] By the time she testified in front of Senator Paul Douglas's National Commission on Urban Problems four years later, she was clearly feeling less confident and more bruised as the BRA's partner. After proudly reciting the many achievements of urban renewal, including a new shopping center, YMCA, Boys and Girls Club, police station, courthouse, branch library, refurbished parks, improved housing, and the recently approved Trotter Elementary School, she acknowledged that "nobody but a bloody idiot would claim that all of this has happened without pain, without struggle, without conflict, without error and without gaps."[49] The BRA likewise received mounting criticism for doing business with the elite of Washington Park.

The Snowdens' position would get only more difficult the next month when Roxbury experienced Boston's comparatively tame, but still troubling, race rebellion, escalating racial tensions in the city. On June 2, 1967—a month before the major riots in Newark and Detroit and two months before New Haven's—more than fifty members of Mothers for Adequate Welfare (MAW) occupied the Grove Hall Welfare Office in Roxbury. They called for welfare reform and an end to what they charged was insulting treatment by social workers and welfare department staff. For three days angry sympathizers carried the protests into the streets—looting, torching, and throwing stones at riot-geared, fiercely retaliating police. The rioters "vented their anger on . . . anything that represented an intrusion into the community," according to an editorial in *The Bay State Banner*, the major African American newspaper in Boston.[50] After the protests ended, some of MAW's original demands were met. Although urban renewal was not an issue in the protests per se, three state representatives presented a nine-point program that included physical improvements such as demolishing abandoned buildings; constructing playgrounds, swimming pools, and a skating rink; and removing trash from streets and vacant lots. A new generation of assertive black activists would gain greater prominence after these June days, though their demands would mostly be faced by Boston's next mayor, Kevin White. John Collins publicly announced that he would not seek reelection only days after the Roxbury riots ended, encouraging speculation that the revolt had spurred his decision, though insiders knew he had made up his mind months earlier.[51]

The November election would also bring the first African American into the city council since it had become an at-large body in 1951. Roxbury's Thomas I. Atkins, a Harvard Law School student and the executive director of Boston's NAACP, not only became a city councillor but also assumed the leadership of the council's Urban Renewal Committee, providing a friendly platform for grassroots groups to get a hearing at city hall.[52] This generational and political changing of the guard within Roxbury coincided with Logue's departure from the BRA, breaking the negotiated pact between the Washington Park elite and the BRA from both sides. As neighborhood redevelopment went in other directions under Mayor White and federal dollars became scarcer, Otto Snowden despairingly told a *Globe* reporter in 1976 that from his point of view, "it's just a matter of time until all the money spent here will have gone down the drain . . . It will fail because it was never finished . . . and we never received the necessary city and social services [that were promised]." The reporter concluded, "Fifteen years and 70.4 million dollars later, the renewal of Washington Park is considered a failure by many of those involved."[53] Although the passage of time had altered prospects for the Snowdens and their neighbors, in their heyday they had been able to marshal substantial community support for the urban renewal plan of their choice, making them the winners of the Washington Park rehabilitation planning game.

A VERY DIFFERENT LOWER ROXBURY

Middle-class individuals like the Snowdens did not always become the BRA's negotiating partner in the city's major black community of Roxbury. In Madison Park, a neighborhood much poorer and more deteriorated than Washington Park, which was about one and a half miles south, low-income residents were the ones to gain recognition as community spokespersons and to fight for changes in the BRA's plan to build the new Campus High School, later renamed Madison Park High School. Over the course of a year, the Lower Roxbury Community Corporation (LRCC), the organizational voice of low-income residents, managed to win favor as the bargaining agent for the neighborhood, including gaining prominence over mostly white, middle-class advocacy planners who had volunteered to help them. Organizers from Urban Planning Aid had originally been invited by the LRCC to represent it to the BRA. But when a memorandum of agreement was finally signed in January 1967, adding more than four hundred units of new housing to the high school plan, its parties were only the LRCC and the BRA, judged by each side to be its best negotiating option, even as tension persisted between them.

The community's engagement with the BRA grew out of the Boston School Committee and BRA's joint plan to build a large integrated high school in the low-income neighborhood of Madison Park.[54] The issue was not that local residents objected to a new high school. Roxbury's schools were in desperate shape, as the Boston School Committee's failure to conform with Massachusetts's Racial Imbalance Act of 1965 was blocking all efforts to construct vitally needed new schools throughout the city—and what was bad in white Boston was worse in black Roxbury. The state feared the creation of more segregated schools and wanted to keep the pressure on the Boston School

Committee to integrate. A 1962 Ford Foundation study had found conditions so appalling that it recommended tearing down at least seventy-one aged elementary schools, constructing fifty-five new schools and twelve additions, and building a city-wide high school for fifty-five hundred pupils, all to the tune of $132 million.[55] The BRA decided to move forward with the high school, whose diverse geographical enrollment would exempt it from the building ban.

Residents of the Madison Park neighborhood had already begun to organize when they learned about the BRA's plans for the new high school in spring 1966. Their action was first prompted by mounting garbage in Madison Park, which had become an unsupervised dumping ground for individuals and even construction company trucks from all over Greater Boston seeking to avoid paying proper waste disposal fees. In March 1966, fed-up residents, aided by clever community organizers, took matters into their own hands, loading a truck with trash and depositing it on the steps of city hall. A few months later, they gathered more refuse and lit a big bonfire in the park. When summoned firemen turned their hoses on protesters as well as flames, they stoked the neighborhood's anger by invoking emotional images of the high-pressure hoses used on civil rights marchers in the American South.[56]

When the BRA presented plans that required using fifty-seven acres of the Madison Park area for a high school and athletic fields, dislocating an estimated 385 families, the stage was set for residents to demand that affordable replacement housing be built—and be ready in time—for the displaced. The LRCC, created in May 1966, became the neighborhood's voice of opposition. It involved many of Roxbury's most important community organizers—Andrea Ballard, Daniel Richardson, Alex Rodriguez, Byron Rushing, and Chuck Turner—but meetings also attracted many concerned citizens who elected the local residents Ralph Smith and Shirley Smolinsky as leaders. Smith was an African American night-shift baker who was about to lose the two-family red-brick rowhouse he had bought in 1946. Smolinsky was a Polish American homemaker whose family was among the shrinking number of whites still living in the neighborhood.[57]

Fearful that it would need help dealing with the experts and bureaucrats in the BRA, the LRCC approached a group of mostly white advocacy planners known for their effective organizing against the Inner Belt and the Southwest Expressway, new proposed highways that were expected to intersect at the Madison Park High School site. These housing and planning activists, many of them young faculty from Harvard and MIT, had met up while protesting the North Harvard urban renewal plan as well as the highways. They had just recently incorporated as a nonprofit advisory group called Urban Planning Aid (UPA).[58]

The LRCC contracted with UPA in July 1966 to come up with an alternative plan for Madison Park and to conduct a community survey to investigate residents' needs and desires.[59] The founding UPA members were an impressive group. The lone African American was Denis Blackett, a project designer at the BRA. Others included Gordon Fellman, an assistant professor of sociology at Brandeis; Robert Goodman, an assistant professor of architecture at MIT; Chester Hartman, an assistant professor of city planning at Harvard; Daniel Klubock, a young activist lawyer; James Morey, the full-time UPA executive director, who, as a psychologist and a systems analyst, had recently left the defense industry in disillusionment; Lisa Peattie, an anthropologist and associate professor of urban affairs and regional planning at MIT; and Fred Salvucci, a BRA transportation planner.[60] Over the spring, summer, and fall of 1966, a fascinating, well-documented three-way struggle transpired between Logue's BRA, the Madison Park community as represented by the LRCC, and UPA, with UPA carrying the torch for the LRCC with the BRA, while the LRCC's mostly African American organizers and members grew increasingly distrustful of their advisers.

During summer 1966, the BRA held several public meetings where Logue and the project director John Stainton explained the plans to mounting neighborhood opposition. Meanwhile, the LRCC was meeting on its own and with the UPA to develop an alternative approach that provided for twenty-five acres of replacement housing. In October, UPA's inner circle requested a private meeting with Logue in his office, without LRCC representatives present, to explain their advocacy planning work with the community and request a four-month delay to allow them to undertake a community survey.[61] Detailed notes written by Fellman provide an almost word-for-word report of this meeting, including prior discussions about who should attend centered particularly on Blackett as a BRA employee and Hartman as a known Logue foe.

As the result of several testy encounters in the past, including a very public dispute over the BRA's relocation record, Hartman clearly "irritate[d] Logue," who felt that his attacks on urban renewal in print and in person undermined confidence in the local government and the BRA. At the meeting, which both Blackett and Hartman in the end attended, UPA members pushed Logue to entertain "more satisfactory representation of divergent views and incorporation of them into the planning process." Logue responded in controlled but angry tones that the BRA was already taking all views into account, "including the interests of low-income people," and criticized the UPA's negative response to the Campus High relocation plan as "irresponsible." The meeting ended with UPA charging Logue with depriving neighborhood people of the "power they would like to have," and Logue dismissing UPA as liking "conflict for its own sake."

Soon, frustrations grew between the UPA and the LRCC. Fellman reported to UPA's board about a well-attended LRCC meeting in early December to hammer out a proposed memo of understanding to submit to the BRA. After a variety of views were expressed, including many by non-community members, the LRCC's leaders asked everyone to leave except for the residents. According to Fellman, "After a closed door session, Mr. Smith (LRCC's Chair) advised UPA the situation had to change for the group was being pulled and advised from too many directions. He requested just one UPA member act as advisor to the new coordinating committee they would establish." Fellman took on that role. Then, revealing honest self-reflection, UPA's minutes continue, "The Board generally agreed that the Madison Pk. project has taught them much. Unfortunately, the LRCC people did not trust them, they have not seen UPA as their advocates but acting more as their directors rather then [sic] advisors. And like the BRA (incorrectly or not) was perceived as telling what was 'good for them.'" Fellman concluded positively, however, that "as a result of all that happened, it forced LRCC closer together as a group that now wanted to make its own decisions. This is an important aspect of a group's maturing process."[62] Further tensions developed between UPA and the LRCC over UPA's dissatisfaction with the quality of work performed by the community volunteers recruited by the LRCC to help with UPA's neighborhood survey.[63]

This triangular contest played out in four days of contentious hearings in front of the city council's Urban Renewal Committee and then in a memorandum of understanding, dated January 5, 1967, between the BRA and the LRCC, with no mention of UPA. It reserved at least fifteen acres for no less than four hundred new or rehabilitated housing units.[64] In some ways the invisibility of UPA in this final negotiation could be viewed as a desirable outcome by advocacy planners who defined their mission as helping communities articulate their own needs and preferences. But more was at play here. Logue deeply disliked what he considered the challenges of troublemaking radicals to his liberal planner's agenda. Discrediting them as "academic amateurs" during the city council hearings, he made it clear that he preferred to deal directly with the community and proceeded to cut out UPA. As *The Boston Globe* reported: "Noting the presence of Chester Hartman, a Harvard assistant professor of city planning and a Logue critic, the Boston Redevelopment Administrator said sharply, 'I question whether Mr. Hartman and his colleagues (in UPA) are interested in solving this problem or having a little fun. I'm of the opinion they want to have a little fun.'" Although it was not UPA's intended strategy, its presence so irritated Logue that he bent over backward to deal directly with the LRCC, and in that respect UPA indirectly helped to further empower the LRCC.[65]

Eventually, after more wrangling with the BRA post-Logue, new housing did come to Madison Park, along with a new Madison Park High School designed by the prominent modernist architect Marcel Breuer.[66] The LRCC won the right to be the housing developer and renamed itself the Madison Park Development Corporation, claiming with its LRCC founding date of 1966 to be "one of the country's first Community Development Corporations" and describing itself as "a community-based, non-profit that independently developed affordable housing for low and moderate-income residents."[67]

When LRCC members and Roxbury community organizers were interviewed years later about the historical background to the revised Madison Park plan, they rarely made mention of UPA, mostly taking pride in the indigenous neighborhood leaders who emerged, particularly Ralph Smith and Cameron Vincent Haynes, for whom the new buildings would be named.[68] Moreover, the housing constructed in Madison Park reflected as much in appearance as in origin the independent vision of the neighborhood's residents. After carefully checking out what they liked and disliked in nearby Marksdale Gardens, Charlame, and Academy Homes and then working closely with a committed community architect named John Sharratt, "they wound up," according to Fellman, "with the housing they wanted. We all thought it was rather unimaginative, but that's what they wanted. I mean, we had visions of compounds and inner courtyards and so on. They wanted housing with their front on the street and a backyard."[69]

The negotiated cityscape of Madison Park revealed not what Logue's BRA originally intended—the experts' plan to devote all the acreage to an exemplary Campus High School—nor what UPA's advocacy planners desired— an innovative approach to subsidized housing—but rather exactly what the residents of Madison Park themselves wanted: a new high school plus new homes with front doors and backyards, developed by and for the neighborhood. The LRCC alone won the rehabilitation planning game in this low-income Roxbury community.

CORRALLING CHARLESTOWN

If any neighborhood in Boston epitomized community opposition to urban renewal during the Logue era, it was Charlestown. The BRA had fairly easily identified its negotiating partners in both the Washington Park and Madison Park neighborhoods. In Washington Park, middle-class pluralist Democrat leaders, organized around an established institution like Freedom House and recognized by city hall as official community spokespersons, welcomed the BRA as their ally and urban renewal as their strategy for preserving the middle-class character of their neighborhood. In Madison Park, the grassroots LRCC insisted on making its own case as participatory democrats unwilling to let elites—whether the BRA or UPA—speak for them. In the end, they won a compromise that incorporated their vision of housing into the BRA's plans. Charlestown was a different story. For most of Logue's administration, the BRA struggled to find a viable negotiating partner in Charlestown that could rally enough support to make the rehabilitation planning game work there at all.

Charlestown was a physically isolated and socially insular community that was not doing well by any measure. Separated from the mainland by the Charles River and Boston Harbor, it was the oldest settled land in the Boston area and only legally annexed to the city in 1873. Apart from an attractive historic residential core around the Revolutionary-era Bunker Hill monument, much of Charlestown consisted of blocks of deteriorating three-decker wooden tenements crisscrossed with highways, access ramps, bridges, railways, and transit lines. Charlestown also featured the nation's oldest navy yard, steadily being abandoned; big areas of open-lot truck storage and waning industrial plants; a huge public housing project, dating from the 1940s and containing 1,150 units, housing 20 percent of the community's inhabitants in 1960; and the "El," a relic of the circa 1900 Elevated Street Railway system that bisected Main Street and cast a dark and sooty shadow over Charlestown's paltry downtown. No surprise that the population had plummeted by a third from 1950 to 1960—to 20,000—and by 1965 would fall still further to 17,400. Charlestown's residents were overwhelmingly Irish Catholic, divided into three parishes with shrinking congregations, including the one where Monsignor Lally, chair of the BRA board, resided. Many Townies dwelling in Charlestown in the early 1960s struggled financially, as its median income of $2,700 was among the lowest in Boston, due in large part to the many public housing residents.[70]

Whereas Charlestown's physical deterioration might have cried out for greater investment of public resources, its residents' history of political infighting and suspicion of outsiders was a hindrance. This conundrum made the BRA's task both pressing and precarious. In the end there were three organizations vying to represent Charlestown in negotiations with the BRA. First to emerge was the Self-Help Organization of Charlestown (SHOC), a grassroots citizens' group that initially expressed great enthusiasm for renewing the neighborhood, spurred by what had happened across the river in the West End. As the group's founder, Leo Baldwin, wrote in a letter to the weekly *Charlestown Patriot*, "The people of the West End formed their committee when the West End was doomed. Have you seen the West End lately?"[71] But after some early success working with SHOC, the BRA's staff became concerned that the group was too volatile and not attracting a wide-enough cross section of the community, excluding in particular important groups such as the pro-renewal Catholic clergy, local business leaders, the longshoremen's union, and many other established civic, fraternal, and religious organizations. In its place, the BRA encouraged the creation of a broader umbrella organization, the Federation of Charlestown Organizations (FOCO), in which SHOC would be only one of many voices.

This insult to SHOC and other errors of judgment by multiple parties turned the BRA's first public meeting, on January 7, 1963, into a fiasco. The BRA's Charlestown staff—led by Pat McCarthy and Joe Vilemas—expected enthusiastic approval of the BRA's plans, including early land acquisition to begin construction on replacement housing, but they had thoroughly misread community sentiment and not done nearly enough to rally supporters to attend the meeting.[72] What they got—ironically only a week before the lovefest hearing in Washington Park—was "a defeat, a rout, a retreat," in the words of Frank Del Vecchio, who would soon replace McCarthy as project director when the BRA began to pick up the shattered pieces of its Charlestown project after the disastrous meeting.[73] More than a thousand Townies crammed into the Clarence Edwards Junior High School auditorium, many of them brought out by SHOC sound trucks blaring "Save your homes" and "Come fight the BRA." When Logue tried to present the plan, he was booed. FOCO supporters who spoke were greeted with hoots and catcalls. When Catholic priests gave their blessing, they met stony silence, and when Monsignor Lally finally called for a show of hands, the BRA's plan was overwhelmingly voted down.

Furious that "we were clobbered," Logue took a step back.[74] After having failed with two negotiating partners, the BRA now cast its fate with a third, the Moderate Middle (MM), headed by a former, more temperate member of SHOC who hoped to thread a reasonable path between an increasingly radicalized SHOC and a discredited, ineffective FOCO. Even more importantly, Logue changed BRA staff leadership in Charlestown, replacing outsiders Vilemas and McCarthy with Del Vecchio, whose standing as a native of the West End gave him community credibility. As Del Vecchio told it, a day or two after the failed hearing, "I went in to see Logue. I said, 'You can have this project. It's not over. You've just got to go to the people, and you didn't. I know how to do it . . . I'll do it for you.'"[75]

Under Del Vecchio, the BRA shifted strategy, seeking new ways of connecting directly to Charlestown residents and not relying on any one organization in this politically fragmented community. SHOC was hopeless at this point, having alienated even founder Baldwin, but FOCO and MM held some promise. To counter the situation he inherited, where "the only people who came out were against," Del Vecchio established a site office in the basement of the public library; hung maps of the renewal plans on the wall rather than keeping them secret; distributed an enticing, well-illustrated booklet, *The Urban Renewal Plan for Charlestown, an Opportunity for Every Resident*; held block meetings week after week for an estimated four thousand residents; and did surveys and planning from a van that traveled through the streets of Charlestown. "I would get out of the van, and knock on the door, and tell them who we were and what we were doing there . . . I took slides, put together a slide show . . . We would open the doors, people would come in ready to fight, but instead they sat down and they saw a slideshow [titled 'Your Home, Your Future, Your Charlestown']. We pre-empted [them]."[76]

Most significantly, selling urban renewal to Townies forced the BRA to improve the deal it was offering. By the time the second public hearing was held, in March 1965, Charlestown residents were being promised that there would be only 10 percent demolition, much less than the 20 to 30 percent elsewhere. All dislocated residents would be rehoused within Charlestown in new or rehabbed subsidized buildings, with special provision for the elderly and assurances that there would be no more public housing, which

Townies feared would attract unwanted outsiders, particularly nonwhites. Homeowners would receive grants and cheap loans for renovation and free architectural and construction advice. New construction would include three schools, parks, playgrounds, a recreation center, two fire stations, a library, a shopping center, and what would later be called Bunker Hill Community College. Traffic would be rerouted away from pedestrian areas, while roads, sidewalks, and utilities would be improved. Last—as the big deal clincher—the long-hated El would be removed to the tune of $12 million, as a result, according to Keyes, of "the BRA invest[ing] enormous quantities of time and money lobbying the Urban Renewal Administration to convince it that removal of the 'El' represented a valid expenditure of federal renewal funds." Until they had that promise in hand, Logue and Del Vecchio knew there was no point in even considering another public hearing.[77]

With what seemed like progress, Logue decided to try again for a public hearing and endorsement, and this time he was better prepared. On Sunday, March 14, 1965, a little more than two years after the first calamitous meeting, twenty-eight hundred Townies gathered at 1:00 p.m. in the largest inside public space available, the cavernous Charlestown Armory. Many arrived in buses chartered by the BRA to bring them directly to the armory from High Mass at the three local churches, where they were encouraged to attend from the altar. Forty-five Boston police were on hand to keep peace. Even Mayor John Collins made a short, rare appearance, making his way slowly down the center aisle in his braces and then urging the tense community not to turn down a precious $41 million to regenerate Charlestown. Said Logue: "That was the one, with his instinct for Boston, where he knew showing the flag would make a difference."[78]

The plan for the meeting was to alternate on an hourly and then half-hourly basis between proponents and opponents until everyone who wanted to got a chance to speak. The first hour of supporter testimony went smoothly enough, but the mood became more inflammatory when an emotional leader of SHOC incited the crowd with, "It's my home and that's what I'm fighting for. You can stick the money up your ass." After hours of debate, broken by occasional fistfights, including the punching of a priest, and emotional testimony by Charlestown native daughter and city councilwoman Kitty Craven, Monsignor Shea from Saint Catherine's suddenly shocked the crowd by calling for a vote: "All those in favor of a renewal plan for Charlestown, stand. Stand for Charlestown!" Pandemonium broke out, as opponents who were standing dove for the floor and Logue stood on a table to count. No one was sure what the actual vote breakdown was, though most observers gave the "yes" vote a clear edge, and the renewal-friendly *Charlestown Patriot* estimated it won by a 3-to-1 margin. Logue, in any event, declared victory and left the armory with other city officials under a tight police escort.[79] Even after this outcome, over four hundred SHOC opponents carried the fight through twelve raucous sessions of city council hearings in April and May 1965, though the mayor and the BRA had already locked up seven of the nine votes.[80]

With NBC's cameras rolling at the armory meeting, gathering footage later included in the Chet Huntley television documentary titled *America the Beautiful* on the urban crisis in Detroit and Boston, a national audience would soon see what some would consider American democracy in action and others another urban renewal travesty like Boston's West End.[81] Members of SHOC would nurse grudges against urban renewers as the latest in a litany of outside threats and land takers—the Boston Elevated in the early 1900s, the Boston Housing Authority in the 1940s, and the Mystic Bridge builders in the 1950s—and carry them into the anti-busing battles of the next decade.[82] Logue and Collins, on the other hand, were both convinced that as a result of pressure exerted by vocal opponents, Charlestown in the end got the best urban renewal deal of all Boston neighborhoods, winning more concessions from the BRA than anywhere else. The biggest one was the BRA's abandonment of Logue's hope for a more socially mixed neighborhood, as Irish working-class Charlestown sought assurances that new housing would not encourage African American newcomers beyond those few families already living in public housing, which now by law required a modicum of integration. In the mid-1960s, there were only about one hundred blacks among the approximately seventeen thousand living in Charlestown, and many

Townies were determined to keep it that way. It was hard to say who won the rehabilitation planning game in Charlestown. But all involved would have agreed that the New Charlestown resulted from a complex negotiation among many parties and not the adoption of any one side's agenda, certainly not the BRA's.

MULTIPLE SOUTH ENDS

The South End could not have been more different from Charlestown. Where Charlestown had clearly defined boundaries and a strongly identified, homogenous Irish Catholic population, the South End hardly functioned as a coherent neighborhood. Rather, it was a large, amorphous six-hundred-acre area bounded by downtown to the north, the Back Bay on the west, Lower Roxbury to the south, and rail yards, highways, and warehouses to the east. Moreover, within the South End dwelled many kinds of South Enders. The status-seeking newly wealthy Bostonians who built handsome bow-front houses in the 1850s and 1860s on filled land had quickly moved on to the more impressive Back Bay, a saga well captured in William Dean Howells's novel *The Rise of Silas Lapham* (1885). But they left behind blocks of substantial homes that, by the turn of the twentieth century, had mostly been converted into tiny apartments and lodging houses, resided in by wave upon wave of new, poor immigrants to Boston. In 1960 almost 28 percent of the once-grand homes and more modest rowhouses of the South End were still functioning as rooming houses, many operating on strict ethnic lines. At least a third of the area's thirty-five thousand inhabitants lived in them.

The South End remained a diverse port of first entry in Logue's era, so different from most of Boston's ethnically homogeneous and insular neighborhoods. Residents identified themselves as coming from forty different ethnic groups, with 41 percent of the community nonwhite—mostly African Americans with growing numbers of Puerto Ricans. Nearly a quarter of the population was made up of single-person households, due partly to the neighborhood's very visible Skid Row. And not surprisingly, the district was among the very poorest in the city, accounting for a third of Boston's welfare caseload. Danny Soltren, who was born in Puerto Rico but grew up mostly in the South End, remembered that around 1960 "everybody was poor; there were poor Syrians, poor Chinese, poor Irish, poor blacks, poor Greeks, and poor Puerto Ricans. We were the new minority coming in. There was a little bit of everything."[83]

But the decade of the 1960s would see significant transformation in the South End, fragmenting the area into even more subcommunities. As the Prudential Center neared completion in 1964, the red-brick and brownstone houses on the nearest South End streets attracted urban homesteaders eager and financially able to convert rooming houses into single-family dwellings. Another group who found opportunity and tolerance in the diversity of the South End were gays and lesbians, always there but now venturing farther out of the closet in the more culturally liberal 1960s. In Boston's South End, as in many cities, they often brought their two-earner household incomes and their sweat labor to renovating run-down properties. No surprise that with all these changes under way in a neighborhood so close to downtown, in a city determined to reinvent itself as the New Boston, working-class families living in low-rent apartments or public housing were feeling increasingly anxious about their futures.[84]

This was the heterogeneous South End that Logue's BRA made the third site of its tripartite neighborhood renewal initiative. The diffuseness of the neighborhood proved both an asset and a liability for the BRA. Mostly, it led to a long struggle to find organizational vehicles and participatory procedures that gave the BRA sufficient community support to move forward with an urban renewal plan. At first the BRA contracted with the United South End Settlements (USES) as the BRA's representative and the ABCD base in the community, an arrangement not unlike the one with Freedom House in Washington Park. USES established the forty-member South End Urban Renewal Committee (SEURC) for community input. When South End activists like Mel King condemned that organization as too limited in reach—particularly as too homeowner dominated—the BRA encouraged structured consultation with sixteen neighborhood associations. But even that process seemed to overrepresent homeowners and local businesses, who, as property owners, voiced the strongest support for the renewal project and not surprisingly wanted less public or subsidized housing than the lower-income renters who feared getting squeezed out.

In response, community activists like King began mobilizing tenants through new organizations such as his Community Assembly for a United South End (CAUSE), the Emergency Tenants Council (later Inquilinos Boricuas en Acción), and the South End Tenants Council (SETC).[85] Meanwhile, Logue, worried that if left to the private market the South End might gentrify too quickly and undermine his hope for socioeconomic balance, tried to interest nonprofit developers in building housing in the South End. In June 1966, soon after receiving a $37 million federal grant for renewal of the South End, he wrote to one nonprofit prospect, "It is our belief that the South End should be a balanced community, too. It should continue to contain a fair share of housing which low income families now living in the area can afford." He stressed the urgency of creating some five hundred units. "The problem in the South End is that middle and upper-income families are moving in, and their demand for housing is escalating acquisition prices. If the [nonprofit] corporations do not succeed in buying now, they may be unable to purchase later at a price which permits low-cost housing."[86]

King and his fellow activists also felt the clock ticking, and they pushed hard for—and eventually won—a more representative, elected rather than appointed SEURC, a victory for promoters of participatory democracy over pluralist democracy. And in the years after Logue left the BRA, they launched grassroots actions designed to pressure Mayor White's city hall to build more low- and moderate-income housing to allow longtime renters to remain. Following a series of occupations of the BRA's South End site office that mocked the BRA as "Blacks Run Again," CAUSE became even more ambitious. On April 26, 1968, King led picketing around a temporary parking lot on land that once had housed a hundred low-income families and now was slated for a parking garage and market-rate apartments. Hundreds joined the protest over the next few days, creating a festive "tent city" encampment of tents and scrap-wood shanties that drew wide attention to the neighborhood's tremendous need for affordable housing. It took twenty years, but finally community persistence resulted in a 269-unit mixed-income project rising on the site bearing the name Tent City Apartments, with three-quarters of the units affordable for low- and moderate-income tenants.

The most substantial affordable housing project to emerge in the South End was Villa Victoria (Victory Town), begun in 1968 and completed in 1982, developed by Inquilinos Boricuas en Acción (IBA). This nineteen-acre project contained almost 750 mixed-income housing units combining new 221(d)(3) townhouses, renovated rowhouses, and a high-rise for the elderly, along with stores, playgrounds, a cultural center, social service offices, and a paved, tree-sheltered public plaza reminiscent of outdoor gathering spaces in Puerto Rico. It became home to about three thousand people. IBA worked closely with the Madison Park architect John Sharratt on the design, secured seed money from a local Episcopal church and sizable grants from the federal and state governments, and sold three hundred units to the Boston Housing Authority to help support the lowest-income renters.[87] In the 1980s, the momentum created by all this South End neighborhood housing activism carried over to a successful campaign to demand jobs for local, particularly minority, residents and the allocation of retail space for community-oriented stores in the newly planned Copley Place retail-hotel-office complex at the border of the Back Bay and the South End, adjacent to the Prudential Center.[88]

By the end of urban renewal, the dogged, demanding struggle of the South End lower-income community had forced the BRA to make concessions, much as eventually had happened in Charlestown. As a result, the South End that emerged out of the turbulent 1960s and 1970s was, despite the relentless pressures of gentrification, a surprisingly diverse neighborhood, given its proximity to downtown and affluent Back Bay. Private homes and condos continued to skyrocket in price, but they existed alongside a substantial amount of subsidized housing such as Tent City and Villa Victoria, still tenant-managed under the IBA and employing fifty residents. Ironically, considering the intense conflict between the BRA and the community, the South End perhaps more than any other Boston neighborhood came to embody the mixed class and racial profile that Logue desired, though little provision was made for the single residents of lodging houses from pre–urban renewal days. They had few advocates in the New South End.

The community's success in fending off total gentrification did not escape Mel King. In fact, rather than condemn the urban renewal of the South End out of hand, King instead credited it with successfully mobilizing the less privileged in the area and ultimately providing a channel through which the community could negotiate with the city for greater resources. The South End of the twenty-first century is testimony to King of the survival of "a lot of buildings" and "folks allowed to remain here or their counterparts that wouldn't have happened if urban renewal hadn't taken place." In a world where "development . . . was city, state, or federally supported," rather than privately driven, there was an opportunity "to include a percentage of folks who were public housing eligible" in a diverse neighborhood that included "low-, moderate-, and market-income folks."[89] To a surprising extent, King and Logue shared a common vision, though King was much more convinced that community activism was required to safeguard it.

NONNEGOTIABLE

The rehabilitation planning game did not always work, and when it didn't, both the BRA and a neighborhood could suffer. In the North Harvard part of Allston, a small community directly across the river from Harvard University and adjacent to its stadium and business school, Logue and Collins dug in their heels and insisted on honoring a commitment the city had once made to a developer for a 1950s tower-in-the-park-style, ten-story luxury apartment building. The urban renewal project required the taking and demolition of fifty-two wood-frame houses, many run-down, but home to seventy-one predominantly Irish and Italian families. Logue admitted it was "a bad project," but he and Collins feared that backing down would demonstrate weakness and force the BRA to capitulate to anti-renewal forces in other neighborhoods like Charlestown and the South End. They told themselves they were compensating the owners at fair market value. It is also likely they calculated that if Harvard was actively acquiring land in the area for future expansion (the university already owned ten of the fifty-two homes, the ones, in fact, in the worst condition), then the university might be planning eventually to clear the land for its own nonprofit development, which would take the land off the city's tax rolls. Privately owned luxury apartments would appeal to Harvard employees now and protect the city's property tax income into the future.

The outraged residents of North Harvard were enthusiastically supported by radical students and young faculty at Harvard, including some of UPA's founders, in a strange alliance with the right-wing John Birch Society, which saw an ideal opportunity to blast urban renewal as a violation of private property rights. At Chester Hartman's instigation, nine members of the Boston chapter of the American Institute of Planners sent an open letter to the mayor and the BRA registering disapproval of this "throwback to the bulldozer type of urban renewal . . . essentially a West End in miniature" and urging low-rent housing on any vacant land. Vocal protests took place at every public hearing and attracted national media coverage. Large signs reading "To Hell with Urban Renewal: It Is Legalized Theft of Private Property, We Shall Defend Our Homes with Our Lives," "Mayor Collins: We Want Our Homes!" and "Urban Renewal Belongs in Russia" went up for all to see. Picketers jeered outside the mayor's residence in Jamaica Plain. Elected officials in Boston and Washington, D.C., were persistently lobbied. And the sheriff and his agents were forced reluctantly to drag the holdouts from their condemned houses. Finally, unable to ignore the firestorm of angry protests any longer, Collins appointed a blue-ribbon committee to arbitrate and then agreed to its recommendation that those houses still standing be allowed to remain. But it was too late. Urban renewal officials in Washington senselessly insisted that their funding was contingent on full clearance of the site.[90]

In the end Logue learned a lesson about the high price to be paid for failing to negotiate with a neighborhood. He never got the planned apartment tower, and his personal—and the BRA's—reputation suffered irreparably. In Del Vecchio's words, "It was totally unnecessary in the big picture for Boston and a political black eye for Logue."[91] Logue later admitted the huge mistake in his testimony during the Ribicoff hearings and in fact explained it exactly that way, as an unfortunate failure to negotiate. In a rare admission of his failings, Logue uncharacteristically admitted, "I would like to say it started before my time, because in fact it did, but I didn't disavow it. That project was more famous, that small seven acres, than the whole rest of the program . . . I would like to say that we negotiate. It is our policy to negotiate the urban renewal plan, and develop it jointly with the people who live in the community. Where we did not do that in North Harvard, we paid and paid dearly for it."[92]

When Logue set out to write his memoirs in the 1990s and plotted a chapter on his greatest mistakes, sure enough, number one on the list was "The North Harvard Street Project."[93] The BRA did eventually change the proposed housing from luxury apartments to a low-rise 221(d)(3) cooperative sponsored by the Committee for North Harvard, an interfaith collaboration of five Allston-Brighton congregations, which the community welcomed. In 1969–70, the affordable, 213-unit Charlesview Apartments rose in Barry's Corner, at the intersection of North Harvard and Western Avenue. Today, three of these congregations—Catholic, Methodist, and Jewish—continue to sponsor the project, even as it has been rebuilt nearby in a deal struck with Harvard University, which after many years of delaying had begun to expand its campus into Barry's Corner.[94] In North Harvard, the unwillingness by both sides to negotiate led to a standoff in which neither party got what it wanted.

TAKING STOCK OF NEIGHBORHOOD RENEWAL

The Boston that Logue left in 1968 was a very different city from the one he entered in 1960. Although still struggling, downtown seemed poised to host an economic revival built around FIRE (finance, insurance, real estate) and knowledge industries. The Prudential Center, Government Center, and other rising modernist monuments would stand alongside the rehabilitated Quincy Market, Sears Crescent, and other historic landmarks to create an eclectic skyline, embodying a compromise between the BRA and historic preservationists that gave a distinctive visual signature to the New Boston. That negotiated cityscape, moreover, would also reflect a mix of public and private investment. Logue, looking back in the mid-1980s when Boston was booming, was convinced that market forces could never have done it alone and he in fact feared that any tilting toward the private side could threaten the public interest. "The public sector created the New Boston and the public sector must control it," he insisted.[95] Langley Keyes, student of Logue's Boston, cast back with similar eyes. "Logue took a city that was flat on its back and got it up on its feet." Comparing Boston of the 1960s to Athens constructing its Acropolis, he claimed, "It was the golden age of federal largesse, and Logue was the Pericles. You can't understand the city today without saying 'Collins and Logue did it.' Without those guys—nothing."[96]

In the neighborhoods, however, Logue's ambition to foster modernized, socially mixed communities proved more controversial and less uniformly successful. Logue admitted as much in 1985 when he described the two-part series he was commissioned to write by the *Boston Observer*: "One part would focus on downtown whose revitalization has earned Boston worldwide renown . . . The second part would focus on the neighborhoods where the story is equally interesting, far more complex and where the results are very much a mixed bag."[97] Nonetheless, what happened in Boston's neighborhoods was not the 1950s top-down style of urban renewal that took place in Logue and Lee's New Haven and Simonian and Hynes's South and West Ends. Rather, as with downtown, the renewal that resulted reflected a compromise between the BRA and Bostonians, a negotiated cityscape that bore the marks of tense give-and-take between the BRA and community residents. This was the case whether the outcome was 221(d)(3) church-sponsored housing in Washington Park, the new homes alongside Madison Park High School, minimal demolition and maximum rehab in Charlestown, the construction of Villa Victoria and Tent City Apartments in the South End, or the Charlesview Apartments in Allston.

One of the most important legacies of neighborhood urban renewal in Boston was the spur it gave to community organizing, which flourished thereafter in many realms of American society. Intense contestation over what constituted an ideal physical environment and how to best achieve democratic decision-making taught Bostonians to assert themselves in new ways. The Great Society programs would mandate "maximum feasible participation," but the real learning took place on the ground, where the scale of urban renewers' ambition to remake the city would arouse new heights of popular activism and inspire the birth of dozens of grassroots organizations. Just taking the South End of the 1960s alone, the list of organizations that involved ordinary citizens in neighborhood planning included SEURC (South End Urban Renewal Committee); CAUSE (Community Assembly for a United South End); SEFCO (South End Federation of Community Organizations); SEPAC (South End Project Action Committee); SETC (South End Tenants Council), which became TDC (the Tenants Development Corporation); ETC (Emergency Tenants Council), which became IBA (Inquilinos Boricuas en Acción); CATA (Columbus Avenue Tenants Association); PEURC (People's Elected Urban Renewal Committee); and SEDC (South End Development Corporation). A number of these organizations, along with Madison Park Development Corporation and Charlesview Inc. in Allston, became the kernels of the major post–urban renewal vehicle of subsidized housing construction: community development corporations.[98]

Community mobilization became so effective in Boston, in fact, that it led to a major defeat for the BRA by the early 1970s. Logue had left town, but the plan that got killed was his. Two major highways for Greater Boston had been on the drawing board since the late 1940s but were made financially feasible by the Federal-Aid Highway Act of 1956: the Inner Belt (I-695), a mostly elevated ten-mile, eight-lane loop through Charlestown, Somerville, Cambridge, Brookline, Roxbury, and Boston's Fenway; and the Southwest Expressway (I-95), an eight-mile road designed to route traffic onto a major highway instead of through residential streets in Hyde Park, Roslindale, Jamaica Plain, Roxbury, and the South End, connecting Route 128 in Canton, south of Boston, to the Southeast Expressway, with a transit line down the center. Although these roads were projects of the Massachusetts Department of Public Works (DPW), and not technically the BRA, the BRA had a big stake and role to play in clearing land for roadways that would move traffic expeditiously through city neighborhoods. Both Logue and Collins supported this highway construction as the best way to minimize traffic congestion, maximize access to downtown, and secure the New Boston's dominance in its region.[99]

Although rumblings of opposition against these highways had been voiced at the DPW's public hearings as early as 1960, radicalized BRA employees helped intensify the pushback against the highways. One day in 1965, the transportation planner Fred Salvucci and the architect Tunney Lee were studying maps of the proposed Inner Belt alignment and decided to drive the route. In doing so, they discovered to their horror how many buildings would have to be demolished and how many thousands of residents would be displaced.[100] At first they investigated alternatives to the planned route, but then they shifted to rejecting the whole project. Everyone told them, "You're crazy, you can't stop them . . . you're wasting your time." Joined by three others with whom they would soon found UPA, they wrote a letter of protest to a local newspaper and signed it "The Cambridge Committee on the Inner Belt."[101] So began an intense and ultimately successful battle against these highways. As residents of Greater Boston came to understand the destructive impact these roads would have on residential neighborhoods—many of them white and middle class—they joined forces first to reroute the roads and then to stop them entirely. Although there were the inevitable frictions, low-income community activists from Lower Roxbury, suburban environmentalists, and elite professors from Cambridge's MIT and Harvard found common cause in this battle.

The wide swath that these proposed highways would cut throughout metropolitan Boston—endangering even the venerable Museum of Fine Arts Boston and similar cultural institutions in the Fenway—propelled the formation of a broad-reaching, metropolitan-wide opposition. The result was a sophisticated anti-highway campaign orchestrated by the United Effort to Save Our Cities (SOC) and the Greater Boston Committee on the Transportation Crisis (GBC), whose very names reflected their expansive geographic reach. What ensued were hundreds of neighborhood meetings, media outreach, petition drives, and big rallies in Boston Common like "Beat the Belt" and "People Before Highways Day." The protests intensified after Logue and Collins left office, culminating in Governor Francis Sargent's partial moratorium on highway construction in 1970 and, after comprehensive review, his final decision in late 1972 to cancel both projects. Sargent then led a successful effort to amend federal law with the National Mass Transportation Assistance Act of 1974 to allow interstate highway funds to be used instead for mass transit. Sadly, termination came too late to stop substantial clearance in Roxbury and the South End, adding significantly to the total number of demolished homes attributable to urban renewal broadly defined.[102]

When interviewed in 1977, Collins still regretted the state's failure to construct the Southwest Expressway: "It was an example of the most sensible coordinated planning in the country," he insisted.[103] Nor did Logue ever publicly change his mind about the importance of highways for Boston's survival. However, Anthony Pangaro, who had worked for Logue in New York and was recruited to Boston in 1973 to help implement the linear Southwest Corridor Park planned to replace the canceled expressway, felt that Logue eventually came to recognize the value of mass transit over mass highways. Logue continued to tease Pangaro—"You rascal, you; you're undoing all my good work"—but Pangaro felt that "he had some respect for the fact that his idea had been dismantled by a more current one, if not a better one . . . [In the original plan], there was the road and the transit line was down the middle of the expressway . . . It was totally wrong, but it was the only way to get it done at the time."[104] The defeated highways may have been a rare case when public opposition was so strong, so widespread, and so in tune with larger attitudinal changes about the necessity of investing in mass transit. But they also demonstrated that under the right circumstances, mobilized citizens could successfully constrain the actions of a powerful government agency like the BRA, to the point of even eliminating any need for negotiation.

With the exception of Allston, where Logue and Collins stubbornly refused to negotiate, and the highways, where a politicized public warded off any negotiation, how effectively a Boston neighborhood mobilized to make demands of the BRA determined what it got in return. Michael Appleby, the author of "Logue's Record in Boston," the detailed study commissioned by critics in New York City hoping to keep Logue out, astutely observed that "the amount of clearance that takes place [in a neighborhood] appears to be inversely related to neighborhood political strength."[105] So, he elaborated, Washington Park, which cooperated enthusiastically with the BRA, had a 35 percent relocation rate (to some extent at its own request) and less long-term success than Charlestown, whose residents played hardball and in the end experienced only 8.8 percent relocation, all of whom were offered new homes in the community. In a similar vein, Collins lamented a decade after leaving office that "Washington Park and its inhabitants supported renewal and cooperated with the renewal process and it hasn't worked out quite as well as it should have." In contrast, "a vocal minority in Charlestown opposed urban renewal and yet it has worked out far beyond their greatest expectations and beyond even mine."[106] When Logue returned to Boston in the mid-1980s, he was struck in walking around the South End and Charlestown "over and over again about how much physical improvement has taken place. Clearly private initiative fed upon the initial drive and success of the public initiative." But when it came to Washington Park, although "things are much better than they were," they are "not so much improved as in the other two neighborhoods."[107]

Keyes offered a further explanation for the glaring disparity acknowledged by both Collins and Logue. He argued not only that successful negotiation between a neighborhood and the BRA yielded victory in the rehabilitation planning game but also that how the winners managed the competition with other teams in their communities mattered. In neighborhoods where one interest group was powerful enough to control the game alone, and thus marginalized other local groups, it felt little pressure to demand a renewal plan from the BRA that met diverse community needs. This was the case in Washington Park, where the Snowdens and other pluralist democratic leaders paid little heed to low-income protesters. In contrast, in a community like Charlestown, where public opinion was very divided and multiple groups vied, the only way for the BRA to move forward was to accede to the demands of many participatory democrats and deliver less residential upheaval to everyone.[108] Of course, Roxbury also had to shoulder unfair burdens from Boston's racial dynamics. The community that Collins and Logue encountered in the 1980s was coping with a steady stream of poor residents unwelcome in other parts of the city, burdening that neighborhood with more social and economic problems, lower property values, continued discriminatory treatment by mortgage lenders, and other stressors, all of which encouraged the black middle class to leave.[109]

Logue had entered Boston naively waving the flag of "planning with people," but by the time he left, that phrase would carry much greater significance than he ever intended. For example, the African American newspaper *The Bay State Banner* interpreted the resolution of the Madison Park struggle in December 1965 with equanimity in its editorial "A Battle Is Over": "Logue's agreement with the Lower Roxbury Community Committee is a victory for the concept of planning with people. It would never have been achieved if Ed Logue had not been committed to that principle, or if the Madison Park residents had not been resolute."[110] The Madison Park community organizer Alex Rodriguez took a more critical stance toward the BRA, but he—like Mel King—understood that urban renewal created opportunity as well as opposition: "Urban renewal had a negative impact to get a positive impact. It had to hurt before it helped . . . It disrupted before it re-created, and it was in the re-creation that positive came."[111]

The lasting legacy of urban renewal proved quite the opposite of what Logue had sought. He initially wanted pliant communities that were appreciative of the BRA's well-intentioned experts, registering preferences when given specific choices, but not challenging at any fundamental level a hierarchical model of planning. What Boston got instead was community vigilance and empowerment. An investigator who surveyed the long-term impact of Boston's urban renewal a good decade after Logue departed concluded that "Logue's method of operation had implicitly helped to legitimize the notion of neighborhood control over the planning process through intense local citizen participation in it." Logue, he argued, fought against attempts to turn participation into control, "but in practice the two were very difficult to separate from one another."[112] Keyes would himself conclude many years after his fieldwork of the mid-1960s, "Looking back, there had never been anything in Boston like the city-wide engagement of citizens that took place because of urban renewal!"[113]

While there is much to value in the groundswell of community activism stimulated by Boston's urban renewal, its prevalence in the 1960s and 1970s raised crucial questions about the future of urban planning and redevelopment in the city. In the wake of urban renewal, Boston, like many other cities, found itself struggling to implement even good projects with community benefits. Harry Cobb, the Pei partner who planned Government Center and who increasingly recognized urban renewal's limitations, issued a heartfelt warning. As much as he appreciated the populist "cure" to the urban renewal "disease," he worried that "what's been lost is the capacity to think about the city in larger terms as it does need to be thought of." He lamented that in the years after urban renewal, "There's still tremendous resistance to that . . . We still haven't figured out how to reconcile that need to think about some aspects of the city in larger terms with the need to respect and involve local communities. That gap has not been bridged anywhere."[114]

SEEKING CITY HALL

Logue's Boston years came to a surprising denouement. Faced with constant challenges from the neighborhoods to achieving his New Boston and aware of the intensifying drumbeat of participatory democracy in the city, Logue did the logical if unorthodox thing: he sought a popular mandate for his program by running for mayor. During summer 1967 he campaigned to be one of two top vote-getters in the nonpartisan primary election, scheduled for late September, who would then compete in the November runoff. As Logue often told the story, in the late winter of 1967 Collins announced to him privately, "Ed, I'm not going to go again." Collins had taken a bruising beating in the Democratic race for the Senate in 1966, and it seemed to a close adviser like Henry Scagnoli that he was getting bored with the job.[115] Logue

protested, "For Christ's sake, Mayor, we're not through." Collins stood firm—
"I'm not one of these guys [who] hangs on too long"—and added, "Ed, you'll
never be through." Then, in Logue's telling, Collins suggested that Logue run
himself.[116]

This conversation may indeed have been the final spark, but Logue admitted elsewhere that he had been considering a run for mayor for several
years, as would "anybody that works for a chief elected official in a responsible, highly visible job."[117] *Life* magazine's profile of Logue back in December 1965 in fact had suggested that Collins's possible victory in the Senate
race might push Logue to run for mayor. Around this time, he began to act
increasingly like a candidate for office, sending notes of condolence and con-
gratulation and undertaking other acts of solicitousness learned at the knee
of the master, his old New Haven boss Dick Lee.[118] Publicly Logue claimed
that with Collins out of the mayoral race, he saw no one he could imagine
working for in the emerging field of candidates. So he decided to run himself. As he later put it, "In 1967 I looked at it all—the city, and where we were,
and where we had to go, and who would be in charge—and before the [city
hall] building was even occupied, I attempted my leap from the top floor [BRA
offices] to the fifth floor [mayor's suite]. And that is how my seven years in
Boston came to an end."[119]

This was the first time that Logue abandoned his administrator's back
room for the elected official's front office, and he failed miserably at it. To
his great disappointment, in a very large field of ten, he finished fourth, following the top vote-getter Louise Day Hicks, who, as a member and former
chair of the Boston School Committee, was the notorious defender of the
segregated Boston public schools; and the then secretary of the commonwealth Kevin White and the Brahmin scion John Winthrop Sears,
whom he trailed by only 158 votes. A number of factors explain Logue's poor
showing when he, and many others, thought he had an excellent shot at
winning. First, White and Sears were Logue's neighbors in Beacon Hill
and competed for the same elite support Logue needed. White was already
well known as a holder of state office, and even more crucially, he was extremely well connected politically, his father, grandfather, and father-in-

law all being influential Boston Irish politicians. Sears, a Rhodes scholar, was a moderate Republican state representative with a decent civil rights record, a long Brahmin pedigree he traced back to Massachusetts Bay Colony governor John Winthrop, and enough wealth to amply fund his own campaign. His great-great-grandfather David Sears had built the granite mansion on Beacon Street that housed the elite Somerset Club and the Sears Crescent, now incorporated into Government Center. If Yankee Boston wanted its own man in city hall, Sears was the one.[120]

Second, Logue ran a poor campaign. He had limited funds at first to launch his run, with only a bank loan guaranteed by a well-off cousin. Trusting, as usual, in his fraternal networks, Logue brought his inexperienced brother Frank from New Haven to direct the campaign. A newcomer to Boston politics, Frank proceeded to alienate local movers and shakers like Collins's right-hand guy Scagnoli, who had run all Collins's campaigns and knew everyone in town. Collins asked Scagnoli to help Frank Logue, but when Scagnoli and the corporation counsel Arthur Coffey offered their assistance, "We were treated rough by him. We were practically told that he didn't need us . . . And as a consequence, I didn't lift a finger, even though I liked Ed Logue," explained Scagnoli.[121] It likely didn't help the candidate's image that Logue's wife, Margaret, eager to have a well-deserved summer vacation after her year of teaching but not to become the First Family of Boston, took off with the children for their usual summer in Martha's Vineyard. Logue was disappointed: "It was very upsetting, but that's the way it was."[122] Looking back, Logue also blamed his loss on not starting early enough. He was the last candidate to announce, leaving him only the summer to build support and requiring him to depend extensively for campaign help on willing BRA staffers, who, though not civil servants, were often relative newcomers to the city. It was rumored that "the BRA was empty during the election."[123]

Third, and what Logue did not mention, was his lack of talent as a politician. Robert Litke, BRA project manager for the waterfront area, recalled how Logue asked to be introduced to all the Italian businessmen he knew in the nearby North End: "Ed, myself, and a couple of others are walking the streets, and I'm walking next to him, and little old ladies are coming down and old men, and I said, 'Ed, say hello, tell them who you are.' . . . So he'd walk up to somebody and say, 'Hi, I'm Ed Logue,' and he'd pull his hand back. 'This is not working, Ed. Go up to them and say, "Hello, I'm Ed Logue, I'm running for mayor, I'd like your vote." ' "[124] Logue's forté— to be forceful, opinionated, and strategic behind the scenes—did not serve him well as office-seeking glad-hander; one reporter observed that "he seems to prefer discussion to slap-happy greetings."[125] The *Globe* journalist and political insider Marty Nolan blamed Logue's defeat mostly on the flush Sears campaign, though he couldn't help noting that "here's a guy who runs a huge bureaucracy and can't run a campaign."[126] There was more consistency than Nolan recognized. The flaws in how Logue ran that BRA bureaucracy—micromanaging, avoiding clear lines of authority, and registering his strong personal views with little filtering—came back to haunt him in the campaign.

Fourth, Logue's high profile in Boston also contributed to his defeat. After seven years in the city, "Mr. New Boston" was both extremely visible and still considered an outsider by many multigenerational Bostonians, elite and working class alike. Even the strategic green and white coloring on all Logue's campaign material, and the deliberate mention of his Irish parents in his personal biography, failed to help.[127] Building his candidacy around the slogan "One man stands out," Logue emphasized that he was a "proven capable administrator" and not a politician, who had brought over $200 million in federal funds to Boston and would "keep the rebuilding program going while tackling the other needs of Boston," particularly improving the city's schools. But despite his frequent reminder to voters that "Ed Logue pioneered the principle of 'planning with people,'" his pitches only served to remind some voters of the anger and frustration that urban renewal had sowed in the neighborhoods.[128] Logue admitted as much in a campaign swing in Charlestown: "I have to go around and show them I don't have horns." In an op-ed quite favorable toward Logue, the *New York Times* columnist Tom Wicker put it drily as "his name is known everywhere, not always favorably."[129] The reality was crystal clear to the politically well-connected BRA staffer Arthur Reilly: "Louise Day Hicks, family in South Boston for a hundred years. Kevin White, West Roxbury, living in Beacon Hill, a hundred years. And Ed Logue from New Haven who took my grandmother's house."[130]

Fifth, and perhaps most damaging of all, Logue's campaign made what turned out to be a fateful error when, after consulting with handwriting experts, it challenged Kevin White's nomination signatures in hopes of knocking him out of the race or at least discrediting him. There were good reasons to doubt the accuracy of White's petitions and embarrass the state official responsible for overseeing the election laws. But the devious way that Logue's campaign handled the situation—setting up an unknown, shadowy figure to lodge a complaint of forgery who then disappeared until he was tracked down and traced back to a denying Logue campaign—opened it up to accusations of "dirty politics" and hurt Logue more than White in the end.[131] On Logue's handwritten list of career mistakes prepared for his memoir, "Challenging White's signatures" appeared second after "The North Harvard Street Project."[132]

Finally, Logue's pursuit of the mayoralty suffered as Louise Day Hicks's campaign—with its barely disguised racist message "You Know Where I Stand"—gathered steam. Liberals in the city increasingly felt pressure to coalesce around one candidate judged to have the best chance of beating her in November. Although Logue was clearly identified as a progressive candidate—labeled a "New Deal liberal" in the *Globe*'s series of candidate profiles and positioned at "the other end of the pole" from Hicks, who called him "the enemy" and "the intruder"—hometown boy White, with one foot in Irish Boston and the other in elite Beacon Hill, seemed like the safest choice.[133] On primary day September 26, 1967, it was White in the number two slot, with 30,789 votes to Hicks's 43,722. Sears and Logue received 23,924 and 23,766, respectively.

Hicks's electoral strength, garnering over 28 percent of the vote in this large field of candidates, shocked the anti-Hicks forces into rallying behind White in November, prompting *The Boston Globe* to make its first mayoral endorsement ever and carrying White to a 12,552-vote victory (out of 192,673 cast). (Although the *Globe* didn't endorse any candidate in the primary, Logue's good friend, the editor in chief Tom Winship, kept him company at home on election night, along with several other close associates.)[134] White would go on to serve four terms as mayor of Boston from 1968 to 1984, trying periodically for higher office such as Massachusetts governor in 1970 and the nation's vice president in 1972. Hicks, blocked from the mayoralty, would go on to be elected four times to the Boston City Council and once to Congress. Her greatest visibility would come with her rabble-rousing leadership of the anti-busing campaign in the mid-1970s.

Logue described his primary loss as leaving him "broke but not broken." His BRA colleague Litke detected a "little bit of funk" that "took a little while to get out of." His BRA assistant, Janet Bowler, detected quite a bit more: "He was devastated . . . He was a real optimist, in the sense that I think he always thought that anything was doable. And this was the first time that he had really failed in a very public way."[135] Logue was also saddled with a $60,000 campaign debt to pay off.[136] There were compensations, however. Logue took pride that he won the support of the architects who had helped him build the New Boston. Architects for Logue, with Carl Koch, designer of Roxbury's Academy Homes, serving as secretary and a roster of twenty other major names, reminded designers that "he has fought for architecture and architects and in turn we have been more aware of our responsibilities for improving design in the urban center."[137] Some of the downtown business leaders who had backed the New Boston, like the Brahmin Henry Shattuck, supported Logue over Sears because they felt he'd do a better job, much to Sears's annoyance at being abandoned by his own kind.[138] Developers who had benefited from Logue at the helm of the BRA came through as well, anticipating continued prosperity under Mayor Logue.

But the support Logue prized the most came from Boston's Twelfth Ward, the only one he won outright with a healthy 37 percent of the vote, in the heart of Roxbury's black community. The Snowdens and their Washington Park neighbors did not forget that Logue had responded to their call for neighborhood renewal and they rewarded him with campaign support and their votes.[139] Interestingly, at least two UPA board members acknowledged backing Logue, and there likely were other community activists—similarly engaged in negotiations with the BRA—who feared rocking the boat and jeopardizing their deals.[140] Even the BRA employee Fred Salvucci, often a Logue critic, understood the favorable conditions for community negotiation that existed under Logue's BRA. At the first UPA board meeting after Logue was defeated in the primary, Salvucci reported that "the BRA is taking a turn to the right. People taking over will be worse than those there now (many [are] looking for new jobs)."[141]

What should Ed Logue do next? Holed up in his West Cedar Street home, he contemplated options ranging from joining a Boston law firm to plotting another run for mayor or even governor to pursuing one of the job inquiries coming his way from cities like Los Angeles, San Francisco, Baltimore, and Cleveland.[142] In the end, ironically, it was Joe Slavet—who had recruited Logue to Boston seven years earlier, who had battled him as head of Action for Boston Community Development, and who was now establishing an urban affairs program at Boston University—who arranged for Logue to become the first Visiting Maxwell Professor of Government. This temporary post required very little beyond a set of public lectures and gave Logue an office and a secretary. He hired the Radcliffe graduate Janet Murphy, then working at Harvard Law School. She would work closely with him for the rest of his professional career. A $20,000 travel study grant from his loyal patron, the Ford Foundation, put a little extra cash in his pocket, which he used to visit India, Russia, and New Towns in Sweden and Finland, gaining insights that would soon prove influential in his work.[143] But the permanent solution to "What next?" came with an unexpected phone call in January 1968. Janet Murphy came into his office to say, "The Governor is on the phone." "Which governor?" inquired Logue. "The Governor of New York, Nelson Rockefeller," she replied, and so began the next period of Edward Logue's career and a new, state-level phase in the nation's quest to renew its still troubled cities.[144]

PART III

New York in the 1970s and 1980s: Winning and Losing an Empire in the Empire State

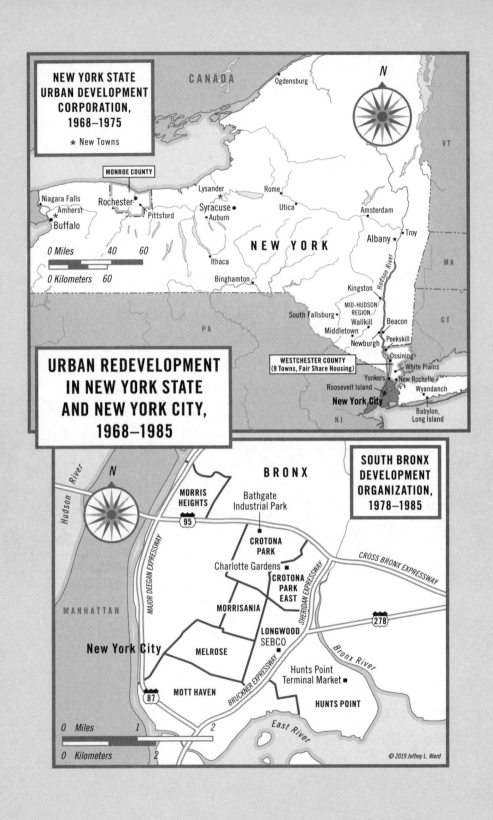

NEW YORK STATE URBAN DEVELOPMENT CORPORATION, 1968–1975

∗ New Towns

CANADA

Ogdensburg

MONROE COUNTY

Niagara Falls
Amherst
Buffalo

Rochester
Pittsford

Lysander ∗

Syracuse
Auburn

Rome

Utica

NEW YORK

Amsterdam

Albany ★
Troy

VT

MA

0 Miles   40   60

0 Kilometers   60

Ithaca

Binghamton

Kingston

MID-HUDSON REGION

South Fallsburg

Wallkill

Middletown

Newburgh

Beacon

Peekskill

Ossining

CT

PA

URBAN REDEVELOPMENT IN NEW YORK STATE AND NEW YORK CITY, 1968–1985

WESTCHESTER COUNTY
(9 Towns, Fair Share Housing)

White Plains

Yonkers
Roosevelt Island

New Rochelle

Wyandanch

New York City

Babylon,
Long Island

NJ

SOUTH BRONX DEVELOPMENT ORGANIZATION, 1978–1985

Hudson River

N

BRONX

MORRIS HEIGHTS

Bathgate
Industrial Park

95

CROSS BRONX EXPRESSWAY

MANHATTAN

MAJOR DEEGAN EXPRESSWAY

CROTONA PARK

Charlotte Gardens

CROTONA PARK EAST

SHERIDAN EXPRESSWAY

MORRISANIA

278

New York City

LONGWOOD
SEBCO

MELROSE

BRUCKNER EXPRESSWAY

Bronx River

Hunts Point
Terminal Market

87

MOTT HAVEN

HUNTS POINT

East River

0 Miles   1   2

0 Kilometers   2

© 2019 Jeffrey L. Ward

7. Constructing a "Great Society" in New York

When Nelson Aldrich Rockefeller surprised Ed Logue with his phone call in January 1968, he expected an immediate response: "Can you come down tomorrow to take a look at a bill?" The next day, Logue was in Rockefeller's New York City office, meeting first with members of Rockefeller's inner circle, particularly his top legislative aide Stephen Lefkowitz, and then alone with the governor. Rockefeller's goal was to persuade Logue to come to New York to serve as president and CEO of a soon-to-be-announced, $6 billion ($44.1 billion in 2019 dollars), powerful state-level urban renewal agency, the New York State Urban Development Corporation (UDC).[1] For many years, this long-serving liberal Republican governor had been trying to revive depressed urban areas and build new subsidized housing in

New York State; the urban riots of the mid-1960s had made that goal seem only more urgent. But state bond issues, the tool to fund such initiatives, required voter approval, according to the state's constitution, and in frustration Rockefeller had watched five of them go down to defeat.[2] Now he and his team had come up with a new scheme to skirt the referendum problem: a state-level public benefit corporation (the legal term for public authority) with the ability to self-finance through issuing its own tax-exempt bonds. Special state appropriations and federal housing programs would supplement private-sector funding.

Rockefeller was attracted to Logue's deep experience and outsize reputation, though the two men had never met. Rockefeller was pushing hard for his UDC in the New York state legislature, and Logue was a free agent since being defeated in Boston's mayoral contest. Rockefeller, used to getting his way, turned his famous charms on Logue to woo him to New York. As Logue later remembered the courting at a commemorative event for Rockefeller, "He just pours it on. Remember the way? I suspect each of us has never been more flattered by anybody, including our spouses, in our whole lives. So he tells me I'm the greatest thing since whatever."[3]

But Rockefeller had met his match in Logue. After carefully reviewing the draft legislation Rockefeller intended to submit to the New York state legislature, Logue congratulated the governor for his ambition ("This is the greatest development bill that I've ever seen") and then told him bluntly, "But it won't work." "What the hell do you mean?" the governor shot back. Logue proceeded to explain that without the ability to acquire property through eminent domain, to reduce or exempt projects from local real estate taxes, and, most radically, to override exclusionary local zoning and outdated building codes, he doubted the UDC would get anywhere. Then, in a strategy to hammer home his point, which Logue later admitted may have taken unfair advantage of the infamous rivalry between Rockefeller and New York City's mayor John V. Lindsay, he added, "If Mayor Lindsay doesn't like what you want to do, he won't do it. It will get stuck in his building department or zoning board, and it will never come out." Logue continued, "You'll never know why you're not getting it, but you won't get it." "You've got a point," admitted Rockefeller.[4] By day's end, Logue was heading back to Boston, Rockefeller's staff had begun revising the legislation to Logue's specifications, and the two men agreed to keep talking. Logue was truly reluctant at first to accept the governor's offer. He and his family were happy in Boston, and their beloved Martha's Vineyard, where the Logues had summered for many years, was nearby. But in time, Logue was seduced by Rockefeller's persuasive powers as well as the unique professional opportunity that the UDC offered: to create on a grand scale an extraordinary "one-stop service" that could acquire project sites and then develop, finance, design, build, and sell or own the resulting structures.[5]

By the end of April, Logue and Rockefeller had come to an agreement, and by summer, Logue was installed as the UDC's president and CEO. He lived at the Yale Club and commuted back to Boston until the Logues found an apartment the next spring, moving in time for the children—Kathy now fifteen, Billy eleven—to begin at a new school in the fall. Once the family settled in, Margaret would restart her career as a teacher and then middle-school principal at Saint Ann's School in Brooklyn Heights. These two men—one, a fifty-nine-year-old privileged heir to the greatest of American family fortunes, who had been serving as Republican governor of mighty New York State for nine years; the other, a forty-seven-year-old Irish Catholic Democrat from Philadelphia who was a self-made pioneer of postwar urban redevelopment—soon discovered that they had a great deal in common. Both were socially committed promoters of monumental projects who believed that the troubles of their time—poverty, poor housing, unemployment, inferior education—could be solved by major interventions in the physical environment. And they were both doers, ambitious and confident executives impatient to turn big, innovative plans quickly into even bigger realities.[6] Logue had undertaken large-scale rebuilding of a New Haven and Boston in steep decline. For his part, Rockefeller had aimed to enhance the state's much neglected capital city of Albany by constructing a massive civic center, the Empire State Plaza; to improve health care delivery by adding thousands of new hospital and nursing home beds; and to strengthen higher education by vastly expanding the multi-campus State University of

New York (SUNY) system.[7] Rockefeller's penchant for building was so great that his critics had a field day satirizing his "edifice complex" and "whim of iron," to which Rockefeller retorted, "All they see is steel and concrete . . . I see jobs. Not only construction jobs, but clerical jobs, service jobs, all kinds of jobs for all kinds of people."[8]

Together Logue and Rockefeller forged a potent partnership that would last until Rockefeller stepped down as governor of New York in December 1973. Although Rockefeller left office voluntarily to better position himself to secure the Republican nomination for president in 1976—perhaps this liberal Republican's last shot at the long-coveted prize that had eluded him in 1960, 1964, and 1968—the UDC would forever be credited to him. For almost six years, Rockefeller and Logue collaborated to build much-needed new housing, a great deal of it subsidized for low- and moderate-income tenants; to revitalize crumbling downtowns; and to jump-start the state's sputtering industries to create new jobs, as New York's economic growth seriously lagged behind the nation's. Rockefeller and Logue had a symbiotic relationship. Margaret Logue described it as not so much a friendship as a mutual respect, closer to the kind of partnership Ed had experienced with John Collins than with father-figure Chester Bowles or brother-like Dick Lee.[9]

Rockefeller put his distinctive ideological stamp on the new agency's structure, combining a deeply held social liberalism with an embrace of Republican orthodoxy that states should play a larger part in governance and that enlightened capitalists should assume a significant role in addressing public needs.[10] Empowering states and private capital presented a stark alternative to President Lyndon Johnson's urban policy, in which federal funding and grassroots engagement (labeled "maximum feasible participation") expanded under his Great Society initiatives. Moreover, urging more public-private sector collaboration aligned Nelson with his banker brother David, president and soon the CEO and chairman of Chase Manhattan Bank. In a Washington speech in early 1967, David had proposed a plan whereby every dollar of government money would be matched by four dollars of private capital, after which Nelson picked up the phone to say, "David, I've got the twenty cents if you've got the eighty cents."[11]

Nelson Rockefeller's description of himself as having "a Democratic heart with a Republican head" was never more apt than when it came to his urban strategy.[12] His liberal profile would later be overshadowed by repressive policies in the last years of his governorship, such as the storming of the Attica Prison in 1971 that left forty-three dead and the passage of tough mandatory sentencing laws for drug sale and possession—which became known as the "Rockefeller Drug Laws"—in 1973. But for much of his administration, Rockefeller advocated for state government to play a progressive role in American society, including directing private capital to socially worthy causes.[13]

The UDC also grew out of Nelson Rockefeller's long-standing interest in architecture, a passion he shared with Logue.[14] As an undergraduate at Dartmouth, Rockefeller had seriously considered becoming an architect until discouraged by his family. "With the responsibilities the family had," Nelson concluded, "I didn't see how I could justify giving way to a personal whim." He also feared that he could never have an independent practice: "I thought what would happen would be I'd get projects that the family was doing. It wouldn't be a genuine operation. I wanted to get out on my own."[15] Although he did not pursue professional training as an architect, much of what Rockefeller did in later life reflected his twin passions for building and artistic expression. Soon after graduating from Dartmouth, Nelson supervised the construction and leasing of his family's Rockefeller Center in New York City. He then went on to oversee development projects in Latin America first as watchdog for the family's Standard Oil Company and then as assistant secretary of state for Latin American affairs.[16] Throughout his adult life, Rockefeller remained a devoted art collector and an aficionado of architecture.

Figuring out how to implement a public benefit corporation to work around taxpayers' opposition to bonds for subsidized housing required another kind of creativity. State-created public authorities with the powers to spend, borrow, collect rent, enter contracts, and sue or be sued had a history going back to the early twentieth century. Some considered them a fourth branch of government beyond the tripartite executive, legislature, and judiciary. These independent quasi-public, quasi-private authorities grew in national importance during the 1930s, when bodies like the Reconstruction Finance Corporation, the Public Works Administration, and the Tennessee Valley Authority, with their autonomous powers, offered a new, welcome tool to navigate the ravages of the Great Depression. After World War II, the use of authorities mushroomed. Defenders praised their administrative flexibility, especially their potential to insulate important public services from political roadblocks, while giving the municipalities and states that created them freedom from annual budget cycles, debt ceilings, and archaic regulations. With their ability to borrow against anticipated future revenues, they made possible more effective long-term planning than public agencies typically enjoyed. Detractors complained that self-financing authorities were less accountable than a normal government agency was, subjecting public needs to the vagaries of the private sector and to governance by independently appointed boards of directors rather than democratically elected officials.[17] The UDC was in fact unusual among New York's public benefit corporations for having its president appointed by and reporting to the governor, not the board, which tied its agenda more closely to Rockefeller's, while also reducing Logue's dependence on his directors.[18]

Rockefeller enthusiastically embraced the public authority structure as a way of delivering on his grand ambitions for New York State—and not incidentally the national attention he sought for himself—without the need for voter approval or deep state coffers. He began by expanding authorities already in existence. When brother David and his Downtown–Lower Manhattan Association pushed hard for the World Trade Center to bolster lower Manhattan's attractiveness to finance, Nelson convinced the Port Authority of New York and New Jersey, the nation's first modern independent authority, created in 1921, to take on this new ambitious building project in return for a covenant that the Port Authority would never be asked to invest in deficit-heavy mass transit.[19] He went on to create a staggering number of new authorities. By the time he stepped down as governor, there were forty-one semiautonomous statewide authorities in operation—twenty-three created under his watch—each empowered to raise its own funds through bond sales.[20] Typical was the State University Construction Fund to expedite building of the state's public university system.

Even before creating the UDC, Rockefeller had used the authority structure to encourage more housing construction when he established the state's Housing Finance Agency (HFA) in 1960, essentially a bank charged with attracting private developers to build below-market-rate, limited-profit projects. Making use of the powers granted by the state's almost-moribund Mitchell-Lama program, created in 1955 to incentivize the construction of low- and middle-income housing, the HFA acquired sites by eminent domain, provided low-cost financing, and granted tax abatements. The resulting lower-cost rentals or cooperatives were protected for up to thirty years and available only to tenants and purchasers who qualified under an income cap. Large-scale, high-density middle-income projects like Co-op City and Lincoln Towers aimed at keeping middle-class New Yorkers in the city.[21] The HFA—deeply invested in upholding the legal requirement that all its projects be self-supporting to pay off revenue bonds and proud of its reputation for financial prudence—strictly focused on housing for the middle class and avoided the greater uncertainties involved in building for low-income and elderly tenants. When the UDC's treasurer compared his own bolder organization with the HFA, where "social purposes never override financial considerations," he concluded dismissively, "Taking risks is our mode. Avoiding them is theirs."[22] Once Rockefeller's team committed to building a wider range of subsidized housing than was possible under the restrained HFA and to revitalizing the state's industry and infrastructure, the question became how to do it.

The solution they came up with was to give the UDC the independence of an authority but to structure it financially to maximize nimbleness and minimize caution. That commitment led to two key decisions. Like the HFA, the UDC would be funded with "moral obligation bonds" that the state assured private investors had its backing, even if not the state's official "full faith and credit," which required voter approval as part of the state's legal debt. In the case of any revenue shortfall, the state pledged to meet its moral obligation by replenishing the UDC's reserve fund. This bonding strategy was sanctioned by the prominent Wall Street municipal bond lawyer John Mitchell (later Richard Nixon's ill-fated attorney general during Watergate), who assured Rockefeller in 1960 that investors would be satisfied with the state's declaration of good intentions. Rockefeller hoped this unsecured moral obligation would suffice to lure large amounts of private money into the subsidized housing market. As Rockefeller told the readers of his 1968 self-promotional book, *Unity, Freedom and Peace*, "government can[not] do it alone." We must have "faith in and commitment to the private enterprise system."[23]

The second crucial decision was proposed by George Woods, former chair of First Boston Corporation and the World Bank, who was Rockefeller's choice to head the nine-member UDC board. To make the UDC as agile as possible, Woods argued for the unusual step of issuing its bonds as "general purpose," not tied to specific projects as those of the HFA and most other authorities were. The logic was that bonds backing the UDC as a whole rather than individual projects would make funds available for ordinary operating expenses, could be issued when market conditions were advantageous, and, most importantly, would allow for more variation and less scrutiny of particular ventures, "pooling the risk," so to speak. With an aggressive UDC, Woods predicted, "you're going to have good ones and bad ones."[24] Logue agreed: "The UDC spread-of-risk factor is one of its great financial strengths."[25] He thus barely focused on the danger that too many bad projects in a bond's bundle could bring down the good ones, now under pressure to produce extra profits, or that careless budgeting on an individual project could cause the full general-purpose bond to come up short. "We were funding as we went, in effect," Lefkowitz later admitted. "And so when we ran out of money, . . . we had forty projects that were not finished," awaiting the next general-purpose bond issue.[26]

Although Logue was not a Republican, inclined toward the virtues of federalism and private sector investment for public purposes, and in fact had long put his greatest trust in federal programs, he had his own reasons for embracing Rockefeller's new UDC. Logue had watched in frustration as federal budgets for housing and urban redevelopment were slashed, mostly as a result of the high costs of the Vietnam War. He like other critics never tired of pointing out that the entire 1970 budget request of $2 billion from the Department of Housing and Urban Development (HUD) was less than one month's expenditure for the war.[27] As Logue searched for alternatives, he welcomed Rockefeller's promise of untapped sources of funding that could become forever self-sustaining through revolving bond funds, sales of projects to private developers or nonprofit sponsors, and retention of some properties for a dependable rental-income stream.

The opportunity to work at the state level greatly intrigued Logue. As he told a Boston University audience in spring 1968, "Although by now it should be clear that I do not expect miracles, I continue to seek for them. My newest hope is that our state governments will respond to the challenge presented by the urban crisis." This crisis had stubbornly persisted. No less than three major government reports detailing it would appear that year.[28] In March, the Kerner Commission warned of dangerous racial divides in America rooted in persistent segregation and economic inequality. In early December, the Kaiser Committee on Urban Housing called for twenty-six million new units by 1978, a quarter federally subsidized for low-income residents. And in late December, Paul Douglas's National Commission on Urban Problems—to which Logue had testified in Boston in May 1967—concurred, arguing for a minimum of two million new units of housing annually, with at least a quarter targeted at low- and moderate-income tenants. Logue acknowledged that states had been "in relative eclipse as an urban problem solver," content to be the "junior partners of the federal government," but he urged them now to play a new role. Cities "which I have put fifteen years of my life into rebuilding . . . cannot solve this problem by themselves."[29]

Although Logue had encountered a Boston hamstrung for lack of home rule by its controlling Massachusetts legislature, he now argued that excessive home rule could deprive a city of a valuable helping hand from state government. While the Republican Rockefeller ideologically applauded the devolution of authority and funding from the federal government to the state level, the Democrat Logue found more alluring the opportunity provided

by a state-level program to operate beyond the boundaries of any one local-
ity to achieve the kind of ambitious metropolitan solutions to urban problems that had eluded him in New Haven and Boston. From the earliest
days of the UDC, Logue expressed hope that small-scale residential projects in suburbia would "create opportunities for low-income families to
share in the good schools, the safe streets, the fresh air and open space other
Americans like so well without unsettling or unbalancing the suburban
communities."[30]

Logue's willingness to support Rockefeller's plan to tap private-sector
funding was likewise a pragmatic choice as federal domestic budgets declined and bureaucracy grew. Although he remained a staunch defender of
government at all levels, Logue was never a lover of cumbersome red tape.
Perhaps private-market bond sales and rent revenues would come with fewer
strings attached and lesser bureaucratic demands. Logue viewed the UDC's
public-private partnership more as a marriage of convenience than as a revolution in how to do the public's business. He recognized that the private
sector had always played a role in conventional urban renewal, as federal
grants that wrote down the cost of urban land had aimed at attracting private developers. But then and still now, Logue considered private investors
more a font of finance than an agent of authority. He fully intended to run
the show, whether the money came from Washington, D.C., Albany, or Wall
Street.[31]

Once Rockefeller decided that Logue was the right man to lead his UDC,
he pulled out all the stops to make it happen. He promised Logue a substantial salary of $50,000 a year ($65,000 by 1972), and in a private deal that became public only in autumn 1974, when Rockefeller was up for confirmation
as Gerald Ford's vice president, he offered Logue what, it turned out, he had
extended to many other high-level associates and friends, including Henry
Kissinger: monetary gifts and loans. To help Logue repay his mayoral campaign debt, which would have been much harder to do if Logue left Boston,
Rockefeller made him a gift of $31,389. So that the Logues could buy a co-
op apartment in the high-priced real estate market of Manhattan, Logue
received a loan of $145,000, of which $100,000 remained unpaid in 1974.

(That apartment, at 1 East End Avenue, turned out to be conveniently located for Ed and Margaret to pin their binoculars on one of the UDC's most important projects, the development of Roosevelt Island in the East River.) Logue never publicly expressed regret at having availed himself of Rockefeller's financial favors, insisting to the Senate Rules Committee holding hearings on Rockefeller's nomination that no New York State statutes had been violated and that without the governor's assistance, "I would not have been able to leave Boston to accept the appointment he offered."[32] But Margaret acknowledged that privately he was embarrassed and worried that some might perceive Rockefeller's assistance as unethical.[33]

Luring Logue to head the UDC proved a lot easier for Rockefeller than getting it past leery New York State legislators who understood only too well the substantial, independent powers being granted to this well-funded state superagency. They complained that it threatened home rule and would impose unwanted physical changes on their legislative districts. Despite the governor's agreement to add further safeguards for localities, such as requiring that the UDC work closely with community advisory committees and leaders, the fate of the UDC did not look promising until Rockefeller shrewdly transformed tragedy into opportunity.[34] On April 4, 1968, civil rights leader Martin Luther King, Jr., was assassinated in Memphis, Tennessee, while supporting the city's striking sanitation workers. Soon, riots erupted in black neighborhoods all over America. Rockefeller, long a promoter of civil rights and a trusted ally of King's, quickly offered his personal support to the King family. His staff helped organize—and he paid for—much of the funeral, and he chartered a plane to fly eighteen leading black legislators with him from New York to Atlanta to attend. While still in Atlanta, Rockefeller called on state legislators to pass the UDC as a tribute to King that would improve the lives of poor black New Yorkers, insisting that "the true memorial to Martin Luther King cannot be made of stone. It must be made of action."[35]

Even with this pressure, the first vote on the UDC passed the state senate but failed in the assembly, as conservative upstate Republicans allied with liberal New York City Democrats, both fearing growing state power.[36] Rockefeller was furious and took to the phones. With a dazzling display of arm-twisting and threats to withhold favors, the governor turned an 86-to-54 defeat into a decisive 86-to-45 victory close to midnight on April 9.[37] One Rockland County legislator was told by a close Rockefeller aide, "I know you don't like the bill, but you're on the list of guys who are going to vote for it." The alternative, he promised, "was to wake up one morning to find the runway of Stewart Air Force base extended right through your goddamn district."[38] The UDC was thus born in an emotional time of racial anxiety and political urgency, but many of its backers in Albany remained deeply skeptical. This approval under duress would shadow the UDC throughout its existence. Years later Logue would candidly acknowledge, "I didn't get a mandate, but I did get the legislation."[39]

Another kind of suspicion more of Logue's making than Rockefeller's would accompany his entry into New York. Logue had had two major involvements in New York City while he was running the Boston Redevelopment Authority. In 1966, soon after Logue's college and law school classmate John Lindsay was elected mayor of New York, Lindsay asked him to head a task force—funded, like so many other urban initiatives of the era, by the Ford Foundation—to study the enormous housing challenges facing New York City and make recommendations for addressing them. Logue threw himself into the assignment, assembling a blue-ribbon panel of national urban leaders and a staff drawn mostly from the BRA, headed by Logue's right-hand man Bob Hazen. Seven months later, Logue's commission delivered a report titled *Let There Be Commitment*, which was highly critical of the status quo in New York City. It called for a $1.5 billion attack on the city's slums, and urged, among many proposals, the construction on scattered sites of fifteen thousand new public housing units a year, in addition to many more thousands of subsidized ones. Lindsay's next move was to try to hire Logue to implement the ambitious program, a proposal that met opposition from Logue skeptics in New York, such as the planning critic Jane Jacobs and the Columbia sociologist Herbert Gans, author of the 1962 book *The Urban Villagers* about Boston's West End.[40]

But the real obstacle to Logue accepting Lindsay's job proved to be the mayor's inability or unwillingness to grant Logue the same extensive, consolidated powers over planning and redevelopment that he considered so fundamental to his Boston success.[41] Without this commitment, Logue refused Lindsay's offer. The mayor was unhappy to be turned down by Logue, but the disappointment turned to outright fury when in 1968 Lindsay learned that his archrival Nelson Rockefeller had succeeded where he had failed. Logue would never forget Lindsay's raving-mad late-night call upon learning of Logue's hiring—"You'll never do anything in New York if I don't tell you exactly where, when, and why"—or the disastrous press conference in May 1969 to announce the signing of a general memorandum of understanding between New York State and New York City over the UDC. Held at the mayor's Gracie Mansion residence, it took an embarrassing turn when Rockefeller insulted Lindsay by saying he would support for mayor whichever candidate won the Republican Party's primary, abandoning Lindsay if he received only the Liberal Party's endorsement. Logue vowed never again to bring these bickering foes together in the same room.[42] Logue was thus greeted in New York City by distrustful urban activists and a mayor already on the defensive against the UDC, which he considered a trespasser sent into his backyard by his meddling adversary in Albany. Lindsay officially made Rockefeller his opponent when he changed his party affiliation to Democrat in 1971.[43]

Another New York experience prior to the UDC burdened Logue with unhelpful notoriety. This was the work he did in 1967 with the Bedford Stuyvesant Restoration Corporation (BSRC), the pet project of New York senator Robert F. Kennedy that is generally considered the nation's first federally funded community development corporation.[44] The Bedford-Stuyvesant experience introduced Logue to a new structure of urban development also beginning to emerge in Boston's Roxbury and South End neighborhoods. Bedford-Stuyvesant was a huge six-hundred-block area with over four hundred thousand residents, 90 percent of whom were black or Puerto Rican. Activists had been organizing in the community already for a number of years and political consciousness ran high. Logue was selected as a part-time consultant—the Ford Foundation once again paying—by Kennedy, who boldly set out to promote his own alternative to President Johnson's War on

Poverty and Model Cities Program that would combine employment, job training, community economic development, and neighborhood rehabilitation. Public and private parties ranging from neighborhood residents to philanthropic foundations to corporate executives were all expected to play a role. Federal dollars would be tapped as well. Logue's assignment was to establish a comprehensive plan for the physical rebuilding of this impoverished community.

Logue made several miscalculations. He brought in a team including two veterans of Boston redevelopment, the architects I. M. Pei and David A. Crane, and the equally high-profile planner George M. Raymond, who together proposed a "macro-scale" concept that resembled Crane's "capital web" proposal for Boston, a linear spine punctuated with clusters of commercial and community development. Undeniably, Logue received ambiguous and conflicting guidance from the CDC's leaders, but his proposal still proved too big, too long-term, too top-down, and too far from the incremental, consultative approach that the local community, itself quite factionalized, demanded.[45] One community-oriented board member, Judge Thomas R. Jones, complained, "We were supposed to accept the Gospel According to St. Logue, and we weren't ready to do that." In the end, the call of Boston's mayoral primary gave Logue a convenient way to bow out of the increasingly fraught project, but he drew the disapproval of the same kind of participatory democrats in New York as he had alienated in New Haven and Boston.

Despite the shadow cast by these previous New York involvements, Logue arrived in New York City on July 1, 1968, eager to make a success of this new, thrilling, well-funded opportunity.[46] He expected New York's UDC to become a model that other states would emulate, the first statewide semi-autonomous urban renewal agency supported by two underutilized sponsors—state government and private capital. According to the well-respected planner Louis K. Loewenstein, who was funded by the Ford Foundation to assess the UDC, officials in the other forty-nine states were indeed watching closely what Loewenstein judged to be "the boldest effort of any state to match the size of its housing and urban problems with an agency of comparable authority."[47] The other major chronicler of the UDC during its lifetime, Dr. Eleanor Brilliant, concurred, claiming that few new public authorities since the Tennessee Valley Authority in the 1930s "have aroused more interest among social reformers and planners . . . After a decade of *immobilisme* in urban affairs, the UDC presented a welcome possibility for authoritative decision making and action." Brilliant, publishing in the midst of the UDC's unraveling in 1975, was not blind to the enormous risks involved as well.[48] She understood that the scale of Logue's ambitions for the UDC and a worsening economic and political environment in New York State and nationally were converging to bring the UDC to a spectacular downfall. An urban renewal superagency that its founders conceived to be forever self-renewing would in the end last only seven years.

FRUITS OF UDC LABOR

Once Logue arrived in New York, he lost little time getting the UDC's operation up and running. Both Logue and Rockefeller understood how important it was for the UDC's shaky political fortunes to disperse its riches widely upstate and downstate. A letter soon went out under Governor Rockefeller's signature to each of the more than sixty mayors and city managers in New York State, urging them to take advantage of this "new instrument to help you" and requesting a list of possible projects. Logue and top staff then traveled the state, often by helicopter, meeting local officials and checking out potential sites. Barely a month in, during August 1968, Logue reported having visited nineteen towns in ten days.[49] The requests for UDC help—and money—started rolling in fast, from all over the state. By the end of the UDC's first year, Logue was well on his way to identifying most of the locations for its future projects.[50]

Between 1968 and 1975, the UDC produced nothing short of a whirlwind of building in the state. As a result of an IRS ruling early on that only 10 percent of the UDC's tax-free bonds could go toward the industrial and commercial development that had been central to the UDC's original mandate, most of the UDC's building ended up being residential, along with schools, parks, and other civic projects.[51] The score sheet was still impressive. Over seven years the UDC launched 117 separate housing developments in forty-nine cities and towns, comprising more than 33,000 dwelling units for 100,000 people, about a third low-income, the rest subsidized for moderate- and middle-income residents. In addition, the UDC developed sixty-nine commercial, industrial, and civic projects and three brand-new communities. Armed with an authorization to sell $1 billion in bonds (eventually increased to $2 billion), as well as start-up funds and interest-free loans from New York State, the UDC by early 1975 had launched $1.5 billion worth of projects (over $7 billion in 2019 dollars), with more in the works.[52] Logue and his team were confident that the combined revenue streams of bond and property sales, state and federal government funding, and rental income would cover all costs.[53] Moreover, the UDC expected its own investments to catalyze even greater private development in New York State. In the case of Utica, for example, the city's downtown renewal had been abandoned seven years earlier by a developer, leaving the city in 1969 with not only vacant land but also "the lack of confidence of developers and real estate investors." Now with the UDC, a city official hoped for renewed interest: "It's a wonderful thing . . . where you have New York State behind you like that."[54]

During its lifetime, the UDC's handprints could be found on an extraordinarily wide range of projects throughout the state, varying in location, scale, and type. A very partial list includes a major $60 million facelift to the old, depressed Hudson River town of Newburgh; construction of six thousand units of housing in metropolitan Rochester, half of them low income and on scattered sites in the suburbs; an expansive low-and-moderate-income residential project, the Shoreline Apartments, with a school and shops along Buffalo's Lake Erie, designed by Paul Rudolph; Schomburg Plaza, located at 5th Avenue between West 110th and 111th Streets in Harlem, consisting of two award-winning thirty-five-story octagonal apartment towers with six hundred mixed-income units, stores, and a day care center, developed in collaboration with the prominent black psychologist and UDC board member Kenneth Clark and his wife, Mamie Phipps Clark; new housing and a convention-tourism complex to help buoy the off-season economy of

Niagara Falls; remediation and future planning for six upstate communities in the Chemung River Valley devastated by Hurricane Agnes in June 1972; and the replacement of dilapidated shacks without indoor plumbing in a migrant labor camp in Kent, Orleans County, with the townhouse apartments of Carlken Manor.[55] The UDC's most ambitious and innovative undertaking was the creation of three New Towns on undeveloped land—Audubon, in Amherst, near the new campus of SUNY Buffalo; Lysander, renamed Radisson, twelve miles north of Syracuse; and the transformation of Welfare Island into Roosevelt Island in New York's East River. These New Towns were intended to increase the state's supply of decent housing; to create model, socially integrated communities; and to address an anticipated population increase of five to eight million between 1970 and 2000 (which turned out to be overly optimistic, as New York State's population barely grew by one million).[56]

It looked for a while like New York City would stubbornly refuse help from the UDC. Mayor Lindsay's contentious rivalry with Governor Rockefeller was a factor, but the city also had a long tradition of jealously guarding its home rule from Albany, convinced that the state rarely compensated the city fully and fairly for burdens on transportation, education, or the environment. Snapped Lindsay, "Our cities cannot be renewed by state-operated bulldozers which move into local communities without their consent and without knowledge and concern about the increasing need for supportive services connected with all development."[57] But once Logue "sent word to Lindsay, through an intermediary, that, you know, at the rate we're going, we're going to have all our funds committed upstate and there won't be anything left for New York," the Lindsay administration buried its pride in favor of addressing its huge need.[58] New York's housing supply was shrinking, with new construction at a standstill and landlord abandonment growing. One hundred thirty thousand were on the waiting lists for public housing. And the severe cuts in federal funding that had alarmed Logue were hitting New York hard. According to a despairing Jason R. Nathan, the New York City housing and development administrator, "'Crisis' is an understatement. 'Disaster' may be more appropriate."[59] After tough negotiations, where Nathan pressured Lindsay "to lock arms, not horns, with the UDC . . . to harness UDC's talents and powers . . . to make them work for the city," the UDC and New York City struck a deal in May 1969. The UDC would agree not to launch any projects in New York City without the mayor's prior approval but would pledge to build at least twelve thousand units.[60] In return, the city would protect the UDC by promising to clear the sites and handle any required relocations.

By 1971, half the UDC's total housing starts would be located in New York City, encompassing 30 percent of the city's publicly assisted housing construction that year.[61] What Logue valued most in the deal was securing the land for what became the UDC's crown jewel: the development of two-mile-long Welfare Island in the middle of the East River between Manhattan and Queens as the mixed-income, pedestrian-only New Town of Roosevelt Island. In return for this prize, Logue agreed to take on building sites in the South Bronx and Coney Island that the city found too difficult to develop. Logue was willing to live with that. As he gleefully exclaimed, "I got the goat sites but I got the island."[62]

OPERATING THE UDC

The UDC established an infrastructure statewide to support its ambitious program. At the start, in July 1968, there were only three staff: Logue; his personal assistant Janet Murphy, who moved with him from Boston University and acted, Lefkowitz joked, as "the interpreter of the words of God to man"; and Lefkowitz himself, who officially became the UDC's general counsel but unofficially served as Rockefeller's eyes and ears, put there by the governor, Lefkowitz readily acknowledged, "to watch Ed!"[63] But very quickly new staff were added. At its height, the UDC employed over 550 personnel in seventeen offices, with central functions like executive, design, construction, finance, and legal located in its New York City headquarters, and project-oriented regional and field offices fanning out across the state in a more expansive version of the decentralized organization in Logue's BRA.

In New York, even more so than in New Haven and Boston, the work attracted young and idealistic professionals. Many were trusted veterans of past Logue projects who flocked to the UDC like homing pigeons once the word was out that he was launching an ambitious new venture. The architect Ted Liebman recalled Logue presenting him with a copy of the UDC Act of 1968 and saying, "'Read it. This is where I'm going. I think I'm going to want you to come . . . This is going to be really important.'"[64] New blood soon arrived as well. Lawrence Goldman was twenty-eight in 1973, with an almost-completed Princeton Ph.D. dissertation on a planned town outside London, when he jumped at the chance to become Logue's special assistant and join a "veritable children's brigade of smart—and sometimes smart-assed—uncontainable young professionals . . . , the best and the brightest."[65] Richard Kahan was a Columbia law student in 1971 when he started working at the UDC: "There was this great sense of momentum and everybody feeling they were part of something historic and wanting to kill for this guy . . . He was a two-fisted, roll-up-your-sleeves, let's-get-down-in-the-dirt-and-make-things-happen kind of progressive."[66] Paul Byard, a graduate of Yale College and Harvard Law, was hungry for a job with more social value than his current one at a prestigious New York law firm. "It was thrilling—hours, risks, adventures—but above all, the conviction of the worth of what we were doing. We thought of it as the public business—I think of that as Ed's phrase—not because it was so businesslike but because the phrase made clear . . . the public good we sought to do."[67] Christine Flynn, who began as a staff attorney at the UDC and later served as the executive vice president of Roosevelt Island, summed it up this way: "It was like no other place I've ever worked. Logue had a genius for motivating people."[68] Flynn was one of the few women in a position of authority at the UDC. Urban redevelopment had emerged as a new profession more than a decade earlier, but it was still a male club into which few women gained entry, other than as staff assistants. Janet Murphy exerted substantial influence and kept track of everything and everyone at the UDC, but she did so from a traditional role.

As in Boston, Logue invested in a headquarters intended to convey the stature and ambition of his new superagency. The UDC took over a full floor (later expanding onto two others) of a new skyscraper, the Burlington House, at 1345 6th Avenue, between 54th and 55th Streets. The Burlington Company had re-created a full-scale working textile mill for visitors to its lobby, celebrating the company's loyalty to its industrial roots even as it inserted itself in the postindustrial economy of midtown Manhattan—a mix reflected in the UDC's own economic development activities in New York State. Higher up, the UDC's offices on the forty-sixth floor afforded spectacular views of the vast land awaiting the UDC's imprint. "I could look out my window and see Central Park . . . and see the mountains up in the Catskills," said Logue. And lest he forget less-visible upstate areas, a giant relief map of New York State sat opposite his desk.[69] As in Boston, Logue spared no expense decorating these offices. Though critics condemned them as "Logue's Lush Lair," he defended the modern décor as "well-designed, but not luxurious."[70] To further inspire his staff aesthetically, the Museum of Modern Art, with its well-respected architecture and design department, was just down the block. The UDC found it the perfect venue for its fifth anniversary celebration in 1973.[71]

With the aid of big money, the Rockefellers' well-flexed political muscle, a powerful new toolkit, and a gung-ho staff, Logue took off on a tear to make a big difference in New York State and beyond. Never one to be modest in his self-confidence or his goals, Logue aimed not only to change the physical face of New York but also to pioneer new solutions to the nation's severe housing shortage and its ailing cities. This was the opportunity that Logue had been waiting for his whole career.[72]

MAKING A FAST TRACK

The UDC's power to take a project all the way from land acquisition, finance, and construction to its opening as a home, school, police station, library, or factory made it possible to avoid what had long troubled many in the redevelopment business: the frustratingly slow completion of projects due to time-consuming coordination among multiple parties. Rockefeller and Logue both frequently lamented that it could take five to seven years under normal conditions to build a new residential project. Urban renewal ventures took even longer—an average of eight years in the state and thirteen in New York City.[73] The thicket of funding and regulatory requirements from different levels of government slowed down progress to the point of discouraging private developers from even trying to work in New York State. When a group of major builders were queried about why they hadn't constructed more affordable housing in New York City despite the enormous demand, they uniformly complained about lack of subsidies but even more passionately about horrific delays from red tape.[74] The developer of a project in New York City, for example, had to obtain official approvals from ten separate departments or agencies of the city, state, and federal governments, seven serially.[75] Logue despaired at the problem. "This is hurting us. Some of the builders and developers are [instead] going to Florida."[76]

The UDC was equipped with extensive capabilities in part to address this logjam in housing construction, but even within the UDC's comprehensive operation Logue felt the need to institute a practice he called "fast-tracking." This meant avoiding delays by moving ahead with projects before all the final funding, permitting, designing, and bidding were securely in place. Logue had confidence that they would all come through in the end, and rather than lose valuable time, he began construction using funds already in hand. Interestingly, even Logue's harshest critics, who would later fault the UDC for many abuses, admired what fast-tracking made possible: substantial cost-savings given the constant escalation in construction prices, a reduction in red tape, avoidance of panic selling by project neighbors, and quicker availability of construction jobs.[77] The real estate developer Richard Ravitch, no fan of Logue's UDC and the person Logue most blamed for its downfall, agreed that "he was right to do that. Time is money. If you delay the start of construction, it's going to cost you more." Ravitch stressed, however, that this approach worked only if projects were held tightly to budget, which was not always the case at the UDC.[78] Years later Logue took pride in the boldness of his fast-tracking strategy, which could shorten the time to construction to eighteen months: "Since we had the power of eminent domain, had the resources to hire plans, and to build it ourselves if necessary, I would start a project on land we didn't yet own, with subsidies that were not yet tied up in contract . . . But I had commitments, and I relied on that."[79]

Fast-tracking made it possible for the UDC not only to undertake steps simultaneously rather than sequentially on any one project, but also to launch a multitude of projects concurrently, which Logue felt was crucial to the agency's success. As he once put it: "I wouldn't want to make the people of Harlem think we can solve their problems by nibbling at them, nor would I go to Bedford-Stuyvesant and say, 'Look, you nice people, we'll be working over in the South Bronx for the next ten years, but we'll get to you eventually.' You either do them all at once and on a large scale, or you don't bother."[80] To make fast-tracking work, the UDC operated with a system perhaps best described as "robbing Peter to pay Paul," utilizing funds raised from general-purpose bonds and government grants secured for one set of projects to jump-start others and complete unfinished ones. So long as the faucet kept flowing—and there was no reason to suspect it would not—the UDC could continue to set construction records.

Fast-tracking worked as well as it did because Logue once again proved himself a wizard at securing federal dollars. Although the UDC created great fanfare around tapping into state and private sources of capital, funding from HUD in fact remained key. While the resources available to him were by no means sufficient—Logue constantly called for greater federal funding to write down the price of land and to provide more rent supplements to low-income tenants—he made extensive use of the Section 236 subsidy program created by the 1968 Housing Act, which replaced the Section 221(d)(3) mortgages that he had relied on so heavily in Boston. This Section 236 program, available to state as well as municipal agencies, reduced the interest on mortgages for new or rehabilitated multi-unit dwellings from the conventional market rate down to 1 percent, making the construction of low- and moderate-income housing more feasible. Used for more than 90 percent of the UDC's construction, Section 236 subsidies could reduce the cost per room from $78 to $43.[81] The UDC managed remarkably to get over 60 percent of all Section 236 funding available nationally, receiving at least 90 percent of New York State's share. Logue's shrewd strategy was to come in at the end of the year with fully completed forms to claim uncommitted Section 236 money, counting on the fact that HUD would not want to return unused appropriations to Congress. One could even say that a mutual dependency developed between HUD and the UDC, where Logue brought to New York State $2.7 billion in federal subsidies from write-downs and direct grants and HUD in turn benefited from the high visibility of the UDC.[82]

AVOIDING CLEARANCE

Fifteen years in the redevelopment business in New Haven and Boston had taught Logue that urban renewal's reputation suffered its greatest damage from the criticism that it too aggressively demolished existing buildings and displaced current residents. Logue's own thinking had evolved over time from advocating massive clearance during his early years in New Haven to rehabilitating older structures in Wooster Square by the time he left that city. In Boston, he had carefully distanced himself from the old-style leveling of the West End and sought greater balance, coming to value the preservation of historic buildings downtown as well as in neighborhoods like Charlestown and the South End. But still Logue had battled justifiable, and growing, popular disapproval of urban renewal. He now hoped that the UDC, operating on the much larger terrain of a whole state, might find new ways to meet the huge need for decent housing without requiring excessive clearance. As he told a conference of colleagues in 1970, "We cannot repeat the mistake of the Housing Act of 1949," which "put all of the emphasis on rebuilding, tearing down and rehabilitating in the inner city . . . And city solutions alone will not work."[83]

Logue's desire to build big—and without controversy—drove him to seek out two new sources of land for UDC projects. The first were languishing former urban renewal sites that existed in many cities, where clearing had taken place but no developer had come forward with a project. Eleanor Brilliant estimated that by 1967 more sites had remained leveled for urban renewal in New York State than had been rebuilt.[84] As Logue explained it, "We were not, at UDC, seriously in the relocation business," which had taken so much time and effort in New Haven and Boston, "because we either took open land outside the cities, or we took urban renewal sites, which had long since been cleared and nothing had ever happened to them."[85] This salvaging of sites that had been eyesores in New York's cities for years, "collecting garbage and defeating incumbents while awaiting a developer with cash in hand," as one journalist evocatively put it, meant the UDC was often received with open arms rather than local opposition.[86]

When the UDC did target an occupied urban site, Logue insisted that the city involved clear it first. So, for example, low- and moderate-income housing projects that the UDC undertook early on in New York City—in Coney Island, at Twin Parks in the Bronx, and at Harlem River Park—were on parcels already scheduled for clearance by the city. As Brilliant explained the strategy: "He could therefore hardly be accused of tearing down the homes of poor people to build projects that would benefit the white upper classes, as had been the case in Boston," referring here to the notorious West End.[87] There was irony, of course, in the UDC adopting a tactic for avoiding conflict with communities that took advantage of the glaring scars left behind from an earlier, more disruptive era of urban renewal.

The other major source of UDC land—more conducive to large-scale projects than abandoned inner-city urban renewal lots—consisted of sizable tracts of open land outside major cities that could be turned into New Towns. What soon became the UDC's most distinctive program had been percolating in Logue's mind for quite a while. Decentralizing people and jobs from crowded, poorly serviced urban neighborhoods had long made sense to him. He had promoted it unsuccessfully in Boston when he argued for building subsidized housing in suburbia and even carving the city into multiple New Towns. Once in New York, he had seized every opportunity to encourage investment in the outer boroughs of Brooklyn and the Bronx, even at the expense of developing midtown.[88] But the New Town concept involved dispersal at a much larger scale, promising plentiful new housing, community amenities, and jobs in self-contained communities touted as more satisfying social environments than typical suburbs. Particularly appealing to Logue, a New Town could be built on undeveloped land: "I don't have to condemn it. I don't have to relocate any families. I don't have to demolish any buildings."[89] New Towns also marked another kind of break with ideas that

Logue had once enthusiastically embraced: a turn away from the modernist orthodoxy of separating functions, promulgated by Le Corbusier and his followers. New Towns aimed instead to integrate living, working, schooling, shopping, and recreating all in one planned community, with each activity placed in close proximity to, not apart from, the others.

New Towns historically had been rare in the United States. The British Garden City Movement of the late nineteenth and early twentieth centuries had led to only a handful of American replicas in the United States, such as Radburn, New Jersey, and Sunnyside Gardens and Forest Hills Gardens in Queens, New York. Under the auspices of the New Deal during the 1930s, a few more ambitious New Towns had emerged—Greenbelt, Maryland, and Roosevelt (originally Jersey Homesteads), New Jersey, most prominently. And in the postwar years before Logue arrived at the UDC, three privately planned communities were founded by prominent commercial developers: Reston, Virginia, by Robert E. Simon; Columbia, Maryland, by James W. Rouse; and Irvine, California, by the Irvine Company.[90] The real action had occurred in Europe in the aftermath of World War II, where governments looked to New Towns to replace heavily damaged infrastructure and provide desperately needed new housing. New Towns, combining residences, public buildings, and work sites in a totally new planned environment, offered an ideal solution. Prime examples were the twenty-eight New Towns built in postwar Britain, the most well-known being Stevenage and Milton Keynes; Tapiola in Finland; Vällingby and Farsta outside Stockholm; Cergy-Pontoise in France; and Nordweststadt near Frankfurt, Germany. (The concept spread to developing countries in Latin America, the Middle East, Africa, and South Asia as well.)[91] Logue had carefully tracked these New Towns worldwide and visited many of them, most recently in spring 1968 when he had stopped in Sweden and Finland on his Ford-funded travels during his stint as Visiting Maxwell Professor of Government at Boston University.[92]

Not long before, after his electoral defeat in fall 1967, Logue had gained hands-on experience with the New Town concept when he accepted a consulting job at the invitation of his old New Haven Redevelopment Agency deputy Tom Appleby, now executive director of the District of Columbia

Redevelopment Land Agency. Here Logue, as principal development consultant, helped plan a new community to be built on a 335-acre federally owned parcel in northeast Washington, formerly the site of a fort protecting the city during the Civil War and more recently a youth detention center run by the Department of Justice, soon to be vacated. President Lyndon Johnson himself had initiated this project, hoping it would serve as a prototype for the nation of a well-designed, "balanced" urban community, integrating residents of different economic and racial groups. Here they would interact as neighbors and share local amenities such as new schools, a mini-rail transportation system, recreational facilities, and open space. Although the project faltered over conflicts with neighbors and Johnson's departure from office, the Fort Lincoln New Town project, as it was called, remained a touchstone for Logue when he moved to the UDC.[93] Johnson's interest in the mixed-income New Town idea, moreover, led to the New Communities Act of 1968, which provided modest amounts of federal money that Logue would later tap at the UDC.

Logue began implementing his New Town strategy soon after arriving in New York. Within a year, progress on three New Towns was under way. Although they had much in common with European models, which Logue sent senior staff to visit, the UDC's New Towns struggled with distinctly American challenges.[94] All three were built on unoccupied land, though legally they existed within the jurisdiction of a larger town or city, a fraught relationship given the power of localities in the United States. The UDC's dealings with New York City over Welfare Island were part of its larger agreement with the city. But in upstate New York, both the town of Amherst, future home of Audubon, and the village of Baldwinsville, future home of Radisson, initially resisted the UDC's plan, mostly out of fear that such a large population increase would encumber local services and require higher property taxes. Lawsuits were brought, and ultimately dismissed, in both cases, but it remained difficult to convince current residents that these New Towns within their boundaries would be a boon, not a burden. Inhabitants were also anxious about the new residents who would be flooding their semi-rural, white communities. The *Syracuse Herald-Journal* editorialized that local residents of Baldwinsville "feel put upon by the plans for 20 percent of the projected rental housing to go to low income individuals and families ... some of whom might be clients of the social services department." The *Buffalo Evening News* put it even more bluntly. Homeowners, it claimed, feared "moving the ghetto to Amherst."[95]

Despite common challenges, each New Town was unique. The New Town of Radisson (at first named Lysander) was located twelve miles northwest of Syracuse, on 2,800 acres (4.5 square miles) purchased from the old Baldwinsville Army Ordnance Depot, which had been used for manufacturing explosives in World War II and then abandoned. As he so often did, Logue brought in a familiar face to plan the project: David Crane, his former director of planning and design in Boston, who had also consulted on the Bedford-Stuyvesant and Fort Lincoln projects and was now practicing and teaching in Philadelphia. Crane's plan, to be implemented over ten years, called for five thousand units of mixed-type housing, intended to accommodate sixteen thousand to eighteen thousand residents, with a town center featuring offices, retail stores, a medical center, and recreational facilities, including parks, a golf course, and an Olympic-size swimming pool. Eight hundred acres were reserved for industrial use, testament to the "jobs first" commitment of the project and intended to provide ten thousand to fifteen thousand jobs. Although Radisson, when completed, did not fulfill all of Crane's plan, one of its major successes was attracting the Schlitz Brewing Company to build a $100 million regional brewery, employing almost a thousand workers. UDC staff joked about "Schlitz—the beer that made Radisson feasible." In time, State Farm Insurance also opened a regional headquarters, which employed another thousand.[96]

The other upstate New York New Town was Audubon, in Amherst, four miles east of Buffalo near where the $650 million, one-thousand-acre SUNY Buffalo campus was under construction. This branch of the state university was expected to eventually enroll tens of thousands of students and increase the area's overall population by two hundred thousand. To plan Audubon— smaller in area but larger in anticipated residents than Radisson—the UDC hired the British planner Richard Llewelyn-Davies, whose firm was developing the second-generation British New Town of Milton Keynes north of London. With twenty-four hundred acres to work with, Llewelyn-Davies called for nine thousand units to house around twenty-five thousand people of diverse incomes—a third reserved for low-income families and university students and staff—along with shops, offices, light industry, research facilities connected to the university, community recreational facilities, and substantial open space.[97]

The third and quite different New Town—in that it integrated residential, commercial, civic, and recreational buildings but less so work sites—was Roosevelt Island, the UDC's largest project statewide.[98] Dubbed a "New-Town-in-Town" for its location in the middle of New York City, this community was the latest use of the 147-acre semi-abandoned Welfare Island, which beginning in the 1820s—when the city acquired it from the Blackwell family—had housed institutions mainstream society sought to keep at a distance: prisons, almshouses, workhouses, insane asylums, and chronic disease hospitals. By the late 1960s, only two hospitals remained operative, along with a training facility for the New York Fire Department. The island—stretching for two miles from 50th to 86th Streets in Manhattan and eight hundred feet at its widest—had long attracted development interest, including twice by Robert Moses. That attention grew now that the city struggled with a housing crisis; the Metropolitan Transportation Authority (MTA), newly under state control, pledged to expand the subway connections between Manhattan and Queens with a new tunnel under Welfare Island; and Logue's UDC was flush with ambition and capital. On December 23, 1969, New York City gave Logue just the Christmas gift he most wanted: a ninety-nine-year lease to develop Welfare Island. Planning had already begun under the auspices of a Lindsay-appointed citizens group, the Welfare Island Planning and Development Committee, on which Logue sat as the likely developer. Earlier that fall, an exhibition at the Metropolitan Museum of Art titled *The Island Nobody Knows* and its accompanying catalog unveiled a master plan commissioned by the committee from the well-known architect Philip Johnson and his then partner John Burgee.[99]

Johnson and Burgee's plan took advantage of Welfare Island's natural strengths—plentiful waterfront and impressive panoramas of Manhattan and Queens—in proposing a mixed-use, urban-style, car-free community of five thousand apartments to house approximately eighteen thousand residents of diverse economic status. Not far from the bright lights of Manhattan by subway, it offered New Yorkers a quieter, more spacious living environment. Flats ranged in size from efficiencies to four-bedrooms for large families. Johnson and Burgee's plan called for a town square facing the waterfront with shops in a glass-roofed arcade, a three-hundred-room hotel, offices, restaurants, and a marina. Apartment buildings with retail, schools, a library, community rooms, and fire and police services embedded in them were to be located along a Main Street spine, which was curved for aesthetics and built densely to leave large areas of the island free for parks, playing fields, tennis courts, and a swimming pool. Buildings were taller along the street, stepping down in height as they grew closer to the river. U-shaped buildings with grassy courtyards preserved water views for all residents, as did promenades circumnavigating the island to give low- and moderate-income tenants access to the stunning skylines of Manhattan, since their buildings faced grittier Long Island City, Queens. The island was to be served by a new subway stop on a line that traveled between Manhattan and Queens.

Philip Johnson had often been dismissed as an uninspiring establishment modernist, so his Roosevelt Island plan surprised the major architectural critics in New York City.[100] Ada Louise Huxtable considered the project the UDC's "showpiece and star performance," and Johnson himself "a late-blooming urbanist of notable sensibilities" who had created "a genuine urban environment." The critic Peter Blake concluded, "I can't think of a more exciting site for a new town anywhere in this country. If we botch this one, we might as well give up on urban design altogether." Paul Goldberger praised the island as "exhilarating . . . Finally . . . an urban space of real quality in New York . . . Main Street has the potential of becoming one of the city's most pleasurable, if briefest, urban experiences. Its bends and curves are just enough to provide interest, but not so much to be cute." As others chimed in with similar enthusiasm, even Johnson himself acknowledged how much his plan for an intimate, walkable, mixed-use community differed from his former work and from the typical modernist emphasis on isolated towers, superblocks, and car-dependent residences and commerce. He proclaimed wryly, "This is my Jane Jacobs period."[101]

Roosevelt Island became Logue's pride and joy, the ultimate fulfillment of his utopian vision for a socially diverse and architecturally distinctive New Town. He could barely keep away from it during construction. As a *New York Times* reporter told it, "Logue is to be seen at least once a week plunging in his bearlike way around the site—old corduroys, green Shetland sweater, shirttail hanging out and no hard hat covering his stack of grey hair; slow-speaking, fast-thinking, an interesting mixture of charm and combativeness; fussing about the color of tiles and asking awkward, probing questions of his staff. He is proud of what he is doing on the island."[102]

Logue brought to this project a sensibility honed in Boston to value a negotiated cityscape that both conserved the historic and showcased the modern. As Johnson and Burgee said in *The Island Nobody Knows*: "It is an integral part of the plan for this island that its important landmarks be saved . . . [so that] any new community that may rise on this island will have tangible symbols of the past upon which to build its future . . . Wherever possible, we have tried to juxtapose the old and the new—historic landmarks and new housing."[103] Although some original island buildings were in fact lost, the Gothic-style Chapel of the Good Shepherd (1889) became a meeting space and interfaith religious home; the restored clapboard Blackwell House (1796) served as a community center for small social events; the James Renwick–designed lighthouse (1876), on the northernmost tip of the island, was repaired; the Strecker Memorial Laboratory (1892) was adapted by the MTA as a power-conversion center for the subway; and the Octagonal Tower (1840s), once the entrance to the country's first municipal lunatic asylum, was integrated into a new apartment building.[104]

The decision to rename Welfare Island for the former New York governor and later president Franklin Delano Roosevelt, who surprisingly had no other major monument in the state, similarly embedded the new project in the state's past and particularly in the nation's history of progressive government. Logue commissioned the prominent modernist architect—and fellow Roosevelt admirer—Louis I. Kahn to design an FDR memorial for the southern tip of the island in 1972. It was long delayed by an unfortunate series of events. Kahn flouted the project's $4 million budget (to Logue's great annoyance) and then died suddenly in 1974. A search followed for a colleague to finish the drawings. Mitchell Giurgola Architects agreed, but their work was further postponed by a shortage of funds and litigation brought by foundation donors over public crediting. The Four Freedoms Park finally opened in 2012. One of Kahn's last designs, it is a four-acre memorial park consisting of a garden and a roofless roomlike space enclosing a sculpted Franklin Roosevelt.[105]

Roosevelt Island's nod to the past was well matched by its embrace of futuristic, environmentally friendly new technology. A Swedish-inspired automated vacuum sanitation system (known as AVAC) whisked all domestic trash through giant pneumatic vacuum tubes buried under the street to a central refuse disposal site for compacting. Free, quiet, nonpolluting, battery-powered electric minibuses transported residents around the car-free island to and from the central thousand-car Motorgate garage, near the only bridge access, from Queens. This complimentary public transit and plentiful pedestrian pathways eliminated any social distinctions based on automobile ownership, putting all residents on an equal footing. When it became clear that the subway would be delayed beyond the opening of the first apartments (it didn't actually operate until 1989), Logue's team came up with the clever idea of installing a gondola-style aerial tramway—which soon became the island's icon—from there to Manhattan's East 60th Street, its first use in an urban environment worldwide. This $7 million innovation created a 3,100-foot-long, three-and-a-half-minute soaring ride.

As with the other UDC New Towns, Roosevelt Island as built did not fully realize its visionary plan. Some found the architecture too forbidding, constructed as it was in the austere concrete and brick typical of the 1960s and 1970s, not unlike the brutalist buildings of Boston's Government Center. Completion was also slow. By the end of 1978, three years after the UDC's downfall, only 2,139 of the anticipated 5,000 dwelling units were available, about half of them low- and moderate-income units built with Section 236 funds, with three hundred of those offering additional rent supplements. The other half consisted of 761 middle-income units with Mitchell-Lama state funding and 375 upper-middle-income cooperative apartments. Five schools with a total capacity of 850 children in grades kindergarten through ninth were open, falling short of Logue's goal of thirteen. Nonetheless, they were operating, which Logue later considered "one of the best things I've ever done in my life." And although the marina was never built and the lack of a sub-way limited retail and offices, by late 1978, the 5,500 Roosevelt Island residents had a U.S. post office, bank, supermarket, drugstore, stationery and liquor stores, an Italian restaurant, and a delicatessen. The two remaining hospitals merged to become Coler-Goldwater Specialty Hospital and Nursing Facility, with room for almost two thousand patients and long-term-care residents.[106]

Despite its incompleteness, Roosevelt Island in name, conception, and planned memorial paid homage to the ideal of Roosevelt's New Deal and its successor, Lyndon Johnson's Great Society, that government could help improve lives and make the nation more just. Ironically, however, just as Roosevelt Island underwent construction, President Nixon began unraveling the federal programs needed to realize it. Cuts in funding necessitated compromises in the Johnson-Burgee plan, which had already miscalculated in providing for only four thousand rather than the five thousand units of housing needed to balance the books.[107] To ensure that the project's finances still worked out despite this mistake, the height of the buildings along narrow Main Street was increased, which gave it a more cavernous feel, and a fourth side was added to some apartment courtyards along the river, blocking views. Amenities like air-conditioning were also scaled back in the lower-income housing, which widened the gulf in accommodations between social classes.

Logue complained bitterly about the impact of the Nixon White House's urban policies on Roosevelt Island in June 1973: "I think they are trying to make clear, in a variety of ways, that the idea of government as a solver of social problems is an idea that has been around long enough . . . This Administration does not really feel that the users of low and moderate income housing are a part of its constituency."[108] Logue's New Town utopia on the

East River may have pioneered a new model of an urban neighborhood—being both a part of and apart from a great city—but its survival as originally conceived faced mounting challenges.

ESTABLISHING DIVERSE COMMUNITIES

Logue looked to New Towns to achieve his long-standing ambition of creating communities integrated along the lines of income, age, and race. Over the years, Logue had become convinced that a mix of residents was the key to ensuring more stable and better-resourced urban communities. Efforts to implement this goal in previous redevelopment efforts, however, had gotten Logue into trouble. Too often, integrating centrally located, predominantly low-income black communities like Dixwell in New Haven or the South End in Boston had meant that more white, middle-class residents moved in, understandably antagonizing current inhabitants. In contrast, Logue hoped, constructing new socially mixed communities from scratch would achieve greater residential diversity without displacement or gentrification. As he wrote for the large readership of the popular *Saturday Review* magazine, the danger of "destructive confrontations with opponents already on the turf" would thus be much diminished, "since all the occupants of the new community are, so to speak, volunteers," meaning "no outside force is imposing a change in the character of an already existing community." Logue further dismissed his critics with, "And if they don't like our mix, well don't bother to come."[109]

Roosevelt Island held the greatest promise. Describing it during construction in characteristically immodest, even grandiose, terms, Logue told an interviewer, "It is perhaps our last chance to demonstrate that people of different incomes, races, and ethnic origins can live together . . . and that they can send their children to the same public schools, and that two things are possible—racial and economic integration and the public schools can be a magnet."[110] The original plan had called for day care centers and mini-schools to be scattered throughout the various residential buildings, each containing only a few grades to encourage family-teacher interaction and to draw children of different incomes and races together. As he had in his Boston work, Logue put faith in schooling to create more socially integrated New York communities.

After a great deal of internal discussion and debate, the UDC decided on its ideal social mix for residential projects, an allocation formula of 70-20-10: 70 percent subsidized moderate and middle income, 20 percent low income, and 10 percent elderly, who usually were also low-income. Their rationale was to ensure that only about a third of the residents were at the lowest end of the income scale while the other two thirds fell at different points along the spectrum. All needed assistance, but in differing amounts. Eligibility requirements for the various categories were left to local housing authorities to set, with federal monitoring.[111]

Primarily focused on filling the gap in affordable housing, the UDC built only a very small number of market-rate units. Those were in the most desirable locations, such as on Roosevelt Island, where spectacular vistas of the Manhattan skyline made it possible to stretch the income span further. Everywhere the UDC worked, it promoted some version of socially and economically heterogeneous residential communities for what it argued was broad mutual benefit. As Logue explained the philosophy in a UDC prospectus in July 1972, although "our lowest income families have the greatest need for housing, in today's market an acute need also exists for families with moderate and middle incomes." Moreover, "It is our view, based on long American experience, that developments which cater exclusively to low-income families are undesirable. They will likely produce large-scale, institutionalized, apartheid projects of questionable value either to society as a whole or to the low-income families so housed."[112]

Creating diverse communities was easier said than done, however. Roosevelt Island, for example, was plagued by a major dispute over how best to sequence the construction and rental of low-income versus middle-income units. Logue had hired an old American Veterans Committee pal from Yale, Adam Yarmolinsky, as executive director of the Welfare Island Development Corporation, the UDC subsidiary established to oversee the project. Yarmolinsky brought little experience with urban development, but had impeccable liberal credentials. Logue also believed that he had gained administrative and technological know-how from having spent the last several years working in the Kennedy and Johnson administrations, most recently for the Department of Defense under secretary Robert McNamara, where he had pushed for the desegregation of military bases. Yarmolinsky had worked as well with Sargent Shriver on drafting LBJ's signature anti-poverty programs, until anti-communist smears by southern congressmen whose support Johnson sought booted him out.[113] Once in place overseeing Roosevelt Island, Yarmolinsky hired as his construction consultant an experienced developer in New York City, Richard Ravitch, whose family-owned HRH Construction was already well established as a builder of affordable housing. Ravitch insisted that the only way to make Roosevelt Island succeed financially was to construct upper-income housing first and recruit a satellite branch of a prestigious New York private school like Dalton. Otherwise, he argued, upper-income residents would resist moving into a low-income community and enrolling their children in public school.

Logue minced few words when he angrily rejected Ravitch's approach and dismissed him as a consultant, insisting, "Dick, this is my island, not your island. I'm sorry this had to come to that, but as far as I'm concerned one of my basic goals in this project is to prove that I can get people in that income level to go to these public schools, and for you to deny that destroys one of the basic reasons for my wanting to do this project." In forcing out Ravitch for attacking "the heart of my social engineering," Logue took a political risk that would later contribute to the UDC's and Logue's own downfall when Ravitch took his revenge. Soon after the departure of Ravitch, Logue fired Yarmolinsky as well, on the ostensible grounds that he was "junketing off," more focused on advancing his career in international affairs than on developing Roosevelt Island, and for insulting their boss, Governor Rockefeller, by publicly endorsing his opponent, Arthur Goldberg, in the 1970 gubernatorial race. With his opponents out of the way, Logue went forward with his plan to start with the subsidized buildings, convinced that if the well-to-do arrived first they would never permit the low-income renters to follow. Robert Litke, Logue's trusted lieutenant back to their Boston days, took over management of the project, resigned to having a deeply invested and sometimes intrusive Logue "looking over his shoulder, . . . driv[ing] him crazy," Logue only half joked.[114]

On Roosevelt Island, Logue broadened his definition of desirable diversity to include people with disabilities. This breakthrough, twenty years before passage of the Americans with Disabilities Act of 1990, was likely inspired by the presence of patients in the island's long-term-care hospitals who had remained there only because they couldn't otherwise get around the city. The UDC not only built apartments for the disabled but also made their mobility around and off this pedestrian-oriented island possible with accessible transportation. Logue explained that he had learned a lot about the challenges of managing in a wheelchair from his former boss, the Boston mayor John Collins.[115]

Logue's notion of a diverse community included fostering "a cross-section of age groups . . . where the elderly are not isolated from the young."[116] Incorporating the elderly into UDC projects also became a strategy for expanding the low-income population to a third without burdening local schools and antagonizing middle-class residents. Roosevelt Island's Eastwood building, for instance, had low- and moderate-income units, including specially equipped apartments for the elderly and a senior citizens' center.[117] Although mixing elderly tenants with families at first seemed to UDC planners an uncontroversial benefit to both groups, it turned out to be problematic in some locations. In Coney Island, "the old people were largely Jewish and the young people were largely black and the kids harassed the bejesus out of the elderly Jews," recounted Logue. The UDC ultimately decided they had to separate these populations in different buildings.[118]

Although the UDC paid most attention to income and age diversity, it carefully considered race as well, to a more explicit extent than is common today in an era of greater caution about racial quotas since the landmark *Regents of the University of California* v. *Bakke* Supreme Court decision of 1978. According to Louis Loewenstein's assessment: "The UDC also sought to establish guidelines to preclude a project's becoming identified with only one race or color. As a consequence of the policy, UDC attempted to have about 70 percent of each project rented to whites in the belief that if the figures were less, then it would be exceedingly difficult to rent units to white families and, therefore, the projects would quickly rent to minorities which would fill them completely. UDC was not able to adhere to either the racial or financial guidelines in every instance and it was criticized whenever it deviated from the policy." Roosevelt Island did, in fact, manage to meet this goal of 30 percent minorities.[119] Worried that its search for racial balance might be misunderstood as a lack of commitment to minorities, the UDC sought to publicly associate its projects with high-profile black celebrities such as jazz musician Lionel Hampton and baseball star Jackie Robinson, who was now a developer. Hampton, for example, not only lent his name and fame to a UDC apartment complex in Harlem; he willingly participated in a parade up 8th Avenue celebrating the ribbon cutting.[120]

But the UDC policy of creating racially integrated communities was not always welcomed. In minority neighborhoods, Logue encountered the same kind of criticism as he had in Boston: that not enough housing was going to needy low-income residents of color. So, for example, the dedication of the Cathedral Parkway Houses in Harlem in 1972 attracted a picket line of neighborhood residents wielding signs reading "Logue Must Go" and "Down with Rockefeller" to protest that an inadequate number of units had been reserved for local people who had been removed from urban renewal areas.[121] Nor did whites always cooperate. When the psychologists Kenneth and Mamie Clark idealistically tried to create a racially integrated UDC project at Schomburg Plaza at the southern edge of Harlem, they could not find enough low- and moderate-income whites willing to move in and were forced to settle for balancing African American and Puerto Rican tenants.[122]

The UDC's dedication to social mixing could also exacerbate racial tensions. A notorious case was Twin Parks in the Bronx, where a cluster of architecturally distinguished buildings by major designers (Richard Meier, James Stewart Polshek, Giovanni Pasanella, and Prentice & Chan, Ohlhausen) became the site of racial strife so intense that tenants hesitated to move in despite their desire for better housing. This UDC project of more than two thousand apartments aimed to attract low- and moderate-income residents—divided, it was hoped, into a third each of whites, blacks, and Puerto Ricans—to a neutral oasis sitting on the boundary between Italian and black neighborhoods. Instead, open central plazas designed to encourage interaction became war zones for teenage gangs, forcing the UDC to install gates and other physical barriers to separate groups from one another and to make other residents feel more secure. By mid-1973, Logue opted for simply filling the vacancies rather than trying to socially integrate Twin Parks, and he became much more wary of including large public spaces in future housing designs.[123]

Not surprisingly, the social engineering required to integrate UDC projects like New Towns by income and race offended Jane Jacobs and her followers, even when they sympathized with Logue's goal. Jacobs explained her critique this way: "You take a clean slate and you make a new world. That's basically artificial. There is no new world you can make without the old world . . . The notion that you could discard the old world and now make a new one. This is what was so bad about Modernism."[124] Counterbalancing Jacobs, however, was enthusiasm from one of the era's most prominent anthropologists, Margaret Mead. In an epilogue that Mead wrote to a 1976 book on New Towns, she argued, "New Towns are necessary to a society that has lost its way." Lamenting segregated suburbs, disrupted old neighborhoods, and other forms of social isolation, she considered New Towns a welcome corrective, "a kind of light that beckons us ahead . . . that can tell us how to . . . bring a slum to life, how to turn a suburb from a bedroom town where people are alienated and separated from their neighbors into a place where people work and meet and know each other."[125]

Despite these many challenges, the UDC nevertheless exceeded its goals for diversifying communities. By 1975, 33 percent of UDC residents statewide were low income and 42 percent were minority.[126] For many residents of a place like Roosevelt Island—white and nonwhite—this social mix was part of the attraction. The journalist Mark Lamster recalled visiting his uncle, "a liberal among liberals [who] was one of the first to move in. He loved it there, as did my aunt. I think they felt they were part of a new and more egalitarian society."[127] And when the feedback was less favorable, Logue and his idealistic, determined staff learned to take the hits in stride. Concluded Logue, "If you think you are going to be warmly welcomed and enthusiastically supported by all elements of the community which you are seeking to change, don't bother. That is not how it works."[128]

Logue recognized the limitations in what the UDC could do to counter the inequities of American society. For one thing, HUD rules required that units with different modes of financing be put in separate buildings. But Logue didn't disagree. He told an interviewer when discussing Roosevelt Island, "To an extent I believe you can mix moderate and low income families, but the price of housing is such that you can't mix low income and middle income in the same building because I, for one, can't justify giving lower income families the same quality of accommodations that people get who pay two or three times as much for it. On the other hand, you can't work it the other way. You can't get the upper income families, who have the widest range of housing choices, to take less than they otherwise deserve."[129] Faced with these obstacles, Logue believed that well-designed and commonly shared neighborhood schools and public spaces, like sidewalks, parks, libraries, transit, and the like, would have to do much of the work. In its physical planning, as with its financing structure, the UDC had to content itself with pushing a socially liberal agenda within the constraints of the capitalist marketplace.

OTHER RACIAL INITIATIVES

"Negro removal" had long been a major criticism of urban renewal and one that Logue was particularly sensitive to. In an interview in 1985, he acknowledged honestly that "many black leaders believe that urban renewal was primarily 'Negro removal,' and sometimes it was."[130] Logue hoped that the UDC would act and be perceived differently. After all, it was born in the wake of the assassination of Martin Luther King, Jr., and promoted by its midwives, Rockefeller and Logue, as an innovative way to redress racial and class disparities. In explaining why he had accepted the UDC job, in fact, Logue pointed to the Kerner Commission Report, released in late February 1968 while he was in negotiations with Rockefeller. The report had motivated him to "get involved again in solving various urban problems," he told a journalist, continuing, "New concepts must be tried, instead of the same old approaches snarled in red tape as are most of the federal urban-aid programs."[131]

Despite Logue's conviction that the UDC had a key role to play in improving New York State's troubled racial landscape—both material and attitudinal—figuring out how to navigate this politically charged terrain was not easy. Black communities everywhere in the state, but particularly in the capital of black America, Harlem, were the opposite of the blank slate Logue had sought with his New Towns. Not only were the late 1960s a time when urban residents were encouraged to participate actively—and often did combatively—in shaping federal programs like Model Cities or to weigh in on urban renewal schemes through now-mandatory community advisory committees, but African American neighborhoods like Harlem were becoming politicized in another way. Younger, more militant activists were challenging the integrationist black political elite, along with the white power structure, by calling for Black Power and community control. Harlem in fact had been the site of the first struggle for community control of New York City's schools two years before the more infamous months-long confrontation in 1968 between the community board of Brooklyn's Ocean Hill–Brownsville and the United Federation of Teachers. In spring 1968, tensions exploded in Harlem with an angry response to King's assassination and protests over Columbia's encroachment into city-owned Morningside Park to build a new gymnasium. The growing polarization of racial politics in the late 1960s forced Logue, who in Boston had been more comfortable with the established black middle class of Washington Park than with Roxbury's radicals, to revisit his expectation that the UDC could promote a liberal, integrationist civil rights agenda.

Tensions would explode dramatically in Harlem during 1969.[132] Three years earlier, the Urban League president Whitney Young had proposed that Governor Rockefeller locate the new World Trade Center, where all state offices in New York City were to be consolidated, in Harlem. Though the state declined to give up the downtown site—key to its ambitions for Lower Manhattan—pressure from Young and other Harlem leaders won the concession of a smaller building for state offices uptown. In time, officials chose 125th Street and 7th Avenue for a combined office tower and community cultural center. The project was welcomed by establishment interests like Harlem's major newspaper, *The Amsterdam News*, which proclaimed the State Office Building "the herald of Harlem's economic revival."[133] Clearing of the site began during the summer of 1967, with efforts made to hire black firms for everything from design to demolition. When it came to approving the construction budget, however, the state legislature dragged its feet, appropriating funding for the twenty-three-story office building only under pressure in 1969 and withholding it from the community building. The state's abandonment of the locally oriented part of the project not only was an affront but also played into the political conflicts raging within Harlem.

Opponents calling themselves the Harlem Committee for Self-Defense and the Ad Hoc Committee for a Better Harlem decried the project as an act of colonization by exploitative outside interests. They charged that the building neither reflected a community decision-making process nor responded to what the neighborhood actually needed, which they identified as a high school, low-income housing, and a day care center. Just as construction was about to begin in July 1969, protesters, now united as the Harlem Community Coalition, shut down the project, establishing a tent city on the cleared lot—which they labeled "Reclamation Site #1," a warning of more to come— in an act of defiance against the state as well as the many establishment leaders who still backed the State Office Building as a valuable public investment in Harlem. The squatters also allied with a community design group known as the Architects Renewal Committee in Harlem, which had opposed Lindsay's hiring of Logue back in 1966. Together, they developed a more neighborhood-oriented alternative to the state project, now dubbed the "SOB." Faced with the occupation of the site, Rockefeller called a halt to construction. After three months of standoff and with the Harlem community's leadership deeply divided, Rockefeller finally decided in September 1969 that there was enough support to go forward and he sent in police to oust the protesters.

Meanwhile, Logue had offered the governor his and the UDC's services to mediate the dispute and oversee the construction of a community-oriented structure next to the State Office Building, which he unsubtly named the Harlem State Service Center to emphasize its potential contributions to the neighborhood.[134] For months, Logue and a few widely trusted local leaders met privately with the various sides in a sincere search for a consensus or at least a compromise. Highlighting the intractability of this highly factionalized conflict, *The New York Times*'s Ada Louise Huxtable called the crisis "Rockefeller's Vietnam" and compared Logue's negotiations to the Paris peace talks, which were going on—unproductively—at the same time.[135] Resolution proved as difficult in Harlem as in Paris. No broad-based agreement was ever reached, and Logue's UDC gained little of the local credibility it had hoped for. By the time the State Office Building opened in 1974, however, militance had receded, and the project was widely praised for at least showcasing the work of African Americans in many professions.

Logue's longer-term answer to the challenge raised by the State Office Building controversy was to propose in December 1969 the creation of a new subsidiary of the UDC, not unlike what existed for Welfare Island, to provide for more community self-determination in the redevelopment of Harlem. The protesters had sent a blunt message when they posted a sign at their occupied site: "Stop the colonizer . . . Don't let Harlem be invaded."[136] But in the months that followed, Logue found it difficult if not impossible to implement the kind of negotiations with neighborhoods that he had become accustomed to in Boston, because he could not identify a partner to speak for all parts of the community. He had hoped that the Harlem Urban Development Corporation (HUDC) would become that representative group, but it soon became clear that the board and top staff he recruited—individuals he thought could both work with the UDC and be broadly accepted in Harlem—gave much greater voice to the business, professional, political, and church leaders who had supported the State Office Building than to their opponents. They were establishment figures. The seasoned civil rights leader

John "Jack" E. Wood, Jr., formerly the director of the National Committee Against Discrimination in Housing and not from Harlem, became president and chief executive officer; Percy E. Sutton, a civil rights activist and the first African American to serve as Manhattan borough president, was named honorary chair; and Judge Herbert Evans, director of the Freedom National Bank, took on the leadership of the thirty-one-member board.[137] Confronted with a fractious political landscape and convinced that he had given a fair chance to critics calling for more participatory democracy, Logue grew exasperated and fell back on the pluralist democrats who represented traditionally organized interests in the community.

Over the years, the HUDC racked up a mixed record. On the positive side, it did give local black leaders an unprecedented degree of control over state redevelopment in Harlem. And it gave the UDC a partner on the ground to work with in a politically fragmented community starved for resources. By the end of 1974, the HUDC had overseen UDC investments of $150 million in nine residential projects delivering more than three thousand dwelling units and a fourteen-hundred-seat elementary school.[138] On the other hand, the HUDC hardly challenged mainstream planning and development. Despite Logue's encouragement, he couldn't even get his subsidiary to take the lead on planning a community facility for the State Office Building site. And in its worst moments, particularly in the years after the UDC collapsed and the HUDC continued to exist as an autonomous community development corporation, it made reckless decisions and often operated as a patronage machine for board members pursuing their own self-interest, taking advantage of HUDC's access to public and private investment dollars.[139]

The UDC's effort to mount a robust affirmative action program proved less controversial and brought more acclaim than the Harlem project. Not only did it fit better with Logue's integrationist orientation, but he could control it fully through his power as UDC president rather than having to negotiate with a politically complex set of actors, as in Harlem. Governor Rockefeller had sent a strong message that New York State was committed to affirmative action, but Logue—more than most agency heads—took that charge to heart. Of the UDC's 500 employees, 23 percent were minority, including 15 percent of the 330 professional and technical staffers.[140] As early as 1970, nine of the UDC's fifty-four projects had been designed by minority architects, although only 1 percent of New York State's architects were black or Puerto Rican.[141] By 1973, 16 percent of the UDC's total construction contracts, worth more than $55.5 million, had gone to minority builders. The rate was much higher in New York City, where more firms were located.[142] That same year, in a detailed discussion of affirmative action, which had become a regular feature of the UDC's annual reports, Logue claimed that 26 percent of construction workers on projects statewide were minorities.[143]

At the same time as he trumpeted these successes, Logue lamented the persistent obstacles to minority entrance into the skilled trades. The UDC did what it could to work around discriminatory labor unions, with the goal of having at least the same percentage of minority workers on a project as were present in the local municipality. In the case of the State Office Building, for example, 60 percent of the workforce was black or other minority, along with the architects, the civil engineering firm, one of the construction companies, an electrical subcontractor, and the construction superintendent, *The Amsterdam News* proudly reported.[144] To reach that number of construction workers, training was provided on the job. This wasn't unusual. The UDC contracted with a minority-run operation called the Recruitment and Training Program (R-T-P, formerly the Workers Defense League) to offer technical assistance and job counseling to minority workers on many project sites and with the Contractors' Training and Development Office to help minority-owned contracting firms acquire skills including bookkeeping, writing proposals, and securing bank loans, all required when working with a state agency like the UDC.[145]

That Logue made affirmative action a UDC priority was clear in his instructions to Donald Cogsville, the UDC's African American affirmative action officer. "I want you to go out and look at those sites and make a judgment about whether there are enough minorities on these jobs. If there aren't, complain . . . tell him you'll be back in four weeks more and if you don't see improvement, the contractor's not going to get paid."[146] Cogsville indeed credited the agency's well-recognized success with affirmative action to hav-ing "a guy at the head of the organization who says 'God damn, it's going to be done,' and then gives the freedom to do whatever is necessary to get things done."[147] Other developers and even a black activist in fact complained that the UDC was monopolizing the state's very small number of minority sub-contractors and black construction workers. One white-owned electrical company, Public Improvement Inc., brought a suit against the UDC, claim-ing that an electrical contract went to a higher bidder who was a minority.[148] Aggressively implementing affirmative action practices on UDC sites, much like setting quotas to ensure diversity in residential projects, was the kind of progressive racial policy that suited Logue's top-down management style. He found much harder the messy negotiations and uncertain outcomes that accompanied a more participatory decision-making process demanded by challengers in Harlem, as had their counterparts in the Hill neighborhood of New Haven and Boston's Lower Roxbury.

REDESIGNING MASS HOUSING

During Logue's time in New Haven and Boston, architects had benefited greatly from the federal government's investment in urban renewal. Now, with the visibility and resources of the UDC at his disposal, Logue felt he had an even greater opportunity to engage architects in design innovation. At the top of his list stood finding viable alternatives to the high-rise public housing that for years he had dismissed as dehumanizing and ghettoizing. Although he estimated that it might cost 5 to 10 percent more to hire better architects to do good design, Logue said, "I thought it was worth it. And when you look at the public housing that Bob Moses built as against the parks he built, for example, it's outrageous . . . He set a [disastrous] national model."[149] Quality design, Logue was confident, could also help "remove the stigma attached to housing built under public assistance programs."[150]

The architect Werner Seligmann—architecture professor at Cornell and Harvard in the era of the UDC, later dean of the School of Architecture at Syracuse University, and the designer of a prominent, moderate-income UDC project, Elm Street Housing, in Ithaca—described the dire situation in 1974: "Less than 10 years ago most schools of architecture considered the topic of housing hardly worthy of investigation . . . This lack of concern explains the few significant housing innovations and dearth of housing models in the United States." Seligmann went on to argue that "improvement of housing can only be accomplished by a persistent and thoroughly informed effort," and he commended the UDC for being "remarkable in giving opportunities to talented and responsive architects and in encouraging their contribution." While Seligmann acknowledged that "this has not been a bed of roses for either the UDC or the architects," he concluded that "the results speak for themselves: each project addresses a particular set of issues, and collectively they produce a backlog of solutions and models to build on."[151] Seligmann's endorsement of the UDC's housing program drew attention to one of its chief features: developing prototypes in housing design and construction for broader adoption.

The first challenge Logue faced in creating prototypes of subsidized housing that were attractive, livable, and economical was identifying architects to design them. He often lamented that "if you let architects alone they will make a statement," rather than address the social concerns he felt were so crucial. Logue pursued a number of other goals as well. He wanted a balance of high-profile architects and young up-and-coming talent. Conveniently, soon after the UDC launched, Philip Johnson invited Logue and some of his top staff to a party he threw at his glass house in New Canaan, Connecticut, to introduce them to the young crowd of architects in New York.[152] Over time Logue's roster came to include an eclectic mix of the Architects Collaborative; Max Bond; Davis, Brody & Associates; Kenneth Frampton; Ulrich Franzen; Gwathmey Siegel; Lawrence Halprin; Philip Johnson; Dan Kiley; Richard Meier; James Stewart Polshek; Prentice & Chan, Ohlhausen; and Edward Durell Stone, among many others. Having a large stable of architects was important if the UDC was to avoid a cookie-cutter look to its buildings and any resemblance to typical public housing.[153]

Logue valued architects who had already proved themselves good partners, which brought him back time and again to some of the same designers. John Johansen and Paul Rudolph were veterans of New Haven, while numerous architects had helped in Boston (in such numbers that I. M. Pei and his partner Harry Cobb felt shut out by "so many Boston architects!"): Gerhard Kallmann and Michael McKinnell, Carl Koch, Josep Lluís Sert, Chloethiel Woodard Smith, Don Stull, and Ben Thompson, among others.[154] McKinnell recalled that every working architect was well aware of the "big, big schemes" of this "incredible powerhouse" that was the UDC, though to keep getting work you had to prove that you were "an architect with a social conscience."[155] Rolf Ohlhausen concurred that membership in organizations like Architects/Designers/Planners for Social Responsibility was a ticket to the UDC.[156] But even the best architects, the UDC felt, required coaching from the agency's inside design team. Tony Pangaro, who worked closely with the UDC's chief architect, Ted Liebman, recalled the challenge of collaborating with "all of these fancy architects that Ed decided he wanted to hire," when few of them "had ever done a shred of housing in their lives."[157]

Relations between the UDC and its architects were not always easy. When the UDC told John Johansen that his buildings on Roosevelt Island were designed with too many entrances, complicating security and increasing operating expenses, Johansen threatened to walk off the job.[158] Sert and his partner Huson Jackson complained that the UDC's fees, dictated by HUD guidelines, were frustratingly low.[159] When James Stewart Polshek specified alternating black and white stripes on the facade of his Twin Parks building in the Bronx, Logue wrote in anger that they would give it "the design distinction of the Bronx Hall of Detention" and demonstrated "the failure of a designer to deliver what was promised and accepted."[160] Charles Hoyt, writing in the *Architectural Record* in 1975, complained that Logue's interventions "infringed upon architects' designs."[161] Many of these conflicts were common to the frequently fraught architect-client relationship. But often the problems stemmed from unique pressures the UDC exerted on architects to keep quality high, budgets low, and the pace fast, while still demonstrating innovation in design and materials.[162]

In the search for ideal prototypes, the UDC "spent a lot of time . . . analyzing what had already been built, figuring out where it succeeded and where it was not fulfilling the goal," Pangaro remembered. Their early efforts became "guidelines for future projects, where we had a great deal more control over what the architect was producing than in the first round."[163] Some improvements were as simple as incorporating common spaces— meeting rooms, medical services, schools, senior centers, and day care—into housing to enhance community vitality.[164] But often the goal was more ambitious, such as developing a new approach to elderly housing.[165] The UDC surely benefited from its controversial power to ignore the local building codes that often blocked housing innovation. Sert was able to use skip-stop elevators in the low-income Eastview on Roosevelt Island, for example, only because the UDC overrode the city's building code. With skip-stop, the elevator stopped only on every third floor, permitting the apartments above and below to run as "floor-throughs" with windows at each end providing natural cross-ventilation. Private corridors on the elevator floor and internal staircases leading up and down to the apartments on the other two floors provided residents with unusual amounts of privacy.[166]

In its effort to keep improving the quality of its housing, the UDC in 1972 introduced an unusual process for gaining feedback: requiring UDC staff as well as architects to live in the buildings with their families for one or two weeks as projects neared completion. Insights gained from "live-ins" complemented surveys of residents as well as an in-depth study of tenant satisfaction in eight projects that the UDC commissioned in 1973 from the Cornell sociologist Franklin D. Becker. "Design aids" gathered through all these evaluation tools were then compiled into a set of "livability criteria," arranged in a loose-leaf notebook handed to each architect at the outset of a new project.[167] The UDC also used the evidence behind these design aids to bolster its requests to the FHA and HUD to revise standards when existing ones, such as for room sizes and amenities, proved overly stringent.[168]

Logue believed strongly that those planning housing for others should experience it for themselves. Design changes inspired by the architects' live-ins included adding more telephone booths to building lobbies, providing better screening between residences and streets, improving noise insulation between apartments, and making bedrooms larger. Liebman remembered asking his secretary to order the kind of bedroom set that she would choose for her own home—"not the modern stuff." Lo and behold, the headboards didn't fit. Ed and Margaret set an example by living in three projects—in the Bronx, Coney Island, and Yonkers. After one of these stays, Margaret argued for a larger second bedroom and a pass-through between the kitchen and living room.[169] Live-ins and other evaluation mechanisms did not cure all the problems with UDC projects. Complaints remained, but the UDC tried to balance the often-competing demands of architects, tenants, budget watchers, and the Feds.

The UDC's prototypes frequently used new technology to make housing construction easier, quicker, and cheaper. Applying the methods of mass production to creating "industrial housing" had long been a dream of prominent modernists including Le Corbusier, Walter Gropius, Jean Prouvé, R. Buckminster Fuller, Charles and Ray Eames, Moshe Safdie, and Paul Rudolph. But supply and demand for the concept had been weak in the United States, except for occasional bursts like the short-lived Lustron homes experiment immediately after World War II.[170] Logue nonetheless remained intrigued, particularly in efforts to shift prefab production from single-family houses to multi-family dwellings. In Boston, he had worked with Carl Koch, a pioneer anointed by *Progressive Architecture* as "the Grandfather of Prefab," to utilize precast wall panels and long-span, prestressed floor planks in Roxbury's Academy Homes.[171]

In New York State, technological innovation became fundamental to the UDC's agenda. The UDC even launched its own state-level Operation Breakthrough, thereby cashing in on the HUD secretary George Romney's pet project launched in May 1969. A former American Motors Corporation executive, Romney, too, was eager to apply state-of-the-art mass production methods to a recalcitrant housing industry.[172] A columnist for *Harper's* expressed cautious optimism a year into the UDC's existence that Logue had "started to lay the groundwork for a revolution in the building industry, notoriously the most backward of industries, . . . still us[ing] handicraft methods essentially unchanged since the time of the Pharaohs, and . . . still organized (if one can use that word) in thousands of small, inefficient firms."[173]

The UDC established the Housing Technology Office in its headquarters in New York City with a mission to expand the use of industrialized methods. The UDC also developed a factory to produce precast concrete components such as hollow-core floor slabs, load-bearing and non-load-bearing wall panels, and stairs, landings, and balconies. Other technological experiments, in addition to the AVAC refuse system on Roosevelt Island, included various kinds of modular construction; high-bond mortar to allow pre-assembly of brick walls; plumbing improvements such as single-stack plumbing systems to avoid vent piping, low-flow fixtures that reduced water consumption, and premade "plumbing walls" complete with all fittings and pipes; spray-on painting; solar-power systems; and even the application to housing of electrical wiring panels developed by NASA.[174] In publicizing their Roosevelt Island work, Johansen and his partner Ashok Bhavnani boasted about using, for the first time in the United States, a three-inch extruded cement-asbestos panel erected from within the building that, they claimed, required one-tenth of the labor force to erect than conventional brick and block, needed no scaffolding, and came very cheap.[175]

But despite Logue and his staff's enthusiasm for technical innovation, there were many obstacles to achieving it, including finding manufacturers that could stay in business with a limited volume of orders and the resistance of contractors and building trades unions to changes that might undermine their long-established practices.[176] It also proved time-consuming and expensive to develop these new approaches, which was disappointing, given that a major motive for them was to combat the spiraling costs of construction. Logue even became exasperated with his friend Paul Rudolph when Rudolph's effort to use prefabricated twelve-by-sixty-foot modular units in his Buffalo waterfront housing led to long delays: "My report on your first design for Phase III Buffalo Waterfront is that it will win a P.A. [*Progressive Architecture*] award and that is about it. After the length of time you have been working on this job, it seems to me that we ought to be able to get down to the real world without a waste of time, money, and your own unique talents."[177] These frustrations aside, Logue would remain committed to the holy grail of industrializing housing construction into his next job in the South Bronx during the 1980s.

Probably the most important prototype that the UDC undertook was aimed at developing an alternative to the much-maligned high-rise public housing. In 1973, the UDC's own inside designers Liebman and Pangaro joined Michael Kirkland, Kenneth Frampton, Peter Eisenman, Arthur Baker, Lee Taliaferro, and Peter Wolf of the Institute for Architecture and Urban Studies (IAUS), a recently founded nonprofit organization of theoretically inclined young New York architects, to invent a new kind of low-income housing: "low-rise, high-density." Together they designed Marcus Garvey Park Village, a 626-unit project of four-story, four-unit buildings spread across six devastated city blocks in the Ocean Hill–Brownsville section of Brooklyn, part of a larger Model Cities area. Resembling traditional rowhouses in scale but more modern aesthetically, they achieved the same density of fifty-five units per acre as a high-rise tower, but without the drawbacks. The units, intended particularly for families, featured mostly two- and three-bedroom (with fewer one-, four-, or five-bedroom) duplex apartments, some facing the street and others a public mews, with each household having its own private stoop, entrance, and outdoor space.

The designers were influenced by the architect and planner Oscar Newman's recently published book *Defensible Space* (1972), which attributed the high crime rate in housing projects to residents' feeling that they had little control over, or personal responsibility for, the space. In response, Marcus Garvey's designers strove for greater clarity in distinguishing private, semi-private, semi-public, and public spaces to make tenants feel more secure as families and more invested as community members. The high density on this 2.5-acre site was achieved by eliminating the large setbacks from the street common in public housing towers, instead respecting the urban grid and increasing the number of bedrooms per unit. A second version of the prototype was planned for the more suburban location of Fox Hills, Staten Island, but was never built. Nor were the seven other low-rise, high-density projects on the UDC's docket when it collapsed.

It was important to Logue not simply to build prototypes like Marcus

Garvey, but also to draw public and professional attention to them. One of the reasons he chose the IAUS as a partner was that he knew its architects had close connections with Arthur Drexler, director of the Department of Architecture and Design at the Museum of Modern Art. Just as Logue hoped, on the day of the ground breaking for Marcus Garvey—June 11, 1973—an exhibition showcasing the project opened at MoMA, titled "Another Chance for Housing: Low-Rise Alternatives," with an accompanying catalog. From MoMA it traveled to the U.S. embassy in London.[178] Opinions varied on Marcus Garvey Park Village. Upon its completion, eager tenants flocked to move in, delighted at the unique design features, despite the elimination of some due to budget; chain-link fences had replaced walls between gardens, and the promised day care was never built. Over time, some tenant enthusiasm dimmed in response to management's neglect of community spaces, poor maintenance, and security problems like drug dealing, which sadly thrived in the off-street areas originally intended for protected gathering and play. But an observer who decades later visited the village noted that residents still were "pretty amazed . . . at the quality of the housing they were living in," particularly that as relatively poor people "they lived in a duplex," usually a privilege reserved for the middle class.[179]

With this celebrated low-rise, high-density experiment behind him, Logue moved on to an even greater challenge: seeking high-rise alternatives to the public housing towers that so often failed their residents. Still committed to the prototype strategy, Logue took the unusual step in 1974 of launching a major architectural competition for the design of a mixed-income, high-rise project that would complete the north end of Roosevelt Island. He knew that a competition would garner a great deal of attention. It had certainly worked for Boston City Hall a decade earlier. Logue turned out to be right. The competition attracted more than 700 entrants, of whom 250 made final submissions.

This competition for a thousand units of housing on a 9.2-acre site opposite the Motorgate garage was planned to proceed in two stages, first winnowing the large pool down to eight finalists who would then compete for first, second, and third prizes. Logue explained in the call for proposals that despite success with the low-rise, high-density concept, the UDC wanted a new prototype, because "if we can be convinced that elevator dependent housing can serve families, as well as elderly and childless households, with maximum livability, it will give us much more flexibility in our housing program."[180] Calling on prominent figures to bring wise counsel and public attention to the competition, Logue appointed a jury chaired by Josep Lluís Sert that included fellow architects Paul Rudolph, Joseph Wasserman, and Alexander Cooper; Sharon Lee Ryder, the interior design editor at *Progressive Architecture*; the Cornell sociologist Franklin D. Becker, who had analyzed tenant responses to UDC projects; and the prominent New York real estate developer and philanthropist Frederick Rose.

All the bases were covered, except the most important one: the survival of the UDC. It crashed a couple of months before the competition was completed. Liebman became so concerned the prize money would be canceled that he threatened to go to *The New York Times*. Instead he was kept on for three additional months at the UDC to see the competition through. The planned two stages were telescoped into one, but after all that, the jury divided, splitting the prize among four young firms rather than declaring one winner.[181] The day after the results were announced, Liebman left his post as chief architect of the UDC, and the competition's contribution to high-rise subsidized housing remained more theoretical than real. A design innovation that Liebman had once believed "in his mind's eye that every magazine on earth would say is the future of high-density housing" instead definitively marked the end of the UDC's prototype program.[182]

Despite UDC successes in developing prototypes to improve the quality and quantity of housing in New York State, the strategy had its pitfalls. Some critics argued that the UDC's commitment to developing universal prototypes downplayed the importance of context. The topographical challenges of a particular building site were impossible to ignore, of course, but promoting ideal housing types minimized the importance of each project's unique social and aesthetic setting. In a discussion many years later, with the distance of time, Robert Campbell and Tony Pangaro acknowledged this weakness in the UDC projects that they personally had worked on as young architects. "I don't think they were conceived as parts of something larger. They were conceived as prototypes that could stand alone and could be on one site or perhaps on another site and perhaps on another site," admitted Campbell, who had worked with Sert on several UDC projects. Pangaro agreed, referencing his own work on Marcus Garvey: "We were a bunch of kamikaze architects, you know dropping this project into Brownsville, in the best way we could."[183]

The *New York Times* architecture critic Paul Goldberger may have offered the most balanced assessment when he took stock of the UDC's impact on housing design as the agency came under fire in 1975. He wrote that although the UDC's architectural record was "far from unblemished, and there are some notable failures," over seven years the corporation "built nothing that resembles the banal oppressive buildings customarily considered suitable for public housing." With the UDC's aspiration for architectural quality, "it managed to produce some of the finest housing New York State has seen in recent times."[184] Goldberger might have added that the UDC managed to use its unusual powers, plentiful resources, and public visibility to inspire an atmosphere of experimentation greatly needed in a field that had become stultified, too often content to build either conventional market-rate single-family homes or formulaic high-rise public housing.

THE BIGGEST CHALLENGE OF ALL

The UDC provided Logue with new tools for combating the most serious charges brought against federally funded and locally implemented urban renewal as it was practiced from the late 1940s through the 1960s. He invented a fast track to push projects to completion more quickly. He experimented with ways of avoiding clearance and displacement, utilizing previously leveled urban renewal sites and building New Towns on open land. He tried to make the UDC's urban redevelopment program one that advanced rather than set back the nation's civil rights agenda through creating more diverse residential communities, establishing a semiautonomous

UDC subsidiary in Harlem, and wielding the UDC's contracts as a weapon to promote affirmative-action hiring. He worked to accelerate the nation's slow progress in building more and better housing for all Americans by encouraging design innovations and construction efficiencies, many made possible by adopting the latest technology. And he never gave up on the search for alternatives to failing high-rise public housing. Logue achieved some of these goals more successfully than others, but he made headway on all of them, even as he struggled with participatory democracy's calls for greater grassroots involvement in the planning process.

There was one goal of Logue's, however, that towered above all others in the importance he attached to it and the potential he felt it held to change how American cities were developing. This was Logue's long-standing ambition to solve urban problems at the metropolitan level. In New Haven and Boston, Logue had felt frustrated that his authority stopped at the city's borders when, he judged, so many of its challenges—and certainly the best solutions—were metropolitan-wide. And still now, "The day seems no closer when the New York metropolitan area, covering three states, will take a unified approach to the problems of housing, jobs, transportation, recreation, pollution, and even taxation," he lamented in 1972. Finding this effort "unquestionably the most difficult part of our work," he went on to complain that "despite repeated studies demonstrating substantial needs for new housing for families with low and moderate incomes in all the counties making up the New York metropolitan region, there is great resistance to facing this reality."[185]

Over time, Logue had watched with growing dismay as suburbs provided safety valves for escaping middle-class urban residents, who then raised the ramparts behind them to prevent others from following and disinvested from the cities whose economies made their own lives so comfortable. Finally, he thought, the UDC's statewide mandate and extraordinary powers would make possible an assault on the barriers dividing city and suburb and open up new housing options for people with low incomes. As Logue looked north out the huge windows of his forty-sixth-floor UDC office, his eyes inevitably fixed on Westchester, the wealthiest of New York's suburban counties and, not coincidentally, the historic seat of the Rockefeller family.[186] What became known—and notorious—as the UDC's Fair Share Housing program would soon emerge as its greatest and most controversial challenge to the socioeconomic status quo in New York State. Logue would risk a great deal in making this high-stakes bet, and the outcome would have repercussions far outside this one county's borders, deciding the fate of both the UDC and its tenacious leader, Ed Logue.

GOVERNOR NELSON ROCKEFELLER SIGNING THE UDC LEGISLATION, 1968.
Rockefeller created, with Logue's advice, the New York State Urban Development Corporation (UDC) to construct badly needed subsidized housing and redevelop the state's troubled cities. He then named Logue president of the UDC, with enormous powers to employ eminent domain, override local zoning and building codes, and exempt projects from taxes. (DIGITAL COLLECTIONS OF THE NEW YORK STATE ARCHIVES)

ROBERT MOSES, INSPIRATION AND NEMESIS. Logue rejected any equivalence made between him and New York's once powerful city builder, Robert Moses. Although sharing Moses's conviction that physical interventions could improve people's lives, Logue considered himself much more committed to progressive social change than Moses. As Yale graduates, the two men occasionally met up at football games, like this one in November 1968. (COURTESY OF FAMILY OF EDWARD J. LOGUE)

NEW YORK CITY MAYOR JOHN LINDSAY, RELUCTANT UDC PARTNER, 1969.
Lindsay at first resisted what he saw as state interference in New York City. But he
finally relented out of desperate need for the UDC's resources and proven ability to
produce subsidized housing quickly. This press conference announced the signing
of an agreement between city and state. Logue is at far left. (URBAN DEVELOPMENT
CORPORATION)

New Technology

To contend with spiraling construction costs and to improve the quality of housing, UDC established a special office for technology. This office has begun work in the following areas:

(1) Evaluating new building methods and materials and working with architects, engineers, builders and manufacturers to expedite the introduction of innovations into the design and construction of UDC projects.

(2) Developing criteria for judging the health and safety aspects of new technologies.

(3) Working with State and local officials, building and industry groups and unions to resolve problems regarding standards and work practices as they relate to the introduction of innovations.

UDC's large-scale housing projects throughout New York State provide a unique opportunity for private industry to utilize innovations that promise to reduce construction costs and improve housing quality.

UDC has engaged Tishman Research Corporation and the architectural research office of Goody, Clancy & Associates to evaluate new building products, systems and subsystems. These consultants will make their recommendations in spring, 1970.

Housing Technology—The Shelley System, with on-site factory, San Juan, Puerto Rico.

EXPERIMENTING WITH NEW TECHNOLOGY FOR HOUSING.

As early as its *1969 Annual Report,* the UDC promoted innovation in building methods to make housing construction more efficient and affordable. Examples included preassembled modular units that saved time and labor on-site and electrical wiring panels developed by NASA. (*NEW YORK STATE URBAN DEVELOPMENT CORPORATION ANNUAL REPORT, 1969*)

PRESERVING HISTORIC STRUCTURES ON NEW ROOSEVELT ISLAND. Historic buildings already on the island, like the Chapel of the Good Shepherd here being repurposed as a meeting and interfaith facility, were incorporated into the UDC's "New-Town-in-Town," a commitment to preservation that Logue had learned in Boston. (*THE ROOSEVELT ISLAND HOUSING COMPETITION, NEW YORK STATE URBAN DEVELOPMENT CORPORATION* [BOOKLET], 1974)

ROOSEVELT ISLAND, LOGUE'S UTOPIA IN THE EAST RIVER. Roosevelt Island embodied Logue's idealistic goals for the UDC. Like the other two New Towns that the UDC built in upstate New York, it aimed to mix residents along income and racial lines. It was also car-free and handicap accessible, long before the latter was common, and it used technology in innovative ways. (*THE ROOSEVELT ISLAND HOUSING COMPETITION, NEW YORK STATE URBAN DEVELOPMENT CORPORATION* [BOOKLET], 1974)

PLANNING MARCUS GARVEY PARK VILLAGE, 1972. Long opposed to high-rise public housing, Logue experimented with developing a low-rise, high-density alternative at Marcus Garvey Park Village in Brooklyn. Here Logue is discussing a housing prototype with the UDC architects Ted Liebman (left) and Tony Pangaro (next to Logue), and with Peter Eisenman (farther right) and Kenneth Frampton (not in photo) from the nonprofit Institute for Architecture and Urban Studies, contracted by the UDC to design Marcus Garvey. (COURTESY OF ROBERT PERRON PHOTOGRAPHY)

LIVING IN MARCUS GARVEY. Logue and his colleagues hoped to demonstrate that low-rise housing could achieve the same density per acre as high-rise towers, while also creating an environment where families felt safe and in control. The project's 626 units were organized in four-story, four-unit buildings, each with private entrances and outdoor space. (THEODORE LIEBMAN, FAIA)

THE UDC IN HARLEM. The distinguished psychologist Kenneth B. Clark (second from left), a longtime UDC board member and friend of Logue's, and his accomplished psychologist wife, Mamie Phipps Clark, worked with the UDC to develop Arthur A. Schomburg Plaza at 110th Street and Fifth Avenue. Twin thirty-five-story octagonal towers contained six hundred mixed-income apartments and the Clarks's Northside Center for Child Development, the first facility to offer psychological services to families in Harlem. At this cornerstone ceremony in 1973, the Clarks are flanked to the right by Logue and William H. Hayden, director of the UDC's New York City Region field office. A subsidiary, the Harlem Urban Development Corporation, initiated other projects nearby. (URBAN DEVELOPMENT CORPORATION)

PROMOTING AFFIRMATIVE ACTION. Logue made a strong commitment to affirmative action, requiring that minorities' participation in all aspects of UDC projects be proportional to their presence in a local area. UDC-sponsored loans and technical assistance programs helped minorities compete. Here, the architectural firm Castro-Blanco, Piscioneri & Feder is working with Gruzen & Partners on Schomburg Plaza. (*ANNUAL REPORT OF THE NEW YORK STATE URBAN DEVELOPMENT CORPORATION, 1972*)

THE BATTLE OVER FAIR SHARE HOUSING IN WESTCHESTER, 1972. Logue welcomed the opportunity provided by the state-level UDC to solve racial and income inequities with metropolitan solutions. But the UDC's effort to build one hundred units of garden apartment–style subsidized housing in nine Westchester towns met with ferocious rejection, evident at this Bedford public hearing. (*ANNUAL REPORT OF THE NEW YORK STATE URBAN DEVELOPMENT CORPORATION, 1972*)

UDC COLLAPSE IN WINTER 1975. After the defeat of the Fair Share Housing proposal, problems continued to plague the UDC that neither Logue nor his board of directors, pictured here, could overcome. When the newly elected governor Hugh Carey discovered the precarious financial condition of New York State, he targeted the UDC as a prime offender, firing Logue in anticipation of the UDC's default on notes and bonds in February 1975. (URBAN DEVELOPMENT CORPORATION)

JIMMY CARTER'S SOUTH BRONX TOUR BEGETS THE SBDO. On October 5, 1977, President Carter (center) visited the most ravaged parts of the South Bronx with the New York mayor Abraham Beame (right) and Carter's Secretary of Housing and Urban Development (HUD), Patricia Harris (left). Shocked at the devastation on Charlotte Street, he vowed to help. His promised federal dollars never came through, but that failure prompted the next mayor, Ed Koch, to create the South Bronx Development Organization (SBDO) and hire Logue to lead it.
(PHOTO BY BETTMANN ARCHIVE / GETTY IMAGES)

SBDO COLLABORATES WITH NEIGHBORHOOD GROUPS. Without the big government subsidies of the past, Logue tapped small surviving pockets of public funding for housing, human services, and economic development in the South Bronx. He also built alliances with local community development corporations (CDCs) and community planning boards, like the one he is meeting with here. The SBDO practiced a more grassroots participatory democracy rather than the pluralist democracy of Logue's earlier career. (© BOLIVAR ARELLANO)

GROWING IMPORTANCE OF PRIVATE FUNDING. The CHEMICAL BANK sign hanging below the one crediting the City of New York and the SBDO for this Crotona-Mapes housing signaled the increasing role being played by the private sector during the Reagan administration. New intermediaries like the Local Initiatives Support Corporation, an offshoot of the Ford Foundation, helped channel private resources into projects sponsored by the public and nonprofit sectors. (COURTESY OF PETER BRAY)

MANUFACTURED HOMES FOR CHARLOTTE GARDENS. The best-known project of the SBDO was Charlotte Gardens, ninety single-family, detached, suburban-style ranch homes prefabricated in a factory in Pennsylvania and trucked to the site where Jimmy Carter had walked in horror. Logue hoped that invested homeowners would provide just the anchor needed to revitalize the South Bronx. (COURTESY OF PETER BRAY)

PRE-FAB DREAM HOUSES FOR LOGUE AND PROSPECTIVE BUYERS. Charlotte Gardens fulfilled Logue's ambition to use technology to make quality housing more affordable. These houses gave black and Latino police, firemen, teachers, and others in the lower middle class access to the kinds of homes that whites could buy in the suburbs, communities where nonwhites did not feel welcome or comfortable. (COURTESY OF PETER BRAY)

POLITICIANS DEDICATE CHARLOTTE GARDENS, APRIL 17, 1983. Although Logue's SBDO got minimal government help, all the politicians showed up at the opening, from the United States senator Alfonse D'Amato down to the New York State assemblywoman Gloria Davis. To the right of Logue are the congressman Mario Biaggi, the Bronx borough president Stanley Simon, and the speaker, Mayor Ed Koch, whose support for Charlotte Gardens grew when he saw its enormous popularity. (COURTESY OF PETER BRAY)

GENEVIEVE BROOKS AND HER MID BRONX DESPERADOES. Logue's indispensable partner in Charlotte Gardens was a neighborhood CDC called the Mid Bronx Desperadoes (MBD), co-led by the organizational dynamo Genevieve Brooks (here talking with resident Donald Gould) and a local priest, Father William Smith. Relations between the SBDO and the MBD were sometimes tense, but they respected each other's unique contributions. (© SUSAN FARLEY)

UILDING THE SOUTH BRONX

SEBCO HOUSES-FATHER LOUIS GIGANTE-CHAIRMAN

FATHER LOUIS GIGANTE'S SEBCO. Ten years before Logue arrived, Father Louis Gigante had founded the South East Bronx Community Organization (SEBCO) to renovate housing and provide much-needed social services in the poor Hunts Point neighborhood of his Saint Athanasius Church. Logue grew to admire the parish-level priests like Gigante and Smith, who devoted themselves to neighborhood improvement, displaying a more grassroots level of Catholic Church commitment to urban renewal than seen in Boston, where the Archbishop had taken the lead. (PHOTO BY BETTMANN ARCHIVE / GETTY IMAGES)

THE (PHOTO) SHOT SEEN 'ROUND THE WORLD. When this image of Logue standing behind the white picket fence of a Charlotte Gardens home appeared in *New York* magazine in June 1984, it was just one of hundreds of photos publicizing this unique project. Charlotte Gardens helped to turn around the South Bronx, inspiring many of the strategies that would bring thousands of new and rehabbed housing units to New York City through Mayor Koch's ten-year plan, more than sixty-five thousand to the Bronx alone. (© JON LOVE, 2018)

A BUS TOUR THAT WENT NOWHERE. Logue depended on an annual $1 million technical assistance grant from HUD to cover salary and administrative costs. Despite his best efforts to impress the HUD secretary Samuel Pierce with this tour of the SBDO's accomplishments, Pierce remained hostile and invited other Bronx community groups to compete for the funds. (© BOLIVAR ARELLANO)

VELEZ BEATS OUT LOGUE FOR SCARCE HUD DOLLARS. The $1 million from HUD that had kept the SBDO afloat ultimately went to four other Bronx organizations, with the largest amount going to the corrupt Ramon Velez in return for delivering the Latino vote to the Republicans in the 1984 election. When Logue and Koch's protests failed, Logue resigned in disgust, departing in January 1985. (PHOTO BY TOM CUNNINGHAM / NY DAILY NEWS ARCHIVE VIA GETTY IMAGES)

PURSUING THE PUBLIC GOOD WITH THE PRIVATE PURSE, 1980S ONWARD.
When Logue resettled in Boston in 1985, he worried that the absence of generous public funding was allowing private developers to dictate too much of the city's development. This cartoon by Dan Wasserman in *The Boston Globe* in 1987 expressed a similar concern that the current director of the BRA, Stephen Coyle, was increasingly beholden to private interests.

(DAN WASSERMAN © *THE BOSTON GLOBE*, 1987)

A GRASSROOTS COMMUNITY ACTIVIST IN HIS RETIREMENT. After Logue returned to Boston, he was admired more for what he had accomplished in the past than for what he was doing in the present. It was at his summer retreat on Martha's Vineyard, where he gradually retired in the 1990s, that he had his greatest impact, advocating for land conservation, affordable housing, and a more robust county government. He died there in January 2000, just before turning seventy-nine.

(PHOTO BY KIRSTEN ELSTNER)

8. From Fair Share to Belly-Up

Logue began hatching plans for the Urban Development Corporation to build affordable housing in suburban communities very soon after he became its president. Only months into the job in fall 1968, he delivered a characteristically blunt message to a national audience of housing and redevelopment officials, provocatively targeting by name—for impact—one of the most elite communities in Greater New York. "In the enlightened state of New York," he promised, "New York City is going to be able to count on the services of the state development corporation in rehousing some of its low-income families in Scarsdale." In the same speech, Logue left no ambiguity that he meant to provide housing not only for the economically disadvantaged, but for racial minorities as well. "We have to face directly, in any way we can, the proposition that until the nation decides that low-income black people can have a place to live that they can afford, a place to send their children to school, outside Cleveland, outside Boston, we are just kidding ourselves."[1]

Fearing the hardening of racial lines on the parts of whites as well as blacks, who were increasingly attracted to Black Power and community control in place of integration, Logue called for urgent action. "Each year that goes by makes residential integration more difficult," he warned in 1968.[2] Logue took advantage of every opportunity to make this point, particularly with white audiences. For example, he titled his commencement address at Smith College "Fair Sharing—or Why Don't We Do Something About It," and asked the overwhelmingly white assembly if they were doing their "fair share" as suburban residents, employers, consumers, and Americans.[3] Logue was reprising the message of white responsibility that he had first sent in his 1953 treatise, "Is One Hundred Years Long Enough?" composed in India a decade and a half earlier.

Logue's effort to have the UDC implement changes he considered necessary for the nation proved more difficult to achieve than he ever expected. Although he had anticipated a tough struggle, Logue had hoped that suburban New Yorkers could be convinced to voluntarily embrace a modest housing proposal that integrated their communities economically and racially. After all, similar agendas were very much in the air. The U.S. Commission on Civil Rights called for an end to exclusionary zoning in 1970, and the Republican secretary of Housing and Urban Development, George Romney, had himself initiated an "Open Communities" program to withhold HUD money from suburbs that refused to accept integrated, subsidized low-income housing, though the initiative was short-lived, as Romney's boss, President Richard Nixon, soon pushed him out of office.[4]

Rather than the enthusiasm or even accommodation that Logue had sought, his suburban housing program incited bitter rancor. The UDC had intentionally kept its approach to what it called Fair Share Housing limited in scope, hoping to minimize its impact on any one community. In each of nine Westchester towns, one hundred units of low-income housing were to be built in low-profile structures, allocated according to the usual UDC for-mula of 70 percent moderate income, 20 percent low income, and 10 percent elderly low income. Priority would be given first to current town residents, then to town and school district staff, and finally to employees of local busi-nesses, with Vietnam veterans favored in all categories. In its prospectus, the UDC promised that each development would be "marketed . . . with the objective of achieving a minority occupancy of approximately 20 percent," a goal that the UDC considered conservative.[5] With these stipulations, the UDC intended to put to rest any suburban fears of a large invasion of poor blacks from the Bronx and Harlem. Rather, the agency viewed the plan as a modest contribution to its signature goal of creating socially mixed communities.

But what seemed measured to the UDC was hardly received that way in the nine Westchester towns. It soon became clear that the only way that the Fair Share Housing program could proceed would be if the UDC invoked its controversial power to override town zoning and building codes, which had been authorized for use only when public hearings and informal con-sultation with local officials failed to advance a socially important proj-ect.[6] Literally from day one, Logue had insisted to Rockefeller that the UDC must have this override authority for just such a case as this one, where "the noble tool of zoning has been perverted to maintaining the character of affluent, lily-white suburbs."[7] To Logue's mind, exclusionary local zon-ing laws had proved themselves "among the most powerful forces at work polarizing our society."[8]

Before the "Nine Towns" controversy, the UDC had usually worked col-laboratively with municipal governments, using its eminent domain author-ity and zoning and building code overrides sparingly—and sometimes even at local request.[9] In its 1972 annual report, for instance, the UDC reported that only in 4 developments out of a total of 101 had the agency gone forward with construction against the stated opposition of an elected legislative body.[10] Moreover, the creation of subsidiary boards for the large projects of Roosevelt Island, Harlem, and Rochester had helped involve local commu-nities in UDC decision-making, the agency claimed.[11]

Very quickly, the confrontation escalated from debating the virtues of building low-income housing in affluent suburbs to the larger political question of whether the UDC had the right to impose its plan on a community that strongly objected, thereby making the UDC and its superpowers the issue. Echoing objections raised at the UDC's founding, these Westchester towns and their allies argued that a state agency like the UDC had no standing to violate a community's home rule or right to self-determination. Logue shot back that "a public statewide charter for urban development [could not] condone a policy which promotes, under other banners, an apartheid residential policy."[12] In Logue's view, the UDC could fulfill its statutory mandate *only* if it *did* assert its override power to build low-income multi-family housing in suburban New York, regardless of a community's local zoning. Robert Litke, a veteran of the neighborhood battles in Boston, explained how important this override power was to the UDC: "To be able to do things that we knew were right without the constraints was just very heady stuff."[13] It would turn out, however, that insisting on the UDC's rightful powers was one thing. Exercising them and retaining them in the face of grassroots resistance—this time, not from poor white and black urban residents but from rich and powerful white suburbanites—would prove quite another.

MOVING TO THE SUBURBS

When Logue and his UDC colleagues looked around for the best place to put a Fair Share Housing program in Greater New York, they settled on Westchester for a number of reasons. To start with, the rural character of the central and northern part of the county, where the nine towns selected were located, meant vacant land was available, which was not often the case elsewhere in New York's densely settled suburbs. Moreover, officials in Westchester, particularly County Executive Edwin D. Michaelian, were seeking more economic development to strengthen the county's financial base. The UDC could offer assistance in constructing needed water and sewage infrastructure, while also contributing more affordable housing to accommodate the labor required for economic growth. Although Westchester's population had grown markedly in recent years, its housing supply remained inadequate and so expensive that even middle-income employees often found it difficult to live near their jobs.[14] And, of course, Westchester was Governor Rockefeller's home county, where politicians could, they hoped, be counted on for support. Michaelian, for one, was a Rockefeller ally.

Logue consulted with Rockefeller before going public with the plan and happily received his enthusiastic endorsement. "We haven't bought any land, we've just got it under option. If you want to stop it, you can stop it," Logue recalled saying. To which Rockefeller replied, "Go ahead. What a wonderful idea. It isn't going to hurt anybody too much." During that morning briefing the governor even proposed that the Rockefeller family contribute a twenty-acre parcel of land from its Pocantico estate for a Fair Share development. "I left elated," remembered Logue. But by mid-afternoon, the Rockefeller family's lawyer called to withdraw the governor's offer: "Forget it. It's not Nelson's property; it's the whole family's," which perhaps should have put Logue on notice of the resistance to come.[15] But at least for a while, it seemed that the Westchester initiative held great promise and even the possibility of further expansion in the future.[16]

By the UDC's second summer, in 1969, plans were under way. The agency had commissioned the Regional Plan Association to undertake a report on housing needs and opportunities in the New York metropolitan region, which not surprisingly revealed high demand for low-income housing and the availability of land in Westchester. Logue sought out occasions to speak to planners and reformers in Westchester to line up local allies. Although he asserted that he had "no taste for controversy just for the hell of it," he was adamant that the state could not tolerate what was widely referred to at the time as "snob zoning"—permitting only single-family homes on large lots. Hoping to squelch criticism of too much top-down UDC control, Logue proposed that the Fair Share Housing program be implemented by a UDC subsidiary "to put into the hands of the residents and leaders of Westchester County the powers of the Corporation and the resources of this Corporation."[17]

When plans for the Westchester subsidiary stalled, the UDC decided to proceed without it. In January 1972 Logue met with the Westchester Association of Town Supervisors to unveil the Fair Share program of building a hundred units, mostly townhouses and garden apartments on wooded tracts of ten acres or more, in each of nine towns. In June more details were announced, including naming Bedford, Cortlandt, Greenburgh, Harrison, Lewisboro, New Castle, North Castle, Somers, and Yorktown as the selected sites.

The response varied somewhat in each chosen community, but the overall pattern was much the same. Once word of the UDC project got out, it provoked citizen outcry, large and volatile public meetings, and vigorous organization by opponents. In town after town, something like a civil war broke out. In favor were civic groups like the League of Women Voters; all the black organizations in the county united under the flag of the Coalition of Black Westchester Residents; some local businesses and unions, including the AFL-CIO; and many clergy, inspired by the unequivocal message of the liberal Episcopal bishop Paul Moore, Jr., to his ministers: "You have my total backing in endeavoring to make decent housing possible in Westchester, even when such an effort brings you into conflict with some powerful members of the community or perhaps even the Church."[18]

The opposition was led by newly formed citizens' groups—United Towns for Home Rule being the most visible—and the elected officials they put under increasing pressure. Raucous public meetings—a thousand people showed up at one forum, and police were necessary to keep order—were reminiscent of Logue's Charlestown experiences a decade earlier, despite the dramatic social-class differences between the communities. Hostile speakers charged the UDC with ignoring the views of local communities and incompetence in selecting sites for the housing. They argued that an influx of new residents would put an undue burden on the local schools and school budgets and on the tax base more generally, given the UDC's tax abatement. They claimed that this new housing would change the physical character of their semirural towns and, though rarely said explicitly, their class and racial character as well. Anything that smacked of "urban," starting with the *Urban* Development Corporation, was deemed a dangerous threat. By no coincidence, the effort to emphasize the historical heritage of Bedford by creating a historic district—a move long opposed by residents resistant to restrictions on their property rights—now sailed through with the mission to "maintain the character of the historic district" and "regulate construction of new buildings."[19] It was clear that many ardent opponents feared that the UDC's Fair Share Housing was the opening crack in the zoning wall that would lead to greater development and diversity.[20] Observing the defiance as a young reporter for *The New York Times*, Linda Greenhouse concluded that Logue had "pushed a button they didn't know they had."[21]

Logue acknowledged in the UDC's annual report in 1972 that "the intensity of the opposition was something to behold . . . The clamor, the outrage, the anger—and sadly—the hate displayed were disheartening."[22] Logue was personally targeted with death threats. Once, before an evening hearing, he got a call warning that if he showed up he'd be assassinated. He went nonetheless, bringing the UDC staffers Larry Goldman and Richard Kahan along with him, and sat in a front-row seat, crossing his arms and making himself "just as visible as you could possibly be," recalled Kahan. "It was like, okay, here I am."[23] At one informational meeting called by the UDC, shouts of "Get out, we don't want you in Bedford" drowned out more reasoned discussion.[24] Another meeting had to be adjourned and rescheduled because of excessive "foot stomping and jeering."[25] A suspicious fire destroyed a handsome hundred-year-old barn in Bedford that the UDC had recently purchased to convert into a community center for its proposed housing development nearby.[26]

The UDC struggled to keep the debate on a more civil level. It responded to opponents' concerns about tax shortfalls with reminders that the UDC was making substantial payments in lieu of taxes and with calculations of how state allocations would cover much of the cost of additional students. It also promoted a bill in Albany requiring the state to reimburse communities for any financial losses sustained from a UDC development. Seeking compromise, the UDC conveyed a willingness to reduce the number of units, restrict tenant eligibility to town employees, and investigate alternative sites for the proposed housing. Many spots were in fact poorly located—too far from public transportation, on difficult terrain for building, and in open space—on the only land available for the UDC to buy. In truth, the UDC had made mistakes, such as not communicating sufficiently with towns before announcing its program and not seeking enough input on housing locations. Logue's characteristic drive to fast-track likely rushed the consultation process. But a more politic rolling out of Fair Share Housing would not likely have made a difference. In the heat of battle, the UDC was willing to adjust the plan, but not to back down, arguing that doing so would only obligate more cooperative towns to bear a greater share of the burden. In the hallways of the UDC offices, bitter talk often turned to how racial and class prejudices were really at the root of the resistance.

Many of Logue's closest confidants urged him to give up the fight. The UDC general counsel Stephen Lefkowitz, who usually wielded great influence with Logue, advised, "There is more than enough to do in the cities."[27] The prominent psychologist Kenneth Clark—a close friend, a UDC board member, and chair of the board's Integration Committee—argued against expending political and monetary capital on Fair Share. "They don't want you . . . Don't go!" Clark urged. He had built his academic reputation on exposing the limited opportunity in urban ghettos and was no fan of segregated communities. Nonetheless, he thought the UDC should keep its attention focused on the cities where black people already lived in great numbers and often under inadequate conditions. Harlem leaders, eager for the UDC's resources, not surprisingly sided with Clark.[28] The UDC architect Tony Pangaro recalled that despite the chorus admonishing Logue that "it may be morally correct, but teaching people like that a lesson doesn't really work very well," Logue was unswayed. "He really, really, really wanted to do it. He thought it was absolutely the right thing."[29]

The controversy escalated. Opponents brought numerous legal suits. They lobbied elected leaders, including Rockefeller. Although the governor shared Logue's enthusiasm for more socially integrated communities; valued the Westchester effort as a way of redirecting the UDC's resources away from New York City, with its current claim on 55 percent of the UDC's housing starts; and had expressed his support not only privately to Logue but also publicly, he became more concerned as the summer of 1972 wore on.[30]

Reactions were only growing more negative, particularly among Republican officeholders up for election in November. It should be noted, however, that two liberal Democrats running for Congress from Westchester districts—Ogden "Brownie" Reid and Richard Ottinger—were no more supportive.[31] Typical was the town supervisor who said, "It would be political suicide for me in an election year to support UDC openly."[32] It is not hard to understand why, when anti-UDC supervisors were issuing such nasty statements as "we have some agonizing liberal supervisors in Westchester County who have seen fit to go to bed with the UDC dog and now they're waking up with fleas."[33] In this maelstrom, Rockefeller decided he had no choice but to act. In August, he declared a moratorium on Fair Share Housing until January 15, 1973, giving the towns time to come up with their own alternative plans.

During the interlude, the nine communities continued to discuss the issue, and by January 1973 six of them had issued "positive responses" acknowledging at least some need for low-income housing. Ever optimistic, Logue took that as a good sign. He said on January 16 that the UDC would welcome more conversations with towns and was willing to negotiate further on housing location and other complaints. But pretty soon it became evident that the whole game had changed and the UDC's ability to carry out its Fair Share Housing plan was being seriously undercut. Almost since its creation, enemies in the New York state legislature had been trying to clip the UDC's wings and deprive it of its override powers. But whenever such a bill made it through the legislature, the governor would veto it. "Rockefeller would always beat back the effort to take this override out of the law," Logue later acknowledged in appreciation. "Which is why I loved him, he stood up for me."[34] In October 1972, some New York state representatives had even tried to push a bill through Congress to deny federal funding to any project lacking local community approval, until the House's recess put an end to debate.[35]

Now, in the wake of the tsunami of hostility created by the Nine Towns plan, opposition to the UDC's override grew overwhelming. In June 1973, Rockefeller saw no alternative but to sign a new bill curtailing the UDC's power to override local zoning in New York State's villages and towns, while keeping it in its cities. But he offered Logue a deal as compensation: an additional $3 million appropriation to cover the costs of closing down the project and an increase from $1.5 to $2 billion in bonding authority. Logue didn't blame Rockefeller. "Rockefeller was the last guy to leave that sinking ship, the last guy. And he saw that I got bailed out."[36]

Logue was not happy to have lost the battle against exclusionary zoning in the suburbs. *The Boston Globe*'s Marty Nolan, now the chief of the paper's Washington bureau who had watched Logue successfully manage similar uproars in Boston, called it "a stinging defeat."[37] Indeed, once given permission to ignore the UDC, all nine towns retreated from considering subsidized housing. And the removal of the UDC's override powers had a domino effect in the state. It brought an unhappy resolution, for example, to a long-standing battle on Long Island over building subsidized housing in the unincorporated hamlet of Wyandanch, with its overwhelmingly poor, African American population of fifteen thousand, 68 percent of whom were on public assistance in 1969. The community had begun lobbying the UDC in 1970 to construct urgently needed new housing. By June 1972, designs—by a black architect—were completed for twenty-nine clustered, two-story garden-apartment buildings with 182 units to serve low- and moderate-income tenants. After the state took away the UDC's override, more than a thousand Wyandanch residents turned out for a rally and signed a petition urging continued support for the UDC housing, only to watch the Babylon Town Board, which had legal jurisdiction over Wyandanch, reject it two months later, on the suspect basis of its "adverse impact" on the community's high water table. "The blacks all supported it, 150 percent," Logue fumed, "and the goddamn white bigots killed it."[38]

Logue took some solace in the settlement Rockefeller proffered, appreciating the new resources at his disposal. The whole episode, moreover, entered the UDC's canon of macabre humor when staff members created a satirical book for Logue titled "The Story of 'The Suburban Destruction Corporation' (SDC): E. J. Rogue, President, and the Warm and Wonderful World of Westchester." Large pages featured collages of headlines and illustrations cut out of newspapers and magazines along with text deriding the disaster.

One page carried the headline "Dissatisfaction Guaranteed or Your Zoning Back." Another showed a photo of a large group of men, women, and children in colonial costumes with the caption "Speaking on behalf of the Bedford Historical Society, Mr. Rogue, we have carefully considered your nine towns program, we have considered the alternatives, we have polled our people and it is our collective opinion that you should respectively stick the whole thing up your ass."[39]

The Nine Towns controversy raised some of the same questions that had troubled Logue since his earliest days doing urban renewal in New Haven: Who's in charge, who should have a say, who benefits, and who pays the bill? Once again, Logue found himself contemplating what a democratic process in planning decisions—his much-touted "planning with people"—should really mean. Already skeptical about letting what he considered excessive participatory democracy overshadow professional expertise, his Nine Towns experience only discouraged him further. He wondered anew what form of community consultation might make more possible the kind of social change he judged to be legal and moral.

Logue was not alone in this rumination. Even progressive critics of top-down planning struggled with the conflict between valuing grassroots democratic participation and breaking the seemingly intractable hold of racial segregation. Paul Davidoff, the chief theorist of "advocacy planning" (a movement committed to giving communities, particularly their low-income and minority members, a greater voice), had established the Suburban Action Institute in White Plains, the county seat of Westchester, in 1969. As its executive director, he vigorously battled exclusionary zoning in the courts, his greatest victory in later years being the Mount Laurel decision of the New Jersey Supreme Court requiring all towns to build low- and moderate-income housing. Davidoff applauded the UDC's efforts in Westchester and followed its struggle closely, convinced that the greater good was being served.[40]

In contrast, an eighty-four-year-old, increasingly reactionary Robert Moses, who appeared in Northern Westchester in the midst of the crisis to receive a distinguished service award from a conservative arts organization, took the opposite view, ironically—given his own past insistence on top-down control—siding with the people against the big planner. He accused Logue of trying "to force projects into the suburbs . . . No wonder local people are embittered." And he urged the residents of Northern Westchester to "go slow," "acquire more parkland," and if necessary "consider [yourselves] a separate county."[41] When it came to Fair Share Housing, Davidoff and Moses endorsed the strategy most consistent with their attitudes toward civil rights, not the mode of decision-making that they had promoted throughout their careers.

As the difficult year of 1973 came to a close, Logue fought to contain the damage from the Nine Towns setback. There remained much for the UDC still to tackle. Despite the victory scored by the UDC's enemies, Logue had no intention of letting Westchester become his Waterloo.

THE MAKING OF A CRISIS

The Fair Share fiasco would probably not have doomed the UDC were it not for its unfortunate convergence with a number of other problems—only some within the UDC's control. Looking back, it may seem obvious that the Nine Towns defeat marked the beginning of the end for the UDC. But at the start of 1974, no one could know whether this defeat was simply a rough patch in the road or the first steps in a death march. "It may not have ever come to that [end] except for this terrible, perfect storm of horrible events," lamented the UDC staffer Pangaro.[42]

The first winds of the gathering storm had actually hit earlier in the year, just as the UDC was readying to renew its discussions with the Westchester towns when Rockefeller's cooling-off period came to an end on January 15, 1973. A week before, on January 8, the Nixon administration had announced that it was impounding all congressionally appropriated federal funding for housing, regardless of whether projects had already been approved, were under consideration, or had not yet advanced to review. Following his first election in 1968, Nixon had allowed HUD secretary Romney to continue and even expand Johnson-era federal housing programs, biding his time. But now, emboldened by his landslide reelection victory against the Democratic opponent George McGovern two months earlier, Nixon made his move. With

little notice, the White House proclaimed a national moratorium on housing subsidies of all kinds for eighteen months, to last until July 1, 1974, when
Nixon promised a more cohesive housing and community development program that would replace what he felt was the federal government's ineffective and excessive involvement in urban renewal and housing provision.[43]
Although Romney had agreed to stay on as HUD secretary until Nixon's second inauguration in late January, he had submitted his resignation the day
after Nixon's election, deeply opposed to where Nixon's policies were headed
and angrily feeling undercut. Over the next two months, he railed against
the "message to me that all the good we have accomplished is to be undone."
The White House, he complained, was "discriminating against central cities" in a "hard headed, cold hearted indifference to the poor and [with] racial prejudice."[44] With Romney's departure in January 1973, the UDC lost a
friend in a high place.[45]

Nixon's moratorium was the opening salvo in his larger agenda to de-
volve the locus of policymaking from Washington to the states and localities,
a major break with the postwar American welfare state that had developed
gradually from Roosevelt's New Deal and Truman's Fair Deal to Kennedy's
New Frontier and Johnson's Great Society. At every stage, the federal government had expanded its funding and strengthened its control. Whether
Nixon's reorientation was labeled the "New Federalism," revenue-sharing,
or block grants, his administration's intent was to give states, and less so more
Democratic municipalities, greater discretion in spending and weaker oversight from Washington. This approach aimed to appeal to Nixon's growing
number of southern, suburban, and white working-class voters. The White
House also intended for this restructuring to decrease spending on social
programs like housing. Now, "power, funds, and responsibility will flow from
Washington to the States and to the people," Nixon promised. "The high-cost,
no-result boondoggling by the Federal Government must end."[46]

This devolution of authority should not theoretically have penalized a
state-level agency like the UDC. But Nixon's impoundment created a severe,
eighteen-month drought in the dispersal of federal subsidies, and then once
new policies were in place, urban-oriented agencies like the UDC found
themselves beholden to state legislatures dominated by unsympathetic

rural and suburban interests. The constituents of suburban legislators, Logue argued, will always demand "that state aid to local government be maintained intact at whatever the human cost to programs which serve primarily the poor, the powerless, and the minorities."[47] Despite Nixon's assertion that funds would now flow more directly to states and their cities, big-city mayors were quick to recognize a threat, huddling within weeks of the president's announcement at the New York mayor John Lindsay's Gracie Mansion to consolidate their opposition.[48] Logue at first held out a small hope that there might be some way of using Nixon's draconian measure to cut back on Washington's top-down control over local priorities and to increase the dollars going directly to housing subsidy programs. But he concluded, "One thing is entirely certain to us. There is no way to reduce Federal expenditures and still meet America's housing needs. If anything, additional funds will be required."[49]

That was not to be. The replacement legislation, the Housing and Community Development Act of 1974, with its Community Development Block Grant program, amplified the thrust of the State and Local Assistance Act of 1972, which had implemented revenue sharing. Federal spending now was steered away from the nation's major northern cities toward suburban population centers and the new cities of the Sunbelt.[50] In an essay penned in 1976, Logue complained that the "whole new approach of federal assistance . . . called the 'block grant' program" had "purported to minimize red tape" but was raising "serious doubts . . . about the adequacy of federal funding." He pessimistically concluded, "There is little reason to believe that troubled central cities will be able to reverse their present period of decline."[51] A new era had indeed arrived. Federal urban renewal—in existence for twenty-five years since the Housing Act of 1949—had enjoyed a decidedly mixed record, but it had kept federal attention on cities and had served as the lodestar for many careers in urban redevelopment, including Logue's. And now it was effectively ended. Regardless of whether a Republican or a Democrat was president, the federal government would no longer ensure a uniform set of national policies for American cities.

In place of direct federal funding for urban redevelopment and sub-sidized housing, the new approach would channel money further down the command chain, ranging from states to highly localized community development corporations, and depend more on private-market solutions to help needy households. Some programs still worked well, but they were part of a regime change that sought greater decentralization in programs, less redistribution of financial resources, and more decision-making au-thority by local politicians than urban experts. There would be little con-struction of new public-sector housing, reduced attention to racial inequality and poverty through federal programs like Model Cities and Community Action, wider dispersal of spending throughout the nation with less going to major cities, significant fragmentation—at times non-coordination—in urban policy and practice, and a shift in balance from the public to the private sector through rental vouchers and subsidies to developers. If they were aggressively entrepreneurial, the private, nonprofit community de-velopment corporations could secure federal funds, though given their limited, often neighborhood-based scale and scope, their efforts rarely cohered sufficiently to add up to a citywide or even broader metropolitan strategy for combating deep-seated urban problems.[52]

As Logue feared, Nixon's moratorium proved devastating for the UDC. Predicting that only luxury housing would now be built, Logue warned of a "drastic slowdown and cutback in publicly assisted housing," with far-reaching ramifications, including "widespread unemployment in the con-struction industry."[53] Despite the fanfare the UDC had made over its state funding and bond revenue, the agency depended on regular infusions of fed-eral dollars. At least 90 percent of all UDC projects used Section 236 mort-gage subsidies to keep rents affordable, even for middle-income families, while also making use of other federal programs like the New Communi-ties Act. In fact, if the New York state legislature had not already revoked the UDC's override powers, it is very likely that the lack of federal funding would have prevented construction of the controversial Fair Share Housing in sub-urban Westchester anyway.

Frustratingly for Logue, his innovations at the UDC aimed at remedying long-standing flaws in federal urban renewal practices only worsened the impact of the Nixon moratorium. Such inventive strategies as fast-tracking projects before all financing was officially in place and bundling together partly finished projects in general-purpose bonds to spread the risk worked only so long as federal dollars kept flowing in. When Nixon shut off the funding faucet, innumerable housing developments were left high and dry at various stages of incompletion. Uncertainty about future subsidies, moreover, made it impossible to project whether rental revenues would cover costs. "Here I am hanging out half naked," Logue said. "I've got these houses under construction, they'll be bankrupt from the day they open without the subsidy."[54]

Once again, Nelson Rockefeller came to the rescue. "As soon as it happened," Logue recalled, "I called up . . . the Governor's office and said, 'Hey, I've got a problem. You have a problem. And I can't solve it. The Governor's got to solve it.'"[55] Flashing his Republican bona fides, Rockefeller convinced the White House to reinstate funding for UDC projects already in the pipeline. *The New Republic* later estimated that "as a result of a much vaunted full-speed ahead, mode of operation known as 'fast-track' construction, UDC had had 58 projects underway without having gotten formal federal commitments." In the magazine's view, the "UDC would have collapsed had Rockefeller not had enough clout to get John Ehrlichman in the White House and persuade him to waive the moratorium on those projects."[56] Although the immediate crisis was averted, severe damage remained. The UDC was forced to implement a spending freeze and a 10 percent staff cutback.

With the UDC's once-promising future looking bleak, Logue and his team frantically searched for alternative sources of funding.[57] Selling more bonds was one option, except that the moratorium shook investor confidence because, Logue lamented, auditors felt obligated to disclose on offering statements that "we were building on land we didn't own and that our subsidy contracts were not in place."[58] Nonetheless, when several months later Rockefeller offered Logue an extra half a billion dollars of bonding authority after the UDC's loss of override power, he grabbed it to help soften the blow. But more bonding also meant taking on greater debt and dealing more with bankers and investors, who were growing increasingly skeptical about the UDC's prospects.[59] Logue made no secret of his final judgment about the moratorium. Writing in 1974, he blasted the "federal decree" for forcing the UDC into a "year of consolidation" rather than planned expansion, limiting housing starts to less than 3,500 units instead of the 15,000 expected, a pace one-fourth that of 1972.[60] In October 1975, *Architectural Record* found Logue still storming over what he called "the most outrageous piece of public policy I have ever seen."[61]

The UDC's dependence on Rockefeller in coping with the Nixon moratorium crisis explains why the next squall in the perfect storm proved so damaging. In December 1973, Rockefeller announced that he was stepping down as governor, thirteen months before his term was set to expire, and passing the job on to his long-serving lieutenant governor, Malcolm Wilson. Rockefeller had both generous and selfish motives. Wilson had stood loyally by Rockefeller's side for fifteen years, forever the best man and never the groom. As Rockefeller prepared to leave the office of governor, he thought that Wilson's chances of succeeding him would increase with a year as governor under his belt. But Rockefeller was also still chasing his personal dream of becoming president. This would be his last shot. He was now sixty-five years old, and Nixon would not be able to run again in 1976. In search of more national exposure, Rockefeller left office to become chair of the Commission on Critical Choices for Americans, a bipartisan, politically centrist collection of forty-two prominent citizens who committed themselves to studying the national and international problems confronting the United States. Rockefeller handpicked the politicians, academics, and business leaders who served as commission members, including Logue in this elite group; set up shop in his privately owned former governor's office in midtown Manhattan with former staff he convinced to join him; and provided the initial funding to get the operation off the ground.[62] A year later, in December 1974, Rockefeller would move on once again, this time to become Gerald Ford's vice president when a disgraced Richard Nixon stepped down.

Rockefeller's resignation was a huge blow to Logue. Not only was his great defender departing Albany, but Lieutenant Governor Wilson had never been a great fan of the UDC. Rather, he was often a conservative voice in Rockefeller's ear. He had adamantly opposed granting the UDC override powers at its founding ("over my dead body," he initially said), and Logue was convinced that had Wilson—for many years a state legislator from Westchester—been present when he briefed Rockefeller on the Fair Share Housing program, Wilson would have significantly curbed the governor's enthusiasm.[63] John Stainton, who worked with Logue in Boston and New York, understood how crucial powerful political protectors were to Logue's success and, by extension, the devastating impact of their retreat. "Lee, Collins, and Rockefeller all were pretty strong people, and he used their strength to accomplish what he wanted."[64]

The timing could not have been worse for securing alternative funding. Economic conditions were deteriorating in the United States, New York State, and New York City in ways that directly affected the UDC. At the national level, the United States was undergoing a major reorientation from domestic manufacturing to more globalized production and a postindustrial economy built around finance, insurance, and real estate (FIRE) and other service and corporate employment. Eventually prosperity would come to those cities—like New York—that headquartered this new economy. But many American communities would never make the shift, and even those that did underwent a difficult transition during the 1970s. New York City, for example, lost more than five hundred thousand jobs, many in industry, from 1969 to 1976; by mid-1975, the unemployment rate had reached 12 percent. Other, more immediate problems added to the pain of this restructuring, such as a severe stock market crash during 1973 and 1974; the OPEC oil embargo from October 1973 to March 1974, which sent energy costs through the roof; and destabilizing political crises: Vice President Spiro Agnew's resignation in fall 1973 following corruption charges and the Watergate scandal culminating in President Nixon's resignation in August 1974.

Faced with these many pressures, the American economy experienced a period of what became known as "stagflation," a paralyzing combination of low economic growth, high inflation, and stubborn unemployment that made remedies difficult. As investors' confidence flagged and interest rates climbed perniciously, cities and states—and entities such as the UDC—struggled to sell the bonds that they needed to survive. New York State and especially New York City neared bankruptcy as public spending continued at levels that rising costs and declining tax revenues could no longer support.[65]

Not alone in encountering these financial difficulties, the UDC nonetheless suffered greatly. The Section 236 subsidies that it had managed to hold on to had no provision for inflation, depressing their value as expenses rose.[66] Interest rates on UDC bonds shot up from an average of 6.5 percent in the summer of 1974 to 9.37 percent in September, increasing the burden of repaying investors, which, in turn, made investors more wary of buying. That soaring interest rate reflected not only the troubled economic times but also the fact that many bankers considered the UDC an especially risky investment. Some of that distrust went back to the UDC's origins as a public benefit organization expected to self-finance through moral obligation bonds, without the state's full legal backing. Its general-purpose rather than project-specific bonds, furthermore, made close tracking of revenues and expenditures difficult.[67] Rockefeller's ironclad support for the UDC had gone a long way toward reassuring investors—until 1974, when Rockefeller was no longer governor and money had grown even tighter. Then, all the concerns that had been long smoldering erupted, including complaints about laxness in the UDC's accounting and Logue's single-minded determination to keep building regardless of calls for caution. At base, bankers bristled at what they considered Logue's arrogant refusal to acknowledge that he was running a for-profit operation with investors' money, behaving instead as if the bond market should bankroll a state social welfare program.

By March 1974, the crisis had taken on new urgency.[68] Morgan Guaranty Trust Company, the lead underwriter for the consortium of banks that had promoted UDC bonds enthusiastically for years, refused to sponsor any more sales unless the UDC curtailed future projects and agreed simply to finish what it had started. The withdrawal signaled a damaging lack of confidence in the UDC. Morgan and other banks had long enjoyed robust profits from municipal and state bond sales—as underwriters collecting generous fees and as investors benefiting from high-interest returns and tax exemptions—but they now balked at their exposure from public securities deemed too risky, like the UDC's.

Then, later in the spring, New York, following the lead of neighboring New Jersey, repealed the 1962 bond covenant Rockefeller had made with the Port Authority of New York and New Jersey and its bondholders to never burden them with supporting deficit-heavy mass transit. That reversal not only threatened the Port Authority's reserves earned from lucrative airports, tunnels, and bridges, but convinced bankers that they now had irrefutable proof of the worthlessness of New York State's promises. Doubt deepened that the state would ever live up to its moral obligation to back the bonds of public benefit organizations like the UDC, a debt that was now more than $6 billion for the state's sixteen public authorities. In Logue's telling, "Wall Street was outraged" and was determined "to find some way of teaching the state a lesson and testing this moral obligation." Alarmed by the "avalanche of hostility" from the investment community, Logue thought with trepidation, "I have a feeling which agency is going to be the guinea pig."[69]

That summer, Chase Manhattan Bank CEO David Rockefeller, anxious to keep his brother Nelson's prized UDC viable, rallied fellow bankers to commit to supporting the UDC, at least in the short term. But increasingly, bankers expressed an unwillingness to lend to the UDC and echoed Morgan Guaranty's demand that Logue complete projects already under way and take on no more. Logue refused, insisting that the UDC's finances were sound, that every day more UDC revenue-producing projects were being completed, and that the agency was unfairly being made into a whipping boy by bankers out to score a point with the state. Instead, faced with operating expenses of $1 million a day, Logue anxiously cast about for other remedies, such as transferring some incomplete UDC projects to the state's more solvent Housing Finance Authority (the effort failed), raising the rents on completed developments to generate more revenue (he did so regretfully), and urging the passage of legislation mandating that huge pension funds invest in the state's obligations to buy some independence from the money markets (it never happened, though months later, New York City would be bailed out by unions doing just that). Logue also pleaded for a bailout from the state legislature, but after the Westchester Nine Towns defeat, his friends in Albany were few.[70]

Governor Wilson, confronted with a distressing stalemate and bankers' calls to fire Logue (which he had promised Rockefeller he would never do), finally won a UDC concession not to commit to any new projects without his approval and appointed a six-person task force to make recommendations about the UDC's future, with the goal of strengthening the financial community's support for the UDC. Wilson timed the task force report to come out after the November 1974 gubernatorial election, to highlight his vigilance without revealing any negative findings that might damage his candidacy.[71] Wilson's careful scheming hardly mattered. On November 5, Wilson was soundly defeated by the Democrat Hugh Carey, a longtime Brooklyn congressman who carried 58 percent of the vote in this first post-Watergate election.

After the election, Governor Carey became increasingly aware that he had inherited a state in deep financial trouble. At first, he reassured Logue that he backed the UDC. But within weeks he changed his mind, joining those who fingered the UDC as the agency most guilty of irresponsible financial practices and thus most deserving of public punishment. In his inaugural State of the State address on January 9, 1975, Carey set the stage by declaring, "This government and we as a people have been living far beyond our means," and went on to promise that "the times of plenty, the days of wine and roses, are over."[72] He then proceeded to castigate the UDC for running out of money and barreling toward a catastrophic default on maturing notes and loans in late February, going so far as to call for "an immediate change in the top management of UDC." Less than a month later, right around Logue's fifty-fourth birthday, Carey officially requested his resignation. For years Logue had proudly argued against civil service protection for himself or any of his staff, insisting that all should serve at the pleasure of an elected boss. For the first time ever, he and his closest colleagues would personally pay the price for his principles.

Logue felt angry and betrayed at his dismissal, convinced that he and the UDC had been scapegoated for problems that went far beyond their control.[73] In a farewell letter to the UDC staff, Logue minced few words about where he placed the blame. After thanking them for their "competence, integrity and dedication," he shared his judgment "about the real cause of UDC's crisis." Not misconduct. Nor fiscal irresponsibility. Rather, Nixon's mismanagement of the economy, leading to stagflation, compounded the "the reluctance of the major New York banks to make a continuing commitment to social housing . . . for low and moderate income families in the communities where such families tend to live."[74] With no bailout on offer from the banks or the state legislature, on February 25—another "Black Tuesday" like the stock market crash of 1929—the UDC indeed defaulted on $105 million in short-term notes and two days later on $30 million worth of loans. In what *Time* magazine called "one of the biggest defaults by a public agency since the 1930s," the UDC's credit was destroyed, eighty-five projects remained unfinished, and what was already a dire financial situation in New York now looked even worse, as the UDC's default signaled more trouble for a nearly insolvent New York City and a financially fragile New York State.[75] During the months ahead, the five-hundred-strong UDC staff would steadily shrink—"well-informed heads rolling every which-way," one dismayed observer lamented—with only those deemed essential for completing projects kept on. Ted Liebman and Robert Litke were among the last of the old guard to leave, charged as they were with finishing the first phase of Roosevelt Island.[76]

Parsing blame for the UDC debacle preoccupied its staff and supporters for months, if not years. Immediately, the agency's leaders wrote a spirited defense of the UDC, titled a "Preliminary Memorandum on Behalf of Certain Officers, Former Officers and Directors of the Urban Development Corporation," which denied any "fiscal irresponsibility and mismanagement." Instead, it put the blame on external factors such as fallout from the nation's inflationary financial environment, the city and state debt crisis, the erosion of confidence in moral obligation bonds, and the uncertainties surrounding the gubernatorial election year.[77] In some ways, Logue would never get over losing the UDC presidency. The defeat became even tougher to take when Governor Carey put at the UDC's helm as unpaid chair of the board Logue's old foe Richard Ravitch, the forty-one-year-old construction executive whom Logue had fired for challenging his vision for Roosevelt Island.[78]

Over time and in close collaboration with Governor Carey, Ravitch would secure the hundreds of millions of dollars from the state and the banks needed to finish major UDC projects—to be channeled through a new agency, the New York Project Finance Agency—but not without continued difficulty. Ravitch inherited a challenging situation, to say the least, and worked hard to salvage it. At one point that winter, he would in fact echo Logue by complaining with exasperation to state legislators, "The banks of New York have closed their doors to the people of New York."[79] Nonetheless, Logue and his many loyalists would always believe that Ravitch had savored gaining, perhaps even sought out, Carey's ear in vengeful payback for being dismissed by Logue. His goal, Logue was convinced, was "to embarrass me personally as deeply as possible."

Ravitch's version was that Carey reached out to him in January 1975 for help with the UDC's looming bankruptcy, after being besieged by indignant bankers worried that the UDC was putting the city's and state's access to credit at risk.[80] Ravitch's memory of their tangling over Roosevelt Island also differed from Logue's, but in a way that suggests he might have harbored even deeper anger that motivated him to help Carey. As Ravitch told it, rather than being recruited by Adam Yarmolinsky and fired by Logue, he had been enlisted from the start by Logue, who offered the Ravitch family's HRH Construction a $3 million contract (equivalent to almost $20 million today) to become "the agent and overseer of Roosevelt Island's development," supervising construction of the island's public infrastructure of roads and utilities and managing the residential projects.

Ravitch at first embraced Logue's proposition enthusiastically, as it arrived at a particularly difficult time financially for the firm. But once Ravitch dug more deeply into the numbers, he later claimed, he became worried that the UDC's projections of its operating costs were understated and its revenues overstated to the extent that they "likely would not cover the estimated interest and principal in the bonds financing the project." That anxiety may very well have propelled Ravitch to recommend prioritizing the building of market-rate over subsidized housing, which had so angered Logue. To protect HRH, Ravitch requested a clause in the contract "stating explicitly that HRH was making no representations about the economic success of the project." Logue, insulted at Ravitch's lack of confidence in the UDC, refused and angrily withdrew his offer. According to Ravitch, few at the UDC or HRH knew about Logue's making and rescinding this proposal.

Logue may have linked Ravitch's firing instead to his lack of sympathy with the fundamental social goals of the Roosevelt Island project, but the Logue team's suspicions that Ravitch sought to malign the UDC in fact proved not far off the mark. Ravitch admitted that soon after his dismissal by Logue several years earlier, he had shared with the Chase Manhattan Bank CEO David Rockefeller his dire prediction that the "UDC was headed for financial catastrophe," because it "would have trouble meeting the debt service obligation of its bonds."

Whether driven by personal animus or political and financial calculus, Ravitch insisted that Carey convene a Moreland Act Commission to thoroughly investigate—and make recommendations about the future of—the UDC before he would agree to take its reins, to spare him the uncomfortable necessity, he argued, of suing Logue and others for malfeasance.[81] New York State's Moreland Act of 1907 was a product of Progressive Era reform. It authorized the creation of powerful blue-ribbon commissions to review any state agency suspected of wrongdoing and to propose legislative reforms where needed. A month before announcing a Moreland Act Commission for the UDC, for example, Governor Carey had called for another one to inquire into New York State's notoriously shady nursing home industry, long plagued by allegations of fraud and political corruption. The UDC's Moreland Act Commission was chaired by the prominent New York attorney Orville H. Schell, Jr., well known to be liberally minded and a recent president of the New York City Bar Association, whose headquarters on West 44th Street hosted the public hearings.[82] The commission did its work between February 1975 and March 1976. Armed with a staff of thirty lawyers, accountants, and housing specialists, it interviewed at least a hundred witnesses and examined more than five hundred thousand documents, issuing a lengthy final report on March 31, 1976, titled *Restoring Credit and Confidence: A Reform Program for New York State and Its Public Authorities*. This report, combined with the UDC staff's defense of the agency's record and extensive coverage by a battalion of journalists who recognized the significance of the UDC's collapse, illuminates what went right and wrong in the short but ambitious career of the New York State Urban Development Corporation.[83]

MORELAND ACT HEARINGS

The Moreland Act Commission investigation proved an extremely trying time for Logue. He and his loyal assistant Janet Murphy holed up with Logue's extensive files in the historic Blackwell House on Roosevelt Island to prepare his case. Poignantly, Logue's pet UDC project was now providing a safe haven from which to mount his defense against an aggressive team of commission lawyers headed by Chief Counsel Sheldon H. Elsen, who had made it clear that he intended the proceedings to last a year and to require testimony from prominent witnesses, including former governors Rockefeller and Wilson and former attorney general John Mitchell, promulgator of the moral obligation bond concept. Logue knew to expect an inquisition of sorts—he was convinced Elsen's goal was "to put me in jail." (Whether or not Ravitch meant to go this far, he did acknowledge "spending a lot of time with Shelly Elsen, . . . educating him.") It was thus welcome news to get a call from Edward Costikyan, a politically well-connected senior litigating partner in the prominent firm of Paul, Weiss, Rifkind, Wharton & Garrison, offering pro bono legal services. According to Margaret Logue, he was a "big gun," who was a "sweet guy, but not in court."[84]

During its thirteen months of deliberations, the Moreland Act Commission on the UDC regularly made the headlines, with the question of Ed Logue's personal culpability always front and center. The onetime staffer

Pangaro concluded that "because he had made it [the UDC] such a crusade, the attacks were directed at Ed personally, rather than the agency." Logue's sister, Ellen, recalled that normally tough Ed was under a strain so great that he secretly threw up every day he testified. The press more often described his public demeanor as alternately "feisty" and "angry," such as when—in vintage Logue combative style—he charged that "Morgan Guaranty wants the freedom to fatten off America but not share in the solution to its problems."[85]

Logue and the UDC's greatest vulnerability going into the Moreland hearings was whether there had been outright financial fraud or simply poor fiscal management and reporting. In the end, the commission concluded that charges of corruption were groundless. The most that the UDC administration could be faulted for was accounting sloppiness and indulging its ambition to build over its responsibility to its investors.[86] For Logue, neither a numbers man nor deeply knowledgeable about the bond business, addressing the great need for housing had justified any number of finance sins, or at least poor practices. These included making commitments that exceeded the UDC's debt ceiling and then borrowing to meet these obligations at such a slow pace that the interest the UDC had to pay to finance them surpassed that of the mortgages issued.[87] When the first UDC treasurer, Robert Moss, originally recommended by Rockefeller, expressed concerns over exceeding the debt ceiling, Logue dismissed them in a memo introduced into evidence at the Moreland hearings: "We are going to build as much as we can. The need is there now. When, having prudently managed our affairs, we have gone as far as we can go, and we can't borrow any more, that is another day . . . We will of course be making our best judgments . . . in other words, that's my problem."[88] John Stainton recalled Logue's frequent use of the expression "It's a fail-smash system," in place of "fail-safe," meaning, "I'm going to go for broke and as hard as I can because time is short and you want to accomplish as much as you can." Even when Frank Kristof, the UDC housing economist who was affectionately nicknamed "Dr. No," warned Logue about potential problems, Stainton remembered, "Ed found some of it [his advice] useful, but he didn't necessarily follow it."[89] Eventually as criticism of the UDC's bookkeeping mounted, Logue fired the treasurer Moss, in whom he had lost all confidence, replacing him with Robert Adelman, who most everyone, including Logue, agreed did a much better job balancing the UDC's mission with good accounting practices. Years later, the UDC staffer Litke was still defending the trade-off the agency had made: "Had he been more concerned about the financial structure, we would not have built half of what we built. Which is better? . . . Thirty-three thousand housing units in six years—how can you best that?"[90]

The Moreland Commission focused much of its attention on the structural problems behind the UDC's crash and then recommended remedies applicable to many other state authorities also caught between "the social needs of the state and the state's ability to pay for them," in Chairman Schell's words. Most fundamentally, the commission judged the moral obligation bonds, of which the UDC had sold $1.1 billion through early 1975, an imperfect concept that should be abandoned, even as it appreciated that Governor Rockefeller had sought to sidestep the difficult-to-pass referenda required to build affordable housing with regular state bonds. The commission concluded that both sides were too quick to make assumptions: the state that it would never have to back moral obligation bonds, and bankers that they could depend on the state fulfilling its commitment.[91] In place of moral obligation bonds, the Moreland report called for a two-thirds vote of the state legislature to set the debt ceiling for all public authorities, a recommendation Logue applauded as a more reasonable approach than a ballot referendum.[92]

Likewise, the commission acknowledged the benefits of the UDC's spread-the-risk general-purpose bond strategy for such a broad and diverse project portfolio, but it criticized management's lack of self-discipline in monitoring these bond packages. This weak internal vigilance was aggravated by lax oversight by the UDC's board, the commission determined. Career banker George Woods, Rockefeller's choice for UDC board chair, should have served as more of a watchdog, but as the UDC general counsel Stephen Lefkowitz explained, he was not a "day-to-day guy."[93] The most deserving of blame in the eyes of the commission was the Rockefeller-era state government—the executive, legislature, and controller—for inadequately supervising the UDC's financial operation: too much partnership, not enough control, particularly from the governor himself. Instead, explained Schell to Governor Carey as he presented the report, "They were like boys playing on a beach, building sand castles with their backs to the tide."[94] The report, therefore, called for an effective public authorities control commission to oversee all such state entities, as other authorities were judged to be insufficiently monitored as well, and to report regularly to the legislature and the public.

The Moreland Commission insightfully recognized that some of the UDC's efforts to improve on past flaws in urban renewal had actually worsened its financial situation. Fast-tracking to complete projects more quickly, to control inflation, and to minimize red tape had significantly shortened the building process from seven years down to eighteen months, but it had also left the UDC in a lurch after Nixon's moratorium and had sometimes led to higher costs due to less-open contract bidding and late modifications.[95] Similarly, Logue's efforts to avoid the often complex and time-consuming coordination among multiple parties by consolidating the responsibilities of developer, lender, borrower, and builder in the UDC often deprived the agency of normal checks, such as lender scrutiny and the help of partners if trouble struck. In other words, by styling itself as a one-stop superagency that did it all, the UDC was stuck holding the bag alone.[96]

Another well-intended innovation that created problems for the UDC was the prioritizing of good design. Intended to improve on the mediocre architecture of much urban renewal, it often made projects more expensive than the funding available, even if architecture critics like Paul Goldberger of *The New York Times* praised how "The UDC's Architecture Has Raised Public Standard," according to a headline published at the height of the crisis.[97] Many UDC opponents, including the more cautious Housing Finance Agency, argued that Logue had gone overboard in hiring ambitious architects and investing in expensive experiments like the low-rise, high-density Marcus Garvey project. Ravitch went so far as to suggest that the UDC might even have survived had it "scaled back" its architectural ambitions and relied less on "fancy schmancy architects."[98]

The UDC's embrace of technological innovation was similarly blamed for budgetary overreach. One frequently cited misjudgment involved the UDC's eager acceptance of Con Edison's proposal to install electrical heating with bulk metering on Roosevelt Island. Promoted as a clean, efficient, and comfortable source of heat that could be controlled building-wide, it promised savings in construction costs equivalent to a capital subsidy of between $1,000 and $2,000 a unit. But when the energy crisis of 1973–74 hit, not only did electric bills skyrocket, but bulk metering left the UDC footing the bill.[99] Likewise, Logue's preference for building on open land to avoid the dislocations that had so tarnished urban renewal's reputation also came in for criticism, as the Moreland Commission urged more attention to the preservation and rehabilitation of existing housing.[100]

The commission concluded that significant though these vulnerabilities were, the UDC's downfall could be attributed mostly to one underlying contradiction: between its social mandate to build for low- and moderate-income tenants and its fiscal mandate to do so at no cost to taxpayers. Project budgets simply could not be kept to a level that the UDC could sustain with the financial resources at its disposal or generated through rents, if they were to be kept affordable.[101] The UDC's sister agency in New York, the Housing Finance Agency, and most housing agencies in other states avoided this conundrum by focusing on middle-class housing. The Council of State Housing Agencies, for instance, reported that more than two-thirds of construction carried out by its member agencies provided for middle- and moderate-income families in suburban locations.[102] The UDC's focus on lower-income clients usually living in urban settings led to riskier projects with higher construction and operating costs, whether for enhanced security, as at the Bronx's Twin Parks, or for amenities that created viable communities in low-resourced areas. Day care and senior centers, schools, community rooms, convenience stores, and other examples of what one New York housing official called "social stuff" were not revenue-producing and thus necessitated subsidies. Responding to criticism of the UDC's record of favoring these features in its projects, John Burnett, the UDC's general manager under Logue, said, "Is it risky to take care of daycare and schools and shops—things which enhance the attractiveness and livability of residential projects? . . . We would have been adding to the margin of risk by *not* taking care to try to make our projects well-rounded, inviting and, of course, rentable by being worthy of the people we were created to serve."[103]

The mismatch between the UDC's social ambitions and its available funding was intensified by Logue's strong conviction that the public good outweighed his responsibilities to private investors if and when they challenged his agency's work. Many observers, including Ravitch, severely criticized Logue's failure to adequately consider the concerns and cultivate the confidence of his investors. But although Logue had embraced the concept of a public-private partnership at the UDC's founding, he resisted the notion that private interests seeking a return on investment should have the right to override the UDC's social mission. "We cannot allow basic public policy of this importance to be made in corporate board rooms and issued to public men by fiat," he insisted.[104] Private investors, he was convinced, were improperly thwarting the foundational social goals underpinning the UDC. "It was too good to last, and that's why I so cordially dislike bankers . . . They feel threatened . . . I was engaged in—bankers said this—social engineering. As if that's a mortal sin. I was very proud of the fact that Roosevelt Island was a total piece of social engineering."[105]

In his own time, Logue expressed an interpretation that some analysts of New York's broader fiscal crisis of the 1970s have elaborated in the years since. They argue that municipal financiers had a more ambitious agenda than simply bringing New York back from the brink of what was undeniably a looming fiscal catastrophe that threatened to bankrupt the largest American city and wreak damage far beyond its borders. Rather, this analysis goes, they used the leverage of their lending and bonding powers to force New York City and New York State to radically reorient themselves from liberal, social democratic public policies to more neoliberal ones. In demanding an austerity budget that scaled back labor union commitments and social welfare services, including the UDC's ambitious housing program, banking and business leaders sought to fundamentally restructure the behavior of elected officials and the expectations of the public about what government could and should deliver. As the CEO of the New York Telephone Company bluntly put it, "To balance the budget, to restore the confidence of the financial community whose resources we need in order to survive, to guarantee the survival of New York City there is an urgent need to alter the traditional view of what city government can and should do. What is required is a fundamental rethinking of the level and quality of services the city provides its citizens."[106] While critics like this one on the Right sought to roll back the public sector altogether, critics on the Left often urged a shifting of costs from the local to the federal government, arguing that Washington was more capable of raising revenue and carrying debt. But the call for government retrenchment at any level in the wake of fiscal crisis was patently rejected by Ed Logue.

A FLAWED CONCEPT?

In identifying a fundamental flaw in the UDC's conception, the Moreland Commission asked in its final report whether a public responsibility could *ever* be discharged by an entity that was funded by private investors whose goal was to make a profit. As the UDC collapse and its postmortem unfolded over many months in 1975, other analysts would chime in with similar doubts, most forcefully articulated by the journalist Joseph Fried. Writing in *The Nation* magazine, Fried claimed that the "fundamental issue raised by the plight of the Urban Development Corporation . . . goes to the heart of the fact—which this country still does not acknowledge—that only a long-range, public effort will make possible the construction and rehabilitation needed if 10 million or more American families are to live in decent housing and decent neighborhoods." Condemning the UDC's funding model, he insisted that the "skittish and volatile" private investment market "can hardly be expected to have the staying power to underwrite a task as difficult" as this one. "Rather," he asserted, "the job must be done by American society generally, and that means sufficient public funds for subsidized housing and redevelopment programs to begin with, as well as a willingness by government to take the ultimate risk when it does seek to draw private capital into the effort." Fried concluded somberly that the fall of the UDC is "testimony to how far we have come from those days in the 1960s when the flames of urban riots crackled in squalid slums" and inspired public officials as well as business leaders to tackle the urban crisis. It should serve as a "harsh and vivid reminder that American society is still a long way from meeting a moral obligation of its own."[107]

As Fried intimated, a lot of wishful thinking had lain behind the UDC, from Rockefeller's initial search for an easily fundable way to build subsidized housing, revitalize cities, and create new jobs to bankers' overconfidence that UDC projects could surely generate sufficient revenues to cover operating expenses and debt service on outstanding bonds. Logue, too, had optimistically signed on, eager to find new sources of housing finance as the federal budget tightened. But none of these expectations proved feasible. It became apparent that it would take years to create a positive cash flow, if one could even be achieved. The UDC itself projected that its operating and debt-service expenses would exceed income until 1981, and had it kept building new projects, that date would have extended further.[108] Moreover, the financial picture was not helped by the IRS's early ruling that the more lucrative commercial and industrial development called for in the original UDC legislation, which might have generated greater income for the agency, must be limited to only 10 percent of the tax-free bonds.

But should anyone have ever expected the UDC to be self-supporting? John Zuccotti, at various points in his career a New York City public official and a real estate developer but long a UDC champion, argued that any assumption of a natural alignment between the goals of private bankers—whose job it was to make money for depositors and stockholders—and affordable housing production was misguided from the start. The UDC, and the nation, needed some other way to create housing.[109] The UDC chronicler Eleanor Brilliant identified other contradictions. The so-called private market for UDC bonds in fact depended on government, whether it was stated explicitly or not. Tax-exempt bonds were subsidized by the federal government, and the State of New York made the bonds marketable through offering its protection. She also identified a contradiction within the UDC itself, contending that "it was not possible for the UDC to enjoy the benefits of being both a public and a private authority at the same time." If it were intended "to do public good, it would have to move in the direction of a recognized public nature," including "assuming continual public funding . . . along with accountability of its staff."[110] Even Frank Smeal of Morgan Guaranty Trust Company, spokesperson for the disapproving banking consortium, concurred about this incompatibility when asked if banks should have demonstrated more concern for the UDC's mission. He declared in no uncertain terms that "social goals are funded one way in this country and economic goals another way." Smeal further acknowledged that "building where others failed to tread, . . . we now know requires a much firmer state commitment, which can only be given by the people."[111]

Even as recognition of the need for public subsidy for low-income housing grew, the ideal level of government to provide it remained a matter of contention. Brilliant was convinced not only that localities were ill equipped financially but also that "clearly, local level decisions are not necessarily the best since they tend to affirm the status quo at the expense of those outside who want to come in." As the Nine Towns failure showed, "it was not possible to develop a metropolitan view of urban problems at the local level."[112] Nor, despite Rockefeller's best efforts to the contrary, had state-level funding of the UDC proved adequate to provide housing at a cost that low- and moderate-income residents could afford. In truth, federal assistance had always been necessary for the UDC to succeed. Subsidies from Washington were crucial to making the math work, which is why more than 90 percent of UDC projects were federally supported until jeopardized by Nixon's moratorium. In fact, as one analyst put it, the UDC's creators had made a losing gamble in 1968 when they mistook the setting sun for the dawn.[113]

In assessing the UDC for the Ford Foundation, Louis Loewenstein aimed for balance. The UDC suffered an unlucky convergence of many unfortunate events, he acknowledged. And it had made some serious misjudgments, such as expanding in a contracting money market and not distinguishing well enough between abstract housing "need" and real "demand," if that included the ability of low-income tenants to pay. Nonetheless, it could claim significant achievements. It brought an estimated $2.7 billion in federal subsidies in write-downs and payments through Section 236 contracts to New York State, which amounted to well over half the national federal Section 236 awards. It furnished housing for some one hundred thousand people in fifty cities and towns and developed three New Towns. All told, the UDC was responsible for about a quarter of all government-aided housing constructed in New York State from 1969 to 1975, including 40 percent of what was built in upstate New York and New York City's suburbs and 15 percent of New York City's units.[114] It had created many new jobs—through its own construction projects as well as by building new industrial and commercial facilities in the state.

In the heat of the UDC crisis, a *New York Times* op-ed headline reminded readers "It Built Where Nobody Else Would" and urged that the question now should not be "'What is wrong with the U.D.C,' but rather, 'if not the U.D.C. what?'"[115] In a way, even Logue's archenemy Ravitch agreed. Ravitch did not so much reject the UDC's lofty goals as argue that in taking them all on, the agency was trying to accomplish the impossible—subsidized housing, racial integration, great architecture, open space, first-rate education, community involvement—and pay for it by combining inadequate state and private-sector funding with a federal requirement to keep rents affordable. The difference was that Ravitch, a man of business, did not assume that the state or federal governments must step up or that bankers must take more responsibility. Ravitch was a pragmatist who felt that the UDC had no choice but to live within its means, as limited or unfair as they might be, and adjust its ends accordingly. In contrast, Logue—hard-nosed as he often seemed—was actually the idealist, driven by what he felt could and should be.[116]

Logue's bold UDC undertaking to revitalize cities in a new way ultimately went bust. But he could take some solace in what he had managed to build and how colleagues in the urban policy and architecture fields would long applaud the UDC's valiant efforts. Reviewing the UDC debacle in fall 1975 while the Moreland investigation was under way, *Architectural Record* concluded, "In all events, the Urban Development Corporation set fresh solutions and strategies in motion, establishing a benchmark by which other efforts, across the country, will be measured for a long time."[117] Even the

Moreland Commission concluded that the "UDC was led and staffed by creative and highly motivated persons who conceived and built many projects of which the citizens of the State can be proud."[118] And indeed, for decades after 1975, the UDC would remain a touchstone for advocates of building affordable housing and breaking through the suburban zoning barrier, inspiring any number of conferences, exhibitions, and idealistic new efforts to provide all Americans with a decent home.[119]

THE FUTURE FOR THE UDC AND LOGUE

The infamous default and subsequent demise of Logue's UDC, after having been the largest developer of subsidized housing in the country, created shock waves nationwide. Directly affected were the dozens of states that, inspired by the UDC, were funding housing with moral obligation bonds or similar instruments now coming in for closer scrutiny.[120] Logue's projects were eventually finished under Ravitch, who remained the UDC's chair until 1977. Ironically, given that New York taxpayers' lack of support for subsidized housing had inspired the creation of the UDC, they ended up footing the bill, as private investors were repaid in full to preserve the state's credit.[121] Logue's UDC would survive in name only, barred from building any more housing and reconstituted as a more conventional economic development agency for New York State—"a cautiously run real-estate enterprise rather than a daring spearhead for social betterment," in the journalist Fried's brutal assessment—until it even lost the name in 1995 and was relabeled the Empire State Development Corporation.[122]

Ed Logue had his own rocky recovery from the loss of the UDC. Some critics were quick to blame him, taking a cue from Carey and Ravitch. Others were more appreciative. The analyst Brilliant, for example, concluded that "Logue had made enemies for some of the best of reasons. He wanted to develop New Towns for integrated economic and social goals, and he wanted to build housing in the suburbs and in the most troubled inner-city areas. He developed major minority employment programs; and he had upgraded the architectural style of publicly assisted housing, if not always the livability of individual units." She acknowledged, "It might be argued that Logue was too ambitious or too tempestuous in his style," but she insisted that even if Logue "had been the most superlative politician and the most charming of entrepreneurs, it seems doubtful that UDC could have conquered the forces against it."[123] Logue agreed and felt unfairly scapegoated. "I would never want to say that we didn't make any mistakes," he freely admitted, "but the blame that I acquired was somewhat disproportionate, I think."[124] The chorus of criticism and the sullying of his reputation were particularly stinging for a public servant who, his staff all agreed, prided himself on being "an ethical guy . . . and a very careful guy," in the words of the UDC staff assistant Larry Goldman. He was someone, said his longtime friend Penn Kimball, who deeply valued "his reputation for being on the side of right and justice, . . . a powerful man of principles."[125]

Professionally, Logue tried to keep his hand in the urban field that had been his life's work, piecing opportunities together with the help of loyal friends and colleagues. At first he set himself up in Rockefeller's Critical Choices Commission, until he was invited to share offices with his friends Kenneth and Mamie Clark at 60 East 86th Street, where he opened a consulting firm, the Logue Development Company. A typical project enlisted George Raymond and Robert Litke in an assessment for HUD of why some New Towns had failed and what could be done about it.[126] Sympathetic and still-admiring associates also offered him part-time teaching opportunities— at Yale and NYU law schools, Princeton's School of Architecture, and the University of Pennsylvania's City and Regional Planning Program.[127]

Personally it was a dark period. The journalist Fried reported that initially "Logue was bitter and depressed at the way he was expelled from the top ranks of his profession." Once the lion king presiding over "Logue's Lush Lair" and driven around in a chauffeured car, he was now operating out of a modest ground-floor office in a small building surrounded by mementos of better days—awards, citations, aerial photographs, redevelopment maps, and a 3-D model of Roosevelt Island. From his desk he looked out at the tiny backyards of houses on 85th Street rather than sprawling majestic vistas of New York all the way to the Catskills.[128] Drinking that previously had greased the wheels of male sociability and aided unwinding at the end of hard-driving workdays now threatened to become more than that, a fear that his brother Frank had voiced a few years back in an intimate letter. "I don't know what demon makes you treat yourself so badly," Frank had written. "I'm sure it's not negative self-image. You like yourself. You do indeed do important public work and do it surprisingly well. But you won't do it long at the rate at which you are drinking."[129] Longtime associates like Litke and Stainton who stayed in touch with Logue after the UDC debacle worried that his drinking was worsening.[130] With Margaret Logue working at Saint Ann's School, the Logues moved to Brooklyn Heights, leaving behind their posh East End Avenue address for what Ed described to Ted Liebman as "a smaller, less expensive place, . . . not as grand as what we had" but, Ed added, "we like it."[131] For the first time in their marriage, Margaret's job, not Ed's, dictated where they would live.

Through it all, however, Ed kept in mind the negative example of Fred Rodell, his Yale Law School mentor who had let the university's retaliation against his unpopular political stances make him, in Logue's words, "a hater," someone "who blighted his own life terribly, . . . inflicting more damage on himself" than anyone had inflicted on him. Reflecting back on those years, Margaret felt confident that despite the injustice Ed felt, he in fact succeeded in not becoming bitter like Rodell.[132] Nonetheless, in a revealing interview that Logue gave in October 1976 to Jean Joyce, a former colleague from the Indian embassy days who was documenting the career of their common mentor Chester Bowles, Logue interpreted Bowles's defeat for the Connecticut Democratic Senate nomination in 1958 in terms that reflected his own fears. "In '58 he was at the end of the road of personal, political power . . . I've had to go through a lot of this myself, in the last couple of months. This happens, and what does it mean? And even your best friends don't always tell you . . . As far as being a major dominant force, with not only a power base but a place in which to use it—that's when he lost it."[133]

What was next for Ed Logue? At the time of his resignation from the UDC, he was still a relatively young man, in his mid-fifties, with twenty years of intense city-building experience under his belt. But if the future was unknown, one thing was certain: if Logue ever got another chance to do significant work in his chosen field of urban redevelopment, it would be under very different conditions, and not only because of the black mark he bore as a result of the UDC's downfall. Clearly, the end had come to the era of large-scale government programs of which Logue had been a master. While it lasted, the UDC—although far from perfect—had given Logue rare opportunities to experiment with making subsidized housing more plentiful, affordable, and livable; better designed and technologically advanced; further integrated by race, income, age, and physical disability; and built by a more racially integrated workforce. If Logue were to continue to grapple with the still-pressing problems of urban America, particularly the dire need for decent housing, he would have to find some other way.

9. Ashes to Gardens in the South Bronx

E d Logue was making a decent living piecing jobs together, but "I was bored with what I was doing," he admitted as he watched and waited for what might be his next opportunity in urban redevelopment. In an uncanny foreshadowing, during the winter of 1976 he tried using his connections to Vice President Rockefeller to pitch an idea to President Gerald Ford's secretary of Housing and Urban Development, Carla Anderson Hills, and HUD's New York regional administrator, S. William Green. Logue proposed to use Section 8 subsidies and FHA insurance to build extensive low-rise rental housing on vacant land already owned by New York City, particularly in the fast-deteriorating South Bronx. But despite Logue's dogged efforts to sell the idea in Washington and New York, it went nowhere.[1]

The next year, however, fate intervened. When Vernon Jordan, president of the National Urban League, rebuked the new Democratic president, Jimmy Carter, for shirking his responsibilities to American cities, an abashed Carter and his staff secretly planned a visit to the Bronx, the northernmost borough of New York City and one of the most poverty-stricken areas in the United States, while Carter was in town to address the United Nations. On October 5, 1977, the president and his entourage drove through the South Bronx, stopping for a photo opportunity amid the ruins of Charlotte Street. In what became an internationally infamous photograph, a horrified Carter stood, hands in pockets, amid acres of rubble with the haunting shells of abandoned, burned-out apartment buildings looming in the distance. (The site had actually been cleared for a new school that was never built, but the photo became known for portraying a South Bronx so devastated that it resembled bombed-out London or Dresden.) Shocked at the evidence of overwhelming urban poverty and devastation, Carter turned to his HUD secretary, Patricia Harris, and instructed her, "See which areas can still be salvaged . . . Get a map of the whole area and show me what can be done."[2]

New York City officials lost no time taking advantage of the South Bronx's moment of infamy and urged a major White House initiative to address the deteriorated housing, huge unemployment, and multiple other social problems confronting the South Bronx. Soon after Ed Koch took over as mayor from Abraham Beame in January 1978, he gave Deputy Mayor Herman Badillo, a former Bronx borough president and congressman and the most visible Puerto Rican politician in the city, the assignment of preparing a plan. By April, Badillo had formulated an ambitious preliminary $1.5 billion proposal to rehab and build 26,500 units of housing in two- and three-story buildings over seven years. Aimed at a population of 750,000, "it was to be a massive redevelopment project to rebuild . . . the whole South Bronx, and in the process to show how we could rebuild all the slums in this country," Badillo explained. The centerpiece would be a 732-unit low-income housing co-op on Charlotte Street, heavy with symbolism as the site of Carter's visit. At the suggestion of the New York area HUD administrator Alan Wiener and through no lack of lobbying on his own, Logue emerged as Badillo's consultant on the project.[3] In September 1978, Mayor Koch, seeking to win the confidence of the White House for a major investment in the South Bronx, established a South Bronx Development Office with Logue—still working as a consultant—at its helm.[4] The *Washington Post* architecture critic Wolf Von Eckardt wrote that "Logue, try as he will, can hardly contain his excitement over getting back into harness . . . 'The area is bigger than all of New Haven,' he says like a boy bragging about all the gadgets on this new bicycle."[5]

The eighteen months between Carter's Bronx excursion in October 1977 and the rejection of Badillo's plan by the powerful New York City Board of Estimate in February 1979 unfolded as a series of misleading cues and back-pedaling by the White House, grandiose and wishful thinking by some New York officials, and mistrust of the plan and its promoters by other city leaders. By the time the eleven-member Board of Estimate—made up of the mayor's representatives, the city council president Carol Bellamy, the city comptroller Harrison Goldin, and all the borough presidents—finally scuttled the plan in a 7-to-4 vote, the case against it was manifold: fear that it would isolate poor people without the services they needed; well-founded concern that a cautious, cash-strapped White House would never come through with the money; and resentment by other borough presidents over the Bronx getting so many new resources. As the Brooklyn borough president cynically put it, "If President Carter's chauffeur had taken a right turn instead of a left turn on his trip here, we'd have all the money going to Bushwick now."[6]

The council president Bellamy's opposition to the plan—likely at the urging of an apprehensive White House—proved particularly damaging. A furious and disgraced Badillo, convinced that Koch had failed to put his full weight behind the proposal, immediately resigned from the project and, before long, from being deputy mayor, sufficiently embarrassing Mayor Koch that he kept Logue on to signal that something would still happen in the South Bronx. Even if the Carter White House had made it clear that it favored job programs over housing and above all wanted to reduce the price tag, Koch calculated that launching a planning process for revitalizing the

South Bronx would at least buy some time and assuage proponents.[7] Brooded Logue, "So I'm left with a job and this hopeless place of ground, the South Bronx, with no program, nothing for anybody."[8]

But never one to be daunted for long, by April 1979, a year after Badillo's initial unveiling of his billion-dollar Bronx dream, Ed Logue had pieced together a modest budget of $4 million from the Feds, the state, and a half-heartedly committed and still fiscally crippled city (its contribution almost all in-kind—office space and the use of a few official cars) to undertake an eighteen-month comprehensive planning effort.[9] So it was that Logue became director of the South Bronx Development Office (SBDO, renamed in January 1981 as the South Bronx Development Organization, a nonprofit with Logue now president rather than director). The SBDO emerged as an unusual operation that functioned as an administrative unit in the New York City Planning Department but had minimal authority, few development tools like the power of eminent domain, and little dependable funding. All it had for its mission to improve the South Bronx was a "hunting license," according to Logue, and a leader eager to redeem himself because, said Logue, "I'm not going to let that son-of-a-bitch Hugh Carey write the last chapter in my public life."[10]

Thus began the fourth and last major chapter of Ed Logue's career in urban redevelopment. After remaking New Haven and Boston in the heyday of federal urban renewal and leading the New York Urban Development Corporation in a groundbreaking but ultimately imperfect experiment in public-private and federal-state collaboration, Logue was now taking on the South Bronx at the dawn of a new era of small-scale, neighborhood-oriented, market-based urban interventions. After Nixon had effectively killed federal urban renewal, Carter's Urban Development Action Grant (UDAG) program aimed to incentivize private investment. His successor, Ronald Reagan, went even further in promoting private-sector solutions to cities' problems.

In the South Bronx, Logue would face the worst urban devastation of anywhere he had worked, with fewer resources than he had ever before had at his disposal. "In retrospect, it makes the challenges I faced years ago with Dick Lee in New Haven and John Collins in Boston seem very modest indeed!" Logue was the first to admit.[11] Once having prided himself on being an effective rebel in the belly of the establishment beast—whether fighting to reform tradition-bound Yale University or lobbying in Washington to improve HUD policies—he now had to content himself with being a pesky fly on the back of a hostile establishment. But ironically, it would also be here, with much less support from those in power in the city, the state, or the nation, and in a South Bronx hobbled by impoverishment, arson, and population loss, where he would come closest to fulfilling his long-touted but at times empty promise of "planning with people." This once-powerful pluralist Democrat who previously had consulted with handpicked representatives of organized interests would now, by necessity, work closely with grassroots groups, collaborating with the kind of participatory democrats with whom he had previously jousted. When Logue brought this last major stage of his career to an end in 1985, he would leave behind a scorecard of gains and losses that would prove complex to tally.

THE SOUTH BRONX, CAULDRON OF URBAN ILLS

It was no accident that Jimmy Carter's White House staff picked the South Bronx for the president's public display of concern for urban poverty in fall 1977. It won the contest hands down. The 1980 census would identify these twenty square miles, with more than six hundred thousand residents, as the poorest area in the nation.[12] The Bronx had undergone rapid growth in the 1920s, with the northern expansion of the city's subways, to become an attractive residential area for working-class white ethnics—the Irish as well as more recent Jewish and Italian immigrants making a leap out of the ghetto—and middle-class families in search of larger, more affordable apartments like those on the Grand Concourse. But after World War II, a combination of factors conspired to propel the Bronx toward a dramatic descent. More than its fair share of low-income public housing projects were located here. The redlining of heavily ethnic neighborhoods discouraged investment in what had been—and often still were—blocks of decent six-story brick apartment houses. Cheap mortgages through the GI Bill and the Federal

Housing Administration made homes in the suburbs an attractive option for white, upwardly mobile returning veterans, particularly when there were relatively few opportunities for homeownership in the rental-dominated Bronx. And the development from 1966 to 1973 of Co-op City—the largest cooperative residential community in the world, with more than fifteen thousand units in thirty-five high-rise towers—lured lower-middle-class residents away from their old Bronx neighborhoods to a new, state-subsidized, affordable alternative nearby in the far northeastern reaches of the borough. The ultimate blow was the construction of Robert Moses's Cross Bronx Expressway—the first American highway built in a crowded urban environment. It slashed through viable Bronx neighborhoods, displacing sixty thousand residents and depressing the value of the remaining homes nearby.[13]

As property values plummeted and, landlords claimed, rent control constrained their profits, building owners often found insurance payments more lucrative than rents, leading to an epidemic of arson. The journalist Bill Moyers laid out the brutal truth: you could buy a large occupied apartment house in the Bronx for less than $1,000, take advantage of the city's three-year tax moratorium while collecting several thousand dollars a month in rents, provide minimal heat and services, and when enough tenants gave up in disgust, you could buy a first-class arson job for $200 and collect on the federally subsidized fire insurance to walk away with $70,000 to $80,000.[14] In the 1970s, the Bronx averaged twelve thousand arson fires a year, over thirty a day, making the local New York Fire Department Engine Company No. 82 the busiest by far in the city. *The New York Times* even ran a daily box, what came to be called the "Ruins Section," to record the latest fire tally.[15]

This dramatic decline in the South Bronx made it an affordable if greatly troubled destination for low-income newcomers to New York City, particularly African Americans from the South and Puerto Ricans, contributing to a major racial transition in the borough. As in so many other places, they arrived just as factories that once had provided good working-class jobs moved out. With gainful employment scarce, poverty grew, bringing all the usual attendant social problems of landlord disinvestment, poor city services and retail options, drug dealing, crime, failing schools, huge unemployment, high rates of infant mortality, and somewhere between a third and 40 percent of residents requiring welfare assistance. This downward spiral sent long-standing inhabitants fleeing, resulting in the Bronx losing 40 percent of its population between 1970 and 1980 alone, as entire blocks emptied out.[16] When the ABC sportscaster Howard Cosell famously interrupted his reporting of game two of the October 1977 World Series in Yankee Stadium to exclaim that the Bronx was burning, he was only confirming to a national audience what local observers had noted with alarm for a long time and what a week earlier Jimmy Carter had seen for himself.

The deteriorating conditions of the South Bronx had not escaped city officials, but they had made little progress addressing them. Mayor Beame's housing and development administrator, Roger Starr, and the investment banker Felix Rohatyn, who was leading the fiscal rescue of New York City as chair of the Municipal Assistance Corporation, went so far as to seriously float the idea of "planned shrinkage," by which they meant focusing resources on areas of strength in the city and abandoning others they deemed hopeless, their top candidate being the South Bronx. It was in fact Starr's and Rohatyn's "callous disregard for human lives" that had outraged Badillo and spurred him to propose such an ambitious housing plan to rebuild the South Bronx.[17] Soon after assuming office, the Koch administration would take a different—albeit equally infuriating to some Bronx residents—tack. In a notorious effort to distract from the borough's decline, the city put decals of curtained windows with flower pots and other signs of domestic stability on abandoned buildings visible from major highways crisscrossing the Bronx.

All was not hopeless within the South Bronx, of course. There were impressive pockets of resilience and creativity during the otherwise discouraging 1970s. A resourceful, charismatic priest, Father Louis Gigante, had founded a nonprofit community development corporation tied to his Saint Athanasius Church in 1968. His South East Bronx Community Organization (SEBCO) pioneered efforts to renovate housing and provide social services to the poor Hunts Point neighborhood, soon nicknamed Gigante Land.[18] The invention of hip-hop music, break dancing, and graffiti art by young residents of the Bronx's housing projects would achieve national, even international fame. In 1978, a group of community-minded artists opened a storefront arts space in Mott Haven called Fashion Moda, "a museum of Science, Art, Invention, Technology, and Fantasy," which helped promote the local arts of hip-hop and graffiti.[19]

But residents also had a hand in worsening rather than in improving conditions when they fought over meager spoils. Corrupt Bronx politicians (many of whom would eventually serve jail time and were labeled by Logue as "the crummiest [of] political leadership, operat[ing] the place like a dime store") put lining their personal pockets above their public duty.[20] And a cunning, streetwise operator named Ramon Velez, a Puerto Rican immigrant and former welfare caseworker, opportunistically used federal antipoverty funding intended for poor people to run a political machine out of his Hunts Point Multi-Service Corporation. By the early 1970s, Velez was running the largest antipoverty empire in New York City, controlling a thousand jobs and managing $12 million in funds. Velez earned the enmity of many honest figures in the South Bronx, including Gigante, Badillo, and later Logue, with whom he would eventually have a showdown.[21]

It was no surprise that when the photographer Lisa Kahane arrived in the South Bronx in 1979 to document the devastation, she found it "an unimaginable wasteland. It was frightening and fascinating, not just another neighborhood but another realm, visible but incomprehensible, an urban wilderness actively populated by ghosts . . . Seventy-five thousand buildings abandoned in one place in twentieth-century America? Now that's scary."[22] It was here that Logue sought his comeback.

TAKING ON THE SOUTH BRONX

Despite these dreadful conditions—perhaps because of them—Logue lobbied hard for the job heading the South Bronx Development Office. Although Logue faced few competitors for such a formidable challenge, it was still not easy for him to get hired, given his well-known history at the UDC. Badillo had had to convince Koch to hire Logue; "I was imposed on him," Logue later admitted to an SBDO staff member. Koch, in turn, felt he had to reassure critics not to worry, that Logue would not have financial autonomy.[23] It helped that as New York City, Yonkers, and New York State faced financial crises similar to those faced by the UDC, the agency's default became less easily attributable to Logue's mismanagement. But still, many city officials remained wary. When Logue walked into his final meeting with Koch to seal the deal for the SBDO, he was surprised to find twenty commissioners of various ranks in the room, until he realized, he later said, "I know why they're here. The idea is to keep an eye on me so I won't get out of control." And even after Badillo assured New York governor Hugh Carey, Logue's former adversary, "You know, Hugh, he's all right, he'll do the job," Carey still insisted, "I don't want any of my money to go to him."[24]

Logue would never fully overcome this skepticism, which surely contributed to the limited cooperation he got from the city and the state throughout his years at the SBDO. "They did their best to marginalize him," said Stephen Lefkowitz, who remained well connected in New York politics following his years as general counsel at the UDC.[25] But Logue made up his mind to ride the waves, attracted to the challenge, convinced of the worthiness of the cause, and eager for the opportunity to get back in the game, working first with Badillo until his ambitious plan went down in flames and then accepting Koch's invitation to run a more modest operation.[26]

Many of Logue's friends and colleagues were far less enthusiastic about him taking the job. "Everyone thought I was going to get eaten alive," Logue mused.[27] Even if he survived in this near-impossible position, they thought it was humiliating for him to accept it. "It was really a huge comedown for him, to run the world and then run this," said Larry Goldman from UDC days.[28] Richard Kahan, another UDC staffer, was convinced that "he was not going to be happy up in the Bronx with no staff, no power, and a mayor that didn't really care about his success, . . . and we tried to talk him out of it."[29] John Stainton, at his side in Boston and at the UDC, fretted that whereas once Logue had worried about thousands of units of new housing, now "he is talking about 250."[30] Joseph Fried, the journalist who had sympathetically chronicled Logue's fall from power at the UDC, was more sanguine. He argued rather poetically that the South Bronx and Ed Logue were well matched for a joint redemption, the defeated man and the defeated community both poised for rehabilitation.[31]

Others close to Logue understood why Ed was honestly attracted to this job. They knew it had always been as much the mission as the power that had motivated him. His wife, Margaret, acknowledged the lesser status but felt "he thought he was doing something important." His sister, Ellen, claimed, "He never talked about it as a comedown . . . It was something he viewed as a horrendous challenge. He was engaged in it. And he felt he was giving the people their hope." His old friend Allan Talbot recognized that others "thought it was a sad ending to a meteoric career," but Logue personally considered the job "relevant to everything he had done in his life." And Logue's Boston and UDC collaborator Robert Litke felt that Logue was being offered a historic opportunity "to create a social and physical mechanism that would [remake] the South Bronx from the bottom up."[32]

It took a while for the SBDO to become a functioning operation. After a short stint in the small 86th Street office occupied by Logue Development Company, the SBDO set up shop in two New York City locations: in the South Bronx at 529 Courtlandt Avenue between 148th and 149th Streets and in Manhattan at 1250 Broadway, at 32nd Street. Stalwart Janet Murphy, who had accompanied Logue from Boston to New York a decade earlier, now returned to his side. After working for a banking consortium in the years since the UDC's collapse, she happily took up her familiar role as Logue's gatekeeper. And she did her job well. Even in this much smaller office, a staff member recalled, "We were all scared of Janet."[33]

Reaching back even deeper into his network of contacts, Logue got help with hiring staff from Sally Bowles, an old friend since Logue had worked with her father, Chester, in Connecticut and India.[34] As he had in the past, Logue sought out idealistic young talent eager for a public service opportunity and mentoring.[35] Two of the earliest recruits were Jennifer Raab and Rebecca Lee. They fit the profile perfectly. They had both grown up in working-class neighborhoods of New York City, Raab in Washington Heights, Lee in a Queens housing project. After completing graduate school in public policy—Princeton's Woodrow Wilson School for Raab, Harvard's Kennedy School of Government for Lee—they accepted Logue's job offer from among several other options, attracted, as many had been before them, to the chance to make significant social change and be tutored by an experienced veteran in the field.[36] Other young idealists would follow them to the SBDO. For example, Peter Bray, a master's candidate in the city planning program at MIT, heard Logue lecture there about his work in the South Bronx and then sought him out to ask for a job.[37] By fall 1980, the SBDO staff had grown to seventy, split between the two offices. Here it basically remained while Logue was at the helm, though he perpetually struggled to make payroll. Notably, for the first time women filled many of the important jobs, reflecting a new era when women like Raab and Lee were getting graduate degrees in the urban field and expecting to have serious careers. But it shouldn't be overlooked that as a small, local operation, the SBDO might have seemed less attractive to ambitious men and thereby offered women more opportunity.

Mayor Koch's initial charge to the SBDO to undertake a comprehensive plan for the South Bronx fit well with Logue's usual approach. He had begun his work in New Haven, Boston, and New York State with similar surveys that evolved into blueprints for future redevelopment programs. *Areas of Strength, Areas of Opportunity* was released in December 1980 and became known in-house as "the Red Book" for its bright red cover and importance as the gospel according to Chairman Logue (albeit much larger in format than Chairman Mao's then popular *Little Red Book*). It was wide-ranging in scope, with separate sections on economic development, housing, human services, parks and recreation, transportation, and land revitalization, and politically savvy in organizing itself according to the South Bronx's six community districts, honoring the existing channels for neighborhood input into the city's planning process. The Red Book set out to identify present points of strength and then to build the SBDO's ambitious plans for action around them.[38] With none of the combined planning and development powers that Logue had previously demanded in every other city he had worked in, he nonetheless pushed forward.

THE SBDO AGENDA

Economic development in the South Bronx was a major focus for the SBDO. Logue had long made job creation a priority in redevelopment, convinced that the availability of decent work was the key to revitalizing a city for all its residents. In the South Bronx, the situation was dire, the very worst in a New York City that was hemorrhaging manufacturing jobs in general. Of the 2,000 manufacturers operating in the Bronx in 1959, 650 had left by 1974, taking an estimated 17,688 jobs with them; and the situation was only getting worse. Between 1976 and 1980, 5,500 more jobs disappeared.[39] To encourage investment by potential employers, the SBDO oversaw a South Bronx Economic Development Coordinating Committee (EDCC), made up of representatives from New York State, New York City, and Bronx Borough economic development offices, in hopes of bringing all the key players to the same table. The EDCC met monthly to review proposals and to try to create a one-stop development agency to attract customers.[40]

The economic development strategy also involved developing industrial parks in the South Bronx to entice potential employers away from alluring suburban locations, viewed by many manufacturers as a safer choice than New York City. Bathgate Industrial Park, a 21-acre site adjacent to the Cross Bronx Expressway developed in conjunction with the nonprofit New York City Public Development Corporation and the Port Authority of New York and New Jersey, was the first to be completed. Logue raised $4.3 million from the federal government and $3.1 million from New York City, with the promise of creating one thousand jobs. Bathgate's first tenants were Aircraft Supplies Company and Majestic Shapes, a shoulder-pad manufacturer. Here, and in the 10.5-acre Mid-Bronx Industrial Park (and the planning for Intervale, which was never built), the SBDO oversaw the preparation of land, including demolishing unwanted buildings; expedited any needed rezoning for light manufacturing; relocated utility easements; consulted with local community boards; redirected traffic, and more. Logue was proud that when he "first came to this job in 1978, the attitude of business was 'Get the hell out before you get burned.' There were three million square feet of empty industrial space." And by 1984, he thought, probably too optimistically, "We have convinced industry that the South Bronx is a safe place to remain in, grow in, and come into." Logue's strategy? "Give business as much as they can get in the suburbs."[41]

The last piece of the SBDO's economic development program involved sponsoring the annual South Bronx Industrial Fair with all the EDCC partners to sell the borough to prospective tenants, promising to accelerate the labyrinthine approval process that too often discouraged commercial and industrial companies from entering New York City. Rebuilding the industrial base of the South Bronx was a much bigger, longer-term project than Logue's modest organization could realistically undertake, but despite the hard sell and the limitations of being more of a broker than an active redeveloper, the SBDO made some important inroads.

Shifting its attention from the economic health of the Bronx to the personal health of its residents, the SBDO focused as well on human services. As far back as New Haven and Boston, Logue had insisted that social service interventions must accompany physical redevelopment. With Gray Areas funding from the Ford Foundation, Logue had launched Community Progress Inc. in New Haven and Action for Boston Community Development in Boston to coordinate social service delivery that too often, he felt, was balkanized. Both these agencies, however, had met a mixed community reception in the anti-paternalistic political atmosphere of the 1960s. Later, at the UDC, without the same local orientation as his New Haven and Boston redevelopment agencies, Logue nonetheless had prioritized creating social service spaces in new housing, whether schools, senior centers, clinics, or recreational facilities. By the 1980s in the South Bronx, human service work met less grassroots resistance than it had previously, partly because administrators like the SBDO's Karolyn Gould had previously learned important lessons about how to involve community members in decision-making and partly because by the 1980s, as the government safety net was shrinking, any and all available services were valued. The SBDO's attentiveness to job training, along with more traditional social service programs addressing poor health, addiction, disability, and teenage pregnancy, made its work all the more appreciated by struggling South Bronx residents.[42]

Another SBDO initiative was land reclamation and revitalization, since block after block of the South Bronx was strewn with rubble from buildings crumbling out of neglect and abandonment. Any efforts to turn them to new purposes or even to create usable open space for recreation would require stabilization first. The SBDO experimented with various approaches, settling on soil compacting as far cheaper than rubble removal. The Bathgate Industrial Park first introduced the problem and the solution. The "dynamic compaction technique" developed there, in which a crane dropped a six-ton ball with a flat bottom from a height of forty feet to pound the rubble, was later used to prepare all other SBDO sites, including for housing.[43]

By far the most important SBDO undertaking, however, was the one that had mattered most to Logue throughout his career: the construction and rehabilitation of housing. The housing program in fact claimed so much of Logue's time and attention that the staffer Jennifer Raab, who was assigned to human services, lamented that she missed out on more of Logue's mentoring than did her colleague Rebecca Lee, who worked closely with Logue on physical development. Not surprisingly, it was in the area of housing that the SBDO would make its most significant contribution to turning around the South Bronx.

MAKING CHARLOTTE GARDENS GROW

It was such a startling idea that it made headlines not just in New York City but nationally and even internationally. In the middle of decimated Charlotte Street—President Carter's stomping ground—Logue's SBDO constructed Charlotte Gardens, a new neighborhood of ninety freestanding single-family homes with white picket fences that were heavily subsidized for purchase. It was nothing less than the suburban American dream plopped down in the middle of one of the worst neighborhoods in the city, if not the nation. As Logue had familiarized himself with the South Bronx, he had noticed that amid ravaged blocks, a few homeowners persisted in caring lovingly for their homes. He had also learned, as he told Mayor Koch, that many new arrivals to New York, "Southern Blacks, Island Blacks and Island Hispanics[,] do not consider a row house a home! A home has to have a back yard and a garden, and you have to be able to walk around it!" Homeown-ership, it occurred to Logue, offered just the stability needed in South Bronx neighborhoods. (To ensure their permanent commitment, in fact, buyers of homes in Charlotte Gardens had to agree not to sell their subsidized homes for ten years or encounter substantial penalties.)[44] In a statement that surely would have amused his nemesis Jane Jacobs for how it echoed her own preaching, Logue declared, "We need front stoops again." In truth, however, Logue's commitment to Jacobs's "eyes on the street" had been evolving for some time, particularly in the UDC's low-rise, high-density experiment of Marcus Garvey Park Village, where every unit had its own exterior entrance.[45]

Logue's strategy was practical as well. In the dawning age of privatized solutions to social problems, Logue calculated that subsidies for home purchase would be easier to secure than the public funding needed to put up large-scale multiple dwellings with rental units. Detached homes would also cost less to build, because they could make use of existing sewer con-nections and would avoid the expensive masonry firewalls required by the city's building codes for attached units.[46]

Even so, delivering affordable, single-family homes for purchase would surely be challenging, particularly given the elimination of the Section 235 mortgage subsidies to owners. So Logue turned to a cost-saving strategy that had long intrigued him, first in Boston and then in more significant ways at the UDC: manufactured housing. Labor and materials for prefabricated structures, Logue figured, would be far cheaper, with better quality con-trol, than more conventional building in New York's high-cost construction market. Moreover, production in a factory eliminated the risk of vandalism and the high security costs that scared home builders away from jobs in rough neighborhoods like Charlotte Street.[47] The clincher: Logue argued that using manufactured housing to repopulate the South Bronx provided a way of simultaneously advancing the borough's economic development. If a factory for building manufactured homes was opened in one of the SBDO's industrial parks, it would create many new jobs along with new residences.[48]

Defying the vocal skepticism of the New York City Department of

Housing Preservation and Development commissioner Anthony Gliedman, Charlotte Gardens was a huge hit.[49] Early on, Logue had realized that he was up against the common view that, in the words of one observer, "there's no way in hell that anyone is going to buy a single-family house in the middle of the South Bronx when you look outside and all that you can think of is 'I'm going to be dead in the next twenty-four hours.'" Responding to these concerns, Logue cooked up the idea of opening model homes, much like those in new suburban developments.[50] The gamble paid off. When the first two model houses opened in April 1983, thousands of curious visitors snaked in long lines for a chance to take a look. After only three weeks of active marketing, more than 360 potential buyers applied for a home. After six weeks, there were 500; and in time, there was a waitlist of over 2,000—far more than could be accommodated.

The basic Charlotte Gardens house was a conventional, 1,152-square-foot raised ranch with three bedrooms, one and a half baths, and a full basement dug on-site, which was partly aboveground for later finishing as living space. It was constructed in one of the few factories producing prefab houses, the Deluxe Manufactured Homes plant in Pennsylvania, and then trucked in modular halves during the dead of night over the George Washington Bridge, flanked by Port Authority police and met at the other side by the New York Police Department.[51] Homeowners could customize such design options as the color of the house's exterior siding and bathrooms, type and color of the wall-to-wall carpeting, and whether they wanted a bay window, though getting the factory to meet these specifications accurately proved a huge headache for the SBDO. The purchase price for a quarter-acre lot and a home was highly subsidized through various sources, so that the price tag of about $50,000 was at least $30,000 below the actual construction cost (and if all expenses were included, less than half the full $114,000 sticker price). With the requirement of a down payment of 10 percent, a buyer needed to scrape together around $5,000.[52] With philanthropic funding, the Cooperative Extension of Cornell University offered workshops at local schools and churches attended by hundreds of potential purchasers to teach basic lessons in insurance, home maintenance, landscaping, and the budgeting and cash flow needed to pay taxes and a mortgage. Help from the Community Development Legal Assistance Center cut closing costs. And phased tax abatements from the city cushioned the burden of real estate taxes for the first eight years.[53]

It is hard to convey the amount of attention that Charlotte Gardens' model houses attracted. An illustrated article on one of them appeared on the front page of *The New York Times*, and it took off from there.[54] This publicity was no accident, of course, as Logue's SBDO had geared up to maximize the potential of its fourteen-acre Charlotte Gardens project to revitalize the South Bronx. Most brilliant was the ribbon-cutting ceremony on April 17, 1983, which included bigwig elected officials—Senator Alfonse D'Amato, Congressmen Mario Biaggi and Robert Garcia, the Bronx borough president Stanley Simon, the state assemblywoman Gloria Davis, and Mayor Ed Koch—photographed whitewashing a picket fence Tom Sawyer-style in front of the model houses. All this enthusiasm won over even the formerly reluctant Mayor Koch. Koch recalled, "As we were getting dragged in, I was saying to myself, 'What am I getting into?'" But as the publicity mounted, he called up Logue to stake his claim. "'This is my project, right Ed? This was my idea, wasn't it?'" recalled Logue, with amusement. When at the dedication of the model homes, a heckler in the crowd cynically yelled out his prediction that in no time these houses would surely be destroyed, as so much else in the neighborhood had been, Koch responded combatively, "These people will defend their houses with their lives!" Eventually Koch concluded, "This was the best thing we could have done. It anchored the community."[55]

To an impressive degree, Charlotte Gardens attracted just the population that the SBDO had hoped for—skilled workers and lower-middle-class public employees from the area.[56] Robert Litke recalled that early on, "Ed would take me there and we would look at the land, the raw land, and he would paint his vision . . . I mean he was in heaven thinking about the opportunities he was creating for working stiffs, a cop, a single mother."[57] Of the 507 applicants who were processed before the list was closed, most were the "working families" Logue had targeted: policemen, firemen, truck and bus drivers, transit conductors, foremen, mechanics, plumbers, secretaries, teachers, and nurses and other hospital workers. A quarter were employed by the city or one of its independent agencies such as the Transit Authority or Public Housing Authority; 15 percent worked for the state or federal governments, many of the latter for the post office. On average, households had 1.65 wage earners. Forty-nine percent were local, from the South Bronx; 30 percent were from the North Bronx; 11 percent were from Manhattan, mostly Harlem and East Harlem; and the remaining were from working-class communities in New Jersey or neighboring towns like Mount Vernon, most originally from the South Bronx and eager to return.[58] Forty-seven percent of the prospective buyers were black, 45 percent Latino, 7 percent Asian, and 1 percent white. None of these hopeful buyers had owned a house before.[59]

When the ninety homeowners who succeeded as purchasers were surveyed in 1985, there were slight alterations in the totals, reflecting both who actually qualified to buy and the priorities of the screeners. Notably a larger number (82 percent) were Bronx residents, particularly from the South Bronx (68 percent). Most (slightly less than three-quarters) were employed by private companies rather than the public sector. The median household income of $33,000 was slightly higher than among the applicants and, in 60 percent of the households, made possible by at least two wage earners. A very large proportion of Charlotte Garden residents were under eighteen. None of the actual buyers had owned a home before, and residents were fairly evenly split between blacks and Latinos.[60] Charlotte Gardens seemed to be helping to retain—even lure back—the lower middle class of the Bronx. And they stayed, taking pride in their neighborhood and improving their homes—often through their own labor—with finished basements, patios, above-ground swimming pools, gardens, carports, and the like.

As the SBDO had hoped, there was remarkably little turnover in homes in Charlotte Gardens, even long after the penalty for selling had expired. Twenty-five years later, two-thirds of the original owners were still there, and when an owner had left, in two out of three cases the house had changed hands only once.[61] Interviews with three original owners—Josephine Cohn and Preston Keusch, Carmen and Rafael Ceballo, and David and Irma Rivera—revealed how hard they had lobbied to get a house (in some cases bugging the sales office weekly or monthly), how frustrated they became over endless construction delays, and ultimately how much pride they took in being part of this unique community in the South Bronx. In Josephine Cohn's case, the fact that she was white, living in Manhattan, and had no kids were strikes against her, she feared. "So I worked really, really hard to charm everybody in sight," Cohn recalled laughingly. The day she moved into her new home was "one of the best days of my life next to my wedding . . . I walked into my own house, brand new, untouched, cream carpeting. And I was just so excited and tearful."[62]

Not everyone was so enthusiastic about Charlotte Gardens. Some critics charged that the neighborhood needed housing for low-income residents, not those who could afford to buy a single-family house, however much it was subsidized. Logue's response was that in the long run the entire community would benefit from buyers willing to commit their hard-earned dollars and their family's security to becoming pioneering homeowners with a financial stake. Options for the less well-off in a mixed-income community would follow later.[63] Moreover, even better-off Charlotte Gardens homeowners still experienced economic insecurity. For example, David Rivera, the very first resident to move in, owned a local shoe store when he was accepted as a buyer, but by the time he sold his house in 1995, he identified himself as a "peddler," claiming he had been forced out of his store by rising rent and other expenses.[64]

The most common criticism of Charlotte Gardens was that single-family suburban-style housing was inappropriate in density and architecture for an urban setting. Logue was not unaware of how far he had strayed from the cutting-edge modernism that he had promoted through his UDC housing. He freely admitted, "This stuff will not win the architectural awards that I have so enjoyed receiving in the past."[65] It was painful for him to lose the approval of the national community of planners and architects he had so carefully cultivated through much of his career when they criticized this project as a hare-brained scheme, too low in density and too low-brow in aesthetics. Close Logue associates like Ted Liebman, who had been chief architect at the UDC, found it so difficult to stomach the look of Charlotte

Gardens that he strictly avoided the topic whenever he met up with his much-admired former boss.[66] Still today, a recent American Institute of Architects guide to New York City's architecture describes Charlotte Gardens as "another kind of destruction: that of valuable, close-in, urban land through underutilization. Silly."[67]

As surreal as Charlotte Gardens may have looked for the South Bronx, Logue was convinced that he needed to embrace a different set of priorities to help overcome the stigma of Charlotte Street. Here, Logue the pragmatist won out over Logue the modernist. Even the contrast in names between Logue's very different New York ventures—Roosevelt Island versus Charlotte Gardens—suggested the replacement of his heroic, male monumental modernist project with a domesticated, female-gendered alternative. And it is noteworthy that the esteemed architecture critic Ada Louise Huxtable, a self-described "unrepentant modernist," praised Logue for "put[ting] up little houses in the rubble on Charlotte Street that symbolized hope and renewal when the South Bronx had become the poster child for terminal urban decay. You could say they were the right thing in the right place at the right time."[68]

More than anything else, the shift from the publicly subsidized housing that Logue had been able to build with federal urban renewal funds in New Haven, Boston, and New York State to projects more dependent on the private marketplace affected the architecture of what got built. The bold, innovative, modernist designs of the UDC, promoted by an architecturally adventurous, independent public official like Logue, gave way to conventional styles that appealed to ordinary homebuyers and conservative mortgage lenders. "Real houses for real people," was how Litke described it. In fact, many of the blacks and Latinos who signed up to buy Charlotte Gardens homes aspired to own the kind of new houses that were blanketing suburban areas of New York, which they couldn't afford and which, as minorities, they were not welcome in. Logue had learned that lesson only too well in his failed UDC experiment with Fair Share Housing. Their tastes, one journalist confirmed, were "nothing unusual here, nothing that seemed experimental, trendy, or less than the suburbia these buyers wanted."[69]

Whereas architects had enjoyed great importance in the hierarchy of professionals who propelled federal urban renewal, in this new era of private-market approaches to housing they frequently found themselves sidelined. In a project like Charlotte Gardens, architects were only minimally involved.[70] Taking their place in influence were developers and nonprofit and private-sector financiers, often local bankers lending money to private borrowers, incentivized or mandated by the government under antidiscrimination legislation, such as the Fair Lending Act of 1974, the Home Mortgage Disclosure Act of 1975, and the Community Reinvestment Act of 1977. These laws required banks to disclose where they were lending and to help meet the credit needs of the communities in which they did business.[71] As the federal government's role shifted from direct sponsorship of affordable housing to encouraging the private sector to invest in it, architects who had once enjoyed shaping "social housing," as it was often called, saw their impact decline along with the public dollars that had supported it.[72]

NEW PARTNERS IN CHARLOTTE GARDENS

Charlotte Gardens and other housing constructed by the SBDO in the South Bronx marked important shifts in how Logue went about practicing urban redevelopment. He collaborated with a different set of partners than he had before. And he depended on a substantially altered business model to fund his work.

In the past, Logue had often resisted pressure to submit his redevelopment projects to grassroots review, whether in Boston's Allston or in the suburbs of Westchester. He now found himself looking to community groups well rooted in the South Bronx and not to his former allies in high places. Given the political changes in Washington, HUD bureaucrats were increasingly hostile, and officials in city hall were notably ambivalent. A stranger to the area with neither local ties nor external backing, Logue knew he needed the legitimacy that would come from being supported by well-known and trusted neighborhood groups. Accordingly, Logue developed his closest working relationship with a nonprofit community development corporation, the Mid Bronx Desperadoes (MBD), so named by its African American founder Genevieve "Gennie" Brooks, "because we were desperate. Our streets were lined with garbage, we had drug trafficking and arson. We needed everything, especially decent housing."[73]

Brooks had moved to the South Bronx from a farm in South Carolina at the age of seventeen to live with an uncle. Over time, she watched her stable neighborhood deteriorate, and finally decided as a widow in her forties that she had to take action. She first organized a tenants' association in her apartment building, then a block association on Seabury Place, and finally a day care center, which soon grew into a more multifaceted community organization, the MBD. By the time that Logue arrived in the South Bronx to head the SBDO, Brooks was sharing the leadership of the MBD with a Catholic priest from the neighborhood, the Reverend William J. Smith.[74] A few years later, Brooks and Smith were joined by a young Julie Sandorf, who became the MBD's project director for Charlotte Gardens.

To ensure Charlotte Gardens' success, Logue contracted with the MBD, tapping its deep knowledge of the community for help soliciting, screening, and selecting buyers for the much-sought-after homes. Brooks herself interviewed every one of the hundreds of families who applied, did home visits, gave counseling sessions, encouraged buyers to get involved in the community, and in every way possible tried to make Charlotte Gardens successful. Other aspects of the project were also shared with the MBD—designated by Community Board No. 3 as the SBDO's official community cosponsor—in what was a complex, deeply interwoven division of labor between the two organizations.[75]

Relations between Logue's SBDO and the MBD were not without tensions. When Peter Bray arrived to work on the Charlotte Gardens project, he was shocked to "get an absolute earful" from Gennie Brooks "along the lines of we're not going to come in and tell them what to do." Bray understood that, but he also learned it was a delicate balance, that if "they thought they could push us around, if we let them do it, shame on us. We had to push back . . . In that environment . . . a strong offense is the best defense." Sometimes MBD members thought Logue went too far, operating as if he were still the big boss of the UDC.[76] And the goals of the SBDO and the MBD were not always the same. They agreed on the importance of prioritizing current South Bronx residents who were not yet homeowners and recruiting stable families with dependable incomes and low debt as buyers. But the SBDO pushed for greater social and economic diversity among the homeowners selected for Charlotte Gardens, out of Logue's long-standing commitment to create socially mixed communities. The MBD, perhaps more aware of the fragility of prospective buyers' finances, worried more about homeowners not keeping up their payments and thereby jeopardizing the whole project. In internal discussions, the SBDO at one point fretted that the MBD was too "seduced by extremely high income, or perhaps factors such as the length of time a candidate has been living at his current residence," while also favoring Hispanics over blacks and established households over young ones whose children would populate the local school and give a "family feel" to the neighborhood.[77] But in the end Logue and Brooks, and their respective organizations, found a way of working together successfully. The MBD acknowledged that Logue did listen and was getting them what they couldn't get on their own.[78] Father Smith frequently went out of his way to convey his great respect for Logue, who reciprocated, repeatedly expressing enormous affection and respect for Brooks, Smith, and their colleagues.[79]

Logue's local collaborations in the South Bronx extended beyond the MDC. The SBDO worked closely with the six community boards in the area, attending meetings, coordinating with district managers, and seeking to win over suspicious residents. By 1983, the chairpersons of five of the six boards sat on the SBDO's nineteen-member board of directors. SBDO's human services director, Karolyn Gould, felt that Logue's genius "was to position himself as the community's advocate and prove this consistently and to dispel fears that this master urban planner would be their nemesis, another Robert Moses," who—thanks to the Cross Bronx Expressway—was truly the enemy in the South Bronx. Logue's message to community boards, according to Gould, was "Tell me what you want me to do."[80] That assessment was confirmed by an insider, Jack Flanagan, a board member and former local cop who was executive director of the Bronx Frontier Development Corporation, a grassroots activist organization promoting urban greening: "Logue is, contrary to popular belief, working with the local planning boards."

The Community District 3 manager Veralyne Hamilton recounted how the situation in her own district evolved into a collaboration between her board and the SBDO. When outsider Logue first arrived, her constituents "were ready to lynch him," insisting, "I don't want anything built unless I have input into it." She feared that her community district would "get left out altogether because they were bogged down in that debate." Over time, however, Hamilton convinced her members to work with Logue, telling them, "I respect him because of his knowledge." While placating Logue's critics with "Okay, Ed Logue may be a racist," she went on to urge them to appreciate that he "knows how to push projects. You see this vacant land around here, ladies and gentlemen? Well, it could be like this forever if you don't hook up with this new situation."[81] Community boards like Hamilton's realized that so long as Logue listened to them, they would benefit from his ability to tap into resources otherwise inaccessible or even unknown to them. As Peter Cantillo, district manager of Community Board No. 2, put it, "When he's on your side, he just makes life a lot easier."[82]

The Charlotte Gardens project manager Bray attributed the successful partnerships that eventually emerged not just to Logue's learning from past mistakes but also to the fact that the SBDO had more in common with community boards than with city agencies downtown, as they both had to work from the margins to influence the city's planning decisions.[83] Brooks concurred: "Logue came in very optimistic and he soon found out the . . . heartache the local activist groups were feeling." The real problem, according to Brother Patrick Lochrane of Board No. 6, was not Logue: "He's spoken to everyone in the community, not just to the power brokers. When they [SBDO] came up with a plan for Board No. 6, it was what everyone wanted . . . Compared to Logue, it's the City Planning Commission that's the absolute horror."[84] Logue himself, of course, consistently battled city officials who enjoyed more official power than he did, though many came to appreciate the value to them of the SBDO's deep connections to the South Bronx community.[85] In a stunning reversal of Logue's history of relationships elsewhere, when the Ford Foundation commissioned a confidential report on Logue's work in the South Bronx in late 1980, it predicted that the SBDO's success or failure would depend not on community support, which Logue seemed to have, but on "the degree of commitment coming from the opposite direction: the willingness and ability of the Mayor, Governor, and federal agencies to give Logue the kind of support he needs." And two years later, in 1982, when the Fund for the City of New York did its own assessment of the SBDO, it concluded that the SBDO deserved higher marks for its impressive (and improving) relations with notoriously hard-to-please community boards in the South Bronx than with city agencies.[86]

Over time, Logue also developed strong working relationships with Banana Kelly Community Improvement Association, founded in 1977 with the motto "Don't Move, Improve," and particularly with SEBCO's founder, Father Gigante.[87] At first, Gigante was suspicious of Logue, considering him an interloper and perhaps judging him as a potential rival, but they learned to trust and help each other.[88] Gigante eventually came to share Logue's view that adding some homeowners would help stabilize low-income rental communities with residents who had a financial investment. "We must balance our neighborhood. We love the poor. We are working with the poor. But we have to bring an economic class in that can sustain the neighborhood," Gigante explained.[89] When Logue needed to protect the two model homes, fully furnished with donations from the nearby Kelly's Furniture Store and now sitting vulnerable in the midst of a rough Charlotte Street neighborhood, Gigante assisted in the hiring of the Nighthawk gang members he had trained as a security force, with the goal of turning their street smarts to more benevolent ends. When Koch asked Logue how he protected the site at night, Logue took pleasure in replying, "We hire the people who steal it to be guards!"[90]

This was a very different Ed Logue from the redevelopment czar of New Haven, Boston, and New York State. Logue's transformation is particularly well captured in how he collaborated with the Catholic Church. In Boston, Logue allied with the highest levels of the archdiocese, Cardinal Richard Cushing and his right-hand adviser, Monsignor Francis Lally, who served for a decade as chair of the Boston Redevelopment Authority board, which theoretically made him Logue's boss. But while Boston's urban renewal had united the highest ranks of church and state, in the South Bronx Logue's Catholic partners were parish-level priests and nuns—such as Fathers Smith and Gigante and the latter's colleague Sister Thomas—and the community activists with whom they worked. He was convinced that these local religious leaders made the Catholic churches of the South Bronx, with their twenty-four parishes, seventeen parochial schools, and priests residing in neighborhoods—90 percent of them bilingual—a vital force for social stability and positive community change. They sat on community planning boards, built low-income housing, and ran social services. In fact, when *The New York Times* published a laudatory profile of Cardinal Terence Cooke of New York in March 1983, Logue wrote a letter to the editor criticizing the article's omission of the "priests, nuns and brothers" of the South Bronx Catholic religious community who were "a very important element of strength," so much so that he "wish[ed] they could be cloned." These locally oriented Catholics were more likely to challenge the church hierarchy in New York with their activism and independence than to speak for it.[91]

Another major way that Logue's experience at the SBDO differed from his past efforts in urban redevelopment lay in how his work was now financed. In contrast to the 1950s and 1960s, when urban renewal money flowed plentifully from Washington, the 1970s and 1980s marked a steady decline in the federal government's support for housing construction and other urban projects that benefited low- and moderate-income Americans. For example, the Section 235 deep mortgage subsidies created in 1968 that Logue had at first counted on to finance homes in Charlotte Gardens were effectively eliminated by President Ronald Reagan in 1981.[92] The next year, Reagan canceled Section 8 subsidies designed to encourage construction of buildings for low-income tenants through guaranteeing developers and landlords the difference between fair-market rent and 25 (later 30) percent of occupants' income. Reagan kept only the cheapest part, the vouchers for individual renters.[93] The Reagan administration also cut the Urban Development Action Grant program, aimed at leveraging government funding to spur private investment and jobs, though Logue managed to secure $14,500 for each Charlotte Gardens house out of remaining funds. Likewise, Reagan halved financing available under the Community Development Block Grant program. By one estimate, the $2.6 billion a year in federal funds that flowed to community development projects at the end of the Carter administration had shrunk to $1.6 billion (inflation adjusted) by 1985. Reagan cut HUD funding for assisted housing from $30.9 billion in Carter's last budget to $18.2 billion in his own first budget. All told, over the period 1981 to 1987, housing programs were slashed by two-thirds, more than any other part of the Reagan budget, the latest chapter in the assault on federal spending and responsibility that had begun with Richard Nixon's New Federalism a decade earlier.[94]

This severe reduction in federal dollars by the 1980s forced redevelopers like the SBDO to piece together what remained of funding at the federal, state, and municipal levels to make projects work. The Community Reinvestment Act of 1977 helped. Between 1977 and 1997, total annual lending by banks to low-income communities grew from $3 billion to $43 billion a year.[95] In Charlotte Gardens, the SBDO benefited from the New York State Mortgage Agency's Forward Commitment Program, which made below-market mortgages available to first-time home buyers and specified neighborhoods by insuring banks against risk. With that protection, Chemical Bank was willing to provide $4 million worth of mortgages to Charlotte Gardens home buyers at low rates.[96] But the funding was never enough, deepening Logue's frustration with this shift in reliance from the public to private sector. In a 1983 speech to the National Housing Conference, he railed against the now reigning philosophy of "Let the market forces prevail."[97] Stephen Coyle, a successor of Logue's at the helm of Boston's BRA who would go on to run the AFL-CIO Housing Investment Trust, visited Logue in the South Bronx that same year and felt he was witnessing "the master builder surrounded by urban decay, with the federal government abandoning [him]."[98]

Filling part of the gap left by the retreat of the federal government and performing a novel role that connected private-sector funders to nonprofit recipients was a new player in the world of urban redevelopment: the "third sector," dominated by foundations. Foundations had long been important to urban initiatives. The Ford Foundation had funded many of Logue's projects over the course of his career. But with public support on the wane, nonprofit intermediaries grew even more important. Logue's South Bronx work had already benefited from philanthropy; the Bathgate Industrial Park received funding from the Vincent Astor Foundation as well as the International Ladies' Garment Workers Union, which hoped to encourage the creation of more jobs in the apparel industry. But the major source of non-profit support for the SBDO came from a brand-new spin-off from the Ford Foundation, the Local Initiatives Support Corporation (LISC), founded and headed by Logue's former colleague in New Haven, Mike Sviridoff. After establishing CPI in New Haven, Sviridoff went first to New York City to set up Mayor John V. Lindsay's Human Resources Administration and then became a vice president of the Ford Foundation for thirteen years. LISC emerged out of Ford's recognition under its new president, Franklin Thomas, who had been the founding president of the pioneering Bedford Stuyvesant Restoration Corporation, that past failures in urban policy and this dawning era of greater dependence on the private sector called for the foundation to invent new ways of intervening in the nation's still-troubled cities.[99]

Born about the same time and building on the strong ties between Logue and Sviridoff, LISC and the SBDO grew up together. Although Ford had already given a little money to the Bronx's SEBCO and Banana Kelly community development corporations, "the real commitment had to be to an organization like the South Bronx Development Organization that would begin to do some planning and putting in the financing for the rehabilitation," explained Anita Miller, a top LISC staff member.[100] LISC, in its role as financial intermediary, contributed about $300,000 to Charlotte Gardens—underwriting a feasibility study, financing the construction of the two model houses when no conventional lender would touch it, and providing other loans at key moments, which Miller's assistant Richard Manson felt "tipped Charlotte Street forward to get done."[101] In turn, the South Bronx became an important laboratory for LISC as it developed into a significant player in

the new regime of public-private financing of affordable housing, channel-
ing dollars as well as working to develop greater managerial capacity in
CDCs, which were bearing increasing responsibility.

By 1984, LISC had opened thirty-one branch offices nationwide and
raised more than $70 million from 250 corporations and foundations and
3 federal agencies. In the South Bronx alone, its loans and grants leveraged
$60 million of investment.[102] LISC was soon joined by similar nonprofit or-
ganizations, such as the real estate developer and philanthropist James
Rouse's Enterprise Foundation and the civic-minded banker David Rockefeller's New York City Housing Partnership.[103] Meanwhile, the Reagan administration continued to promote incentives that encouraged the private
sector to invest, such as enterprise zones and tax relief, necessitating all the
more intermediary groups who could direct private money into the hands
of nonprofit housing developers.[104] Almost three decades after Logue and
Sviridoff had collaborated with Mayor Dick Lee to make New Haven a showcase for federal urban renewal both physical and social, they were once again
teaming up, but this time to devise new strategies for coping with federal
withdrawal from cities.

SCORING LOGUE'S FOURTH ROUND

Assessing the failures and successes of Logue's SBDO is complicated. Logue
acknowledged that "nothing I've done was as difficult as building those two
goddamn houses on Charlotte Street," referring to the two model homes.[105]
At one point, funding got so tenuous after only ten houses were built that
Logue ordered all the remaining foundations to be poured—"to remove any
doubt."[106] Charlotte Gardens as a whole should have taken a couple of years
to complete; instead it stretched out to eight.[107] Problems ranged from the
technical challenge of building on ever-present rubble to political obstacles
at almost every level of decision-making. New York City's housing commissioner Gliedman fought whatever Logue proposed, the State of New York
was no great friend, and the Reagan administration's HUD secretary, Samuel
Pierce, was openly hostile to the SBDO. Nor did it help that under Pierce,

HUD became increasingly mismanaged, with some officials later convicted of corruption and influence-peddling serious enough to be sent to prison. Pierce himself was investigated but never prosecuted.[108] Faced with these obstacles, Logue was constantly worried about funding. The days of having a Lee, a Collins, or a Rockefeller watching Logue's back, and loyal friends in Washington looking favorably on his proposals, were far in the past.

Ultimately, the death knell for Logue came in May 1984 when the meager $1 million of federal money that for five years the SBDO had received annually from Washington—HUD Technical Assistance Funds, relied on to cover salary and administrative costs—was eliminated by the Reagan administration's Pierce, out of a little spite and a lot of political expediency.[109] Adding insult to injury, when the money was reallocated to four community groups in the Bronx, the big winner was the notoriously unethical Ramon Velez in return for his support of Reagan in the 1984 election and delivery of the Latino vote. No effort was made to hide the deal. Announcement of the HUD awards took place at a Hunts Point facility operated by Velez. Logue and Koch protested angrily at Velez's muscling in, but it made no impact.[110] Logue, denouncing the award as "straight whoredom," submitted his resignation on May 22, 1984, setting a departure date of October 1.[111] But when buyers of Charlotte Gardens homes, fearing for the project's future, objected, Logue agreed to stay on until the end of the year, optimistically hoping that by then Charlotte Gardens would be "pretty much in place." Logue even indicated some willingness to remain longer if the city made a concerted effort to keep him.[112]

Apparently no one took him up on the offer. With Margaret Logue already ensconced as principal of the Carroll School for dyslexic children, in Lincoln, Massachusetts, outside of Boston, Logue said a bittersweet farewell to his staff at a party on January 10, 1985 (where the cake was decorated with a Charlotte Gardens house with a picket fence and the message "Our One and Only Edward J. Logue"), and headed north. Margaret's career advancement this time dictated the Logues' relocation away from New York. A skeletal staff remained at the SBDO to complete Charlotte Gardens under the newly appointed president, Jorge Batista, a smart, politically visible Puerto Rican attorney who had served as a deputy borough president of the Bronx and turned out to have ties to Velez. Bray, who stayed on as a consultant to the SBDO, was very critical of Batista's leadership, claiming "his real agenda was apparently to put SBDO to sleep," which was interrupted, Bray felt, only when the Charlotte Gardens homebuyers publicly raised holy hell. Given the extent to which Logue *was* the SBDO, this retreat was not surprising, nor was Batista's closing down of the SBDO in March 1987, upon running out of funds. Seeking independence, Karolyn Gould had already spun off the human services division of SBDO as the South Bronx Human Development Organization.[113] Logue left the South Bronx reluctantly, but with pride that "the most important thing we [did] is to help change people's attitudes . . . We have spread a new commandment around. We should not speak ill of the South Bronx." By this, Logue meant changing how Bronx residents, not just outsiders, viewed the borough's future prospects.[114]

The passage of time would reveal that the SBDO had another major impact: providing the model for a more extensive turnaround of the South Bronx and for building affordable housing in New York City more broadly. Not long after Logue left the South Bronx, Mayor Ed Koch made a historic commitment to renovate and upgrade more than 100,000 (later 250,000) units of housing over ten (in the end fifteen) years at the cost of $4.2 billion (eventually $5.12 billion) to deal with a growing crisis of homelessness and deteriorating housing.[115] It was soon clear how formative the SBDO's experiments had been. Koch said as much. He told an interviewer that after he recovered from the shock of President Carter pulling out of his commitment to the South Bronx, "I decided that I would go forward anyway, first with Charlotte Street . . . and then ultimately expanded that into a ten-year program." Even if Koch's historical rendering was oversimplified, the clear link he made between the two projects is significant.[116]

The Bronx historians Lloyd Ultan and Barbara Unger concurred in their history of the borough that "the effective rebuilding of The Bronx began when Mayor Edward I. Koch placed Edward J. Logue in charge of the South Bronx Development Organization."[117] LISC's Anita Miller likewise contended, "I believe that Charlotte Gardens turned the South Bronx . . . That was really, I think, the beginning of creating a new image." The message it sent New York City and far beyond, she continued, was that "you can have this kind of economic integration that everybody wanted to see happen but nobody knew how to achieve. We have to thank Ed Logue for that."[118] A later LISC president, Paul Grogan, credited Charlotte Gardens' "very strangeness" with "a symbolic wallop" that "reverse[d] the hopelessness." He concluded, "Absent Charlotte Gardens, it's hard to imagine the extensive revitalization happening."[119] Even MBD's Julie Sandorf, who was not without her criticisms of Logue as a project and money manager, was thoroughly convinced of the impact of Charlotte Gardens: "I always felt it was, Anita and me, and Ed and Gennie, to do this, was the gutsiest thing I've ever known. And it was the loss leader. It created so much attention and so much heat and so much excitement, and the reality is there were six hundred families lined up to buy these houses, and 90 percent of them came from the South Bronx."[120]

With the SBDO as inspiration, Koch's ten-year plan took advantage of the very large number of buildings and vacant lots that had come to New York City through tax default, what was called in rem housing, to make possible the widespread construction and renovation of residential units. A core tenet of Koch's plan was that housing would be developed through onetime capital subsidies, low-interest loans, and tax abatements, and in the end would be owned by nonprofits, individuals, landlords, and tenants in some cases, but, crucially, not by government, which had cut its subsidies way back. Building on SBDO precedents, the city worked with neighborhood-based CDCs. It partnered with "third sector" nonprofits like LISC, Rouse's Enterprise Foundation, Rockefeller's New York City Housing Partnership, and the Community Preservation Corporation (founded in 1974 but now much expanded in scope and resources). It pioneered homeownership in struggling neighborhoods and more generally aimed to create mixed-income neighborhoods with a variety of housing types, though usually not single-family homes. It made use of manufactured housing, now available in townhouses and rowhouses. It combined multiple sources of funding—public and private—some in quite small amounts. And it pressured banks to step up. All these strategies had proved essential ingredients in the SBDO's formula for developing affordable housing in this new era of privatization.

The SBDO's impact on the Koch plan can, of course, be exaggerated. There were surely other inspirations. But when in 1998, after fourteen years away, Jill Jonnes, a keen observer of the South Bronx's fall and revival, revisited the places where from 1981 to 1984 she had spent many a day researching her book *South Bronx Rising*, she couldn't believe "the size and scope of the renaissance," how "the Bronx had roared back to life." Drawing a direct line between the SBDO and the success of Koch's ten-year plan, she wrote, "As we drove up towards Charlotte Street and the blocks and blocks of ranch houses came in sight, . . . I felt a great wave of emotion at seeing Logue's dream flourishing."[121]

It was no surprise that Jonnes observed so much improvement in her old haunt of the South Bronx. Continuing the SBDO's momentum in another way, the greatest share of new housing provided under the Koch plan— 36 percent—went to the Bronx, creating what came to be called the "Bronx Miracle." In the South Bronx in particular, often in small-scale two- or three-family houses, LISC financed 4,182 units, the Enterprise Foundation 2,949 units, and the Community Preservation Corporation 9,000 units. The New York City Housing Partnership built 6,000 units, and Nehemiah Houses, working with South Bronx churches, 2,000 units. All told, between 1987 and 2000, the Bronx gained 57,361 new units in rehabbed apartment buildings and 9,557 units in new, two- and three-family townhouses, equivalent to remaking 15 percent of the Bronx's total housing stock. Much of it was low density, given the prohibitive cost of erecting larger multi-family units without substantial government financing.[122] When another president, this time Bill Clinton, visited Charlotte Street in October 1997 on the twentieth anniversary of Carter's fateful tour, he found a thriving community with residents whose homes were now worth on average $200,000. By the time reporters returned for the thirtieth anniversary in October 2007, that value had grown to $500,000.[123] For a few lucky Bronx residents, Logue's SBDO had delivered the American dream of a home that was a growing capital asset, not simply a shelter. For many more Bronx residents, the SBDO provided a blueprint and the inspiration for building thousands of units of affordable housing.

TAKING STOCK

Many observers saw the South Bronx as Ed Logue's resurrection. "His comeback came in the South Bronx," the reporter Jim Yardley told *New York Times* readers in 1997. The sociologist Herbert Gans, who had been a critic of Logue's work in Boston and did everything he could to block Lindsay's hiring of Logue back in the 1960s, acknowledged, "He did a lot of good by my standards toward the end of his career when he was building affordable houses in the Bronx."[124] But in many ways, Logue was doing the same thing he always had, constantly adapting his strategy for building affordable housing and improving cities to changing policy and funding environments. Whether it was New Haven in the 1950s, Boston in the 1960s, New York State in the 1970s, or the South Bronx in the 1980s, it was always about improvisation. Lassoing the private market to subsidize homeownership for lower-income, particularly minority, families was just Logue's latest approach, and one that would reverberate in President Clinton's National Homeownership Strategy of the 1990s and President George W. Bush's Ownership Society of the early 2000s—culminating in the overreach that produced the 2008 subprime mortgage crisis.[125]

Logue left the South Bronx in January 1985 a humbler urban redeveloper than he'd been earlier in his career: more modest and incremental in his goals, more collaborative in how he achieved them, and more realistic about what was now possible. He was surely frustrated with the glaring limitations in what he could achieve but was never apologetic, self-pitying, or defeatist. Logue had regretfully abandoned his utopian visions of plentiful federal funding, idealistic New Towns for living and working, and cutting-edge experiments in technologically and architecturally innovative modernist architecture. A greater departure from the ambition—some would say hubris—of New Haven's massive urban renewal of some thirty years earlier is hardly imaginable. As Litke put it drily, "You don't go from the high-rise concept of redevelopment [in 1961] to single-family housing in the South Bronx [in 1983] without evolving."[126]

When Logue left New York in early 1985, he acknowledged his difficulties turning around the South Bronx, yet he was confident he had made a positive difference. Only sixty-four, Logue headed back to Boston, the place where he had felt most effective and valued. He now hoped to add a final chapter to his career that would make use of his many years of experience seeking a healthier urban America. But he knew, too—better than he had at other transitional junctures—that there were limits both to what he could achieve at this stage in his life and what America in the last decades of the twentieth century was willing to support.

Conclusion: The End of a Life and an Era

During the last fifteen years of Ed Logue's life, he sought to extend his influence in the field of urban redevelopment by teaching as a senior lecturer at MIT's School of Architecture and Planning and taking on various projects through the small consulting business he set up in Boston. He also spent considerable time in his cherished Martha's Vineyard, particularly after he and Margaret built a new year-round house in West Tisbury and Margaret retired there in 1989. Logue would not join her full-time until he retired himself in 1996 after suffering a small stroke the year before. But he became increasingly involved over these years in volunteer activities on the Vineyard that called on his professional expertise, whether conserving undeveloped land as a principal founder of the Vineyard Open

Land Foundation, advocating for affordable housing, strengthening Dukes County government, or defending the Steamship Authority, the primary means of transport between the mainland and the island, from legislative attack. For the first time in his life, Logue was on the other side of the fence as a grassroots community activist.[1]

Logue remained in frequent touch with many of his former compatriots from India, New Haven, Boston, and New York, even recruiting some of them—like Al Landino from New Haven days; John Bok, John Ryan, and the architects Don Stull and Paul Rudolph from his Boston Redevelopment Authority period; Rebecca Lee from the South Bronx Development Organization; and the ever loyal Janet Murphy—to help with his consulting work.[2] His most important contracts involved trying (and failing) to relocate Emerson College to economically depressed Lawrence, Massachusetts; exploring moving Suffolk University from its valuable Beacon Hill property into the State Service Center in Government Center that he had helped build in the 1960s—and when Suffolk bailed out, making it a new home for the Boston University Law School (also unsuccessful); overseeing the development of a multimillion-dollar medical complex to revitalize downtown Worcester; and counseling the Atlanta mayor Maynard Jackson on how the city might profit from the Summer Olympics of 1996.[3] Bill Tuttle, one of the handful of employees who worked in Logue's consulting business (in his case, for two and a half years after he graduated from MIT in planning), noted that even in Logue's position as a private developer he sought less to make money and more to make deals that helped nonprofits like universities and cultural institutions leverage their real estate holdings to enhance their economic survival. As Tuttle put it, "This was private development with the most public minded person you could think of running it . . . I'm working for a private developer who is probably more of a public servant than most of the people who are actually in public service."[4] Needless to say, Logue's consulting business did not prove terribly profitable.

Despite Logue's involvements, it was no surprise that a *New York Times* headline in 1997, three years before Logue's death, said of him, "Forgotten by the Public, 'Mr. Urban Renewal' Looks Back."[5] During his last years, Logue receded in relevance, considered a vestige from an earlier era, invited to speak when a symposium revisited the urban past but rarely its future, and greeted more with affection than awe at his old Boston haunts like the Tavern Club. When Lawrence Vale, today a professor of urban design and planning at MIT but then a student, attended one of Logue's classes, "Development Delivery Systems," in fall 1986, it was more to observe the once powerful man up close than to learn new redevelopment techniques from him.[6] Robin Berry worked for Logue as a research assistant while a master's student at MIT from 1985 to 1987 and then for a short time afterward at his consulting office. She observed that by the time Logue returned to Boston in the mid-1980s, he no longer knew the players and they didn't know him. "Ironically, years earlier when he arrived in Boston, he had had to get to know all the old families and firms," Berry explained. But now, twenty years later, Logue's successful efforts to revive Boston "had yielded new blood to whom he was invisible."[7]

Logue still sought ways to make an impact, writing letters to the editor and communicating, often unsolicited, with those he still knew at *The Boston Globe* or in city government.[8] But even an old, admiring associate like John Stainton, who had worked with Logue in Boston and at the New York Urban Development Corporation, acknowledged Logue's marginality. "In a way he tried to go about doing things the same way he had done when he had the power. He did it fairly gracefully. I never heard grumbling." But Stainton concluded, "I think it was hard for him. I don't think it was an easy time."[9]

Logue's contributions were far from forgotten by those who had worked closely with him over the years or benefited from his efforts. Conferences and events marking anniversaries of the emergence of the "New Boston" or the opening of Roosevelt Island still paid homage to Logue's pivotal role.[10] He always attended with enthusiasm and appreciation. When he showed up at BRA headquarters to pitch a project to convert the South End's Benjamin Franklin Institute into condos and a new home for the Boston Shakespeare Company, the room was packed with worshipful former BRA staff, "who wanted to see the old lion at work again," recalled an observer.[11] And he took tremendous pride in receiving the American Planning Association's Distinguished Leadership Award in April 1998, particularly knowing that the recognition resulted from a letter-writing campaign by colleagues from New Haven onward. When Logue died unexpectedly on the morning of January 27, 2000, at almost seventy-nine, he had been planning to meet the next day with someone who was traveling to the Vineyard to interview him about his work at the BRA.[12] The final tribute, which he would have loved for how it gathered together his friends and associates from a lifetime in the city building business, was a memorial service at Faneuil Hall on April 12, 2000. At least two hundred people attended, despite a raging storm that prohibited some, including scheduled speakers, from making it to the event.[13] His pals were quick to note that Logue went out of this world at the turn of a new twenty-first century with the same ferocity that he had brought to redeveloping cities in the second half of the twentieth.

PERSISTENT AND SHIFTING GOALS

Taking measure of a life's work as complex as Ed Logue's raises challenges. He described his career to an oral historian from the Library of Congress in 1995 as "a helluva ride."[14] It was a career of continuities fueled by unwavering personal passions and ideological convictions, and of changes resulting from significant shifts in his thinking as well as strategic adaptations made to the evolving rules of urban redevelopment.

Some of Logue's commitments he never compromised. Keeping American cities viable was the first commandment for this Philadelphia-born, New Haven–educated, Boston- and New York–devoted urban professional. Next, the goal of providing all Americans with decent housing propelled him to redevelop neighborhoods, even when it seemed—particularly in the early days in New Haven—that he was tearing down more buildings than he was putting up. He never doubted that there was method to what some thought was madness. A great deal of Logue's neighborhood renewal—New Haven's Dixwell and Wooster Square, Boston's Roxbury and Charlestown, Roosevelt Island and the Nine Towns in New York's Westchester County, and Charlotte Gardens in the South Bronx—was motivated by his conviction that the highest hope for cities and their residents lay in creating mixed-income and mixed-race communities. He was convinced that even if there was some displacement in the short term, the segregation of urban populations in distinctive neighborhoods of cities and in separate municipalities across metropolitan areas only fed inequity in public services and life chances. Otherwise, the better-off always got the best.

As far back as Logue's student days at Yale College and Law School, he had devoted himself deeply to racial integration. The pursuit of racial, not just income, diversity in residential projects animated all his work, from New Haven to Boston to all over New York State. Logue held to this ideal, even when its opponents came to include not just entrenched whites but also separatist-oriented African Americans in the era of Black Power. In the South Bronx, although white buyers were scarce for Charlotte Gardens homes, Logue sought a balance between black and Latino residents. Everywhere he worked, he insisted that minorities be well represented among contractors and their subcontractors and that school integration be made a top priority.[15]

Segregated living by class and race, Logue insisted, was not just a problem within cities. As suburbanization boomed in the postwar era, whole communities became differentiated and unequal in the opportunities they offered their residents. To address this segmentation, Logue tried to plan for entire metropolitan areas in New Haven and Boston, but it was only at the UDC where he finally enjoyed enough statewide authority to push it. The result was his Fair Share Housing program. He promoted it with passion and forbearance, but it created so much opposition that in a backlash, the UDC lost its extraordinary zoning-override powers.

To achieve all these goals, Logue kept lifelong faith in the role, responsibility, and resources of the federal government. Although he felt that urban planning and execution were most successful when handled by locals who knew their cities well, only the federal government could supply sufficient financial and other support to help cities and their residents prosper. He knew no better vehicle for achieving what he enthusiastically referred to as "social engineering" that challenged the status quo, though some of his contemporaries disparaged it.[16]

As loyal as Logue was to these enduring ambitions throughout his life, he did evolve over time. Probably the most significant shift was his recalibration of the ideal relationship of urban redevelopers to the communities they set out to "improve." Despite his adoption of the motto "planning with people" in New Haven during the 1950s, there Logue considered himself the expert who needed to consult only with representatives from established interest groups to serve the public interest. I have labeled this mode of community input pluralist democracy. In those days Logue and his colleagues Dick Lee and Mike Sviridoff felt it unnecessary, if not unwise, to collaborate with more grassroots participatory democratic organizations like the Hill Parents Association. But in Boston, in the throes of the politicized 1960s, Logue by necessity learned to negotiate with community groups like the Lower Roxbury Community Corporation and South End housing activists, giving them more of what they wanted for their neighborhoods in return for advancing his own redevelopment agenda. The *Boston Herald* reported that the South End community organizer Mel King objected to Logue's prioritizing of downtown over the neighborhoods but "credits Logue with setting the stage for neighborhood groups to get involved in housing development."[17]

By the time Logue was embedded once again in a local community during the late 1970s and 1980s in the South Bronx, he made an even bigger adjustment, recognizing that his only chance for success resided with working closely with neighborhood CDCs, community planning boards, and other grassroots vehicles advancing participatory democracy. Without the kind of backing he had once enjoyed from the federal government, the statehouse, and city hall, his best bet rested in allying with residents who were deeply invested in the fate of their neighborhoods. Somewhat to his own surprise, Logue came to value those relationships and to recognize their importance for everyone involved. One might be tempted to argue that Logue's greater openness to community input resulted simply from the breakdown of the pipeline from Washington. But this explanation does not sufficiently account for Logue's evolution from renewal czar of New Haven to collaborative colleague in the South Bronx.

Another shift in Logue's redevelopment strategy lay in his approach toward architecture. In New Haven during the 1950s, he and his partner Mayor Lee were convinced that building in a cutting-edge modernist style would send just the signal needed that New Haven was viable in the post-war economy and open for business. Logue even wanted the house that he and Margaret constructed for themselves to convey this up-to-dateness. Only in his last years in New Haven did Logue begin to experiment with reha-bilitating existing housing rather than demolishing the old and building anew. The exemplary Wooster Square project would remain a source of great pride forever after.

In Boston, Logue persisted with his conviction that the latest modern-ist architecture provided the perfect way to announce a declining city's re-birth. Government Center in particular, with its new city hall chosen by international architectural competition, appropriately symbolized the New Boston. Logue's confidence that there were rewards for good modern archi-tecture extended to the point that in the late 1980s, long after the opening of Boston's Government Center, Logue tried unsuccessfully to complete Paul Rudolph's State Service Center as planned, with its pinwheeling tower, even bringing in Rudolph himself to help.[18] Back in the 1960s, however, Logue had already begun to soften his exclusively modernist vision. Recalling New Ha-ven's Wooster Square, he came to appreciate even more the importance of preserving some of the historic fabric of Boston alongside the new buildings, which led to the preservation of the Sears Crescent and Quincy Market. In Boston, too, he lived in a nineteenth-century rowhouse on historic Beacon Hill. What I have called Logue's embrace of a more "negotiated cityscape" between the old and new would influence later projects like Roosevelt Island, where Logue went out of his way to preserve historic structures.

At the UDC, Logue welcomed what he considered his mission to cre-ate architecturally innovative housing prototypes for use anywhere.[19] He adapted European New Towns to the American physical and political landscape. He pioneered applying the latest technology to residential construction. And he hired prominent architects to design new types of subsidized housing, such as an innovative model for low-rise, high-density living in Brooklyn's Marcus Garvey Park Village. Logue later launched a competition for a fresh approach to high-rise subsidized housing on Roosevelt Island, until the UDC's downfall kept him from seeing it to completion. Although some of the UDC's critics blamed the agency's financial woes on Logue's hiring of high-profile architects, he stubbornly defended the importance of experimentation in housing design and sought to make improvements based on insights that emerged from the UDC staff's famous live-ins. Not all UDC housing succeeded, of course. Some was judged poor in quality, due to overly experimental design, cost constraints, and Logue's rush to get it up quickly with his fast-tracking schemes.

When Logue arrived in the South Bronx and was faced with the challenge of redeveloping the devastated Charlotte Street neighborhood with a minimum of public resources, he abandoned his previous prioritizing of creative design and searched for another approach that would appeal to the prospective residents and private financers whose buy-in he now needed. Charlotte Gardens, a suburban-type development of ninety conventional, architecturally uninspired, ranch houses was groundbreaking only in its use of prefabricated construction. To Logue's credit, although he knew that he was inviting condemnation from the planners and architects whose admiration he had long cultivated, he chose to put a viable future for Charlotte Street above his own architectural predilections and personal reputation. In the realm of design, as in the way he learned to consult more broadly with community members, Logue adjusted to the requirements of the moment and brought flexibility rather than ideological rigidity to his work.

As opportunities allowed it, Ed Logue enjoyed being what I have described as a rebel in the belly of the establishment beast, using his powerful position to pursue his goals and, if necessary, impose his own standards and values on projects and people. But over time Logue learned that this role did not always serve him well. At the UDC, when Logue's social mission sharply conflicted with the economic interests of his establishment sponsors, he was ousted. In the South Bronx, by necessity, Logue accomplished more as an outsider operating from the city's far north reaches than as a mouthpiece of the political authorities downtown. At the height of his influence, Logue's insider stance likely had blinded him to some of the limitations of federal urban renewal that only in later life did he fully understand. But although his passage from star performer to cast extra was not easy, Logue's ability to shift ultimately helped him preserve his sense of self-worth and not withdraw into defeatism or alienation. Even if out of the mainstream toward the end of his career, Logue remained effective.

THE LEGACY OF LOGUE'S STORY

In 1987, a few years after Logue returned to Boston from New York, he publicly criticized the trend toward privatization that had gained momentum over the twenty years since he had left the leadership of the BRA. Lamenting that "the lead role of the BRA in planning and development [has] diminished" while "the role of the private sector [has] increased," Logue insisted that "when purely private interests make development proposals, their overwhelming concern is private profit, not the public interest." He called fervently for Boston to resume "an active public leadership role instead of a re-active one."[20] Logue wasn't naive about the inescapable necessity for public-private partnerships to help achieve urban projects. He had depended on a private developer for the downtown Church Street shopping mall in New Haven, on the support of the business-dominated Vault in redeveloping downtown Boston, on bondholders to fund the UDC, and on banks to provide mortgages for new Charlotte Gardens homeowners. He did expect, however, that public officials would be in the driver's seat, not the back seat.

The shift from public to private funding and initiative in city development that Logue decried would only expand after he left the South Bronx and following his death. It mattered little if Democrats or Republicans governed in Washington. Although Logue lived to see Boston and New York City benefiting from growth in private investment, and even the South Bronx turning the corner, New Haven continued to struggle. Like other deindustrialized cities in the United States, it was largely ignored by investors and the young talent who flocked to places with vibrant, new economies. But in all his cities, prosperous or not, affordable housing—as it was now universally called rather than "public," "low-income," or "subsidized"—was in devastatingly short supply. Today Logue would be deeply disturbed to observe the years-long wait lists in almost every American city for affordable rental units, apartments in aging public housing, and Section 8 vouchers—now officially named Housing Choice vouchers—that recipients theoretically could take into the private rental market.[21]

In the urban policy regime of market-based solutions with few direct government provisions that prevailed by the end of Logue's career and still persists, there are two major tools for making housing more affordable: housing vouchers and the Low-Income Housing Tax Credits (LIHTC) program, which arrived on the scene in 1986, a year after Logue departed the South Bronx.[22] LIHTC, the predominant method today of financing subsidized housing in the United States, established a more expansive and efficient way than was available to Logue's SBDO of mobilizing the private sector's investment in affordable housing. It works by allocating tax credits to states, which then award them to selected low-income housing projects. Private investors gain valuable tax credits by making equity investments in the housing, which in turn reduces the cost of construction and the rents of tenants. Although this approach has encouraged a major scaling up of private investment in much-needed affordable housing, it also has serious vulnerabilities. Most obvious is its dependence on the vagaries of corporate need for tax credits to offset profits. In tough economic times, when struggling individuals are most desperate for decent housing, corporate participation often declines along with earnings, introducing uncertainty and limitations into the system. And if and when corporate taxes are lowered and companies have less need to shelter profits, demand drops for credits and less capital is available for building.[23] Most fundamentally, in an echo of the debate that raged at the UDC's demise, a public responsibility to house needy Americans gets fulfilled only by giving private corporations and banks financial breaks, at the sacrifice of tax monies that would otherwise have gone into government coffers.[24]

Housing vouchers have likewise become a more significant provider of affordable housing, particularly as units in public housing have disappeared, but again the demand wildly outstrips the supply. Based on a compelling argument that low-income families benefit from moving to middle-class communities with better services and safer environments—an ideal that Logue himself endorsed—the voucher program has been undermined by holders' shrinking buying power and the unwillingness of many landlords to accept vouchers in a competitive rental market. The resulting *lack* of choice that recipients have in using Housing Choice vouchers only perpetuates the economic and racial segregation that flourishes when the private market faces few constraints. Even with mounting evidence documenting the advantages, particularly to children, of living and schooling amid diversity and away from concentrated poverty, Logue's dream of a more socially integrated America continues to fade.[25] So, too, has Logue's hope for metropolitan planning that better distributes low-income residents in a region, as power and responsibility for planning have devolved from the federal and state governments to municipalities and even more narrowly focused neighborhood-based CDCs.[26] Only Logue's pioneering effort to integrate the disabled into residential communities like Roosevelt Island has achieved universal acceptance, helped by the passage of the Americans with Disabilities Act in 1990 and successful litigation to enforce it thereafter.

CDCs, such as the Mid Bronx Desperadoes—the SBDO's partner—have only grown in importance since Logue's days in the South Bronx. Here, as with the LIHTC, there are strengths and weaknesses. Many CDCs provide valuable affordable housing, frequently utilizing LIHTCs.[27] As Logue learned, small-scale, locally oriented CDCs not only get the job done, but they do so in a way that increases community participation often missing in the more top-down federal urban renewal of Logue's earlier days. On the other hand, neighborhood-based CDCs, many thinly staffed with dedicated but overworked housing activists, spend a lot of their time patching together funding from multiple sources, including tax credits, and have limited ability to provide housing on the scale needed or to plan beyond the neighborhood at the city and metropolitan levels.

When Julie Sandorf asked MBD's leaders Gennie Brooks and Father William Smith at their first meeting, as she looked around in disbelief at what seemed like miles of abandoned buildings and vacant lots in the South Bronx,

"How in the world are you going to rebuild this neighborhood?" they replied with conviction, "Building by building, person by person, block by block."[28] Those were inspiring words, but they also conveyed a limitation that Felice Michetti, a longtime housing insider in New York City who oversaw Mayor Ed Koch's ten-year housing program, recognized. She noted that the South Bronx's CDCs, like MBD, SEBCO, and Banana Kelly, each "had their area . . . And generally, the groups respected the boundaries of each other," making them "highly organized" in their own territories and less competitive with one another. But in turn, she lamented, they were also "less global."[29] In the shift from large-scale, citywide federally supported programs to the more piecemeal grants and smaller turfs of CDCs, community residents may have gained in influence, but they lost in access to financial resources, predictability, and reach. These were tough trade-offs.

In addition to depending on limited LIHTC credits, housing vouchers, and CDCs, American cities have adopted new strategies of their own to squeeze public benefits out of the private real estate market. These include collecting linkage fees from developers seeking approval for new downtown ventures that are then used to build affordable housing elsewhere and passing inclusionary zoning laws that require developers to designate a certain percentage of units in new market-rate residential projects as affordable. Admirable as these tactics are, they do not come close to meeting the enormous demand for affordable housing nor creating socially balanced neighborhoods. Moreover, the necessity for cities to fend for themselves to solve their problems encourages them to use tax forgiveness and other financial incentives to lure investors promising needed resources. These baits often set off races to the bottom among cities, which all ultimately lose, as winning cities encounter new costs while their tax revenue is reduced and inequality among cities is accentuated.[30]

The history of urban redevelopment since the end of World War II, as told through Logue's career, yields many insights. The overarching message of Logue's "Tale of a City Builder," as he considered titling his never-completed book, is that urban renewal was not one undifferentiated mistake from the Housing Act of 1949 to President Richard Nixon's moratorium on federal spending for housing in 1973. Rather, the career of this urban redeveloper demonstrates that there were gains and losses, failed and successful experiments, times of breakthrough and moments of disgrace. Some of Logue's work improved the cities and neighborhoods he labored in, and some did not. But there can be no denying that Logue learned lessons in doing one project that he carried to the next. He revised his strategies to adapt to changing times, shifting political realities, and his own evolving understanding of what it took to save America's cities. Urban renewal was driven as much by improvisation as by orthodoxy.

Like Logue, we, too, can learn lessons from urban renewal's past successes and failures. Here are only a few. Architecture can be more than a means to an end; it carries within it the potential to improve the social and aesthetic quality of urban environments and to deliver better and cheaper housing when innovative design and technology are prioritized. The private sector has a significant role to play in expanding the capacity of American society's investment in housing and other urban amenities and necessities, but that does not mean that government can abandon its responsibility for the general welfare. There is much lost in a neoliberal world where the most robust activity is local and global. The intervening levels of state and national governance are crucial tools of redistribution within vast and diverse territories. Only policy and program at that scale can counteract the inequalities that flourish in a society consisting of islands of poverty and privilege. Moreover, when government does assert itself, it must involve community residents in decisions that affect their homes, neighborhoods, and cities, seeking to avoid the extremes of both nonconsultative command and community NIMBYism. Development by increment rather than through mega plan often yields greater success and more citizen participation over the long term. And cities thrive by providing dynamic pedestrian- and transit-oriented alternatives to suburbia, not mimicking its sprawl and car-orientation.[31]

This history of city building in the United States over almost three-quarters of the last century suggests two final aspirations. First, there is no one right or wrong way to remake a city, but rather it requires above all a spirit of experimentation and a process of negotiation where every interest has a seat at the table—public officials as well as private investors, urban planners and architects, multiple levels of government, and residents. As Logue learned from hard experience over his career, the fate of cities cannot be left solely to top-down redevelopers or government bureaucrats or market forces or citizens' groups. Rather, the goal should be a negotiated cityscape built on compromise, an approach that Logue came to accept in Boston, after failing to do so in New Haven, and that he eventually promoted in the South Bronx. Second, a better understanding of this history will hopefully reawaken from a long slumber the will and wherewithal to revitalize cities that still struggle for economic survival, to invest in neighborhoods still lacking adequate services, and to improve the prospects for those Americans still poorly housed or, in the worst cases, homeless. This would be the legacy of urban renewal that Ed Logue would want us to honor and that he would consider the highest tribute we could pay to his lifetime of public service, imperfections and all.[32]

NOTES

Abbreviations Used in the Notes

AAPSS—American Academy of Political and Social Science

AB—*Architecture Boston*

AF—*Architectural Forum*

AR—*Architectural Record*

BG—*Boston Globe*

BH—*Boston Herald*

BM—*Boston Magazine*

Bowles—Chester Bowles Papers, Yale University Library Manuscripts and Archives, New Haven, CT

Bray—Peter Bray Papers, private collection

BSB—*Bay State Banner*, Boston, MA (Boston's major African American newspaper)

BW—*Business Week*

COH—Columbia Center for Oral History Archives, Edward I. Koch Administration Oral History Project, Butler Library, Columbia University, New York, NY, transcripts

Collins—Papers of John Collins, Boston Public Library, Boston, MA

CR—*City Record*, Boston, MA

Crimson—*Harvard Crimson* newspaper, Harvard University, Cambridge, MA

CSM—*Christian Science Monitor*

CT—*Chicago Tribune*

Dahl—Robert Dahl Papers, Yale University Library Manuscripts and Archives, New Haven, CT, transcripts

EJL—Edward J. Logue Papers, Yale University Library Manuscripts and Archives, New Haven, CT

FH—Freedom House Papers, Northeastern University, Archives and Special Collections, Boston, MA

HGSD—Harvard Graduate School of Design, Cambridge, MA

JAIP—*Journal of the American Institute of Planners*

JH—*Journal of Housing*

JJ—John Johansen Papers, Avery Library, Columbia University, New York, NY

Jones—Frank Jones, interview with Edward J. Logue, April 1999, Martha's Vineyard, MA, Edward J. Logue Papers, 2007 Addition, Box 2, Yale University Library Manuscripts and Archives, New Haven, CT, transcript

JPH—*Journal of Planning History*

JUH—*Journal of Urban History*

LAT—*Los Angeles Times*

MBD—Mid Bronx Desperadoes Community Housing Corporation

MDL—Margaret DeVane Logue Papers, Martha's Vineyard, MA; some of this material moved to Edward J. Logue Papers, 2007 Addition, Yale University Library Manuscripts and Archives, New Haven, CT

MLogue—Margaret DeVane Logue, interview by Lizabeth Cohen, July 18, 2007, Martha's Vineyard, MA

NAACP—National Association for the Advancement of Colored People

NHR—*New Haven Register*

NYDN—*New York Daily News*

NYPL—New York Public Library, New York, NY

NYSA—New York State Archives, Albany, NY

NYSUDC—New York State Urban Development Corporation

NYT—*New York Times*

PA—*Progressive Architecture*

PD—Paul Davidoff Papers, Rare and Manuscript Collections, Carl A. Kroch Library, Cornell University, Ithaca, NY

PT—*Patent Trader* (Mount Kisco, NY, newspaper)

RCL—Richard C. Lee Papers, Yale University Library Manuscripts and Archives, New Haven, CT

Rotival—Maurice E. H. Rotival Papers, Yale University Library Manuscripts and Archives, New Haven, CT

Ruben—Gregory Ruben interviews, 2006, New Haven County Bar Association Centennial Celebration Oral History Project, New Haven, CT, transcripts

Schussheim—Morton Schussheim, interview with Edward J. Logue, May 24, 1995, Pioneers in Housing Oral History Project, Library of Congress, Washington, DC, transcript

SEP—*Saturday Evening Post*

Steen—Ivan Steen, ten interviews with Edward J. Logue, 1983-91, Edward J. Logue Papers, 2002 Addition, Box 21, Folder "EJL Rockefeller Oral History," Yale University Library Manuscripts and Archives, New Haven, CT, transcripts

UPA—Urban Planning Aid Records, 1966-82, University of Massachusetts, Boston, MA

WM—*Washington Monthly*

WP—*Washington Post*

WSJ—*Wall Street Journal*

WWD—*Women's Wear Daily*

YULocal35—Yale University of Union Employees Local 35, AFL-CIO, Papers, 1941-81, Yale University Library Manuscripts and Archives, New Haven, CT

YMA—Yale University Library Manuscripts and Archives, New Haven, CT

Introduction: Cities in Crisis

1. These totals vary slightly from source to source, likely because of inconsistencies in tallying; see Louis K. Loewenstein, *The New York State Urban Development Corporation: Private Benefits, Public Costs, an Evaluation of a Noble Experiment* (Washington, DC: Council of State Planning Agencies, 1980), 38-39, 123-24; Steven R. Weisman, "Nelson Rockefeller's Pill: The UDC," *WM*, June 1975, 35; Lawrence Goldman, "Federal Policy and the UDC," *Planner* 61, no. 5 (May 1975): 177; William Marlin, "After the Pratfall: UDC Dusts Off the Debris of Default," *AR* 158, no. 6 (Mid-October 1975): 107-24; Jim Yardley, "A Master Builder's Mixed Legacy: Forgotten by the Public, 'Mr. Urban Renewal' Looks Back," *NYT*, December 29, 1997; *New York State Urban Development Corporation Annual Report 1974*, 5.

2. Louis K. Loewenstein, "The New York State Urban Development Corporation—a Forgotten Failure or a Precursor of the Future?," *JAIP* 44, no. 3 (July 1978): 262; Eleanor L. Brilliant, *The Urban Development Corporation: Private Interests and Public Authority* (Lexington, MA: Lexington Books, D. C. Heath, 1975), 184.

3. Weisman, "Nelson Rockefeller's Pill," 35; Loewenstein, "Forgotten Failure," 262. Loewenstein, *Private Benefits, Public Costs*, 112, calculated that the default affected forty-four state housing finance agencies. Franziska Porges Hosken, in "Planning and Urban Renewal: A Discussion with Edward Logue," in *The Functions of Cities* (Cambridge, MA: Schenkman, 1973), 109, singled out Massachusetts, Connecticut, New Jersey, Pennsylvania, West Virginia, and Ohio for having particularly strong interest in the UDC model.

4. "Big daddy government" was a phrase that Logue attributed to critics of the UDC's effort to build affordable housing in Westchester County; Logue handwritten statement, no title, no date, EJL, 2002 Accession, Box 22, Folder "Notes, Misc., 1980s," 10.

5. Linda Greenhouse, "Logue Sees U.D.C. as 'Whipping Boy,'" *NYT*, October 21, 1975; Logue, interview, Jones, Tape 3:38.

6. Logue, interview, Steen, July 11, 1991, Boston, MA, 39.

7. Nicholas von Hoffman, "Ed Logue—the Master Rebuilder," *WP*, April 15, 1967; Logue, "New York: Are Cities a Bust?," *Look*, April 1, 1969, 70-73; Richard Schickel, "New York's Mr. Urban Renewal," *NYT Magazine*, March 1, 1970; "Housing: How Ed Logue Does It," *Newsweek*, November 6, 1972.

8. Alice O'Connor, "The Privatized City: The Manhattan Institute, the Urban Crisis, and the Conservative Counterrevolution in New York," *JUH* 34, no. 2 (January 2008): 333–35; Michael B. Katz, *The Undeserving Poor: America's Enduring Confrontation with Poverty*, 2nd ed. (New York: Oxford University Press, 2013).

9. Bryce Covert, "Give Us Shelter," *Nation*, June 18–25, 2018, 15.

10. William Lucy, "Logue on Cities," *Planning* 1, no. 8 (August 1985): 15. On memory versus the reality of urban renewal, see J. Rosie Tighe and Timothy J. Opelt, "Collective Memory and Planning: The Continuing Legacy of Urban Renewal in Asheville, NC," *JPH* 15, no. 1 (February 2016): 46–67.

11. Richard Rogin, "New Town on a New York Island Named Welfare," *City* 5, no. 3 (May–June 1971): 43.

12. Critiques of top-down planning for valuing rational expertise over local, indigenous knowledge include James Scott, *Thinking Like a State: How Certain Schemes to Improve the Human Condition Have Failed* (New Haven, CT: Yale University Press, 1999); and Eric Avila, *The Folklore of the Freeway: Race and Revolt in the Modernist City* (Minneapolis: University of Minnesota Press, 2014).

13. Logue, "The Head Table—Briefly," March 21, 1981, EJL, 2002 Accession, Box 23, Folder "Recognition to Friends."

14. A classic statement of the growth-machine argument is J. R. Logan and H. L. Molotch, *Urban Fortunes: The Political Economy of Place* (Berkeley: University of California Press, 1987).

15. The masterful and comprehensive, if highly critical, book on Robert Moses is Robert A. Caro, *The Power Broker: Robert Moses and the Fall of New York* (New York: Vintage, 1975); for a revisionist account that acknowledges more of his contributions, see Hilary Ballon and Kenneth T. Jackson, eds., *Robert Moses and the Modern City: The Transformation of New York* (New York: W. W. Norton, 2007).

16. Jane Jacobs, *The Death and Life of Great American Cities* (New York: Vintage, 1961); for a critique along these lines at her death, see Nicolai Ouroussoff, "Outgrowing Jane Jacobs," *NYT*, April 30, 2006. For other recent considerations of Jacobs, see Peter L. Laurence, *Becoming Jane Jacobs* (Philadelphia: University of Pennsylvania Press, 2016); and Robert Kanigel, *Eyes on the Street: The Life of Jane Jacobs* (New York: Knopf, 2016).

17. Martin Anderson, *The Federal Bulldozer: A Critical Analysis of Urban Renewal, 1949–1962* (Cambridge, MA: MIT Press, 1964); *Reason* website, http://www.reason .com, particularly Jacobs's obituary, "Jane Jacobs, RIP," http://reason.com/blog /2006/04/25/jane-jacobs-rip, and "Jane Jacobs at 100," http://reason.com/blog/2016 /05/04/jane-jacobs-at-100, which labels her "the great defender of urban freedom." Peter Laurence offers a careful analysis of where Jacobs's thinking overlapped with that of prominent conservatives like Friedrich Hayek and Karl Popper and where she recognized that government action was needed; Laurence, *Becoming Jane Jacobs*, 289–305.

18. Lawrence P. Goldman, "Eulogy, Edward J. Logue, Memorial Service, April 27, 2000," Faneuil Hall, Boston, MDL, 4. For Logue's opinion of Moses, see Logue, interview, Steen, December 13, 1983, New York, NY, 31, where he called him a "high-handed son-of-a-bitch"; January 16, 1991, Boston, MA, 34, where he railed against Moses's

public housing as an "outrageous" national model, with "no redeeming qualities," "no sense of community"; and July 11, 1991, 22–23, where he said Moses "could be the most charming guy in the world. But you don't have to read more than two chapters of Caro to know that he had another side to him."

19. Robert Moses to Edward Otis Proctor, Esq., October 17, 1966, New York, NY, and Edward Otis Proctor to Robert Moses, October 21, 1966, Boston, MA, Robert Moses Papers, Box 84, NYPL, Rare Books and Manuscript Division, with thanks to Adam Tanaka.

20. Ada Louise Huxtable, "New York's 9/11 Site Needed Not a Moses but a Logue," *WSJ*, August 27, 2008.

21. Logue, "The View from the Village," in "American Cities: Dead or Alive?—Two Views," *AF* 116, no. 3 (March 1962): 89. Also see Walter McQuade, "Architecture," *Nation*, March 17, 1962, 241–42, on the Logue-Jacobs debate at MoMA; Logue, interview, Steen, December 13, 1983, New York, NY, 44, where Logue said, "The only thing I have any respect for Jane Jacobs for is that when her son became a CO in the Vietnam War, she said, 'The hell with this, I'm going to go to Canada with him.'"

22. "Godmother of the American City," interview by James Howard Kunstler expanded from *Metropolis*, March 2001, in *Jane Jacobs: The Last Interview and Other Conversations* (Brooklyn, NY: Melville House, 2016), 73–75, 95. Also, Yardley, "Master Builder's Mixed Legacy," *NYT*. Logue claimed that he wrote to Jacobs "and offered to take her on a tour of any neighborhood [he] worked in, in New Haven or Boston"; Logue, "Reflections of 'Mr. Urban Renewal, the Forgotten Master Builder,'" 1998, MDL.

23. John Zuccotti, interview by Lizabeth Cohen, December 10, 2007, New York, NY.

24. Joint Center for Housing Studies of Harvard University, *The State of the Nation's Housing 2018* (Cambridge, MA: Joint Center for Housing Studies, 2018), 1–6; Covert, "Give Us Shelter," and Jimmy Tobias, "The Way Home," *Nation*, June 18–25, 2018; Mathew Desmond, *Eviction: Poverty and Profit in the American City* (New York: Crown, 2016); "Reach for the Sky: Running San Francisco," *Economist*, June 2, 2018. "Moving to Opportunity" was the name of a demonstration research project implemented in the 1990s by the U.S. Department of Housing and Urban Development to assess the impact of mobility in housing achieved through Section 8 vouchers on the social and economic prospects of low-income families.

25. Housing Act of 1949, Section 1441, Title 42, 3891, https://www.gpo.gov/fdsys/pkg/USCODE-2010-title42/pdf/USCODE-2010-title42-chap8A-subchapI-sec1441.pdf.

1. The Making of an Urban Renewer

1. Quote from Logue to John M. Golden, September 25, 1953, EJL, Series 4, Box 26, Folder 56. For more on Logue's involvement in the Lee campaign, see Chester Kerr to Logue, October 7, 1953, EJL, Series 4, Box 27, Folder 67; and Logue to Chester Bowles, October 19, 1953, EJL, Series 3, Box 13, Folder 10, where Logue is listed as a member of the Executive Committee of Independents for Lee.

2. Mayor Richard C. Lee, Speech to the New Haven Board of Aldermen, November 11, 1960, in Fred Powledge, *Model City: A Test of American Liberalism; One Town's Efforts to Rebuild Itself* (New York: Simon and Schuster, 1970), 42. Lee used versions

of this phrase frequently; also see Allan R. Talbot, *The Mayor's Game: Richard Lee of New Haven and the Politics of Change* (New York: Harper and Row, 1967), 88. So did Logue; see Logue, interview, Schussheim, 20.

3. Logue frequently described his home as "without racial prejudice" in oral histories; see, for example, Logue, interview, Schussheim, 2.

4. Logue quote in Ruth Knack, "Edward Logue, AICP," *Planning* 64, no. 4 (April 1998): 16.

5. Ellen Logue (sister), interview by Lizabeth Cohen, April 13, 2008, Berkeley, CA. Later in life, Logue credited Philadelphia with sparking his interest in urban design, "a city not without style and grace" where "I went to school in Rittenhouse Square and learned at a formative age what a delightful place a modest public square can be"; Logue, "The Education of an Urban Administrator," in *The Universitas Project: Solutions for a Post-Technological Society*, conceived and directed by Emilio Ambasz (New York: Museum of Modern Art, 2006), 177.

6. Ellen Logue, interview; "Requiem Mass Celebrated for Sister Maria Kostka," *Catholic Standard and Times* (Philadelphia), January 10, 1958.

7. On Logue's youth in Philadelphia, see Logue, interview, Jones, Tape 5:13–34; Paul Hogan, *Philadelphia Boyhood: Growing Up in the 1930s* (Vienna, VA: Holbrook and Kellogg, 1995); Ellen Logue, interview; Frank Logue, "From Yale to City Hall, and Back Again," *Yale Herald*, December 6, 2002; Seymour "Spence" Toll to Margaret Logue, January 28, 2000, MDL. Toll, a high school friend of brother John, recalled "the years of terrible financial stress" during the Logues' youth.

8. On religious and class discrimination at Yale, see George Wilson Pierson, *A Yale Book of Numbers: Historical Statistics of the College and University 1701–1976* (New Haven, CT: Yale University, 1983), 85, 87, 89, 96, 127; Dan A. Oren, *Joining the Club: A History of Jews and Yale* (New Haven, CT: Yale University Press, in cooperation with the American Jewish Archives, 1985), 70–71, 91–93, 181–82, 348n19; Jerome Karabel, *The Chosen: The Hidden History of Admission and Exclusion at Harvard, Yale, and Princeton* (Boston: Houghton Mifflin, 2005), 200–219; Marcia Graham Synnott, *The Half-Opened Door: Discrimination and Admissions at Harvard, Yale, and Princeton* (Westport, CT: Greenwood Press, 1979), xviii, 14, 128, 131–32, 218; Geoffrey Kabaservice, "The Birth of a New Institution: How Two Yale Presidents and Their Admissions Directors Tore Up the 'Old Blueprint' to Create a Modern Yale," *Yale Alumni Magazine*, December 1999, http://www.yalealumnimagazine.com/issues/99_12/admissions.html, and the appreciative response by Frank Logue, http://www.yalealumnimagazine.com/issues/00_02/letters.html; Frank Logue, "From Yale to City Hall, and Back Again"; Frank Logue, interview by Lizabeth Cohen, February 15, 2006, Hamden, CT. On discrimination against Jewish faculty at Yale, which particularly hurt the sciences, see Brooks Mather Kelley, *Yale: A History* (New Haven, CT: Yale University Press, 1974), 416. William Horowitz, a local New Haven businessman and politician (and father of the historian Daniel Horowitz), was the first Jewish member of the Yale Corporation, elected in the mid-1960s by alumni petition. As of 1974, no Catholic had ever been a member, according to Raymond E. Wolfinger, *The Politics of Progress* (Englewood Cliffs, NJ: Prentice-Hall, 1974), 27–28. Daniel Horowitz's fascinating study of the Yale College Class of

1960 shows how slowly the social order changed at Yale: *On the Cusp: The Yale College Class of 1960 and a World on the Verge of Change* (Amherst: University of Massachusetts Press, 2015).

Thomas Bergin (Class of '25, Ph.D. '29), a New Haven High School graduate who attended Yale in the 1920s and felt excluded from the dominant prep-school culture, appreciated how much the college system improved the social experience of "the plebian class" when he returned as a professor in 1948. Nonetheless, when Anthony Astrachan ('52), a Jewish student from Stuyvesant High School in New York City, arrived that same year, he still encountered discrimination: "If you did not request specific roommates, the Yale of 1948 automatically put four Jewish strangers together. This concern for our comfort discomfited us by telling us we were all outsiders"; Thomas Bergin, "My Native Country," and Anthony Astrachan, "Class Notes," in *My Harvard, My Yale*, ed. Diana Dubois (New York: Random House, 1982), 160–67, 212.

9. John Arcudi, interview by Deborah Sue Elkin, December 16, 1997, "Bridgeport Working: Voices from the 20th Century Oral History Project," Bridgeport Public Library, transcript, 6, 10–13, 56; for the La Guardia rally and Winchester strike, Logue, interview by Deborah Sue Elkin, September 18, 1993, New Haven, CT, transcript from Elkin, 28–30; Bud Scher to Margaret, Frank, and John Logue, February 4, 2000, MDL.

10. On the Labor Party of the Yale Political Union, see Deborah Sue Elkin, "Labor and the Left: The Limits of Acceptable Dissent at Yale University, 1920s to 1950s" (Ph.D. dissertation, Yale University, 1995), 51.

11. FBI, Report from New Haven, November 1, 1951, for United States Civil Service Commission, Security Clearance File, obtained under a Freedom of Information Act (FOIA) request on April 20, 2009, received on September 18, 2009, 3; Hood to FBI Washington Field, cable November 19, 1951, FOIA; Logue, Elkin interview, 15–16.

12. Logue, interview, Schussheim, 10. Arcudi felt a similar connection to New Haven: "I go to New Haven in 1939, and I don't have any money, you know? But I had great entertainment, walking around the streets of New Haven"; Arcudi, interview, 56.

13. Quote from Logue, Elkin interview, 2. On Logue's support of the union cause while a student, see letter to the editor, *Yale Daily News*, November 4, 1941. At a debate at the Yale Political Union, "Laborite" Logue defended the resolution "Resolved, That Yale C.I.O. employees should have a union shop"; "Moderates Pull Coup; P.U. Upholds 'Protective Shop,'" *Yale Daily News*, November 27, 1941.

14. Ellen Logue, interview.

15. MLogue, interview.

16. On Logue's work as a labor organizer, see YULocal35, Boxes 1 and 3, including Logue to A. D. Lewis, September 8, 1948, Box 1, Folder 3; Elkin, "Labor and the Left," 48–228; Logue, Elkin interview, 16–18. For conditions of Yale workers, see George Butler, "Yale Needs the C.I.O.," *Nation* 146, no. 3 (January 15, 1938): 67–68. On labor in New Haven more broadly, see Frank E. Annunziato, William Carey, and Nick Aiello, *Labor Almanac: New Haven's Unions in the 1990s*, a joint project of the Greater New Haven Labor History Association and the Greater New Haven Central Labor Council, AFL-CIO, 1995.

17. Logue to Franklin D. Roosevelt, September 29, 1942, EJL, Series 1, Box 6, Folder 94; Military Intelligence Service, War Department, Washington, DC, to Honorable J. Edgar Hoover, Director, FBI, July 3, 1943, with accompanying report by Intelligence Division, Army Service Forces, June 10, 1943, FOIA.

18. From YULocal35, Box 1, Folder 7: Logue to Member, January 29, 1942; Logue to A. D. Lewis, January 26, 1943: "I am more than happy," he wrote in his resignation letter, "to fight as a member of the Army Air Corps for our democracy and for the cause of free labor everywhere."

19. "Master Pieces: Ed Logue Talks with Rebecca Barnes AIA," *AB* 1, no. 2 (1998): 32; Logue, "Life as a City Builder—'Make No Little Plans,'" March 26, 1991, written for Yale Reunion Book, *The Yale '42 Story: 50 Years Out*, MDL, 2; "Another Droops-noot Bombardier Checks In," *Crosshairs*, September 1994, 15.

20. On Le Corbusier, see M. Christine Boyer, "Aviation and the Aerial View: Le Corbusier's Spatial Transformations in the 1930s and 1940s," *diacritics* 33, nos. 3–4 (Fall–Winter 2003): 93–116; quotation in Le Corbusier, trans. Edith Schreiber Aujame, *Precisions on the Present State of Architecture and City Planning* (Cambridge, MA: MIT Press, 1991, originally published 1930), 236.

21. Logue to Mary Nelles, November 4, 1944, EJL, Series 1, Box 5, Folder 77; Max Page and Timothy Mennel, eds., *Reconsidering Jane Jacobs* (Chicago: American Planning Association, 2011), 5–6. For Maurice Rotival's bird's-eye viewing, see Rachel D. Carley, "Tomorrow Is Here: New Haven and the Modern Moment," report prepared for New Haven Preservation Trust, June 2008, 16.

22. Logue's work as a union organizer from 1946 to 1948 in YULocal35, Box 1, Folders 11, 12, 13, and EJL, Series 1, Box 7, Folders 110–23. For Logue's appointment as a part-time organizer, see Logue to A. D. Lewis, October 7, 1946, and A. D. Lewis to Logue, November 1, 1946, EJL, Series 1, Box 6, Folder 109, and a detailed paper Logue wrote for Fred Rodell about his efforts, "Organizational Techniques," April 21, 1947, EJL, Series 1, Box 6, Folder 102.

23. MLogue, interview; Logue's references for jobs included Rodell, Dean Wesley Sturges, Harry Schulman (a labor arbitrator), and Thomas I. Emerson, probably the most politically radical member of the Yale Law faculty; Glenn Fowler, "Thomas I. Emerson, 83, Scholar Who Molded Civil Liberties Law," *NYT*, June 22, 1991.

24. Laura Kalman, *Legal Realism at Yale, 1927–1960* (Chapel Hill: University of North Carolina Press, 1986); Laura Kalman, "Legal Realism," in *The Oxford International Encyclopedia of Legal History*, ed. Stanley L. Katz (New York: Oxford University Press, 2009); Neil Duxbury, "In the Twilight of Legal Realism: Fred Rodell and the Limits of Legal Critique," *Oxford Journal of Legal Studies* 11, no. 3 (Autumn 1991): 354–95; Charles Alan Wright, "Goodbye to Fred Rodell," *Yale Law Review Journal* 89, no. 8 (July 1980): 1455–62; "Journals of Opinion and the Work of Democracy: A Conversation with Victor S. Navasky," Institute of International Studies, University of California, Berkeley, http://globetrotter.berkeley.edu/people5/Navasky/navasky -conl.html. At an August 1944 union meeting, Rodell said, "I'm even more grateful for the honorary membership you have given me than for the honor of belonging to the University Faculty"; clippings: "Union Will Seek Contract Revision with University" and "Law Professor Joins Employees Union," scrapbook, YULocal35,

Box 3, Folder 1. I am grateful to Laura Kalman for guiding me through the complexities of legal realism at Yale.

25. As early as 1942, Logue spoke out against redbaiting: Logue to A. D. Lewis, October 21, 1942, YULocal35, Box 1, Folder 3: "It is my belief that the labor movement in general can gain nothing by a policy of redbaiting. I don't like Communists, but there are other ways of getting them out of their positions of power than crying 'Bolsheviks' to the general public." For his efforts to expose Yale's discriminatory quotas against blacks, Jews, Catholics, and other minorities, as well as politically motivated hiring and firing, see EJL, Series 1, Box 6, Folder 101; Logue to Margaret DeVane, April 23, 1946, EJL, Series 1, Box 3, Folder 31; also Ellen W. Schrecker, *No Ivory Tower: McCarthyism and the Universities* (New York: Oxford University Press, 1986), 67–68, 250–53; and Seymour quote, *Crimson*, June 4, 1949, 111.

26. On factionalism in the AVC: Logue, "Citizens First, Veterans Second," *Progressive* 10, no. 48 (December 16, 1946): 4, 11; Logue, Elkin interview, 32–33. Also, John S. Atlee, "A.V.C. Sets the Pace," *Nation*, June 22, 1946, 740–41; "Veterans: 'Citizens First,'" *Time*, June 24, 1946, 23–24; Julian H. Franklin, "Why I Broke with the Communists," *Harper's*, May 1947, 412–18; Robert L. Tyler, "The American Veterans Committee: Out of a Hot War and into the Cold," *American Quarterly* 18, no. 3 (Fall 1966): 419–36; Robert Francis Saxe, "'Citizens First, Veterans Second': The American Veterans Committee and the Challenge of Postwar 'Independent Progressives,'" *War and Society* 22, no. 2 (October 2004): 75–94. At nearby Columbia University, the freshman and later prominent sociologist Emmanuel Wallerstein found the AVC to be "the most vibrant political organization on campus" but "torn apart (and destroyed) by this . . . split"; http://iwallerstein.com/intellectual-itinerary/.

27. Logue, "Negro Labor: A Call to Action," *Progressive* 10, no. 13 (April 1, 1946): 10; Philip Burnham to Edward Logue, April 24, 1946, EJL, Series 1, Box 1, Folder 13.

28. Harold Grabino, interview, March 22, 2006, by telephone, Ruben, transcript, 2.

29. Logue's "Grades for 1946 Fall Term" included "Property I"; "Grades for 1947 Spring Term" included "Legal Aspects of Community Planning and Development," EJL, Series 1, Box 6, Folder 98. Logue also took "Law, Science and Policy" under Harold Lasswell in spring 1946; EJL, Series 1, Box 6, Folder 100. In May 1947, he wrote a paper proposing a "labor law firm" to service the legal needs of workers, which began, "The law is a thing that makes rich men richer and poor men poorer"; EJL, Series 1, Box 6, Folder 106. Also, Kalman, *Legal Realism at Yale*, 176–87.

30. FBI, Report from New Haven, November 1, 1951, FOIA, 4; "Logue, 1942, Succeeds John Clark, as Head of Yale Employees Union," *Yale Daily News*, July 6, 1942. Logue's sister, Ellen, remembered that when his union activity angered Yale alumni in Philadelphia who had funded his scholarship, Ed's response was, "It's the right thing to do"; Ellen Logue, interview.

31. Logue to Ellen Logue, April 24, 1947, EJL, Series 1, Box 3, Folder 45.

32. Milton DeVane, interview, April 13, 2006, Ruben, transcript, 26.

33. Allan Talbot, email message to author, June 13, 2007.

34. "Interrogatory No. 5" in "Interrogatory for Edward J. Logue," eleven questions with responses by Logue, June 23, 1952, to Conrad E. Snow, Chairman, Loyalty Security

Board, U.S. Department of State, 1-7, in response to request from Mr. Snow, May 27, 1952, MDL.

35. Logue to M. H. Goldstein, September 15, 1947, EJL, Series 1, Box 2, Folder 28, expressing determination "to take a long look at the Philadelphia City Planning Exhibition." More on Logue's visit to the exhibition in EJL, Series 1, Box 5, Folder 83. Quote from "The Better Philadelphia Exhibition: What City Planning Means to You," 1947, General Pamphlets, Box 521, Temple University Urban Archives, cited in Scott Gabriel Knowles, ed., *Imagining Philadelphia: Edmund Bacon and the Future of the City* (Philadelphia: University of Pennsylvania Press, 2009), 87, also see 29-31, 86-91. In addition, "Philadelphia Plans Again," *Newsletter, Citizens' Council on City Planning*, EJL, Series 1, Box 5, Folder 83.

36. Quote from "Philadelphia Plans Again," *AF* 87, no. 6 (December 1947): 66-88.

37. Logue, interview, Schussheim, 12.

38. Logue's concern over poor housing conditions is in Logue to Richardson Dilworth, November 15, 1948, EJL, Series 1, Box 5, Folder 76. For Logue on the Philadelphia Citizens' Council on City Planning, see EJL, Series 1, Box 5, Folders 82-83. On the election, see G. Terry Madonna and John Morrison McLarnon III, "Reform in Philadelphia: Joseph S. Clark, Richardson Dilworth, and the Women Who Made Reform Possible, 1947-1949," *Pennsylvania Magazine of History and Biography* 127, no. 1 (June 2003): 57-88.

39. Logue to Fred Rodell, July 31, 1948, Fred Rodell Papers, Haverford College Special Collections, Addition 1927-80, Box 11, Item 105, a remarkable letter in which Logue acknowledges the limitations of Goldstein's practice and declares, "What I really want to do eventually is get into politics."

40. Rodell got Logue the job offer from Chester Bowles; Logue, interview by Jean Joyce, May 27, 1974, Bowles, transcript, 2. On the job offer from Humphrey, Logue to Hubert Humphrey, February 16, 1953, Series 3, Box 15, Folder 54. Humphrey's speech is at http://www.americanrhetoric.com/speeches/huberthumphey1948dnc.html.

41. Chester Bowles, "The Role of the States," in *Two-Thirds of a Nation: A Housing Program*, ed. Nathan Straus (New York: Alfred A. Knopf, 1952), 236-55; Logue, interview, Steen, December 13, 1983, New York, NY, 3; on Logue's work on Bowles's staff, see EJL, Series 2, Boxes 9-12.

42. Logue's candid assessment of Chester Bowles's strengths and weaknesses in Logue, second interview by Jean Joyce, October 2, 1976, Essex, CT, Bowles, transcript, passim but particularly 62-63.

43. Bowles wanted Logue's help in India, but he also wanted Logue to keep an eye on Connecticut politics, "something we must definitely not let slip away from us"; Chester Bowles to Logue, September 18, 1951, EJL, Series 1, Box 1, Folder 12. Logue's work in India—and the entire Bowles operation there, including a great deal about Point Four and community development—is documented in EJL, Series 3, Boxes 13-22.

44. Conrad E. Snow to Logue, May 17, 1952; quotation from Logue to Conrad E. Snow, June 23, 1952; and attached "Interrogatory for Edward J. Logue," MDL; Margaret Logue quote from email message to author, December 21, 2005. Finally, in November 1952, Logue received an official letter declaring that he was no security risk to

the United States; Carlisle H. Humelsine to Logue, November 3, 1952, EJL, Series 3, Box 15, Folder 62.

45. Logue to Tom [?], July 19, 1953, EJL, Series 4, Box 29, Folder 113, 2. The following spring, Logue shared harsh criticisms of McCarthy with his mother: "It is distressing to hear supposedly informed people talking about McCarthy in the way you report. He is a menace to the freedoms all our wars have been supposed to protect. He is a dishonest, immoral man who has brought nothing but evil into American life"; Logue to Resina Logue, May 3, 1954, EJL, Series 4, Box 28, Folder 86.

46. Chester Bowles, *Ambassador's Report* (New York: Harper and Brothers, 1954), 31.

47. "Is One Hundred Years Long Enough?," Winter 1953, MDL; Penn Kimball to Logue, January 12, 1953, EJL, Series 3, Box 15, Folder 59; Logue to Paul Hoffman, May 30, 1953, EJL, Series 3, Box 15, Folder 52, and Logue to Dyke Brown, July 18, 1953, EJL, Series 3, Box 15, Folder 36, on the hope that the Ford Foundation's Fund for the Republic will sponsor his idea. Logue was not easily discouraged and reminded Bowles of it when he became a board member of the fund: Logue to Chester Bowles, December 23, 1954, EJL, Series 4, Box 23, Folder 10. While in India, Logue chastised the editor of the embassy's publication, *American Reporter*, for failing to tell the whole truth about racial discrimination in America; Logue to Jean Joyce, September 10, 1952, EJL, Series 3, Box 13, Folder 1.

Two civil rights activists of the 1960s also became inspired by their time in India: Harris Wofford, intimate of John F. Kennedy and Martin Luther King, Jr., and Kathleen Neal Cleaver—a Black Panther Party member and the wife of Eldridge Cleaver—who grew up in India while her father, Ernest Neal, a rural sociologist from Tuskegee, worked in community development there. See Ernest Neal to Logue, February 10, 1953, and Logue to Ernest Neal, April 15, 1953, EJL, Series 3, Box 16, Folder 78, where they discussed Logue's "Is One Hundred Years Long Enough?"

48. Harry S. Truman, Inaugural Address, January 20, 1949, Harry S. Truman Library and Museum, https://www.trumanlibrary.org/whistlestop/50yr_archive/inagural 20jan1949.htm.

49. On Truman and Point Four, see Bowles, *Ambassador's Report*, 323. The Ford Foundation had recently reinvented itself after the death of Henry Ford, Sr., in 1947 as a more ambitious, activist, and international-oriented philanthropy, with a strong commitment to India and Pakistan. A Ford office opened in New Delhi just as the Logues arrived in January 1952; Alice O'Connor, "Community Action, Urban Reform, and the Fight Against Poverty: The Ford Foundation's Gray Areas Program," *JUH* 22, no. 5 (July 1996): 586–95.

50. On Etawah, Faridabad, and Nilokheri, see Bowles, *Ambassador's Report*, 197–98, 202; Robert McGill, *Report on India*, reprints of articles from the *Atlanta Constitution*, December 1951, 11, 12, 18, 21, 29. The "Guide to Albert Mayer's Papers on India" (hereafter Mayer) in the University of Chicago's Special Collections, available online at http://www.lib.uchicago.edu/e/su/southasia/mayer.html, provides a useful outline to Mayer's involvement in India. Also see his account: Albert Mayer and Associates, *Pilot Project, India: The Story of Rural Development at Etawah, Utttar Pradesh* (Berkeley: University of California Press, 1959). Logue described Nilokheri as "a development project which has been created out of a swamp in three

years. One of the most remarkable things in my life," in Logue to Don Herzberg, February 18, 1952, EJL, Series 3, Box 15, Folder 53. Margaret Logue described both sites vividly in a letter home: Margaret Logue, Letter III, February 23, 1952, EJL, Series 3, Box 16, Folder 70.

51. Saunders Redding, *An American in India* (New York: Bobbs-Merrill, 1954), 21–29. Redding, an African American English professor at Hampton Institute, urged Bowles and Logue to accept Indian neutrality. Bowles elaborates on not requiring too strident an anti-communism from the Indians in *Ambassador's Report*, 343. On his personal anti-communism, see Chester Bowles, "'The Most Powerful Idea in the World,'" *NYT Magazine*, May 13, 1951, 9, 29, 30.

52. Quotation from Chester Bowles, "Asia Challenges Us Through India," *NYT Magazine*, March 23, 1952, 53 (italics in original); Chester Bowles to George V. Allen, March 7, 1953, MDL. On the community development program in India, also see Bowles, *Ambassador's Report*, 195–214, 322–47; Cynthia Bowles, *At Home in India* (New York: Harcourt, Brace, 1956), 130–55; Chester Bowles, *Promises to Keep: My Years in Public Life, 1941–1969* (New York: Harper and Row, 1971), 548–50; Chester Bowles, *The Makings of a Just Society: What the Postwar Years Have Taught Us About National Development* (Delhi: University of Delhi, 1963), 56–62. For progress reports from 1953, see Jonathan B. Bingham, "The Road Ahead for Point Four," *NYT Magazine*, May 10, 1953, 12, 65, 67; and from 1955, Chester Bowles, "India Revisited: 'Spectacular Progress,'" *NYT Magazine*, April 3, 1955, 13, 63–67; Howard B. Schaffer, *Chester Bowles: New Dealer in the Cold War* (Cambridge, MA: Harvard University Press, 1993), 63–79. For an excellent overview, see Dennis Merrill, *Bread and the Ballot: The United States and India's Economic Development, 1947–1963* (Chapel Hill: University of North Carolina, 1990), 76–93, 121–25, 141–43, 162–79, 206–7. A thorough collection of sources is *Action for Rural Change: Readings in Indian Community Development* (New Delhi: Munshiram Manoharlal, 1970). For astute analyses of the failures of community development, see Bipan Chandra, Aditya Mukherjee, and Mridula Mukherjee, *India After Independence* (New Delhi: Penguin Books India, 2000), 146–48; and Lane E. Holdcroft, "The Rise and Fall of Community Development in Developing Countries, 1950–65: A Critical Analysis and an Annotated Bibliography," *MSU Rural Development Paper No. 2* (1978), Department of Agricultural Economics, Michigan State University. A more strident condemnation of community development, with some useful insights, is Garvin Karunaratne, "The Failure of the Community Development Programme in India," *Community Development Journal* 11, no. 2 (1976): 95–118. On the larger context of American development activities, see Nick Cullather, *The Hungry World: America's Cold War Battle Against Poverty in Asia* (Cambridge, MA: Harvard University Press, 2010), particularly 75–107 on community development in India. Other works offering important discussions are Daniel Immerwahr, *Thinking Small: The United States and the Lure of Community Development* (Cambridge, MA: Harvard University Press, 2015), particularly 66–100; Nicole Sackley, "The Village as Cold War Site: Experts, Development, and the History of Rural Reconstruction," *Journal of Global History* 6, no. 3 (November 2011): 481–504; and Subir Sinha, "Lineages of the Developmentalist State: Transnationality and Village India, 1900–1965," *Comparative Studies in Society and History* 50, no. 1 (2008): 57–90.

53. EJL, Series 4, Box 25, Folder 43: Logue to Douglas Ensminger, January 15, 1955; Logue to Ensminger, August 21, 1956; Logue to Allen Wagner, May 8, 1957; "Rough Draft to Hon. Chester Bowles," May 15, 1957, EJL, Series 4, Box 23, Folder 13, 3-4. In 1956, Logue wrote to two Indian graduate students at Yale, "The program [urban renewal] has very much in common with your country's community development program, which my wife and I had firsthand opportunity to observe when we were in India three years ago"; Logue to Gurherdial S. Grewal and Kulbir Singh Gill, September 28, 1956, EJL, Series 4, Box 26, Folder 56.

54. The classic text on the agricultural reformers in the New Deal is Richard S. Kirkendall, *Social Scientists and Farm Politics in the Age of Roosevelt* (Columbia: University of Missouri Press, 1966). More recent literature on them and their move to the developing world is extensive; see Jess Gilbert, "Agrarian Intellectuals in a Democratizing State: A Collective Biography of USDA Leaders in the Intended New Deal," in *The Countryside in the Age of the Modern State: Political Histories of Rural America*, ed. Catherine McNicol Stock and Robert D. Johnston (Ithaca, NY: Cornell University Press, 2001), 213-39; Jess Gilbert, "Low Modernism and the Agrarian New Deal: A Different Kind of State," and Mary Summers, "The New Deal Farm Programs: Looking for Reconstruction in American Agriculture," in *Fighting for the Farm: Rural America Transformed*, ed. Jane Adams (Philadelphia: University of Pennsylvania Press, 2003), 129-59. Also see Douglas Ensminger, interview by Harry S. Taylor, June 16 and July 7, 1976, Harry S. Truman Library, Columbia, MO. I have benefited enormously from an extensive email exchange with Jess Gilbert, Clifford Kuhn, and Mary Summers.

55. For the Logues' stay in Japan, see Logue to Ensminger, July 8, 1953, EJL, Series 3, Box 15, Folder 48; Logue to Bowles Family, July 8, 1953, EJL, Series 3, Box 13, Folder 10; Logue to Dyke Brown, July 18, 1953, EJL, Series 3, Box 15, Folder 36.

56. "Time of Trial for Wolf Ladejinsky, Land Reform Expert Ousted from Job," *NHR*, December 31, 1954; Wolf Ladejinsky to Logue, January 14, 1955; Logue to Ladejinsky, February 6, 1956; Ladejinsky to Logue, February 15, 1956; and Logue to Ladejinsky, March 20, 1956, EJL, Series 4, Box 27, Folder 69; Logue to Ensminger, March 20, 1956, EJL, Series 4, Box 25, Folder 43; Logue to Paul Appleby, March 20, 1956, and Appleby to Logue, March 22, 1956, EJL, Series 4, Box 23, Folder 2; Logue to Chester Bowles, March 27, 1956, EJL, Series 4, Box 23, Folder 12. On Wolf Ladejinsky and his land reform work, see Bowles, *Ambassador's Report*, 181, 185, 374; Wolf Isaac Ladejinsky and Louis J. Walinsky, eds., *Agrarian Reform as Unfinished Business: The Selected Papers of Wolf Ladejinsky* (New York: Published for the World Bank by Oxford University Press, 1977), particularly introduction, 2-22; Al McCoy, "Land Reform as Counter-Revolution: U.S. Foreign Policy and the Tenant Farmers of Asia," *Bulletin of Concerned Asian Scholars* 3, no. 1 (Winter–Spring 1971): 24; Cullather, *Hungry World*, 94-105.

57. Bernard Loshbough quoted in Albert Mayer, "Transplantation of Institutions in Both Directions: Examples from India and the U.S.A.," Duke University seminar, February 2, 1962, 19, Mayer, Folder 41, in Immerwahr, *Thinking Small*, 145; on Loshbough's Pittsburgh work, O'Connor, "Community Action, Urban Reform," 603, 622n46. Much of the attention to ideas moving from the developing world back to the United States focuses on the poverty programs of the 1960s, not urban

renewal and infrastructural improvements; see Immerwahr, *Thinking Small*; Alyosha Goldstein, *Poverty in Common: The Politics of Community Action During the American Century* (Durham, NC: Duke University Press, 2012).

58. Ed Logue wrote something similar in "Life as a City Builder—'Make No Little Plans'": "Looking back, my training at Yale, in college and law school, my war-time experience, my service with Chet Bowles in Hartford and New Delhi, prepared me to be a city builder in a new and different way," 5.

59. This description of New Haven is based on Elizabeth Mills Brown, *New Haven: A Guide to Architecture and Urban Design* (New Haven, CT: Yale University Press, 1976); New Haven Colony Historical Society, *New Haven: Reshaping the City, 1900–1980* (Charleston, SC: Arcadia Publishing, 2004); Vincent Scully, Catherine Lynn, Erik Vogt, and Paul Goldberger, *Yale in New Haven: Architecture and Urbanism* (New Haven, CT: Yale University Press, 2004); and Douglas W. Rae, *City: Urbanism and Its End* (New Haven, CT: Yale University Press, 2003).

60. Logue to Margaret DeVane, January 1946, EJL, Series 4, Box 4, Folder 56.

61. Robert J. Leeney, *Elms, Arms, and Ivy: New Haven in the Twentieth Century* (Montgomery, AL: Community Communications, in cooperation with the New Haven Colony Historical Society, 2000), 61, 108.

62. Talbot, *Mayor's Game*, 16.

63. Robert A. Dahl, *Who Governs? Democracy and Power in an American City* (New Haven, CT: Yale University Press, 1961), 120.

64. Talbot, *Mayor's Game*, 16–17.

65. On Ivy-style dress: "Report by Dahl and Wolfinger, Mayor Richard C. Lee," May 2, 1958, Dahl, Box 1, Folder "Special Interviews," 1, 3; Paul Moore, Jr., "A Touch of Laughter," in *My Harvard, My Yale*, 20; Horowitz, *On the Cusp*, 45–53.

66. Quote from John P. Kotter and Paul R. Lawrence, *Mayors in Action: Five Approaches to Urban Governance* (New York: John Wiley and Sons, 1974), 137.

67. NAACP support from Mandi Isaacs Jackson, *Model City Blues: Urban Space and Organized Resistance in New Haven* (Philadelphia: Temple University Press, 2008), 65.

68. Logue, interview, Schussheim, 9.

69. Maurice E. H. Rotival to Logue, memorandum, January 15, 1954, "Confidential," Rotival, Box 37. Lee and Logue began talking to Rotival about assisting with ambitious redevelopment within weeks of Lee's election; see Logue to Rotival, December 16, 1953, and Rotival to Logue, December 23, 1953, Rotival, Box 37.

70. On the Federal Housing Acts of 1937, 1949, and 1954 and the Federal-Aid Highway Act of 1956, see Susan S. Fainstein and Norman I. Fainstein, "Economic Change, National Policy and the System of Cities" and "New Haven: The Limits of the Local State," in Susan S. Fainstein, Norman I. Fainstein, Richard Child Hall, Dennis R. Judd, and Michael Peter Smith, *Restructuring the City: The Political Economy of Urban Redevelopment*, rev. ed. (New York: Longman, 1986), 13, 15, 37, 47.

71. Linda Corman, "Former BRA Head Takes Another Look at the City He Helped Plan," *Banker and Tradesman*, October 21, 1987, 6.

72. Logue, "Can Cities Survive Automobile Age? New Haven Used as a Test Case," *Traffic Quarterly* 3, no. 2 (April 1959): 175.

73. Talbot, *Mayor's Game*, 159–61.

74. William Finnegan, *Cold New World: Growing Up in a Harder Country* (New York: Alfred A. Knopf, 1998), 34.

75. Talbot, *Mayor's Game*, 152.

76. Logue, "Can Our Cities Survive?" [1958], EJL, Series 4, Box 23, Folder 19 (draft of what would appear in *NYT Magazine*, November 9, 1958, as "Urban Ruin—or Urban Renewal?"). Draft text is slightly different than final published version. These quotes from draft, 3.

77. Logue, "Urban Ruin—or Urban Renewal?," 17.

78. Henry E. and Katharine Pringle, "New Haven," *SEP*, May 28, 1949, 126.

79. "Slum-Cut New Haven Sizes Up Logue," *CSM*, April 26, 1960; Talbot, *Mayor's Game*, 38.

80. Joe Alex Morris, "He Is Saving a 'Dead' City," *SEP*, April 19, 1958, 118.

81. Logue, "A Marshall Plan for Our Cities," *BG*, August 7, 1960.

82. MLogue, interview.

83. Logue, "Can Cities Survive Automobile Age?," 178. A couple of years earlier, Logue wrote to the architect John Follett, who, with John Graham, was designing the new Malley's department store: "This opportunity which you as architects and we as administrators now have comes to us in large part from the genius of Maurice Rotival . . . We have great confidence in his judgment"; Logue to John Follett, July 2, 1957, Rotival, Box 35, Folder "N.H. City, 1956–7."

84. In a helpful analysis of the multiple Rotival plans, Rico Cedro argues that Rotival's proposals for New Haven were inspired by Le Corbusier and Manhattan, the epitome for Europeans of the modern city in the 1920s; Rico Cedro, *Modern Visions: Twentieth Century Design in New Haven* (New Haven, CT: New Haven City Arts Gallery, 1988), 255. Many of Rotival's plans were rendered in aerial perspective. On Rotival's career, see Carola Hein, "Maurice Rotival: French Planning on a World-Scale (Part I), *Planning Perspectives* 17 (2002): 247–65; and Hein, "Maurice Rotival: French Planning on a World Scale (Part II)," *Planning Perspectives* 17 (2002): 325–44.

85. "New Haven: Test for Downtown Renewal," *AF* 109, no. 1 (July 1958): 80.

86. Maynard G. Meyer and Maurice E. H. Rotival, *Master Plan, Report to the City Plan Commission* (New Haven, CT: New Haven City Plan Commission, 1941); New Haven City Plan Commission, *Tomorrow Is Here*, 1944; Lloyd B. Reid and Maurice E. H. Rotival, *Short Approach Master Plan with Particular Reference to Highway Design and Urban Redevelopment* (New Haven, CT: New Haven City Plan Commission, 1953); "Map of New Haven, Including Redevelopment and Renewal Boundaries," New Haven Redevelopment Agency Records, YMA, Box 319, in Francesca Ammon, "'Town Living in the Modern Manner': A History of the Postwar Redevelopment of Downtown High-Rises in New Haven, CT" (seminar paper, Yale University, 2006), 43, in possession of the author.

87. Logue, "Can Cities Survive Automobile Age?," 176, also passim; on road mileage, Kenneth A. Simon, "Suburbia: The Good Life in Connecticut?," http://www.simonpure.com/suburbia_print.html, 4.

88. Leeney, *Elms, Arms, and Ivy*, 58.

89. Jane Jacobs, *The Death and Life of Great American Cities* (New York: Vintage, 1961), 365–68.

90. Quote in "Richard C. Lee, 86, Mayor Who Revitalized New Haven," *NYT*, February 4, 2003.

91. Promotional brochure, "The Distinguished Apartment Residence in New Haven: University Towers, 100 York Street," RCL, Box 29, Folder 29, in Ammon, "'Town Living in the Modern Manner,'" 17 for quote; 28, 31–33, 48–50 on parking.

92. JJ Papers, Boxes 2, 3, 11, 12 on the Dixwell Project; John M. Johansen, *John M. Johansen: A Life in the Continuum of Modern Architecture* (Milan: L'Arca Edizioni, 1995), 38; Brown, *New Haven*, 173, 176; John Johansen, interview by Lizabeth Cohen, November 13, 2010, Wellfleet, MA; Don Metz and Yuji Noga, *New Architecture in New Haven* (Cambridge, MA: MIT Press, 1966), 18–19; Sherman Hasbrouck, "Transformation: A Summary of New Haven's Development Program" (M.A. thesis, Yale University, 1965), 55, which notes that utilities were placed underground, common in suburban developments.

93. Lizabeth Cohen, *A Consumers' Republic: The Politics of Mass Consumption in Postwar America* (New York: Alfred A. Knopf, 2003).

94. Harry Barnett, interview by Robert Dahl, August 13, 1957, New Haven, CT, Dahl, Box 1, Folder "Interviews A–H," 1.

95. On the condition of New Haven retail and competition from suburban stores, see retail trade statistics and details about Hamden Plaza in Jeff Hardwick, "A Downtown Utopia? Suburbanization, Urban Renewal and Consumption in New Haven," *Planning History Studies* 10, nos. 1–2 (1996): 43–44; Wolfinger, *Politics of Progress*, 298–99, 342; and Dahl, *Who Governs?*, 139. For the breakdown of changes in sales by category of merchandise, see the chart (based on the U.S. Census of Business) in Daniel W. Kops to Mayor Richard C. Lee, May 23, 1957, EJL, Series 5, Box 71, Folder 595. For New Haven's small share of the area's growth in retail sales, see "CBD Data from Census Report," EJL, Series 5, Box 71, Folder 595. Clearly, Logue's office undertook extensive analysis of New Haven's retail position. Also, "2 New Haven Stores Battle to Boost Downtown Role," *WWD*, December 6, 1961; Samuel Feinberg, "From Where I Sit," *WWD*, November 8, 1963.

96. For the Harris survey of 1956, see Wolfinger, *Politics of Progress*, 299; Logue to Richard C. Lee, memorandum RE: Louis Harris Survey, November 21, 1956; Lee Comments, December 7, 1956; and "A Proposed Study of What the People of New Haven Think of Their Downtown Shopping Facilities" with sample questionnaire, all in EJL, Series 5, Box 57, Folder 395.

97. On vacant stores and the CBD tax burden, see Wolfinger, *Politics of Progress*, 298–99; "Malley's, the New Haven Central Business District, and the South Central Renewal Project," May 23, 1957, EJL, Series 5, Box 72, Folder 608, 2.

98. "Malley's, the New Haven Central Business District, and the South Central Renewal Project," EJL, 2; Nick Wood to Logue, memorandum, February 26, 1958, EJL, in Hardwick, "Downtown Utopia?," 47. On the effort to lure women shoppers, see City of New Haven, *New Haven: New England's Newest City—Pulling Power, Buying Power, Growing Power* (New Haven, CT: City of New Haven, 1960), n.p., RCL, Box 60, Folder 1183. See Alison Isenberg on the effort to lure female shoppers in *Downtown America: A History of the Place and the People Who Made It* (Chicago: University of Chicago Press, 2004), 175–87.

99. Macy's quote in "Paul Rudolph Designs a Place to Park in Downtown New Haven," *AR* 133, no. 2 (February 1963): 148; *Macy's Annual Report for the Fiscal Year Ended August 1, 1964*, 26; "Downtown Goes Up in Macy Estimation for New Stores," *WWD*, November 13, 1964; Richard Longstreth, *The American Department Store Transformed, 1920–1960* (New Haven, CT: Yale University Press, in association with the Center for American Places at Columbia College Chicago, 2010), 232. On Macy's strategy, see *WWD*: "Macy Deals for Unit in New Haven," September 18, 1962; "New Macy's in New Haven: Big Store, Big Competition," December 20, 1962; Samuel Feinberg, "From Where I Sit: No Sacred Precincts for Any Retailers," November 8, 1963; Samuel Feinberg, "From Where I Sit: What's in Macy's Star over New England?," November 13, 1963; and "Government Aid Stressed to Redevelop Downtown," May 27, 1964.

Logue's papers contain a marked-up article discussing the desire of downtown merchants to help shoppers bring cars downtown: Mabel Walker, "The Impact of Outlying Shopping Centers on Central Business Districts," *Public Management* 39, no. 8 (August 1957): 170–74.

100. Daniel W. Kops to Richard C. Lee, May 23, 1957, EJL, Series 5, Box 71, Folder 595; Louis Harris and Associates, "A Survey of the Race for Mayor of New Haven," February 1959, EJL, Series 4, Box 26, Folder 59, 27. Norris Andrews, head of the New Haven Planning Department, pointed out that downtown also faced serious competition from the new-style, freestanding professional building; Norris C. Andrews to Logue, memorandum, April 28, 1959, Rotival, Box 38, Folder "#1," 2.

101. Alexander Garvin, *The American City: What Works, What Doesn't*, 2nd ed. (New York: McGraw-Hill, 2002), 154–55.

102. Marshall Berman, *All That Is Solid Melts into Air: The Experience of Modernity* (New York: Penguin Books, 1988), 169, 302, 306–7. On Brasilia, James Holston, "The Modernist City and the Death of the Street," in *Theorizing the City: The New Urban Anthropology Reader*, ed. Setha Low (New Brunswick, NJ: Rutgers University Press, 1999), 245–75; Jonathan Barnett, "The Modern City," in *The Elusive City: Five Centuries of Design, Ambition and Miscalculation* (New York: Harper and Row, 1986), 107–56.

103. Milton Cameron, "Albert Einstein, Frank Lloyd Wright, Le Corbusier, and the Future of the American City," *Institute Letter* (Spring 2014): 8–9.

104. Dolores Hayden, "'I Have Seen the Future: Selling the Unsustainable City in 1939,'" Presidential Address to the Urban History Association, October 2010; Robert W. Rydell and Laura Burd Schiavo, eds., *Designing Tomorrow: America's World Fairs of the 1930s* (New Haven, CT: Yale University Press, 2010); Folke T. Kihlstedt, "Utopia Realized: The World's Fairs of the 1930s," in *Imagining Tomorrow: History, Technology, and the American Future*, ed. Joseph J. Corn (Cambridge, MA: MIT Press, 1986), 97–118; Stanley Appelbaum, *The New York World's Fair 1939/1940 in 155 Photographs by Richard Wurts and Others* (New York: Dover Publications, 1977).

There is a large literature on the impact of automobiles and highway building on U.S. cities. See, for example, Clay McShane, *Down the Asphalt Path: The Automobile and the American City* (New York: Columbia University Press, 1994), and

Owen Gutfreund, *20th Century Sprawl: Highways and the Reshaping of the American Landscape* (New York: Oxford University Press, 2004).

105. Edward Malley Co. brochure, November 21, 1962, Malley's Clipping File at New Haven Free Library, in Hardwick, "Downtown Utopia?," 49.

106. New Haven Plan Commission, *Tomorrow Is Here*, n.p.

107. Seon Pierre Bonan to Richard C. Lee, March 15, 1960, RCL, Box 38, Folder 809; Edward J. Logue to Seon Pierre Bonan, March 22, 1960, RCL, Box 38, Folder 809; both in Ammon, "'Town Living in the Modern Manner,'" 20; also Ray Wolfinger, memorandum, November 2, 1958, Dahl, Box 1, Folder "Special Interviews," 9–10.

108. New Haven Redevelopment Agency, *Redevelopment and Renewal Plan for the Wooster Square Project Area* (New Haven, CT: 1958; revised 1965); Leeney, *Elms, Arms, and Ivy*, 67.

109. Film footage of downtown market taken by Ted Gesling, from RCL, 1985 March Accession. Also see Gregory Donofrio, "Attacking Distribution: Obsolescence and Efficiency of Food Markets in the Age of Urban Renewal," *JPH* 13, no. 2 (May 2014): 136–59.

110. Logue, "Urban Ruin—or Urban Renewal," 28; Rachel D. Carley, "Tomorrow Is Here: New Haven and the Modern Movement," report prepared for the New Haven Preservation Trust, June 2008, 34–40.

111. Scully, "Modern Architecture at Yale," 294–95.

112. Robert Stern made the case in 1969 that a second generation of modern architects, then the leaders of the profession, had split into two camps: the "exclusive approach," which retained the orthodox modernist commitment to the abstract "prototypical solutions" of Le Corbusier, Sigfried Giedion, and the Bauhaus (with Mies van der Rohe as its emissary to the United States), and the "inclusive approach," more attuned to the individual case and the realities of context. However one parses the evolution of modernism after World War II—and there are many analyses—the style became increasingly diverse from the 1960s onward, culminating in the split-off of postmodernism; Robert A. M. Stern, *New Directions in American Architecture* (New York: George Braziller, 1969).

113. Scully, "Modern Architecture at Yale," 296.

114. Albert Mayer, "Report on Master Plan of the New Punjab Capital," May 12, 1950, Mayer, Box 18, Folder 30, in Cullather, *Hungry World*, 82, 84; R. J. Chinwalla, "Chandigarh: Breakthrough from the Past," *Times of India*, April 15, 1962, A7, in Manish Chalana, "Chandigarh: City and Periphery," *JPH* 14, no. 1 (February 2015): 62; Maristella Casciato, "Modern Chandigarh," in *The City and South Asia* (Cambridge, MA: Harvard South Asia Institute, 2014), 23–25. For more examples, see Daniel Immerwahr, "The Politics of Architecture and Urbanism in Postcolonial Lagos, 1960–1986," *Journal of African Cultural Studies* 19, no. 2 (December 2007).

115. Hardwick, "Downtown Utopia?," 49. For similar connections between modern architecture and values of rationality and progress, as made by universities, see Michael H. Carriere, "Between Being and Becoming: On Architecture, Student Protest, and the Aesthetics of Liberalism in Postwar America" (Ph.D. dissertation, University of Chicago, 2009). Yale is one of his case studies.

116. Carriere, "Between Being and Becoming," 61.

117. "Death of the Gargoyle," *Time*, November 15, 1963, 80–85.
118. For a thorough, if opinionated, treatment of modern architecture on the Yale campus, see Scully, "Modern Architecture at Yale," 293–353.
119. Scully, "Modern Architecture at Yale," 301.
120. Margaret Logue to Logue, April 15, 1948; April 28, 1948; May 2, 1948; and January 25, 1949, in EJL, Series 1, Box 4, Folder 54; Kimberly Konrad Alvarez, "The Lustron House: The Endangered Species of the Post-war Prefab Industry," *Docomomo US Newsletter*, Summer 2008, 1, 8–9.
121. Logue to Louis Laun, March 21, 1958, EJL, Series 4, Box 27, Folder 68; "Logue Leaves New Haven with a Record of Success," *New Haven Journal-Courier*, November 24, 1960; "Margaret and Edward Logue House, 8 Reservoir Street," http://newhaven modern.org/margaret-and-edward-logue-house; Margaret Logue, email message to author, November 2, 2005. When designed, the Logues' house at 8 Reservoir Street was considered so avant-garde that they had trouble securing a mortgage. Times have changed. Recently, the New Haven Preservation Trust has singled out the Logue house as one of the city's most important modernist buildings.
122. Hugo Lindgren, "New Haven," *Metropolis* 13 (January–February 1994): 27–28.
123. Talbot, *Mayor's Game*, 233 for Lee's office, 138 for the fire chief's.
124. Quote in WNBC-TV documentary, *Connecticut Illustrated: A City Reborn*, 1966, RCL.
125. It took a long time for New Haven's significant modernist architecture to be fully appreciated. Recently, the New Haven Preservation Trust has undertaken thorough surveys of buildings erected during the period 1931 to 1980, is encouraging their careful renovation, and has launched an informative website; see http://newhaven modern.org, which includes an extensive report by Rachel D. Carley, "Tomorrow Is Here: New Haven and the Modern Movement," June 2008, and "Survey of Modern Architecture in New Haven, Connecticut, Phase II Inventory of Historic Resources," June 2011. Mies van der Rohe was commissioned to design Church Street South, but he withdrew in 1967, soon replaced by Charles Moore, another prominent architect who was the newly named dean of the Yale School of Art and Architecture; Carley, "Tomorrow Is Here," 31–33.
126. Talbot, *Mayor's Game*, 116.
127. *NHR*, February 19, 1960, in Wolfinger, *Politics of Progress*, 296.
128. Talbot, *Mayor's Game*, 80. Before the auction to select the developer, Ralph Taylor "emphasized [to all potential developers] the interest of New Haven in having top architectural execution of the apartment buildings within Blocks A, B & C"; "Minutes of Staff Meetings, August 15 and August 17, 1956, 9 a.m. each day," EJL, Series 5, Box 55, Folder 363. Logue described the design difficulties with the apartment buildings in "About Jerry Rappaport," n.d., MDL; also Ray Wolfinger, memorandum, 8–9.
129. Logue to Roger Stevens, September 19, 1958, EJL, Series 5, Box 88, Folder 826, 1; draft of a letter by Logue to Stevens, September 12, 1958, EJL, Series 5, Box 88, Folder 826, 1.
130. Richard C. Lee to Logue, memorandum, May 21, 1958, EJL, Series 5, Box 81, Folder 732; Talbot, *Mayor's Game*, 53; Ray Wolfinger described the negotiation between Lee and Logue over prominent versus local architects in Ray Wolfinger, memorandum, 15.

131. Rudolph's Church Street Redevelopment drawings in "Unprocessed in PR 13 CN 2001:126," Paul Rudolph Archive, Library of Congress Prints and Photographs Division; Logue to Paul Rudolph, October 9, 1958, EJL, Series 5, Box 88, Folder 826.

132. Margaret Logue, email message to author, January 11, 2009. "Sensual" was used in a review of the garage in the architectural press: "Sensually Structured Parking Garage by Rudolph," *PA* 41, no. 9 (September 1960): 51.

133. Walter McQuade, "Rudolph's Roman Road," *AF* 118, no. 2 (February 1963): 108. For more on the garage, see Carley, "Tomorrow Is Here," 26–27.

134. "Paul Rudolph: How One of the Great Young Architects Lives and Works," *Vogue*, January 15, 1963, 85–91.

135. Logue, "Education of an Urban Administrator," 177–78. After the telephone company building debacle, Logue wrote a clause into all subsequent contracts giving the city final approval of design; Jeanne R. Lowe, *Cities in a Race with Time: Progress and Poverty in America's Renewing Cities* (New York: Random House, 1967), 451.

136. Margaret Logue, email message to author, January 11, 2009. On Rudolph, see Paul Rudolph, *Writings on Architecture*, foreword by Robert A. M. Stern (New Haven, CT: Yale School of Architecture, 2008), particularly "Six Determinants of Architectural Form," originally published in *AR* 120, no. 4 (October 1956): 21–29; John C. Cook and Heinrich Klotz, with a foreword by Vincent Scully, *Conversations with Architects* (New York: Praeger, 1973), 90–121.

137. Logue, interview, Jones, Tape 3:42; Logue, interview, Steen, April 9, 1990, Boston, MA, 20; also see Logue to Paul Rudolph, May 17, 1965, EJL, Series 6, Box 150, Folder 443, where Logue thanks Rudolph for sending *Perspecta* (a publication of Yale School of Architecture): "It will improve my education." Logue wrote an enthusiastic letter supporting Rudolph's nomination as a fellow of the AIA; Logue to Jury of Fellows, December 3, 1969, EJL, Series 5, Box 99, Folder 974. For quote, Logue, remarks in "Rethinking Designs of the 60s," *Perspecta* 29 (1998), 11. For more on Rudolph's work in urban renewal, see Lizabeth Cohen and Brian D. Goldstein, "Paul Rudolph and the Rise and Fall of Urban Renewal," in *Reassessing Rudolph*, ed. Timothy M. Rohan (New Haven, CT: Yale School of Architecture, 2017), 14–29.

138. Logue, "Education of an Urban Administrator," 179.

139. Emerson Goble, "Horrors! A Handsome Garage," *AR* 133, no. 2 (February 1963): 9, and in same issue "Paul Rudolph Designs a Place to Park in Downtown New Haven," 146; also, "Paul Rudolph, Temple Street, New Haven, 1959–63," in Simon Henley, *The Architecture of Parking* (London: Thames and Hudson, 2007), 56–61. The challenge of creating monumental urban space had long preoccupied Rudolph. He argued for giving greatest scale to the governmental and institutional (and in an earlier era, religious); Cook and Klotz, *Conversations with Architects*, 114–15; Paul Rudolph, "The Six Determinants of Architectural Form," *AR* 120, no. 4 (October 1956): 183–90; Paul Rudolph, "A View of Washington as a Capital—or What Is Civic Design?," *AF* 118, no. 1 (January 1963): 70; Paul Rudolph, "Architecture and Society," *L'arca*, no. 62 (July–August 1992): 1–5, in Rudolph, *Writings on Architecture*, 156.

140. "Statement by Edward J. Logue," Boston, Massachusetts, May 26, 1967, *Hearings Before the National Commission on Urban Problems*, vol. 1, May–June 1967 (Washington, DC: Government Printing Office, 1968), 191.

141. Samuel Zipp, *Manhattan Projects: The Rise and Fall of Urban Renewal in Cold War*

New York (New York: Oxford University Press, 2010), 19. An exception to the criticism of superblock residential projects is Danielle Aubert, Lana Cavar, and Natasha Chandani, eds., *Thanks for the View, Mr. Mies: Lafayette Park, Detroit* (New York: Metropolis Books, 2012).

142. Lowe, *Cities in a Race with Time*, 451.

143. Wolfinger, *Politics of Progress*, 157–58, 163; Dahl, *Who Governs?*, 143–46; U.S. Department of Housing and Urban Development, "The Old and the New in New Haven," *Urban Renewal Notes*, 13.

144. Leeney, *Elm, Arms, and Ivy*, 59; Talbot, *Mayor's Game*, 209; Lowe, *Cities in a Race with Time*, 520–21, on the plan to double salaries by 1953 to make them competitive with suburban school systems.

145. On school modernization, New Haven Redevelopment Authority, *1961 Annual Report*, "Education and Schools"; Garvin, *American City*, 262; Leeney, *Elms, Arms, and Ivy*, 60, 65; Lowe, *Cities in a Race with Time*, 514–21; Robert Hazen, interview by Lizabeth Cohen, June 14, 2007, New York, NY.

146. On Lee's view of the Conté School, Talbot, *Mayor's Game*, 140; on Logue's view, "Can Cities Survive Automobile Age?," 182. On the Grant School, see Mary Hommann, "Symbolic Bells in Dixwell," *AF* (July–August 1966): 54–59, particularly 58–59; from Johansen: "The Dixwell School, New Haven, Connecticut," Box 12, Folder 7; photographs of the model of Dixwell School, Box 2, Folder 10; Dixwell Project New Haven Development Office, "Dixwell Renewal News," September 1964, Box 11, Folder 22; Johansen, interview.

147. U.S. Department of Housing and Urban Development, "Profile of a City," *Urban Renewal Notes*, July–August 1966, 4. New Haven's urban renewal also gained increasing international attention: "Foreign Officials Observe City Renewal," *NHR*, September 27, 1966; "Turkish Officials View City Answer to Some Shared Social Problems," *NHR*, October 8, 1966, cited in Carriere, "Between Being and Becoming," 232n47.

148. WNBC-TV documentary, *Connecticut Illustrated*. Excerpts are also incorporated into two more-recent documentaries: Ted Gesing, *Model City* (MFA thesis film, University of Texas, Austin, 2003), and American Beat Film produced by Elihu Rubin and directed by Stephen Taylor, *Rudolph and Renewal*, Yale School of Architecture, 2008 (made to accompany the exhibition "Model City: Buildings and Projects by Paul Rudolph for Yale and New Haven," November 3, 2008–February 6, 2009), copies of all in possession of the author.

149. Wirtz quote in "An Old Industrial City Wages Dramatic War on Poverty," *Trenton Sunday Times Advertiser*, July 12, 1964; Weaver quote in "New Haven Pursuing the American Dream of a Slumless City," *NYT*, September 7, 1965, both in Powledge, *Model City*, 90.

150. "Cities: Forward Look in Connecticut," *Time*, June 24, 1957; Jeanne R. Lowe, "Lee of New Haven and His Political Jackpot," *Harper's*, October 1957; *Life*, March 22, 1958; Logue, "New York: Are Cities a Bust?," *Look*, April 1, 1969; Joe Alex Morris, "He Is Saving a 'Dead' City," *SEP*, April 19, 1958; totals from Powledge, *Model City*, 25.

2. Urban Renewal as a Liberal Project

1. "Antipoverty Expert Mitchell Sviridoff," *NYT*, June 14, 1966.

2. Logue-Ylvisaker reminiscence in Logue, interview by Noel A. Cazenave, July 17,

1992, EJL, 2002, Box 21, Folder "Noel A. Cazenave, Ph.D., University of Connecticut," 2–7.

3. Preface by Mayor Richard Lee, "Opening Opportunities: New Haven's Comprehensive Program for Community Progress" (City of New Haven, New Haven Board of Education, and Community Progress, April 1962), in Fred Powledge, *Model City: A Test of American Liberalism; One Town's Efforts to Rebuild Itself* (New York: Simon and Schuster, 1970), 55 and 45–64, passim. For more on the Gray Areas Program, CPI, Paul Ylvisaker, and Mitchell Sviridoff, see William Lee Miller, *The Fifteenth Ward and the Great Society: An Encounter with a Modern City* (Boston: Houghton Mifflin, 1966), 221–43; Douglas W. Rae, *City: Urbanism and Its End* (New Haven, CT: Yale University Press, 2003), 348–49; Jeanne R. Lowe, *Cities in a Race with Time: Progress and Poverty in America's Renewing Cities* (New York: Random House, 1967), 517–18, 522–44; Robert Halpern, *Rebuilding the Inner City: A History of Neighborhood Initiatives to Address Poverty in the United States* (New York: Columbia University Press, 1995), 89–97; Karen Ferguson, *Top Down: The Ford Foundation, Black Power, and the Reinvention of Racial Liberalism* (Philadelphia: University of Pennsylvania Press, 2013), 49–64; Edward Zigler and Sally J. Styfo, *The Hidden History of Head Start* (New York: Oxford University Press, 2010), 9–10; "Antipoverty Expert Mitchell Sviridoff," *NYT*; "Mitchell Sviridoff, 81, Dies; Renewal Chief," *NYT*, October 23, 2000. A very rich source is Mitchell Sviridoff, ed., *Inventing Community Renewal: The Trials and Errors That Shaped the Modern Community Development Corporation* (New York: Milano Graduate School, New School University, 2004), passim but particularly 21–25, 27–35, 105–11, 121–29, 149–50, 160–96.

The title "Gray Areas Program" was intended to be racially neutral, aiming instead at the older, often deteriorating sections of cities bordering downtowns; Wendell E. Pritchett, *Robert Clifton Weaver and the American City: The Life and Times of an Urban Reformer* (Chicago: University of Chicago Press, 2008), 197–99. For an excellent history suggesting a longer incubation for Gray Areas than Logue's version, Alice O'Connor, "Community Action, Urban Reform, and the Fight Against Poverty: The Ford Foundation's Gray Areas Program," *JUH* 22, no. 5 (July 1996): 586–625. O'Connor explains how Ford wanted to avoid an explicitly racial agenda. In addition to New Haven, the other Gray Area sites were Boston, Oakland, Philadelphia, Washington, D.C., and the North Carolina Fund, a statewide agency.

4. For extensive background on Sviridoff, see *Inventing Community Renewal*, particularly the interview with him, 160–96.

5. Logue, interview by Cazenave, 2.

6. "Interrogatory for Edward J. Logue," eleven questions with responses by Logue, June 23, 1952, to Conrad E. Snow, Chairman, Loyalty Security Board, U.S. Department of State, 1–7, in response to a request from Mr. Snow, May 27, 1952, MDL, response to question 11.

7. Linda Corman, "Former BRA Head Takes Another Look at the City He Helped Plan," *Banker and Tradesman*, October 21, 1987, 6; "I have never met a developer I trusted" was a typical Loguism; from Robert Geddes, interview by Lizabeth Cohen, May 25, 2006, Princeton, NJ.

8. William Lee Miller and L. Thomas Appleby, "'You Shove Out the Poor to Make Houses for the Rich,'" *NYT Magazine*, April 11, 1965, 68.

9. Robert A. Dahl, *Who Governs? Democracy and Power in an American City* (New Haven, CT: Yale University Press, 1961); Nelson W. Polsby, *Community Power and Political Theory: A Further Look at Problems of Evidence and Inference* (New Haven, CT: Yale University Press, 1963; 2nd, enlarged ed. 1980); Raymond E. Wolfinger, *The Politics of Progress* (Englewood Cliffs, NJ: Prentice-Hall, 1974).

10. C. Wright Mills, *The Power Elite* (New York: Oxford University Press, 1956); Floyd Hunter, *Community Power Structure: A Study of Decision Makers* (Chapel Hill: University of North Carolina Press, 1953). For a useful discussion of the elitism and democracy debate, see Phillip Allan Singerman, "Politics, Bureaucracy, and Public Policy: The Case of Urban Renewal in New Haven" (Ph.D. dissertation, Yale University, 1980), 3–36.

11. G. William Domhoff, *Who Really Rules? New Haven and Community Power Reexamined* (New Brunswick, NJ: Transaction Books, Rutgers University, 1978), which is dedicated to Floyd Hunter. Also see "Who Really Ruled in Dahl's New Haven?," originally posted September 2005 but continually updated, http://www2.ucsc.edu/whorulesamerica/local/new_haven.html.

12. Dahl looks back on *Who Governs?* in "A Conversation with Robert A. Dahl," interview by Margaret Levi, *Annual Review of Political Science* 12 (2009): 1–9; Douglas Martin, "Robert A. Dahl Dies at 98; Yale Scholar Defined Politics and Power," *NYT*, February 7, 2014.

13. Wolfinger, *Politics of Progress*, 228; "Mayor Appoints Action Commission Headed by C of C Past Pres. Freese," *New Haven News Letter* (published by the New Haven Chamber of Commerce) 9, no. 6 (September 1954), Dahl, Box 1, Folder "Redevelopment"; "How to Get Renewal off Dead Center," *AF* 105, no. 4 (October 1956): 167–69.

14. Dahl, *Who Governs?*, 136–37, 200–201.

15. Ralph Taylor, interview by Robert Dahl, September 4, 1957, New Haven, CT, Dahl, Box 1, Folder "Interviews S–Z," 8; Max Livingston, interview by Robert Dahl, August 5, 1957, New Haven, CT, Dahl, Box 1, Folder "Interviews I–R," 9.

16. New Haven Citizens Action Commission, *Third Annual Report* (New Haven, CT, 1957), 1, quoted in Dahl, *Who Governs?*, 122–23.

17. Dick Banks, interview by Robert Dahl, July 23, 1957, New Haven, CT, Dahl, Box 1, Folder "Interviews A–H," 2.

18. Wolfinger, *Politics of Progress*, 305.

19. Powledge, *Model City*, 28, 29, 37, 38–39, 42, 44, 66–67, 112–13, on Lee's election results.

20. Logue, interview by Robert Dahl and Nelson Polsby, September 3, 1957, New Haven, CT, Dahl, Box 1, Folder "Interviews I–R," transcript, 16.

21. Wolfinger, *Politics of Progress*, 285; Louis Harris and Associates, "A Survey of the Race for Mayor of New Haven," February 1959, EJL, Series 4, Box 26, Folder 59, 16. Also see the Harris Poll, identified as "Post Election Survey—November 1954," in EJL, Series 4, Box 24, Folder 27. A survey of registered voters in summer 1959 on the popularity of Lee and redevelopment found varying degrees of support but almost no outright opposition; Memo to Mayor Richard Lee from William Flanigan, September 2, 1959, Dahl, Box 3.

22. Allan R. Talbot, *The Mayor's Game: Richard Lee of New Haven and the Politics of Change* (New York: Harper and Row, 1967), 126.

23. In interview after interview, Logue would insist that little if any opposition was raised at public hearings, whether in the neighborhood or downtown in the alderman chambers. See, for example, Logue, interview, Steen, December 13, 1983, New York, NY, 7-8.

24. Talbot, *Mayor's Game*, 161.

25. *The Hartford Courant* quote in Lowe, *Cities in a Race with Time*, 407. The Connecticut Democratic National committeeman John M. Golden told *Time*, "I'm for Dick Lee for anything," in recognition of his strong voter appeal; "Cities: Forward Look in Connecticut," *Time*, June 24, 1957.

26. Hugo Lindgren, "New Haven," *Metropolis* 13 (January-February 1994): 29.

27. Talbot, *Mayor's Game*, 89, 157; Joe Alex Morris, "He Is Saving a 'Dead' City," *SEP*, April 19, 1958, 118.

28. Quoted in Powledge, *Model City*, 90.

29. Logue referred to trying to "keep my dearly beloved wife sullen rather than mutinous" from "all the overtime that I have been putting in and expect to put in between now and election," in requesting four days off to sail back from Maine with the Bowleses; Logue to Richard Lee, August 23, 1955, EJL, Series 4, Box 27, Folder 70. Ralph Taylor's wife, Henny, had vowed never to marry a doctor like her father, because of the demanding hours away from home; she had not expected that urban redevelopment work would prove much the same; H. Ralph Taylor, interview by Lizabeth Cohen, April 21, 2006, Chevy Chase, MD. Dick Banks, who worked closely with the mayor on public relations, told Dahl that Logue was "probably the hardest working guy in the city administration"; Banks, interview, 10. Frank O'Brion, the Tradesmen's Bank president who chaired the New Haven Redevelopment Agency Board, observed to Dahl about Logue, Taylor, Grabino, and Appleby: "It's amazing. These fellows work ten and twelve hours a day and Saturdays and Sundays"; Frank O'Brion, interview by Robert Dahl and Nelson Polsby, September 23, 1957, New Haven, CT, Dahl, Box 1, Folder "Interviews I-R," transcript, 1.

30. Harold Grabino, interview by Lizabeth Cohen, November 23, 2007, New York, NY.

31. Allan Talbot, interview by Lizabeth Cohen, June 13, 2007, New York, NY. Talbot also recounted how one staff member got such a dressing-down at a weekend staff meeting held at Logue's modern house that he "literally walked into the [glass] door, trying to get out of there."

32. Grabino, interview.

33. Quoted in Margaret Logue, email message to author, April 25, 2011.

34. Taylor, interview.

35. Talbot, *Mayor's Game*, 21. Staff member Harry Wexler made his own list of Logue's contradictory personality traits: "brilliant, visionary, felt deeply about issues" as well as "arrogant, unforgiving, confrontational"; Harry Wexler, interview by Lizabeth Cohen, October 24, 2005, New Haven, CT; Harry Wexler, email message to author, September 12, 2005. Ed Logue's brother-in-law, Milton DeVane, made similar observations: "He made up his mind fast," "he was busy bringing all kinds of knowledge to bear on the questions that he had before him on a daily basis," "he was absolutely an open person about . . . equality and not judging anyone on ethnic

grounds," and "he didn't suffer fools gladly"; Milton DeVane, interview, April 13, 2006, New Haven, CT, Ruben, transcript, 15, 24, 25.

36. Grabino, interview.

37. Wolfinger, *Politics of Progress*, 198–99; Singerman, "Politics, Bureaucracy, and Public Policy," 117–23; "Slum-Fighting Funds Requested by Cities," *NYT*, October 2, 1958; Logue résumé, May 29, 1958, EJL, Series 4, Box 27, Folder 72; Logue quote from Logue, interview by Jean Joyce, October 22, 1976, Bowles, Part 9, Series 3, Subseries 3, Box 398, Folder 199b, transcript, 81. On JFK's urban platform, see Roger Biles, *The Fate of the Cities: Urban America and the Federal Government, 1945–2000* (Lawrence: University Press of Kansas, 2011), 87.

38. Mitchell Sviridoff, interview by Robert Dahl, September 18, 1957, New Haven, CT, Dahl, Box 1, Folder "Interviews S–Z," transcript, 5–6.

39. Taylor, interview by Dahl, 6, 24.

40. Talbot, *Mayor's Game*, 23.

41. "'Dying City' Label Stirs New Haven," *NYT*, May 22, 1955; Robert J. Leeney, *Elms, Arms, and Ivy: New Haven in the Twentieth Century* (Montgomery, AL: Community Communications, in cooperation with the New Haven Colony Historical Society, 2000), 60; Talbot, *Mayor's Game*, 122–23, 247.

42. Richard Lee, interview by Ray Wolfinger, February 12, 1958, New Haven, CT, Dahl, Box 1, Folder "Special Interviews and Reports by Ray Wolfinger," transcript, 3.

43. Memorandum from Richard C. Lee to Logue, January 30, 1956; Memorandum from Logue to Richard C. Lee, February 6, 1956; EJL, Series 5, Box 51, Folder 309.

44. New professional expectations had also arisen in the foreign service after the war; on the Foreign Service Act of 1946, see https://www.encyclopedia.com/history /encyclopedias-almanacs-transcripts-and-maps/foreign-service-act-1946. For the range of skills needed by new urban experts, see Singerman, "Politics, Bureaucracy, and Public Policy," 138–39.

45. Ambassador Chester Bowles, "Efficiency Report for Edward Joseph Logue for Period 1/28/1952 to 3/15/1953," EJL, Series 3, Box 15, Folder 63, "Summary Comments," 1.

46. Logue to Douglas Ensminger, August 21, 1956, EJL, Series 4, Box 25, Folder 43.

47. Two interrelated historical dynamics were under way here: a growing embrace of rational state planning as the American welfare and warfare state developed from the New Deal on, and the rise of broadly trained administrative experts to implement these new state functions.

On the expansion of state planning, see Rexford G. Tugwell and Edward C. Banfield, "Governmental Planning at Mid-Century," *Journal of Politics* 13, no. 2 (May 1951): 133–63 for emerging consensus by 1950 that "the kind of government which had now arrived necessitated planning. For the role of government was no longer merely rule-making," 135. Otis L. Graham, Jr., traces the vicissitudes of a commitment to planning by the federal government from the 1930s to the 1970s in *Toward a Planned Society: From Roosevelt to Nixon* (New York: Oxford University Press, 1976), but even when he argues that it slowed under Eisenhower, he singles out the Housing Acts of 1949 and 1954 as exceptions: 124, 162.

There is a substantial literature on experts in twentieth-century America, but much less on the post–World War II era than on the first half of the century, particularly on the generalist administrator. What exists tends to focus on more specialized experts, such as scientists and social scientists who brought their technical knowledge to solving the nation's problems within narrowly defined areas. Christopher Klemek includes many of these same people in his notion of the "urbanist establishment"; his protagonists are mostly connected to academia. See his *Transatlantic Collapse of Urban Renewal: Postwar Urbanism from New York to Berlin* (Chicago: University of Chicago Press, 2011). Also useful is Brian Balogh's *Chain Reaction: Expert Debate and Public Participation in American Commercial Nuclear Power, 1945–1975* (New York: Cambridge University Press, 1991), 1–20; Balogh argues that scientists shifted from a wariness toward the state to greater embrace of its funding and patronage, only to see their authority undermined by the 1970s.

    On social scientists becoming policy experts in the postwar era, see Nicole Sackley, "Passage to Modernity: American Social Scientists, India, and the Pursuit of Development, 1945–1961" (Ph.D. dissertation, Princeton University, 2004); Ian Hart, "The Quest to Institutionalize a Social Report in American Government" (D.Phil. dissertation, University of Oxford, 2009); Alice O'Connor, *Poverty Knowledge: Social Science, Social Policy, and the Poor in Twentieth-Century U.S. History* (Princeton, NJ: Princeton University Press, 2001); and James Allen Smith, *The Idea Brokers: Think Tanks and the Rise of the New Policy Elite* (New York: Free Press, 1991).

48. David Ekbladh, "'Mr. TVA': Grass-Roots Development, David Lilienthal, and the Rise and Fall of the Tennessee Valley Authority as a Symbol for U.S. Overseas Development, 1933–1973," *Diplomatic History* 26, no. 3 (Summer 2002): 335–74; Balogh, *Chain Reaction*.

49. Senator Hubert H. Humphrey, *War on Poverty* (New York: McGraw-Hill, 1964), 14.

50. Logue, notes for speech to AVC, 1948, EJL, Box 1, Folder 7.

51. Powledge, *Model City*, 22. Logue used the term himself as late as 1998; Logue, "Mike Sviridoff Tribute, March 26, 1998," EJL, 2002 Accession, Box 23, Folder "March 1998 Mike Sviridoff," 3.

52. Wolfinger, *Politics of Progress*, 402, 406.

53. Talbot, *Mayor's Game*, 217.

54. Logue quoted in the Ford Foundation, *Metropolis* (booklet, 1959), EJL, Series 4, Box 25, Folder 47, 13.

55. See, for example, New Haven Redevelopment Agency, *Redevelopment Plan for the Oak Street Redevelopment Area* (New Haven, CT: 1955; revised 1966), 20; criteria for blight in New Haven Redevelopment Authority, "Application for a Preliminary Advance of Planning Funds, submitted by NHRA, New Haven, Connecticut," December 28, 1950, 20, Rotival, Box 37, in Francesca Ammon, "'Town Living in the Modern Manner': A History of the Postwar Redevelopment of Downtown High-Rises in New Haven, CT" (seminar paper, Yale University, 2006), 5–6, in possession of the author.

56. Talbot, *Mayor's Game*, 51.

57. On the deterioration of the meritocratic intentions of civil service, see Nicholas Thompson, "Finding the Civil Service's Hidden Sex Appeal," *WM*, November 2000.

58. Wolfinger, *Politics of Progress*, 274–75, 362.

59. Similar arguments continue to be made that the city is the most promising level for progressive policy and the revival of liberalism; see Harold Meyerson, "The Revolt of the Cities," *American Prospect*, May–June 2014, 30–39; and Meyerson, "Why Democrats Need to Take Sides," *American Prospect*, July–August 2014, 22–24.

60. "What Is Urban Renewal" and "Planners, Politicians and People: New Haven, Connecticut, 'Bulldozed' by Urban Renewal," in "Special Supplement: The Case Against Urban Renewal," *Human Events*, April 1963, 1, 12–13.

61. Laura Kalman, *Legal Realism at Yale, 1927–1960* (Chapel Hill: University of North Carolina Press, 1986), 158–64.

62. Harold Grabino, interview, March 22, 2006, by telephone, Ruben, transcript, 12.

63. Wexler, interview.

64. Jane Jacobs, *The Death and Life of Great American Cities* (New York: Vintage, 1961), 410–13.

65. Logue, interview, Steen, December 13, 1983, New York, NY, 6.

66. Talbot, *Mayor's Game*, 161; Singerman, "Politics, Bureaucracy, and Public Policy," 138–39. New Haven alderman William Lee Miller put it this way: "The great trick in urban renewal appears to be to have people working for the city who know how to forage in its behalf out in the nation's bureaucratic jungles. It is not enough that the federal government pass city-helping laws; there must also then be hunters for the city who can make their way through all the Titles I and Titles II to find the meat"; Miller, *Fifteenth Ward and the Great Society*, 154.

67. Robert Hazen, interview by Lizabeth Cohen, June 14, 2007, New York, NY; Taylor, interview by Dahl, 7, 18.

68. Taylor, interview by Dahl, 7, 18.

69. Dahl, *Who Governs?*, 130.

70. Singerman, "Politics, Bureaucracy, and Public Policy," 154–59, on what he calls "the Redevelopment Bureaucrats"; Grabino, interview.

71. Logue to Richard Lee, September 6, 1957, EJL, Series 4, Box 27, Folder 70, 2.

72. Logue, Memo to Richard C. Lee, September 6, 1957, "RE: 1958 Executive Salary Scale," EJL, Series 5, Box 64, Folder 503.

73. Logue, interview, Steen, December 13, 1983, New York, NY, 6.

74. Quoted in Powledge, *Model City*, 90.

75. Ensminger to Logue, May 13, 1957, EJL, Series 4, Box 25, Folder 43; Ensminger to Logue, December 28, 1957, EJL, Series 4, Box 25, Folder 46.

76. "The Ford Foundation Program Letter, India: A Master Plan for India's Capital," Report No. 95, February 12, 1958, EJL, Series 4, Box 26, Folder 53; "The Ford Foundation Program Letter, India: Report of a Pilot Project in Urban Community Development," Report No. 112, May 23, 1960, EJL, Series 4, Box 26, Folder 54, with memo attached from Logue, dated September 1960.

77. Paul N. Ylvisaker, interview by Charles T. Morrissey, September 27 and October 27, 1973, Folder 15, Box 5, Ylvisaker Papers, Harvard University, in Daniel Immerwahr, *Thinking Small: The United States and the Lure of Community Development* (Cambridge, MA: Harvard University Press, 2015), 145–46.

78. Mary Hommann to Margaret Logue, February 2, 2000, MDL.

79. Grabino, interview.

80. Ellen Logue, interview by Lizabeth Cohen, April 13, 2008, Berkeley, CA. A young Larry Goldman marked his acceptance in the inner circle at the UDC when he "began to be included in the 6:00 or 6:30 'Come into my office and have a drink'"; Lawrence Goldman, interview by Lizabeth Cohen, May 3, 2010, Newark, NJ.

81. Joseph Slavet, interview by Lizabeth Cohen, May 31, 2007, Boston, MA; Herbert Gleason, interview by Lizabeth Cohen, May 31, 2007, Cambridge, MA; Martin Nolan, interview by Lizabeth Cohen, May 24, 2007, Cambridge, MA.

82. Richard Kahan, interview by Lizabeth Cohen, June 15, 2007, New York, NY.

83. Richard Bell, interview, February 24, 2006, Ruben, transcript, 23, 25.

84. Talbot, *Mayor's Game*, 42–43.

85. Logue, interview by Dahl and Polsby, Dahl, 29. Logue continued to boast throughout his career, as, for example, when he claimed that the UDC "had half the state allocation [of 236 money] for the whole country; Logue, interview, Jones, Tape 3:39.

86. Wexler, interview, and Wexler, email message to author.

87. "Bold Boston Gladiator—Ed Logue: Planner Stirs Up a Ruckus and Battles Opposition to Build the Place of His Dreams," *Life*, December 24, 1965, 126–34; "What's Happening in Proper Old Boston?," *Newsweek*, April 26, 1965, 78.

88. Talbot, *Mayor's Game*, 22–24, 43.

89. Maurice Rotival to Steve Carroll, Confidential Memo, February 21, 1955, Rotival, Box 37, no folder number; Talbot, *Mayor's Game*, 37–38.

90. "Report by Dahl and Wolfinger, Mayor Richard C. Lee," May 2, 1958, Dahl, Box 1, Folder "Special Interviews," 1.

91. MLogue, interview.

92. Ray Wolfinger, April 14, 1959, Dahl, Box 1, Folder "Special Interviews and Reports by Ray Wolfinger," 2; Wolfinger, *Politics of Progress*, 274.

93. Talbot, *Mayor's Game*, 42.

94. Talbot, *Mayor's Game*, 41.

95. MLogue, interview.

96. Logue, interview, Steen, March 3, 1986, Lincoln, MA, 29.

97. Theodore "Ted" Liebman, interview by Lizabeth Cohen, October 15, 2006, New York, NY.

98. Taylor, interview by Dahl, 6. Larry Goldman, a young staff assistant to Logue later at the UDC in New York, still remembers with pride when Logue openly expressed his affection toward him: "He once told me how precious I was to him, and that was great. I remember he met my mother, my father, and said something like, . . . 'We like having Larry here' . . . There [was] a lot of tough love, but there was more tough than love a lot of the time . . . I think we all wanted his approval. He was a very strong father figure . . . There were certain circumstances under which he could tell you that he cared"; Goldman, interview by Cohen.

99. Taylor, interview by Cohen; Howard R. Moskof, interview by Lizabeth Cohen, April 21, 2006, Chevy Chase, MD.

100. On the common use of "urban housekeeping," see, for example, Rebecca Sherrick, "Their Fathers' Daughters: The Autobiographies of Jane Addams and Florence Kelley," *American Studies* 27 (Spring 1986): 50.

101. Michael H. Carriere, "Between Being and Becoming: On Architecture, Student Protest, and the Aesthetics of Liberalism in Postwar America" (Ph.D. dissertation, University of Chicago, 2009); Vincent Scully, "Modern Architecture at Yale: A Memoir," in Vincent Scully, Catherine Lynn, Erik Vogt, and Paul Goldberger, *Yale in New Haven: Architecture and Urbanism* (New Haven, CT: Yale University Press, 2004), 315–16.

102. Dahl, *Who Governs?*, 130.

103. Taylor, interview by Dahl, 5.

104. Maurice E. H. Rotival to Logue, February 4, 1959, and Rotival to Logue, October 26, 1959, Rotival, Box 35, Folder "N.H. City 1956–57." Correspondence between Logue and Rotival in New Haven conveys constant tension, particularly Logue's frustration that Rotival's office was not completing assignments adequately and on time and Rotival's complaint that Logue was not giving his firm work worthy of their full capacities as planners; see correspondence between the two in Rotival, Boxes 35 and 37, and EJL, Series 5, Box 100, Folder 991.

105. Logue to Maurice Rotival, Memorandum, December 8, 1954, Rotival, Box 36, Folder "N.H. City, 1954–55." Also see Carl Feiss to Maurice Rotival, May 9, 1955, Rotival, Box 37, no folder title or number; "Carl Feiss, a Pioneer of Urban Preservation, Dies at 90," *NYT*, October 27, 1997.

106. "How to Get Renewal off Dead Center," 169.

107. Robert Fishman, ed., *The American Planning Tradition: Culture and Policy* (Washington, DC: Woodrow Wilson Center Press, 2000); Mary Corbin Sies and Christopher Silver, *Planning the Twentieth-Century American City* (Baltimore: Johns Hopkins University Press, 1996), particularly Thomas W. Hanchett, "Roots of the 'Renaissance': Federal Incentives to Urban Planning, 1941 to 1948," 283–304; Mel Scott, *American City Planning Since 1890* (Chicago: American Planning Association, 1995); Louise Nelson Dyble, "The Continuing Saga of Zoning in America," *JPH* 9, no. 2 (May 2010): 140–46. Andrew M. Shanken makes a convincing case for the war's impetus toward more planning, though he argues for a precipitous collapse of its most utopian aspects once the war ended; *194X: Architecture, Planning, and Consumer Culture on the American Home Front* (Minneapolis: University of Minnesota Press, 2009).

108. Dahl, *Who Governs?*, 116–18; Talbot, *Mayor's Game*, 18, 34–35, 38, 241.

109. Wolfinger, *Politics of Progress*, 276. It is quite clear that Rotival's firm, not the New Haven Planning Department, was doing the technical planning work for New Haven redevelopment, much of it out of an office adjacent to the New Haven Redevelopment Agency. Even with all Logue's frustrations with Rotival's firm, he never discussed giving the work instead to the city's staff planners; see EJL, Series 5, Box 100, Folder 991 for correspondence between Logue and Rotival's office.

110. Paul Davidoff, "Advocacy and Pluralism in Planning," *JAIP* 31, no. 4 (1965): 331–38; Tom Angotti, "Advocacy and Community Planning: Past, Present and Future," *Planners Network*, April 2007, http://www.plannersnetwork.org/publications/2007 _spring/angotti.htm.

111. In a provocative essay, Thomas Campanella contends that planners today continue to see their profession as low status and of trivial significance. He holds Jane Jacobs responsible, arguing that her critique of planners "diminished the disciplinary

identity of the planning profession" and "privilege[d] the grassroots over plannerly authority and expertise." He laments "the seeming paucity among American planners today of the speculative courage and vision that once distinguished this profession." While Campanella shares my view of planners' professional decline, his blaming of Jacobs suggests that he misses how planners also lost out to development administrators; Thomas J. Campanella, "Jane Jacobs and the Death and Life of American Planning," in *Reconsidering Jane Jacobs*, ed. Max Page and Timothy Mennel (Chicago: Planners Press of the American Planning Association, 2011), 141–60.

112. Logue, "View from the Village," on Jane Jacobs's *Death and Life of Great American Cities*, "American Cities: Dead or Alive?—Two Views," *AF* 116, no. 3 (March 1962): 90.

113. Ieoh Ming Pei, interview by Lizabeth Cohen, June 11, 2007, New York, NY.

114. John M. Johansen, *John M. Johansen: A Life in the Continuum of Modern Architecture* (Milan: L'Arca Edizioni, 1995), 37.

115. Quote from I. M. Pei in the exhibition "Beyond the Harvard Box: The Early Works of Edward L. Barnes, Ulrich Franzen, John Johansen, Victor Lundy, I. M. Pei, and Paul Rudolph," curated by Michael Meredith, October 5–November 15, 2006, HGSD.

116. See the graph in Lizabeth Cohen and Brian D. Goldstein, "Paul Rudolph and the Rise and Fall of Urban Renewal," in *Reassessing Rudolph*, ed. Timothy M. Rohan (New Haven, CT: Yale School of Architecture, 2017), 16, based on data from Tony Monk, *The Art and Architecture of Paul Rudolph* (West Sussex, UK: John Wiley and Sons, 1999), 122–24.

117. Ray Wolfinger, "This is Ray on November 2 dictating a number of items dating from my stay in the Mayor's Office," November 2, 1958, Dahl, Box 1, Folder "Special Interviews," 8–9. After this conflict, Logue watched University Towers closely. In December 1958 he wrote in a memo to staff members, "I heard a rumor that changes had been made in the plans which down-graded them. Is this rumor true? Please let me know immediately"; Logue to Norris Andrews, John Maniatty, and Tom Appleby, December 10, 1958, Rotival, Box 38, Folder "#2."

118. Natalie de Blois, interview by Betty J. Blum, March 12–15, 2002, West Hartford, Connecticut, Chicago Architects Oral History Project, Art Institute of Chicago, transcript, 47–48, http://digital-libraries.saic.edu/cdm/compoundobject/collection/caohp/id/15893/rec/.

119. Liebman, interview. Larry Goldman concurred: "He loved to hang out with architects"; Goldman, interview.

120. Logue, "Work of the Boston Renewal Administration in the Urban Core," address to the Harvard Graduate School of Design eighth annual Urban Design Conference, "The Role of Government in the Form and Animation of the Urban Core," May 1, 1964, 5, 8; proceedings in Papers of Josep Lluís Sert, Special Collections, HGSD.

121. Charles Abrams, "Some Blessings of Urban Renewal," in *Urban Renewal: The Record and the Controversy*, ed. James Q. Wilson (Cambridge, MA: MIT Press, 1966), 561–62, originally published in Abrams, *The City Is the Frontier* (New York: Harper and Row, 1965), chapter 9.

122. Robert A. M. Stern, *New Directions in American Architecture* (New York: George Bra-

ziller, 1969), 8, 10, 80–108; for "piazza compulsion," 91–94; for towers, 94–98; on technologically inspired mega-structures, 105–8.

123. Stern, *New Directions in American Architecture*, 15, 17; also see discussion of Rudolph, 12.

124. Logue to Eugene Rostow, December 5, 1961, EJL, Series 6, Box 150, Folder 445.

125. Quotes from Logue, interview, Schussheim, 20; Talbot, *Mayor's Game*, 127, 131, also see 117–18, 126–34. In addition, see Grabino, interview, on Stevens's experience as a real estate investor and inexperience as a real estate developer. For more on Stevens's eclectic career, see E. J. Kahn, Jr., "Profiles: Closings and Openings—I," *New Yorker*, February 13, 1954, 37–56; E. J. Kahn, Jr., "Profiles: Closings and Openings—II," *New Yorker*, February 20, 1954, 41–59; Duncan Norton-Taylor, "Roger Stevens, a Performing Art," *Fortune*, March 1966, 152–204 (with page breaks). On Stevens's unsuccessful Boston effort, see Elihu Rubin, *Insuring the City: The Prudential Center and the Postwar Urban Landscape* (New Haven, CT: Yale University Press, 2012), 167–72.

126. Norton-Taylor, "Roger Stevens, a Performing Art," 202.

127. Jerome Rappaport, interview by Lizabeth Cohen, September 17, 2007, Boston, MA. For more on the auction, see Taylor, interview by Dahl, 5; "New Haven: Test for Downtown Renewal," *AF* 109, no. 1 (July 1958): 81. The city had agreed without protest to the auction to avoid politically damaging charges of a land "giveaway" to Yale, which would have been deeply resented by locals. But Lee and Logue expected that Yale would prevail, which would assist with its current faculty housing crunch while also helping to hook Yale and Stevens for the big job of Church Street.

128. Logue, interview by Dahl and Polsby, Dahl, Box 1, Folder "Interviews I–R," 29. That purchase price was then converted to an annual rental, per University Towers Inc.'s agreement; "Construction Expected to Start Next Week on 16-Story University Towers Structure," *NHR*, July 22, 1958.

129. Bernard J. Frieden and Lynn B. Sagalyn, *Downtown, Inc.: How America Rebuilds Cities* (Cambridge, MA: MIT Press, 1989), 44. Martin Anderson, a conservative critic of urban renewal based on the government's violation of private property rights, also objected to it for the difficulty that private developers had turning a profit in their renewal activities; *The Federal Bulldozer: A Critical Analysis of Urban Renewal, 1949–1962* (Cambridge, MA: MIT Press, 1964), 107–23.

130. H. Ralph Taylor, interview by David G. McComb, March 25, 1969, Washington, D.C., General Services Administration, National Archives and Records Service, Lyndon Baines Johnson Library, transcript, 6–8; "13-Term N.Y. Congressman James H. Scheuer Dies at 85," *WP*, September 1, 2005; "Capitol Park," The Cultural Landscape Foundation, https://tclf.org/content/capitol-park-washington-dc; Pritchett, *Robert Clifton Weaver and the American City*, 175, 195–96, 214 on Scheuer's progressive stands on integrated housing. For more on Scheuer's involvement in Southwest Washington and the challenges facing the developer in urban redevelopment, see Lowe, *Cities in a Race with Time*, 175–95.

131. Pei, interview. For more on Zeckendorf's involvement with Southwest Washington, see Lowe, *Cities in a Race with Time*, 174–200.

132. Pei, interview.

133. Quote from Ed Zelinsky in Rob Gurwitt, "Death of a Neighborhood," *Mother Jones*, September–October 2000, http://motherjones.com/politics/2000/09/death -neighborhood, 4.
134. Quoted in Talbot, *Mayor's Game*, 137. New Haven was the first city to make use of the new provision in the Housing Act of 1954 for rehabilitation of existing structures; Powledge, *Model City*, 39.
135. Logue to Chester Bowles, letter draft, May 15, 1957, EJL, Series 4, Box 23, Folder 13, 1.

3. Trouble Right Here in Model City

1. *Building the American City: Report of the National Commission on Urban Problems to the Congress and to the President of the United States* (Washington, DC: Government Printing Office, 1968), preface, vii–viii; introduction, 1–31, with final quote 31; statistics on poor progress on building housing from Howard E. Shuman (executive director of the commission), "Behind the Scenes and Under the Rug," *WM*, July 1969, as quoted in Fred Powledge, *Model City: A Test of American Liberalism; One Town's Efforts to Rebuild Itself* (New York: Simon and Schuster, 1970), 121. For Johnson's reaction to the commission's report, see Roger Biles, *The Fate of Cities: Urban America and the Federal Government, 1945–2000* (Lawrence: University Press of Kansas, 2011), 155–59.
2. Description of the New Haven hearing of the National Commission on Urban Problems is based on *Hearings Before the National Commission on Urban Problems*, vol. 1, May–June 1967: Baltimore, New Haven, Boston, Pittsburgh (Washington, DC: Government Printing Office, 1968), 110–86, quotes on 111; Mandi Isaacs Jackson, *Model City Blues: Urban Space and Organized Resistance in New Haven* (Philadelphia: Temple University Press), 109–13; Douglas W. Rae, *City: Urbanism and Its End* (New Haven, CT: Yale University Press, 2003), 349–51.
3. *National Commission Hearings*, 111.
4. *National Commission Hearings*, 187–265; Douglas quote on 188.
5. *National Commission Hearings*, 113, 128, 138.
6. Frank O'Brion, president of New Haven's Tradesmen's Bank and chair of the New Haven Redevelopment Agency, acknowledged that "there's just no comparison" between New Haven and Pittsburgh, with its "hundreds of multi-million corporations who have their headquarters" there; Frank O'Brion, interview by Robert Dahl and Nelson Polsby, September 23, 1957, New Haven, CT, Dahl, Box 1, Folder "Interviews I–R," transcript, 6–7. For a thorough discussion of urban redevelopment in Pittsburgh and the role played by the private sector, see Jeanne R. Lowe, *Cities in a Race with Time: Progress and Poverty in America's Renewing Cities* (New York: Random House, 1967), 110–63. It should be noted that although Pittsburgh's downtown redevelopment did not involve federal funding, the slum clearance of the Lower Hill, begun in 1955, did. And recent scholarship has suggested that there was more ideology than reality to Pittsburgh's crediting of the private-sector for its renewal success; "Forum: Pittsburgh's Renaissance Revisited," *JUH* 4, no. 1 (January 2015): 3–46.
7. On pro-growth coalitions, see John Mollenkopf, *The Contested City* (Princeton, NJ: Princeton University Press, 1983); Andy Jonas and David Wilson, eds., *The Urban*

Growth Machine: Critical Perspectives, Two Decades Later (Albany: State University of New York Press, 1999); John R. Logan and Harvey L. Molotch, *Urban Fortunes: The Political Economy of Place* (Berkeley: University of California Press, 1987).

8. Richard C. Lee, interview by Robert Dahl, September 13, 1957, New Haven, CT, Box 1, Folder "Special Interviews and Reports by Ray Wolfinger," transcript, 7, also 9; see in addition, Logue, interview by Robert Dahl and Nelson Polsby, September 3, 1957, New Haven, CT, Dahl, Box 1, Folder "Interviews I–R," transcript, 1–2; Ray Wolfinger, "This is Ray on November 2 dictating a number of items dating from my stay in the Mayor's Office," November 2, 1958, Dahl, Box 1, Folder "Special Interviews," 33.

9. Neil Brenner, "Is There a Politics of 'Urban' Development? Reflections on the U.S. Case," in *The City in American Political Development*, ed. Richardson Dilworth (New York: Routledge, 2009), 126, 130.

10. Logue, interview, Schussheim, transcript, 22.

11. Lowe, *Cities in a Race with Time*, 546–47.

12. Allan R. Talbot, *The Mayor's Game: Richard Lee of New Haven and the Politics of Change* (New York: Harper and Row, 1967), 150–52.

13. Powledge, *Model City*, 127. By 1970, 44 percent of New Haven's grand list of taxable property was tax-exempt; Peter Hall, "Is Tax Exemption Intrinsic or Contingent? Tax Treatment of Voluntary Associations, Nonprofit Organizations, and Religious Bodies in New Haven, Connecticut, 1750–2000," in *Property-Tax Exemption for Charities*, ed. Evelyn Brody (Washington, DC: Urban Institute Press, 2002), cited in Nikolas Bowie, "Poison Ivy: The Problem of Tax Exemption in a Deindustrializing City, Yale and New Haven, 1967–1973," *Foundations* 3, no. 2 (Spring 2009): 5. For years the city tried unsuccessfully to get Yale to contribute to the city's revenues; finally, in 1978, the state instituted a PILOT (payment in lieu of taxes) program that required colleges to reimburse municipalities like New Haven for 25 percent of what local property taxes would have yielded. In 1990, Yale also agreed to make a separate annual payment to the city for fire service, so long as no Yale nonacademic properties like dormitories and skating rinks were assessed for taxes. Patrick Flaherty, "An Analysis of PILOT (Payment in Lieu of Taxes), Windham, Connecticut," May 15, 2007, Connecticut Center for Economic Analysis, University of Connecticut, 7–8; the state gradually raised the percentage of payment required. Conflict continues to rage between the city and Yale over PILOT payments.

14. Wolfinger, "This is Ray on November 2," Dahl, 30. The Harris Poll of 1959 revealed a good deal of worry among respondents about tax increases; Louis Harris and Associates, "A Survey of the Race for Mayor of New Haven," February 1959, EJL, Series 4, Box 26, Folder 59, 15, 24, 27.

15. Logue, interview by Jean Joyce, October 22, 1976, Bowles, Part 9, Series 3, Subseries 3, Box 398, Folder 199b, transcript, 64–65.

16. *National Commission Hearings*, 124. During the many years before Connecticut implemented an income tax, it depended on the property tax, the main source of income for cities and towns, and the sales tax, which was at the highest rate in the country for a long time; from the *NYT*: "Resistance to a Connecticut Income Tax Is Strong," March 20, 1971; "Tax Increases Are Adopted in Connecticut, an 8 Percent Sales Levy

Will Be Highest in U.S.," May 31, 1989; "Connecticut's Precarious Tax Solution," June 11, 1989; "Region Rethinks Its Dependence on the Sales Tax," March 27, 1992.

17. Lee, interview by Dahl, 23; also see "Cities: Forward in Connecticut," *Time*, June 24, 1957, on Lee's ambitions for increasing tax assessments. Ralph Taylor made the same arguments to Dahl about how the increase in property tax revenue would make urban renewal self-supporting; H. Ralph Taylor, interview by Robert Dahl, September 4, 1957, New Haven, CT, Dahl, Box 1, Folder "Interviews S–Z," transcript, 23. On substantial increases in tax assessment in the Oak Street area between 1959 and 1970, see Raymond E. Wolfinger, *The Politics of Progress* (Englewood Cliffs, NJ: Prentice-Hall, 1974), 297, and Lee testimony, *National Commission Hearings*, 124. The Fainsteins concluded in their analysis, however, that the increases in property assessments resulting from urban renewal were hardly impressive, particularly when one took into account the city's cash and in-kind contributions to urban renewal; Norman I. Fainstein and Susan S. Fainstein, "New Haven: The Limits of the Local State," in Susan S. Fainstein, Norman I. Fainstein, Richard Child Hall, Dennis R. Judd, and Michael Peter Smith, *Restructuring the City: The Political Economy of Urban Redevelopment*, rev. ed. (New York: Longman, 1986), 49–50.

18. Eugene Rostow, interview by Robert Dahl, October 31, 1957, New Haven, CT, Box 1, Folder "Interviews S–Z," transcript, 15. The literature is extensive on the Housing Acts of 1949 and 1954; for a short summary, see Jewel Bellush and Murray Hausknecht, eds., *Urban Renewal: People, Politics and Planning* (New York: Anchor Books, 1967), 3–16. Public housing survived the House of Representatives by only five votes, and progress was very slow on building the units authorized; Eugene J. Meehan, "The Evolution of Public Housing Policy," in *Federal Housing Policy and Programs, Past and Present*, ed. J. Paul Mitchell (New Brunswick, NJ: Center for Urban Policy Research, Rutgers University, 1995), 299.

19. On Lee's objection to public housing, quote in William Lee Miller, *The Fifteenth Ward and the Great Society: An Encounter with a Modern City* (Boston: Houghton Mifflin, 1966), 88; Robert A. Solomon, "Symposium: Building a Segregated City: How We All Worked Together," *Saint Louis University Public Law Review* 16, no. 2 (1996–97), 21.

20. "New Haven Pursuing the American Dream of a Slumless City," *NYT*, September 7, 1965.

21. *National Commission Hearings*, 191.

22. *National Commission Hearings*, 115.

23. For Logue's pride in the relocation effort, Logue, interview, Schussheim, 29. Logue claimed that New Haven was the first urban renewal program in the county to establish a business-relocation office; Logue, "In Defense of Urban Renewal," letter to the editor, *NYT*, September 25, 1994, in Robert C. Ellickson, *Urban Legal History: The Development of New Haven; Class Materials*, vol. 2, Yale Law School, Course Pack Spring 2005, 712.

24. Mitchell Sviridoff, ed., *Inventing Community Renewal: The Trials and Errors That Shaped the Modern Community Development Corporation* (New York: Milano Graduate School, New School University, 2004), 162.

25. Bernard Asbell, "They Said It Wouldn't Happen in New Haven: Dick Lee Discovers How Much Is Not Enough," *NYT Magazine*, September 3, 1967. On 221(d)(3), see

Talbot, *Mayor's Game*, 141–43. Also, Powledge, *Model City*, 71–74, and Wolfinger, *Politics of Progress*, 196–97, on subsidies, loans, and rental programs.

26. Catherine Bauer Wurster published her classic *Modern Housing* in 1934 and co-authored the Housing Act of 1937 with its provision for public housing. She remained a vocal advocate for public-supported housing until her death in 1964. Correspondence between Logue and Bauer Wurster in the Catherine Bauer Wurster Papers, Bancroft Library, University of California, Berkeley, Box 21, Folder 21, containing letters with Logue from 1957 to 1963. Ralph Taylor studied with her at the Littauer School at Harvard in 1947 and credited her with inspiring him to undertake a career in housing and city building; H. Ralph Taylor, interview by Lizabeth Cohen, April 21, 2006, Chevy Chase, MD. I am grateful to Nancy Cott for alerting me to the Bauer Wurster correspondence with Logue. Also see Samuel Zipp, "The Roots and Routes of Urban Renewal," *JUH* 39, no. 3 (May 2013): 359–65.

27. Asbell, "They Said It Wouldn't Happen in New Haven," *NYT Magazine*; Wolfinger, *Politics of Progress*, 197; Phillip Allan Singerman, "Politics, Bureaucracy, and Public Policy: The Case of Urban Renewal in New Haven" (Ph.D. dissertation, Yale University, 1980), 205–6, which has slightly different figures.

28. Rae, *City*, 339; New Haven Redevelopment Agency, "Housing Report," February 20, 1969, in Powledge, *Model City*, 119. Rae acknowledges that not all moves were under compulsion; some people welcomed the help in moving.

29. *National Commission Hearings*, 117.

30. U.S. Census Bureau, *Census of Population 1950 and 1960*, in Jeff Hardwick, "A Downtown Utopia? Suburbanization, Urban Renewal and Consumption in New Haven," *Planning History Studies* 10, nos. 1–2 (1996): 42; Fainstein and Fainstein, "New Haven," Tables 2.1 and 2.2, 31; Wolfinger, *Politics of Progress*, 16.

31. *National Commission Hearings*, 123; also 128–29, 134, 145. Sviridoff agreed; *Inventing Community Renewal*, 145.

32. *National Commission Hearings*, 207.

33. *National Commission Hearings*, 129.

34. Harris quote in Richard Balzer, *Street Time* (New York: Grossman, 1972), 32, and in Jackson, *Model City Blues*, 110–11. For more on Harris and the HPA before and after these hearings, see Powledge, *Model City*, 152–77; Yohuru Williams, *Black Politics/White Power: Civil Rights, Black Power, and the Black Panthers in New Haven* (New York: Brandywine Press, 2000), 68–105; Harold Antonio Neu, "The Hill Parents Association and the Challenge of Community Action" (senior essay, Yale College, 1989), in possession of the author.

35. *National Commission Hearings*, 142–43.

36. Wolfinger, "This is Ray on November 2," Dahl, 19–21; Wolfinger, *Politics of Progress*, 284–85.

37. Lowe, *Cities in a Race with Time*, 425. Also see Polsby, *Community Power and Political Theory: A Further Look at Problems of Evidence and Inference* (New Haven, CT: Yale University Press, 1963; 2nd enlarged ed. 1980), 75, and Linda Prokopy, "Talking with State Street Businessmen," *AIM: The Bulletin of the American Independent Movement* 2, no. 8 (November 25, 1967): 6, 8, which recounts public hearings where the city's side went on so long "that by the time it comes to the citizens'

chance to speak, they're either exhausted or feel inadequate to confront all these officials." A draft plan for the public hearing on the Church Street Redevelopment Project, to take place July 24, 1957, reveals this orchestration as well as the community leaders and renewal committees asked to testify; "Aldermanic Committee on Streets and Squares, Public Hearing," July 24, 1957, EJL, Series 5, Box 72, Folder 611.

38. Quoted in Dane Archer, "New Haven: Renewal and Riots," *Nation*, June 3, 1968, 731. Established community leaders were often hired by the Redevelopment Agency to serve as neighborhood staff. For example, in Wooster Square, Theodore De Lauro, who had grown up in the area and had been a neighborhood leader most of his adult life, was hired for the important post of "neighborhood representative." Anthony Paolillo, another neighborhood leader, was hired as project assistant to help in the field office; *Wooster Square Design: A Report on the Background, Experience, and Design Procedures in Redevelopment and Rehabilitation in an Urban Renewal Project*, prepared by Mary Hommann (New Haven, CT: New Haven Redevelopment Agency, 1965), 29.

39. Russell D. Murphy, *Political Entrepreneurs and Urban Poverty: The Strategies of Policy Innovation in New Haven's Model Anti-Poverty Project* (Lexington, MA: D. C. Heath, 1971), passim, with particular attention to 41, 51–53, 151–52 for quotes. Quotation from the CPI deputy director in Howard W. Hallman, "Planning with the Poor: A Discussion of Resident Participation in the Planning of Community Action Programs" (paper delivered at the Conference on Community Development), Ford Foundation Archives, PA #62–29, cited in Alice O'Connor, "Community Action, Urban Reform, and the Fight Against Poverty: The Ford Foundation's Gray Areas Program," *JUH* 22, no. 5 (July 1996): 614. Also see Peter Marris and Martin Rein, *Dilemmas of Social Reform: Poverty and Community Action in the United States* (New York: Atherton Press, 1967), passim on CPI and New Haven.

40. *National Commission Hearings*, 155–58. This sea change in the political environment was noted by many involved in New Haven's urban renewal; see Talbot, *Mayor's Game*, 211–12, where he called it "direct citizen action"; Powledge, *Model City*, 68–69, 145–46, 251.

41. *National Commission Hearings*, 185–86; on Cook and AIM, see Jackson, *Model City Blues*, 127, 166–72. AIM published *AIM: The Bulletin of the American Independent Movement* twice a month from April 1966 to March 1970, and it is now in the Yale Library. Urban renewal—or "urban removal," as the *Bulletin* referred to it—was frequently the topic. A special issue published August 31, 1967, covered the New Haven riot. "A Position Paper on Urban Renewal—Prepared by the American Independent Movement Sub-Committee on Urban Renewal" appeared in November 1967. Several months later, another organization, the Coalition of Concerned Citizens (CCC), was organized by Dr. William Ryan and his wife, Phyllis, relative newcomers to New Haven, who, as social activists, were frustrated with the political status quo in their new home. (In 1971, Dr. Ryan would publish an important work of sociology, *Blaming the Victim*.) The CCC criticized "the unchecked continuation of injustice and inequality in this city . . . These are only symptoms of the real disease that grips New Haven: the decline of democracy." On CCC, see Powledge, *Model City*, 183–90, quotes on 183–84.

42. *National Commission Hearings*, 115.

43. *National Commission Hearings*, quotes from 147, 148, 151, 152, 153. Other critics amplified Harris's comments. The commission's executive director, Shuman, would later write, "Unknown to us until the end of our day of hearings there, the New Haven police had been stationed inside and outside the hall in case our hearings got out of hand. We prevented that by welcoming the views of unscheduled as well as scheduled witnesses. In fact, the 'walk-in' witnesses talked with a fire and an eloquence which the others did not match"; Shuman, "Behind the Scenes," *WM*, in Powledge, *Model* City, 121.

44. *National Commission Hearings*, 178–80; Miller, *Fifteenth Ward and the Great Society*, 244–59. On Papa's long, mostly unsuccessful career in New Haven politics, see Singerman, "Politics, Bureaucracy, and Public Policy," 304.

45. Asbell, "They Said It Wouldn't Happen in New Haven," *NYT Magazine*, 31.

46. U.S. Census Bureau, *Census of Population, New Haven, Connecticut, 1950, 1960, 1970*.

47. Logue, "Can Cities Survive Automobile Age? New Haven Used as a Test Case," *Traffic Quarterly* 3, no. 2 (April 1959): 175. See Christopher S. Schell, "Oak Street Unearthed: The Households in New Haven's Low-Income Housing 1913–1957" (term paper, Yale Law School, 1998; New Haven Museum and Historical Society), 67, which documents that blacks had greater difficulty than Jews moving out of the Oak Street neighborhood.

48. New Haven Human Rights Committee, "Report of Findings and Recommendations 12–14," 1964, in Ellickson, *Urban Legal History*, 590.

49. Rae, *City*, 340–43. Also, Family Relocation Office, "Report of the Progress of Family Relocations in Oak Street Redevelopment Area," March 10, 1957, cited in Gregory Ruben (paper for Robert Gordon on lawyers in urban renewal of New Haven, June 2006 draft), 36n184, in possession of the author.

50. For a thorough investigation of the state of black organizations in New Haven, see Williams, *Black Politics/White Power*, chapters 1–3. The Reverend Edwin Edmonds, a civil rights activist from North Carolina, criticized the moderate views of New Haven's civil rights leaders when he became the minister of the Dixwell Avenue Congregational Church in 1959: "This was one backward town"; Rev. Edwin Edmonds, interview by Sarah Hammond, February 16, 2004, New Haven, CT, New Haven Oral History Collection, YMA.

51. NAACP, "The Urban Renewal Program and NAACP Guidelines to Integration," n.d. but c. 1963, 2, cited in Jennifer Hock, "Race and Class on the Drawing Boards," paper for the American Society of City and Regional Planning History Conference, October 22, 2005, 7, in possession of the author. Andrew R. Highsmith found many of the same racial dynamics at work in Flint, Michigan's, urban renewal in *Demolition Means Progress: Flint, Michigan, and the Fate of the American Metropolis* (Chicago: University of Chicago Press, 2015).

52. Jennifer Hock, "Political Designs: Architecture and Urban Renewal in the Civil Rights Era, 1954–1973" (Ph.D. dissertation, Harvard University, 2012), 44–46, 50–51, 53–55, 63–66, 73–74; see 51 for quote from Memo from Logue to Richard Lee, August 23, 1960, New Haven Redevelopment Authority Papers, Box 36, Folder 791.

Redevelopment Agency staff members claimed that the final city hearing on the Dixwell renewal plan, which "climaxed hundreds of smaller meetings with neighborhood residents and businessmen" organized by the Dixwell Renewal Committee, was "attended by over 600 persons from the neighborhood" and "the only criticism of the plan at that time was that it did not include enough acquisition of properties for demolition"; Melvin J. Adams, Donald Kirk, and Louis Onofrio, "The Wooster Square and Dixwell Projects in New Haven, Connecticut," in *Residential Rehabilitation*, a compilation of papers presented at the Training Institute in Residential Rehabilitation, ed. M. Carter McFarland and Walter K. Vivrett, University of Minnesota, Minneapolis, July 19–30, 1965 (Minneapolis: School of Architecture, University of Minnesota, 1966), 294–96.

53. Harris and Associates, "Survey of the Race for Mayor of New Haven," EJL, 6.

54. "A Post-Election Analysis of Voter Opinion in New Haven," December 1965, 21–25, in Singerman, "Politics, Bureaucracy, and Public Policy," 253–54.

55. Irving L. Allen and J. David Colfax, *Urban Problems and Public Opinion in Four Connecticut Cities* (Storrs: Institute of Urban Research, University of Connecticut, 1968), 58, also 49, 59, 170; Singerman, "Politics, Bureaucracy, and Public Policy," 252.

56. The most vocal critics of urban renewal in the neighborhoods during the 1950s were those displaced by the redevelopment of the Oak Street area. Although there was very little organized resistance to the project before it happened, within a few years of the razing, former residents, mostly white ethnics, began holding annual reunions to reminisce about the old days; see Ted Gesing's documentary film *Model City* (2003) for footage of one of these reunions.

57. Alvin A. Mermin, *Relocating Families* (Washington, DC: National Association of Housing and Redevelopment Officials [NAHRO], 1970), 4, in Rae, *City*, 338. Mermin became the second director of the Family Relocation Office and would serve for ten years, according to Doug Rae "with decency and ingenuity, attempting to mitigate the trauma of relocation." On Redevelopment Agency concerns about finding relocation housing for nonwhites ineligible for public housing, see S. Carroll to Mr. Logue, Mrs. Craddock, Mr. Sweet, Mr. Feiss, June 10, 1955, Rotival, Box 36, Folder "N.H. City, 1954–55."

58. Logue, interview by Deborah Sue Elkin, September 18, 1993, New Haven, CT.

59. On Wooster Square urban renewal in general, see New Haven Redevelopment Agency, *Redevelopment and Renewal Plan for the Wooster Square Project Area* (New Haven, CT: 1958, amended 1965); Mary Hommann, *Wooster Square Design: A Report on the Background, Experience, and Design Procedures in Redevelopment and Rehabilitation in an Urban Renewal District* (New Haven, CT: New Haven Redevelopment Agency, 1965), in which she claims that there was a racial mix on rehabbed Court Street, 60; Sherman Hasbrouck, "Transformation: A Summary of New Haven's Development Program" (M.A. thesis, Yale University, 1965), 37–48; Talbot, *Mayor's Game*, 136–45; Powledge, *Model City*, 39–41; Mary S. Hommann, "New Haven Skid Row Rowhouses Being Rehabilitated as Link in Renewal Chain," *JH* 18, no. 7 (July 1961): 337–39, 57; Mary S. Hommann, "Neighborhood Rehabilitation Is Working in Six Projects in New Haven; Here's How," *JH* 19, no. 4 (May 1962):

185–89; Lowe, *Cities in a Race with Time*, 463–89. The 80 percent homeowner figure is from Adams, Kirk, and Onofrio, "Wooster Square and Dixwell Projects in New Haven, Connecticut," in *Residential Rehabilitation*, 268–69.

60. On Dixwell urban renewal, see New Haven Redevelopment Agency, *Dixwell Redevelopment and Renewal Plan* (New Haven, CT: 1960); Hasbrouck, "Transformation," 49–56; Talbot, *Mayor's Game*, 146–47; Lowe, *Cities in a Race with Time*, 489–506. The New Haven Redevelopment Agency used its leverage with the local Tradesmen's National Bank, where it deposited its federal urban renewal funds, to pressure the bank to make money available for rehab in Dixwell; Logue, interview, Schussheim, 18; "Master Pieces: Ed Logue Talks with Rebecca Barnes AIA," *AB* 1, no. 2 (1998): 33–34; Adams, Kirk, and Onofrio, "Wooster Square and Dixwell Projects in New Haven, Connecticut," 286, 298. Mary Hommann gave even more details: before renewal, because of their race, "Dixwell homeowners were denied equitable financing and often carried two mortgages at 12 percent each. Now they can get 25-year mortgages at 5 ¾ per cent, cutting payments in half even after the principle is increased for renovations. Dixwell is also using the new Federal rehabilitation grants of up to $1,500 for low-income owners and 3 percent mortgages. Each owner is given rehabilitation advice of all kinds, from architectural to financial, by the project staff"; Mary Hommann, "Symbolic Bells in Dixwell," *AF* (July–August 1966): 56.

61. "Florence Virtue Housing, New Haven, Connecticut," JJ, Box 3, Folder 2.

62. Criticism of Florence Virtue Homes in Jackson, *Model City Blues*, 54–56, 58–59; refuted by Bass, "Write Your Own Caption," *New Haven Independent*, May 16, 2008. The 55-to-45 black-white racial balance comes from Hommann, "Symbolic Bells in Dixwell," 56; other reports put it at 60-to-40. Talbot, *Mayor's Game*, 147, explains that when the Dixwell Avenue Congregational Church's low-key outreach to potential white buyers failed to deliver enough white customers, the Redevelopment Agency hired an ex-newspaperman to market the project more aggressively as "University Park–Dixwell" and attracted greater interest. Talbot was optimistic about the integration of Dixwell: "There are few cities genuinely attempting to use renewal as a means of transforming a Negro ghetto into an integrated neighborhood with integrated schools."

63. Talbot, *Mayor's Game*, 166; Ed Logue, "Mike Sviridoff Tribute," March 26, 1998, EJL, 2002 Accession, B23, Folder "March 1998 Mike Sviridoff," 2. Although blacks had been living in Elm Haven, New Haven's first public housing project, since its opening in 1940, individual buildings were racially segregated; Solomon, "Symposium: Building a Segregated City," 16, a very good history of public housing in New Haven.

64. Talbot, *Mayor's Game*, 191–92.

65. Talbot, *Mayor's Game*, 179–81.

66. Remarks of Richard C. Lee, "Occasion: International Sunday School Convention of Church of God in Christ," July 28, 1960, EJL, Series 5, Box 110, Folder 1114; Talbot, *Mayor's Game*, 171, 257; Jackson, *Model City Blues*, 52–54.

67. Miller, *Fifteenth Ward and the Great Society*, 40–49; Talbot, *Mayor's Game*, 182–88.

68. Miller, *Fifteenth Ward and the Great Society*, 84–98. That expansion was never easy. Miller's white, middle-class Fifteenth Ward was the contested site of one of the first

"scattered houses." The neighborhood Congregational church had inherited the house and, after some soul searching, made it available to the New Haven Housing Authority. After the uproar, the city returned the house to the church.

69. Wolfinger, *Politics of Progress*, 199.

70. Miller, *Fifteenth Ward and the Great Society*, 66–67 for quote, also see on busing 50–83, 126–143, 22; Talbot, *Mayor's Game*, 189–210.

71. "The Vote in New Haven," editorial, *NYT*, October 30, 1965; Miller, *Fifteenth Ward and the Great Society*, 260–63; Talbot, *Mayor's Game*, 223–24.

72. Logue to Chester Bowles, letter draft, May 15, 1957, EJL, Series 4, Box 23, Folder 13, 2; Logue to Walter P. Reuther, November 16, 1953, requesting that he take a leadership role in a movement to put pension funds "to socially useful ends, such as moderate rental housing. Eisenhower is not going to do the housing job. We will have to do it ourselves." Logue also tried to get Mike Sviridoff's help lining up a progressive union to take the mortgage on the first of the Oak Street apartment buildings, which "will be the first one in the United States in which there is a specific and binding agreement between the developer and the municipality for insuring that the apartments will be open to all, regardless of race, creed, or color"; Logue to Mitchell Sviridoff, September 15, 1958, EJL, Series 5, Box 85, Folder 786.

73. On the divisions, generational and ideological, within New Haven's black community organizations, see Williams, *Black Politics/White Power*, 14–18, 24–43, 49–64.

74. *National Commission Hearings*, quotes from 147, 148, 151, 152, 153.

75. "Cities: No Haven," *Time*, September 1, 1967.

76. Rae, *City*, 351–55, quote on 354; Hugo Lindgren, "New Haven," *Metropolis* 13 (January–February 1994): 30. Additional sources on the riot informing my discussion include Powledge, *Model City*, 91–93, 109–14, 215; Jackson, *Model City Blues*, 138–52; Asbell, "They Said It Wouldn't Happen in New Haven"; Williams, *Black Politics/White Power*, 81–105; and Robert J. Leeney, *Elms, Arms, and Ivy: New Haven in the Twentieth Century* (Montgomery, AL: Community Communications, in cooperation with the New Haven Colony Historical Society, 2000), 67–70. Observers on the Left often linked the rioting to the city's urban renewal and poverty programs: "Urban Planning and Urban Revolt? A Case Study," *PA* 49, no. 1 (January 1968): 134–56; and Archer, "New Haven: Renewal and Riots," 729–32. Jane Jacobs told the *NYT*, "Logue tosses people and small business around ruthlessly. If you want to know what he does, ask the rioters in New Haven"; *NYT Magazine*, March 1, 1970. In contrast, the conservative local paper, the *NHR*, emphasized youth violence and praised the police. To the extent that "costly and 'expert' programs" were mentioned, it was to claim that the protests showed the "waste and carelessness of the do-good bureaucracy"; *NHR*, front pages and editorials, August 20–27, 1967, passim.

77. "A Survey of the Political Climate on New Haven, Connecticut" (October 1967), Study #619, and "A Scouting Survey of the Political Climate in New Haven, Connecticut" (November 1967), Study #630, cited in Singerman, "Politics, Bureaucracy, and Public Policy," 249–51.

78. On the end of the Lee regime, see Powledge, *Model City*, 256–57, 296–98, 304–6.

79. Charles Abrams, "Some Blessings of Urban Renewal," in *Urban Renewal: The Record and the Controversy*, ed. James Q. Wilson (Cambridge, MA: MIT Press, 1966),

571. Also see in the same volume, Basil Zimmer, "The Small Businessman and Relocation," on a study of three hundred businesses displaced by urban renewal and highway building in Providence, Rhode Island, from 1954 to 1959. Nearly seven out of ten employed fewer than three workers; 380–403. On the active campaigning of large chains and department stores against smaller businesses, see Alison Isenberg, *Downtown America: A History of the Place and the People Who Made It* (Chicago: University of Chicago Press, 2004), 195.

80. William N. Kinnard, Jr., and Zenon S. Malinowski, *The Impact of Dislocation from Urban Renewal Areas on Small Business* (Storrs, CT: University of Connecticut School of Business Administration, 1960), 63, cited in Wolfinger, *Politics of Progress*, 319, also 332–37; Hardwick, "A Downtown Utopia?": 47–49.

81. On the Savitt suit, see Talbot, *Mayor's Game*, 120–21.

82. Leo S. Gilden to Richard C. Lee, June 15, 1957; Logue to Mayor Richard C. Lee, August 12, 1957; and L. S. Rowe to Leo S. Gilden, August 13, 1957, all in EJL, Series 5, Box 7, Folder 596. Also see in same folder: "Merchants Bid for Help on Project Data," *NHR*, July 18, 1957; "Sound Redevelopment—but No 'Railroading,'" editorial, *NHR*, July 21, 1957. On the CCA suit, see Talbot, *Mayor's Game*, 119. The detailed story of the small merchants and the city is well told in Wolfinger, *Politics of Progress*, 315–24, and in a candid memo he wrote to Dahl, "City Hall Memos from RW," July 7, 1958, Dahl, Box 1, Folder "Special Interviews–Wolfinger 1958," 4–7.

83. One of the small businesses that did survive the redevelopment of downtown New Haven is Louis' Lunch, which claims to be the birthplace of the hamburger. When the small restaurant moved four blocks to its current location at 261–63 Crown Street, the owner constructed a "wall of tears": "I decided to collect the bricks. So on that wall there is a brick for every shop torn down from the Green all the way to the end of the parking garage"; interview in Gesing, *Model City* film.

84. 1963 Campaign "Downtown Campaign Q&A" (120 seconds), film footage, RCL.

85. Jane Jacobs, *The Death and Life of Great American Cities* (New York: Vintage, 1961).

86. Interview with Richard Lee quoted in Powledge, *Model City*, 250–55. The Kerner Commission concurred in its report released in February 1968, drawing a "lesson" from New Haven and Detroit, "where well-intentioned programs designed to respond to the needs of ghetto residents were not worked out and implemented sufficiently in cooperation with the intended beneficiaries"; quoted in Archer, "New Haven: Renewal and Riots," 732. More openness to citizen participation did not keep the Lee administration from trying to discredit Harris and other HPA leaders after the riot, however. Harris was arrested for possession of drugs and stolen goods, charges he claimed were part of a campaign of police harassment; Neu, "Hill Parents Association," 39–46.

87. Powledge, *Model City*, 133–42; *Inventing Community Renewal*, 180–92, on Sviridoff's personal resistance to implementing a great deal of popular participation at CPI.

88. Jean Joyce, "Grassroots Democracy Comes to Rajasthan," in "The Ford Foundation Program Letter: India," Report No. 109, March 21, 1960, EJL, Series 4, Box 26, Folder 54, 1.

89. John Barber, "Black Power in New Haven: Problems of Land and Police," *AIM Bulletin* 3, no. 11 (October 29, 1968): 16.

90. Rae, *City*, 361–63; Logue, interview by Joyce, Bowles, 46. Many people I interviewed noted how renewal efforts were undermined by the city's steady bleeding of jobs; see Allan Talbot, interview by Lizabeth Cohen, June 13, 2007, New York, NY; Howard R. Moskof, interview by Lizabeth Cohen, April 21, 2006, Chevy Chase, MD.

91. As early as September 1954, a mere six months into Lee's first term, Logue was already scheming how to get more help from Yale; see Spence Toll to Logue, September 11, 1954, Rotival, Box 36, Folder "N.H. City, 1954–55." For Logue's criticism of Yale's inaction in New Haven, see, for example, Logue, "Life as a City Builder— 'Make No Little Plans,'" written for the Yale Reunion Book, March 26, 1991, MDL; Logue to Linda Lorimer, Secretary, Yale University, May 12, 1995, MDL.

92. Rob Gerwitt, "Death of a Neighborhood," *Mother Jones*, September 1, 2000, 8–9.

93. Ellen Herman, *The Romance of American Psychology: Political Culture in the Age of Experts* (Berkeley: University of California Press, 1995); Fred Turner, *The Democratic Surround: Multimedia and American Liberalism from World War II to the Psychedelic Sixties* (Chicago: University of Chicago Press, 2013).

94. Insert in *AIM Newsletter* 4, no. 20 (November 15, 1969), in Jackson, *Model City Blues*, 156.

95. Logue, "The Boston Story—Getting Started," draft chapter for memoir, "Tales of a City Builder, Compared to What," January 2000, MDL, 6–v7.

4. Sizing Up the Old Boston

1. Logue, "The Boston Story—Getting Started," draft chapter for memoir, "Tales of a City Builder, Compared to What," January 2000, MDL, 6–8v7. For more on the recruitment of Logue to Boston, Joseph Slavet, interview by Lizabeth Cohen, May 31, 2007, Boston, MA; Lewis H. Weinstein, *My Life at the Bar: Six Decades as Lawyer, Soldier, Teacher and Pro Bono Activist* (Hanover, MA: Christopher Publishing House, 1993), 139–41. Amusingly, Logue wrote to a girlfriend from the military during World War II, after she had visited Boston: "Have much trouble finding your way around Boston? It's the only town I have been in twice and still had a great deal of difficulty orienting myself"; Logue to Babe, October 5, 1944, EJL, Series 1, Box 3, Folder 44.

2. Logue, "The Boston Story," 8v7; also Logue, interview by Richard Heath, December 7, 1990, in Heath, *An Act of Faith: The Building of the Washington Park Urban Renewal Area, 1960–1975*, booklet originally published 1990, reprinted 2005, part 5, 2; Logue, "Boston, 1960–1967—Seven Years of Plenty," *Proceedings of the Massachusetts Historical Society* 84 (1972): 84.

3. "Logue Remains Silent on $40,000 Mass. Post," *NHR*, January 22, 1960; "People," *AF* (March 1960).

4. Logue, "Boston, 1960–1967—Seven Years of Plenty," 84; on the issue of Logue's salary, see Janet Bowler Fitzgibbons, interview by Lizabeth Cohen, June 21, 2007, Cambridge, MA; Ellen Logue, interview by Lizabeth Cohen, April 13, 2008, Berkeley, CA; MLogue, interview. Logue took pride that he was the highest-paid public official in New England; Logue, interview, Schussheim, transcript, 26.

5. See correspondence from Collins, Box 172, Folders 13 and 14: Logue to Jock Saltonstall, Jr., December 31, 1959; Saltonstall, Jr., to John F. Collins, January 4, 1960;

Memos "Development Administrator—City of Boston" and "Development Program for the City of Boston," January 26, 1960; Logue to Collins, February 2, 1960; Memo "Development Administrator—City of Boston," February 2, 1960; Logue to Collins, February 5, 1960; Logue to Collins, February 23, 1960, with attachment "Development Program Outline, City of Boston."

6. "What's Happening to Proper Old Boston?," *Newsweek*, April 26, 1965; "Bold Boston Gladiator—Ed Logue: Planner Stirs Up a Ruckus and Battles Opposition to Build the Place of His Dreams," *Life*, December 24, 1965, 126–34; "Meet Boston's Mr. Urban Renewal," *CSM*, December 18, 1965, 126–34; Nicholas von Hoffman, "Ed Logue—the Master Rebuilder," *WP*, April 15, 1967.

7. Edward J. Driscoll, Jr., "Edward Logue Is Dead, Gave Boston New Face," *BG*, January 28, 2000; Logue, interview by Heath, 1.

8. Irene Saint, "What Makes Logue Tick: He Has Wheedled $200 Million out of the Federal Government to Help Build the New Boston," *BH*, December 5, 1965.

9. Logue, "The Boston Story," 13–17v7, 26v7, 35v7, 39v7, 47v7; Logue, "Boston, 1960–1967—Seven Years of Plenty," 89–90; "$90 Million Development Program for Boston," *CR*, September 24, 1960; Robert B. Hannan, "Huge Renewal Plan Offered by Collins," *BG*, September 22, 1960; "Remarks of Mayor John F. Collins at a public meeting on the Proposed Development Program in the Old South Meeting House, October 7, 1960, 7 p.m.," EJL, Series 6, Box 148, Folder 374.

10. Barry Bluestone and Mary Huff Stevenson, *The Boston Renaissance: Race, Space, and Economic Change in an American Metropolis* (New York: Russell Sage Foundation, 2000), 81.

11. For more details and statistics on Boston's economy in 1960, see Walter McQuade, "Boston: What Can a Sick City Do?," *Fortune*, June 1964; "Boston Bonds' Rating Slips a Notch," *BW*, December 19, 1959; Nancy Rita Arnone, "Redevelopment in Boston: A Study of the Politics and Administration of Social Change" (Ph.D. dissertation, MIT, 1965), 14–17; John Stainton, *Urban Renewal and Planning in Boston: A Review of the Past and a Look at the Future*, consultant study directed by John Stainton, commissioned by the Citizens Housing and Planning Association and Boston Redevelopment Authority, November 1972, 3, 24–35; Jeffrey P. Brown, "Boston," in *Cities Reborn*, ed. Rachelle L. Levitt (Washington, DC: Urban Land Institute, 1987), 9–27; Lawrence W. Kennedy, *Planning the City upon a Hill: Boston Since 1630* (Amherst: University of Massachusetts Press, 1992), 168; Thomas H. O'Connor, *Building a New Boston: Politics and Urban Renewal, 1950–1970* (Boston: Northeastern University Press, 1993), 42–43, 146–47; Gerard O'Neill, *Rogues and Redeemers: When Politics Was King in Irish Boston* (New York: Crown, 2012), 120; John H. Mollenkopf, *The Contested City* (Princeton, NJ: Princeton University Press, 1983), 142–45.

12. Quote from *CSM*, August 2, 1960, cited in Timothy Francis Rose, "Civic War: People, Politics, and the Battle of New Boston, 1945–1967" (Ph.D. dissertation, University of California, Berkeley, 2006), 45.

13. Logue, "The Boston Story," 36v7.

14. Quotes from *BG*, November 3, 1949, and William Shannon, "Boston's Irish Mayors: An Ethnic Perspective," in *Boston 1700–1980: The Evolution of Urban Politics*, ed.

Ronald Formisano and Constance Burns (Westport, CT: Greenwood Press, 1984), 205, cited in Rose, "Civic War," 82–83. Another source put the 1959 figure of city income from real estate taxes at 69.1 percent; George Sternlieb, *The Future of the Downtown Department Store*, mimeographed (Cambridge, MA: Joint Center for Urban Studies of MIT and Harvard University, 1962), 141. Jon Teaford cited a 1963 statistic from the U.S. Census Bureau of 61 percent of general revenue coming from the property tax, but even that made it far higher than in eleven other major cities, Cleveland being next highest at 53.3 percent; Teaford, *The Rough Road to Renaissance* (Baltimore: Johns Hopkins University Press, 1990), 144. For the definitive biography of James Michael Curley, see Jack Beatty, *The Rascal King: The Life and Times of James Michael Curley (1874–1958)* (Reading, MA: Addison-Wesley, 1992).

15. Harvey Cox, *The Secular City: Secularization and Urbanization in Theological Perspective* (New York: Macmillan, 1965), 95–97; the Brandeis quote is attributed to Lewis Mumford, *The City in History* (New York: Harcourt, Brace and World, 1961), 495. The Cox quotation was brought to Logue's attention; Stonewall J. McMurray III to Logue, August 11, 1965, EJL, Series 6, Box 150, Folder 433, 1.

16. "Urban Development Prospects as Seen by Edward Logue," speech given to a Boston College Citizen Seminar, April 12, 1960, *CR*, April 16, 1960, 318.

17. O'Connor, *Building a New Boston*, 43, 91; for more on the lack of home rule, see Martin Meyerson and Edward C. Banfield, *Boston: The Job Ahead* (Cambridge, MA: Harvard University Press, 1966), 11–16; David J. Barron, Gerald E. Frug, and Rick T. Su, *Dispelling the Myth of Home Rule: Local Power in Greater Boston* (Cambridge, MA: Rappaport Institute for Greater Boston, John F. Kennedy School of Government, Harvard University, 2004); and Gerald E. Frug and David J. Barron, *City Bound: How States Stifle Urban Innovation* (Ithaca, NY: Cornell University Press, 2008).

18. Henry Scagnoli, interview by Lizabeth Cohen, June 20, 2007, Boston, MA.

19. Opposition to Curley's machine went beyond Yankees. Joe Slavet's father was a socialist-leaning Jewish Democrat who said he "never voted Irish" and always supported Republicans to deprive Curley of support; Slavet, interview.

20. Ryan quoted in "Is Boston 'Beginning to Boil?'" *Fortune*, June 1957; "Route 128 Opens Boston's High Tech Age, August 24, 1951," *Mass Moments*, https://www.massmoments.org/moment-details/route-128-opens-bostons-high-tech-age.html; William Holt, "The Man Behind Route 128," *BG*, January 11, 2015; Massachusetts Advisory Committee to the U.S. Commission on Civil Rights and the Massachusetts Commission Against Discrimination, *Route 128: Boston's Road to Segregation*, January 1975, 37–42; "Urban General: James McCormack" and "Transportation: 'If It Gets Any Worse, It May Never Get Better,'" *AF* 120 (June 1964): 85, 111.

21. William J. Poorvu, "Yale, New Haven, and Me," in *Class of 1956 Book*, Yale University, 2006, 75.

22. On the redlining of lower-class, ethnic, and racial urban neighborhoods beginning in the 1930s, see Kenneth Jackson, *Crabgrass Frontier: The Suburbanization of the United States* (New York: Oxford University Press, 1985), 197–218; and Lizabeth Cohen, *A Consumers' Republic: The Politics of Mass Consumption in Postwar America* (New York: Vintage, 2003), 170–72, 214, 221.

23. Scagnoli, interview.

24. Dero A. Saunders, "Department Stores: Race for the Suburbs," *Fortune*, December 1951; "Downtown Loads Its Heavy Guns," *BW*, November 23, 1957; Sternlieb, *Future of the Downtown Department Store*, particularly 162–70; "Downtown Boston Slips; Branches Up," *WWD*, March 5, 1963; "Boston Makes a Comeback: A Look at an Old Metropolis 'On the Move,'" *U.S. News and World Report*, September 21, 1964; "Boston Retailers Gain 5% for 1963; Downtown Lags," *WWD*, February 25, 1964; "The Downtown Area: How to Clean It Up—and Make It Pay," *AF* 120 (June 1964): 99; U.S. Department of Housing and Urban Development, "Profile of a City—Boston," *HUD Notes*, September–October 1966, 4.

25. O'Neill, *Rogues and Redeemers*, 98, also 115–41; O'Connor, *Building a New Boston*, 21–149, passim.

26. "Boston Makes a Comeback"; also James Aloisi, "The New Boston Was a Mix of Good and Bad," *CommonWealth*, 2–3, September 26, 2013, https://commonwealth magazine.org/politics/007-the-new-boston-was-a-mix-of-good-and-bad/.

27. Logue, "The Boston Story," 38v7.

28. John Collins, interview by José de Varon, Tape 12, March 24, 1977, EJL, 1985 Accession, Box 3, Folder "Oral History John Collins," transcript, 2–4; Scagnoli, interview.

29. On Kane Simonian, see articles on Simonian soon after his death in *West Ender* 15, no. 3 (September 1999); Slavet, interview; O'Neill, *Rogues and Redeemers*, 151–55, 173–74.

30. James A. Aloisi, Jr., *The Big Dig* (Beverly, MA: Commonwealth Editions, 2004), 5–9.

31. For a detailed, insightful history of the Prudential Center, Elihu Rubin, *Insuring the City: The Prudential Center and the Postwar Urban Landscape* (New Haven, CT: Yale University Press, 2012); Benjamin Waterhouse, "'Through the Ordinary Operations of Private Enterprise': The Prudential Insurance Company's Corporate Renewal in Boston" (seminar paper, Harvard University, May 18, 2005), in possession of the author. In an otherwise laudatory column about Boston's urban renewal, the *NYT* architecture critic Ada Louise Huxtable condemned the Prudential Center as "a flashy 52-story glass and aluminum tower" that was "a Back Bay behemoth," part of an "over-scaled megalomaniac group" of buildings, "shockingly unrelated to the city's size, standards or style"; Huxtable, "Renewal in Boston: Good and Bad," *NYT*, April 19, 1964.

32. On the long negotiation with the federal government over placement of the federal building, see Richard Wallace Nathan, "The Government Center of Boston" (unpublished manuscript), Inter-University Case Program, October 1960.

33. Wolf Von Eckardt, "Architectural Commentary on Boston Today," *Ekistics* 18, no. 105 (August 1964): 88, 93. An earlier, more architecturally successful design for the site—then called the Back Bay Center—by an illustrious group of Boston architects headed by Walter Gropius, had been promoted by the downtown New Haven developer Roger Stevens during the 1950s, but it failed; Rubin, *Insuring the City*, 114–20, 167–72. As early as 1963, George Sternlieb cautioned that the construction of the Prudential Center in the Back Bay could speed the decay of downtown retail; George Sternlieb, "The Future of Retailing in the Downtown Core," *JAIP* 29, no. 2 (May 1963): 111; for early discussion of Back Bay retail, see "Major Changes Affect Boston Retail Scene," *WWD*, June 11, 1957.

34. Mel King, *Chain of Change: Struggles for Black Community Development* (Boston: South End Press, 1981), 20–21.

35. Emilie Tavel, "Debate Mounts in Boston Over Plan to Rebuild West End District," *CSM*, July 9, 1956; Joseph A. Keblinsky, "Favoritism on Contract Denied in West End Row," *BG*, December 8, 1956; Daniel M. Abramson, "Boston's West End: Urban Obsolescence in Mid-Twentieth Century America," in Daniel M. Abramson, Arindam Dutta, Timothy Hyde, and Jonathan Massey, *Governing by Design: Architecture, Economy, and Politics in the Twentieth Century* (Pittsburgh: University of Pittsburgh Press, 2012), 47–69; Robert Campbell, "Boston's Old West End Persists as a Palace," *BG*, January 8, 2012, for historic and contemporary photographs of the West End.

   As with New Haven's Oak Street neighborhood, the West End has an organization of active former residents who sponsor reunions; a newspaper, *The West Ender*, with the tagline "Printed in the Spirit of the Mid-Town Journal and Dedicated to Being the Collective Conscience of Urban Renewal and Eminent Domain in the City of Boston"; and a museum and archive (the West End Museum); see Barry Newman, "West End Story: A Neighborhood Died, but One Bostonian Refuses to Let It Go," *WSJ*, August 23, 2000; Joe Battenfeld, "West End Story," *BH Magazine*, February 15, 1987; Peter Anderson, "West End Story: A Neighborhood in Exile and Its Efforts to Go Home," *BG Magazine*, May 24, 1987; Michael Kenney, "The Museum Feels Their Pain: A Lost 'Hood Gets Its Belated Due," *BG*, October 21, 2007.

36. On how Rappaport got the West End project, see Frank Del Vecchio, *City Streets: A Memoir* (North Andover, MA: Leap Year Press, 2016), 209–10; also Anthony Yudis, "West End Sidewalk Plan Set Off Logue-Rappaport Feud," *BG*, August 12, 1963, on the state legislature's frustration over the developers' decision not to build subsidized housing. Joseph Lee provided Logue with a list of inappropriate actions by Kane Simonian and the BRA in the transaction of the West End's urban renewal: Joseph Lee to Logue, February 14, 1961, EJL, Series 6, Box 148, Folder 375. The estimates of how many residents were dislocated vary wildly, from 1,729 to 7,000; many residents departed on their own over the many years that the project was in planning; O'Connor, *Building a New Boston*, 125; Kennedy, *Planning the City upon a Hill*, 164.

37. Herbert J. Gans, *The Urban Villagers: Group and Class in the Life of Italian-Americans* (Glencoe, IL: Free Press, 1962); Marc Fried, *The World of the Urban Working Class* (Cambridge, MA: Harvard University Press, 1973); Chester Hartman, "The Housing of Relocated Families," *JAIP* 30, no. 4 (November 1964): 266–86. Logue responded to Hartman, who then had a rejoinder; Logue, "Comment on 'The Housing of Relocated Families,'" *JAIP* 31, no. 4 (November 1964): 338–40; and Hartman, "Rejoinder by the Author," 340–44. The whole debate is analyzed in Jay Curtis Getz, "The Progressive Technician and Mr. Urban Renewal: Lawrence Veiller, Edward Logue, and the Evolution of Planning for Low-Income Housing" (M.A. thesis, University of Illinois at Urbana-Champaign, 1990), 87–99. The urban historian Alexander von Hoffman recalled asking Logue how he would like to be introduced at an American Planning Association conference session years later; Logue replied,

"Tell them I wasn't responsible for the West End!" Alexander von Hoffman, email message to author, May 18, 2015.

38. Yudis, "West End Sidewalk Plan Set Off Logue-Rappaport Feud"; also Logue, "The Boston Story," 4v7.

39. Collins, interviews by de Varon: Tape 17, May 13, 1977, 3; Tape 30, October 25, 1977, 4–8, 11–12; Tape 31, October 26, 1977, 1–3.

40. Collins, interview by de Varon, Tape 30, October 25, 1977, 2, 9–11.

41. On John Collins and the 1959 election, see Murray B. Levin, *The Alienated Voter: Politics in Boston* (New York: Holt, Rinehart and Winston, 1960); O'Neill, *Rogues and Redeemers*, 159–69; O'Connor, *Building a New Boston*, 150–61; Scagnoli, interview, on television in campaign; John Patrick Ryan, interview by Lizabeth Cohen, June 18, 2007, Cambridge, MA.

42. Slavet, interview. On the Boston Municipal Research Bureau, see Boston Urban Study Group, *Who Rules Boston? A Citizen's Guide to Reclaiming the City* (Boston: Institute for Democratic Socialism, 1984), 53–54. Slavet had made a study of urban renewal programs nationwide in 1959, including visiting New Haven, where he first met Logue; he was appalled at how much Boston lagged in per capita federal urban renewal spending; Joseph S. Slavet, *Charting the Future of Urban Renewal* (Boston: Boston Municipal Research Bureau, July 1959).

43. Collins, interview by de Varon, Tape 31, October 27, 1977, 9–10; also see Martin Nolan, "Ex-Mayor Collins Dead at 76, Fought to Restore City's Pride, Image," *BG*, November 24, 1995.

44. On the history of the Coordinating Committee, or Vault: Mark I. Gelfand, *Trustee for a City: Ralph Lowell of Boston* (Boston: Northeastern University Press, 1998), 268–73; Boston Urban Study Group, *Who Rules Boston?*, 14, 36–37.

45. Scagnoli, interview, 22.

46. A 3 percent sales tax finally passed in 1966, after an expensive lobbying campaign financed by the Vault; Gelfand, *Trustee for a City*, 272. In 1967, the state increased the income tax and began covering the welfare costs of cities and towns; Collins, interview by de Varon, Tape 13, March 28, 1977, 3, 8. Collins also won back the authority to appoint the city's police commissioner and control that department's budget in 1962.

47. "State vs. the City: The Painful Politics of Obstruction," *AF* 120 (June 1964): 107.

48. "The Inaugural Address of Mayor Collins," *CR*, January 9, 1960; "Business Leaders Hail Collins' Program for Hub," *BG*, January 5, 1960.

49. Quotes from "The New Boston: Men, Projects, and an End to Despair," *AF* 120 (June 1964): 82; lack of confidence quote from Logue, "Boston, 1960–1967—Seven Years of Plenty," 82.

50. Logue to Catherine Bauer Wurster, June 13, 1960, Papers of Catherine Bauer Wurster, 1931–1964, Bancroft Library, University of California, Berkeley, Box 21, Folder 21.

51. Logue, "The Boston Story," 49v7.

52. "The New Boston: Men, Projects, and an End to Despair"; McQuade, "Boston: What Can a Sick City Do?," 136.

53. Many individuals, including Logue, took credit for devising the legislative strategy

that made the Prudential Center possible; see Logue, "The Boston Story," 20v7–25v7; Waterhouse, "'Through the Ordinary Operations of Private Enterprise,'" 18–20; Daniel Golden and David Mehegan, "Changing the Heart of the City," *BG*, September 18, 1983; McQuade, "Boston: What Can a Sick City Do?," 135; Rubin, *Insuring the City*, 124–26.

54. Logue, interview by Lawrence Kennedy, November 23, 1987, Boston, MA, notes, 2.

55. When Logue, to his surprise, earned automatic tenure after five years of city service, he delivered a letter of resignation to Collins to file and use whenever he wished: Logue to Joseph Dunlea, City Clerk, October 19, 1965, and Logue to Mayor John Collins, October 19, 1965, EJL, Series 6, Box 149, Folder 400; Logue to Rt. Rev. Msgr. Francis J. Lally, October 19, 1965, EJL, Series 6, Box 150, Folder 424.

56. Logue, "The Boston Story," 42v7.

57. Logue, "Boston, 1960–1967—Seven Years of Plenty," 91.

58. Ken Hartnett, "A Conversation with Monsignor Francis J. Lally," *BM*, October 1984.

59. O'Connor, *Building a New Boston*, 197; on the job offer from the Kennedy administration, Logue, "Boston, 1960–1967—Seven Years of Plenty," 91. Logue's struggles with the BRA board over a year's time were documented blow-by-blow in *BG*; for the highpoints, see "New Haven Expert Offered $30,000 to Head Hub Renewal," January 28, 1960; "A Key to Boston's Future," January 29, 1960; "Key Problems Dog Logue on Boston Redevelopment," April 28, 1960; "B.R.A. Calls Logue to Face Quiz Today," October 20, 1960; "Top Renewal Post After 90-Day Test Offered to Logue," October 21, 1960; "Renewal Wins—Logue Stays, Gains Full Power on 3–2 Vote; Accepts an Indefinite Term," January 25, 1961; "Collins' Renewal Program Wins Hub Authority Vote," January 26, 1961.

60. Telegram from Carl Koch, Concord, MA, January 24, 1961, to Logue, EJL, Series 6, Box 150, Folder 420. Logue's files are filled with letters of support sent to him and to the BRA board from ministers, social service workers, business leaders, architects, neighborhood activists, and others; see EJL, Series 6, Box 148, Folders 374 and 375. The *BG* and *BH* also editorialized in his favor.

61. Melnea A. Cass to Mr. Joseph Lund, with copies sent to five other BRA board members, January 24, 1961; Francis G. Reith to Boston Redevelopment Authority, January 21, 1961, EJL, Series 6, Box 148, Folder 375. Also Russ Lopez, *Boston 1945–2015* (Boston: Shawmut Peninsula Press, 2017), 83, on support of Cass and the Snowdens.

62. On the rally outside the BRA, see "Boston Bar Group Insists Logue's Plan Is Legal," *BG*, January 25, 1961.

63. Michael Liuzzi, "Heavy Seas Subside for Logue," *CSM*, January 25, 1961; also see similar statement in "Turning Point for a City, 9:30 a.m. Today—73 Tremont Street," *BG*, January 25, 1961.

64. "I wanted no part of that project" in Logue, "A Boston Story," 42. For more on the tensions between Logue and Simonian, and Simonian's suit, see "*Kane Simonian v. Boston Redevelopment Authority and Another*," Suffolk, April 5, 1961–May 5, 1961, *Massachusetts Report, Decisions of the Supreme Judicial Court of Massachusetts, February 1961–June 1961* (Boston: University Press of Cambridge, 1962): 573–86; "Simonian Airs Charges on Logue in High Court," *BG*, April 5, 1961; "Simonian Suit to Oust Logue Is Dismissed," *BG*, May 5, 1961. For insights into this stormy re-

lationship: Paul McCann, interview by Lizabeth Cohen, June 1, 2007, Boston, MA; and John "Jack" Reardon, interview by Lizabeth Cohen, February 17, 2010, Cambridge, MA. Controversy swelled around Simonian to the end. He finally retired at age eighty with a pension and a three-year renewable consulting contract that paid him more than his former salary, to the outrage of critics; Adrian Walker, "'Retirement' Sweet for Power Broker; Pension, Fee, Exceed Previous Pay at BRA," *BG*, February 28, 1994. Rappaport was likewise delighted to avoid more testy interactions with Logue; Jerome Lyle Rappaport, interview by Lizabeth Cohen, September 17, 2007, Boston, MA.

65. Ryan, interview; Arnone, "Redevelopment in Boston," 95, noted that Logue often presented the BRA board with faits accomplis when major decisions were involved.

66. Quoted in Daniel Pool, *Politics in New Boston, 1960–1970: A Study of Mayoral Policy Making* (Waltham, MA: Brandeis University Press, 1974), 84, cited in Rose, "Civic War," 170.

67. Logue, "The Boston Story," 53–54v7.

68. See the Tavern Club website; Anthony Pangaro, interview by Lizabeth Cohen, June 24, 2009, Boston, MA. Many of the people in Logue's circle were Tavern Club members, including the *Globe* reporter Martin Nolan and the BRA board chair, Monsignor Frank Lally.

69. Quoted in Jim Vrabel, *When in Boston: A Time Line and Almanac* (Boston: Northeastern University Press, 2004), 322.

70. Cleveland Amory, *The Proper Bostonians* (New York: Dutton, 1947), 354. Many observers commented on the insularity of the Boston elite. For example, John Zuccotti noted that when he graduated from Yale Law School in 1963, "it was said that you could not be a successful lawyer in Boston unless you had been born there or gone to school there." John Zuccotti, interview by Lizabeth Cohen, December 10, 2007, New York, NY.

71. Robert Campbell, interview by Lizabeth Cohen, June 18, 2009, Cambridge, MA; Margaret Logue, email message to author, April 28, 2011; Logue, "The Boston Story," 37v7; Herbert Gleason, interview by Lizabeth Cohen, May 30, 2007, Cambridge, MA; also see Bowler Fitzgibbons, interview; Robert Hazan, interview by Lizabeth Cohen, June 14, 2007, New York, NY; Ellen Logue, interview.

72. Logue, "The Boston Story," 36v7.

73. Huxtable, "Renewal in Boston: Good and Bad."

74. Robert C. Weaver to Logue, September 30, 1960, EJL, Series 6, Box 151, Folder 457; Arthur Reilly, interview by Lizabeth Cohen, June 25, 2009, Brookline, MA.

75. Examples of the personal antagonisms displayed by city council members, particularly Foley and Craven, abound: "Foley, McCloskey Spar with Logue," *BG*, March 17, 1961; "Young Old Pol William Foley," *AF* 120 (June 1964): 86; Robert B. Kenney, "Political Circuit, Mrs. Craven Slapped," *BG*, March 26, 1964; "Boston Makes a Comeback," *US News*; Irene Saint, "The Changing Face of Boston," *BH*, November 28, 1965; "Bold Boston Gladiator—Ed Logue," *Life*; "Exhibit 199, Minority Report of Councilor Katherine Craven, Member of the Committee on Urban Renewal," November 29, 1966, Federal Role in Urban Affairs (Senator Abraham

Ribicoff's Subcommittee on Executive Reorganization of Senate Committee on Government Operations, November–December 1966), 2876; Kirsten A. Petersen, Carol Hardy-Fanta, and Karla Armenoff, "'As Tough as It Gets': Women in Boston Politics, 1921–2004," *Publications from the Center for Women in Politics and Public Policy* (McCormick Graduate School, University of Massachusetts Boston) (2005): 10–11. Also see minutes of almost any city council meeting when BRA business was discussed.

76. Lavinia M. Underwood to Logue, November 17, 1966, EJL, Series 6, Box 151, Folder 455; for others, see Lois Henderson Bayliss to Logue, January 25, 1966, EJL, Series 6, Box 149, Folder 388; Peter W. Beacham to Logue, August 23, 1963, EJL, Series 6, Box 149, Folder 388; Kevin M. Flatley to Logue, August 1965, EJL, Series 6, Box 149, Folder 403.

77. Logue, "The Boston Story," 45–48v7. Many observers agreed that the Feds needed an urban renewal success: Frank Del Vecchio, "Topical Notes," November 18, 2006, prepared for interview November 27, 2006, 8; Robert Litke, interview by Lizabeth Cohen, May 25, 2006, Somerset, NJ; Langley Carleton Keyes, Jr., interview by Lizabeth Cohen, May 30, 2007, Cambridge, MA.

78. John Stainton, interview by Lizabeth Cohen, May 30, 2007, Jamaica Plain, MA; Logue, interview, Jones, Tape 1: v–vi.

79. "The New Boston: Men, Projects and an End to Despair," 82; Associate Professor Joseph L. Bower and John W. Rosenblum (research assistant), "Harvard Business School Case on the Boston Redevelopment Authority," 1969, State Library of Massachusetts, State House, Boston, sets the number of staff at "more than 500" in August 1967, 12, 14; Logue recalled it numbering "about 550" when he left in the summer of 1967; Logue, interview, Steen, March 3, 1986, Lincoln, MA, 35.

80. Anthony Yudis, "B.R.A. Reports 'Seven-Year Progress,'" *BG*, August 11, 1967; Litke, interview; Arnone, "Redevelopment in Boston," 75, 238; minority staff members in visible positions included Reginald Griffith, Denis Blackett, and Tunney Lee.

81. Esther Maletz Stone, email message to author, July 16, 2015.

82. MLogue, interview.

83. Arnone, "Redevelopment in Boston," 75.

84. McQuade, "Boston: What Can a Sick City Do?," 132, 169; also Frederick Salvucci, interview by Lizabeth Cohen, June 16, 2009, Cambridge, MA; Del Vecchio, "Topical Notes," 3, 5.

85. Reilly, interview.

86. Michael D. Appleby, "Logue's Record in Boston: An Analysis of His Renewal and Planning Activities, with a Foreword and Summary by Herbert J. Gans for the Steering Committee, Council for New York Housing and Planning Policy, Funded by the Normal Foundation, May 1966," EJL, 2002 Accession, Box 22, Folder "Logue's Record in Boston by Michael Appleby," 11.

87. Reginald Griffith, interview by Lizabeth Cohen, April 7, 2010, Washington, DC; Frank Del Vecchio, email message to author, July 23, 2006; Ted Liebman, interview by Lizabeth Cohen, October 15, 2006, New York, NY.

88. Stainton, interview.

89. Arnone, "Redevelopment in Boston," 194–97; Nathan Leventhal, "Citizen Partici-

pation in Urban Renewal," *Columbia Law Review* 66, no. 3 (March 1966): 578–79; Appleby, "Logue's Record in Boston," 11–12; Del Vecchio, interview.

90. "What's Happening to Proper Old Boston?," 78. Logue explains "planning with people" in "Logue on Boston: 'Never Satisfied,'" *CSM*, April 20, 1962.
91. Del Vecchio, "Topical Notes," 5.
92. Margaret Logue, email message to author, March 21, 2011. The *BG* reporter Martin Nolan also recalled how much Logue loved Beacon Hill and the "walkable city" it was a part of; Martin Nolan, interview by Lizabeth Cohen, May 24, 2007, Cambridge, MA.
93. Logue, interview by Kennedy, 2. Logue discussed Collins's strengths on many occasions; see for example, Logue, "Boston, 1960–1967—Seven Years of Plenty," 83.
94. Arnone, "Redevelopment in Boston," 143.
95. Collins, interview by de Varon, March 24, 1977, 26; Del Vecchio, *City Streets*, 136. Many others confirmed Collins's surveillance of Logue's activities: Gleason, interview; Scagnoli, interview; Bowler Fitzgibbons, interview; Ryan, interview; Arnone, "Redevelopment in Boston," 94, 142–43.
96. Langley Carleton Keyes, Jr., *The Rehabilitation Planning Game: A Study in the Diversity of Neighborhood* (Cambridge, MA: MIT Press, 1969), 29. Also see McQuade, "Boston: What Can a Sick City Do?," 137. To criticism that he was trying to do too much at once, Logue replied, "I thought it was the only way to get momentum going"; Linda Corman, "Former BRA Head Takes Another Look at the City He Helped Plan," *Banker and Tradesman*, October 21, 1987, 87.
97. Huxtable, "Renewal in Boston: Good and Bad." This discussion of ABCD is based on the following sources: Stephan Thernstrom, *Poverty, Planning, and Politics in the New Boston: The Origins of ABCD* (New York: Basic Books, 1969); Peter Marris and Martin Rein, *Dilemmas of Social Reform: Poverty and Community Action in the United States* (New York: Atherton Press, 1967), 124–26, 181–83; Robert Halpern, *Rebuilding the Inner City: A History of Neighborhood Initiatives to Address Poverty in the United States* (New York: Columbia University Press, 1995), 98–100; Leventhal, "Citizen Participation in Urban Renewal," 556–58; Robert C. Hayden and Ann Withorn, eds., *Changing Lives, Changing Communities: Oral Histories from Action for Boston Community Development* (Boston: Action for Community Development and the University of Massachusetts, 2002); and primary documents in Action for Community Development Grant Files, Ford Foundation Grant #0620457, Microfilm Reels 2, 633–34, Ford Foundation Records, Rockefeller Archive Center, Sleepy Hollow, NY (hereafter Ford); Paul Ylvisaker Papers, Harvard University Archives, Cambridge, MA, Boxes 19 and 27; Mel King, interview by Lizabeth Cohen, June 17, 2009, Boston, MA; Scagnoli, interview.
98. "Energetic Reformer: Joseph Slavet," *AF* 120 (June 1964): 83–84.
99. Slavet, interview.
100. Slavet, interview.
101. Clifford J. Campbell, Consultant, Department of City Planning, City of Chicago, to Paul N. Ylvisaker, Director of Public Affairs Program, Ford Foundation, February 5, 1963, Ford, 7.
102. Clifford J. Campbell to Paul N. Ylvisaker, May 2, 1964, Ford, 8–10.
103. Marris and Rein, *Dilemmas of Social Reform*, 125–26.

104. U.S. Department of Housing and Urban Development, "Profile of a City—Boston," 8–9.
105. Paul Ylvisaker to Michael Phillips, September 11, 1973, provided to me by daughter Elizabeth Ylvisaker.
106. Boston Redevelopment Authority, *1965/1975 General Plan for the City of Boston and the Regional Core* (Boston: Boston Redevelopment Authority, 1965), cover letter, passim, but 58–59 in particular; Keith Morgan, "City of Ideas: Structure and Scale in the Boston General Plan," in *Heroic: Concrete Architecture and the New Boston*, ed. Mark Pasnik, Michael Kubo, and Chris Grimley (New York: Monacelli Press, 2015), 62–77; Golden and Mehegan, "Changing the Heart of the City"; Saint, "What Makes Logue Tick," *BH*; McQuade, "Boston: What Can a Sick City Do?," 137; U.S. Department of Housing and Urban Development, "Profile of a City—Boston," 4, 14. Mayor Collins also sought metropolitan solutions to the city's economic woes; see "Remarks of John Frederick Collins, Facing Up to the State's Financial Commitments," February 27, 1968, in *Proceedings of the 1966–67 and 1967–68 Series of Citizen Seminars on the Fiscal, Economic, and Political Problem of Boston and the Metropolitan Community* (Chestnut Hill, MA: Boston College, 1968).
107. "Testimony of Mr. Edward J. Logue, Administrator, Boston Redevelopment Authority, Boston, Massachusetts," *Hearing Before the United States Commission on Civil Rights: Hearing Held in Boston, Massachusetts, October 4–5, 1966*, 234–51; "Statement of Edward J. Logue, Administrator, Boston Redevelopment Authority," *Federal Role in Urban Affairs* (Senator Abraham Ribicoff's Subcommittee on Executive Reorganization of Senate Committee on Government Operations, November–December 1966), Logue testimony, December 12, 1966, 2804–6, 2819.
108. "Meet Boston's Mr. Urban Renewal," *CSM*; Logue, interview by Franziska Porges Hosken, 1971, audiotape, Rotch Architecture and Design Library, MIT.
109. Logue testimony, *Hearing Before the United States Commission on Civil Rights in Boston*, 236, 240; also see on Logue's busing proposal: John Chaffee, Jr., "'Scatteration' Wins Support," *BH*, September 5, 1965; "Urges Suburb Schooling for Slum Children," *CT*, April 27, 1965; Logue, op-ed, *BG* (adapted from a speech given at MIT), May 2, 1983; Ronald P. Formisano, *Boston Against Busing: Race, Class, and Ethnicity in the 1960s and 1970s* (Chapel Hill: University of North Carolina Press, 1991), 229–30, 307n15; Lily Geismer, *Don't Blame Us: Suburban Liberals and the Transformation of the Democratic Party* (Princeton, NJ: Princeton University Press, 2015), 79–95.
110. Katherine M. Shannon, interview by Ruth Batson, December 27, 1967, Boston, MA, Civil Rights Documentation Project, Batson Papers, Schlesinger Library, Box 1, cited in Geismer, *Don't Blame Us*, 81. Logue lamented the lack of support for his busing proposal and the limited scale of the METCO voluntary plan in Logue, "Crisis in the City: Lectures at Boston University 1968," Boston University Urban Institute, 1970, 48.
111. In 1970, Logue would make the radical proposal that Greater Boston learn from the example of Greater London and reorganize government on a two-tier metropolitan basis, with a metropolitan government assuming all assessing and taxing powers and local communities—Boston proper and a dozen small-scale town units within Routes 128 or 495—keeping control over services and facilities; Logue,

"What Sort of Future for Boston? A Look at Home from Abroad," *Boston University Journal* 18, no. 1 (Winter 1970): 49–51.

112. Jane Jacobs, *The Death and Life of Great American Cities* (New York: Vintage, 1961); Logue, "The View from the Village," in "American Cities: Dead or Alive?—Two Views," *AF* 116, no. 3 (March 1962): 89–90; Walter McQuade, "Architecture," *Nation*, March 17, 1962, 241–42; Anthony J. Yudis, "Logue Replies to Author-Critic of City Planning," *BG*, April 5, 1962; Christopher Klemek, *The Transatlantic Collapse of Urban Renewal: Postwar Urbanism from New York to Berlin* (Chicago: University of Chicago Press, 2011), 117, 119.

5. Battling for a New Boston

1. "The Past and Future of Planning in Boston," *The Taubman Center Report* (John F. Kennedy School of Government, Harvard University) (1999): 12; also see Linda Corman, "Former BRA Head Takes Another Look at the City He Helped Plan," *Banker and Tradesman*, October 21, 1987, 9.

2. Martin Meyerson and Edward C. Banfield, *Boston: The Job Ahead* (Cambridge, MA: Harvard University Press, 1966), 68. The same U.S. Census of Housing determined that 90.7 percent of Boston's housing units were built before 1939, indicating little new construction in the neighborhoods; "Monograph, City of Boston," Massachusetts Department of Commerce and Development, revised December 1964, "Boston: III. Housing—U.S. Census, 1960," EJL, Series 6, Box 148, Folder 380.

3. Janet Bowler Fitzgibbons, interview by Lizabeth Cohen, June 21, 2007, Cambridge, MA.

4. Langley Keyes, *City Builder: An Interview with Ed Logue, Administrator of the Boston Redevelopment Authority from 1960–67*, 1983, video, Rotch Architecture and Design Library, MIT.

5. John Collins, interview by José de Varon, Tape 6, December 21, 1976, EJL, 1985 Accession, Box 3, Folder "Oral History John Collins," transcript, 5.

6. Logue, interview, Steen, December 13, 1983, New York, NY, 28.

7. "The Old Seaport: Planning a Window on the World," *AF* 120 (June 1964): 95–96; the plan was enthusiastically endorsed by the architecture critic Wolf Von Eckardt in "Architectural Commentary on Boston Today," *Ekistics* 18, no. 105 (August 1964): 90–92.

8. Kevin Lynch Papers, MIT Archives and Special Collections (hereafter Lynch), contain important documentation on the waterfront project. These quotes from "Memorandum Preliminary to the Conference on the Downtown Waterfront Faneuil Hall Renewal Area," Quincy Market, 1 p.m., October 17, 1961, prepared by Daniel J. Ahern and Samuel E. Mintz, Box 2, Folder "Waterfront"; also see "BRA with C of C Presentation to Logue," Thursday, March 15, 1962, 8:30 p.m., and numerous meeting minutes from "Waterfront—BRA Staff & Logue"; "Downtown Waterfront-Faneuil Hall Renewal Area, Progress Report on Food Market Relocation Including a Recommended Site for a New Food Distribution Center," December 1962; and Anthony Yudis, "B.R.A. Vows Waterfront Aid," *BG*, June 27, 1962; Yudis, "New Look Waterfront Faces Major Hurdles," *BG*, July 5, 1963.

9. Timothy Orwig, "Concrete Solutions: Tad Stahl's Urbanism," *Historic New England*, Spring 2012, 19–20, on early involvement of Tad Stahl and Roger Webb in proposing the rehabilitation of the historic markets.

10. Logue, "The Boston Story—Getting Started," draft chapter for memoir, "Tales of a City Builder, Compared to What," January 2000, MDL, 31v7; Corman, "Former BRA Head Takes Another Look at the City He Helped Plan," 9; Walter McQuade, "Boston: What Can a Sick City Do?," *Fortune*, June 1964, 166.

11. "Boom Moves into the Hub," *BW*, June 9, 1962, 116.

12. On the CCBD and its planning, see Irene Saint, "Downtown Business Area Changes Made Cautiously," *BH*, November 30, 1965; "$400 Million Plan for Downtown Revitalization Called Creative, Bold, Realistic," *CR* 59, no. 21 (May 27, 1967): 409; Boston Redevelopment Authority, "Progress Report on the Central Business District Project," March 12, 1962; and BRA, "Central Business District Project—Informational Memo," August 27, 1962, EJL, Series 6, Box 152, Folder 481; "Statement by Charles A. Coolidge, President, The CCBD, Inc. before the Boston City Council," September 26, 1962, EJL, Series 6, Box 153, Folder 501; Memo from Logue to Mayor John F. Collins, February 5, 1963, "Status Report—Downtown Plan," EJL, Series 6, Box 152, Folder 482; CCBD and BRA, "Recommendations Concerning the Interim Report for the Central Business District Project," February 19, 1963, EJL, Series 6, Box 152, Folder 485; Memo to Ed Logue from Robert Hazen, October 22, 1963, "CBD Status and Recommendations," EJL, Series 6, Box 152, Folder 485; Memo from Brimley Hall to Robert G. Hazen, "CCBD Executive Committee Meeting with Victor Gruen—August 10, 1964," and Memo to Logue from Robert G. Hazen, December 11, 1964, EJL, Series 6, Box 153, Folder 501; "The Downtown Area: How to Clean It Up—and Make It Pay," *AF* 120 (June 1964): 100–101; "CCBD," EJL, Series 6, Box 153, Folder 501; Memo to Board of Directors, CCBD from Robert G. Hazen, March 15, 1965, "Status Report—CBD and Related Development and Transportation Projects," EJL, Series 6, Box 153, Folder 502; Memo from Robert G. Hazen to Logue, March 16, 1965, "Filene's," Series 6, Box 152, Folder 483; Memo to CBD Executive Committee from Robert G. Hazen, "Draft Central Business District Urban Renewal Plan," February 11, 1966, EJL, Series 6, Box 153, Folder 503; Minutes of CCBD Board of Directors' Meeting, December 12, 1966, EJL, Series 6, Box 153, Folder 513; draft and news releases for *A General Plan for the Central Business District*, 1967, EJL, Series 6, Box 152, Folder 484.

On retailers' concerns about the present and future of Boston's retail center, see "'Where to Park' Guide Published by Chamber," *CR* 55, no. 7 (February 16, 1963): 149; "Statement by Charles A. Coolidge, Esq., President of the CCBD, Inc. to the BRA Public Hearing, October 7, 1965, Faneuil Hall, Boston on the Central Business District Renewal Project," EJL, Series 6, Box 153, Folder 502; Remarks of Harold D. Hodgkinson, Chairman of the Board of William Filene's Sons Co. at the First Citizens Seminar on the Fiscal, Economic and Political Problems of Boston and the Metropolitan Community, "A Look at the Record and Unfinished Business," November 19, 1963, sponsored by the College of Business Administration and Bureau of Public Affairs, Boston College; "Downtown Garage," *CR* 57, no. 41 (October 9, 1965): 726.

Robert Gladstone's report was *Downtown Boston Market Studies*, 1963. For an astute observation of the work of the CCBD and the general situation in Boston's downtown, see McQuade, "Boston: What Can a Sick City Do?," 166.

13. Victor Gruen, *The Heart of Our Cities: The Urban Crisis—Diagnosis and Cure* (New York: Simon and Schuster, 1964), 321–26. For Gruen's stillborn plan for Fort Worth, see M. Jeffrey Hardwick, *Mall Maker: Victor Gruen, Architect of the American Dream* (Philadelphia: University of Pennsylvania Press, 2004), 166–92.

14. Saint, "Downtown Business Area Changes."

15. My argument resembles that of John H. Mollenkopf, *The Contested City* (Princeton, NJ: Princeton University Press, 1983), who suggests that "political entrepreneurs" like Collins and Logue used government intervention to draw capitalists to their own objectives and did not simply do their bidding.

16. Robert Hazen, interview by Lizabeth Cohen, June 14, 2007, New York, NY; Nancy Rita Arnone, "Development in Boston: A Study of the Politics and Administration of Social Change" (Ph.D. dissertation, MIT, 1965), 130; Robert Litke, interview by Lizabeth Cohen, May 25, 2006, Somerset, NJ.

17. "Governor, Private Sectors Have Failed to Aid Mayors in Big Urban Crisis," *CR*, August 5, 1967.

18. "Boom Moves into the Hub," *BW*, June 9, 1962, 118; "Young Promoters: Wood and Stahl," *AF* 120 (June 1964); Henry Scagnoli, interview by Lizabeth Cohen, June 20, 2007, Boston, MA.

19. John Quincy, Jr., *Quincy's Market: A Boston Landmark* (Boston: Northeastern University Press, 2003), 188–93, 215–19; "Faneuil Hall Markets: Operation Restoration," *CR*, March 31, 1975.

20. Gerald Gamm, *Urban Exodus: Why the Jews Left Boston and the Catholics Stayed* (Cambridge, MA: Harvard University Press, 1999).

21. "Boston's Prince of the Church," excerpt from John H. Fenton, *Salt of the Earth: An Informal Profile of Richard Cardinal Cushing* (New York: Coward-McCann, 1965), 3–13, in *The Many Voices of Boston: A Historical Anthology, 1630–1975*, ed. Howard Mumford Jones and Bessie Zaban Jones (Boston: Little, Brown, 1975), 431–37.

22. Logue, "The Boston Story," 21. The archdiocese gave enthusiastic support to the hiring of Logue in 1961; "New Brooms," reprinted from *The Pilot* in the *BG*, March 14, 1961.

23. Ken Hartnett, "A Conversation with Monsignor Francis J. Lally," *BM*, October 1984. For evidence of Monsignor Lally's Progressivism before Vatican II, likely shared with Cushing, see "A Mike Wallace Interview with Francis J. Lally," produced by ABC in association with the Fund for the Republic, 1958, http://www.hrc.utexas.edu /multimedia/video/2008/wallace/lally_francis_t.html. For Lally's views on urban renewal: "Churchly Chairman: Monsignor Lally," *AF* 120 (June 1964): 86; Francis J. Lally, *The Catholic Church in a Changing America* (Boston: Little, Brown, 1962); and his Boston College Citizen Seminars speeches, including "Remarks of Rt. Rev. Msgr. Francis J. Lally, Editor of *The Pilot*, at the Eighth Annual Conference on Economic Problems of Greater Boston Area, May 23, 1961" and "Remarks of Rt. Rev. Msgr. Francis J. Lally, Editor of *The Pilot*, Chairman of the Boston Redevelopment Authority, at the Third Citizens Seminar on the Fiscal, Economic, and Political Problems of Boston and the Metropolitan Community, 'Youth-Education-Employment,' January 28, 1964" (Chestnut Hill, MA: Boston College, 1964).

24. Quoted in Hartnett, "Conversation with Lally."

25. Philip Denvir, "Cardinal Officiates at West End Dedication; Priests' Residence Blessed," *BG*, December 28, 1964. On the El location, Gerard O'Neill, *Rogues and Redeemers: When Politics Was King in Irish Boston* (New York: Crown Publishers, 2012), 199; Frederick Salvucci, interview by Lizabeth Cohen, June 16, 2009, Cambridge, MA.

26. My discussion of the Boston Catholic Church and Vatican II and urban renewal is based on the following sources: "The Unlikely Cardinal," in "Catholics in the U.S.: A Surge of Renewal," special issue, *Time*, August 21, 1964; Xavier Rynne, "Letter from Vatican City," *New Yorker*, December 25, 1965; Patrick Allitt, *Religion in America Since 1945: A History* (New York: Columbia University Press, 2003), 67, 80–86, 107–11; John T. McGreevy, *Catholicism and American Freedom: A History* (New York: W. W. Norton, 2003), 205, 236–38, 256, 269, 283–84; James Carroll, "The Catholic Church's Lost Revolution," *BG*, September 30, 2012. On Boston specifically: Thomas H. O'Connor, *Boston Catholics: A History of the Church and Its People* (Boston: Northeastern University Press, 1998), 239–82; John T. McGreevy, *Parish Boundaries: The Catholic Encounter with Race in the Twentieth-Century Urban North* (Chicago: University of Chicago Press, 1998), 125–26, 128–32, 145, 151, 158–64, 178–80, 209; Thomas H. O'Connor, *Building a New Boston: Politics and Urban Renewal 1950 to 1970* (Boston: Northeastern University Press, 1993), 13–14, 37, 42, 45, 49, 92–98, 102–6, 116, 127–31, 177, 196–97, 216–19; and J. Anthony Lukas, *Common Ground: A Turbulent Decade in the Lives of Three American Families* (New York: Alfred A. Knopf, 1985), 354–56, 385.

27. This discussion is drawn from my published essay "Re-viewing the Twentieth Century Through an American Catholic Lens," in *Catholics in the American Century: Recasting Narratives of U.S. History*, ed. R. Scott Appleby and Kathleen Sprows Cummings (Ithaca, NY: Cornell University Press with the Cushwa Center, Notre Dame, 2012), 43–60. Also see McGreevy, *Parish Boundaries*, 178–80; and William Leonard, "The Failure of Catholic Interracialism in Boston Before Busing," 228–45, and James E. Glinski, "The Catholic Church and the Desegregation of Boston's Public Schools," 246–69, in *Boston's Histories: Essays in Honor of Thomas H. O'Connor*, ed. James M. O'Toole and David Quigley (Boston: Northeastern University Press, 2004); Joseph Marr Cronin, *Reforming Boston Schools, 1930–2006* (New York: Palgrave Macmillan, 2008), 78–80.

28. Logue, "The Boston Story," 11v7.

29. Arnone, "Redevelopment in Boston," 89–91, 144.

30. With an eye on its burgeoning suburban readership, the *Globe* moved in 1958 from its urban headquarters on Newspaper Row to a more sprawling complex on Morrissey Boulevard closer to highways; Dan Adams, "Globe to Move to State Street Offices," *BG*, December 11, 2015.

31. Logue, "The Boston Story," 10v7.

32. On the *Globe* and Tom Winship, see Boston Urban Study Group, *Who Rules Boston?: A Citizen's Guide to Reclaiming the City* (Boston: Institute for Democratic Socialism, 1984), 88–92; "Thomas Winship, 81; Editor," *LAT*, March 15, 2002; Mary McGrory, "The Crusader Who Put the Boston Globe on the Map," March 15, 2002; Lukas, *Common Ground*, 478–92; for affectionate notes between Logue and Winship, see EJL, Series 6, Box 151, Folder 460.

33. Martin Nolan, interview by Lizabeth Cohen, May 24, 2007, Cambridge, MA. The *Globe* supported urban renewal throughout the Collins-Logue era. See, for example, Thomas Winship, "The Most Attractive City in America Is Our Goal and We Will Make It," *BG*, May 21, 1967, signed editorial.

34. Logue, interview by Richard J. Lundgren, April 18, 1990, in Lundgren, "Edward J. Logue: Public Entrepreneur" (paper submitted to Richard E. Cavanaugh, instructor, Kennedy School, Course M-484, n.d.), EJL, 2002 Accession, Box 22, Folder "EJL: Public Entrepreneur, Richard Lundgren, Kennedy School," 13.

35. Nicholas von Hoffman, "Boston Is an Ingrate," *WP*, April 9, 1967.

36. Nolan, interview; Nolan disapproved of the merger of news and editorial at Winship's *Globe*, which was unlike the *NYT*, the *WP*, and the *WSJ*.

37. Christopher Lydon, conversation with Lizabeth Cohen, April 11, 2015, Cambridge, MA. The Appleby report did, however, get covered in Robert F. Hannan, "Logue's Moves Blunt Criticism," *BH*, December 11, 1966. Jane Jacobs told the *Village Voice* that Logue "is just a slightly smoother Robert Moses" and that his coming to New York would be "New York's loss and Boston's gain"; Mary Perot Nichols, "Boston City Planner Rumored Lindsay Choice," *Village Voice*, November 11, 1965.

38. Thom Duffy, "A City Planner Shares His Values," *NHR*, November 24, 1985.

39. David A. Crane, "Mayor Richard S. Daley Lights the Way for the Boston Renaissance," 1989, EJL, 2002 Accession, Box 22, Folder "Mayor Daley . . . ," unpublished manuscript, 1–17, with quote on 4, intended for Ann L. Strong and George E. Thomas, *The Book of the School: 100 Years* (Philadelphia: Graduate School of Fine Arts of the University of Pennsylvania, 1990), where it appeared in a shorter version, 188–89. For Crane's urban vision, see *1965/1975 General Plan for the City of Boston and the Regional Core*, 23–30 on the "capital web" and "broken seams"; Crane, "The Public Art of City Building," *Annals*, AAPSS 352, "Urban Revival: Goals and Standards" (March 1965): 84–94; Kenneth Halpern, *Downtown USA: Urban Design in Nine American Cities* (New York: Whitney Library of Design, 1978), 187. Tunney Lee described his Boston experience with Crane at his memorial service, Cambridge, MA, August 19, 2005, written remarks, in possession of the author; Lee discussed the "capital web" concept in Tunney Lee, interview by Lizabeth Cohen, July 13, 2007, Wellfleet, MA.

40. Jonathan Barnett, *Redesiging Cities: Principles, Practice, Implementation* (Chicago: American Planning Association, 2003), 281.

41. Philip Sinclair Will, "Design Review in Urban Renewal: A Case Study of the Boston Redevelopment Authority" (M.A. thesis, MIT, 1966); Logue, "Boston, 1960–1967— Seven Years of Plenty," 87, 94–95. The Architectural Advisory Committee to the Boston City Planning Board had already issued a report on the Government Center project in October 1959. Its members were much the same. Logue's papers contain extensive documentation related to this committee, beginning with the invitation to architects to serve; see EJL, Series 6, Box 151, Folder 471, 472, for meeting summaries, memos, and correspondence.

42. *Design and Urban Renewal* (BRA, n.d. but c. mid-1960s), last page; Chloethiel Woodard Smith to Logue, August 19, 1963, EJL, Series 6, Box 151, Folder 446.

43. Lee, interview. The documents related to Logue's Design Advisory Committee reveal constant discussion about defining the role of the committee versus the BRA's

design staff, and benefiting from members' experience without overly burdening them or creating serious conflicts of interest.

44. Logue and David Crane both spoke at the Harvard Graduate School of Design, eighth annual Design Conference, "The Role of Government in the Form and Animation of the Urban Core," May 1–2, 1964; proceedings in Papers of Josep Lluís Sert, Special Collections, HGSD.

45. Stephen Diamond to Logue, "Memorandum: Housing Design Review Panel," July 25, 1963, EJL, Series 6, Box 151, Folder 472; "Carl Koch, 86; Noted Architect; of Prefab Homes, Cluster Housing," *BG*, July 10, 1998; David Fixler, "Hipsters in the Woods: The Midcentury-Modern Suburban Development," *AB* 12, no. 1 (Spring 2009): 27–29. Logue and Koch communications after Koch's initial telegram in 1960 include other congratulatory notes to Logue, April 18 and November 18, 1966, in EJL, Series 6, Box 150, Folder 414.

46. David Kruh, *Always Something Doing: Boston's Infamous Scollay Square*, rev. ed. (Boston: Northeastern University Press, 1999), for an overview of Scollay Square before and during the construction of Government Center. Also Frank Del Vecchio, *City Streets: A Memoir* (North Andover, MA: Leap Year Press, 2016), 68; Daniel A. Gilbert, "'Why Dwell on a Lurid Memory?': Deviance and Redevelopment in Boston's Scollay Square," *Massachusetts Historical Review* 9 (2007): 103–33; Stephanie Schorow, *Inside the Combat Zone: The Stripped Down Story of Boston's Most Notorious Neighborhood* (Boston: Union Park Press, 2017); Kevin Lynch, *The Image of the City* (Cambridge, MA: MIT Press, 1960), 173–81.

47. John King, "How the BRA Got Some Respect," *Planning Contents* 56, no. 5 (May 1990): 6; *Building Boston*, video, Bob Nesson Productions and WGBH Educational Foundation, 1985. For the long-term history of locating a civic center on this site, see Boston Redevelopment Authority, "Research Report: A History of Boston's Government Center," June 1970, 12–16.

48. "Statement of Edward J. Logue, Administrator, Boston Redevelopment Authority," Federal Role in Urban Affairs (Senator Abraham Ribicoff's Subcommittee on Executive Reorganization of Senate Committee on Government Operations, November–December 1966), Logue testimony, December 12, 1966, 2796, 2798.

49. Mayor Collins received letters from Bostonians urging a traditional city hall "with pillars in the front and Bulfinch style and all the rest"; Collins, interview by de Varon, Tape 6, December 21, 1976, 10.

50. This style of modernism, which emerged in France and Britain in the 1950s and 1960s through the inspiration of Le Corbusier, was long referred to as "brutalist," in reference to *béton brut*, meaning "raw concrete." Recently, some Boston architects and architectural historians have rejected that label for its disparaging connotations and have urged the renaming of Boston's substantial examples of concrete modernism as "heroic"; Mark Pasnik, Michael Kubo, and Chris Grimley, eds., *Heroic: Concrete Architecture and the New Boston* (New York: Monacelli Press, 2015); also Robert Campbell, "Brutalism Gets a Reworking on UMass Campus," *BG*, November 25, 2012.

51. Albert Bush-Brown, "Critic Hails Prizewinner: No Copy Cat of Hub Styles," *BG*, May 4, 1962.

52. John Collins to Rt. Rev. Msgr. Francis J. Lally, November 14, 1960, EJL, Series 6, Box 148, Folder 374; the federal government's willingness to shift from the Back Bay to

the Scollay Square site depended on the State of Massachusetts also agreeing to build in the area; "City Council Meets Logue," *BH*, April 2, 1960.

53. *A Competition to Select an Architect for the City Hall in the Government Center of the City of Boston* (Boston: Government Center Commission, 1961), with an introduction by Mayor John F. Collins; Anthony J. Yudis, "And Here's New City Hall, Apt to Stir Controversy," *BG*, May 4, 1962; Bush-Brown, "Critic Hails Prizewinner"; "Three Columbia Faculty Members Win Boston City Hall Competition," *AR* 132, no. 1 (July 1962): 14–15; Hélène Lipstadt, ed., *The Experimental Tradition: Essays on Competitions in Architecture* (New York: Architectural League of New York, 1989), 10–11, 96, 99, 160–61; Logue, "Boston, 1960–1967—Seven Years of Plenty," 95–96.

54. "Boston Government Center. Its Evolution Described by Charles Hilgenhurst. Appraisal by Henry Millon," *Architectural Design* 41 (January 1970): 11–23, "jewel" quote on 16. For more on Government Center and Boston City Hall, see "Government Center Urban Renewal Plan, April 3, 1963, Revised May 29, 1963"; Paul D. Spreiregen, "The Boston Government Center: A Study in Urban Design," *Art and Architecture* 82, no. 10 (October 1965): 21–23; "The New Boston City Hall," *PA* 44, no. 4 (April 1963): 132–52; Brian M. Sirman, "Concrete Dreams: Architecture, Politics, and Boston's New City Hall" (Ph.D. dissertation, Boston University, 2014); David A. Crane, "The Federal Building in the Making of Boston's Government Center: A Struggle for Sovereignty in Local Design Review," in *Federal Buildings in Context: The Role of Design Review*, ed. J. Carter Brown, Studies in the History of Art, vol. 50 (Washington, DC: National Gallery of Art, 1995), 21–38; Martin Nolan, "City Hall Debate Has Been Raging for 300 Years," *BG*, May 6, 1962; Ada Louise Huxtable, "Boston's New City Hall: A Public Building of Quality," *NYT*, February 8, 1969; Alex Krieger, ed., *The Architecture of Kallmann McKinnell & Wood* (Cambridge, MA: Harvard Graduate School of Design, 1988), 21–37; David Dillon, *The Architecture of Kallmann McKinnell & Wood* (New York: Edizioni Press, 2004), 12–19.

55. Harold D. Hodgkinson, "Miracle in Boston," *Proceedings of the Massachusetts Historical Society* 3, no. 84 (1972): 78; Logue, "Boston, 1960–1967—Seven Years of Plenty," 96; also Scagnoli, interview.

56. Scagnoli, interview.

57. Michael McKinnell, interview by Lizabeth Cohen, June 15, 2010, Cambridge, MA; "Concrete Is Patient," McKinnell, interview in *Heroic*, 22; Jack Thomas, "'I Wanted Something That Would Last': At 89, an Architect Stands by His Plan for City Hall After Four Decades of Both Condemnation and Praise," *BG*, October 13, 2004; Leon Neyfakh, "How Boston City Hall Was Born," *BG*, February 12, 2012.

58. On the State Service Center, see Ada Louise Huxtable, "Complex in Boston Is Radically Designed," *NYT*, November 7, 1963; Timothy M. Rohan, "The Rise and Fall of Brutalism, Rudolph and the Liberal Consensus," *CLOG: Brutalism*, 2nd ed. (June 2013), 60–61; Rohan, *The Architecture of Paul Rudolph* (New Haven, CT: Yale University Press, 2014), 116–28; Tony Monk, *The Art and Architecture of Paul Rudolph* (Chichester, UK: Wiley-Academy, 1999), particularly "Boston State Service Center, Boston, Massachusetts, 1962–71"; Carol John Black, "A Vision of Human Space, Paul Rudolph: Boston State Service Center," *AR* 154, no. 1 (July, 1973): 105–16; Hilgenhurst, "Evolution of Boston's Government Center," 14–15; "1st Draft, Health, Welfare

and Education Building," Paul Marvin Rudolph Papers, Library of Congress, Box PMR-3022-4, File "Governor's Report"; James McNeely, interview by Lizabeth Cohen, May 31, 2007, Boston, MA; McNeely, "Architecture: The Training of an Architect," *Beacon Hill Paper*, August 26, 1997; Rohan, "The Dream Behind Boston's Forbidding State Service Center," *BG*, September 7, 2014; and correspondence among Logue, Stubbins, and Rudolph in EJL.

59. Logue, "Work of the Boston Renewal Administration in the Urban Core," Address to the Harvard Graduate School of Design eighth annual Urban Design Conference, "The Role of Government in the Form and Animation of the Urban Core," May 1, 1964, 5; "Government Center: Symbolic Showpiece of a New Boston," *AF* 120 (June 1964): 92; McNeely, interview; Rudolph's scale comment from Paul R. Kramer, "Summary of an Interview with Paul Rudolph, New York," *Werk* 60, no. 4 (1973): 457.

60. Jeanne M. Davern, "Conversations with Paul Rudolph," *AR* 170, no. 4 (March 1982): 90–97, in Paul Rudolph, *Writings on Architecture* (New Haven, CT: Yale School of Architecture, 2008), 121.

61. "Final Plan Unveiled for Boston's New Government Center," *AR* 133, no. 6 (Mid-May 1963): 14; "Winner Announced in Boston Competition," *AR* 137, no. 3 (March 1965): 316.

62. Logue, "Boston, 1960–1967—Seven Years of Plenty," 94; Hilgenhurst, "Evolution of Boston's Government Center," 20; Daniel Golden and David Mehegan, "Changing the Heart of the City," *BG*, September 18, 1983. Logue admired the building's design and remained grateful to the Leventhals for stepping up when their support was so needed; Keyes, *City Builder*; Robert Campbell, interview by Lizabeth Cohen, June 18, 2009, Cambridge, MA; Bryan Marquard, "Norman Leventhal at 97; Enhancer of Lives and Landmarks," *BG*, April 5, 2015; Norman Leventhal, interview by Lizabeth Cohen, June 21, 2007, Boston, MA. Weak demand for new office space prompted Logue to pressure Joseph Slavet to consider moving ABCD to the Central Plaza building.

63. On the Parcel 8 controversy, see McQuade, "Boston: What Can a Sick City Do?," 137, 163; "Winner Announced in Boston Competition," *AR* 137, no. 3 (March 1965): 12–13, 288, 300, 308, 316; Hilgenhurst, "Evolution of Boston's Government Center," 18; advertisement, "Boston Redevelopment Authority Announces a Competition for the Selection of a Developer for Parcel 8, Government Center," *WP*, July 1, 1964; Irene Saint, "Government Center," *BH*, November 29, 1965; "Government Center Shaping Up Despite Setbacks," *BH*, November 29, 1965; Arnone, "Development in Boston," 105; O'Connor, *Building a New Boston*, 202, 212; "Government Center: Symbolic Showpiece of a New Boston"; Henry N. Cobb, interview by Lizabeth Cohen, June 8, 2010, New York, NY; Lewis H. Weinstein, *My Life at the Bar: Lawyer, Soldier, Teacher and Pro Bono Activist* (Hanover, MA: Christopher Publishing House, 1993), 143–45. There was a lot of public criticism of the city council tying up the Government Center project; see, for example, Paul Benzaquin's program on WEEI-CBS radio, July 30, 1963, where he complained, "However you look at it, the five angry men have created a spectacular embarrassment for Boston"; EJL, Series 6, Box 148, Folder 378.

64. Boston Redevelopment Authority, *1965/1975 General Plan for the City of Boston and the Regional Core*, 1965, 20.

65. The Charles Center was a large-scale redevelopment project in central Baltimore's downtown business district built in the late 1950s and early 1960s to stem decline; see Nicholas Dagen Bloom, *Merchant of Illusion: James Rouse, America's Salesman of the Businessman's Utopia* (Columbus: Ohio State University Press, 2004), 37–43. This strategy of a city encouraging its workers to patronize local restaurants persists today; Nellie Bowles, "San Francisco Officials to Tech Workers: Buy Your Lunch," *NYT*, July 31, 2018.

66. McKinnell, interview by Cohen; also see Ellen Perry Berkeley, "More Than You May Want to Know About the Boston City Hall," *Architecture Plus* 1, no. 1 (1973): 72–77.

67. Hilgenhurst,"Evolution of Boston's Government Center," 11 on workforce size, 22 on tax assessments.

68. Walter Muir Whitehill, *Boston: A Topographical History*, 2nd ed. (Cambridge, MA: Harvard University Press, 1968), 215–17; Paul McCann, a longtime BRA staffer all the way back to Logue's time, credited Government Center with being a catalyst for intense private development on its periphery; Paul McCann, interview by Liza- beth Cohen, June 1, 2007, Boston, MA.

69. "Uses of the Past," *AF* 137, no. 2 (February 1972): 24–33; Kathryn Welch, "Boston's Old City Hall," *Antiques* 107, no. 6 (June 1975): 110–15; Charles Lockwood, "An 1860's City Hall Survives," *CSM*, December 8, 1972, 13. "Maison Robert" closed in 2004 and has been replaced.

70. Logue insisted that the "Friends of old Scollay were few, really non-existent" and that he recalled "few, if any, of the nostalgic comments about old Scollay Square that I occasionally hear today"; Logue, "The Boston Story," 14, 31v7.

71. On Logue's appreciation for Beacon Hill and the North End, Logue, "Work of the Boston Renewal Administration in the Urban Core," Harvard Graduate School of Design eighth annual Urban Design Conference, 5; "Urban Development Prospects as Seen by Edward Logue," *CR* 52, no. 16 (April 16, 1960): 315. On the earliest historic preservation campaign in Boston, "Urban Preservation and Renewal: Designating the Historic Beacon Hill District in 1950s Boston," *JPH* 16, no. 4 (November 2017): 285–304.

72. "Scholars Join Forces to Rescue Sears Crescent from Developers," *BG*, November 19, 1961; Anthony Yudis, "Cornhill May Be Blended with Modern Boston," *BG*, Febru- ary 26, 1962; Thomas H. O'Connor, *Building a New Boston: Politics and Urban Re- newal, 1950–1970* (Boston: Northeastern University Press, 1993), 199–201; Nolan, interview, on impact of his *Globe* story on threatened Brattle Book Shop in fall 1961. Whitehill informed Logue of his other preservation activities, including the Old Corner Book Store Building "to make it a tangible asset to the city"; quote from Walter Muir Whitehill to John Crosby, November 21, 1960; also Walter Muir White- hill to Logue, November 21, 1960, and Logue to Whitehill, November 22, 1960; EJL, Series 6, Box 151, Folder 459; on Charlestown, see Whitehill to Logue, February 9, 1961, EJL, Series 6, Box 151, Folder 459. The Government Center planner Cobb claimed that a "marriage of old and new" was always the goal; Cobb, testimony to Boston City Council, June 1963, in Henry N. Cobb, *Words and Works, 1948–2018: Scenes from a Life in Architecture* (New York: Monacelli Press, 2018), 74.

73. Scagnoli, interview.

74. George J. Gloss to Logue, February 7, 1964, EJL, Series 6, Box 149, Folder 405; also Alexander Burnham, "Struggle Is Under Way to Save Intellectual Landmark in Boston," *NYT*, June 10, 1962.

75. The architect Tad Stahl was involved in the restoration of many of Boston's historic buildings; see Orwig, "Concrete Solutions: Tad Stahl's Urbanism," 19–20.

76. Logue, "Boston, 1960–1967—Seven Years of Plenty," 93; Logue, "Don't Blame Me for the Old Howard's Demise," letter to the editor, *BG*, July 2, 1998.

77. Logue, "The Boston Story," *Planning 1964: Selected Papers from the ASPO National Planning Conference, Boston, Massachusetts, April 5–9, 1964* (Chicago: American Society of Planning Officials, 1964), 5, 7.

78. Stephanie Ryberg-Webster, "Urban Policy in Disguise: A History of the Federal Historic Rehabilitation Tax Credit," *JPH* 14, no. 3 (August 2015): 204–23; Jon Gorey, "As Filing Deadline Looms, a Look at How Taxes Have Shaped Our Architecture," *BG*, April 12, 2018.

79. Kruh, *Always Something Doing*, 141–42; "Foley Blasts Logue Plan for Historical Site," *BG*, July 25, 1961.

80. Ada Louise Huxtable, "Renewal in Boston: Good and Bad," *NYT*, April 19, 1964.

81. Ada Louise Huxtable, "Why You Always Win and Lose in Urban Renewal," *NYT*, September 19, 1976. It would take until December 1976 for Boston to establish a Landmarks Commission; Halpern, *Downtown USA*, 195.

82. Logue, "The Future of Boston, Its Architecture and Architects," in *Boston Society of Architects: The First Hundred Years, 1867–1967*, ed. Marvin E. Goody and Robert P. Walsh (Boston: Boston Society of Architects, 1967), 101.

83. Logue, "The Education of an Urban Administrator," *The Universitas Project: Solutions for a Post-Technological Society*, conceived and directed by Emilio Ambasz, from a symposium January 8–9, 1972 (New York: Museum of Modern Art, 2006), 176–79.

84. Logue, "Could Growth Kill Boston's Boom?," Boston College Citizen Seminars, State Street Bank, May 19, 1987; also see Logue, "Garrity's Impact and Other Thoughts on Boston," op-ed, *BG*, May 2, 1983, and "A City Planner Shares His Values," *NHR*, November 24, 1985, in which Logue argued that he and Collins "created the framework" for Boston's "current downtown boom," but in a way that put government in the position to monitor "the abuses of private enterprise—its selfishness, its greed, its unconcern for what we value—seems to me that businessmen alone are not to be trusted."

85. "Former BRA Director Logue Issues a Report Card," *BG*, June 8, 1986; Logue, "Boston, 1960–1967—Seven Years of Plenty," 95; Webb Nichols, "Rerooting Boston's Skyline," *BG*, March 1, 2006; the architecture critic Paul Goldberger shared a number of Logue's concerns in "Urban Building Trends Lend Boston an Odd Mix," *NYT*, June 16, 1985.

In 1984 a columnist for the *CSM* expressed hope that the newly elected mayor, Raymond L. Flynn, and his new director of the BRA would live up to the standards set in "the mid-1960s, when Edward J. Logue, a man of vision for tastefully blending of the old with the new, was running the redevelopment agency"; George B. Merry, "No Room for Haphazard Development in Reshaping Boston of Tomorrow," *CSM*, September 6, 1984. In 2015, the then mayor Martin J. Walsh called for a renewed effort to "balance the old and new." Speaking in familiar language, he said, "We should aim for world-class design. Our historic buildings reflect our unique past. New buildings should project the values and aspirations of our growing city"; Rachel Slade, "Why Is Boston So Ugly? How We Built the Most Mediocre Architecture in History, and How We're Going to Fix It," *BM*, May 2015, 111.

86. Cobb, interview; Cobb by 2010 regretted that "a kind of engagement of the existing fabric . . . is totally missing from Government Center."

87. Nelson W. Aldrich, Pietro Belluschi, Henry R. Shepley, and Hugh Stubbins, Chairman, Memorandum to the Boston Redevelopment Authority, October 2, 1961; Logue to the Architectural Advisory Board, October 2, 1961, EJL, Series 6, Box 151, Folder 471. At a city hall hearing in January 1962, Logue publicly expressed his support for keeping the Sears Crescent building; Elvira Johnson, shorthand reporter, "Status of Government Center Project, Before Committee on Urban Redevelopment, Rehabilitation, and Renewal," Boston, MA, vol. 1, January 25, 1962, 24. But in April 1962, *The Harvard Crimson* was still reporting that the Sears Crescent was slated for demolition; Russell B. Roberts, "Boston Redevelopment Will Claim Historic Sites in Cornhill Vicinity," *Crimson*, April 9, 1962. The final plan would not be published until April 1963.

88. "Barbarians Strip the Palace," *Cityscapes of Boston: An American City Through Time*, Text by Robert Campbell, Photographs by Peter Vanderwarker (Boston: Houghton Mifflin, 1992), 154; "What It Took to Bring About the Best Public Building of Our Time," *Contract Interiors* 128, no. 9 (April 1969): 115–33; from the *BG*: Matt Viser and Donovan Slack, "Mayor Says He'll Build Waterfront City Hall," December 13, 2006; Adrian Walker, "City Hall Takes the Fall," December 14, 2006; Martin Nolan, "The Urban Reality of City Hall, Then and Now," February 5, 2007; Matt Viser, "It's Unique, But Is It a Landmark?," April 25, 2007; George Thrush, "Clean Slate," May 13, 2007.

89. Ada Louise Huxtable, "New Boston Center: Skillful Use of Urban Space," *NYT*, September 11, 1972; McKinnell, interview by Cohen; for more self-criticism from McKinnell and other designers about the plaza, see "50 Years: A Retrospective Symposium on Government Center and Boston City Hall," extracts, in *Re-Making Government Center, Boston Design Lab, Spring 2008* (Cambridge, MA: School of Architecture and Planning, MIT, 2009), 56–63, particularly 60.

90. Ieoh Ming Pei, interview by Lizabeth Cohen, June 11, 2007, New York, NY.

91. City hall and City Hall Plaza have long invited frustrations and proposed remedies; see, for example, Hilgenhurst, "Evolution of Boston's Government Center," 19; Kruh, *Always Something Doing*, 159–68; Gretchen Schneider, "The Never-Ending Story: City Hall Plaza," *AB* 4, no. 5 (May 2001): 16–19; "Reimagining City Hall," special issue, *AB* 10, no. 5 (September–October 2007); Gary Wolf, "Boston City Hall Plaza: A Modern Space for the City upon a Hill," *Docomomo US Newsletter* 3, 10 (Winter 2008); "City Hall Plaza Should Go for the Green—as in Grass," editorial, *BG*, October 1, 2010; Casey Ross, "A 10-Year Plan for City Hall Plaza: New Incre-

mental Approach Starts with Remodeled T Station, Trees," *BG*, March 16, 2011; Martine Powers, "Government Center Closing for 2 Years for Upgrades," *BG*, March 22, 2014; Harry Bartnick, "Give Boston's City Hall a Much-Needed Makeover," *BG*, July 26, 2015; "Boston City Hall Adding Beer, Dogs, Ice Cream to Plaza," BG, April 20, 2018; "Boston Winter Is Canceled Amid Plans to Renovate City Hall Plaza," *BG*, July 3, 2018. Harry Cobb has pushed to open up the ground floor of city hall "and bring some life into it" and the plaza; Cobb, interview.

92. On poor maintenance, Logue, "What's So Bad about City Hall?," *BG*, May 1, 1998.

93. Boston Redevelopment Authority, *Government Center Urban Renewal Plan, April 3, 1963, Revised May 29, 1963*, 5. When the AIA awarded Boston's Government Center a citation for excellence in community architecture in 1972, it praised how the center "combines new buildings superbly sited and designed with worthy old buildings artfully preserved and converted to new uses" and singled out John Collins, Edward Logue, and I. M. Pei as "inspired leaders at the decisive moments, assur[ing] the high quality of the development"; in Collins, interview by de Varon, Tape 6, December 21, 1976, 11.

94. "BRA with C of C Presentation to Logue," Thursday, March 15, 1962, 8:30 p.m., Lynch, Boxes 2, 6, 9.

95. Esther Maletz Stone, email message to author, July 19, 2015.

6. Negotiating Neighborhoods

1. "Testimony of Mr. Edward J. Logue, Administrator, Boston Redevelopment Authority, Boston, Massachusetts," *Hearing Before the United States Commission on Civil Rights: Hearing Held in Boston, Massachusetts, October 4–5, 1966*, 243–46. Even Michael Appleby, who investigated Logue's Boston record to undermine Mayor Lindsay's effort to hire him in New York, reported that Logue's goal was to achieve more socioeconomic mixing in cities and suburbs; Michael D. Appleby, "Logue's Record in Boston: An Analysis of His Renewal and Planning Activities, with a Foreword and Summary by Herbert J. Gans for the Steering Committee, Council for New York Housing and Planning Policy, Funded by the Normal Foundation, May 1966," EJL, 2002 Accession, Box 22, Folder "Logue's Record in Boston by Michael Appleby," 19.

2. Logue, "Power of Negative Thinking," *BM*, February 1969, 60.

3. Logue, "The Boston Story—Getting Started," draft chapter for memoir, "Tales of a City Builder, Compared to What," January 2000, MDL, 17–19v7; Logue, interview, Schussheim, 13; Logue, interview, Steen, July 11, 1991, Boston, MA, 12.

4. "Statement by Edward J. Logue," Boston, Massachusetts, May 26, 1967, *Hearings Before the National Commission on Urban Problems*, vol. 1, May–June 1967 (Washington, DC: Government Printing Office, 1968), 193. On the three options for clearance, Appleby, "Logue's Record in Boston," 37; Logue, interview, Steen, August 3, 1989, Boston, MA, 291.

5. Walter McQuade, "Boston: What Can a Sick City Do?," *Fortune*, June 1964, 164; Evarts Erickson, "Boston Rehabilitation Gets Summer 'Work Camp' Assistance," *JH* 21, no. 9 (October 15, 1964): 468–70; "Once Neglected House Becomes Show Place," *BH*, September 17, 1965.

6. Nancy Rita Arnone, "Redevelopment in Boston: A Study of the Politics and Administration of Social Change" (Ph.D. dissertation, MIT, 1965), 193.

7. Logue, interview, Schussheim, 28.

8. Arnone, "Redevelopment in Boston," 125–26, 131–32; McQuade, "Boston: What Can a Sick City Do?," 168 on incentives to commercial developers to build 221(d)(3) projects.

9. "Can Urban Renewal Make Everybody Happy?," *AF* 120 (June 1964): 104.

10. John Collins quoted in McQuade, "Boston: What Can a Sick City Do?," 168.

11. Logue, "A Look Back at Neighborhood Renewal in Boston," *Policy Studies Journal* 16, no. 2 (Winter 1987): 343; Logue testimony, *National Commission Hearings*, 199; Timothy Francis Rose, "Civic War: People, Politics, and the Battle of New Boston, 1945–1967" (Ph.D. dissertation, University of California, Berkeley, 2006), 223, including n366, on the limited supply of public housing.

12. Logue, "Power of Negative Thinking," 61; "Can Urban Renewal Make Everybody Happy?," 104; McQuade, "Boston: What Can a Sick City Do?," 168; Logue, "The Boston Story," 34.

13. John Stainton, interview by Lizabeth Cohen, May 30, 2007, Jamaica Plain, MA.

14. Chester W. Hartman, "The Housing of Relocated Families," *JAIP* 30, no. 4 (November 1964): 266–86; and in *JAIP* 31, no. 4 (November 1965): Logue, "Comment on 'The Housing of Relocated Families,'" 338–40; and Hartman, "Rejoinder by the Author," 340–44.

15. Anthony Yudis, "B.R.A. Reports 'Seven-Year Progress,'" *BG*, August 1, 1967.

16. Alan Lupo, "Boston: 10 Years Have Changed It," *BG*, February 19, 1967.

17. Quoted in Daniel Golden and David Mehegan, "Changing the Heart of the City," *BG*, September 18, 1983.

18. Logue testimony, *National Commission Hearings*, 193–95.

19. Arthur Reilly, interview by Lizabeth Cohen, June 25, 2009, Brookline, MA.

20. McQuade, "Boston: What Can a Sick City Do?," 168.

21. Joseph W. Lund to Logue, May 25, 1967; Logue to Joseph Lund, June 1, 1967; EJL, Series 6, Box 150, Folder 416.

22. Logue, "A Look Back at Neighborhood Renewal in Boston," 340–41; McQuade claimed that Boston banks pledged some $20 million toward new mortgages to finance rehabilitation in "Boston: What Can a Sick City Do?," 164; Logue testimony, *National Commission Hearings*, 213–15, 255–57, 263–65.

23. "Can Urban Renewal Make Everybody Happy?," 104; McQuade, "Boston: What Can a Sick City Do?," 164.

24. For the full history of B-BURG and its impact, see Hillel Levine and Lawrence Harmon, *The Death of an American Jewish Community: A Tragedy of Good Intentions* (New York: Free Press, 1992); and Golden and Mehegan, "Changing the Heart of the City."

25. "Meet Boston's Mr. Urban Renewal," *CSM*, December 18, 1965.

26. Langley Carleton Keyes, Jr., *The Rehabilitation Planning Game: A Study in the Diversity of Neighborhood* (Cambridge, MA: MIT Press, 1969). For another helpful treatment of these three major neighborhood renewal projects, see Jim Vrabel, *A People's History of the New Boston* (Amherst: University of Massachusetts Press, 2014).

27. Nicholas von Hoffman, "Ed Logue—the Master Rebuilder," *WP*, April 15, 1967; also see Appleby, "Logue's Record in Boston," 30–31.

28. James Q. Wilson, "Planning and Politics: Citizen Participation in Urban Renewal," in *Urban Renewal: The Record and the Controversy*, ed. Wilson (Cambridge, MA: MIT Press, 1966), 418.

29. Armone, "Redevelopment in Boston," 20–21, 44–45; Nicholas von Hoffman, "Boston Is an Ingrate," *WP*, April 9, 1967.

30. Keyes, *Rehabilitation Planning Game*, 13. Keyes specifically targeted James Q. Wilson, Staughton Lynd, and Herbert Gans, who assumed that lower-income people were always excluded from urban renewal; Keyes, *Rehabilitation Planning Game*, 8–12.

31. Logue, "The Boston Story," 28v7.

32. Heath, *Act of Faith*, part 1, 8. The Snowdens joined with the NAACP in endorsing Logue's appointment; Melnea A. Cass, President, NAACP, to Joseph Lund, Chairman of BRA, January 24, 1961; Melnea A. Cass to Logue, January 27, 1961; Logue to Melnea A. Cass, EJL, Series 6, Box 150, Folder 420.

33. On Washington Park urban renewal, see Keyes, *Rehabilitation Planning Game*, 143–90; Heath, *Act of Faith*; John H. Spiers, "'Planning with People': Urban Renewal in Boston's Washington Park, 1950–1970," *JPH* 8, no. 1 (August 2009): 221–47; Jennifer Hock, "Bulldozers, Busing, and Boycotts: Urban Renewal and the Integrationist Project," *JUH* 39, no. 3 (May 2013): 433–53; David R. Gergen, "Renewal in the Ghetto: A Study of Residential Rehabilitation in Boston's Washington Park," *Harvard Civil Rights–Civil Liberties Law Review* 3 (1967–68): 243–310; *Report to the Community: Urban Renewal Reaches Midway Point in Washington Park*, BRA, 1965; Walter L. Smart, *The Washington Park Relocation Story, 1962/1966*, BRA, April 1966; Benjamin Feit, "Freedom House and Boston's Urban Renewal: The Determining Role of a Civic Organizing Institution in the Reshaping of Washington Park" (senior thesis, Yale University, April 2006).

34. On the Snowdens and Freedom House, see "Interview with Muriel S. Snowden," January 21, October 30, November 20, 1977, in *Black Women Oral History Project*, ed. Ruth Edmunds Hill, vol. 9, Schlesinger Library on the History of Women in America (Westport, CT: Meckler, 1991), 1–120; Bradford Paul Meacham, "Black Power Before 'Black Power': Muriel Snowden and Boston's Freedom House, 1949–1966" (senior thesis, Harvard University, March 2005).

35. Thomas O'Connor, interview by Lizabeth Cohen, June 16, 2009, Boston, MA.

36. Heath, *Act of Faith*, part 1, 13.

37. *BG*, February 6, 1962, quoted in Rose, "Civic War," 241.

38. Wolf Von Eckardt, "Bulldozers and Bureaucrats: Renewal and the City," *New Republic*, September 14, 1963, 17. For more evidence of community residents' optimism about urban renewal, see Lewis Watts et al., *The Middle-Income Negro Family Faces Urban Renewal* (Waltham, MA: Research Center of Heller School, Brandeis University, for the Department of Commerce and Development, Commonwealth of Massachusetts, 1964).

39. Logue, interview, Steen, August 3, 1989, Boston, MA, 288–89; Logue, interview by Heath, December 7, 1990, Boston, MA, in Heath, *Act of Faith*, 3; Otto Snowden and Muriel Snowden, "Citizen Participation," *JH* 20, no. 8 (September 30, 1963): 435–39;

Anthony J. Yudis, "Renewal Project Goes Over Big with Roxbury; Logue Cheered," *BG*, January 15, 1963, which said that only three voted against the plan. For more on CURAC, see CURAC Files, FH, Box 30.

40. "Statement of Edward J. Logue, Public Hearing of the BRA Concerning the Washington Park Urban Renewal Area," January 14, 1963, 7:30 p.m., Boston Technical High School, 1, MDL. Community outreach by phone, mail, and personal conversations by Freedom House and CURAC was extensive; see "Freedom House and Urban Renewal—the Task Accomplished and the Task Ahead," February 25, 1963, FH, Box 28, Folder 945 (Freedom House and Urban Renewal—Pinterhughes) for documentation.

41. Heath, *Act of Faith*, part 1, 17.

42. Julius Bernstein and Chester Hartman, letter to the editor, *BG*, June 1, 1966. For more discussion of the difficulties of low-income residents, see Irene Saint, "Washington Park Plan's 4-Year Life Half Over, Problem of Low-Income People Remains," *BH*, December 1, 1965.

43. Arnone, "Redevelopment in Boston," 102; "tea-drinking Negroes" in Logue, interview, Steen, February 4, 1985, Lincoln, MA, 38; Chuck Turner quoted in Rose, "Civic War," 247; "Uncle Tom's Cabin" in "Otto Snowden Obituary," *BG*, September 30, 1995.

44. Washington Park Steering Committee, Minutes, November 13, 1961, in Keyes, *Rehabilitation Planning Game*, 175; Heath, *Act of Faith*, part 1, 9–10.

45. "Statement of Edward J. Logue, Administrator, Boston Redevelopment Authority," "Federal Role in Urban Affairs" (Senator Abraham Ribicoff's Subcommittee on Executive Reorganization of Senate Committee on Government Operations, November–December 1966), Logue testimony, December 12, 1966, 2824; Keyes, *Rehabilitation Planning Game*, 226–27; anger at this decision was recorded in "Low Income Housing Badly Needed," *BSB*, June 4, 1966; the vote was 45 to 29.

46. Appleby, "Logue's Record in Boston," 32; also Arnone, "Redevelopment in Boston," 193.

47. Frederick Salvucci, interview by Lizabeth Cohen, June 16, 2009, Cambridge, MA.

48. Muriel Snowden, "Planning with People: Finding the Formula," Boston College Seminar, April 23, 1963, FH, Box 28, in Rose, "Civic War," 247–48.

49. "Statement by Mrs. Muriel Snowden," *National Commission Hearings*, 232. For details on these civic projects, see Heath, *Act of Faith*, part 3, 1–8. For growth of organized opposition to Freedom House and the Washington Park renewal plan, see Spiers, "'Planning with People,'" 237–41; Mel King, *Chain of Change: Struggles for Black Community Development* (Boston: South End Press, 1981), 73–78; Meacham, "Black Power Before 'Black Power,'" 75–77.

50. "Police Riot in Grove Hall, Scores Injured," "Roxbury Fights Police Attack," "Roxbury Residents Brutalized," all in *BSB*, June 10, 1967; many other articles in *BG*, June 3–8, 1967. Also, Akilah Johnson, "The Forgotten Riot That Sparked Boston's Racial Unrest," *BG*, June 2, 2017.

51. "Mayor Declines 3rd Term; Reviews Stewardship; Urges Continued Progress," *CR*, June 10, 1967, 457, on the Grove Hall Welfare Office incident and ensuing protests.

52. King, *Chain of Change*, 82–84.

53. *BG*, December 11, 1976, quoted in Heath, *Act of Faith*, part 4, 2; Logue, interview by Heath, part 5, 7.

54. Stainton, interview; Martin Nolan, interview by Lizabeth Cohen, May 24, 2007, Cambridge, MA.
55. "Can Urban Renewal Make Everybody Happy?," 103; discussion of the state's position on Boston's schools in Logue testimony, *Hearing Before the United States Commission on Civil Rights in Boston*, 246.
56. "Filth Litters Roxbury Streets," *BSB*, July 23, 1966; Ronald Bailey with Diane Turner and Robert Hayden, preface by Danette Jones, *Lower Roxbury: A Community of Treasures in the City of Boston* (Boston: Lower Roxbury Community Corporation by the Department of African-American Studies, Northeastern University, 1993), 24–25, 33; after the bonfire and the anger it stirred, the city did clean up the garbage and put up barriers to prevent further dumping.
57. On the LRCC, see Lower Roxbury Community Corporation Records, 1968–1978, Northeastern University Archives and Special Collections (hereafter LRCC), particularly the history in "Urban Renewal in Madison Park," c. 1970, *Washington Park Urban Renewal Area Bulletin*, Box 1, Folder 8; LRCC, *The Future of Lower Roxbury Depends on You*, printed pamphlet, n.d. but c. 1968; Bailey, *Lower Roxbury*, 19–26, 29, 32–47, 57–63; Gordon Fellman, interview by Lizabeth Cohen, December 18, 2010, Cambridge, MA.
58. On Urban Planning Aid and its involvement in Madison Park, see UPA Records, 1966–82, particularly its mission statement in "Attachments to Form 1023," n.d. but c. 1966, Box 1, Folder 7; Gordon Brumm, "Urban Renewal in Washington Park and Madison Park," *Dialogues Boston* 1, no. 2 (March 1968), Box 12, Folder 1. Also, "Roxbury Leaders Blast Renewal Plan," *BSB*, May 28, 1966, for how Goodman presented UPA; Robert Goodman, interview by Lizabeth Cohen, April 24, 2010, Amherst, MA; Fellman, interview.
59. "Contract Between Urban Planning Aid and the Lower Roxbury Community Committee on Urban Renewal," July 25, 1966; and Dr. Forrest L. Knapp, Massachusetts Council of Churches, to Professor Robert Goodman, November 30, 1966, UPA, Box 1, Folder 7.
60. "Contract Between UPA and the LRCC," July 25, 1966.
61. "10/18/66, Tuesday meeting with Edward J. Logue," UPA, Box 12, Folder 3.
62. UPA Meeting Minutes, December 14, 1966, UPA, Box 12, Folder 5, 2. At some point, the LRCC also asked the community organizers to leave as well. Alex Rodriguez recalled, "And we knew it was gonna work then, because once they threw us out, we knew they were gonna make the decisions. They weren't going to listen to Alex Rodriguez, Val Hyman, Dan Richardson, Byron Rushing, or anybody else. They were gonna make the decisions and that's what we wanted"; Bailey, *Lower Roxbury*, 35. The sensitive relationship between advocacy planners and community groups was debated at the time in Frances Fox Piven, "Whom Does the Advocate Planner Serve?," *Social Policy* (May–June 1970), and responses in the next issue (July–August 1970) by Sumner Rosen, Sherry Arnstein, Paula and Linda Davidoff, Clarence Funnye, Sylvia Scribner, Chester Hartman, and Piven.
63. UPA Meeting Minutes, August 23, 1967, UPA, Box 12, Folder 5, for a discussion of giving LRCC an ultimatum if more surveyors were not provided; survey materials, UPA, Box 12, Folder 3. For continued tensions between the LRCC and the UPA after the memorandum of understanding was signed, see UPA Meeting Minutes,

April 19, 1967, UPA, Box 12, Folder 5, where Andrea Ballard comments that the "LRCC feels let down by UPA . . . Community organizers in L.R. distrust UPA," and Gordon Fellman says, "Original agreement about working relationship between LRCC and UPA has not been kept by LRCC."

64. "Madison Park—Campus High School Before Committee on Urban Renewal," November 16, 17, 23, 29, Stenographic Record; Anthony J. Yudis, "City Ends Roxbury Hearings," *BG*, November 30, 1966; "City Votes Yes on Park Madison," *BSB*, January 2, 1967; Paul J. Corkery, "BRA and Roxbury Citizen Group Reach Urban Renewal Agreement," *Crimson*, January 6, 1967.

65. Anthony J. Yudis, "Madison Park Leader Denies Logue's Representation Charge, 350 Roxbury Names Support Claim," *BG*, November 24, 1966; also Robert Hannan, "Logue Hits 'Academic Amateurs,' Renewal Chief Doubts Group Can Speak for Community," *BG*, November 18, 1966; Melvin B. Miller, "Agreement Ends Four-Year Fight: Madison Park Battle Nears End," *BSB*, December 3, 1966, which states "Logue refused to negotiate with the U.P.A."

66. "Roxbury High School, Boston, Massachusetts, 1967, Marcel Breuer and Tician Papachristou, architects," in Tician Papachristou, *Marcel Breuer: New Buildings and Projects* (New York: Praeger, 1970), 196–97; design described in Keith Morgan, "City of Ideas: Structure and Scale in the Boston General Plan," in *Heroic: Concrete Architecture and the New Boston*, ed. Mark Pasnik, Michael Kubo, and Chris Grimley (New York: Monacelli Press, 2015), 72–73. Madison Park High School opened in 1977.

67. "Our Mission Statement," Madison Park Development Corporation, http://www .madison-park.org/about-us.

68. Bailey, *Lower Roxbury*; "We Saved a Community," panel discussion and viewing of film *Making of Madison Park: A Shared Vision*, October 19, 2011, Madison Park Development Corp, Roxbury, MA.

69. Fellman, interview; on checking out the Washington Park 221(d)(3) models, LRCC, *Future of Lower Roxbury Depends on You*, 12. At the September 20, 1967, UPA board meeting, Andrea Ballard mentioned that "a number of LRCC officers would like to have private single-family homes in Madison Park." When she was told that anyone who could afford that "will be too affluent for 221(d)(3) housing," she asked for "a short paper explaining problems of private single homes on site, to put to rest this endless discussion at LRCC meetings"; UPA Meeting Minutes, September 20, 1967, UPA, Box 12, Folder 5, 2. The discussion of single-family houses continued at the October 4, 1967, meeting.

70. For descriptions of Charlestown, see Keyes, *Rehabilitation Planning Game*, 87–102; Frank Del Vecchio, memo to Lizabeth Cohen, "Vision: Ed Logue's Audacious Campaign for the Economic Resuscitation of Boston," n.d. but late November 2006, 6; J. Anthony Lukas, *Common Ground: A Turbulent Decade in the Lives of Three American Families* (New York: Alfred A. Knopf, 1985), 149–54; Irene Saint, "Charlestown Dissenters Battled for Every Inch," *BH*, December 2, 1965; "Charlestown: Proud but Neglected Renowned Homeland," *BG*, July 25, 1967, for black population.

71. Leo Baldwin, letter to the editor, *Charlestown Patriot*, April 28, 1960, in Keyes, *Rehabilitation Planning Game*, 104.

72. It hurt that both Vilemas and McCarthy were outsiders, Vilemas a Lithuanian

American from Chicago, where he had organized with Saul Alinsky and the Chicago Catholic archdiocese, and McCarthy, a middle-class Irishman, most recently director of redevelopment operations for the City of San Leandro, California; Logue to Catherine Bauer Wurster, April 10, 1961, Papers of Catherine Bauer Wurster, 1931–1964, Bancroft Library, University of California, Berkeley, Box 21, Folder 21; Patrick E. McCarthy to Edward Logue, March 19, 1965, EJL, Series 6, Box 148, Folder 381.

73. Frank Del Vecchio, interview by Lizabeth Cohen, November 27, 2006, Cambridge, MA.

74. BRA: Charlestown, "Proposed Renewal Project: Before BRA Board," Stenographic Transcript, January 7, 1963, 7, in Keyes, *Rehabilitation Planning Game*, 121; Arnone, "Redevelopment in Boston," 136–37.

75. Del Vecchio, interview; also Frank Del Vecchio, *City Streets: A Memoir* (North Andover, MA: Leap Year Press, 2016), 151.

76. Del Vecchio, interview; *The Urban Renewal Plan for Charlestown, an Opportunity for Every Resident: Charlestown/A Residential Neighborhood*, pamphlet, BRA, n.d.

77. Keyes, *Rehabilitation Planning Game*, 139. Jack Kennedy and Tip O'Neill had both promised to remove the El, but there it still was, contributing to Charlestown's sense of isolation, in Logue's view; Logue, "The Boston Story," 27v7. Also see "When the 'El' Comes Down, a Way of Life Goes with It," *BG*, March 24, 1975. Michael Appleby noted Charlestown residents' fear that racial integration would accompany more government housing programs; Appleby, "Logue's Record in Boston," 22. Although the Boston Housing Authority began to integrate public housing in 1963, four years later only twenty-seven black families lived in Charlestown's projects; *BSB*, July 27, 1967, in Rose, "Civic War," 498. On the revised urban renewal plan, John Stainton, *Urban Renewal and Planning in Boston: A Review of the Past and a Look at the Future*, a consultant study directed by John Stainton, commissioned by the Citizens Housing and Planning Association and BRA, November 1972, 4.

78. Logue, "Boston, 1960–1967—Seven Years of Plenty," *Proceedings of the Massachusetts History Society* 84 (1972): 82.

79. For descriptions of this notorious meeting: Keyes, *Rehabilitation Planning Game*, 132–34; Logue, interview, Jones, Tape 3:20; "2500 Jam Hearings on Bunker Hill," *BG*, March 15, 1965; "Charlestown Supports Urban Renewal Plan" and "Yes Vote Means Rebirth for Town," *Charlestown Patriot*, March 25, 1965; Del Vecchio, *City Streets*, 164–66.

80. Craven and Foley were the negative votes. Among the many articles by Anthony J. Yudis in the *BG*: "Charlestown Hearing Explodes: Wildest Renewal Battle Rocks Council Chamber," April 28, 1965; "Charlestown Foes Challenge Council," May 6, 1965; "Charlestown Renewal Wins Council OK, 7–2," June 8, 1965. Also, Del Vecchio, *City Streets*, 166–70.

81. NBC, *America the Beautiful*, Chet Huntley reporter, Ted Yates producer-author, 52-minute documentary, broadcast October 3, 1965, available at Paley Center for Media, New York, and online at NBC Universal Archives; "N.B.C. to Examine U.S. City Growth," *NYT*, July 29, 1965.

82. For links between urban renewal and the Boston busing struggle: Lukas, *Common*

Ground, 153–56, 355–56; J. Brian Sheehan, *The Boston School Integration Dispute: Social Change and Legal Maneuvers* (New York: Columbia University Press, 1984), 196–238; Ronald Formisano, *Boston Against Busing: Race, Class and Ethnicity in the 1960s and 1970s* (Chapel Hill: University of North Carolina Press, 1991), 121–22, where he calls urban renewal the "dress rehearsal" to busing.

83. Danny Soltren, interview, and Chris Hayes, interview, in *The South End*, Boston 200 Neighborhood History Series (Boston: Boston 200 Corporation, 1975), 24, 27.

84. For descriptions of the South End and urban renewal there: Keyes, *Rehabilitation Planning Game*, 35–86; Vrabel, *People's History of the New Boston*, 101–3; Herbert H. Hyman, "Organizational Response to Urban Renewal" (Ph.D. dissertation, Brandeis University, 1967); "The South End: Ever-Changing Neighborhood of Many Different People," *BG*, August 1, 1967; "A Special Report: The South End Today," *BM* (October 1965): 34–59; Joan Colebrook, "A Reporter at Large: The Renewal," *New Yorker*, January 1, 1966, 35–45; *South End Urban Renewal*, BRA, 1963.

85. "Mel King," in *Changing Lives, Changing Communities: Oral Histories from Action for Boston Community Development*, ed. Robert C. Hayden and Ann Withorn (Boston: Action for Community Development and the University of Massachusetts, 2002), 154–55.

86. Logue to E. C. Struckhoff, June 30, 1966, EJL, Series 6, Box 149, Folder 383.

87. Mario Luis Small, *Villa Victoria: The Transformation of Social Capital in a Boston Barrio* (Chicago: University of Chicago Press, 2004); Vrabel, *People's History of the New Boston*, 104–11; King, *Chain of Change*, 64–72, 111–18, 203–6; "Building Activism," *BG Magazine*, October 10, 2004, 94; Robert Goodman, *After the Planners* (New York: Touchstone, 1971), 193–96; Peter G. Rowe, *Modernity and Housing* (Cambridge, MA: MIT Press, 1993), 244, 246–53; John Sharratt, "Urban Neighborhood Preservation and Development," *Process, Architecture*, nos. 14–15 (1980): 28–30; Micho Spring, "When a Community Embraces Both Progress and Heritage," *BG*, May 10, 2008; Peter Medoff and Holly Sklar, *Streets of Hope: The Fall and Rise of an Urban Neighborhood* (Boston: South End Press, 1994), 19–22; Lawrence J. Vale, *Changing Cities: 75 Years of Planning Better Futures at MIT* (Cambridge, MA: MIT School of Architecture and Planning, 2008), 52–53; "Hispanic Bostonians Mark a Rebirth," *NYT*, May 10, 1983; Johnny Diaz, "Villa Victoria Welcomes a New Leader," *BG*, December 3, 2004. The archives of Inquilinos Boricuas en Acción, 1967–2004, are at Northeastern University Archives and Special Collections; see the finding aid for history and chronology as well as records.

88. Bernard J. Frieden and Lynne B. Sagalyn, *Downtown, Inc.: How America Rebuilds Cities* (Cambridge, MA: MIT Press, 1989), 305–6; Paul Goldberger, "Urban Building Trends Lend Boston an Odd Mix," *NYT*, June 16, 1985.

89. Mel King, interview by Lizabeth Cohen, June 17, 2009, Boston, MA.

90. On North Harvard, see from the Brighton-Allston Historical Society and Heritage Museum and Oral History Center at the Brighton Branch Library: Marjorie T. Redgate, "To Hell with Urban Renewal," 1969, an account of the neighborhood's struggle with the BRA by a resident and owner of a luncheonette in the North Harvard neighborhood, and the four-part series excerpted from her manuscript in the *Allston-Brighton Journal*, ed. William P. Marchione; and oral histories with

community activists. The single best analysis is Edward Michael Stone, "Concrete Ambition: Edward J. Logue and the North Harvard Urban Renewal Project, 1960–1967" (senior thesis, Harvard University, 2004). For Logue's communication with the developers, see Logue, Memorandum to the file, September 21, 1961, EJL, Series 6, Box 148, Folder 376; "North Harvard Project" (materials prepared for Yale Law School class, November 1965), EJL, Series 6, Box 151, Folder 464, which states that backing down would be a "dangerous precedent."

Also, Chester Hartman, *Between Eminence and Notoriety: Four Decades of Radical Urban Planning* (New Brunswick, NJ: Center for Urban Policy Research, Rutgers University Press, 2002), 18–19; "An Open Letter to Mayor John Collins and the Boston Redevelopment Authority," 1965, Loeb Library Ephemera Collection, HGSD; Douglas Mathews, "Politics and Public Relations—or, How to Relocate the BRA," *Crimson*, January 7, 1966; "Urban Planning Aid: A Proposal to Provide Planning Assistance to Low-Income Communities," *Dirt and Flowers* 2 (July 30, 1966): 5, UPA, Box 12, Folder 1; Goodman, interview; "What to Do 'Til the Wrecker Comes, Plot by Boston Renewal Authority, Editing by Brainerd Taylor," *Connection: Visual Arts at Harvard*, Spring 1966, Loeb Special Collections, HGSD; "SDS Will Assist in Fight Against Urban Renewal," *Crimson*, March 4, 1965; "The Mess in Brighton—and a Suggestion," editorial, *BG*, August 11, 1965; "Boston's Powerful Model for Rebuilders," *BW*, November 26, 1966; Jim Botticelli, *Dirty Old Boston: Four Decades of a City in Transition* (Boston: Union Park Press, 2014), 78.

91. Del Vecchio, email message to author, July 23, 2006; similar statements were made by others: Salvucci, interview; Joseph Slavet, interview by Lizabeth Cohen, May 31, 2007, Boston, MA.

92. Logue testimony, Ribicoff hearings, 2821; also Appleby, "Logue's Record in Boston," 35–36.

93. Logue, "Tales of a City Builder, Compared to What," memoir draft notes for "Chapter on Mistakes."

94. *Allston Brighton Citizen-Item*, January 12, 1967: "CNH Drives to Meet No. Harvard Housing Deadline," "Out of a Hateful History: Urban Renewal Redeemed," "'It Is Still Stolen Land: We Still Want Our Deeds,'" and the editorial "CNH: A Setback for the Cynics"; Nan Ni, "Profs Weigh In on Charlesview Design," *Crimson*, October 21, 2008; Charlesview, Inc., website, http://charlesviewcommunity.org/.

95. Logue, interview, Schussheim, 24; Linda Corman, "Former BRA Head Takes Another Look at the City He Helped Plan," *Banker and Tradesman*, October 21, 1987, 6; Logue, "The New Boston—Can the City Control Its Future?," *Boston Observer*, c. 1985, EJL, 2002 Accession, Box 22, 6.

96. Langley Keyes quoted in Golden and Mehegan, "Changing the Heart of the City."

97. Logue, "The New Boston—Can the City Control Its Future?"

98. Tunney Lee, interview by Lizabeth Cohen, July 13, 2007, Wellfleet, MA.

99. On the struggle over the Inner Belt and the Southwest Expressway, see Alan Lupo, Frank Colcord, and Edmund P. Fowler, *Rites of Way: The Politics of Transportation in Boston and the U.S. City* (Boston: Little, Brown, 1971); David Luberoff, "The Roads Not Taken: How One Powerful Choice Made All the Difference,"

AB 15, no. 4 (Winter 2012): 28–31; James A. Aloisi, Jr., *The Big Dig* (Beverly, MA: Commonwealth Editions, 2004), 8–12; Hilary Moss, Yinan Zhang, and Andy Anderson, "Assessing the Impact of the Inner Belt: MIT, Highways, and Housing in Cambridge, Massachusetts," *JUH* 40, no. 6 (November 2014): 1054–78; Peter Siskind, "Growth and Its Discontents: Localism, Protest and the Politics of Development on the Postwar Northeast Corridor" (Ph.D. dissertation, University of Pennsylvania, 2002).

100. Fred Salvucci and Tunney Lee were soon joined by Denis Blackett. When Salvucci informed his BRA boss about his organizing activities, he was encouraged to stop. When he remained firm and offered to quit the BRA, his boss and Logue asked him to stay; Salvucci, interview. Tunney Lee said he was never told "to stop and desist"; Lee, email message to author, February 18, 2010.

101. On the highway protests, in addition to the above sources: Gordon Fellman, in association with Barbara Brandt, *The Deceived Majority: Politics and Protest in Middle America* (New Brunswick, NJ: Transaction Books, Rutgers University Press, 1973); Eric Avila, *The Folklore of the Freeway: Race and Revolt in the Modernist City* (Minneapolis: University of Minnesota Press, 2014), 33–36; Lee, interview; Salvucci, interview; Fellman, interview; "Inner Belt—Transportation Study," *Dirt and Flowers* 2 (July 30, 1966): 6, UPA, Box 12, Folder 1; Vrabel, *People's History of the New Boston*, 139–49; Lily Geismer, *Don't Blame Us: Suburban Liberals and the Transformation of the Democratic Party* (Princeton, NJ: Princeton University Press, 2015), 105–16; Jon C. Teaford, *The Rough Road to Renaissance: Urban Revitalization in America, 1940–1985* (Baltimore: Johns Hopkins University Press, 1990), 234–35. Chester Hartman describes the "Open Letter to State and Federal Highway Officials," signed by 528 Harvard and MIT professors, in Hartman, *Between Eminence and Notoriety*, 19.

102. "Inner Belt to Uproot 937 Roxbury Families," *BSB*, December 18, 1965; "6000 in Roxbury Sent Removal Notice," *BSB*, January 15, 1966.

103. John Collins, interview by José de Varon, Tape 7, January 7, 1977, EJL, 2002 Accession, Box 21, Folder "Oral History John Collins," 14–15.

104. Anthony Pangaro, interview by Lizabeth Cohen, June 24, 2009, Boston, MA; Lawrence Harmon, "A Park That Is the Muscle and Bone of the City," *BG*, May 5, 2010. Years later Logue told the historian Lawrence Kennedy: "We laid that [Southwest corridor] out and persuaded Franny Sargent to approve it. He did, took the land, did the relocation, and only after the corridor was cleared did he change his mind. If the Inner Belt and the third harbor tunnel we proposed had been built I wonder if we would have needed the depressed Central Artery"; Logue to Lawrence Kennedy, May 31, 1988, MDL.

105. Appleby, "Logue's Record in Boston," iv, 25–26, 29, 30.

106. Collins, interview by de Varon, Tape 9, January 26, 1977, 7.

107. Logue, "A Look Back at Neighborhood Renewal in Boston," 345.

108. Keyes, *Rehabilitation Planning Game*, 15.

109. Stainton, *Urban Renewal and Planning in Boston*, 4.

110. "A Battle Is Over," editorial, *BSB*, December 3, 1966.

111. Bailey, *Lower Roxbury*, 26.

112. William J. Lasko, "Qualitative Analysis of Urban Renewal in Boston Under John Collins (1959-1967)" (paper submitted to Master's Paper Colloquium, URB 104, Spring 1979, Professor Norman Fainstein), 44, in possession of the author. For a similar conclusion: Associate Professor Joseph L. Bower and John W. Rosenblum (research assistant), "Harvard Business School Case on the Boston Redevelopment Authority," 1969, State Library of Massachusetts, State House, Boston, 19.

113. Langley Keyes, interview by Jim Vrabel, September 27, 2011, in Vrabel, *People's History of the New Boston*, 33.

114. Henry N. Cobb, interview by Lizabeth Cohen, June 8, 2010, New York, NY.

115. Henry Scagnoli, interview by Lizabeth Cohen, June 20, 2007, Boston, MA.

116. On Logue's mayoral run, see Logue, interview, Schussheim, 31; Logue, interview, Jones, Tape 1:1-11, Tape 3:21-24; O'Connor, *Building a New Boston*, 256-63; John Patrick Ryan, interview by Lizabeth Cohen, June 18, 2007, Cambridge, MA; "The Globe Questions the Candidates for Mayor—Edward Logue," *BG*, September 14, 1967.

117. Logue, interview, Steen, December 13, 1983, New York, NY, 35.

118. "Bold Boston Gladiator—Ed Logue: Planner Stirs Up a Ruckus and Battles Opposition to Build the Place of His Dreams," *Life*, December 24, 1965, 132. Communications that discuss Logue's possible run for mayor include in EJL, Series 6: David L. Marx to Logue, April 27, 1966, Box 150, Folder 432, which references two recent newspaper columns mentioning that Logue was considering running for mayor; Howard M. Kahn to Logue, December 28, 1966, Box 150, Folder 415, refers to a Frank Bucci column in the *Boston Herald-Traveler*; Ellen Logue to Margaret Logue, January 15, 1967, Box 150, Folder 425, which says, "Any decision yet re: Collins & the mayoralty? That would make an interesting year!" Much earlier in life, Logue expressed interest in entering politics: Logue to Resina Logue, August 19, 1945, EJL, Series 1, Box 4, Folder 68, in which he floated the idea of running for Philadelphia city councilman; Logue to Fred Rodell, July 31, 1948, Fred Rodell Papers, Haverford College Special Collections, Addition 1927-80, Box 11, Item 105, where Logue wrote, "What I really want to do eventually is get into politics."

119. Logue, "Boston, 1960-1967—Seven Years of Plenty," 96.

120. Logue, interview, Jones, Tape 3:21-24; Jane Howard, "Round One Was a Breeze for Louise," *Life*, October 13, 1967, 89-94; Homer Bigart, "Boston Mayoral Primary Pits Woman Foe of School Busing Against 9," *NYT*, September 24, 1967; Sara Davidson, "John Sears: A Blueblood with Yen for Melting Pot; the Candidates for Mayor III," *BG*, August 13, 1967; "John Winthrop Sears, 83; City Councilor Ran for Governor, *BG*, November 6, 2014; Sara Davidson, "Kevin White Always the Competitor; the Candidates for Mayor V," *BG*, August 27, 1967.

121. Scagnoli, interview.

122. Logue, interview, Jones, Tape 1:10. Logue told Ivan Steen, "And it's the nearest I've ever come to getting divorced"; Logue, interview, Steen, December 13, 1983, New York, NY, 37; Janet Bowler Fitzgibbons, interview by Lizabeth Cohen, June 21, 2007, Cambridge, MA.

123. Bower and Rosenblum, "Harvard Business School Case on the BRA," 12n1; Reilly, interview; Salvucci, interview; "Statement by Monsignor Francis J. Lally, Chairman of the BRA, on the occasion of the acceptance of Edward J. Logue's resignation of

his seven years as Administrator," August 2, 1967, EJL, Series 6, Box 150, Folder 424. The BRA staff held "A Farewell to Ed Logue," with skits and songs satirizing Logue's years at the BRA and anticipating his victory as mayor, which surely spurred campaign volunteering; invitation to "A Farewell to Ed Logue, August 3, 1967," EJL, Series 6, Box 151, Folder 450; Martin Adler and Michael Gruenbaum, "Skits for Ed Logue's Farewell Party," August 3, 1967, MDL.

124. Robert Litke, interview by Lizabeth Cohen, May 25, 2006, Somerset, NJ.

125. John A. Herfort, "Hi there, Gladtoseeya!" *BG*, September 24, 1967.

126. Nolan, interview.

127. I am grateful to John Stainton and Michael Gruenbaum for giving me a wonderful collection of Logue campaign materials, including buttons, bumper stickers, and brochures (hereafter Stainton Campaign Collection). On Irish parentage, "Ed Logue—the Man."

128. See Stainton Campaign Collection, such as *To meet the needs of the people . . . Ed Logue . . . builder of a Better Boston*, pamphlet; "Ed Logue for Mayor, He Can Do Most for Boston," card; *One man stands out . . .* , brochure.

129. Tom Wicker, "In the Nation: Boston Faces a Choice," *NYT*, August 27, 1967.

130. Reilly, interview; Salvucci made a similar point about attitudes in the Italian North End in Salvucci, interview. Collins was very slow to endorse Logue: Robert Kenney, "Collins Won't Seek Re-Election in Boston," *WP*, June 7, 1967; "Mayor Declines 3rd Term; Reviews Stewardship; Urges Continued Progress," *CR*, June 10, 1967; for quote, "Boston Mayor Contest Losing to Pennant Race," *LAT*, September 25, 1967; also see Andrew J. Glass, "Red Sox Upsetting Boston's Election," *WP*, September 24, 1967.

131. Alan Lupo, *Liberty's Chosen Home: The Politics of Violence in Boston* (Boston: Little, Brown, 1977), 97–113; Christopher Lydon, "Plot Charge Heats Mayoral Race," *BG*, September 2, 1967; Joseph A. Keblinsky, "White Stays on Hub Ballot; Logue Admits Role in Row," *BG*, September 6, 1967.

132. Logue, "Tales of a City Builder, Compared to What," memoir draft notes for "Chapter on Mistakes."

133. "Ed Logue: He Lives and Breathes Public Service; first of a series of profiles of candidates for mayor of Boston," *BG*, July 30, 1967; Howard Ziff, "Race for Mayor Chair Sets Political Boston Swinging," *WP*, August 20, 1967; O'Connor, *Building a New Boston*, 261; Andrew Ryan, "How the 1967 Mayoral Race Changed Boston," *BG*, October 21, 2017.

134. Min S. Lee, "Young Billy Logue Thinks of Calcutta," *BG*, September 27, 1967; Robert Hazen, interview by Lizabeth Cohen, June 14, 2007, New York, NY; Nolan, interview. For official election results, see *Annual Report of the Election Department for the Year 1967* (Boston: January 31, 1968), 46, 107.

135. Logue, interview, Jones, Tape 1:11; Litke, interview; Bowler Fitzgibbons, interview.

136. Within a few months he cut half of that debt, repaying the bank loan secured by his cousin. Also, Barry T. Hynes, Chairman, Friends of Ed Logue Committee, to Friend, n.d. but c. October 1967, inviting recipients to a dinner at twenty-five dollars a person to help pay off Logue's campaign debt; Stainton Campaign Collection.

137. The architects signing the 1967 letter were Nelson Aldrich, Ed Barnes, Pietro

Belluschi, Peter Chermayeff, Joseph Eldredge, Norman Fletcher, Samuel Glaser, Victor Gruen, Huson Jackson, Philip Johnson, Eugene Kennedy, Carl Koch, James Lawrence, Michael McKinnell, Sy Mintz, Lawrence Perkins, Joseph Richardson, Paul Rudolph, Edwin T. Steffian, Hugh Stubbins, and Donald Stull; "Architects for Logue" solicitation letter, July 1967, with handwritten Walter Gropius instruction to send one hundred dollars, and Logue to Walter Gropius, August 23, 1967, thanking him for the contribution, with a handwritten note, Bauhaus-Archiv, Berlin, Series GS 19, Folder 400; Peter Lucas, "Architect Rapped for Aiding Logue," *BH*, August 22, 1967; Christopher Lydon, "Hynes and Son Backing Logue," *BG*, August 16, 1967; Ted Liebman, interview by Lizabeth Cohen, October 15, 2006, New York, NY, on making his first political contribution to Logue's campaign.

138. Slavet, interview.

139. Keyes, *Rehabilitation Planning Game*, 158; "A Split Vote," *BSB*, October 5, 1967. The Snowdens were active organizers of the Roxbury–South End–Dorchester Logue for Mayor Committee; their campaign activities are well documented in FH, Box 66, Folder 2726; and Snowden Papers, Box 6/7, Folder 246 (Political Campaigns—Ed Logue), Northeastern University Archives and Special Collections; Herbert Gleason, interview by Lizabeth Cohen, May 30, 2007, Cambridge, MA, where he recounted that by 1967 Melnea Cass was no longer a fan of Logue's and supported White for mayor.

140. UPA Meeting Minutes, July 12, 1967, UPA, Box 12, Folder 5.

141. UPA Meeting Minutes, October 4, 1967, UPA, Box 12, Folder 5; UPA Meeting Minutes, December 13, 1967, UPA, Box 12, Folder 5, where it was announced that John Stainton was leaving the BRA.

142. Logue, interview, Steen, December 13, 1983, New York, NY, 37–38; Anthony Yudis, "Logue Has Decided He'll Stay Here," *BG*, October 22, 1967. Correspondence around Logue applying for admission to the Massachusetts Bar in MDL: Logue to Lewis Weinstein, October 25, 1967; Judge Herbert S. MacDonald to Logue, October 30, 1967; Lewis H. Weinstein to Board of Bar Examiners, November 1, 1967. Logue's papers make reference to job inquiries he received from Los Angeles, San Francisco, Cleveland, and Baltimore; also "Logue Weighs Los Angeles Renewal Job," *BH*, October 4, 1967; George B. Merry, "Logue Heads for Wider Scope," *CSM*, April 30, 1968.

143. Slavet, interview; Logue, interview, Jones, Tape 1:12. Logue was also named one of the first two research associates of the Institute of Politics at the JFK School, Harvard, and a visiting associate of the Harvard-MIT Joint Center for Urban Studies; "Kenny Institute Names Lindsay, Logue Associates," *Crimson*, January 15, 1968.

144. Logue, interview, Schussheim, 32.

7. Constructing a "Great Society" in New York

1. Sydney H. Schanberg, "Governor Offers a $6 Billion Plan to Rebuild Slums; Calls for Legislature to Set Up Agency with 'Drastic' Power Over Localities," *NYT*, February 28, 1968; the article was on the front page, top-left column.

2. Frank Lynn, "Rockefeller Will Propose a Community Bond Issue," *NYT*, January 21, 1971.

3. Logue commentary in *Rockefeller in Retrospect: The Governor's New York Legacy*, ed. Gerald Benjamin and T. Norman Hurd (Albany, NY: Nelson A. Rockefeller Institute of Government, 1984), 207. At a press conference in February 1968, Rockefeller introduced Logue as "the ablest, young, creative, imaginative developer in this country . . . successful . . . because of a tremendous personality and the drive and ability to break through red tape"; transcript of Nelson A. Rockefeller news conference, February 27, 1968, 13–14, quoted in *Restoring Credit and Confidence: A Reform Program for New York State and Its Public Authorities; A Report to the Governor by the New York State Moreland Act Commission on the Urban Development Corporation and Other State Financing Agencies* (hereafter *Moreland*), March 31, 1976, 245.

4. Logue, interview, Jones, Tape 1:14–16; Logue, interview, Steen, December 13, 1983, New York, NY, 51–53; Logue, interview, Schussheim, 32; Stephen Lefkowitz, interview by Lizabeth Cohen, June 14, 2007, New York, NY.

5. *NYSUDC Annual Report 1972*, 68; Louis K. Loewenstein, *The New York State Urban Development Corporation: Private Benefits, Public Costs, an Evaluation of a Noble Experiment* (Washington, DC: Council of State Planning Agencies, 1980), 14, 20–22.

6. Lawrence Goldman, interview by Lizabeth Cohen, May 3, 2010, Newark, NJ; Goldman felt that both favored executive authority over legislative. The reporter Martin Nolan said each was a "get-things-done-kind of guy"; Martin Nolan, interview by Lizabeth Cohen, May 24, 2007, Cambridge, MA.

7. My understanding of Nelson Rockefeller is primarily based on the following sources: Richard Norton Smith, *On His Own Terms: A Life of Nelson Rockefeller* (New York: Random House, 2014); Peter Siskind, "Shades of Black and Green: The Making of Racial and Environmental Liberalism in Nelson Rockefeller's New York," *JUH* 34, no. 2 (January 2008): 243–65; Academy of Political Science, *Governing New York State: The Rockefeller Years* 31, no. 3 (May 1974), particularly Robert H. Connery, "Nelson A. Rockefeller as Governor," and Frank S. Kristof, "Housing." One of his closest advisers, James Cannon, noted that "Rockefeller disdained the legislative process." When often asked to run for the Senate, he sneered that "it's just a bag of wind up there"; James Cannon, interview by Lizabeth Cohen, April 7, 2010, Washington, DC.

8. Michael Kramer and Sam Roberts, *"I Never Wanted to Be Vice-President of Anything!": An Investigative Biography of Nelson Rockefeller* (New York: Basic Books, 1976), 145; Rockefeller quote in Siskind, "Shades of Black and Green," 245.

9. Loewenstein, *Private Benefits, Public Costs*, 64; MLogue, interview; Peter Marcuse, "Comparative Analysis of Federally-Aided Low-and Moderate-Income Housing Programs," *JH* 26, no. 10 (November 1969): 536–39.

10. My discussion of the UDC is based on a large number of sources, including Eleanor L. Brilliant, *The Urban Development Corporation: Private Interests and Public Authority* (Lexington, MA: Lexington Books, D. C. Heath, 1975); Loewenstein, *Private Benefits, Public Costs*; Louis K. Loewenstein, "The New York State Urban Development Corporation—a Forgotten Failure or a Precursor of the Future?," *JAIP* 44, no. 3 (July 1978): 261–73; Yonah Freemark, "The Entrepreneurial State: New York's Urban Development Corporation, an Experiment to Take Charge of Affordable

Housing Production" (Ph.D. dissertation, MIT, 2013); Siskind, "Shades of Black and Green"; Logue, "Goals, Policies, Prospects of the New York State Urban Development Corporation," July 1972; William K. Reilly and S. J. Schulman, "The State Urban Development Corporation: New York's Innovation," *Urban Lawyer* 1 (Summer 1969): 129–46; Steven R. Weisman, "Nelson Rockefeller's Pill: The UDC," *WM*, June 1975, 35–44; Vincent J. Moore, "Politics, Planning, and Power in New York State: The Path from Theory to Reality," *JAIP* 37, no. 2 (March 1971): 66–77. The legislation creating the UDC is New York State Urban Development Corporation Acts of 1968.

11. Robert H. Connery and Gerald Benjamin, *Rockefeller of New York: Executive Power in the Statehouse* (Ithaca, NY: Cornell University Press, 1979), 262; Brilliant, *Urban Development Corporation*, 23, 26, 35 for more on David Rockefeller's philosophy of public-private partnerships.

12. Quoted in Smith, *On His Own Terms*, xxxiv.

13. Julilly Kohler-Hausmann, *Getting Tough: Welfare and Imprisonment in 1970s America* (Princeton, NJ: Princeton University Press, 2017), 29–120; for how the growth of the Conservative Party in New York pressured Rockefeller, "Lindsay the Democrat," *NYT*, August 12, 1971.

14. Loewenstein, *Private Benefits, Public Costs*, 64.

15. Cary Reich, *The Life of Nelson A. Rockefeller: Worlds to Conquer 1908–1958* (New York: Doubleday, 1996), 65; James E. Underwood and William J. Daniels, *Governor Rockefeller in New York: The Apex of Pragmatic Liberalism in the United States* (Westport, CT: Greenwood Press, 1982), 22–23.

16. Daniel Okrent, *Great Fortune: The Epic of Rockefeller Center* (New York: Viking, 2003); Connery and Benjamin, *Rockefeller of New York*, 28; Joseph E. Pepsico, *The Imperial Rockefeller: A Biography of Nelson Rockefeller* (New York: Simon and Schuster, 1982), 59.

17. The most important source on public authorities is Gail Radford, *The Rise of the Public Authority: Statebuilding and Economic Development in Twentieth-Century America* (Chicago: University of Chicago Press, 2013); also see Annmarie Hauck Walsh, *The Public's Business: The Politics and Practices of Government Corporations* (Cambridge, MA: MIT Press, 1980); Brilliant, *Urban Development Corporation*, 5, 41–48.

18. Annmarie Hauck Walsh, "Public Authorities and the Shape of Decision Making," in *Urban Politics, New York Style*, ed. Jewel Bellush and Dick Netzer (Armonk, NY: M. E. Sharpe, 1990), 205.

19. Walsh, *Public's Business*, 98–100; Jameson W. Doig, *Empire on the Hudson: Entrepreneurial Vision and Political Power at the Port of New York Authority* (New York: Columbia University Press, 2001), 282–83.

20. New York State, Office of the Controller, Division of Audits and Accounts, Public Authorities in New York State, December 31, 1974, in Kramer and Roberts, *"I Never Wanted to Be Vice-President of Anything!"* 146, 153. Also, Hilary Botein, "New York State Housing Policy in Postwar New York City: The Enduring Rockefeller Legacy," *JUH* 35, no. 6 (September 2009): 833–52, 842 for new authorities under Rockefeller.

21. Mitchell-Lama, officially the New York State Limited-Profit Housing Companies Act

of 1955, was landmark legislation that lowered the cost of rental housing; Kristof, "Housing," 191; Brilliant, *Urban Development Corporation*, 32–35; Loewenstein, *Private Benefits, Public Costs*, 5; Whitehouse, "Major Builders Determined to Spur Housing in City," *NYT*, April 4, 1971. On the HFA and its mission to support middle-class housing, see Walsh, *Public's Business*, 133–40; Botein, "New York State Housing Policy in Postwar New York City," passim; and Adam Tanaka, "Private Projects, Public Ambitions: Large-Scale, Middle-Income Housing in New York City" (Ph.D. dissertation, Harvard, 2018). New York State's HFA became a national model, inspiring seventy-nine similar authorities in thirty states by 1975; Walsh, "Public Authorities and the Shape of Decision Making," 203.

22. Treasurer Robert Moss quote in *Moreland*, 124.
23. Nelson A. Rockefeller, *Unity, Freedom and Peace: A Blueprint for Tomorrow* (New York: Random House, 1968), 46–49, 39, in Botein, "New York State Housing Policy in Postwar New York City," 837.
24. On Woods and general-purpose bonds, see *Rockefeller in Retrospect*, 208; Logue, interview, Steen, February 4, 1985, Lincoln, MA, 8; Loewenstein, *Private Benefits, Public Costs*, 34–35.
25. Quoted in Weisman, "Nelson Rockefeller's Pill," 38.
26. Lefkowitz, interview.
27. David K. Shipler, "Sense of Crisis Over Housing Grips Officials," *NYT*, November 16, 1969; typical of Logue's frustration with the current levels of funding is Logue, "NAHRO's 1968 Workshops in Community Development," *JH* 25, no. 9 (October 1968): 459–62.
28. National Advisory Commission on Civil Disorders (Kerner Commission), *Report of the National Commission on Civil Disorders* (New York: Bantam, 1968); President's Committee on Urban Housing (Kaiser Committee), *A Decent Home* (Washington, DC: Government Printing Office, 1968); *Building the American City: Report of the National Commission on Urban Problems to the Congress and to the President of the United States* (Washington, DC: Government Printing Office, 1968).
29. Quoted in Samuel Kaplan, "Bridging the Gap from Rhetoric to Reality: The New York State Urban Development Corporation," *AF* 131, no. 4 (November 1969): 73.
30. Kaplan, "Bridging the Gap."
31. For Logue's defense of government, see "Planning and Urban Renewal: A Discussion with Edward Logue," in Franziska Porges Hosken, *The Functions of Cities* (Cambridge, MA: Schenkman, 1973), 116.
32. Quote in Linda Charlton, "Ronan Says Rockefeller Made Loans as a Friend," *NYT*, November 19, 1974; Frank Lynn, "Rockefeller Gives Details of Gifts to 20 Recipients," *NYT*, October 12, 1974; "Text of Rockefeller Letter and a List of Recipients of Gifts and Loans by Him," *NYT*, October 12, 1974; William Greider, "Rocky Gift to Author Reported," *WP*, October 13, 1974; Robert Lanzner, "Logue to Be Sacked by N.Y. Governor," *BG*, January 10, 1975; for $65,000 salary, see Ursula Cliff, "UDC Scorecard," *Design and Environment* 3, no. 2 (Summer 1972): 63; also see Logue, interview, Steen, February 4, 1985, Lincoln, MA, 12–17.
33. MLogue, interview. Colleagues were shocked when the news came out. For example, Larry Goldman said, "I was disappointed in him." Allan Talbot recalled, "Everyone's

jaw dropped when that came out." Goldman, interview; Allan Talbot, interview by Lizabeth Cohen, June 13, 2007, New York, NY.

34. Loewenstein, *Private Benefits, Public Costs*, 10-13.

35. "Statement by Governor Nelson A. Rockefeller, April 5, 1968," *Public Papers of Nelson Rockefeller*, 1968, 1039, in Smith, *On His Own Terms*, 522; for more on Rockefeller's relationship with King, see 371, 395, 457-58, and related to the assassination, funeral, and UDC, 521-25, 527, 628.

36. The struggle against regional and state authorities for usurping the power of local government went on elsewhere as well; see Louise Nelson Dyble, "The Defeat of the Golden Gate Authority: A Special District, a Council of Governments, and the Fate of Regional Planning in the San Francisco Bay Area," *JUH* 34, no. 2 (January 2008): 287-308.

37. Logue, interview, Jones, Tape 3:2; also see Smith, *On His Own Terms*, 525-26; Kaplan, "Bridging the Gap," 71.

38. Sam Roberts, "Robert R. Douglass, Adviser to Rockefellers, Dies at 85," *NYT*, December 7, 2016.

39. Logue, interview, Jones, Tape 1:18.

40. *"Let There Be Commitment": A Housing, Planning, Development Program for New York City, Report of a Study Group of the Institute of Public Administration to Mayor John V. Lindsay* (New York: Institute of Public Administration, 1966), 12; Steven V. Roberts, "One Housing Body Is Urged for City," *NYT*, June 15, 1966; Steven V. Roberts, "Homes for Millions Proposed for City in Next Ten Years," *NYT*, October 2, 1966; Editorial: To Rejuvenate New York," *NYT*, October 2, 1966; Mort Young, "Logue's Committee Outlines Plans to Reorganize Housing," *World Journal Tribune*, November 4, 1966. For Logue's recounting of this failed recruitment, see Logue, interview, Steen, December 13, 1983, New York, NY, 45. For the opposition to Logue: Michael D. Appleby, "Logue's Record in Boston: An Analysis of His Renewal and Planning Activities, with a Foreword and Summary by Herbert J. Gans for the Steering Committee, Council for New York Housing and Planning Policy, Funded by the Normal Foundation, May 1966," EJL, 2002 Accession, Box 22, Folder "Logue's Record in Boston by Michael Appleby"; and a collection of flyers and correspondence opposing Logue from 1966, including a broadside titled "Keep the Boston Bulldozer out of New York City!" in the Papers of the Metropolitan Council on Housing, Box 65, Folder 38, Tamiment Library, New York University.

41. Logue, interview, Steen, December 13, 1983, New York, NY, 39-42; Steven V. Roberts, "Civil Unit Backs Planning Agency," *NYT*, March 14, 1966; Steven V. Roberts, "Boston's Mastermind in Renewal Weighs Lindsay's Offer for a Post in City," *NYT*, May 1, 1966; Steven V. Roberts, "Logue Won't Take City Renewal Job," *NYT*, November 16, 1966; Robert Hannan, "Report: Logue Rejects N.Y. Post; His Reaction: I Like Boston," *BH*, November 16, 1966; Steven V. Roberts, "Mayor and the Slums: Logue's Rejection of Post Underscores City Housing Ills," *NYT*, November 17, 1966.

42. Logue, interview, Steen, March 3, 1986, Lincoln, MA, 40-41, 44-45; also in Logue, interview, Jones, Tape 1:24-25; for a helpful analysis of the triangle of Rockefeller,

Lindsay, and Logue, see Martin Nolan, "3 Strong Wills Converge in New York," *BG*, June 22, 1968.

43. Sydney H. Schanberg, "State's Urban Agency to Be Led by Logue, Who Spurned City Job," *NYT*, April 27, 1968.

44. My treatment of the Bedford Stuyvesant Restoration Corporation and Logue's role is based on Mitchell Sviridoff, ed., *Inventing Community Renewal: The Trials and Errors That Shaped the Modern Community Development Corporation* (New York: Community Development Research Center, New School University Milano Graduate School, 2004), 67–91, 198–240, quote from Judge Jones on 83; Logue, interview by Roberta Greene, January 23, 1976, New York, NY, for the Robert F. Kennedy Oral History Project at the John F. Kennedy Library, Boston, MA; Michael Woodsworth, *Battle for Bed-Stuy: The Long War on Poverty in New York City* (Cambridge, MA: Harvard University Press, 2016), 236–64; Karen Ferguson, *Town Down: The Ford Foundation, Black Power, and the Reinvention of Racial Liberalism* (Philadelphia: University of Pennsylvania Press, 2013), 220–31; Edward R. Schmitt, *President of the Other America: Robert Kennedy and the Politics of Poverty* (Amherst: University of Massachusetts Press, 2010), 146–68; Brian Purnell, "'What We Need Is Brick and Mortar': Race, Gender, and Early Leadership of the Bedford Stuyvesant Restoration Corporation," in *The Business of Black Power: Community Development, Capitalism, and Corporate Responsibility in Postwar America*, ed. Laura Warren Hill and Julia Rabig (Rochester, NY: University of Rochester Press, 2012), 217–44; Tom Adam Davies, "Black Power in Action: The Bedford Stuyvesant Restoration Corporation, Robert F. Kennedy, and the Politics of the Urban Crisis," *JAH* 100, no. 3 (December 2013): 736–60; Kimberley Johnson, "Community Development Corporations, Participation, and Accountability: The Harlem Urban Development Corporation and the Bedford Stuyvesant Restoration Corporation," *Annals*, AAPSS 594 (July 2004): 109–24; "To Save a Slum," *Newsweek*, November 20, 1967; Leroy F. Aarons, "RFK Announces Big N.Y. Anti-Slum Program," *WP*, December 11, 1966; Wolf Von Eckardt, "'Bed-Stuy' and Urban Attitudes," *WP*, October 20, 1970.

45. Logue also got caught in the political crossfires of two boards competing in the early years. Activists cynically referred to them as the "Black Board" (the Bedford-Stuyvesant Renewal and Rehabilitation Corporation, representing the community) and the "White Board" (the Bedford-Stuyvesant Development and Services Corporation, representing the funders).

46. Logue, interview, Steen, February 4, 1985, Lincoln, MA, 17–18.

47. Loewenstein, "Forgotten Failure," 261.

48. Brilliant, *Urban Development Corporation*, 3, 71. She notes that Paul Davidoff, the well-known advocacy planner, opposed the UDC in March 1968 because he feared it would not build enough low-income housing. His view would change.

49. Logue, interview, Jones, Tape 1:21–22; Logue, interview, Steen, February 4, 1985, Lincoln, MA, 27, 31; Schanberg, "State's Urban Agency to Be Led by Logue, Who Spurned City Job."

50. *Moreland*, 103; Loewenstein, *Private Benefits, Public Costs*, 6, 123–24; Brilliant, *Urban Development Corporation*, 50–54, 73–74, 102–3.

51. Logue commentary in *Rockefeller in Retrospect*, 209; "'New Towns' Plan Faces Tax Hurdle," *NYT*, February 8, 1970; Brilliant, *Urban Development Corporation*, 99–100; *Moreland*, 103–4.

52. Loewenstein, "Forgotten Failure," 261, 272; Loewenstein, *Private Benefits, Public Costs*, 38, 124; Peter Kihss, "State Starts Plans for 2 'New Towns,'" *NYT*, August 4, 1969.

53. Logue, "Goals, Policies, Prospects of the New York State Urban Development Corporation," July 1972, 4.

54. David K. Shipler, "Across the State, Renewal Hopes Rise," *NYT*, April 18, 1969; *NYSUDC Annual Report 1969*, 43; *NYSUDC Annual Report 1971*, 67.

55. On Newburgh: Douglas V. Clarke, "State Development Unit Will Assist Newburgh," *NYT*, August 18, 1968; Clarke, "State Urban Aid Agency Maps Newburgh Debut," *NYT*, January 26, 1969; Richard Schickel, "New York's Mr. Urban Renewal," *NYT Magazine*, March 1, 1970; *NYSUDC Annual Report 1974*, 64; Freemark, "Entrepreneurial State," 121–23.

On Rochester: Freemark, "Entrepreneurial State," 124–25, 190–96; Loewenstein, *Private Benefits, Public Costs*, 49–51; Logue, interview, Jones, Tape 2:1; Logue, interview, Steen, April 9, 1990, Boston, MA, 37–42; *NYSUDC Annual Report 1969*, 39–41; *NYSUDC Annual Report 1970*, 47, 60–61; Rochester Public Library, Local History Division, Pamphlet File: "Housing—Projects (Urban Development Corporation)" and "City Planning-Industrial Centers," miscellaneous brochures; *NYSUDC Annual Report 1971*, 38, 45, 47, 49, 51, 70; *NYSUDC Annual Report 1972*, 17, 21, 48, 51–52, 77, 80–81, 84; *NYSUDC Annual Report 1973*, 16–17, 21–22, 24–25, 27, 30, 42–43; *NYSUDC Annual Report 1974*, 13, 36, 63.

On the Buffalo Rudolph project: Logue, interview, Steen, February 4, 1985, Lincoln, MA, 32–33; Logue, interview, Steen, April 9, 1990, Boston, MA, 20; Mark Byrnes, "The Slow Death of a Brutalist Vision for Buffalo," *Atlantic CityLab*, June 10, 2015; *NYSUDC Annual Report 1969*, 24–25, 53; *NYSUDC Annual Report 1970*, 28–29, 68; *NYSUDC Annual Report 1971*, 38; *NYSUDC Annual Report 1972*, 17; *NYSUDC Annual Report 1973*; *NYSUDC Annual Report 1974*.

On Schomburg Plaza: *NYSUDC Annual Report 1971*, 24, 34; *NYSUDC Annual Report 1973*, 35; Hilary Ballon, "Schomburg Plaza," in *Affordable Housing in New York: The People, Places, and Policies That Transformed a City*, ed. Nicholas Dagen Bloom and Matthew Gordon Lasner (Princeton, NJ: Princeton University Press, 2016), 219–23.

On Niagara Falls: Logue, interview, Steen, January 16, 1991, Boston, MA, 27–28; Terence Cooper, "Downtown Urban Renewal Results in Economic, Social, Aesthetic Restoration for Niagara Falls," *JH* 36, no. 1 (January 1979): 25–28; *NYSUDC Annual Report 1969*, 38, 53; *NYSUDC Annual Report 1970*, 45; *NYSUDC Annual Report 1971*, 41, 70; *NYSUDC Annual Report 1972*, 22; *NYSUDC Annual Report 1973*, 12, 17; *NYSUDC Annual Report 1974*, 7, 45, 52.

On Hurricane Agnes: Lawrence Van Gelder, "$72-Million Plan Is Proposed to Redevelop Elmira," *NYT*, October 15, 1972; *NYSUDC Annual Report 1972*, 22–23, 25–33; *NYSUDC Annual Report 1973*, 13, 69; *NYSUDC Annual Report 1974*, 52; Logue, interview, Steen, January 6, 1991, Boston, MA, 29.

On Carlken Manor: *NYSUDC Annual Report 1971*, 50, 70; *NYSUDC Annual Report 1973*, 27.

56. On the anticipated population increase, *New Communities for New York: A Report Prepared by the New York State Urban Development Corporation and the New York State Office of Planning Coordination*, 1970, 3, 11.

57. David K. Shipler, "Across the State, Renewal Hopes Rise," *NYT*, April 18, 1969; Lindsay quote from *NYDN* in Maura Ewing, "Innovation and Neglect: Sea Rise and Sea Park East," *Urban Omnibus*, November 19, 2014, http://urbanomnibus.net/2014/11/innovation-and-neglect-sea-rise-and-sea-park-east/.

58. Quote in Nolan, "3 Strong Wills Converge in New York"; Logue, interview, Steen, March 3, 1986, Lincoln, MA, 42–43.

59. David K. Shipler, "The Changing City: Housing Paralysis," *NYT*, June 5, 1969; Shipler, "Sense of Crisis Over Housing Grips Officials," *NYT*, November 16, 1969; Walsh, "Public Authorities and the Shape of Decision Making," 204; also see Logue, interview, Jones, Tape 2:1–3 on how New York City came around.

60. Richard Rogin, "New Town on a New York Island Named Welfare," *City* 5, no. 3 (May–June 1971): 44.

61. Jay Curtis Getz, "The Progressive Technician and Mr. Urban Renewal: Lawrence Veiller, Edward Logue, and the Evolution of Planning for Low-Income Housing" (M.A. thesis, University of Illinois at Urbana-Champaign, 1990), 115; *NYSUDC Annual Report 1969*, 29; *NYSUDC Annual Report 1971*, 20–21.

62. Logue, interview, Steen, March 3, 1986, Lincoln, MA, 122–23; Logue, interview, Jones, Tape 2:3–4.

63. On Janet Murphy, see Goldman, interview; Lefkowitz, interview. On Lefkowitz and Logue, Lefkowitz, interview; Smith, *On His Own Terms*, 671; Logue, interview, Jones, Tape 1:23 for Logue's awareness that Lefkowitz was sent to watch him.

64. Ted Liebman, interview by Lizabeth Cohen, October 15, 2006, New York, NY. Liebman began working at the UDC in August 1969.

65. Lawrence P. Goldman, Eulogy at Edward J. Logue Memorial Service, April 27, 2000, Boston, 2; Goldman comment, "Operations: How the UDC Program Worked," Panel No. 1, "Policy and Design for Housing: Lessons of the Urban Development Corporation, 1968–1975" conference, CUNY Graduate Center, June 11, 2005, transcript, 33.

66. Richard Kahan, interview by Lizabeth Cohen, June 15, 2007, New York, NY.

67. Paul Byard, "Edward J. Logue, AIA Memorial," at "2nd Annual Ratensky Housing Lecture Celebrating the Work of Housing and Planning Czar Edward J. Logue," Seagram's Tower, New York, NY, May 24, 2000.

68. *Housing New York: Ed Logue and His Architects*, brochure from the exhibition presented by the Architectural League and the Municipal Art Society, Urban Center, New York, NY, February 5–April 14, 2001, 3.

69. Quote in Logue, interview, Jones, Tape 3:28–29; Logue, interview, Steen, March 3, 1986, Lincoln, MA, 38; Joseph P. Fried, "The Roof Falls In," *Nation*, August 16, 1975, 104; John Fischer, "The Easy Chair: Notes from the Underground," *Harper's*, February 1970, 14.

70. Lefkowitz, interview; Logue, interview, Steen, March 3, 1986, Lincoln, MA, 38;

Anthony Pangaro, interview by Cohen, June 24, 2009, Boston, MA; "Legislator Assails 'Logue's Lush Lair,'" *NYT*, March 27, 1971.

71. Alan S. Oser, "Logue Forecasts 1973 Slowdown in U.D.C. Pace," *NYT*, August 12, 1973.

72. Logue, "NAHRO's 1968 Workshops in Community Development," 461.

73. Reilly and Schulman, "State Urban Development Corporation," 137.

74. Franklin Whitehouse, "Major Builders Determined to Spur Housing in City," *NYT*, April 4, 1971.

75. Kristof, "Housing," 192.

76. Logue, interview, Steen, March 3, 1986, Lincoln, MA, 2.

77. Loewenstein, *Private Benefits, Public Costs*, 10–11, 16–19; Allan R. Talbot, "The Easy Chair: Boston's Bristly Mr. Logue," *Harper's*, November 1966, 30; Kristof, "Housing," 196–97; Goldman, interview; Lefkowitz, interview.

78. Richard Ravitch, interview by Lizabeth Cohen, October 22, 2007, New York, NY.

79. Logue, interview, Jones, Tape 4:7; "After the Pratfall: UDC Dusts Off the Debris of Default," *AR* 158, no. 6 (Mid-October 1975): 124; also Loewenstein, "Forgotten Failure," 263.

80. Talbot, "Easy Chair: Boston's Bristly Mr. Logue," 28.

81. Kristof, "Housing," 189, 195; Fischer, "Easy Chair: Notes from the Underground," 22; Brilliant, *Urban Development Corporation*, 109; *Moreland*, 126; Oser, "Logue Forecasts 1973 Slowdown in U.D.C. Pace," *NYT*, August 12, 1973.

82. Brilliant, *Urban Development Corporation*, 37–39, 51, 109; Loewenstein, "Forgotten Failure," 272; Loewenstein, *Private Benefits, Public Costs*, 30, 122; Lefkowitz, interview; Mary Perot Nichols, "On a Shifty Foundation: The Houses Rocky Built," *New Republic*, July 17, 1976, 27.

83. Logue, "A Summing Up," from the New York State Urban Development Corporation, Urban America, "The Proceedings of the Conference at Tarrytown," New York, NY, 1970, 221.

84. Brilliant, *Urban Development Corporation*, 27; also Talbot, interview.

85. Logue, interview, Steen, March 3, 1986, Lincoln, MA, 36, also 4, 46–47.

86. Kaplan, "Bridging the Gap," 72.

87. Brilliant, *Urban Development Corporation*, 75.

88. Logue, "NAHRO's 1968 Workshops in Community Development," 460; Logue, "What Sort of Future for Boston? A Look at Home from Abroad," *Boston University Journal* 18, no. 1 (Winter 1970): 49–50; Logue, interview by Franziska Porges Hosken, 1971, audiotape, Rotch Architecture and Design Library, MIT; "Rockefeller Asks City Plan Liaison," *NYT*, November 19, 1969; "New York Plan Makes Concentration a Virtue," *NYT*, November 23, 1969.

89. Logue, interview, Steen, October 31, 1986, Lincoln, MA, 6.

90. "The New City," in Robert A. M. Stern, *New Directions in American Architecture* (New York: George Braziller, 1969), 105–13; Steven Conn, *Americans Against the City: Anti-Urbanism in the Twentieth Century* (New York: Oxford University Press, 2014), 70–75, 94–113, 245–51, 266–69; Cathy D. Knepper, *Greenbelt, Maryland: A Living Legacy of the New Deal* (Baltimore: Johns Hopkins University Press, 2001); Julie D. Turner, "To Make America Over: The Greenbelt Towns of the New Deal" (Ph.D. dissertation,

Miami University, 2010); Nicholas Dagen Bloom, *Suburban Alchemy: 1960s New Towns and the Transformation of the American Dream* (Columbus: Ohio State University Press, 2001); Carol Corden, *Planned Cities: New Towns of Britain and America* (Beverly Hills, CA: Sage Library of Social Research, 1977); Mark Reinberger, "Peachtree City, Georgia: Progressivism in a Post-War Southern New Town," *JPH* 13, no. 3 (August 2014): 247–72; Logue, interview, Steen, December 2, 1988, Lincoln, MA, 34.

91. For a comprehensive survey of the substantial literature on New Towns, see Rosemary Wakeman, *Practicing Utopia: An Intellectual History of the New Town Movement* (Chicago: University of Chicago Press, 2016). Also D. Burtenshaw, M. Bateman, and G. J. Ashforth, *The City in Western Europe* (Chichester, UK: John Wiley and Sons, 1981), 284–302. For more on British New Towns, see "The New Towns Record, 1946–2002," primary sources compiled by Anthony Burton and Joyce Hartly (London: i-documentsystems, 2002); Frederic J. Osborn and Arnold Whittick, *New Towns: Their Origins, Achievements and Progress* (London: Leonard Hill, 1977); Stephen V. Ward, *Planning and Urban Change*, 2nd ed. (London: Sage Publications, 2004); John R. Gold, *The Practice of Modernism: Modern Architects and Urban Transformation, 1954–1972* (London: Routledge, 2007).

For other countries: Heikki von Hertzen and Paul D. Spreiregen, *Building a New Town: Finland's New Garden City Tapiola*, rev. ed. (Cambridge, MA: MIT Press, 1973); David Pass, *Vällingby and Farsta—from Idea to Reality* (Cambridge, MA: MIT Press, 1973); Kenny Cupers, *The Social Project: Housing Postwar France* (Minneapolis: University of Minnesota Press, 2014), 183–219; Jack A. Underhill with Paul Brace and James Rubenstein, *French National Urban Policy and the Paris Region New Towns* (Washington, DC: U.S. Department of Housing and Urban Development, 1980); Carlos C. Campbell, *New Towns: Another Way to Live* (Reston, VA: Reston Publishing, Prentice-Hall, 1976), "Learning from the Europeans," 233–40; Jennifer S. Mack, "New Swedes in the New Town," and Michelle Provoost, "WiMBY!'s New Collectives," in Kenny Cupers, *Use Matters: An Alternative History of Architecture* (London: Routledge, 2013), 121–37, 183–98.

92. Logue, interview, Steen, December 2, 1988, Lincoln, MA, 35; Logue, "The Need for Urban Growth Politics," *AIA Journal* 5, no. 5 (May 1971): 18–22; Logue, interview by Carlos Campbell, *New Towns: Another Way to Live*, 210.

93. "Fort Lincoln Urban Renewal Area," National Capital Planning Commission Redevelopment Land Agency, 1967; Jared Stout, "NCPC Best Plan for Racially Balanced 'New Town,'" *WP*, August 9, 1968; Wolf Von Eckardt, "Fort Lincoln: Tugging the Bottom Card," *WP*, March 23, 1969; Wolf Von Eckardt, "Holding Down the Fort: The Unfulfilled Promises of Ft. Lincoln," *WP*, January 26, 1980; Martha Derthick, "Defeat at Fort Lincoln," *Public Interest* 20 (Summer 1970): 3–39; Martha Derthick, *New Towns In-Town: Why a Federal Program Failed* (Washington, DC: Urban Institute, 1972); Howard R. Moskof, interview by Lizabeth Cohen, April 21, 2006, Chevy Chase, MD. Fort Lincoln New Town finally did get built by a private developer, with economic diversity in housing types but not race, as it is almost all black, with large representations of Jamaicans and Africans; Linda Wheeler, "Fort Lincoln: Finding a Leafy Enclave," *WP*, July 18, 1992; "LBJ's 'Great Society' Spawned Fort Lincoln Development Plan," *Common Denominator*, May 6, 2002; Clarence Williams,

"Hope Stirs in Fort Lincoln," *WP*, April 30, 2007; "Washington, DC (Fort Lincoln New Town)," NeighborhoodScout, https://www.neighborhoodscout.com/dc /washington/fort-lincoln-new-town.

94. Lefkowitz, interview, on speed of undertaking New Towns and staff tours; John Stainton, interview by Lizabeth Cohen, May 30, 2007, Jamaica Plain, MA. Overviews of the New Town Program in Robert T. Dormer, "Three New Towns," *JH*, February 1979, 87; Freemark, "Entrepreneurial State," 221–69.

95. *Syracuse Herald-Journal*, May 28, 1969, quoted in Harvey H. Kaiser, *The Building of Cities: Development and Conflict* (Ithaca, NY: Cornell University Press, 1978), 82; *Buffalo Evening News*, November 24, 1969, quoted in Ed Durbin, "Contesting Suburbia: The Struggle for Suburban Space in Western New York," Oxford University Paper, May 2012; Logue, "A Summing Up," from "The Proceedings of the Conference at Tarrytown," 1970, 224; Virginia Ross, "UDC: Detour on the Road to 'New Town,'" *Buffalo Magazine*, October 1971, 32; "Some Things Worked, Some Didn't; Subsidized Housing Faltered," *Syracuse Herald-American*, October 11, 2000.

96. On Lysander: *NYSUDC Annual Reports 1969, 1970, 1971, 1972, 1973*, and *1974*; Freemark, "Entrepreneurial State," 257–64; Weisman, "Nelson Rockefeller's Pill," 40 for Schlitz quote; Kaiser, "Lysander (Radisson)" chapter in *The Building of Cities: Development and Conflict*, 68–102; *Radisson: Building Today for Tomorrow*, supplement to *The Baldwinsville Messenger*, n.d.

97. Only a fraction of the scale planned for was actually built. On Audubon: "General Project Plan for the Amherst New Community," Kermit Carlyle Parsons Papers, #15-2-1420, Division of Rare and Manuscript Collections, Cornell University Library; *A New Community in Amherst, Vol. 1: The Plan* (New York: New York State Urban Development Corporation, Planning Consultants: Llewelyn-Davies Associates, n.d.); Durbin, "Contesting Suburbia"; David Foster Parker, "The Audubon Experiment in New Community Development" (DPA dissertation, SUNY Albany, 1980); *NYSUDC Annual Report 1969*, 46, 52; *NYSUDC Annual Report 1970*, 56, 69; *NYSUDC Annual Report 1971*, 40; *NYSUDC Annual Report 1972*, 20, 50–51; *NYSUDC Annual Report 1973*, 12; *NYSUDC Annual Report 1974*, 7.

98. My discussion of Roosevelt Island is based on Philip Johnson and John Burgee, *The Island Nobody Knows* (NYSUDC, October 1969); Yonah Freemark, "Roosevelt Island: Exception to a City in Crisis," *JUH* 37, no. 3 (May 2011): 355–83; Brilliant, *Urban Development Corporation*, 74–82, 110–17, 157; Judith Berdy and the Roosevelt Island Historical Society, *Images of America: Roosevelt Island* (Charleston, SC: Acadia, 2003); Timothy D. Berg, "Reshaping Gotham: The City Livable Movement and the Redevelopment of New York" (Ph.D. dissertation, Purdue University, 1999), 83–119; *Affordable Housing in New York*, 198–201, 234–39; Robert A. M. Stern, Thomas Mellins, and David Fishman, *New York 1960* (New York: Monacelli Press, 1995), 640–59; Municipal Art Society Panel on Logue and Roosevelt Island, March 7, 2001, full transcript, http://www.edlogue.org/docs/Logue-Roosevelet_03 -07-01.pdf. The papers for the Roosevelt Island Operating Corporation are in NYSA.

99. Johnson and Burgee, *Island Nobody Knows*; also see Philip Johnson and John Burgee, "The Plan for Welfare Island," technical report, October 7, 1969, prepared for NYSUDC.

100. Logue, interview, Jones, Tape 2:5. Logue and Johnson were already acquainted professionally; Philip Johnson to Logue, December 8, 1964, and Philip Johnson to Logue, February 21, 1966, EJL, Series 6, Box 150, Folder 413.

101. Ada Louise Huxtable, "This Time They Mean It," *NYT*, October 19, 1969; Huxtable, "Quality Design with Amenities," *NYT*, October 7, 1970; Peter Blake, "The Island Nobody Knows," *New York*, November 10, 1969, 63; Paul Goldberger, "New Urban Environment: Roosevelt Island Is Exhilarating Now but Status as Community Is Years Off," *NYT*, May 18, 1976; also Goldberger, *The City Observed: New York, a Guide to the Architecture of Manhattan* (New York: Random House, 1979), 331–37.

102. Anthony Bailey, "Manhattan's Other Island," *NYT*, December 1, 1974.

103. Johnson and Burgee, *Island Nobody Knows*, 3, 15.

104. Judy Berdy, "Preserving Social History on Roosevelt Island," May 23, 2005, Roosevelt Island Historical Society website, http://rihs.us/?page_id=2.

105. The idea for the renaming was originally proposed in a *NYT* editorial, April 12, 1970; Logue, interview, Jones, Tape 2:9; Stern et al., *New York 1960*, 649. The bust of Roosevelt had been sculpted by Jo Davidson in 1933. Also Logue, "Reflections on Roosevelt Island," July 2, 1998, 4, courtesy of Ivan Steen; Logue to Robert Geddes, September 21, 1992, courtesy of Robert Geddes; Logue, interview, Jones, Tape 2:16–18; Ted Liebman, interview by Yonah Freemark, April 25, 2008, on Kahn and Logue as fans of FDR; "Franklin D. Roosevelt Four Freedoms Park," http://www.fdrfourfreedomspark.org; "Timeline: The FDR Memorial for Roosevelt Island," provided by Cooper Union, *The Main Street Wire*, January 22, 2005; *Coming to Light: The Louis I. Kahn Monument to Franklin D. Roosevelt for New York City* (January 10–February 5, 2005), Irwin S. Chanin School of Architecture, Cooper Union for the Advancement of Science and Art, 2005, which includes in its frontispiece a quote from Kahn with his reasons for a garden and a room.

106. Dormer, "Three New Towns," 86–89; Freemark, "Roosevelt Island."

107. Logue blamed Johnson and Burgee for this "stupid mistake." They were told that the build-out had to be five thousand units of housing, but the plan they produced only accommodated four thousand, which obligated Logue to make changes, including building higher; Logue, interview, Steen, October 31, 1986, Lincoln, MA, 32.

108. Campbell, *New Towns: Another Way to Live*, 211; Logue, interview, Steen, October 31, 1986, Lincoln, MA, 32–33.

109. Logue, "Piecing the Political Pie," *Saturday Review*, May 15, 1971, 29; Logue, interview, Steen, October 31, 1986, Lincoln, MA, 15.

110. Campbell, *New Towns: Another Way to Live*, 209, 214.

111. Brochure, "UDC and Housing Policy," New York State Development Corporation, n.d., Kermit Carlyle Parsons Publications, Rare and Manuscript Collections, Cornell University Library, Collection #6691, Box 2.

112. Logue, "Goals, Policies, Prospects of the New York State Urban Development Corporation," July 1972, 7.

113. Rowland Evans and Robert Novak, *Lyndon B. Johnson: The Exercise of Power* (New York: New American Library, 1966), 429–33; Michael L. Gillette, *Launching the War on Poverty: An Oral History* (New York: Twayne, 1996), 32.

114. Logue, interviews, Steen, Lincoln, MA, October 31, 1986, 16–23, and March 3, 1986, 32, for Logue quotes; Logue, interview, Jones, Tape 4:21; also John Zuccotti,

interview by Lizabeth Cohen, December 10, 2007, New York, NY; Brilliant, *Urban Development Corporation*, 115–16; "'. . . Hung, Drawn and Quartered': The Adam Yarmolinsky Story," *BG*, August 13, 1964; Campbell, *New Towns: Another Way to Live*, 214; "Welfare Island: A Problem for Housing," *NYT*, February 16, 1972; Richard Ravitch, *So Much to Do: A Full Life of Business, Politics, and Confronting Fiscal Crisis* (New York: Public Affairs, 2014), 51–53.

115. Logue, interview, Jones, Tape 2:13–14.

116. Logue, "Goals, Policies, Prospects of the New York State Urban Development Corporation," 7; Logue made similar points for a larger audience in "Piecing the Political Pie," *Saturday Review*, 29.

117. "Roosevelt Island, Eastwood," Josep Lluís Sert Papers, Special Collections, HGSD (hereafter Sert).

118. Logue, interview, Jones, Tape 3:42; Ewing, "Innovation and Neglect: Sea Rise and Sea Park East."

119. Loewenstein, *Private Benefits, Public Costs*, 26.

120. Kahan, interview; *NYSUDC Annual Report 1972*, 39; "Celebration," *NYSUDC Annual Report 1973*, 51.

121. Edith Evans Asbury, "Pickets Mar Housing Dedication Here," *NYT*, July 26, 1972, in Freemark, "Entrepreneurial State," 159. Logue responded characteristically by saying that the protesters were only exercising their rights to "free speech"; Logue, interview, Steen, August 3, 1988, Boston, MA, 10.

122. Hilary Ballon, "Schomburg Plaza," in *Affordable Housing in New York*, 221.

123. "Learning from Twin Parks," *AF* 138, no. 5 (June 1973): 62–67; Freemark, "Entrepreneurial State," 147–48; Mariana Mogilevich, "Designing the Urban: Space and Politics in Lindsay's New York" (Ph.D. dissertation, Harvard, 2012), 169–86; *NYSUDC Annual Report 1973*, 35; Nicholai Ouroussoff, "By the Architects, for the People: A Trend for the 2010s," *NYT*, May 3, 2010; Susanne Schindler and Juliette Spertus, "A Few Days in the Bronx: From Co-op City to Twin Parks," *Urban Omnibus*, July 25, 2012, https://urbanomnibus.net/2012/07/a-few-days-in-the-bronx-from-co-op-city-to-twin-parks/; Yonah Freemark and Susanne Schindler, "Twin Parks," in *Affordable Housing in New York*, 226–30.

124. Jane Jacobs, interview by James Howard Kunstler, "Godmother of the American City," expanded from *Metropolis*, March 2001, in *Jane Jacobs: The Last Interview and Other Conversations* (Brooklyn, NY: Melville House, 2016), 81. In early 1967 on a speaking tour of Britain, Jacobs complained after spending an evening with planners, "These people are tiresome beyond belief about their new towns, etc. I wish they would just leave me alone"; quoted in Robert Kanigel, *Eyes on the Street: The Life of Jane Jacobs* (New York: Alfred A. Knopf, 2016), 260.

125. Margaret Mead, epilogue to Campbell, *New Towns: Another Way to Live*, 267.

126. Freemark, "Entrepreneurial State," 306; minority figure from 1974.

127. Mark Lamster, "Rethinking Roosevelt Island," *Design Observer*, January 14, 2012, http://designobserver.com/article.php?id=32188.

128. Logue, "A Summing Up," from "The Proceedings of the Conference at Tarrytown," 1970, 224.

129. Campbell, *New Towns: Another Way to Live*, 210.

130. William Lucy, "Logue on Cities," *Planning* 51 (August 1985): 15.

131. George M. Merry, "Logue Heads for Statewide Approach in N.Y. Renewal Setup," *CSM*, May 3, 1968.

132. My discussion of Logue and the UDC's involvement in Harlem, including the struggle over the state office building and the creation of the Harlem Urban Development Corporation, is based on the following sources: Johnson, "Community Development Corporations, Participation, and Accountability," 109–24; Louella Jacqueline Long and Vernon Ben Robinson, *How Much Power to the People? A Study of the New York State Urban Development Corporation's Involvement in Black Harlem* (New York: Faculty-Student Technical Assistance Project, Urban Center, Columbia University, 1971); *A Profile of the Harlem Area, Findings of the Harlem Task Force*, December 1973; *Harlem the Next Ten Years: A Proposal for Discussion* (New York: Harlem Urban Development Corporation, June 1974); Brian Goldstein, "'The Search for New Forms': Black Power and the Making of the Postmodern City," *JAH* 103, no. 2 (September 2016): 375–99, and the larger discussion in his book, *The Roots of Urban Renaissance: Gentrification and the Struggle over Harlem* (Cambridge, MA: Harvard University Press, 2017), 47–51, 85–118, 128–35, 143–52; Brilliant, *Urban Development Corporation*, 83–90, 118–32; Siskind, "Shades of Black and Green," 252–56, 260–62; Peter Siskind, "'Rockefeller's Vietnam'? Black Politics and Urban Development in Harlem, 1969–1974," paper presented at Gotham Center, CUNY Graduate Center, October 6, 2001; Ivan Steen, "Edward J. Logue, the New York State Urban Development Corporation, and New York City," paper presented at Gotham Center, CUNY Graduate Center, October 6, 2001, in possession of the author; and relevant *Amsterdam News* articles, 1968–1982.

133. "Harlem Towers Signal New Day," *Amsterdam News*, February 10, 1968.

134. Charlayne Hunter, "State Aide Assailed on Proposed Plan for Site in Harlem," *NYT*, December 12, 1969.

135. Ada Louise Huxtable, "The State Office Building Dilemma," *NYT*, November 2, 1969, in Siskind, "Shades of Black and Green," 255.

136. "State Building Now Postponed; Rocky Gives In to Area," *Amsterdam News*, July 5, 1969.

137. Charlayne Hunter, "Development Unit Set Up for Harlem," *NYT*, July 14, 1971; Bill Kovach, "State Unit Offers Aid on Facilities for Harlem Site," *NYT*, September 19, 1969, on Logue's search for a representative group.

138. Harlem Urban Development Corporation, "The Harlem Urban Development Corporation: A Review of Structure, Programs, Performance," 7, in Steen, "Edward J. Logue . . . and New York City," 8.

139. Temporary Commission of Investigation of the State of New York, *An Investigation into the Creation of the Harlem Urban Development Corporation and Its Operations from 1981–1995* (New York, April 1998).

140. Nelson Rockefeller to Edward Logue, January 15, 1973, EJL, Box 321, Folder "Correspondence: Nelson A. Rockefeller (1973 Jan–Feb)," and Edward Logue to Nelson Rockefeller, September 22, 1971, EJL, Box 321, Folder "Correspondence: Hugh L. Carey (1974–75)" in Freemark, "Entrepreneurial State, 138.

141. Freemark, "Entrepreneurial State," 138.

142. Rudy Johnson, "Less Profit Seen in Ghetto Housing," *NYT*, March 31, 1973.

143. *NYSUDC Annual Report 1973*, 64. It is worth noting that Logue's years at the UDC corresponded with the U.S. Department of Labor's implementing of the Philadelphia Plan, a requirement to set goals and timetables in hiring minority workers within the highly discriminatory construction trades.

144. "Harlem on the Move—State Office Building Opening," *Amsterdam News*, March 16, 1974.

145. *NYSUDC Annual Report 1972*, 72.

146. Logue, interview, Jones, Tape 4:11–12.

147. Campbell, *New Towns: Another Way to Live*, 209.

148. Logue, interview, Steen, August 3, 1988, Boston, MA; *NYT*, July 10, 1973, quoted in Steen, "Edward J. Logue . . . and New York City," 9; *NYSUDC Annual Report 1973*, 9. Many years later, Richard Kahan would claim that Logue's affirmative-action record at the UDC "set a standard for a long period of time"; introduction by Kahan, Municipal Art Society Panel on Logue and Roosevelt Island, March 7, 2001, transcript, 1.

149. Logue, interview, Steen, January 16, 1991, Boston, MA, 34.

150. "Statement by Edward J. Logue, President and Chief Executive Officer," *Roosevelt Island Housing Competition, New York State Urban Development Corporation*, 1974, 3.

151. "Appraisal, by Werner Seligmann," in "Assessing Broadway East," *PA* 55, no. 10 (October 1974): 62. On Seligmann's Elm Street Housing, see Charles Moore, "After a New Architecture: The Best Shape for a Chimera," *Oppositions* 3 (May 1974); "Scattered Site Hill Town," *PA* 54, no. 5 (May 1973): 64–71.

152. Logue, interview, Steen, January 6, 1991, Boston, MA, 35–36; Peter Eisenman, conversation with Lizabeth Cohen, January 23, 2009, New Haven, CT.

153. Huxtable, "Quality Design with Amenities."

154. Chloethiel Woodard Smith was based in Washington, DC, not Boston, but Logue called on her frequently.

155. Michael McKinnell, interview by Lizabeth Cohen, June 15, 2010, Cambridge, MA; Ieoh Ming Pei, interview by Lizabeth Cohen, June 11, 2007, New York, NY; Henry N. Cobb, interview by Lizabeth Cohen, June 8, 2010, New York, NY. John Johansen concurred that Logue picked architects whose work he knew and liked and deliberately avoided others; Johansen, interview by Lizabeth Cohen, November 13, 2010, Wellfleet, MA.

156. "Design: UDC's Emphasis on Design Quality and Livability," Panel No. 2, "Policy and Design for Housing" conference, CUNY Graduate Center, June 11, 2005, transcript, 21.

157. Pangaro, interview.

158. Robert Litke, interview by Lizabeth Cohen, May 25, 2006, Somerset, NJ; Johansen, interview; also see Logue, interview, Steen, January 6, 1991, Boston, MA, 37, where Logue called Johansen "a bit of a disappointment."

159. Huson Jackson to Josep Lluís Sert, July 10, 1970, Sert, Folder E15, "Correspondence, 1970."

160. James Stewart Polshek, Memo to Edward Logue, November 11, 1971, and Edward Logue, Memo to James Stewart Polshek, November 12, 1971, EJL, Box 291, Folder

"Twin Parks, 1971," in Freemark, "Entrepreneurial State," 135–36. Also see Kahan, interview, for another UDC complaint about the Twin Parks windows.

161. Charles Hoyt, "What Did the New Super-Agency Mean for the Architect," *AR* 158, no. 6 (Mid-October 1975): 107; also "Economic/Political Systems," *AR* 149, no. 4 (April 1971): 129–31.

162. Many architects expressed gratitude to the UDC for work but also for backing when conflicts arose with contractors: Andy Leon Harney, "The New York UDC as Client: A Record of Accomplishment," *AIA Journal* 63, no. 2 (February 1975): 33; Joseph Wasserman to Edward Logue, July 19, 1974, and Edward Logue to Herbert A. Tessler, July 22, 1973, EJL, Box 290, Folder "Coney Island, 1971–1973," in Freemark, "Entrepreneurial State," 136.

163. Pangaro, interview.

164. Freemark, "Entrepreneurial State," 137.

165. Theodore Liebman and Alan Melting, "Learning from Experience: The Evolution of Housing Criteria," *PA* 55, no. 11 (November 1974): 72.

166. On skip-stop, see Stern et al., *New York 1960*, 652; "Part I: Projects, B. Roosevelt Island, Uniqueness of the Client," Sert, Folder B87C.

167. Franklin D. Becker, "Design for Living: The Residents' View of Multi-Family Housing; Final Report to the New York State Urban Development Corporation," Center for Urban Development Research, Cornell University, May 1974; *NYSUDC Annual Report 1972*, 57–58; *NYSUDC Annual Report 1973*, 39–43; *NYSUDC Annual Report 1974*, 31; Harney, "New York UDC as Client," 33.

168. Liebman, interview by Cohen; Pangaro, interview.

169. Liebman, interview by Cohen; Logue, interview, Jones, Tape 3:40–41; MLogue, interview; Freemark, "Entrepreneurial State," 140.

170. Barry Bergdoll and Peter Christensen, *Home Delivery: Fabricating the Modern Dwelling* (New York: Museum of Modern Art, 2008); Loren Berlin, "From Stigma to Housing Fix: The Evolution of Manufactured Homes," *Land Lines* 30, no. 1 (January 2018): 4–13; Peter Wolf, *The Evolving City: Urban Design Proposals by Ulrich Franzen and Paul Rudolph* (New York: Whitney Library of Design for the American Federation of Arts, 1974), 57–58 on Rudolph's assessment of modules; Thomas Fetters, *The Lustron Home: The History of a Postwar Prefabricated Housing Experiment* (Jefferson, NC: McFarland, 2002).

171. Tom Long, "Carl Koch, 86; Noted Architect," *BG*, July 10, 1998; Jennifer Hock, "Bulldozers, Busing, and Boycotts: Urban Renewal and the Integrationist Project," *JUH* 39, no. 3 (May 2013): 443.

172. Brilliant, *Urban Development Corporation*, 31; "State to Review Building Methods," *NYT*, December 7, 1969; Logue, interview, Jones, Tape 4:38. On Operation Breakthrough, see Kristin M. Szylvian, "Operation Breakthrough: Manufactured Housing for the City?," paper delivered to the Urban History Association, October 16, 2016; "Operation Breakthrough: Lessons Learned About Demonstrating New Technology," Report to the Congress by the Comptroller General of the United States, November 2, 1976, http://www.gao.gov/products/PSAD-76-173. The National Commission on Urban Problems also recommended prefabrication as a way to improve the quality of urban and suburban housing; *Building the American City*, 431–50, photo insert, 9.

173. Fischer, "Easy Chair: Notes from the Underground," 18–20.

174. On technical innovations: Logue, "The Education of an Urban Administrator," *The Universitas Project: Solutions for a Post-Technological Society*, conceived and directed by Emilio Ambasz, from Symposium January 8–9, 1972 (New York: Museum of Modern Art, 2006), 181; Logue, "New York State Proves the Value of Urban Development Corporation," *The Housing Yearbook, 1971*, 18, National Housing Conference, 45; *NYSUDC Annual Report 1969*, 49, 53; *NYSUDC Annual Report 1971*, 70–71; *NYSUDC Annual Report 1972*, 74–75; "Housing: One Government Agency Reaches for Good Architecture," *AR* 152, no. 3 (September 1972): 151, 159; Ursula Cliff, "UDC Scorecard," *Design and Environment* 3, no. 2 (Summer 1972): 62; "Design Alternatives for Low-to Moderate-Income Urban Housing," *AR* 160, no. 2 (August 1976): 106; Loewenstein, *Private Benefits, Public Costs*, 32.

175. "Statement of the Architect," c. 1976, JJ, Box 12, Folder 7. Johansen discussed the material and its installation in Johansen, interview, 36–38.

176. "Did the UDC Advance Technology?"; "What Did the New Super-Agency Mean for the Architect?," *AR* 158, no. 6 (Mid-October 1975): 108, 110; Logue, "Goals, Policies, Prospects of the New York State Urban Development Corporation," 11; Logue, interview, Steen, August 3, 1988, Boston, MA, 4.

177. Edward Logue to Paul Rudolph, October 21, 1971, EJL, Box 300, Folder 597; Suzanne Stephens, "Standing by the Twentieth-Century Brick," *PA* 55, no. 10 (October 1974): 81.

178. *Another Chance for Housing: Low-Rise Alternatives; An Exhibition at the Museum of Modern Art*, June 12–August 19, 1973, designed by the Institute for Architecture and Urban Studies for the New York State Urban Development Corporation. On Marcus Garvey Park Village more generally, see Pangaro, interview; Liebman, interview by Cohen; *NYSUDC Annual Report 1973*, 44–45; "Low-Rise, High-Density: UDC/IAUS Publicly Assisted Housing," *PA* 54, no. 12 (December 1973): 56–63; "What Did the New Super-Agency Mean for the Architect?," *AR* 158, no. 6 (Mid-October 1975): 109; "Ken Frampton and Friends on Ed Logue," *Oculus* 63, no. 2 (October 2000): 14–15; Kim Förster, "The Housing Prototype of the Institute for Architecture and Urban Studies," *Candide: Journal for Architectural Knowledge*, no. 5 (February 2012): 57–92; Kenneth Frampton, interview by Karen Kubey, October 31, 2008, New York, NY, COH; Karen Kubey, "Marcus Garvey Village," in *Affordable Housing in New York*, 231–34; "Design: UDC's Emphasis on Design Quality and Livability," Panel No. 2, "Policy and Design for Housing" conference, CUNY Graduate Center, June 11, 2005, 27–30; Ada Louise Huxtable, "Another Chance for Housing," *NYT*, June 24, 1973.

179. "Politics: The Role of Developing UDC Projects," Panel No. 3, "Policy and Design for Housing" conference, CUNY Graduate Center, June 11, 2005, 5. Also see Karen Kubey, "Low-Rise, High-Density Housing: A Contemporary View of Marcus Garvey Village," *Urban Omnibus*, July 18, 2012, http://urbanomnibus.net /2012/07/low-rise-high-density-housing-a-contemporary-view-of-marcus -garvey-park-village/; Susan Saegert and Gabrielle Bendiner-Viani, "Making Housing Home," *Places* 19, no. 2 (2007): 72–79; Anna E. J. Fogel, "Marcus Garvey Village: Towards a New Housing Prototype" (senior thesis, Harvard University, 2007); Gina Bellafonte, "A Housing Solution Gone Awry," *NYT*, June 1, 2013.

180. "Statement by Edward J. Logue, President and Chief Executive Officer," *Roosevelt Island Housing Competition*, 3; also see *The Roosevelt Island Housing Competition*, catalog for exhibition at the McGraw-Hill Building, October 15–November 4, 1975, ed. Deborah Nevins (New York: Architectural League of New York, 1975); Paul Goldberger, "U.D.C.'s Architecture Has Raised Public Standard," *NYT*, March 3, 1975; Stern et al., *New York 1960*, 655–56.

181. The winners were Stern & Hagmann of New York; Kyu Sung Woo of New York; Sam Davis and the ELS Design Group of Berkeley, California; and Robert L. Amico and Robert Brandon of Champaign, Illinois; Stern et al., *New York 1960*, 656. Also see Suzanne Stephens, "Roosevelt Island Housing Competition: This Side of Habitat," reprint from *PA* 56, no. 7 (July 1975): 58–59; "Roosevelt Island Competition—Was It Really a Flop?," *AR* 158, no. 6 (Mid-October 1975): 111–20; Hélène Lipstadt, "Transforming the Tradition: American Architectural Competitions, 1960 to the Present," in *The Experimental Tradition: Essays on Competitions in Architecture*, ed. Lipstadt (New York: Architectural League of New York, 1989), 102–105.

182. Liebman, interview by Cohen.

183. Pangaro, "Design: UDC's Emphasis on Design Quality and Livability," Panel No. 2, "Policy and Design for Housing" conference, CUNY Graduate Center, June 11, 2005, 15, 29.

184. Goldberger, "U.D.C.'s Architecture Has Raised Public Standard."

185. Logue, "Goals, Policies, Prospects of the New York State Urban Development Corporation," 9.

186. Nathan Laliberte, "The History of the Rockefeller Family in Westchester," *Westchester Magazine*, October 2012.

8. From Fair Share to Belly-Up

1. Logue, Address in "NAHRO's 1968 Workshops in Community Development," *JH* 25, no. 9 (October 1968): 461–62.

2. Logue, "National Policies and Priorities," *Crisis in the City: Edward J. Logue Lectures at Boston University 1968* (Boston: Urban Institute, Boston University, 1968), 19.

3. Logue, "Fair Sharing—or Why Don't We Do Something About It," Commencement Address, Smith College, Northampton, MA, June 2, 1968, FH, M16, Box 56, Folder 2273, 7–8; Logue, "Only White Society Can Solve Black Problems," Phi Beta Kappa Oration, *Harvard Alumni Bulletin* 70, no. 17 (July 1, 1968); Logue, "Commencement Address—Marlboro College, Marlboro, VT, June 15, 1969.

4. David K. Shipler, "Suburban Zoning Laws: New Frontier in Civil Rights Drive," *CT*, August 23, 1970; Wendell Pritchett, "Which Urban Crisis? Regionalism, Race, and Urban Policy, 1960–1974," *JUH* 34, no. 2 (January 2008): 278–79; Richard Rothstein and Mark Santow, "The Cost of Living Apart," *American Prospect*, August 22, 2012; "America's Federally Financed Ghettos," editorial, *NYT*, April 7, 2018.

5. "Housing: How Ed Logue Does It," *Newsweek*, November 6, 1972.

6. Sydney H. Schanberg, "New York Urban Aid: A New Man May Stir Things Up," *NYT*, May 5, 1968; Sydney H. Schanberg, "State's Urban Agency to Be Led by Logue, Who Spurned City Job," *NYT*, April 27, 1968.

7. Logue quoted in "A Superagency for Urban Superproblems," *BW*, March 7, 1970, 98.

8. Logue, "Piecing the Political Pie," *Saturday Review*, May 15, 1971, 29.

9. Eleanor L. Brilliant, *The Urban Development Corporation: Private Interests and Public Authority* (Lexington, MA: Lexington Books, D. C. Heath, 1975), 4nb; Logue, "Goals, Policies, Prospects of the New York State Urban Development Corporation," July 1972, 7; Louis K. Loewenstein, *The New York State Urban Development Corporation: Private Benefits, Public Costs, an Evaluation of a Noble Experiment* (Washington, DC: Council of State Planning Agencies, 1980), 27; Frank S. Kristof, "Housing," in the Academy of Political Science, *Governing New York State: The Rockefeller Years* 31, no. 3 (May 1974): 199 on the consent of local communities to overrides.

10. *NYSUDC Annual Report 1972*, 48.

11. Brilliant, *Urban Development Corporation*, 57–64; Logue, interview, Steen, March 3, 1986, Lincoln, MA, 18, where Logue explained how subsidiaries created "community partners" and helped avoid the charge that "you've given the store away."

12. Logue, "Can the State Help Save the Suburbs?," *Social Action* 36, no. 8 (1969): 25–31, in Jay Curtis Getz, "The Progressive Technician and Mr. Urban Renewal: Lawrence Veiller, Edward Logue, and the Evolution of Planning for Low-Income Housing" (M.A. thesis, University of Illinois, Urbana-Champaign, 1990), 111.

13. Robert Litke, interview by Lizabeth Cohen, May 25, 2006, Somerset, NJ.

14. On Westchester, Sharon Zukin, "The Mill and the Mall: Power and Homogeneity in Westchester County," *Landscapes of Power: From Detroit to Disney World* (Berkeley: University of California Press, 1991), 135–77.

15. Logue, interview, August 4, 1983, 211, in *Rockefeller in Retrospect: The Governor's New York Legacy*, ed. Gerald Benjamin and T. Norman Hurd (Albany, NY: Nelson A. Rockefeller Institute of Government, 1984), 210–11; Logue, interview, Jones, Tape 3:34.

16. My description of the UDC's Fair Share Housing or Nine Towns program in Westchester is based on Brilliant, *Urban Development Corporation*, 90–99, 132–46, 166; *NYSUDC Annual Report 1972*, 10–11, 53–55; Loewenstein, *Private Benefits, Public Costs*, 55–58; Martin F. Nolan, "The City Politic: Showdown Vote in Northern Westchester," *New York*, June 4, 1973; Stephen Lefkowitz, interview by Lizabeth Cohen, June 14, 2007, New York, NY; Yonah Freemark, "The Entrepreneurial State: New York's Urban Development Corporation, an Experiment to Take Charge of Affordable Housing Production" (Ph.D. dissertation, MIT, 2013), 200–213; and many *NYT* articles, particularly by Linda Greenhouse: "Low-Income State Housing Due in Rural Westchester," June 21, 1972; "Suburbs Fighting State Agency's Plan to Override Local Zoning," July 17, 1972; "Westchester Towns Win a Moratorium on U.D.C. Housing," August 2, 1972; "Housing Delayed in Westchester," September 26, 1972; "State Low-Income Housing Plan Is at a Standstill in Westchester," November 6, 1972; "State to Push Housing in Westchester," January 17, 1973. Also editorials: "Westchester's Test," August 31, 1973; "For a New Westchester," January 26, 1973.

17. Logue, "Remarks at the Bards Award Luncheon," City Club of New York, Roosevelt Hotel, May 23, 1969; and Logue, "The Urban Development Corporation in Westchester County," Address Before the Joint Dinner Meeting of the Westchester Council of Social Agencies and the Westchester Municipal Planning Federation, June 18, 1969, PD, Box 11, 11–12.

18. "Bishop Urges UDC Support Even in Conflict with Church Members," *Harrison Independent*, July 26, 1972.

19. Donald Marshal, "Bedford Historic District First in Westchester," *PT*, August 31, 1972; *Bedford Historic District*, pamphlet, 4; Bedford Town Board Meeting Minutes, August 15, 1972, 286–87.

20. To follow the bitter battles in Westchester towns, see many articles in these local newspapers: *Patent Trader, Harrison Independent, The Yorktowner*, and *Scarsdale Inquirer*.

21. Linda Greenhouse, interview by Lizabeth Cohen, August 2, 2018, Boston, MA.

22. *NYSUDC Annual Report 1972*, 11.

23. Lawrence Goldman, interview by Lizabeth Cohen, May 3, 2010, Newark, NJ; Richard Kahan, interview by Lizabeth Cohen, June 15, 2007, New York, NY. Ted Liebman remembered that at one point Logue needed a bodyguard to go to a Bedford meeting; Ted Liebman, interview by Lizabeth Cohen, October 15, 2006, New York, NY.

24. Elizabeth Simonoff, "UDC Told to 'Get Out' of Bedford," *PT*, August 19, 1972.

25. Linda Greenhouse, "Housing Debated in Westchester," *NYT*, September 10, 1972.

26. "Building Burns at UDC Site," *PT*, October 12, 1972.

27. Stephen Lefkowitz to Logue, December 15, 1971, EJL, Box 271, Folder "Correspondence: Nelson A. Rockefeller (1971 July–December)," in Freemark, "Entrepreneurial State," 189.

28. Logue, interview, Steen, March 3, 1986, Lincoln, MA, 8; Logue, interview, Steen, December 2, 1988, Lincoln, MA, 29; Sydney H. Schanberg, "Clark Named to State Urban Board," *NYT*, August 3, 1968; Daniel Matlin, *On the Corner: African American Intellectuals and the Urban Crisis* (Cambridge, MA: Harvard University Press, 2013), 36–122. Ironically, Clark and his wife lived in the predominantly white suburban town of Hastings-on-Hudson in Westchester.

29. Anthony Pangaro, interview by Lizabeth Cohen, June 24, 2009, Boston, MA.

30. For housing starts in New York City, Alan S. Oser, "Logue Forecasts 1973 Slowdown in U.D.C. Pace," *NYT*, August 12, 1973; 86 percent were in cities large and small.

31. For Logue's disgust with behavior of supposed liberals Reid and Ottinger, see Logue, interview, Steen, August 3, 1988, Boston, MA, 38.

32. Quoted in Brilliant, *Urban Development Corporation*, 142.

33. Elizabeth Simonoff, "Town Will Sue UDC," *PT*, July 13, 1972.

34. Logue, interview, Jones, Tape 3:36.

35. Dan Margulies, "Court Backs UDC," *PT*, September 7, 1972; "UDC Legislation Stalls," *PT*, September 28, 1972.

36. Logue, interview, Steen, August 3, 1988, Boston, MA, 40.

37. Martin F. Nolan, "Staying Out of Suburbia," *BG*, June 1, 1973.

38. Logue, interview, Steen, August 3, 1988, Boston, MA, 40; Logue, interview, Steen, January 6, 1991, Boston, MA, 24–26; Panel "Housing Unbuilt: Politics Over People," in Part 3: "The Current Status of Housing," in the exhibition "Policy and Design for Housing: Lessons of the Urban Development Corporation 1968–1975," http://www.udchousing.org/exhibition_3.htm, Architectural League of New York, Urban Center, New York, NY; *NYSUDC Annual Report 1971*, 55; *NYSUDC Annual Report 1973*, 11, 54, 56, 60; George Vecsey, "Babylon Officials Reject Wyandanch Housing Plan," *NYT*, August 17, 1973.

39. "The Story of 'The Suburban Destruction Corporation' (SDC): E. J. Rogue, President, and the Warm and Wonderful World of Westchester," MDL.

40. Nancy Maron, "A Gingerly Step into Westchester Taken by Logue," *NYT*, February 22, 1970; Joseph Berger, "Paul Davidoff, 54: Planner Challenged Suburbs' Zone Rules," *NYT*, December 28, 1984. Davidoff kept a significant clippings file on the UDC's Fair Share Housing struggle; "UDC Westchester Clippings, 1969-1973," PD.

41. Sidney Eaton Boyle, "Moses: Go Slow on Housing," *Reporter Dispatch* (White Plains, NY), November 2, 1972.

42. Pangaro, interview.

43. On Nixon's moratorium, see Pritchett, "Which Urban Crisis?," 279-82; Brilliant, *Urban Development Corporation*, 145-46, 149-50, 161; Loewenstein, *Private Benefits, Public Costs*, 60-61; Freemark, "Entrepreneurial State," 44-57, 295-96. In a remembrance at an AIA memorial to Logue in May 2000, Paul Byard traced the UDC's collapse back to when "Richard Nixon closed the little spigot of section 236 and our descent began as well"; "2nd Annual Ratensky Housing Lecture, Celebrating the Work of Housing and Planning Czar, Edward J. Logue," New York Chapter, AIA, Seagram Tower, New York City, May 24, 2000.

44. George Romney to Casper W. Weinberger, n.d. but late 1972, and George Romney, "Notes for Speech in Roosevelt Room, December 22, 1972," both in George Romney Archives, Box 10-P, Folder "Office of Management and Budget," in Freemark, "Entrepreneurial State," 56.

45. Michael Kranish, "Nixon, Romney Relationship Came to Frosty End," *BG*, June 27, 2007.

46. Richard Nixon, "Address to the Nation on Domestic Programs," August 8, 1969, *Public Papers of the Presidents, Richard Nixon, 1969*, 637-38, and "Annual Budget Message to the Congress, Fiscal Year 1974," January 29, 1973, *Public Papers of the Presidents, Richard Nixon, 1973*, 46-47, quoted in Pritchett, "Which Urban Crisis?," 278, 280.

47. Logue, "Looking Ahead—Looking Back in Housing, Planning, and Community Development," March 22, 1976, Paper Presented at Plenary Workshop, "Design: Strategies of Habitat," National Congress of Planning, Joint AIP/ASPO National Planning Conference, EJL, 2002 Addition, Box 22, Folder "Looking Ahead," 2.

48. Murray Schumach, "12 Mayors, Alarmed at U.S. Budget, to Meet Here on Monday," *NYT*, January 31, 1973.

49. "Federal Housing Policies and Programs—the Federal Moratorium of January 8, 1973," EJL, 2002 Accession, Box 22, Folder "Federal Housing Policies and Programs, 1973." Logue called for greater federal funding and more flexibility for state and local government implementation in "Testimony of Edward J. Logue, President of the New York State Urban Development Corporation Before the Senate Subcommittee on Banking, Housing, and Urban Affairs," July 27, 1973, NYSA, Series 12309, Subseries 97, Box 23.

50. For analysis of impact of revenue sharing and block grants, see Roger Biles, *The Fate of Cities: Urban America and the Federal Government, 1945-2000* (Lawrence: University Press of Kansas, 2011), 188-91.

51. Logue, "The Idea of America Is Choice," in *Qualities of Life, Papers Prepared for the Commission on Critical Choices for Americans*, vol. 7 (Lexington, MA: Lexington Books, 1976), 18.

52. Pritchett, "Which Urban Crisis?," 281-82; Alice O'Connor, "Swimming Against the

Tide: A Brief History of Federal Policy in Poor Communities," in *Urban Problems and Community Development*, ed. Ronald F. Ferguson and William T. Dickens (Washington, DC: Brookings Institution Press, 1999), 77–137, particularly 108–10; Yonah Freemark, "Roosevelt Island: Exception to a City in Crisis," *JUH* 37, no. 3 (May 2011): 2, 16; National Low Income Housing Coalition, "40 Years Ago: August 22, President Ford Signs Housing and Community Development Act of 1974," http://nlihc.org /article/40-years-ago-august-22-president-ford-signs-housing-and-community -development-act-1974; Nicholas Dagen Bloom and Matthew Gordon Lasner, eds., *Affordable Housing in New York: The People, Places, and Policies That Transformed a City* (Princeton, NJ: Princeton University Press, 2016), 197–98; Susan S. Fainstein, *The Just City* (Ithaca, NY: Cornell University Press, 2010), 92.

53. Edith Evens Asbury, "Hamilton Deplores Housing-Fund Cutoff," *NYT*, January 9, 1973.

54. Logue, interview, Jones, Tape 4:8; Logue similarly told Steen, "I got buildings that are starting, buildings that are three-quarters finished, buildings that are halfway up, and they'll all be bankrupt without these subsidies"; Logue, interview, Steen, August 3, 1988, Boston, MA, 3.

55. Logue, interview, Steen, August 3, 1988, Boston, MA, 2.

56. Mary Perot Nichols, "The Martin Luther King Memorial Ripoff," *New Republic*, July 24, 1976, 21.

57. Schumach, "12 Mayors, Alarmed at U.S. Budget, to Meet Here on Monday"; Edith Evans Asbury, "Federal Freeze Imperils Housing Projects in Area," *NYT*, February 4, 1973.

58. Logue, interview, Jones, Tape 4:8; *Restoring Credit and Confidence: A Reform Program for New York State and Its Public Authorities; A Report to the Governor by the New York State Moreland Act Commission on the Urban Development Corporation and Other State Financing Agencies*, March 31, 1976 (hereafter *Moreland*), 141–42.

59. Logue on how the moratorium "worried a lot of people in the financial community," Logue, interview by Benjamin and Hurd, *Rockefeller in Retrospect*, 211.

60. *NYSUDC Annual Report 1973*, 5.

61. William Marlin, "After the Pratfall: UDC Dusts Off the Debris of Default," *AR* 158, no. 6 (Mid-October 1975): 121.

62. Francis X. Clines, "Rockefeller Gets a Ford Accolade," *NYT*, December 5, 1973; Alfonso A. Narvaez, "2-Year Study Is Projected to Define Critical Choices," *NYT*, December 12, 1973; Frank Lynn, "A Zestful Rockefeller Steers 'Choices' Study," *NYT*, February 27, 1974; Richard Norton Smith, *On His Own Terms: A Life of Nelson Rockefeller* (New York: Random House, 2014), 637–39.

63. Loewenstein, *Private Benefits, Public Costs*, 8, 64–65; Logue, interview by Benjamin and Hurd, *Rockefeller in Retrospect*, 210.

64. John Stainton, interview by Lizabeth Cohen, May 30, 2007, Jamaica Plain, MA. Robert Hazen also stressed that Logue always assumed that Rockefeller would be there to bail him out; Robert Hazen, interview by Lizabeth Cohen, June 14, 2007, New York, NY.

65. On the economic crisis facing the nation, New York State, and New York City, see Seymour P. Lachman and Robert Polner, *The Man Who Saved New York: Hugh Carey and the Great Fiscal Crisis of 1975* (Albany: State University of New York Press, 2010);

Marlin, "After the Pratfall," 122; Robert Bailey, *The Crisis Regime: The MAC, the EFCB, and the Political Impact of the New York City Financial Crisis* (Albany: State University of New York Press, 1984); Ralph Blumenthal, "Prayer for Help: Unusual Ways a City Coped in 70s Crisis," *NYT*, December 27, 2002. On Rockefeller's role as vice president, Smith, *On His Own Terms*, 671–77.

On the restructuring of New York's economy, see Lizabeth Cohen and Brian Goldstein, "Governing at the Tipping Point: Shaping the City's Role in Economic Development," in *Summer in the City: John Lindsay, New York, and the American Dream*, ed. Joseph P. Viteritti (Baltimore: Johns Hopkins University Press, 2014), 163–92; Lachman and Polner, *Man Who Saved New York*, 94; Joshua B. Freeman, *Working-Class New York: Life and Labor Since World War II* (New York: New Press, 2000); Kim Moody, *From Welfare State to Real Estate: Regime Change in New York City, 1974 to the Present* (New York: New Press, 2007).

66. Logue, interview, Steen, July 11, 1991, Boston, MA, 17.

67. On interest rate rise and its causes and consequences, see Marlin, "After the Pratfall," 122; Brilliant, *Urban Development Corporation*, 154–55.

68. For events leading up to the collapse of Logue's leadership of the UDC in February 1975 and its immediate aftermath, see Marlin, "After the Pratfall," 121–22; Brilliant, *Urban Development Corporation*, 149–80; *NYSUDC Annual Report 1974*, 6, 15; Logue, interview, Schussheim, 35–37; John Zuccotti, interview by Lizabeth Cohen, December 10, 2007, New York, NY; Richard Ravitch, interview by Lizabeth Cohen, October 22, 2007, New York, NY; Steven R. Weisman, "Nelson Rockefeller's Pill: The UDC," *WM*, June 1975, 35–44.

69. Logue, interview by Benjamin and Hurd, *Rockefeller in Retrospect*, 212; Linda Greenhouse, "Governor Orders Inquiry to Save Faltering U.D.C.," *NYT*, February 6, 1975; Alan S. Oser, "How the U.D.C.'s Reach Came to Exceed Its Grasp," *NYT*, March 16, 1975; Logue, interview, Steen, July 11, 1991, Boston, MA, 9; Weisman, "Nelson Rockefeller's Pill," 37; Michael Kramer and Sam Roberts, *"I Never Wanted to Be Vice-President of Anything!": An Investigative Biography of Nelson Rockefeller* (New York: Basic Books, 1976), 146–47.

70. Joseph P. Fried, "Urban Development Unit Curbed on New Projects," *NYT*, October 6, 1974; $1 million a day figure from Myer Kutz, "How Could It Happen to the UDC?," *Planning* 41 (May 1975): 14.

71. Richard L. Dunham, Chair, "Report of the Task Force on the Urban Development Corporation," December 26, 1974, NYSA, Series A0507, Subseries 78, Box 1; Paul L. Montgomery, "Wilson Unit Asks Halt in New Financing by U.D.C.," *NYT*, December 27, 1974; Brilliant, *Urban Development Corporation*, 174–75; Weisman, "Nelson Rockefeller's Pill," 40, 43. On Wilson's promise not to fire Logue, see Logue, interview, Jones, Tape 4:16.

72. Lachman and Polner, *Man Who Saved New York*, 82; Greenhouse, interview.

73. Allan Talbot, interview by Lizabeth Cohen, June 13, 2007, New York, NY.

74. Logue, "A Farewell Message to UDC Staff," February 6, 1975, NYSA, Series A0507, Subseries 78, Box 1.

75. "Securities: A Moral Issue," *Time*, March 10, 1975.

76. Marlin, "After the Pratfall," 122; Brilliant, *Urban Development Corporation*, 177; Litke, interview; by spring, the UDC staff had been reduced by more than a third.

77. "Preliminary Memorandum on Behalf of Certain Officers, Former Officers and Directors of the Urban Development Corporation," n.d. but 1975; copy thanks to Robert Hazen.
78. Brilliant, *Urban Development Corporation*, 174. Also see "Carey Considering Developer as Chairman of State's U.D.C.," *NYT*, January 20, 1975.
79. Richard Ravitch, *So Much to Do: A Full Life of Business, Politics, and Confronting Fiscal Crisis* (New York: Public Affairs Press, 2014), 65; for Ravitch's perspective on his role, see 51–70, which includes quotes; also Ravitch, interview, for detailed discussion of his involvement in Roosevelt Island and his efforts to salvage the UDC.
80. Other sources on Ravitch's involvement with the UDC bailout include: Zuccotti, interview; Lefkowitz, interview; Logue, interview, Steen, October 31, 1986, Lincoln, MA, 27.
81. Ravitch, interview.
82. Celestine Bohlen, "Moreland Act of 1907; Governor's Strong Suit," *NYT*, December 15, 1988; Edward Hudson, "Orville H. Schell Jr., 78, Dies; Lawyer and Ballet Chairman," *NYT*, June 19, 1987; Frank Lynn, "Carey Picks a Prosecutor for Nursing Home Inquiry," *NYT*, January 7, 1975.
83. Much of what follows is drawn from *Moreland*. All the files, including hearing transcripts, for the UDC Moreland Act Commission are all in NYSA, Series 11449.
84. Logue, interview, Steen, July 11, 1991, Boston, MA, 43; "Edward N. Costikyan, Adviser to New York Politicians, Is Dead at 87," *NYT*, June 23, 2012; MLogue, interview.
85. Pangaro, interview; Ellen Logue, interview; Logue, interview, Jones, Tape 4:24–27; Ravitch, interview; Brilliant, *Urban Development Corporation*, 173–80; Zuccotti, interview. For Logue testimony, see Statement of Edward J. Logue, October 20, 1975, and transcripts from October 20 and October 21, 1975, in NYSA, Series 11449, Subseries 98, Box 9, and quotes and descriptions in Linda Greenhouse, "Logue Sees U.D.C. as 'Whipping Boy,'" *NYT*, October 21, 1975; "Staff of New York State's UDC Warned of Financial Peril in '71, Hearings Show," *WSJ*, October 21, 1975; "Logue Attributes Collapse of U.D.C. to Miscalculation of City's Bankers," *NYT*, October 22, 1975; Linda Greenhouse, "Lessons to Be Learned from U.D.C.'s Collapse," *NYT*, November 9, 1975; "UDC's Fiscal Woes Wore Beyond Control of Any New Yorker, Rockefeller Testifies," *WSJ*, December 4, 1975.
86. On accounting challenges at the UDC, see Logue, interview, Jones, Tape 4:14; Logue, interview, Steen, January 6, 1991, Boston, MA, 49. Logue also struggled against the conservative and cautious views of New York State controller Arthur Levitt, who never favored moral obligation bonds: David K. Shipler, "Levitt Criticizes Bidding Policy of Unit for Urban Development," *NYT*, April 3, 1972; Logue, interview, Steen, March 3, 1986, Lincoln, MA, 11; Logue, interview, Steen, July 11, 1991, Boston, MA, 7; Lefkowitz, interview.
87. Linda Greenhouse, "Expert Criticizes U.D.C.'s Operation," *NYT*, October 16, 1975; this was called a "negative interest spread."
88. Logue message to Moss, December 9, 1971, quoted in Greenhouse, "Logue Sees U.D.C. as 'Whipping Boy.'" For observations on Logue's lack of sufficient attention to finances, see Annmarie Hauck Walsh, *The Public's Business: The Politics and Practices of Government Corporations* (Cambridge, MA: MIT Press, 1980), 271; Lefkowitz, interview. Logue sometimes admitted as much himself, as when he

recounted Robert Weaver saying, "Oh that Logue, he doesn't give a shit about money," and added, "And in a sense that was true I guess"; Logue, interview, Jones, Tape 1:ii.

89. Stainton, interview; for Moss's feeling that Logue was ignoring his advice, see *Moreland*, 139.

90. Litke, interview.

91. For Schell quote, Linda Greenhouse, "Hearings to Begin on UDC Collapse," *NYT*, October 12, 1975; Kutz, "How Could It Happen to the UDC?," 14.

92. Logue, interview, Steen, July 11, 1991, Boston, MA, 34, 37, where Logue claimed to have "never been a believer in direct democracy."

93. Lefkowitz, interview; Logue, interview, Steen, March 3, 1986, Lincoln, MA, 11. On Woods's testimony and defense of himself, see Linda Greenhouse, "Logue Is Called Deficient in His Grasp of Banking," *NYT*, October 24, 1975. In response to questions about why he did not push harder for reforms, Woods said defiantly, "I had not been put in as a watering can to pour cold water on management's activities."

94. Quoted in Linda Greenhouse, "Panel Reports U.D.C. Collapse Was Result of 3 Wrong Moves," *NYT*, May 27, 1976.

95. *Moreland*, 223–28.

96. Louis K. Loewenstein, "The New York State Urban Development Corporation—a Forgotten Failure or a Precursor of the Future?," *JAIP* 44, no. 3 (July 1978): 270; Loewenstein, *Private Benefits, Public Costs*, 115.

97. Paul Goldberger, "U.D.C.'s Architecture Has Raised Public Standard," *NYT*, March 3, 1975.

98. Ravitch, interview; Marlin, "After the Pratfall," reported spending on architecture a frequent criticism of the UDC but argued for the importance of its contribution in the long run, 123–24; the Wilson Task Force had also found that hiring expensive architects brought about "substantially higher" expenditures.

99. Logue, interview, Steen, January 6, 1991, Boston, MA, 43–44; Logue, interview, Steen, July 11, 1991, Boston, MA, 11; *NYSUDC Annual Report 1972* bragged about the expected savings, 74.

100. *Moreland*, 14, 37–46. Logue was closely questioned on why he had not undertaken more housing rehabilitation in New York. He argued that although he had done a lot of rehab in New Haven and Boston, the UDC lacked the financial and relocation tools of urban renewal, and the private market—owners and lenders—lacked the will to invest in rehabilitation within city limits; Logue testimony, October 21, 1975, NYSA, Series 11449, Sub-series 98, Box 9, 700–725.

101. Greenhouse, "Panel Reports U.D.C. Collapse Was Result of 3 Wrong Moves."

102. Robert C. Alexander, "What Is the Lesson of UDC for Other State Housing Agencies?," *JH* 32, no. 4 (April 15, 1975): 178.

103. Marlin, "After the Pratfall," 124; also see Logue, interview, Steen, July 11, 1991, Boston, MA, 12; Logue, interview, Jones, Tape 2:1.

104. Joseph P. Fried, "Banks Assailed by Head of U.D.C.," *NYT*, January 17, 1975.

105. Logue, interview, Jones, Tape 3:38. Rockefeller took a similar position in his testimony to the Moreland Commission in December 1975. When pressed as to why

there wasn't a better contingency plan, he retorted, "We weren't running a corporation. We weren't running a bank. We were running a social institution trying to help people"; quoted in "UDC's Fiscal Woes Were Beyond Control of Any New Yorker, Rockefeller Testifies," *WSJ*, December 4, 1975.

106. William Ellinghaus Statement on MAC Program, July 31, 1975, Binder: MAC material, Jack Bigel Papers, Baruch College Archives, quoted in Kim Phillips-Fein, "The New York City Fiscal Crisis and the Idea of the State," in Collection of Conference papers for "The New History of American Capitalism," November 17–19, 2011, 193. For a more extensive analysis, see Kim Philips-Fein, *Fear City: New York's Fiscal Crisis and the Rise of Austerity Politics* (New York: Metropolitan Books, 2017).

107. Joseph P. Fried, "The Roof Falls In," *Nation*, August 16, 1975, 102–6. For a similar reminder of how the rebuilding of depressed urban areas and the promoting of housing integration had recently been an important, shared goal, see Oser, "How the U.D.C.'s Reach Came to Exceed Its Grasp."

108. Marlin, "After the Pratfall," 124.

109. Zuccotti, interview.

110. Brilliant, *Urban Development Corporation*, 168–70.

111. Francis X. Clines, "Rockefeller Set Up Urban Development Group on Rebound from Voter Rejection," *NYT*, February 26, 1975; Weisman, "Nelson Rockefeller's Pill," 44. Smeal remained no fan of the UDC. His description, quoted by Clines, of the UDC as a "stylish, highly visible agency, more cooperative with editorial writers than with bankers" that committed to "build, build, and build some more, without regard as to who would pay" was often repeated by him and others.

112. Brilliant, *Urban Development Corporation*, 170; Alan Campbell, "It Has Built Where Nobody Else Would: The Big Goals of the U.D.C.," *NYT*, March 2, 1975.

113. Marlin, "After the Pratfall," 123.

114. Loewenstein, "Forgotten Failure," 269, 271–72; *Moreland*, 104; also see Fried, "Roof Falls In," 103; Kutz, "How Could It Happen to the UDC?," 14.

115. Brilliant, *Urban Development Corporation*, 162–63; Campbell, "It Has Built Where Nobody Else Would," *NYT*, March 2, 1975; Kahan, interview.

116. Ravitch, interview.

117. Marlin, "After the Pratfall," 124.

118. *Moreland*, 11.

119. A sampling includes "Housing New York: Ed Logue and His Architects," exhibition by the Architectural League and Municipal Art Society, the Urban Center, New York, NY, February 5–April 14, 2001; panel discussion on Ed Logue and Roosevelt Island, Municipal Art Society, March 7, 2001, full transcript at http://www.edlogue .org/docs/Logue-Rooservelet_03-07-01.pdf; "Policy and Design for Housing: Lessons of the Urban Development Corporation 1968–1975," exhibition, June 10–September 10, 2005, Architectural League of New York, Center for Architecture, New York, NY, and extensive symposia April 8, 2005, June 10–11, 2005; exhibition also traveled to MIT, September 21–December 22, 2006; Susan Saegert and Gabrielle Bendiner-Viani, "Making Housing Home," *Places Journal* 19, no. 2 (2007); "Friends of Ed Logue" website, http://www.edlogue.org/.

120. On other states influenced by the UDC: Marlin, "After the Pratfall," 123; Loewenstein,

Private Benefits, Public Costs, 112; Kutz, "How Could It Happen to the UDC?," 14; Alexander, "What Is the Lesson of UDC for Other State Housing Agencies?," 177–79.

121. Walsh, *Public's Business*, 139, 161; Loewenstein, "Forgotten Failure," 266–69, which includes details of the resolution of the UDC crisis.

122. Joseph P. Fried, "Goodbye, Slum Razing; Hello, Grand Hyatt," *NYT*, July 15, 1979; Maurice Carroll, "Development Unit Tests Ambitious New Agenda," *NYT*, January 29, 1981; Martin Gottlieb, "U.D.C. Looking to Suburbs and Rural Areas," *NYT*, November 27, 1983; "Who'll Set the Beat for 42nd Street," editorial, *NYT*, October 3, 1984; Ravitch, interview; Hilary Botein, "New York State Housing Policy in Postwar New York City: The Enduring Rockefeller Legacy," *JUH* 35, no. 6 (September 2009): 845–46.

123. Brilliant, *Urban Development Corporation*, 170, also 161–71 more broadly. Wolf Von Eckardt, who had been following Logue's career for many years, agreed that "a good many people will rejoice if and when Logue joins the ranks of the unemployed," but he has been "a dynamic, strong leader who has the arrogance to be an unassailable idealist as well ... They have been calling Ed Logue an S.O.B. ever since he started to get things done in New Haven"; Von Eckardt, "The Housing That Logue Builds," *WP*, January 25, 1975. For discussion of how Logue offended others, Nicholas Katzenbach, interview by Lizabeth Cohen, May 26, 2006, Princeton, NJ.

124. Logue, interview, Steen, July 11, 1991, Boston, MA, 19; Logue wrote to Rockefeller that "to give his position credibility he [Carey] needed a scapegoat. I was rather eligible for that purpose"; Edward Logue to Nelson Rockefeller, January 9, 1975, EJL, 1983 Addition, Box 31, Folder "Rockefeller, Nelson A. 1974–75," quoted in Freemark, "Entrepreneurial State," 303.

125. Goldman, interview; Penn Kimball, interview by Lizabeth Cohen, July 18, 2007, Martha's Vineyard, MA; also Lefkowitz, interview; Kahan, interview. Margaret Logue concurred: "He had felt all his life that his own reputation was his most precious possession"; MLogue, interview.

126. Alan S. Oser, "Logue Asks U.S. Act on Housing," *NYT*, May 7, 1976; Litke, interview; Logue, interview, Jones, Tape 4:44; Raymond, Parish, Pine & Weiner and Logue Development Company, "The Role of Local Government in New Community Development," Washington, DC, U.S. Department of Housing and Urban Development, Office of Policy Development and Research, 1979, project supervised by Edward Logue; Robert Litke, project manager.

127. On what he was doing, see Linda Greenhouse, "Why a Bill with Ardent Backers and Firm Opponents Has Gone Nowhere in 5 Weeks," *NYT*, March 8, 1976; Oser, "Logue Asks U.S. Act on Housing"; Robert Geddes, interview by Lizabeth Cohen, May 25, 2006, Princeton, NJ.

128. Joseph P. Fried, "South Bronx Story: Ed Logue Returns," *New York*, October 16, 1978, "Legislator Assails 'Logue's Lush Lair,'" *NYT*, March 27, 1971.

129. Frank Logue to Edward Logue, November 11, 1971, EJL, Series 6, Box 150, Folder 426, 3.

130. Litke, interview; Stainton, interview.

131. Liebman, interview.

132. Logue, interview, Steen, October 31, 1986, Lincoln, MA, 28; MLogue, interview.

133. Logue, interview by Jean Joyce, October 22, 1976, Bowles, Part 9, Series 3, Subseries 3, Box 398, Folder 199b, 48.

9. Ashes to Gardens in the South Bronx

1. Charles J. Orlebeke, *New Life at Ground Zero: New York, Home Ownership, and the Future of American Cities* (Albany, NY: Rockefeller Institute Press, 1997), 34–39, 231; for "bored" quote, Logue, interview, Jones, Tape 4:55. For other job opportunities that came Logue's way, including the deanship of the University of Pennsylvania School of Fine Arts, see Wolf Von Eckardt, "Baron of South Bronx: Urban Renewer Ed Logue's New Challenge," *WP*, November 4, 1978.
2. Carter's statement and photograph became ubiquitous; for Logue's version, Logue, interview, Jones, Tape 4:53–54. For others, see Von Eckardt, "Baron of South Bronx"; Jill Jonnes, *South Bronx Rising: The Rise, Fall, and Resurrection of an American City* (New York: Fordham University Press, 2002), 310–17; Alexander von Hoffman, *House by House, Block by Block: The Rebirth of America's Urban Neighborhoods* (New York: Oxford University Press, 2003), 34–35. On the Carter administration's cuts in federal funding and devolution of federal responsibility in urban policy, see Thomas J. Sugrue, "Carter's Urban Policy Crisis," in *The Carter Presidency: Policy Choices in the Post–New Deal Era*, ed. Gary M. Fink and Hugh Davis Graham (Lawrence: University Press of Kansas, 1998), 137–57; and Tracy Neumann, "Privatization, Devolution, and Jimmy Carter's National Urban Policy," *JUH* 40, no. 2 (March 2014): 283–300.
3. Logue to Hon. Herman Badillo, May 3, 1978, in "May 5, 1978, Logue Proposal to City," EJL, 1985 Accession, Box 62, Black Binder; Joseph P. Fried, "Logue, Who Led U.D.C., Is Asked to Head Bronx Plan," *NYT*, June 17, 1978.
4. For Badillo's view of his plan, see Herman Badillo, interview by John Metzger, March 8, 1994, COH, 1–7. For details of New York City's response to Carter's visit under Mayors Beame and Koch, see Thomas Glynn, "Charlotte Street, the Bronx," *Neighborhood: The Journal for City Preservation* 5, no. 2 (August 1982; special issue on the South Bronx): 26–31. On Logue's appointment, "Remarks by Mayor Edward I. Koch at a Press Conference Announcing the Appointment of Three Aides for the South Bronx Redevelopment Program, Blue Room, City Hall, Manhattan, Monday, September 11, 1978, 10:30 A.M."
5. Von Eckardt, "Baron of South Bronx."
6. Anna Quindlen, "The Politics of Charlotte Street," *NYT Magazine*, October 7, 1979; Jonnes, *South Bronx Rising*, 324–25; Robert P. Wagner, interview by Jonathan Soffer, August–September 1992, COH, 2–102; Badillo, interview, 5, 8, 10; Peter Bray, interview by Lizabeth Cohen, February 18, 2010, New York, NY; "Statement of Edward J. Logue, South Bronx Director, before the Board of Estimate of the City of New York at its public hearing on November 16, 1978 in support of the request of the New York City Housing Authority for approval of its plan and project for the Charlotte Street Housing Project in the South Bronx," Bray. On the Board of Estimate rejection, Andy Logan, "Around City Hall: Symbols," *New Yorker*, February 26, 1979, 90–95; von Hoffman, *House by House*, 35–36.
7. Badillo, interview, 1–10; Wagner, interview, 2–102; former SBDO staff member Rebecca Lee argued that Koch established the SBDO to show that he was taking

action; Rebecca Lee, interview by Lizabeth Cohen, March 10, 2010, Boston, MA; Lee Dembart, "Koch, in a Reversal, Orders New Plan for South Bronx," *NYT*, February 13, 1979; "South Bronx Debate; Dig It Now or Plan It Later," *NYT*, February 25, 1979.

8. Logue, interview, Jones, Tape 4:59–60.

9. Of this, $1.5 million came from the federal government, $1 million from the State of New York, and $500,000 from the City; see Glynn, "Charlotte Street, the Bronx," 29; Neil R. Peirce and Jerry Hagstrom, "Two Years After Carter's Visit, Islands of Hope Dot the South Bronx," *National Journal*, October 6, 1979, 1644–48.

10. Logue, interview, Jones, Tape 4:58; "hunting license" and city cars from Logue, interview by Peter Bray, April 23, 1982, Bronx, NY; Bray, interview, on SBDO's vulnerability.

11. Logue to Badillo, EJL, May 5, 1978.

12. Joseph P. Fried, "Robert Garcia Dies at 84; Bronx Congressman Undone by Scandal," *NYT*, January 26, 2017.

13. On the growth and decline of the South Bronx, see Patrick Breslin, "On These Sidewalks of New York, the Sun Is Shining Again," *Smithsonian Magazine*, April 1995, 100–111; Thomas Glynn, "The Neighborhood," *Neighborhood: The Journal for City Preservation* 5, no. 2 (August 1982; special issue on the South Bronx): 2–34; Robert Jensen, *Devastation/Resurrection: The South Bronx*, exhibition catalog, November 9, 1979–January 13, 1980, Bronx Museum of the Arts; Constance Rosenblum, "Grand, Wasn't It?," *NYT*, August 21, 2009; Ian Frazier, "Utopia, the Bronx: Co-op City and Its People," *New Yorker*, June 26, 2006.

14. Bill Moyers, "The Fire Next Door," December 5, 1980, in *In the South Bronx of America, Photographs by Mel Rosenthal* (Willimantic, CT: Curbstone Press, 2000), 51.

15. Lisa Kahane, *Do Not Give Way to Evil: Photographs of the South Bronx, 1979–1987* (Brooklyn, NY: Powerhouse Books, 2008), 18; Peter L'Official, "Urban Legends: The South Bronx in Representation and Ruin" (Ph.D. dissertation, Harvard University, 2014); von Hoffman, *House by House*, 22–23; Jonnes, *South Bronx Rising*, 249–67, provides details on arson.

16. On demographic change, displacement, and social problems, see Peirce and Hagstrom, "Two Years After Carter's Visit," 1647; Jonnes, *South Bronx Rising*, 100–102, 111–14, 118–26; Edward J. Logue to Whom It May Interest, Memo with South Bronx Profile, April 27, 1984, Bray. On Puerto Ricans in the South Bronx, see Nicholas Lemann, "The Other Underclass," *Atlantic*, December 1991, 96–110.

17. Nicholas Dagen Bloom and Matthew Gordon Lasner, eds., *Affordable Housing in New York: The People, Places, and Policies That Transformed a City* (Princeton, NJ: Princeton University Press, 2016), 263; quote from *NYT*, March 17, 1976, in Orlebeke, *New Life at Ground Zero*, 33.

18. On Father Louis Gigante, Jonnes, *South Bronx Rising*, 168–70, 302–303; von Hoffman, *House by House*, 24–30.

19. Trisha Rose, *Black Noise: Rap Music and Black Culture in Contemporary America* (Middletown, CT: Wesleyan University Press, 1994); Randy Kennedy, "A Feast of Street Art, Luminous and Legal: Graffiti Art of the City, from the Bronx to Brooklyn," *NYT*, August 29, 2013.

20. Owen Moritz, "Departing Ed Logue Sees Hope for South Bronx," *NYDN*, October 7, 1984.

21. On Velez, Wayne Barrett, "Señor Big: How Ramon Velez Bleeds New York," *Village Voice*, December 31, 1985; David Gonzalez with Martin Gottlieb, "Power Built on Poverty: One Man's Odyssey," *NYT*, May 14, 1993; David Gonzalez and Martin Gottlieb, "The Baron of the Bronx: In an Antipoverty Empire, a Clinic Is an Opportunity," *NYT*, May 15, 1993; Douglas Martin, "Ramon S. Velez, the South Bronx Padrino, Dies at 75," *NYT*, December 3, 2008; David Gonzalez, "A Second Look at a Bronx Baron's Methods," *NYT*, December 5, 2008; David Medina, "Controversy Clouds Projects," *NYDN*, June 27, 1980; Jonnes, *South Bronx Rising*, 164–68, 170–74.

22. Kahane, *Do Not Give Way to Evil*, 10.

23. Logue, interview by Bray; Joseph P. Fried, "South Bronx Story: Ed Logue Returns," *New York*, October 16, 1978, 21–22; Edward I. Koch, interview by Alexander von Hoffman, May 1, 2001, New York, NY; Logue's hiring was covered in all major national papers.

24. Logue, interview, Jones, Tape 4:56–57.

25. Stephen Lefkowitz, interview by Lizabeth Cohen, June 14, 2007, New York, NY.

26. Fried, "South Bronx Story: Ed Logue Returns," 22.

27. Logue, interview by Bray.

28. Lawrence Goldman, interview by Lizabeth Cohen, May 3, 2010, Newark, NJ. Ted Liebman agreed: "I thought it was below [him] . . . I didn't want him to have a lesser job"; Ted Liebman, interview by Lizabeth Cohen, October 15, 2006, New York, NY.

29. Richard Kahan, interview by Lizabeth Cohen, June 15, 2007, New York, NY.

30. John Stainton, interview by Lizabeth Cohen, May 30, 2007, Jamaica Plain, MA.

31. Fried, "South Bronx Story: Ed Logue Returns," 21–22.

32. MLogue, interview; Ellen Logue, interview by Lizabeth Cohen, April 13, 2008, Berkeley, CA; Allan Talbot, interview by Lizabeth Cohen, June 13, 2007, New York, NY; Robert Litke, interview by Lizabeth Cohen, May 25, 2006, Somerset, NJ. Also, Anthony Pangaro, interview by Lizabeth Cohen, June 24, 2009, Boston, MA, who acknowledged that Logue "enjoyed the power . . . and being able to pick up the phone and get something done is a tremendous thrill, but it wasn't, in and of itself, the end. It was a means. It was a tool. It was always about what's the mission. How do we get that done?"

33. Bray, interview; Logue, interview, Steen, March 3, 1986, Lincoln, MA, 34.

34. Lee, interview.

35. Logue said that one of his greatest satisfactions was mentoring the next generation; Bray, interview; Peter Bray, letter to the editor, *NYT*, February 4, 2000.

36. Jennifer Raab, interview by Lizabeth Cohen, February 27, 2009, New York, NY; Lee, interview.

37. Bray, interview.

38. South Bronx Development Office, *Areas of Strength, Areas of Opportunity: South Bronx Revitalization Program and Development Guide Plan*, December 1980.

39. Quote from *Neighborhood*, August 1982, cited in Rosenthal, *In the South Bronx of America*, 89; A. O. Sulzberger, Jr., "Job Growth Since 1976 Is Mostly in Manhattan," *NYT*, October 6, 1981. In this period the Bronx and Brooklyn lost jobs, while

Manhattan, Queens, and Staten Island gained them; Logue to Whom It May Interest, Memo with South Bronx Profile, April 27, 1984, Bray. For a thorough analysis, see Peter Bray, "SBDO's Economic Development Role" and "Private Perspective," chapters 4 and 5, MIT thesis draft, Bray.

40. Bray, "SBDO's Economic Development Role"; Logue to Peter Bray, August 10, 1982, with Logue comments on the Bray case study of SBDO economic development work, focusing on Gabriel Industries, and manuscript, "The South Bronx Development Office 1," Bray, 13–17.

41. Logue, interview by Jill Jonnes, August 9, 1984, quoted in *South Bronx Rising*, 384–85; also "Bathgate Tenants Move In," *South Bronx Developments* (newsletter), March 1982, 1; Glynn, "Charlotte Street, the Bronx," 30; *Bathgate Industrial Park*, promotional brochure, n.d. but c. 1981; *New York City Public Development Corporation*, brochure, n.d., 13; William R. Greer, "South Bronx, Once Symbol of Blight, Draws Industry," *NYT*, January 15, 1984; John Lewis, "Blight Fighter Chalks Up Gains," *NYDN*, February 21, 1984; Alan S. Oser, "Port Authority Fashions a Bronx Industrial Showcase," *NYT*, July 7, 1985. By 2003, Bathgate supported 2,500 jobs; Peter Bray, "Rebuilding the South Bronx: The Role of the Public Entrepreneur," lecture, April 2, 2003, Notre Dame University, Bray.

42. *Meanwhile, in the South Bronx . . .* , (New York: SBDO, 1983), 20–25; "South Bronx Launches Employment Training Program," *South Bronx Developments*, November 1982, 1, 6.

43. On compaction, see Logue, interview by Bray; *Meanwhile, in the South Bronx . . .* , 26–27.

44. Logue to Hon. Edward I. Koch, RE: Charlotte Gardens Marketing, May 12, 1983, EJL, 1985 Accession, Box 111, Folder "Mayor's Office–Koch." One of the first owners in Charlotte Gardens, Herb Sellers, valued how he could "walk around" his house; Michael Winkleman, "The Bronx: High-Rise, No-Rise," *Metropolis*, April 1985, 34; also Carleton Knight III, "Ed Logue, Hard-Nosed Houser," *Architecture* 74, no. 7 (July 1985): 61. See A. K. Sandoval-Strausz, "Latino Landscapes: Postwar Cities and the Transnational Origins of a New Urban America," *JAH* 101, no. 3 (December 2014): 804–31, for Latin American and Caribbean use of yards.

45. Quoted in John J. Goldman, "Master Rebuilder of Cities Hired to Revive the South Bronx, Epitome of Urban Decay," *LAT*, December 26, 1978.

46. Bray, "Rebuilding the South Bronx," 16–17; Bray, interview.

47. Logue, "Charlotte Gardens: Is There a Future for Single Family Homes in New York?," March 17, 1985, EJL, 2002 Accession, Box 22, Folder "Charlotte Gardens," 12.

48. Edward Logue to Hon. Carlos C. Campbell, Assistant Secretary for Economic Development, Economic Development Administration, May 18, 1983, EJL, 1985 Accession, Box 107, Folder "Manufactured Housing–Correspondence"; Logue to William Eimicke, Deputy Secretary for Policy and Programs, Albany, December 16, 1983, EJL, 1985 Accession, Box 112, Folder "NYS"; Logue to Mayor Edward I. Koch, January 27, 1984, EJL, 1985 Accession, Box 111, Folder "Mayor's Office–Koch"; SBDO, "South Bronx Manufactured Homes Program Project Area Description and Market Study," November 10, 1982, Bray; Sandy Ewing to Logue, August 17, 1984, "RE: Housing Factory—My Final Report," including SBDO, "Proposed Housing Factory at the Mid-Bronx Industrial Park," May 29, 1984, Bray; Lee, interview.

49. On Gliedman's opposition to Logue, SBDO, and Charlotte Gardens, Bray, interview; Koch, interview by von Hoffman. Gliedman agreed to certify Charlotte Gardens only after he saw the enthusiasm for it. Logue told interviewer Frank Jones, "It's becoming clear that [Gliedman] despises me and everything I believe in and stand for. It's very mutual, by the way"; Logue, interview, Jones, Tape 4:60–61.

50. Richard Manson, interview by Alexander von Hoffman, March 8, 2001.

51. Bray, "Rebuilding the South Bronx," 20–21; Bray, interview; von Hoffman, *House by House*, 37 for Julie Sandorf's vivid description of the transport.

52. On Charlotte Gardens houses, Bray, "Rebuilding the South Bronx," 18–19. By some accounts, the final unit cost of $114,000 represented a cost overrun of over 100 percent; Peter Bray, "Thesis Outline," February 24, 1988, Bray, 9.

53. "South Bronx: Strength from Unity Reviving an Urban Wasteland," *LAT*, July 26, 198; Thomas Glynn, "Interview with Anita Miller, a Warrior for the South Bronx," *Neighborhood*, 37; *Meanwhile, in the South Bronx . . .* , 15. Also, MBD, "Dear Charlotte Gardens Homebuyer," January 9, 1983, listing workshops offered; Bray. Worksheets and "Some Questions and Answers on Purchasing a Home in Charlotte Gardens" are impressively detailed and clearly presented in the folder "Charlotte Gardens: South Bronx Manufactured Homes Program," Bray; on tax abatements, Julia MacDonnell Chang, "Financing the South Bronx Homeownership Project," *City Limits*, May 1983, 22.

54. Philip Shenon, "A Taste of Suburbia Arrives in the South Bronx," *NYT*, March 19, 1983 (front page). A small sampling of other publicity, chronologically, includes "Ranch Houses? Where?," editorial, *NYT*, March 24, 1983; "Factory-Built Subdivision Opens on Charlotte Street in So. Bronx," *Home Again for Housing and Community Professionals*, Winter 1983, no. 1, 6; "Bronx Cheer," *Economist*, May 14, 1983; "Renewal Project in South Bronx Proves Popular," *BG*, August 19, 1983; "Middle-Class Eager to Buy Homes in Bronx Wasteland," *LAT*, August 15, 1983; "Suburbia Comes to the South Bronx," *Architecture*, October 1983, 65; "'Pioneer' Settlers Bring Glow to South Bronx," *NYT*, January 14, 1984; and Mark Starr with David L. Gonzalez, "Ranch Houses at Fort Apache," *Newsweek*, February 13, 1984.

55. Koch quotes on Charlotte Gardens project from Joyce Purnack, "Metro Matters: He Reshaped the Places We Live," *NYT*, April 24, 2000; Koch quote at dedication in Logue, "Charlotte Gardens: Is There a Future for Single-Family Homes in New York?," 8; Logue quote from Logue, interview, Jones, Tape 4:62. While frustrated that "this has never been on the top of Ed Koch's agenda," Logue also recognized that "if you take office on January 1, 1978, what's your problem? It isn't the revitalization of the South Bronx . . . It's the salvation of the goddamn city financials"; Logue, interview by Bray. Ironically, Koch had spent the first five years of his life in the Charlotte Street area of the Bronx. The invitee list for the Charlotte Gardens ribbon cutting was pages long and included elected officials; city, state, and federal employees from many departments; private-sector and nonprofit representatives; and members of dozens of Bronx community organizations—a testament both to how many people contributed to the project and to the SBDO's ambitious public relations effort; Bray.

56. Logue to Campbell, May 18, 1983, EJL, 36, and described in much of the press coverage.

57. Litke, interview.

58. "Suburbia Comes to the South Bronx," *Architecture*; for more on Charlotte Gardens buyers, see John Lewis, "Blight Fighter Chalks Up Gains," *NYDN*, February 21, 1984; Barbara Stewart, "Market's Nod to a Rebirth," *NYT Magazine*, November 2, 1997; Sandy Ewing to Logue, June 6, 1983, "RE: Charlotte Garden Applicants," Bray.

59. Logue to South Bronx Policy Group, January 13, 1982, EJL, Box 105, Folder "MH Meetings, Agendas"; "Phase 1 Residents," November 16, 1983, EJL, 1985 Accession, Box 111, Folder "First Ten"; Winkleman, "The Bronx: High-Rise, No-Rise," 35; Manny Fernandez, "In the Bronx, Blight Gave Way to Renewal," *NYT*, October 5, 2007; Peter L. Bray, "Charlotte Gardens: Planning a New Community in the South Bronx," September 20, 1984, Bray, 20–21.

60. Julie Sandorf, "Crotona South/Mid-Bronx Homeownership Demand Study," February 1985, Bray, 6–7; Sandy Ewing to Logue, June 15, 1983, "RE: Income Levels of Charlotte Gardens Applicants," Bray.

61. Analysis of Charlotte Gardens residents, prepared by Brian Goldstein, based on New York City Department of Finance—Digital Tax Map Online, http://gis.nyc.gov /dof/dtm/mapviewer.jsf, and information about buyers in EJL, 1985 Accession, Boxes 107, 108, 110, 111; also Stewart, "Market's Nod to a Rebirth," that, by 1997, only eight houses had been put up for sale.

62. Carmen and Rafael Ceballo, interview by Peter L'Official, April 12, 2010, Bronx, NY; Josephine Cohn and Preston Keusch, interview by Peter L'Official, April 16, 2010, Bronx, NY; Riveras interviewed in "'Pioneer' Settlers Bring Glow to South Bronx," and "Urban Homesteaders," *Time*, January 30, 1984.

63. "South Bronx Revival," editorial, *WP*, January 17, 1984; "Suburbia Comes to the South Bronx," *Architecture*.

64. Starr with Gonzalez, "Ranch Houses at Fort Apache"; Sam Roberts, "Charlotte Street: Tortured Rebirth of a Wasteland," *NYT*, March 9, 1987; Goldstein, analysis of Charlotte Gardens residents, 1520 Crotona Park East deed, originally held by David and Irma Rivera, passed to Belia and John Clark, July 1995.

65. Edward J. Logue to John Goldman of *LAT*, May 27, 1982, EJL, Box 107, 1985 Accession, Folder "MH Correspondence, Miscellaneous."

66. Liebman, interview. For other criticism of the low density, see Bradford McKee, "South Bronx," *Architecture*, April 1995, 86–95; Richard Plunz, letter to the editor, *NYT*, November 5, 1997; Roberta Brandes Gratz, *The Living City: How America's Cities Are Being Revitalized by Thinking Small in a Big Way* (Washington, DC: Preservation Press, 1994), 133–34.

67. Norval White and Elliot Willensky, *AIA Guide to New York City*, 4th ed. (New York: Three Rivers Press, 2000), 562. Interestingly, in the 2010 edition, this text was removed and in its place was substituted "President Clinton returned in 1997 to a rebuilt neighborhood, transformed into suburbia"; White and Willensky with Fran Leadon, *AIA Guide to New York City*, 5th ed. (New York: Oxford University Press, 2010), 835.

68. "Her Critical Judgments Were Built to Last," *WSJ*, January 8, 2013; Ada Louise Huxtable, "The Man Who Remade New York," *On Architecture: Collected Reflections on a Century of Change* (New York: Walker, 2008), 342.

69. Litke, interview; Winkleman, "A Slice of the Pie," in "The Bronx: High-Rise, No-Rise," 29. Bray concluded that Logue never intended to make a design statement,

only a social statement: "The house that is the house of choice for millions of white Americans should be available to minorities, who are often excluded by discrimination from buying those houses in the suburbs"; Peter Bray, "MIT Thesis Outline," February 24, 1988, Bray, 14.

70. Edward J. Logue to Melvin Senchak, HUD, December 28, 1982, with attachment "Architects [sic] Services and Responsibilities," EJL, 1985 Accession, Box 113, Folder "MH Tessler, Jul–Dec '82." I. M. Pei concurred that developers, whose "interest is their bottom line," usurped the place of architects: "They want to be celebrities themselves. So the architect becomes secondary"; Ieoh Ming Pei, interview by Lizabeth Cohen, June 11, 2007, New York, NY.

71. Ellen Seidman, "Don't Blame the Community Reinvestment Act," and Mark A. Willis, "Community Reinvestment: The Broader Agenda," *American Prospect*, July–August 2009, A15–17, 26–29.

72. See, for example, my own analysis of the typological breakdown of prominent modernist Paul Rudolph's projects. His public work grew over the 1950s and 1960s, the heyday of federal urban renewal; peaked between 1966 to 1970; and began a steep decline from 1971 to 1975 from which it never recovered; "Paul Rudolph, Projects, 1946–95," graph, in Lizabeth Cohen and Brian D. Goldstein, "Paul Rudolph and the Rise and Fall of Urban Renewal," in *Reassessing Rudolph*, ed. Timothy M. Rohan (New Haven, CT: Yale School of Architecture, 2017), 16.

73. Kathleen Teltsch, "Once Desperate, a Bronx Housing Group Earns Praise," *NYT*, October 30, 1987.

74. On Genevieve Brooks: Teltsch, "Once Desperate, a Bronx Housing Group Earns Praise"; Breslin, "On These Sidewalks of New York," 106; Les Christie, "The Greatest Real Estate Turnaround Ever," *CNNMoney*, November 25, 2009.

75. Julie Sandorf, interview by Alexander von Hoffman, November 9, 2000, New York, NY; Logue, "Charlotte Gardens: Is There a Future for Single Family Homes in New York?," 25; SBDO, "Charlotte Gardens Manufactured Homes Program," March 23, 1983, Bray, 2.

76. Bray, interview.

77. Sandy Ewing to Logue, July 14, 1983, "RE: MBD's Charlotte Gardens Candidates," EJL, 1985 Accession, Box 111, Folder "MH Mid Bronx Desperadoes, 1981–Aug 1983." For more subtle evidence of tension between the SBDO and the MBD, see the published SBDO Report of 1983, *Meanwhile, in the South Bronx . . .* , which contained an erratum slip with an apology that complimentary mention of the MBD's role had inadvertently been left out, suggesting that the MBD had protested. In another example, when Brooks was interviewed upon receipt of a major service award, she made no mention of the SBDO's role in Charlotte Gardens; *Meanwhile, in the South Bronx . . .* , 16, attached erratum slip; interview with Genevieve Brooks, *Makers*, https://www.makers.com/profiles/591f26dea8c7c425e029ca7a/5547c499e4b0f61941cd91f2.

78. Sandorf, interview by von Hoffman; Logue to Xavier Rodriguez, Board No. 3, December 13, 1983, EJL, Box 106, Folder "Community Board No. 3," with his apology for not adequately recognizing community leaders when Governor Cuomo visited and reiterating his respect for them.

79. For Father Smith's praise of Logue as a "visionary" who "if he hadn't pushed for Charlotte Gardens, that wouldn't have gotten done," see Father William Smith,

interview by Alexander von Hoffman, November 28, 2000. For Logue's compliments toward his MBD partners, see MLogue, interview; Logue, "Life as a City Builder—'Make No Little Plans,'" *Yale Reunion Book*, March 26, 1991, 22; Logue, interview, Jones, Tape 5:1, 9.

80. *Meanwhile, in the South Bronx . . .* ; Karolyn Gould, interview by Lizabeth Cohen, June 12, 2007, New York, NY, and Karolyn Gould, email message to author, October 3, 2006; Bray, interview; Peter Cantillo, interview by Peter Bray, n.d.

81. Jack Flanagan quote in Peirce and Hagstrom, "Two Years After Carter's Visit," 1647; Veralyne Hamilton quote in Jonnes, *South Bronx Rising*, 327–28. For Logue's advice on working with community groups, Jack Towe, letter to the editor, *Planning*, September 1984, 26.

82. Bruce Porter, "Ford, Logue and the South Bronx: A Report to the Ford Foundation, Confidential," Ford Foundation Records, Series II: Program and Grant-Related Files, Office Files of Bernard McDonald, Urban Poverty Program, Rockefeller Archive Center, Sleepy Hollow, NY (hereafter Ford), Box 3, Folder 6, November 21, 1980, 9. This report has a lengthy discussion of Logue's interactions with the South Bronx community, 9–19.

83. Bray, interview; Cantillo, interview by Bray, saw the mutual benefit. On the establishment of community boards in 1975 and mayors' dislike of them, see Bruce Berg, *New York City Politic: Governing Gotham* (New Brunswick, NJ: Rutgers University Press, 2007), 277–79.

84. Brooks quoted in Jim Yardley, "Clinton Praises Bronx Renewal as U.S. Model," *NYT*, December 11, 1997; Brother Patrick in Porter, "Ford, Logue and the South Bronx," 12.

85. Bray has a fascinating final chapter in his thesis draft, "Public Sector Assessment," where his interviews with New York City public officials revealed "tremendous ambivalence about Logue" and wariness, based on his history, that "he was seeking or would be provided with an independent power base with control over vast amounts of federal funds." Hence, the SBDO was subject to regular city processes and granted no special dispensations. Nonetheless, over time, officials came to appreciate "SBDO's possession of knowledge regarding the community and its actors . . . [One] official explained that SBDO has been an important resource in terms of assessing the political sentiment of the local community towards certain projects"; Bray, MIT thesis draft, chapter 6, Bray.

86. Porter, "Ford, Logue and the South Bronx," 20; Frederick O'R. Hayes, Sharon L. Franz, Joan M. Leiman, Jerry E. Mechling, "The South Bronx Development Organization: What It Has Accomplished and How It Is Viewed," April 15, 1982, report by the Frederick O'R. Hayes Associates for the Fund for the City of New York, 33–43, 59–60.

87. Von Hoffman, *House by House*, 31; Breslin, "On These Sidewalks of New York," 108; Peirce and Hagstrom, "Two Years After Carter's Visit," 1644; Jensen, *Devastation/ Resurrection: The South Bronx*, 84–85; Neil R. Peirce, "South Bronx Rising," *WP*, October 4, 1979; Gratz, *Living City*, 82–85, 103–10, 127–39.

88. Logue, interview, Jones, Tape 5:10.

89. Louis Gigante quote from conference transcript, "New Homes for New York Neighborhoods," 1984, 58–60, cited in Orlebeke, *New Life at Ground Zero*, 174–75.

90. On Nighthawks: von Hoffman, *House by House*, 39; Bray, interview, 89; Koch, interview by von Hoffman; Logue, interview, Jones, Tape 5:3. Nonetheless, transforming vigilante Nighthawk gang members into vigilant night guards required patience and supervision. Problems included guards sleeping and watching TV on duty, entertaining girlfriends, vandalizing houses and SBDO equipment, playing with firecrackers, and pulling pranks like ordering limousines; EJL, 1985 Accession, Box 112, Folder "Security 1982–Aug. '83"; "Security Sept. '83–Dec. '84."

91. Logue, letter to the editor, *NYT*, April 7, 1983. On Logue's praise for Catholic clergy in the South Bronx, see Joseph Giovannini, "The Appeal of Bronx Living," *NYT*, July 5, 1984; Jonnes, *South Bronx Rising*, 379. On the Catholic Church's impact in the South Bronx, see Porter, "Ford, Logue and the South Bronx," 4–8; Glynn, "Neighborhood," 21. Brother Patrick Lochrane of Saint Joseph's Roman Catholic Church served as chair of Community Board No. 6 and was also an activist partner to SBDO; "Community Profile: Brother Patrick Lochrane," *South Bronx Developments*, May–June 1983, 4.

92. Orlebeke, *New Life at Ground Zero*, 61–65; Logue, interview by Bray, on use of Section 235, 9, 37; Amy Alson, "Broken Promises in the South Bronx," *Crain's New York Business*, November 5, 1985.

93. On Section 8, Orlebeke, *New Life at Ground Zero*, 34–36, 71, 104; *Affordable Housing in New York*, 198.

94. Neal R. Peirce and Carol F. Steinbach, *Corrective Capitalism: The Rise of America's Community Development Corporations; A Report to the Ford Foundation* (New York: Ford Foundation, 1987), 57; Roger Biles, *The Fate of Cities: Urban America and the Federal Government, 1956–2000* (Lawrence: University Press of Kansas, 2011), 255. Also on housing cuts, see Alice O'Connor, "Swimming Against the Tide: A Brief History of Federal Policy in Poor Communities," in *Urban Problems and Community Development*, ed. Ronald F. Ferguson and William T. Dickens (Washington, DC: Brookings Institution Press, 1999), 112–15; on Urban Development Action Grant and Community Development Block Grants, see Orlebeke, *New Life at Ground Zero*, 74–75, 193–94; Lynne B. Sagalyn, "Public/Private Development: Lessons from History, Research and Practice," *Journal of the American Planning Association* 73, no. 1 (Winter 2007): 7–22.

95. Jonnes, *South Bronx Rising*, 397; Camilo Jose Vergara, "A South Bronx Landscape," *Nation*, March 6, 1989, 305; *Meanwhile, in the South Bronx . . .* , 15, 19.

96. Logue, interview, Jones, Tape 5:1; Logue to Peter L. Bray, November 20, 1984, with SONYMA agreement of October 2, 1984, attached, EJL, 1985 Accession, Box 113, Folder "MH SONMYA, 1983–"; "State Funds Come to Aid of S. Bronx Renewal," *New York Tribune*, December 10, 1983. A full summary of the funding tapped to underwrite Charlotte Gardens is in Sandorf, "Crotona South/Mid-Bronx Homeownership Demand Study," February 1985, Bray, 5.

97. Logue, "New Directions for National Housing Policy: Remarks by Edward J. Logue, President, SBDO, Inc.," July 8, 1983, Washington Athletic Club, Seattle, National Housing Conference, sponsored by the Center for National Policy, D.C., and City of Seattle, 1.

98. Edgar J. Driscoll, Jr., "Edward Logue Is Dead: Gave Boston a New Face," *BG*, January 28, 2000.

99. On LISC, see Karen Ferguson, *Top Down: The Ford Foundation and the Reinvention of Racial Liberalism* (Philadelphia: University of Pennsylvania Press, 2013), 210–12, 242–54, 260; Peirce and Steinbach, *Corrective Capitalism*, 61, 75–77; Kathleen Teltsch, "Activist Making Switch to Academia," *NYT*, December 29, 1985; Glynn, "Interview with Anita Miller, a Warrior for the South Bronx," 34–37; Anita Miller, interview by Alexander von Hoffman, December 7, 2000; Manson, interview by von Hoffman; Jonnes, *South Bronx Rising*, 378, 394.

100. Miller, interview by von Hoffman.

101. Manson, interview by von Hoffman; Bray, "Charlotte Gardens: Planning a New Community in the South Bronx," 17; "LISC, South Bronx Program, Summary Status of Program Actions, for Period January 1, 1981 through December 1, 1981," Ford, Microfilm Reel 5488, three entries for SBDO ($150,000 loan, $40,000 grant, with reference to previous $10,000 grant). Correspondence between Logue and LISC was filled with SBDO requests for additional grants and loans to tide it over and meet costs of required services; see, for example, related to financing for South Bronx Manufactured Homes Program, from Bray: "South Bronx Home-ownership Program Manufacturing Homes Feasibility/Marketability," November 22, 1981; Logue to Anita Miller, February 18, 1982; Logue to Miller, March 9, 1982; Logue to Miller, October 29, 1982; Sol H. Chafkin (Executive Vice President, LISC) to Logue, October 25, 1983; Logue to Mitchell Sviridoff, December 27, 1984.

102. Von Hoffman, *House by House*, 15; Jonnes, *South Bronx Rising*, 378. Sviridoff explains the importance of developing technical capacity in local CDC leaders in *Inventing Community Renewal: The Trials and Errors That Shaped the Modern Community Development Corporation*, ed. Sviridoff (New York: Community Development Research Center, Milano Graduate School, New School University, 2004), 241–46.

103. Paul Goldberger, "James W. Rouse, 81, Dies; Socially Conscious Developer Built New Towns and Malls," *NYT*, April 10, 1996; Peirce and Steinbach, *Corrective Capitalism*, 77–81.

104. Nicholas Lemann, "The Myth of Community Development," *NYT Magazine*, June 9, 1994; Ellis Henican, "Urban-Zone Plan Meets Skepticism," Columbia Graduate School of Journalism publication, January 29, 1982.

105. Logue, interview by Jill Jonnes, May 18, 1983, quoted in *South Bronx Rising*, 377. He also said, "In retrospect, building Roosevelt Island, tramway and all, seems easy"; in Alan S. Oser, "Lessons from One-Family Housing in the South Bronx," *NYT*, April 21, 1985.

106. Stewart, "Market's Nod to a Rebirth."

107. Bray, interview.

108. Gliedman went so far as to tell a prospective contractor for Charlotte Gardens that "if you sign that contract, you will never do any work for the City of New York again"; Bray, interview. On the corruption at Pierce's HUD, Biles, *Fate of Cities*, 279–83; Philip Shenon, "Samuel R. Pierce Jr., Ex-Housing Secretary, Dies at 78," *NYT*, November 3, 2000; Robert L. Jackson, "Samuel R. Pierce, Jr.; Reagan HUD Chief Was Investigated but Never Charged," *LAT*, November 4, 2000.

109. Gerald M. Boyd, "H.U.D. Won't Renew Grant for Agency in South Bronx," *NYT*, February 24, 1984; "Reneging on the South Bronx," editorial, *WP*, April 28, 1984.

110. Logue, interview, Jones, Tape 5:7; Dan O'Grady, "4 Groups Share U.S. Grant," *NYDN*, June 11, 1984; Mayor Edward I. Koch to Hon. James A. Baker, III (Chief of Staff, White House), March 6, 1984, EJL, 1985 Accession, Box 92, Folder "Funding March 1–14, 1984," with attachment of "Why Sabotage the South Bronx," editorial, *NYDN*, February 28, 1984. On Velez's support of Reagan, Owen Moritz, "Is HUD Dancing to a Latin Beat in the Bronx?," *NYDN*, March 11, 1984; George Arzt, "Top Hispanic May Bolt Dems for Reagan," *New York Post*, March 27, 1984; Owen Moritz, "Departing Ed Logue Sees Hope for South Bronx," *NYDN*, October 7, 1984; Logue thought he might have offended Pierce when he criticized him in testimony to Congress, prompting Pierce to enter a "cabal with [Stanley] Friedman, [Stanley] Simon, [Robert] Garcia, and Mario Biaggi," all Bronx politicians who would end up serving time in prison. Logue, fearing the worst by late February 1984, started lobbying everyone he could think of—elected officials, journalists, and business leaders—touting the SBDO's accomplishments and attaching comprehensive surveys and clippings that documented SBDO activities and investment in the South Bronx.

111. Logue to Hon. Edward I. Koch, May 16, 1984, Bray; "Planning Chief to Leave in Fall," *NYDN*, May 23, 1984; "Topics: Shaping the Future—City Builder," *NYT*, May 24, 1984.

112. Lawrence Chandler, Charlotte Gardens buyer, handwritten letter to the editor complaining about lack of HUD support, sent to *NYT*, *NYDN*, *New York Post*, Hon. Robert Garcia, Hon. Mario Biaggi, and Hon. Alphonse Demato [*sic*], March 15, 1984, EJL, 1985 Accession, Box 92, Folder "Funding March 1–14, 1984"; Henry Hylton, President, Charlotte Gardens Homeowners/buyers Association, to Mayor Koch, December 20, 1984, EJL, 1985 Accession, Box 108, Folder "Homeowners Association," reiterating that "we demand completion with Edward Logue in charge"; Logue to Robert Esnard (Deputy Mayor for Physical Development), January 3, 1985, EJL, 1985 Accession, Box 111, Folder "CG–Esnard."

113. On SBDO after Logue's departure, Office of the Mayor, City of New York, press release, January 4, 1985, released February 1985, announcing the appointment of Jorge L. Batista as president of SBDO; Bray, interview; Robert Esnard, interview by Lizabeth Cohen, February 19, 2010, New York, NY; Gould, interview; John Lewis, "Batista Replacing Ed Logue," *The Bronx*, January 14, 1985. On ties between Batista and Velez, see Wayne Barrett, "A Bronx Cheer for Ethics," *Village Voice*, December 31, 1985; Philip Shenon, "South Bronx Development Agency Is Target of Investigation by City," *NYT*, February 4, 1986; Jorge L. Batista to SBDO Staff, March 3, 1987, "RE: Closing Down of SBDO," Bray; Bray, "MIT Thesis Outline," 10; Sam Howe Verovek, "After Heated Debate, Vice Chancellor Is Selected to Lead Regents," *NYT*, November 16, 1991, announces that Batista was named vice chancellor of the New York State Board of Regents.

114. Logue, interview by Bray; Logue, interview by Jonnes, August 9, 1984, in Jonnes, *South Bronx Rising*, 388.

115. On Mayor Koch's ambitious ten-year plan and its resemblance to the SBDO's approach, see Jonathan Soffer, *Ed Koch and the Rebuilding of New York City* (New York:

Columbia University Press, 2010), 290-304; *Affordable Housing in New York*, 273-76; Orlebeke, *New Life at Ground Zero*, 117-21; "Housing Policy in New York City: A Brief History," Working Paper 06-01, Furman Center for Real Estate and Urban Policy; Abraham Biderman, interview by John Metzger, August 20, 1992, COH, 1-14; Robert Esnard, interview by John Metzger, April 7, 1995, COH, 2/55-57; von Hoffman, *House by House*, 48-51; Bray, "Rebuilding the South Bronx," 24.

116. Koch, interview by von Hoffman.
117. Lloyd Ultan and Barbara Unger, *Bronx Accents: A Literary and Pictorial History of the Borough* (New Brunswick, NJ: Rivergate Books, Rutgers University Press, 2000), 276.
118. Miller, interview by von Hoffman.
119. Stewart, "Market's Nod to a Rebirth."
120. Sandorf, interview by von Hoffman.
121. Jonnes, *South Bronx Rising*, xv.
122. Jonnes, *South Bronx Rising*, 396, on Nehemiah, 66-67; Glynn, "Interview with Anita Miller, a Warrior for the South Bronx," 37, on low density.
123. Yardley, "Clinton Praises Bronx Renewal as U.S. Model"; Manny Fernandez, "In the Bronx, Blight Gave Way to Renewal," *NYT*, October 5, 2007; Clinton visit described in Jonnes, *South Bronx Rising*, 405.
124. Jim Yardley, "A Master Builder's Mixed Legacy: Forgotten by the Public, 'Mr. Urban Renewal' Looks Back," *NYT*, December 29, 1997; Herbert Gans, email message to Frank Barrett, September 13, 2007, shared by Barrett in email message to author, September 14, 2007; also Herbert Gans, interview by Lizabeth Cohen, February 18, 2010, New York, NY; Raab, interview, for similar view.
125. Michael Lawson and Kat Aaron, "Promoting Home Ownership Through the Years," *Investigative Reporting Workshop*, American University School of Communications, July 21, 2011.
126. Litke, interview.

Conclusion: The End of a Life and an Era

1. On Logue's Vineyard activities: Logue, interview, Jones, Tape 5:41-44; "Edward J. Logue Rebuilt Cities," *Vineyard Gazette*, February 4, 2000; "Ed Logue, R.I.P.," editorial, *Martha's Vineyard Times*, February 3, 2000; "Ed Logue and the Vineyard," biography prepared for County Commissioner Election, October 1994, MDL; Logue, "Affordable Housing: An Urgent Need," guest editorial, *Martha's Vineyard Gazette*, August 20, 1999; Logue, "$7.5 Million Is a Lot of Money," letter to the editor, *Martha's Vineyard Times*, n.d., 1999; Eric L. Peters, Chairman, Vineyard Land Foundation, to Margaret Logue and Family, February 11, 2000, MDL.
2. Rebecca Lee, interview by Lizabeth Cohen, March 9, 2010, Boston, MA. Logue's communications with his friends and former associates were prolific. Of particular note was a celebratory lunch that colleagues gave him in Washington, DC, in May 1995. Details, including guest lists, are in EJL, Accession 2002-M-001, Box 23, Folder "EJL, Bill Slayton's Party." A birthday gathering in May 1994 with the old New Haven gang is documented in the same box.
3. There were actually two companies—Logue Development Company, Inc., revived from the 1970s, and Logue Boston Limited Partnership, which he founded with

John Ryan, John Bok, and David Place as a development company that focused mostly on the State Service Center project. For Logue's consulting projects, see Linda Corman, "Former BRA Head Takes Another Look at the City He Helped Plan," *Banker and Tradesman*, October 21, 1987, 1, 3, 6, 9; William Tuttle, interview by Lizabeth Cohen, March 6, 2010, Belmont, MA, touches on most of his Boston projects; Anthony Pangaro, interview by Lizabeth Cohen, June 24, 2009, Boston, MA, on the failed Emerson College effort; Anupreeta Das, "Out of the Shadows," *BG Magazine*, November 12, 2006; Jerry Ackerman, "Time Catches Up with the New Boston, Government Center Faces Many Changes," *BG*, December 24, 1989; David Nyhan, "When Politics Clash with an Affordable-Housing Plan," *BG*, June 26, 1990, on the BU Law School plan; Matt Carroll and Jerry Ackerman, "Lots and Blocks," *BG*, April 12, 1992, on the Worcester project. For Logue's work in Atlanta, see interviews by Alexander von Hoffman with Clara Axam, August 1, 2000; Randall Roark, August 3, 2000; and Robert Begle, August 3, 2000, all in Atlanta, GA. Also, Alexander von Hoffman, *House by House, Block by Block: The Rebirth of America's Urban Neighborhoods* (New York: Oxford University Press, 2003), 174.

4. Tuttle, interview.

5. Jim Yardley, "A Master Builder's Mixed Legacy: Forgotten by the Public, 'Mr. Urban Renewal' Looks Back," *NYT*, December 29, 1997.

6. Lawrence Vale, interview by Lizabeth Cohen, November 23, 2005, Cambridge, MA.

7. Robin Berry, interview by Lizabeth Cohen, September 19, 2007, by telephone.

8. A good example is Logue, "Former BRA Director Logue Issues a Report Card," *BG*, June 8, 1986.

9. John Stainton, interview by Lizabeth Cohen, May 30, 2007, Jamaica Plain, MA.

10. For examples of conferences Logue attended and addressed: Charles A. Radin, "Boston Architects' Conference Yields Consensus for Growth," *BG*, April 11, 1987; Jim Miara, "Real Estate Experts View the Past as a Guide to the Future," *Boston Business Journal*, November 7, 1997; invitation to "A Reception for Friends of Edward Logue, Winner of the American Planning Association's Distinguished Leadership Award," April 7, 1998, Tavern Club, Boston; and Larry Koff to Sarah Polster (American Planning Association), September 12, 1997, nomination of Logue with seventeen letters of support from colleagues over the years; MDL.

11. Tuttle, interview.

12. Frank Barrett was doing research on Jerome Lyle Rappaport; Barrett, interview by Lizabeth Cohen, July 25, 2007 by telephone; Barrett, email to Kim Heath and Family and Friends of Edward Logue, January 28, 2000.

13. Program for "Memorial Service for Edward J. Logue, February 2, 1921–January 27, 2000, Faneuil Hall, Boston, Massachusetts, Saturday, April 22, 2000, 2:00 p.m.'; MDL.

14. Logue, Schussheim interview, 39.

15. Logue to Herbert A. Tessler, memorandum, March 19, 1984, EJL, 1985 Accession, Box 113, Folder "MH Tessler 1983–": "Our new friends cannot have an all white set of subs either here or anywhere else they expect to do publicly assisted housing in the City of New York." On persistent segregation of schools, Fred Harris and Alan Curtis, "The Unmet Promise of Equality," *NYT*, March 1, 2018.

16. For Logue's continued call for greater federal involvement in housing: Logue, "Housing as a National Responsibility," *Oculus*, April 1989, 4–5, special issue of the publication of New York Chapter of the AIA, "Can New York Afford Affordable Housing?"

17. Quoted in "'New Boston' Planner Comes Back for More," *BH*, January 12, 1988.

18. "'New Boston' Planner Comes Back for More"; Tuttle, interview.

19. On Logue's architectural ambitions for the UDC, *Housing New York: Ed Logue and His Architects*, brochure from the exhibition presented by the Architectural League and the Municipal Art Society, Urban Center, New York, NY, February 5–April 14, 2001.

20. Logue, "Could Growth Kill Boston's Boom?," Boston College Citizen Seminars, May 19, 1987, 2, 3, 5, MDL; Logue: "The public sector created the New Boston and the public sector must control it," n.d., MDL; Logue, "The New Boston—Can the City Control Its Future?," *Boston Observer*, c. 1985, EJL, 2002 Accession, Box 22. Also see the tribute to Logue after his death by the *NYT* architecture critic Herbert Muschamp, who argued that what began as a repudiation of "large-scale, top-down urban renewal associated with the likes of Logue" had the unintended consequence of fostering "the capitulation of city planning to the private sector and its market-driven pressures"; "From an Era When Equality Mattered," *NYT*, February 20, 2000.

21. A tremendous amount has been reported on the shortage of affordable housing of all sorts. See, for example, Conor Dougherty, "Tax Overhaul Is a Blow to Affordable Housing Efforts," *NYT*, January 18, 2018; Glenn Thrush, "With Market Hot, Landlords Slam the Door on Section 8 Tenants," *NYT*, October 12, 2018; Aaron Schrank, "It's a Long Wait for Section 8 Housing in U.S. Cities," *Marketplace,* NPR, January 3, 2018; Laura Sullivan, "Section 8 Vouchers Help the Poor—but Only if Housing Is Available," *All Things Considered*, NPR, May 10, 2017; Emily Badger, "These 95 Apartments Promised Affordable Rent in San Francisco. Then 6,580 People Applied," *NYT*, May 12, 2018. Every year since 1988 the Joint Center for Housing Studies of Harvard University has issued a report, "The State of the Nation's Housing," which documents the difficulties low-income families face in securing affordable housing; http://www.jchs.harvard.edu/state-nations-housing-2018. Also see Susan Saegert, interview by Lizabeth Cohen, February 19, 2010, New York, NY, on limited capacity of CDCs, the problems with Hope VI, and the increasing unmet demand for vouchers and public housing.

22. Nicholas Dagen Bloom and Matthew Gordon Lasner, eds., *Affordable Housing in New York: The People, Places, and Policies that Transformed a City* (Princeton, NJ: Princeton University Press, 2016), 251–52; Orlebeke, *New Life at Ground Zero*, 191–93.

23. Chris Arnold, "How the House Tax Overhaul Bill Could Hurt Affordable Housing," *Morning Edition*, NPR, December 15, 2017.

24. Beryl Satter, "Structural Injustice: A (Teenage) Primer," *Seventeen: Harvard Design Magazine*, no. 4 (Fall–Winter 2017): 125.

25. Raj Chetty, Nathaniel Hendren, and Lawrence Katz, "The Effects of Exposure to Better Neighborhoods on Children: New Evidence from Moving to Opportunity Experiment," *American Economic Review* 106, no. 4 (April 2016): 855–902; John Eligon,

Yamiche Alcindor, and Agustin Armendariz, "Tax Credits to House Poor Reinforce Racial Divisions," *NYT*, July 3, 2017; Barbara Samuels, "'Nowhere to Live Safe': Moving to Peace and Safety," *Poverty and Race* 23, no. 6 (November–December 2014): 1; Thomas B. Edsall, "Does Moving Poor People Work?," *NYT*, September 16, 2014.

26. Sarah Serpas, "For Low-Income People of Color in NYC, Segregation Is a Regional Problem," *City Limits*, August 1, 2016.

27. Robert Jensen and Cathy A. Alexander, "Resurrection: The People Are Doing It Themselves," in Robert Jensen, *Devastation/Resurrection: The South Bronx*, exhibition catalog, November 9, 1979–January 13, 1980, Bronx Museum of the Arts, 83–112; Karolyn Gould, email message to author, March 31, 2008.

28. Julie Sandorf, interview by Alexander von Hoffman, November 9, 2000, New York, NY, quoted in von Hoffman, *House by House*, 33.

29. Felice Michetti, interview by Alexander von Hoffman, March 9, 2001, New York, NY.

30. Edward Luce, "Beauty Contest Reveals Ugly Truths," *Financial Times*, June 6, 2018.

31. Logue cautioned about NIMBYism's excesses; "With the NIMBY . . . attitude [applying to] prisons, homeless shelters, trash disposal, affordable housing, [we] will come to realize that some decisions can't be left to localities. We need a public process, but not a local veto"; Corman, "Former BRA Head Takes Another Look at the City He Helped Plan," 6.

32. "New Data Reveals Huge Increases in Concentrated Poverty Since 2000," August 9, 2015, citing findings of Paul A. Jargowsky, *Architecture of Segregation: Civil Unrest, the Concentration of Poverty and Public Policy* (New York: Century Foundation, 2015), that the number of persons living in high-poverty neighborhoods nearly doubled from 2000 to 2015 and poverty became more concentrated there along racial lines; https://tcf.org/content/commentary/new-data-reveals-huge-increases-in-concentrated-poverty-since-2000/.

ACKNOWLEDGMENTS

It has become commonplace to say "It took a village" when seeking to highlight a great collaborative effort. In the case of this book, the almost fifteen years I have been at work on it and the many people who have helped me along the way suggest that it is more appropriate to say "It took a city." For about half of that time, I had the pleasure and responsibility of serving as dean of the Radcliffe Institute for Advanced Study at Harvard. Although that position undoubtedly delayed my writing, it taught me many things that proved of great value as I inched toward the book's publication. Above all, I became more fully aware of the importance of reaching out broadly with ideas that might otherwise remain within the academic realm. Radcliffe prides itself on bringing the latest scholarship to a wide, intellectually curious audience. Knowing that many Americans share my love for and worries about our nation's cities, I have taken a biographical approach to this book in hopes that it will help engage readers.

I thank my colleagues and advisory board members at the Radcliffe Institute, who worked closely with me for seven years to expand Radcliffe's reach and who were always supportive of "the book" that they knew was long simmering on the back burner.

There are risks and benefits to writing recent history that still lies within some people's recollections. The risk is that surviving participants will contest your interpretation. The benefit is the help they can offer, which I found to far outweigh the risk. I have been particularly fortunate that Ed Logue's family members and associates have been more than generous with their memories, their mementos, and their patience as they awaited the publication of this book. Ed Logue's wife, Margaret; children, Bill and Kathy; sister, Ellen; and late brother, Frank; as well as Ed and Margaret's assistant, Kim Heath, have been enormously helpful over the years, always eager to answer my questions, share family photographs and papers, and connect me with others, while remaining respectful of my independence as a historian. In the course of researching this book, I have interviewed or had substantive conversations with almost one hundred individuals. All enthusiastically welcomed me into their homes and offices or traveled distances to meet me. They often shared precious photos and documents, along with their reminiscences. Some were suffering from serious illnesses when I interviewed them, more than one attached to an oxygen tank. A few are no longer with us. What they had in common was a commitment to having Ed Logue's and their own stories told and made part of American history. This book would have been much the poorer without their voices.

For their willingness to be interviewed, I thank Mel Adams, Robert Beal, Robin Berry, John Bok, Peter Bray, Winifred Breines, Robert Campbell, James Cannon, Carmen and Rafael Ceballo, Harry Cobb, Josephine Cohn and Preston Keusch, Stephen Coyle, Robert Dahl, Frank Del Vecchio, Stephen Diamond, Larry DiCara, Peter Eisenman, Robert Esnard, Gordon Fellman, Janet Bowler Fitzgibbons, Herbert Gans, Alexander Garvin, Robert Geddes, Herbert Gleason, Lawrence Goldman, Robert Goodman, Karolyn Gould, Harold Grabino, Linda Greenhouse, Gail Gremse, Reginald Griffith, William Grindereng, Chester Hartman, Robert Hazen, John Johansen, Richard Kahan, Nicholas Katzenbach, Langley Keyes, Penn Kimball, Melvin King, Rebecca Lee, Tunney Lee, Stephen Lefkowitz, Norman Leventhal, Anthony Lewis, Ted Liebman, Robert Litke, Ellen Logue, Frank and Mary Ann Logue, Margaret Logue, Christopher

Lydon, Paul McCann, Michael McKinnell, James McNeely, Janet Murphy, Howard Muskof, Martin Nolan, Thomas O'Connor, Anthony Pangaro, Lisa Peattie, I. M. Pei, William Poorvu, Jennifer Raab, Jerome Rappaport, John Ryan, Susan Saegert, Frederick Salvucci, Henry Scagnoli, Joseph Slavet, John Stainton, Esther Maletz Stone, Allan Talbot, Ralph Taylor, William Tuttle III, Richard Wade, Harry Wexler, and John Zuccotti.

Although Ed Logue was no longer living when I launched this project in 2005, he having died in 2000, others who had the good fortune of interviewing him when he was alive have provided me with invaluable first-person sources. Many of those interviews are now in Logue's papers at Yale, but other oral histories with Logue and his close associates were generously shared by Peter Bray, Deborah Elkin, Andy Horowitz, Lawrence Kennedy, Greg Ruben, Morton Schussheim, and Alex von Hoffman. During the period from 1983 to 1991, Ivan Steen of SUNY Albany interviewed Logue ten times in order to thoroughly document his work with the New York State Urban Development Corporation. I am grateful to Professor Steen for sharing the audiotapes and transcripts of these interviews with me to complement what was available in Logue's Yale papers. The sociologist Frank Jones interviewed Logue over a two-day period in 1999. Although the transcript is in Logue's papers, I want to thank him for the service he provided by engaging in such a far-reaching, in-depth discussion with Logue about his full career. All of these interviews helped bring Ed Logue and his milieu to life for me. The Columbia Center for Oral History Archives undertook an extensive Edward I. Koch Administration Oral History Project, which was of tremendous help as well.

I have also benefited from the support of many colleagues as well as individuals who participated in or closely observed Logue's life. They have shared advice, insights, and encouragement; reviewed drafts of proposals, lectures, and maps; introduced me to others; shared relevant materials in their possession or stumbled upon while doing their own archival research; and so much more. I am grateful to Alan Altshuler, Hillary Ballon, Frank Barrett, David Barron, Paul Bass, Jonathan Bell, Nicholas Bloom, Peter Bray, Robert Caro, Michael Carriere, Sue Cobble, Nancy Cott, John Davis, Jameson Doig, Claire Dunning, Robert Ellikson, Louise Endel, Susan Fainstein, Justin Florence, Eric Foner, Gerald Frug, John Gaddis, Gary Gerstle, Jess Gilbert, Glenda Gilmore, Edward Glaeser, Brian Goldstein, Linda Gordon, Robert Gordon, Chris Grimley,

Michael Gruenbaum, Dirk Hartog, Dolores Hayden, Diana Hernandez, Jennifer Hock, Andy Horowitz, Ada Louise Huxtable, Ken Jackson, Jerold Kayden, Alice Kessler-Harris, Jim Kloppenberg, Alex Krieger, Michael Kubo, Clifford Kuhn, Matthew Lasner, Stephen Lassonde, Deborah Leff, Neil Levine, David Luberoff, Elisa Minoff, John Mollenkopf, Mitchell Moss, Dan Okrent, Mark Pasnik, Alina Payne, Alan Plattus, Douglas Rae, Tim Rohan, Mark Rose, Lynne Sagalyn, Nick Salvatore, Hashim Sarkis, Chris Schmidt, Jane Shaw, Gaddis Smith, Jonathan Soffer, Tim Stanley, Robert Stern, Tom Sugrue, Mary Summers, Adam Tanaka, Lawrence Vale, Jim Vrabel, David Wylie, and Elizabeth Ylvisaker. From the very first day that Dawn Ling began working as my assistant at Radcliffe in 2015, she went out of her way to facilitate my work on this book. In the final stages of identifying images and securing permissions, she truly became my partner, sharing all the challenges that these tasks involved. We were helped greatly by Jess Brilli, who brought her graphic design talents to photo scanning, and Lisa Albert, who managed the substantial financial bookkeeping required.

The "Friends of Ed Logue," who built a website and mounted an exhibition on UDC housing to ensure that Logue's legacy would not be lost, have become my friends as well, providing me with invaluable documents, sitting for interviews, and introducing me to other friends of theirs and Ed's. I hope that Stephen Diamond, Ted and Nina Liebman, Tony Pangaro, and Tunney Lee know how much they have contributed to this book. Another group of individuals who provided a bridge to the past are the ROMEOS (Retired Opinion-Makers Eating Out), a group of former journalists and public officials who lived through Logue's Boston years. They connected me to several crucial interviewees. Robert Hannan and Edward Quill have worked tirelessly to keep this group going. Although I have long been interested in cities and the built environment, I was not trained as an architect or a planner. Over the years at Harvard, I have benefited enormously from the instruction of colleagues at the Harvard Graduate School of Design (GSD). Some are singled out above, but many more have tutored me and warmly welcomed me into their ranks, including the former dean Mohsen Mostafavi.

Being part of a university has also given me the gift of talented students— undergraduate and graduate—who helped me tremendously as research assistants. Most of them were enrolled at Harvard, but a few Yalies assisted me as well. I hope that they will recognize their contributions throughout the book and that the work they did has helped them as much as it has me. They are now lawyers, professors, planners, school teachers and principals, bankers, and businesspeople, but without exception they proved themselves hard-working, resourceful researchers, digging up nuggets of gold and helping me to assess their value. I owe a great debt to Francesca Ammon, Michael Baskin, Niko Bowie, Lauren Brandt, Christine DeLucia, Claire Dunning, Anna Fogel, Kyle Frisina, Brian Goldstein, Matthew Hartzell, Tammy Ingram, Andrew Kalloch, Erica Kim, Charles Loeffler, Pete L'Official, Andy Malone, Whitney Martinko, Bradford Meacham, Elisa Minoff, Robin Morris, Paul Nauert, Geoffrey Rathgeber, Bekah Glaser Ross, Aditi Sen, Nico Slate, Alex Stokes, Ashley Tallevi, and Clinton Williams.

Friends, colleagues, and my husband, Herrick Chapman, served as invaluable readers of draft chapters of this book. Herrick, Brian Goldstein, Alice O'Connor, Daniel Rowe, and Susan Ware read the whole manuscript and greatly strengthened the book with their penetrating insights. Gareth Davies, Daniel Horowitz, Laura Kalman, Michael Kazin, and members of the Boston Area Twentieth-Century U.S. History Writing Group read one or more chapters, giving me the benefit of their incisive feedback.

Financial support from several sources made possible the time to research and write, and subsidized travel and interview transcriptions. At an early stage of this project, Ed Glaeser and David Luberoff, who were at the helm of the Rappaport Institute for Greater Boston and the Taubman Center for State and Local History at Harvard's Kennedy School of Government, enthusiastically awarded me a research grant, conveying great confidence in the project, which in turn buoyed my own confidence in proceeding. Rick Peiser, who was then running the Real Estate Academic Initiative at Harvard's GSD, similarly offered crucial financial and moral support. Sabbatical leave and research funding from Harvard's Faculty of Arts and Sciences and the Radcliffe Institute helped me complete the book. Receiving the Harold Vyvyan Harmsworth Professorship in American History at Oxford during the 2007–2008 academic year brought many advantages, including immersion in the British postwar urban experience and the stimulating company of the Oxford Americanists under the leadership of Richard Carwardine, the then Rhodes Professor of American History.

Audiences at many universities and conferences have listened attentively as I tried out ideas and, through their challenging questions and comments, helped this book to evolve and improve over its many years of incubation. I am grateful for having had the opportunity to share my work with colleagues on four continents and in a variety of settings, including the American University of Beirut, Boston University (two conferences), Brigham Young University (Russel B. Swenson Lecture), Cambridge University (American History Seminar on two occasions), the Carnegie Museum in Pittsburgh, the Chicago History Museum (Urban History Seminar), the University of Cincinnati (Charles Phelps Taft Memorial Lectures), Columbia University (symposium on Robert Moses), East China Normal University in Shanghai, the JFK Institute at Freie Universität Berlin, the German American Studies Association, the German Historical Institute in Washington, D.C., the Harvard Humanities Center (Architecture and Knowledge Seminar), the Taubman Center for State and Local Government / Rappaport Institute for Greater Boston / Center for American Political Studies jointly sponsored lecture at Harvard, the University of Kentucky, the Lawrence History Center in Massachusetts (urban renewal symposium), Leeds University, University of London, Ludwig-Maximilians-Universität in Munich (conference at Center for Advanced Studies), Manchester University (Postgraduate Conference in American Studies), University of Maryland (Rundell Lecture), University of Massachusetts Boston (Betty and Matt Flaherty Lecture), Massachusetts Historical Society (two events), University of Miami, Northern Illinois University (W. Bruce Lincoln Memorial Lecture), Notre Dame University (conference at Cushwa Center for the Study of American Catholicism), Oxford University (Harmsworth Lecture, American History Research Seminar, and Economic and Social History Seminar), Princeton's Shelby Cullom Davis Center, Society of American City and Regional Planning History Conference, Queen's University Belfast, Radcliffe Institute for Advanced Study (dean's inaugural lecture), Schlesinger Library of the Radcliffe Institute (two symposia on biography), Society of Architectural Historians, Tulane University, University of Wisconsin–Eau Claire, University of Wisconsin–Madison (conference on consumption), Urban History Association, Warwick University, and the Yale School of Architecture (conference on Paul Rudolph).

Libraries and archives, and their dedicated staffs, made my research possible. Foremost were the rich collections in Yale's Manuscripts and Archives, including Ed Logue's papers and those of many of his colleagues in New Haven. In New York, I benefited from archives at Columbia University, New York

University, and the New York State Archives in Albany. In Boston, materials at the Boston City Archives, the Boston Public Library, the University of Massachusetts Boston, Northeastern University, and the always astonishingly wide-ranging holdings of the Harvard Libraries proved indispensable as well, particularly the GSD's Loeb Library, whose diverse collections are a reminder that architects and planners leave behind impressive work in print, not just their imprint on the built environment.

I signed on with Farrar, Straus and Giroux early in this book's development, which has given me the benefit of Eric Chinski's wise counsel for a long time. But it was when I presented him with a full draft that I really understood why he has earned a reputation as such a brilliant editor. He read closely, attentive to everything from argument to word choice. Although I was at first shocked at his request that I cut thirty thousand words from the draft, he showed me how to do it and improved the book. At FSG, I have also benefited from the first-rate support of Julia Ringo; the production editor, Carrie Hsieh; and the jacket and book designers, Alex Merto and Richard Oriolo. M. P. Klier was everything an author hopes for in a copy editor—an appreciative reader with a light but magical touch. Jeffrey L. Ward created handsome maps. Steve Weil has ushered the book out into the world with care and commitment. My agent, Geri Thoma, has been by my side from the very inception of this book, helping to shape it, reading perceptively, and knowing when to keep her distance and when to intervene. Her genuine excitement about the book helped sustain me.

Finally, I want to thank my wonderful family. Since the last time I wrote book acknowledgments, my immediate family has grown. Daughters Julia and Natalie, in marrying, have bought us sons at last with their wonderful husbands, Paul and Nico. And *Saving America's Cities* comes into the world only a few short months after the birth of our grandson, Jesse, who is growing up in Jersey City, where his parents have enthusiastically made their home. The rest of my extended family are also city people, having claimed New York City as home base for generations and caring deeply about its fate. My last thank-you is for my husband, Herrick, who has been my partner in so much over the more than forty years we have been married. Together we have raised children; made and remade homes; explored cities worldwide; endlessly debated issues rooted in the past, present, and future; and taken turns serving as sounding boards, editors, and critics of each other's work. I dedicate this book to him for all these reasons as well as in appreciation for his deep commitment to making cities a home for all. Growing up in Denver during the height of the civil rights movement and attending a big, diverse public high school left a mark that years spent in the Bay Area, Pittsburgh, New York, and Boston have only deepened. I thank him with all my heart for the love and support he has given me over the years.

INDEX

A NOTE ABOUT THE AUTHOR

Lizabeth Cohen received her Ph.D. from the University of California, Berkeley. She is the Howard Mumford Jones Professor of American Studies and a Harvard University Distinguished Service Professor. Until recently, she was dean of the Radcliffe Institute for Advanced Study at Harvard. Previously, she taught at Oxford University, New York University, and Carnegie Mellon University. The author of many articles and essays, Dr. Cohen was a Pulitzer Prize finalist for her first book, *Making a New Deal: Industrial Workers in Chicago, 1919–1939*, which later won the Bancroft Prize and the Philip Taft Labor History Book Award. She is also the author of *A Consumers' Republic: The Politics of Mass Consumption in Postwar America* and coauthor of the popular college and advanced-placement history textbook *The American Pageant*.